The Visual Experience

Teacher's Edition

Second Edition

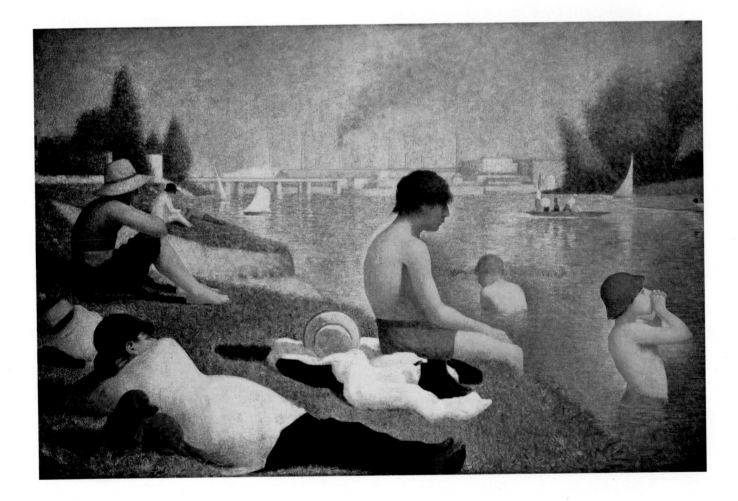

Richard Salome & Jack Hobbs

Davis Publications, Inc.   Worcester, Massachusetts

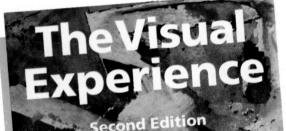

Student Edition:
• Large, dramatic images appeal to students
• Engaging conversational text flows smoothly, makes reading enjoyable
• Exposure to a variety of artworks unlocks students' creative powers
• Carefully developed methods provide students with the means to analyze and enjoy works of art for a lifetime
• Questioning strategies and discovery learning help develop skills in creative and critical thinking
• Creative experiences in art appreciation, studio, history and criticism
• *Try it Yourself* features are ideas for independent student exploration and research
• Colorful maps, diagrams and illustrations aid comprehension
• Glossary, Index

Reproducibles
A separate workbook of reproducible student handouts puts chapter diagrams, study and test questions, report forms and lesson-related visual examples at your fingertips.

Teacher's Edition:
• Provides you with all the information you need to help your students see art, artists and the world around them with new eyes and a fresh, informed perspective
• Clear, colorful presentation makes planning easy and enjoyable
• For ease of use, teaching notes and strategies are integrated with full-size student pages
• Chapter diagrams show you overall content at a glance
• Detailed lesson plans take you step by step through 45 experiences in art appreciation, production, history and

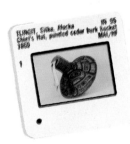

Slides
Over 100 examples, from ancient to contemporary — with a special emphasis on multicultural images. Correlated to lesson plans in the Teacher's Edition.

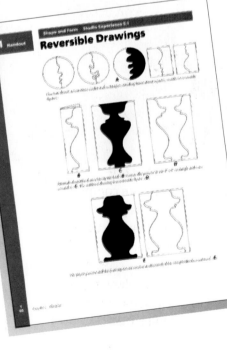

Overhead Transparencies

20 colorful images expand your visual library and provide resources beyond those in the student book. Correlated to lesson plans for ease of use, they are also linked directly to the test questions for assessing students' higher order thinking skills.

Large Reproductions with Teacher's Guide

24 laminated color reproductions (18" x 24") of artworks not found in the text allow you to explore techniques, compare styles, analyze composition — quickly and easily. Reproductions are correlated to lesson plans. Accompanying the reproductions is a Teacher's Guide filled with background information and teaching ideas.

Software

Your own computer disk lets you customize study and test questions to meet your students' unique needs. Available in the following formats: Macintosh, Apple, IBM

National Gallery Laserdisc

Bar codes correlated to the Lesson Plans are printed in *The Visual Experience* Teacher's Edition. Nearly 2,000 images from the National Gallery's extensive collection of world art are yours for display.

A team of experienced authors

Richard A. Salome

Richard A. Salome is Professor Emeritus at Illinois State University where he instructed undergraduate and graduate art education courses for twenty-five years. He also taught at the University of Minnesota and at Stanford University where he received his Ed.D. Dr. Salome has developed and instructed art programs for secondary students enrolled in the Iowa public school system. He served as coeditor and senior editor of the NAEA's publication *Studies in Art Education* and served on its Commission on Research in Art Education.

Jack Hobbs

Jack Hobbs has been a professor of art at Illinois State University for twenty-four years. He taught at Buena Vista College in Iowa and served as Art Supervisor for nine years at Crystal Lake Public Schools in Illinois. He completed his Ph.D. at the University of Iowa. Dr. Hobbs has published several books on art, including *Art in Context; Arts, Civilization, and Ideas;* and *Arts and Civilisation.* He has been active as an artist and has been featured in such shows as the *National Exhibition of Prints* and *The Art in the Embassies Program* held in Washington, DC.

Cynthia Colbert

Dr. Cynthia Colbert is Chair of Art Education and Professor of Art at the University of South Carolina in Columbia. She is a practicing ceramic artist. In 1993, the NAEA selected her as the Most Outstanding Art Educator in Higher Education.

Carolyn Sollman

Carolyn Sollman is the project director for the "Close the Cracks" program sponsored by the Center for Arts in the Basic Curriculum in Washington, DC. She received her B.S. and M.A. from Ball State University. Sollman's drawings and paintings are widely shown and have received numerous awards.

Bonnie L. MacDonald

Bonnie L. MacDonald received her M.A. in Art Education from the Rhode Island School of Design in Providence. She has worked as a microcomputer programmer and as a consultant in computer-aided design, automated publishing and videodisc authoring systems.

John Lidstone

Dr. John Lidstone is Professor Emeritus of Art Education and founding Dean of the School of Education at Queens College of the City University of New York. Born in Canada, he has taught at Pratt Institute, Teachers College, Columbia University and Bank Street College of Education.

Front Cover: Robert Hudson, *Drawing #26,* 1975. Mixed media on paper, 30 1/2" x 25 1/2" (77 x 65 cm). From the collection of Jan Perry Mayer, Denver, Colorado.

Back Cover: Lawrence Beck, *Punk Walrus Spirit (Poonk Aiverk Inua),* 1987. Mixed media, 10" x 17" x 16" (25 x 43 x 41 cm). Photograph: Garry Sutto.

Title Page: Georges Seurat, *Bathing at Asnières,* 1883–1884. Oil on canvas, 6' 7" x 9' 11" (210 x 302 cm). Reproduced by courtesy of the Trustees, The National Gallery, London.

Library of Congress Catalog Card Number: 93–74640
ISBN: 87192–291–6
10 9 8 7 6 5 4 3 2 1

Acknowledgments

We wish to extend our appreciation to the graduate and undergraduate students at Illinois State University who contributed their time, talent and expertise to this project: to Barbara Caldwell who contributed numerous multicultural suggestions as well as photographs; to Linda Willis-Fisher who contributed to the teacher's edition; and to the members of Dr. Salome's classes who permitted us to use their artwork for the "Experiences." We wish to acknowledge those whose counsel we sought while compiling the text: Kent Anderson, David Baker, Laura Chapman, Robert Daugherty, Michael Hagenbuck, Connie Newton, Ronald Silverman and David Henley.

Managing Editor:
Wyatt Wade

Associate Editor:
Claire Mowbray Golding

Production Editor:
Nancy Burnett

Production:
Steve Vogelsang

Copyeditor:
Janet Stone

Editorial Assistance:
Holly Hanson, Amee Bergin, Denise Nephew

Design:
Douglass Scott, WGBH Design

Design Advisor:
Karen Durlach

Electronic Page Makeup:
Carol Hoyle Ballard

Illustrator:
Susan Christy-Pallo

One book that does it all!

The **Teacher's Edition** contains the **complete Student Edition**. You see exactly what your students see **in color** and **at full size**. Convenient, compact, easy to use, it offers opportunities for learning experiences your students will never forget.

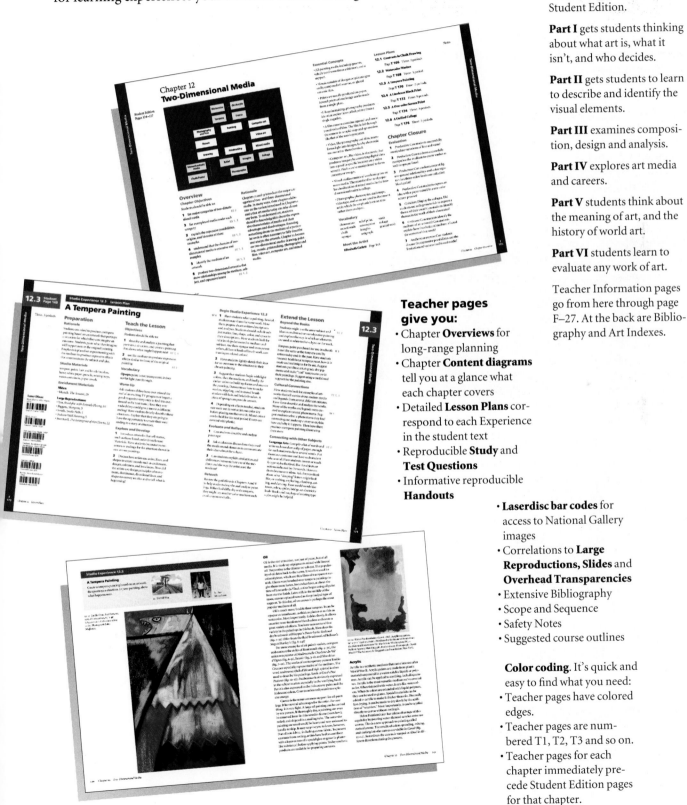

Teacher pages give you:
- Chapter **Overviews** for long-range planning
- Chapter **Content diagrams** tell you at a glance what each chapter covers
- Detailed **Lesson Plans** correspond to each Experience in the student text
- Reproducible **Study** and **Test Questions**
- Informative reproducible **Handouts**

The **Teacher's Edition** has six parts, each identified by the color on the edge of its pages. Each part corresponds to the same part in the Student Edition.

Part I gets students thinking about what art is, what it isn't, and who decides.

Part II gets students to learn to describe and identify the visual elements.

Part III examines composition, design and analysis.

Part IV explores art media and careers.

Part V students think about the meaning of art, and the history of world art.

Part VI students learn to evaluate any work of art.

Teacher Information pages go from here through page F–27. At the back are Bibliography and Art Indexes.

- **Laserdisc bar codes** for access to National Gallery images
- Correlations to **Large Reproductions, Slides** and **Overhead Transparencies**
- Extensive Bibliography
- Scope and Sequence
- Safety Notes
- Suggested course outlines

Color coding. It's quick and easy to find what you need:
- Teacher pages have colored edges.
- Teacher pages are numbered T1, T2, T3 and so on.
- Teacher pages for each chapter immediately precede Student Edition pages for that chapter.

Part I
Introduction

Part II
What To Look For

Part III
How Is It Organized

Part IV
What Is It Made Of

Part V
What Is It Saying

Part VI
In the Final Analysis

F-5

The Chapter Overviews

The **Chapter Overviews** show you what is covered in each chapter of the Student Edition. At a glance, you see the **concepts** and **vocabulary** students learn in this chapter, and how these fit into the text's general aims.

You'll find each chapter's **special features** here, plus **titles** and **estimated times** for each **lesson plan,** a list of **reproducible handouts,** and questions that help you **evaluate what students have learned**.

Color coding, with chapter title, tells you which part and chapter these pages address (This is Part 2, Chapter 4.).

Student Edition pages are clearly indicated; you can turn to them easily yourself, or direct students while referring to Teacher pages.

Student Edition **chapter number** and **title** are plain and easy to read.

Chapter diagrams (also color coded by Part) help you see at a glance what each chapter covers. Can be used as teaching aids, too: overheads, study sheets, discussion supplements.

Meet the Artist lists the artist biographies students encounter in each chapter: personal, personable looks at the lives of artists whose work appears in the text.

Chapter Closure suggests questions — linked to the main pedagogical components of art education — to evaluate what students have learned and discover where they might need some review.

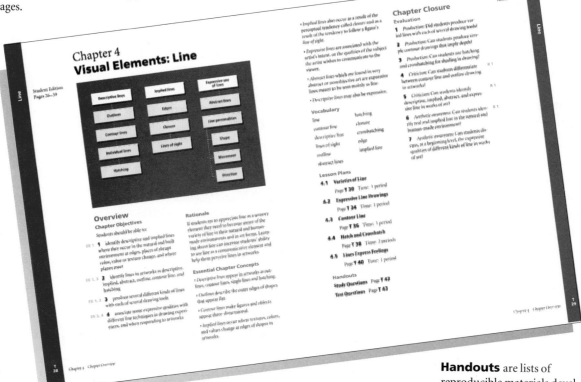

Chapter Objectives tell you clearly and concisely the chapter's instructional aims.

Rationale describes how this chapter's material contributes to students' development as artists, as human beings, as members of an image-rich society.

Essential Chapter Concepts state the chapter's main ideas and define terms, in straight-forward language.

A list of the chapter's **Lesson Plans** shows you the Studio, Aesthetic, Art History and Critical Analysis Experiences that will help students apply what they have learned in the chapter …and the suggested amount of time you'll spend on each lesson.

A **vocabulary list** prepares you for the chapter's main terms.

Handouts are lists of reproducible materials developed for each chapter: guidelines, tips for improving artwork or clarifying concepts, study and test questions.

A blank column lets you **make notes** and jot down reminders related to chapter material.

The Lesson Plans

Each **Lesson Plan** is linked to an Experience found in the student text. Lesson Plans take you step by step through an Experience based on appreciation of art, art history or the criticism and analysis of artworks.

The red tabs on the Lesson Plan pages contain a large easy-to-read number. This number corresponds to one of the numbered **Experiences** in the student text. You can find that Experience (and, in most cases, a representative student artwork) on the student page referred to in the tab. The lesson corresponds to the title in the student book, and tells you the lesson's main idea.

Time indicates the approximate number of periods you'll need to complete this lesson.

Preparation

This section tells you just what you'll need to teach the lesson.

The **Rationale** explains the lesson's fundamental concepts.

The **Studio Materials** list helps you assemble what your students will need to create artwork for the lesson.

Vocabulary for the lesson is listed in boldface italic and defined in simple, straightforward language.

Warm Up takes the class immediately into a dynamic activity or discussion.

Explore and Develop moves into discussion and explanation of the lesson's concepts.

Begin Studio Experience marks the point in the lesson at which students make use of the concepts they've learned and turn to creating artworks of their own.

Student Edition

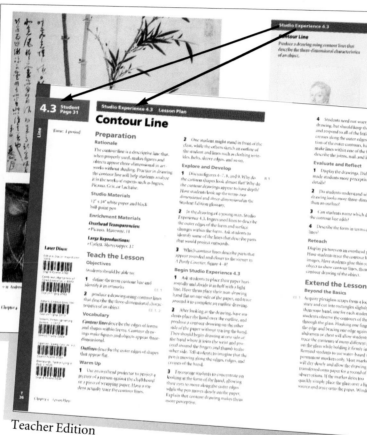

Teacher Edition

Enrichment Materials are additional resources, available separately, that have been chosen to deepen students' understanding of this lesson's concepts.

Teach the Lesson

Step by step, this section explains how you might take your students through the lesson.

Objectives state clearly what students should understand and be able to accomplish upon completion of the lesson.

Evaluate and Reflect asks pointed questions that help you gauge students' comprehension of the lesson and assess work created for it.

Reteach provides alternative teaching strategies for students having difficulty with lesson concepts.

Extend the Lesson

Help your students explore the lesson topic further, discover threads that link the arts with science, language arts and other disciplines.

Beyond the Basics is designed for teachers who want to go further, and for students who easily grasp the lesson's main concepts and are eager to delve more deeply into the subject.

Cultural Connections offer activities, research projects and explorations that help students understand and appreciate the world's many artistic traditions and forms of expression.

Connecting with Other Subjects lets you show students that the study of art easily crosses disciplinary boundaries to literature, history, science, social studies, psychology and the like.

The Handouts

These **reproducible teaching aids** are ready for you to use, and tailored precisely to lesson plans or chapter content.

Study Questions cover fundamental chapter information and prepare students for final assessment.

Name:

Course:

Test Questions
Chapter 5–Visual Elements: Shape and Form

Circle the correct answer in each question.

1 An ellipse is to an ellipsoid as a
a. circle is to a sphere.
b. rectangle is to a cylinder.
c. triangle is to a square.
d. a and b.
e. a, b, and c.

2 Shape constancy refers to the tendency to see
a. all shapes the same no matter what the viewing angle.
b. all objects the same size no matter what the viewing angle.
c. foreshortened shapes.
d. a and b.

Name:

Course:

Study Questions
Chapter 5–Visual Elements: Shape and Form

1 What is the difference between a shape and a form?

2 What is the relationship between lines and shapes?

3 Explain the terms *figure* and *ground*.

4 What are positive and negative shapes?

5 Which artwork in the text is an example of figure-ground reversal?

6 Give an example of closure found in this chapter.

7 Define shape constancy.

8 Define foreshortening.

9 Define size constancy.

10 What can be learned about a three-dimensional object using only the sense of touch?

11 What is the difference between an organic shape and a geometric shape?

12 Give one sculptural example of an open form and one of a closed form pictured in the chapter.

Chapter 5   Reproducible Handout

Study Answers
Chapter 5
Visual Elements:
Shape and Form

Test Answers
Chapter 5
Visual Elements:
Shape and Form

1 A

9.1 Handout

Analyzing American Gothic · Criticism Experience 9.1

Guidelines for Analyzing an Artwork

Analyzing involves identifying relationships among elements in an artwork. It means looking at how the artist organized subject matter and elements including line, shape, form, texture, value, and space so that they interrelate as a composition. The guidelines below will help you analyze an artwork. You may not need all of the items. You may want to add others that you find there.

Shape and Form   Studio Experience 5.3

Foreshortening (continued)

Handout 5.3

Shape and Form

Test Questions on vital chapter content are presented in a variety of forms.

Special Handouts clarify visual concepts, supply guidelines and sample responses for students' reference, suggest possible solutions to creative problems, and provide forms for research reports and group projects.

Contents

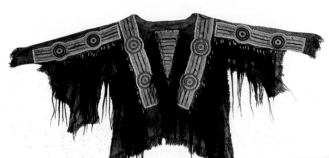

Part I Introduction

Part II What To Look For

Part III How Is It Organized?

Part IV What Is It Made Of?

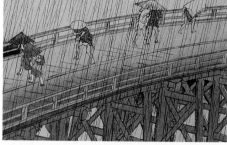

Part V What Is It Saying?

Part VI In the Final Analysis

Philosophy and Features of the Program

Goals and Content

The Visual Experience contributes to students' development in the four content areas of **art production**, **art history**, **art criticism**, and **aesthetics**. The text is organized to help teachers involve every student in:

1. creating art
2. analyzing, interpreting and making judgments about art
3. researching and writing about art history
4. discussing and synthesizing ideas about aesthetics.

The varied modes of learning included in an art appreciation program provide varied opportunities for students to develop critical analysis skills. The value of art production as a way to learn about art is abundantly provided for in studio experiences throughout the text.

Practice with Art Materials and Procedures

Because the study of art is enhanced through experiences in creating art, students explore a variety of two- and three-dimensional studio experiences throughout the text. These studio experiences are presented as lessons in the teacher's edition.

Students are introduced to what artists do, the materials and procedures they use, purposes that motivate them, and the many cultural and social meanings their works convey.

Making art can help students understand the technical, visual and creative problems that artists deal with. Art production when integrated with criticism, history and aesthetics will help them understand the power of visual imagery to convey emotions, feelings, concepts and values. The authors feel strongly that art production is also a means of fostering creative thinking.

Analyzing Art Forms

Students come prepared with subjective responses and opinions about art. The critical process requires them to differentiate between subjective and objective responses.

Art criticism is defined for this program as the systematic discussion of an artwork in four stages:

1. **describing** what is seen in an artwork
2. **analyzing** how the artwork is organized
3. **interpreting** the meaning or mood of the artwork
4. **judging** the success of the artwork

Students are introduced to the four parts of this critical method throughout the text, with a culminating experience provided in Chapter 21, where the complete four-stage model is presented.

The process of art criticism involves critical thinking skills. Students learn how artists manipulate the art elements to achieve effective compositions, and how they use media, procedures and images to communicate ideas. Students who learn to look at art, analyze the composition, offer multiple interpretations of meaning, make critical judgments and talk or write about what they see, think and feel are engaging in art criticism.

Reflecting upon the Experience of Art

Aesthetics — *as the study of the nature of art* — is dealt with in the very first chapter. When confronted with a collection of objects and asked to determine which of them is art, students discover that artworks can take an infinite variety of forms. In the second chapter, to answer the question "When is it art?", students learn about the philosophy of art, the aesthetic experience, and the art world. The study of the nature of art fosters critical thinking by challenging students to ask serious questions.

Aesthetics — *as the study of sensory responses to artworks* — is closely related to criticism and is covered throughout the text. Students analyze the visual and expressive qualities of artworks or objects and examine their personal responses to these forms.

Aesthetic perception involves thinking about the sensory experiences and feelings derived from a work of art, its impact and meaning for the individual or society. Throughout this book, students are encouraged to explore philosophical questions about art, reflect upon their responses to individual works and develop richer experiences with art in general.

Art in Historical Contexts

Art history helps students place artists and artworks in their correct social and chronological context. Students may learn to value the contributions of art in societies and cultures by studying art in historical contexts. Knowledge of the historical context in which an artist lived can help the individual understand the style and work of that artist. The chronology of art history helps students understand the development of art styles. Chapters 16 through 19 cover the history of art in non-Western and Western cultures and include opportunities for research and studio assignments.

Organization of the Teacher's Edition

The first section of the teacher's edition (pages F–1 to F–27) explores the teacher's role in planning instructional objectives, teaching content and thinking skills, providing for students with varied ability levels, and using assessment strategies. Recommendations on how to insure a safe and hazard-free art room are provided. Outlines show the scope and sequence of *The Visual Experience* and the art lessons. Planning charts show how the text chapters and related art lessons can be used over periods of one semester or one year.

The second section, beginning on page T–2, includes 21 teacher edition chapters. Every chapter in the teacher's edition provides the following content and materials:

1. An **overview** including chapter objectives, rationale, essential chapter concepts, a vocabulary list, titles of chapter lesson plans, support materials and chapter evaluation.
2. Complete **lesson plans** for each student experience in the chapter. Each plan includes a rationale statement, a list of resource materials including slides, transparencies and reproductions, lesson objectives, vocabulary with definitions, warm up suggestions, teaching approaches, evaluation, reteach suggestions, ideas for extending the lesson, cultural connections, and connections with other subjects.
3. **Study questions** that can be duplicated and a list of answers.
4. **Test questions** that can be duplicated and answers.
5. **Handouts**, where appropriate, that can be copied and shared with students.

A bibliography of reference materials for each chapter is presented at the end of the teacher's edition.

About the National Gallery of Art Videodisc

The use of videodisc imagery in the art classroom provides an alternative to slides and overhead transparencies. The National Gallery of Art Videodisc introduces students to one of the finest art collections in the world. Numbering 1645, these reproductions are easily accessed by frame number on a laser videodisc player and displayed on a color monitor. Each artwork frame is followed by a catalog frame listing the artist's name, his/her nationality, life span, title of work, date created, medium, size and donor.

In the Enrichment Materials sections of the lessons is a selection of images from the Videodisc Catalogue (Side II, Chapters 2–16). Images were selected to reinforce and augment the key concepts in each lesson. To take advantage of videodisc technology, we have listed close-up images or details and video segments from the gallery tour when appropriate.

Located on the left margin of the first page of a lesson is a column of barcodes which can be scanned with a barcode reader. If you are using a remote control, the search frame number is printed under each barcode. Below are "Some Tips on Using a Laser Videodisc Player" to help you get started.

Exploring the National Gallery of Art Videodisc

Side II, Chapter 1 contains color bars for color adjustment and information about the organization of the disc. You may want to explain to students that a question mark (?) following an artist's name indicates uncertainty about the date and whether that artist did execute the work. To introduce students to the National Gallery, in Lesson 1.1 we recommend that students view Side II, Chapter 17, A Tour of the National Gallery of Art. If time permits, Side 1, The History of the National Gallery of Art is also recommended for background information on art museums and their history.

We encourage you and your students to use the suggested selections as a starting point for discussions and further exploration of the videodisc. Scan forward and backward from a selected work to see related works by the same artist or contemporary artists. Use the chapter index to locate works from the same period, art movement and country. Use the index to painters and their works to locate particular artworks for comparison and contrast.

Some Tips on Using a Laser Videodisc Player

Consult manufacturer's instructions on how to hook up the video and audio cables from the player to the color monitor. Read the section on care and handling of discs. You may want to set up the player where students can consult it anytime as they would a dictionary or any reference book. Explain the operation of the laser videodisc player and care and handling of videodiscs with your students.

Using a Barcode Reader

You may need to practice using the barcode reader to scan the barcodes. Be sure there are no obstacles between the player and the barcode reader. Typically, the range of the barcode reader is within 20 feet of the player.

To scan a barcode, hold the barcode reader like a pencil with your index finger posed above the READ and SEND/REPEAT buttons. Position the barcode reader approximately 1/4 inch to the left or right of the barcode.

Press the READ button. You will see a red light reflected on the page. Keep the READ button pressed as you swiftly move the tip of the reader horizontally across the barcode.

You will hear a beep and see a memory indicator light turn on when the barcode data has been successfully read. If not, try again.

To send a barcode data to the player, point the barcode reader at the barcode sensor on the player and press the SEND/REPEAT button. The selected frame appears or video segment will play.

Suggestions for the Active Teacher

Art provides an understanding of our world and of ourselves. This basic tenet underlies a major role of the art teacher — to develop an art curriculum helps students:

1. learn significant achievements of many cultures
2. creatively express ideas, feelings and experiences through the purposeful use of art materials and visual elements
3. see art as a form of nonverbal communication
4. make reasoned choices based on critical assessment.

Characteristics of Active Teachers

Active teachers recognize that effective learning occurs when students are actively involved in organizing information and finding relationships rather than being passive recipients of teacher-delivered materials. The active teacher is the single most important influence on student development. While teaching strategies vary, there are common characteristics of active teachers. Active teachers:

1. purposefully plan for student learning
2. select teaching strategies that agree with planned goals
3. present content in a form that students understand
4. actively involve students in the learning process
5. employ instructional strategies that allow interaction with students.

The Teacher's Edition Is a Resource

You will find the guidelines and study and test questions in the teacher's edition helpful in planning and presenting an art program of sequential learning experiences. The activities are sequential; some, such as the critical analyses problems, build one-on-another, requiring students to use concepts from earlier lessons. Students can use the completed study questions to prepare for tests. Encourage students to maintain files of the notes and materials they will receive throughout the year.

The student experiences included in each chapter deal with art production, art criticism and art history. The experiences involving *art production* help students apply and synthesize the conceptual material of the chapter. The process of *art criticism* is presented in sequential stages throughout the text. Art criticism provides a core experience to which everything else relates. The criticism activities are especially conducive to the development of *higher order thinking skills*, eventually reaching the evaluation level. *Art history* is presented in four consecutive chapters to preserve the chronology of time periods. In addition, there are references to art from various cultures and time periods throughout the text. The student assignments for the history chapters provide good opportunities for *cooperative group learning. Aesthetic responding* activities encourage students to analyze and interpret the visual and expressive communication of artworks.

Instructional Objectives for Art Experiences

You will find *chapter objectives* at the beginning of every chapter in the teacher's edition, and *objectives* at the beginning of each art lesson plan. The chapter objectives describe desired outcomes. The objectives for the art lessons clarify the purposes of the lessons, and can be used to guide your planning decisions. All objectives are written in reference to the *student*. While the goal and performance behavior are described in the lesson objectives, teachers may adjust the performance level to their specific classroom situation.

The art lessons included in the teacher's edition are planned to help students learn concepts, develop thinking skills and engage in problem solving.

• Clearly stated objectives make it easier to select examples and activities that will help students learn relevant concepts.
• Learning objectives, if *shared* with students, help to focus on problems and encourage creative solutions.
• There should be a relationship between the objectives and the products or images produced during art lessons.
• Some art activities such as the perspective drawing exercises call for an ideal solution that all students should reach if they are to use the skill in future art production or art criticism.
• A few objectives introduce lessons that are meant to increase the student's ability to respond to and criticize art.

Developing Thinking Skills through Visual Experiences

The assumption that art is a means of developing creative self-expression and personal growth underlies the practice of studio art in many schools today. The arts are regarded as dealing with emotions rather than the mind. However, this emphasis on student creativity can result in resistance to structured content and overlooks the fact that art production involves important levels of thinking. *This perspective does not recognize that creation of images is a matter of mind requiring inventive problem solving, analytic and synthetic forms of reasoning, and judgment.*

John Dewey's early 20th century pronouncement that being an artist requires the same intellectual rigor as being a scientist initiated a line of inquiry into how creativity and comprehension in the arts nurtures the intellect.

Howard Gardner has continued this inquiry in his work on the relationship between cognition and art.

Teachers are expected to teach *about* thinking to increase students' awareness of their own mental processes. By *identifying* thinking skills within the curriculum framework, teachers are also teaching students how to strengthen their cognitive abilities.

Educational goals are commonly divided into three domains. **Cognitive** goals address development of the student's intellect. **Affective** goals are concerned with emotional and social development. **Psychomotor** goals address manipulative skills and coordination.

The school curriculum is focused primarily on the cognitive domain to help students acquire bodies of useful information and develop thinking skills that allow them to learn on their own.

Developing Thinking Skills at All Levels of the Cognitive Process

The learning objectives and content provided in *The Visual Experience* contribute to the development of thinking skills at all levels of the cognitive process. The chapter tests and study questions include items at the knowledge, comprehension, application and analysis levels. The suggestions and student exercises located in every chapter involve thinking skills at the **analysis** and **synthesis** levels. For example, the suggestion in Chapter 1 asks students to *originate* a list of things in their environment that might interest a culture in the distant future, and to *imagine* how those objects would look to someone who had never seen them before.

The aesthetic experience for Chapter 2 directs students to select objects from home that they can *defend* as artworks using conditions listed in Chapter 2. The student must *persuade* classmates that the object is art.

Students are introduced to a **four-stage art criticism model** in sequential activities distributed throughout the text, enabling them to develop necessary concepts and skills as they learn to use each stage of criticism.

The first stage of the model involves activities at the **knowledge** and **comprehension** levels as students *identify, describe* and *explain* what is in an artwork.

The second stage of art criticism involves **application** and **analysis skills** as the students *classify* the elements in an artwork and *analyze* the interrelationships between design principles and art elements.

When dealing with the third phase, **interpretation,** students must use synthesis thinking skills as they *generate* possible meanings for the artwork from the information available. Students *speculate* about the meaning and present an argument that supports it.

The **evaluation** stage of art criticism asks for an *appraisal* of the artwork in relation to others of its kind. Information from the three prior categories, art history and personal experiences is considered in evaluation.

As the students read and discuss the text, respond to the study questions and tests, and complete challenges in art production, art history and critical analysis, they are involved in observing, explaining, comparing similarities and differences, predicting and generalizing. **These are skills which contribute to critical thinking and to the primary goal of the text, stimulating creative and critical thinking about art, entertainment, industrial design, graphic design, and the constant display of visual imagery that is used to disseminate information in our culture.**

Research and Writing Skills

Four different report forms are presented in Chapters 16, 17, 18 and 19: 1) an art form significant to a culture; 2) functions of art in a culture; 3) the effects of the social organization on the art of a period; 4) an art style review.

The forms can be used at any time for writing assignments. Additional writing tasks are listed under Extend the Lesson.

Relating Art to Other Subject Areas

Interdisciplinary Connections

The connections in each lesson in the Teacher's Edition provide opportunities for the art teacher to connect the lesson with other subject areas. Art knowledge and skills can contribute to growth across content areas rather than being ends in themselves. Finding connections among subject areas is an integral part of the learning experience. Connections can be found through dates, places, people and events. A primary goal should be to help students to see relationships and make their own connections.

Integration is the process of combining subject matter areas into one unified course, project or unit. For example, the teaching of history, geography, art, music and English language arts can be interrelated in a unit of study on the Renaissance. The art teacher might include objectives dealing with both art history and art production:

1. Students will list major characteristics of Renaissance painting (use of perspective, realistic figures, etc.).
2. Students will name at least three major Renaissance artists.
3. Students will describe changes in Renaissance society which are reflected in art of the era.
4. Students will analyze the perspective techniques used in a Renaissance painting.
5. Students will use one-point perspective in a drawing.

An **integrated program** recognizes the importance of each subject area involved in the study unit. Organizing the curriculum around integrated themes of significant content that students find relevant to their own lives helps students see connections between concepts and information common among different disciplines. The integrated program which includes art encourages students to use other capacities for learning including the nonverbal, spatial, perceptual and production modes.

Multicultural Art Education in Culturally Diverse Schools

The racial and ethnic mix of the American population has changed dramatically in the past decade, with nearly one in every four Americans claiming African, Asian, Hispanic or American Indian ancestry.

Multicultural art education is not just for minority students. It provides a new perspective for everyone to understand that a democratic culture is ever-changing. A multicultural curriculum recognizes the role played by the indigenous peoples of this continent as well as its immigrants.

Multicultural art education can benefit students from all cultural groups equally. The visual arts provide an obvious connection across cultures and with past civilizations. For students more concerned with "becoming an American" than learning about their cultural heritage, the opportunity to access information about their cultural identity may be a source of discomfort. For multicultural education to succeed, teachers must perceive it as dealing with the contributions of all peoples regardless of color or cultural background. A major challenge for the teacher is the identification of art experiences that can create a common ground among students of various cultures.

Multicultural Art Curricula Should Begin with the Students and Community

Utilize the students' knowledge, experiences, skills and values in organizing learning activities. Involve students in examination of their own as well as other cultural groups' values and perceptions concerning art — perhaps in analyzing advertisements in newspapers, magazines and on TV to determine how visual imagery uses gender, race, age and social class to sell products.

Students can gather information about the history of the area, using resources such as galleries, historical societies, local historical sites, libraries and museums that might provide community information. They may interview people in art-related jobs in their community.

A first step in developing multicultural art education experiences is identification of commonalties across different cultures. An example is the use of clay in different cultures to develop pottery. Another is the various historical roles of the mask in the visual arts, theater and literature. Sculpture, metalwork and jewelry can also be explored as commonalties among different cultures. On the other hand, differences do exist and should be recognized. For example, the students might deal with the concept of pattern, and the various ways it has been used in different cultures.

Instructional Strategies for Varied Ability Levels

Students with Special Needs

The Education for All Handicapped Children Act (public law 94–142) and the inclusion of students with special needs into the educational system provides serious challenges for all teachers. Art plays an important role in the development of students in both mainstream and self-contained settings. These young people have the same basic needs as other adolescents, but have individual differences in growth and ability. Their success in developing art skills and behaviors depends greatly upon the teacher's capacity to adapt all art experiences to make them accessible (Henley, 1992).

Approaches currently in practice with special needs students may be described as existing on a continuum including art psychotherapy, art as therapy, art as expression, art as skill development, and studio art. Secondary art education programs should emphasize individual expression and skill development for special needs students.

A common misconception is that students with physical or intellectual challenges cannot achieve more than basic skills. If the teacher provides adaptive tools and materials when needed, proper instruction in processes, patient guidance and encouragement, a structured art education approach is beneficial for most special needs students.

Providing for Special Needs Students

Students with special needs can participate successfully in many of the activities included in *The Visual Experience*. The teacher's best judgment will determine what adaptations for individual needs have to be made.

Students with developmental disabilities have difficulty in understanding abstract concepts and learn at varying paces. They may have difficulty grasping certain techniques, and the teacher must supervise them closely when dangerous tools and equipment are used.
• Provide personally meaningful art activities with different durations and outcomes.
• Provide repeated demonstrations and instructions, emphasizing demonstration rather than excessive talking.
• Encourage students to observe others getting started before they receive individual attention.
• Emphasize projects which are tactile in nature with materials that are solid and have some weight: wood, clay, cardboard boxes, plaster carving.
• Accept emotional responses to artworks shown in class, and integrate them into aesthetic/art historical discussions.

Students with emotional disturbances frequently suffer from behavior problems such as disrupting classes. Others are oversensitive and withdrawn. They may have difficulty following instructions, staying on a task, and frequently display impulse control problems.

• Emphasize structure in all projects assigned, allowing sufficient opportunity for emotional expression.

• Teach proper behavior and demonstrate correct use of tools and equipment, and supervise the student closely.

• Make the student feel wanted in the class; be supportive, praising the good and dealing with the bad quickly and routinely.

• Let the student experience success through projects of short duration that offer immediate results. Work into longer projects.

Students with learning disabilities or attention deficits may have one or more conditions such as perceptual handicap, impulsiveness, or dyslexia and have difficulties following directions and sequences. They are described as easily distracted, inattentive, uncoordinated and poor readers.

• Written materials may have to be read to L. D. students.

• Break lessons into discrete parts; supplement demonstrations with charts and pictures.

• To develop drawing skills, let students complete a picture in any way the individual desires. Have students copy a picture. Move to freehand drawing as the student is ready.

• Emphasize projects which are not dependent upon technical mastery, such as monotype printmaking.

• Let students with L. D. or A. D. D. be part of class discussions about the organization of artworks to help them organize their own.

Henley, David. *Exceptional Children, Exceptional Art.* Worcester, MA: Davis Publications, Inc., 1992.

Artistically Gifted and Talented Students

Who are the artistically gifted and talented? Although it can be argued that it is impossible to provide a true definition of the gifted and talented student, a *general definition subject to change to meet specific situations is offered:* Those students who consistently demonstrate outstanding abilities and unusually high levels of performance with a variety of media in the production of visual artworks are identified as artistically gifted and talented.

Students identified as gifted in art should also demonstrate willingness to acquaint themselves with artists and art history, and demonstrate skill in art criticism. As in all areas of the curriculum, giftedness in art should be recognized, and the school should provide the means for these students to develop their potential.

Identifying the artistically gifted is commonly based on the collective observations of teachers in a school system. If the school system seeks outside funding to support a program for the gifted, tests of scholastic ability and creativity will have to be used to identify gifted students.

Providing for Artistically Gifted Students

The Visual Experience includes art production, history and criticism lessons that can be extended to actively involve both academically and artistically gifted students in enrichment activities. Linkage with art history and art criticism will help gifted students acquire the knowledge necessary for in-depth development of their own skills. Instructional strategies for the gifted might include the following:

1. Completion of the chapter suggestions, many of which require higher order thinking skills, and involve generalizing from observations, or explaining and hypothesizing to acquire relevant information.

2. Introduction of gifted students to the complete criticism model in Chapter 21 early in the semester so they may use it to analyze their own artwork, as well as works by other artists. Again, higher order thinking skills are involved.

3. Development of students' observational skills in art elements in the environment, focusing on similarities and differences, essential features and details.

4. Promotion of sensitivity to the interrelationship between medium, procedure and purpose of the artwork.

Examples of Extended Student Art Experiences

Studio Experience 4.2 asks students to continue their work with linear drawing tools. Extend this investigation of the *interpretative qualities* of line by asking students to analyze how lines developed to interpret weeds might be used to draw a fierce warrior, a graceful dancer, etc.

Student Experience 4.3 involves a contour drawing of the hand. For students adept at contour drawing, give them problems using contour lines in foreshortening, expressive portraits, sports action, etc.

Studio/Aesthetic Experience 4.5 asks students to use line in abstract drawings to communicate an idea or feeling. Extend the activity by assigning students to study the expressive drawings of Paul Klee, Arshile Gorky, William de Kooning, Vincent van Gogh, Ben Shahn, prior to producing expressive drawings of figures or objects.

Studio Experience 6.1 requires students to work with value contrasts to suggest a mood and make objects appear three-dimensional. Have students study how Caravaggio, Gentileschi, Rubens and Rembrandt used light, shadow and atmosphere to create mood and drama in paintings. Students can create a drawing or painting in the style of one of these artists, emphasizing exaggerated value contrasts to suggest movement and dramatic mood.

After reading Chapter 10 on design, ask the gifted student to analyze the composition of a complex painting such as Picasso's *Guernica* or Delacroix's *The Lion Hunt*.

Other enrichment activities for the artistically gifted include independent study contracts with the teacher, the scheduling of a special class in which gifted students may work together, art museum or gallery programs, and college or university classes. Teachers who wish to organize a special program for the gifted may refer to *The Gifted and Talented in Art: A Guide to Program Planning* by Al Hurwitz.

Student Grouping for Art Instruction and Learning

The Visual Experience program involves students with content in art production, art history and art criticism. Students may move more efficiently through the text and with greater learning if they work in cooperative groups.

Numbered Heads Together. (From "The Structural Approach to Cooperative Learning," by Spencer Kagan. Educational Leadership, vol. 47, pp. 12–15.) When discussing study questions or chapter material, or analyzing an artwork, this strategy permits all students to participate. Group the students as follows:

• Organize the students into groups of three or four students (whichever your class divides into best), including a high, two middle and a low achiever in each group.

• Have the students number off within groups so that each student has a number: 1, 2, 3, 4.

• Ask a question. Have students "put their heads together" to make sure that everyone on the team knows the answer.

• Call a number (1, 2, 3, 4) and students with that number can raise their hands to respond.

Art Criticism Interview. This group strategy can be used with one or more of the four stages of art criticism.

• Students form two pairs within their teams of four. Students in each pair take turns being the interviewer and interviewee, asking questions and sharing ideas concerning criticism of the artwork.

• The pairs should write down the information they share for each stage of criticism dealt with.

• The pairs return to their group of four. Using a round-robin approach, each student takes a turn sharing information learned in the interview.

• The group may attempt a consensus of ideas for sharing with the whole class.

Partners. Students may work in pairs to master the content of a chapter, and share their understanding with the other partner pair in their team of four.

Group Investigation. The art history chapters include opportunities for research reports on time periods, cultures and art styles. Group size will depend on the number of projects designated. Suggest that students select a coordinator, determine exactly what they want to find out, and set up subtopics for each member to research. Invite each group to present its findings to the class.

Procedures for Assessing Student Achievement

Self-Evaluation

• Study questions for each chapter help students determine their understanding of text information.

• Every Student Experience includes self-evaluation questions for students to use in analyzing their success in achieving the goals of the project.

Teacher Evaluation

• The study questions provide the teacher with an indication of student understanding of chapter concepts.

• Objective tests are provided for every chapter to provide an indication of text content mastery. The easier questions are placed at the beginning of each test and increase in difficulty. The test questions test student comprehension, application and analysis skills.

• The art production experiences provide an indication of the students' comprehension of content, ability to apply concepts and skills, ability to analyze the interrelationship of elements in a composition, and ability to synthesize the concepts, skills, materials and procedures to create an artwork.

• The sequential art criticism exercises throughout the text provide an indication of students' increasing ability to acquire knowledge about artworks, analyze the elements and their relationships, and synthesize all of the information to defend a hypothesis about the meaning of the artwork.

• Should it be needed, a comprehensive exam can be constructed by using questions from the tests for each chapter.

Safety in the Artroom

• Students can maintain portfolios of their artwork to be used for periodic reviews throughout the program.

The secondary art program utilizes all kinds of specialized equipment, materials and tools. Precautions must be taken to insure that working with art materials does not lead to student illness or injury. **Failure to take necessary precautions may result in litigation if students become ill or are injured in the art room.** While restrictions are necessary, the teacher should be assured that nontoxic materials can usually be substituted for toxic ones with little or no extra cost, and good classroom management will prevent accidents.

Under the art material labeling law passed by Congress in October, 1988, every manufacturer, distributor, retailer and some purchasers (schools) have a legal responsibility to comply with this law. The law amended the Federal Hazardous Substances Act to require art and craft materials manufacturers to evaluate their products for their ability to cause chronic illness and to place labels on those that do.

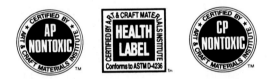

CP, AP, and HL. What do they mean? The Art and Craft Materials Institute, Inc. has sponsored a certification program for art materials, certifying that these products are nontoxic and meet standards of quality and performance.

CP (Certified Product) are nontoxic, even if *ingested*, *inhaled* or *absorbed*, and meet or exceed specific quality standards of material, workmanship, working qualities and color.

AP (Approved Products) are nontoxic, even if *ingested*, *inhaled* or *absorbed*. Some nontoxic products bear the **HL (Health Label)** seal with the wording, "Nontoxic," "No Health Labeling Required." Products requiring cautions bear the HL label with appropriate cautionary and safe use instructions.

Teachers should check with their school administrators to determine if the state board of education has prepared a document concerning art and craft materials that cannot be used in the classroom, and listed products that may be used in all grade levels. If no list is locally available, contact The Art and Craft Materials Institute, Inc., 715 Boylston Street, Boston, MA, 02116 for a list of art products bearing the CP, AP, or HL/Nontoxic Seal.

In addition to determining that only nontoxic media are available in the classroom, the teacher is responsible for instruction in how to use all tools and equipment correctly and safely.

Make sure that the artroom has accident preventing items such as the following:
• Signs on or near all work areas and equipment where injury might occur if students are careless, or should have instruction prior to use of the equipment.
• Protective equipment such as safety glasses, respiratory masks and gloves.
• A first aid kit containing antiseptics, bandages and compresses.
• Adequate ventilation to exhaust fumes from kilns, dust and procedures such as melting wax for batik.
• Safety storage cabinets and safety cans for flammable liquids. You are better off not to keep them in the classroom.
• Self-closing waste cans for saturated rags.
• Soap and water wash-up facilities.
• Lock cabinets for hazardous tools and equipment.
• Rules posted beside all machines.

Precautions the teacher may take:
• Always demonstrate the use of hand and power tools and machines.
• During demonstrations, caution students concerning any potential hazards related to incorrect use of equipment.
• Give safety tests before permitting students to use tools and machines, and keep the tests on file.
• Establish a safety zone around all hazardous equipment.
• Establish a dress code for safety indicating rules about clothing, jewelry and hair in order to prevent accidents.
• Establish a code of behavior conducive to the safety of individuals and their classmates, and enforce it.
• Keep aisles and exits clear.
• Be aware of any special problems among students such as allergy, epilepsy, fainting or handicap.

Some "Do Nots" for the Safety Conscious Art Teacher:
• Do not absent yourself from the art room when pupils are present.
• Do not ignore irresponsible behavior and immature actions in the art room.
• Do not make the use of all tools and machines compulsory.
• Do not permit students to work in the art room without supervision.
• Do not permit pupils that you believe to be accident prone to use power equipment. Check on the eligibility of some mainstreamed students to use power tools.

Teachers should demonstrate constant concern for safety in the art room, and teach by example to help students accept responsibility for accident prevention. For a thorough discussion of health and safety hazards associated with specific media and procedures see *Safety in the Artroom* by Charles Qualley, 1986.

Scope and Sequence

This outline indicates the content focus of the Teacher Edition Lessons that are linked to the Student Edition Experiences. It also indicates the skills and themes that are stressed in the Student Edition. Some aesthetics, studio, history and criticism can be found in every lesson. **The primary focus for each lesson, however, is marked with an *.**

	Chapter 1	2	3	4	
Content Areas by Experience/ Lesson Number — Aesthetics	1.1*	2.1*	3.1	4.1, 4.2, 4.3, 4.4, 4.5	
Studio				4.1*, 4.2*, 4.3*, 4.4*, 4.5*	
History	1.1				
Criticism		2.1	3.1*		
Skills and Themes by Student Book Page — 2-D				28, 31, 32, 39	
3-D					
Visual Elements			20, 21, 22, 23, 24	26–39	
Principles of Design		11, 12			
Critical Thinking	3, 6	10, 11, 12, 13, 14, 15, 16, 17	20, 21, 22, 23, 24, 25	27, 36, 39	
Multicultural Awareness	4, 5, 6	14		29, 30, 33, 34, 36, 37	
Interdisciplinary	6	12, 13, 15, 17		26, 27, 34–5	
Research/Writing			24–5		
Technology					
Careers					
Cooperative Learning	3, 6	14, 17		36	

5	6	7	8	9	10	11
5.1, 5.2, 5.4, 5.5	6.6			9.1	10.4	11.1
5.1*, 5.2*, 5.3*, 5.4*, 5.5*	6.1*, 6.2*, 6.3*, 6.4*, 6.5*, 6.6*	7.1*, 7.2*, 7.3*, 7.4*, 7.5*, 7.6*	8.1*, 8.2*, 8.3*, 8.4*, 8.5*		10.1*, 10.2*, 10.3*	
	6.1, 6.2, 6.3, 6.4, 6.5	7.1, 7.2, 7.3, 7.4, 7.5	8.3, 8.4, 8.5	9.1*	10.1, 10.2, 10.4*	10.3, 11.1
43, 48	60, 63, 64, 65, 66, 72	82, 83, 84, 85, 87	97, 104, 107		121, 126	130–3
50			97, 99		117	130–3
40–55	56–73	74–91	92–107			
	66–7, 68–9			112	116–127	
40, 41, 42, 44–5, 49, 55	60, 72, 73	74, 75, 81, 83, 85, 91	93, 97, 104, 106, 107	111, 112, 114	122–3, 127	132
46, 52–3, 54	59, 70	80, 87, 88	96, 102		118, 124, 125	
40	57, 62–3, 69	75				
	73		104, 107	114	127	132
49	72	85	97			

continued

Scope and Sequence

		Chapter 12	13	14	15	
Content Areas by Experience/ Lesson Number	**Aesthetics**	12.1, 12.2			15.1	
	Studio	12.1*, 12.2*, 12.3*, 12.4*, 12.5*, 12.6*	13.1*, 13.2*, 13.3*, 13.4*, 13.5*, 13.6*			
	History					
	Criticism	12.3, 12.4, 12.5, 12.6	13.1, 13.2, 13.3, 13.4, 13.5, 13.6		15.1*	
Skills and Themes by Student Book Page	**2-D**	134–157	185			
	3-D		158–185			
	Visual Elements				200	
	Principles of Design		160–1			
	Critical Thinking	135, 144, 148, 153, 157	159, 174, 175	197	202–4, 205	
	Multicultural Awareness	137, 140, 142, 145, 146, 151, 152, 154, 156	159, 162, 166, 167, 170–1		202, 203, 204	
	Interdisciplinary	150, 152				
	Research/Writing		175	197	205	
	Technology	134–157	158–185	186–197		
	Careers	134–157	158–185	186–197		
	Cooperative Learning	144	174, 185			

16	17	18	19	20	21	
16.2	17.1	18.1	19.2	20.1	21.1	
16.1*	17.2*, 17.3*	18.2*	19.1*			
16.1, 16.2*	17.1*, 17.2, 17.3	18.1*, 18.2	19.1, 19.2*			
				20.1*	21.1*	
219		273				
	231, 242		276			
		246, 249, 266, 268	277–8, 280, 283, 285, 286–7, 290–3, 294–6, 300–1		312–14, 316–17, 318–19	
		246, 252–3, 266, 269–70, 271, 272–3	283, 285–6,			
206, 215, 223	228, 242	262, 265, 273	279, 293, 302, 304–5	309, 311	312–323	
206–223	260, 263	283				
206–223	224–243	244–273	274–305	309		
223	228	273	302	311	312–323	
210, 214, 218, 219–20	226–7, 228, 230, 234, 235, 237, 238–9, 240, 241–2	244, 245, 248–9, 255–7, 259, 263, 265, 267, 270	279, 288–9, 298–9, 302–3			
				309–311		

Suggested Planning Charts

Purpose of the Charts

The following charts *suggest* how the chapters and related art lessons might be scheduled for a one, or two semester program. Individual teaching situations may require different arrangements, and teachers will use their own judgment to arrange a pace that is most appropriate for their students. The lesson plans which follow these outlines provide full information on how to teach each of the experiences listed.

It was not possible to include all of the student experiences in the one semester plan. Teachers may decide to substitute other lessons that will best meet the needs of their students. Allotted times for some studio experiences or research reports may need to be lengthened, requiring the teacher to eliminate an experience from the schedule. Attention is directed to the suggestions under *Extend the Lesson,* which may work as substitutes, and require less time.

The second chart shows how *The Visual Experience* might be used in a two semester program. All of the student experiences have been included. The content of *The Visual Experience* is sequential, enabling students to build on experiences throughout the program. Some teachers may prefer to introduce the complete criticism model (Chapter 21) earlier in the year to help students understand the gradual unfolding of the model throughout the text, and the student experiences.

Teachers will find that the studio experiences, the various research report forms, and the many suggestions for extending the lessons make it possible to emphasize any one or two of the four content areas should their situation require it. There are plentiful suggestions under *Extend the Lesson* for multicultural and integrated learning experiences. As you become familiar with the material, you should make adjustments to best meet the needs of your program goals and students.

Part I Introduction Chapter	Lesson	1 Semester Days	2 Semesters Days
1 Seeing, Wondering, Enjoying	1.1 Variety in the World of Art	1	1
2 When Is It Art?	2.1 Why Is It Art?	1	2
Part II What To Look For			
3 Describing What You See	3.1 Describing an Artwork	1	2
4 Visual Elements: Line	4.1 Varieties of Line	1	1
	4.2 Expressive Line Drawing	2	2
	4.3 Contour Line	0	1
	4.4 Hatch and Crosshatch	2	2
	4.5 Lines Express Feelings	1	2
5 Visual Elements: **Shape and Form**	5.1 Reversible Drawings	1	1
	5.2 Reversible Patterns	0	3
	5.3 Foreshortening	0	1
	5.4 Distance	2	3
	5.5 Sculpting Without Seeing	1	2
6 Visual Elements: **Value and Color**	6.1 Value Contrasts	3	3
	6.2 Related Colors	0	3
	6.3 Monochromatic Colors	2	3
	6.4 Mixing Bright and Dull Colors	1	2
	6.5 Matching Colors	0	3
	6.6 Warm and Cool Colors	2	4
7 Visual Elements: **Space in Three-Dimensional Art**	7.1 Depth in Collage	2	3
	7.2 Identifying One-Point Perspective	1	1
	7.3 Applying One-Point Perspective	2	3
	7.4 Identifying Two-Point Perspective	1	1
	7.5 Applying Two-Point Perspective	0	2
	7.6 A Landscape with Aerial Perspective	0	3

The Visual Experience

Jack Hobbs & Richard Salome

Davis Publications, Inc.
Worcester, Massachusetts

Paul Cézanne, *Still Life with Apples and Peaches*, (detail), ca. 1905. Oil on canvas, 32″ x 39 ⅝″ (81 x 101 cm). National Gallery of Art, Washington, DC (Gift of Eugene and Agnes Meyer).

Jack Hobbs

Jack Hobbs has been a professor of art at Illinois State University for twenty-four years. He also served as Art Supervisor for nine years at Crystal Lake Public Schools in Illinois. He completed his Ph.D. at the University of Iowa. Dr. Hobbs is also the author of several college texts including *Art in Context.* He has been active as an exhibiting artist and has been featured in such shows as the *National Exhibition of Prints* and *The Art in the Embassies Program* held in Washington, DC.

Richard A. Salome

Richard A. Salome is Professor Emeritus at Illinois State University where he instructed undergraduate and graduate art education courses for twenty-five years. He also taught at the University of Minnesota and at Stanford University where he received his Ed.D. Dr. Salome has also developed and taught art programs for secondary students. He served as coeditor and senior editor of the NAEA's publication *Studies in Art Education* and served on its Commission on Research in Art Education.

Printed in U.S.A.
Library of Congress Catalog Card Number: 93–74640
ISBN: 87192–291–6
10 9 8 7 6 5 4 3 2 1

Acknowledgments

We wish to extend our appreciation to the graduate and undergraduate students at Illinois State University who contributed their time, talent and expertise to this project: to Barbara Caldwell who contributed numerous multicultural suggestions as well as photographs; to Linda Willis-Fisher who contributed to the teacher's manual; and to the members of Dr. Salome's classes who permitted us to use their artwork. We wish to acknowledge those whose counsel we sought while compiling the text: Kent Anderson, David Baker, Laura Chapman, Robert Daugherty, Michael Hagenbuck, Connie Newton and Ronald Silverman.

Managing Editor: Wyatt Wade
Associate Editor: Claire Mowbray Golding
Production Editor: Nancy Burnett
Production: Steve Vogelsang
Copyeditor: Janet Stone
Editorial Assistance: Holly Hanson, Amee Bergin, Denise Nephew

Design: Douglass Scott, WGBH Design
Design Advisor: Karen Durlach
Electronic Page Makeup: Carol Hoyle Ballard
Illustrator: Susan Christy-Pallo

Front Cover: Robert Hudson, *Drawing #26,* 1975. Mixed media on paper, 30 ½" x 25 ½" (77 x 65 cm). From the collection of Jan Perry Mayer, Denver, Colorado.

Back Cover: Lawrence Beck, *Punk Walrus Spirit (Poonk Aiverk Inua),* 1987. Mixed media, 10" x 17" x 16" (25 x 43 x 41 cm). Photograph: Garry Sutto.

Preface

Have you ever wondered about the world of art? Have you ever been stimulated, or turned off, by an artwork? Have you ever liked an artwork, but didn't know why? Did you know that artworks come in all sizes and shapes? Some works are as big as buildings. Some are small enough to fit in the palm of your hand. Some are as new as today. Some are thousands of years old. If you follow the news, you know that some are very expensive. A painting by van Gogh, for example, recently sold for nearly $53,000 a square inch!

Art is much more than just sensational facts and figures, however. If you stop to think about it, art — at least certain kinds of art — is part of your daily life. Consider, for example, the effects of graphic or applied art on your life. Magazine illustrations stimulate you to like everything from clothes to compact discs; movies provide you with fashionable role models that are hard to resist; television lures you to crave everything from pizzas to sunglasses; music video informs you about what is "in" in all kinds of things — music, celebrities, clothes, hairstyles, and much more.

Many people are very critical of commercial imagery. They believe that much of it is so poor in visual quality that it lowers public taste. They disapprove of its content, believing that it sends the wrong message about what is truly important in life. The authors feel that there is both good and bad in commercial imagery. But the point is: *images are powerful.* They can and do influence people's attitudes and desires.

Art images are also powerful, yet they do not try to persuade you to buy products or convince you to be fashionable. They do say things about life, however. Some artworks celebrate modern society, other criticize it; some works arouse our anxieties about life in general, other reassure us. Still other works delight us

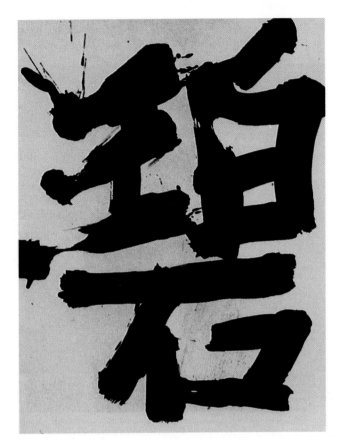

Kazuaki Tanahashi, *Heki,* 1965. Ink on paper, 36″ x 28″ (92 x 71 cm). East-West Center, Honolulu.

by their high standards of originality and visual quality. Did you know that the styles of advertisements and commercials often follow the styles of art?

The pages of this book will introduce you to all kinds of art and ways to look at it, analyze it, judge it, and even make it. After using this book, you will definitely know more about art. But we sincerely hope that you *never* stop wondering about it.

How to use this book . . .

The Visual Experience is made up of many different elements. We hope these elements will help you understand what art is, how it is made, and how it can make your life richer. The next few pages point out important features in the book, and show how to get the most out of your study of the visual world.

The **table of contents** is your map of the entire book. It helps guide you through the textbook. Where was that chapter on color and value? Was Chapter 14 or 17 about careers in art?

The **part titles** are the book's major divisions. Each part is like a small book itself.

Chapters make up each of the parts. Each chapter covers a different aspect of the study of art.

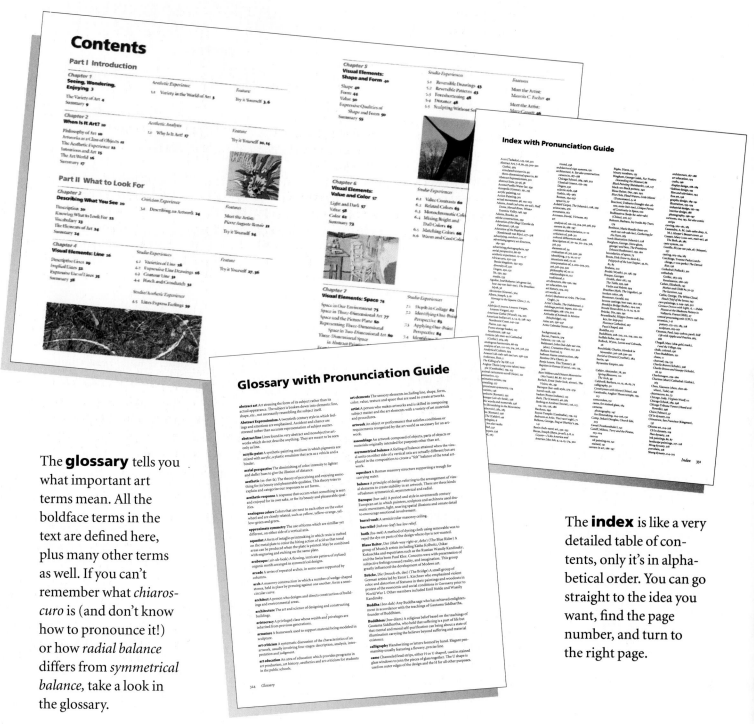

The **glossary** tells you what important art terms mean. All the boldface terms in the text are defined here, plus many other terms as well. If you can't remember what *chiaroscuro* is (and don't know how to pronounce it!) or how *radial balance* differs from *symmetrical balance*, take a look in the glossary.

The **index** is like a very detailed table of contents, only it's in alphabetical order. You can go straight to the idea you want, find the page number, and turn to the right page.

The **captions** are the short bits of text beneath or beside the illustrations in the book. A caption might tell you who created a work of art, when it was created, what it is made of, and who owns it. Pay close attention to the measurements given for artworks — they'll help you imagine whether the art takes up a whole room, or just a sheet of notebook paper. The caption may also mention special things to notice about a work of art or ask you questions about it. Each caption has a number. The number will help you find the images referred to in the text.

The **text** is what we call the words the authors have written in each chapter. The text is like a voice, explaining, defining, asking you questions, helping you think. The voice points out things you might not notice in artwork, in the world around you, in your own thoughts. It might make you laugh, too.

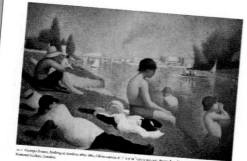

Chapter 10
Design

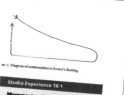

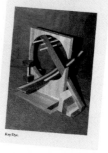

In Chapter 9, you learned that artists compose elements to create a work of art. The final result is called a composition. The artist follows a plan, or **design**, to organize the composition. In the final composition, the different elements should all work together.

There are no exact rules for achieving good composition in works of art. However, there are some principles of design that can be followed. The principles of unity, variety, dominance, rhythm and movement, and balance can be helpful in seeing how the various elements are organized and how they work together.

Unity

Unity in art can be compared with teamwork in sports. A basketball team needs five players. But to be successful, the coach must make the five members play as a unit. Likewise, if an artwork is to be successful, the artist must make the elements work together as a unit. If a work of art does not have unity, it will appear to be a collection of individual parts. If the composition is successful, you are aware of the whole work of art before looking at individual parts. The main purpose of the artist's plan is unity.

Several aspects of design contribute to unity. They can be demonstrated by examining Georges Seurat's painting, *Bathing at Asnières*.

Proximity

One way to make separate objects look unified is to place them close together, or in **proximity**. In Seurat's painting there are groups of people and objects. There are the three boys on the right. A pile of clothing is by the large boy. The man and dog form a group of two. There are groupings of trees and buildings in the distance. Notice how the individual figures and objects along the riverbank are tied together by their proximity. Your eye moves from one to another.

Similarity

A second way to achieve unity is to make things similar in color, texture, shape, or form. Several objects in the painting, even those that are distant from each other, are connected by their similarity in color. Red-orange, for example, appears in the dog, the hat of the boy in the water, and his shorts. Can you identify some other items with red-orange? What other colors are repeated in Seurat's painting?

Several objects in the painting have similar shapes. For example, the dome shape occurs in the hats, the heads of the two hatless bathers, and even in some of the trees. There are many triangle shapes. For example, look at the bent legs of the person sitting on the bank. The arms of the boy holding his hands to his mouth are bent in a triangle. Look for a triangle in the back of the reclining man, and in the shadow behind the large boy's arm. The boat sails are also triangular. Can you identify some other repeated shapes in the painting?

Continuation

When you view an artwork, your eye often follows a certain path. The flow of vision can be caused by a line, edges of shapes, or the arrangement of objects. This is called **continuation**. The edge of the riverbank in Seurat's painting is a good example of a line that directs the flow of vision. The riverbank continues from the lower right corner to the upper left side. Another is the line of the bridge and buildings.

Continuation is often reinforced by the similarity and placement of the forms. For example, your vision tends to move from the large figures in front to the small ones at the far end of the riverbank. Then you look along the buildings, past the boat sail reflected in the water, and back down to the boy with cupped hands. The continuation in *Bathing at Asnières* is shown in figure 10–2.

10–2. Diagram of continuation in Seurat's Bathing.

Studio Experience 10.1

Movement and Unity in Sculpture

Construct a three-dimensional sculpture. Choose wood scraps and organize them to create visual movement and unity throughout the form.

Kay Dye.

10–1. Georges Seurat, Bathing at Asnières, 1883–84. Oil on canvas. National Gallery, London.

108 Chapter 10 Design

Chapter 10 Design 107

The **text** is what we call the words the authors have written in each chapter.

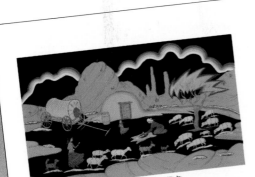

7–27. Andrew Tsinahjinnie, Pastoral Scene. Navajo. Tempera.

Three-Dimensional Space in Abstract Painting

People tend to think that abstract art does not have spatial depth. But this is not true. Painters of abstract works are concerned with more than just the two-dimensional space of the picture plane. For some abstract painters, the suggestion of three-dimensional space is also important.

Look at the depth in Andrew Tsinahjinnie's stylized and semiabstract picture of a Navajo settlement, *Pastoral Scene* (fig. 7–27). Depth is conveyed through variations of size, overlapping, high–low placement, and even some foreshortening.

Hans Hofmann created depth, however, mainly through color variation. Notice how the warm colors tend to come toward the viewer. The cool colors tend to go back.

Foreshortening, overlapping, size variation, and color variation create depth in Irene Rice Pereira's abstract *Oblique Progression* (fig. 7–29). The sense of movement through and around lines and shapes in space is quite visual.

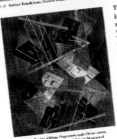

7–29. Irene Rice Pereira, Oblique Progression, 1948. Oil on canvas. Collection of Whitney Museum of American Art, New York.

89 Chapter 7 Space

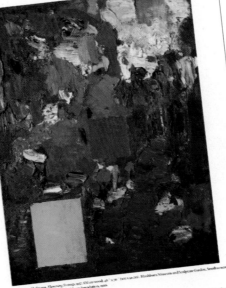

7–28. Hans Hofmann, Flowering Swamp, 1957. Oil on wood. Hirshhorn Museum and Sculpture Garden, Smithsonian Institution. Gift of the Joseph H. Hirshhorn Foundation, 1966.

Chapter 7 Space 90

The **artworks** shown in the book are photographs of actual works of art. They are as large as possible, because they are the most important part of the book, and because we want you to see what the artist wants to show. Most artists create because they have something to say. Their art can speak to you in any language. It might tell you things it doesn't tell anybody else.

How to use this book . . .

You can probably work on the **Experiences** (in the light yellow boxes) without anyone else's help, but they'll mean a lot more to you if you "experience" them with your teacher and the rest of the class. Some ask you to create artwork, others let you experiment with materials or techniques. Some just give guidelines for a report or have you analyze a work of art. Most of them include pictures of artworks done by students your age.

Where's Borobudor, anyway? And were there really more Roman Catholics than Calvinists in Europe in the 1500s? **Maps** will tell you. Each one has an inset globe to help you find out where in the world you are, and an enlarged area to help you see the region being discussed.

If you lose your place in the book, it's easy to find it again. Look in the lower lefthand or righthand corner of almost any page. There you'll find the **folio** (page number) and **running foot** (chapter number and title) for that page.

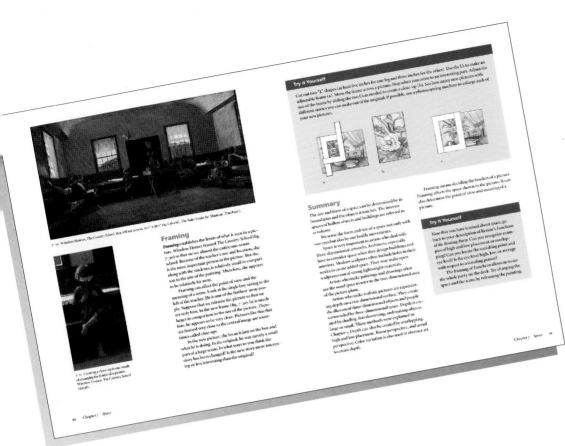

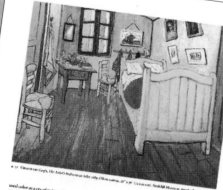

Try it Yourself (in the green boxes) suggests things you can do that will help you understand some of the ideas in the text. You won't be tested on these activities — they're there to get you going, get your mind working on something other than reading. You can "Try it Yourself" without any special materials, besides your mind, a piece of paper and a pencil.

Did you get so involved in the artwork that you forgot the main points of the chapter? Take a look at the **Summary**, which always appears at the end of the chapter. It will help you review the important ideas.

Diagrams and illustrations make complicated ideas clearer. They're used to simplify the information in a work of art, focus your attention on a particular feature, or explain a concept visually.

Which artist created a spoon so large it spans a river in Minnesota? Who found rural Iowa so appealing that he made it the subject of most of his paintings? Find out when you **"Meet the Artist."** These short biographies let you in on what shaped the lives of some of the artists featured in *The Visual Experience.*

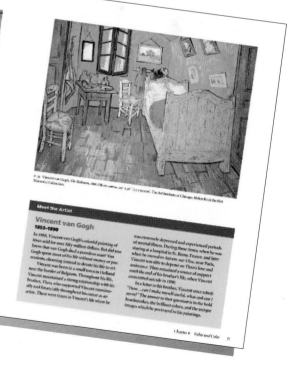

IX

Contents

Part I Introduction

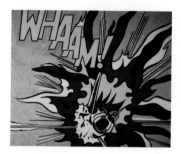

Part II What to Look For

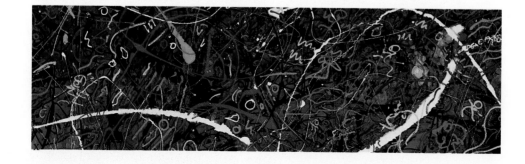

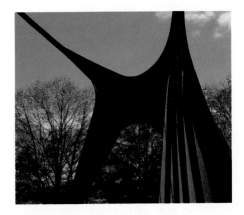

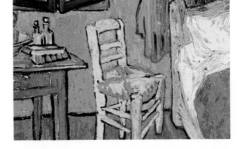

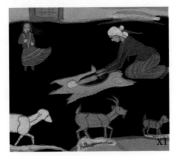

XI

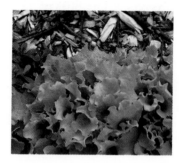

Part III How Is It Organized?

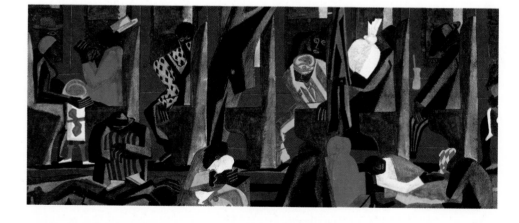

Part IV What Is It Made Of?

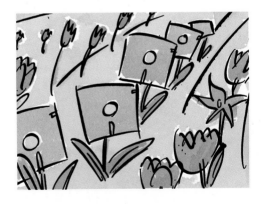

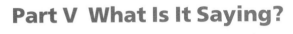

Part V What Is It Saying?

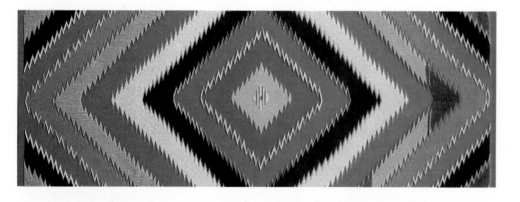

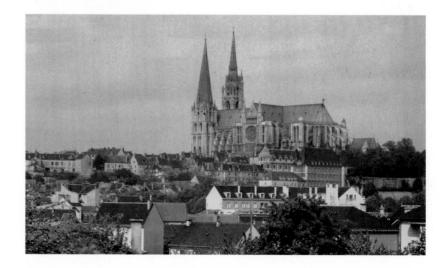

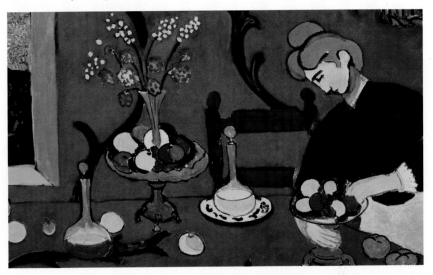

Part VI In the Final Analysis

Part I
Introduction

Robert S. Duncanson, *Blue Hole, Little Miami River* (detail), 1851. Oil on canvas, 29¼″ x 42¼″ (74 x 107 cm). Cincinnati Art Museum, Gift of Norbert Heermann and Arthur Helbig.

Chapter 1
Seeing, Wondering, Enjoying

1 Seeing, Wondering, Enjoying

Student Edition
Pages 3–9

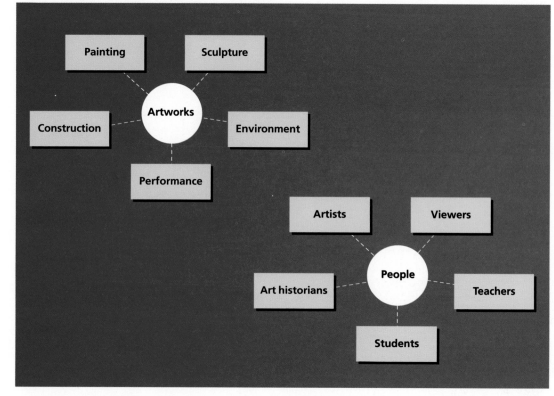

Overview

Chapter Objectives

Students should be able to:

EE 2, 3   **1**   recognize that art today includes an extensive variety of forms produced with many different materials

EE 3, 4   **2**   understand that what we call art is affected by the work of artists, art historians, archaeologists, teachers, viewers, students, museums, and galleries

EE 3   **3**   understand that cultures past and present from all over the world contribute to the expansive variety of today's art

Rationale

In art education, aesthetics is often looked upon as problematic to teach. This book starts with aesthetics in the first chapter by asking students to identify things called art. Students are thus introduced to the fact that art is a broad concept with input from many sources and that it comes in an almost infinite variety of forms. They are also confronted with the issue of *defining* art, a central theme in today's aesthetics.

Essential Chapter Concepts

• Art is a broad concept encompassing artworks and input from artists, art critics, museums and curators, gallery directors, collectors, archaeologists, viewers, teachers, and students.

• Art includes objects from societies all over the world and from throughout history.

• Art takes many different forms, and is created from a wide variety of materials.

Vocabulary

artists   abstract art

contemporary art   viewers

traditional art

Lesson Plan

1.1   Variety in the World of Art

Page **T 4**   Time: 1 period

Handouts

Study Questions
Page **T 6**

Test Questions
Page **T 7**

Chapter Closure

Evaluation

1   *Aesthetic awareness:* Do students demonstrate interest in the variety of art forms produced throughout the world today?

2   *Aesthetic awareness:* Are students aware of the many people whose decisions affect what art is?

3   *Aesthetic awareness:* Are students open to art as a broad concept which takes many different forms?

Notes

Seeing, Wondering, Enjoying

Time: 1 period

Variety in the World of Art

Preparation

Rationale

Art is a broad concept involving not only artworks, artists and museums, but also galleries, viewers, art historians, archaeologists, art critics, viewers of art, teachers, and students. This chapter introduces students to the amazing variety in today's art world.

Discussion Materials

Art Quiz, Student Edition page 4

Enrichment Materials

Slides:
- Chief's Hat, Tlingit, N. America, 1
- Broken Nose Mask, Onandaga, N. America, 3
- Picasso, *Three Musicians*, 6
- Gabo, *Linear Construction*, 16
- Boccioni, *Unique Forms of Continuity*, 23
- Marisol, *Women and Dog*, 45
- Teotihuacán Temple of Quetzalcoatl, Mexico, 69
- Hokusai, *The Wave*, 104

Laser Discs:

Tour National Gallery of Art

Search 3360, Play To 52688

Overhead Transparencies:
- Ernst, *The Eye of Silence*, 1
- Escher, *Circle Limit IV*, 3
- I. M. Pei, *East Building*, 6
- Vasarely, *Edetta*, 7
- *Oni (King) of Ife*, 8
- Adams, *Half Dome*, 12
- Graves, *Diagonals Migrated*, 14
- Oldenburg, *Floor Cake*, 15
- Timilnada, *Siva, King of the Dancers*, 19

Large Reproductions:
- Smith, *Snake Path*, 1
- Catlett, *Sharecropper*, 12
- Yan, *Brushfire with Animals Fleeing*, 16
- Prow ornament, Tlingit war canoe, 17
- Olbinski, *Private Fame*, 13
- Chan, *Wild Thing*, 19

Teach the Lesson

Objectives

Students should be able to:

1 describe ten to twelve different forms that art may take   EE 2, 3

2 list eight to ten different materials that can be used to make artworks   EE 2

3 identify various people and institutions that contribute to our concept of art   EE 3, 4

4 share their interest in a particular artist or art form with their classmates   EE 3

Vocabulary

Artists are people who make artworks. They use many different materials and procedures to create many different kinds of artworks.   R 1

Traditional art has form, style, and subject matter that are familiar as art.

Contemporary art refers to works created in our own day and age.

Abstract art stresses the form of its subject rather than its actual appearance.

Viewers are people like yourself who look at and examine artworks.

Warm Up

1 Ask the class to identify the medium (what it is made of) and subject of as many artworks as they can in two minutes (for example: medium—painting; subject—sunflowers). Make two lists on the chalkboard, one under *medium* and the other under *subject*. Encourage students to name artworks other than paintings.   R 2

2 Have students take the quiz on Student Edition page 4, using a separate piece of paper to indicate whether or not each of the ten photographs is a work of art. Tell them to cover Student Edition page 5, which gives the answers. Compare the media and subjects in their group list with those in the quiz to see if they included as much variety in the group list. The ten artworks in the quiz represent ten different media.

Explore and Develop

1 Discuss any of the ten quiz examples that members of the class did not list as artworks. Were there any surprises in the quiz examples? What media are represented in the quiz examples that were not included in their list?

2 Using Student Edition page 3, determine what *art* involves besides artworks. Identify four groups that are involved in art.

3 Which of the artworks in the examples on page 4 is *traditional*? Which is *abstract*? Which are *contemporary*?

4 Using Student Edition page 4, have students identify three forms generally accepted as art prior to 1900.

5 Use the quiz examples to demonstrate that art has broadened to include many objects because artists work with so many different materials and because of the work of art historians and archaeologists.

6 If you have the transparencies or the slides, show them, and call attention to the variety of forms and media represented. Attend to the different cultures and time periods represented.

7 Give students two minutes to make a second list of art forms and subject matter. Compare with the first list.

Evaluate and Reflect

1 Did students increase their list of forms that art may take and materials that are used to make art?

2 Do students understand why is it so difficult to define art?

3 Can students list the people and institutions that contribute to art?

Reteach

Students may use the study questions to review the chapter information. You may try the cooperative group approach with four students per group if time permits. Give each student in a group a number from 1 to 4. Call a number, 1–4, and direct questions to the groups. Let the four members work together to come up with the answers, but permit only those students from each group with the number you called to answer the question.

Extend the Lesson

Beyond the Basics

Suggest students look at works of art in their texts showing people as the subject. Ask students to find six works of art that remind them of their own culture, their world and their time.

EE 3

Cultural Connections

Direct attention to artworks in the text that are from different cultures. Explain that different cultures may have different ideas about what art is, what is beautiful, and the value of art. Do the students feel it is important to understand how a culture views art when viewing art of that culture? What are the reasons?

EE 1, 3
R 5

Connecting with Other Subjects

Geography The students have learned that museums hold much of the world's art. Make up a list of museums around the world, e. g., the Hermitage, Leningrad; the Louvre, Paris; Rijksmuseum, Amsterdam; and Uffizi Gallery, Florence. Contact the Geography teacher for a world map, and have students locate the major art museums of the world.

Study Questions
Chapter 1–Seeing, Wondering, Enjoying

1 What does art involve besides artworks?

_____

_____

2 Why is the landscape by Duncanson (fig. 1–1) referred to as traditional?

_____

_____

3 What were the three forms generally accepted as art prior to 1900?

_____

_____

4 Define relic.

_____

_____

5 Define archaeologist.

_____

_____

6 Looking at the examples in Chapter 1 (text figures 1–1 through 1–10), name three contemporary artworks.

_____

7 Define abstract art.

_____

_____

8 Art takes a variety of forms. Name two examples presented in this chapter that you were surprised at being considered works of art. Why were you surprised?

_____

_____

9 The idea of what art is has broadened. What are three reasons for this?

_____

_____

Test Questions
Chapter 1–Seeing, Wondering, Enjoying

Circle the correct answers.

1 T F Artworks that are familiar in subject matter, form and style are classified as traditional.

2 T F Objects such as masks, banners, tools, and weapons from ancient cultures can be found in art museums.

3 T F Abstract art tries to capture photographic images.

4 Scientists who explore ancient cities and villages to discover, identify, and catalog relics are called

    a. museumologists.   c. curators.
    b. archaeologists.   d. biologists.

5 Contemporary artworks include those of

    a. today's artists.   c. ancient cave dwellers.
    b. medieval monks.   d. Renaissance patrons.

6 Circle the three forms most commonly accepted as art prior to 1900.

    a. ceramics   d. sculpture
    b. painting   e. architecture
    c. jewelry

7 In addition to artworks, museums, and galleries, the word "art" includes people. Name four groups that are involved in art.

_____

_____

_____

8 A century ago paintings and sculptures were considered works of art. Today what is considered art has broadened to include many objects. Give two reasons why.

_____

_____

Study Answers
Chapter 1
Seeing, Wondering, Enjoying

1 Art galleries and art museums; people, including artists, art historians, viewers, teachers, students.

2 The form (painting) style and subject matter are familiar as art.

3 Painting, sculpture and architecture.

4 Objects from the past that survive or are preserved.

5 Scientists who explore ancient cities and villages to discover, identify, and catalog relics.

6 Answers may include text figures 1–1, 1–2, 1–3, 1–4, 1–6, 1–9, or 1–10.

7 Art that does not resemble things in real life.

8 Answers will vary.

9 Today's artists have added new kinds of art; art historians have added previously undiscovered art from the past; and archaeologists have added objects from other cultures.

Test Answers
Chapter 1
Seeing, Wondering, Enjoying

1 T

2 T

3 F

4 B

5 A

6 B, D, E

7 Artists, art historians, viewers, teachers, and students.

8 Two of three possibilities: Today's artists have added new kinds of art; art historians have added previously undiscovered art from the past; archaeologists have added objects from other cultures.

Teacher Lesson Notes

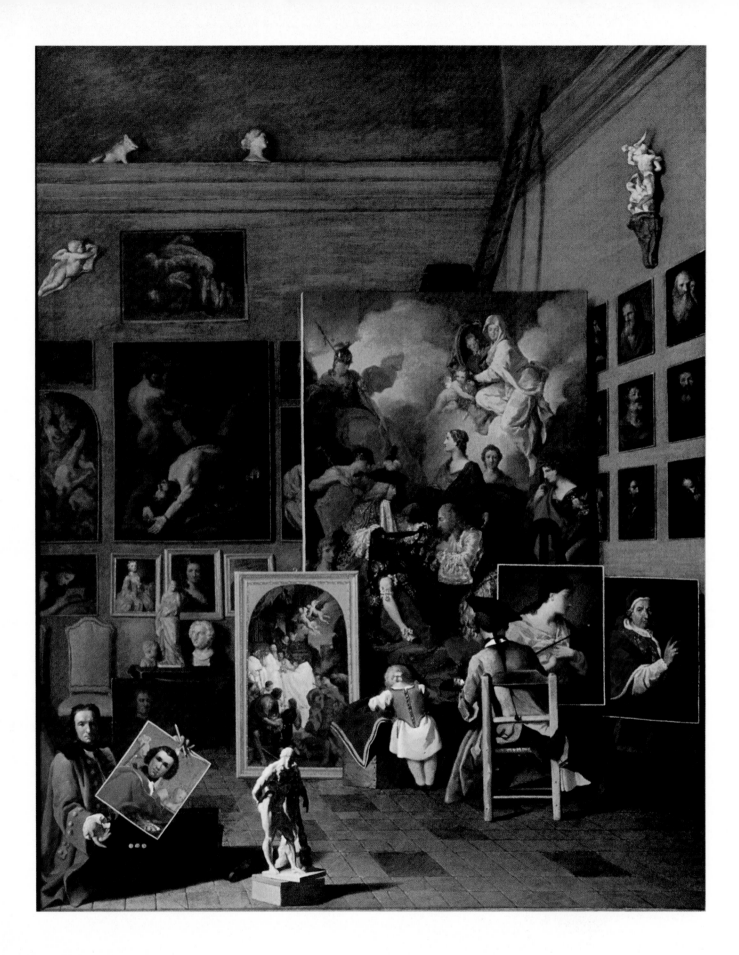

Chapter 1
Seeing, Wondering, Enjoying

What does the word *art* mean to you? Does it remind you of paintings and sculptures—objects that are often called *works of art* or *artworks*? (In a minute or two, you will have a chance to test your knowledge about these kinds of objects.) Does it make you think of an art gallery or art museum where these objects are displayed? Or does art make you think of a classroom full of paints and other supplies where you and your classmates make artworks and talk about them?

If the word *art* made you think about those kinds of objects and places, you were correct. But art is more than that. It is also people. It is **artists** who make art and **viewers** who visit galleries and museums. It is *teachers* who talk about art and *students* like you who study it. All of these people are taking part in *seeing*, *wondering*, and *enjoying*.

Art obviously involves seeing. But effective seeing of art is a special skill. If you know how to see art, art can fill you with wonder—with a sense of curiosity, amazement, or even astonishment. And, finally, art can provide enjoyment, not just because the experience of seeing art is pleasant, but because it is meaningful and worthwhile.

A good place to begin this book is with the artwork itself. What is an artwork? What sets it apart from other objects? You probably already have some ideas about this subject.

1-0 This is a painting about being an artist—a painting about paintings. The artist tells his own life story through works he painted at various times in his career. Early in his life, he painted with his young daughter at his side (can you see her?); an older self may be seen at the bottom left, holding a portrait. What does a painting like this tell you about art's importance? How many different ways to remember a time, a place or a person can you see here? How important is his art to this artist? Pierre Subleyras, *The Artist's Studio*, Fine Arts Academy, Vienna.

The Variety of Art

Test your ability to recognize an artwork by taking the quiz on this page. You will not be graded on this. You can score it yourself for your own information.

Art Quiz

There are ten photographs on this page. Look at each one. Decide whether or not it is a work of art by answering "yes" or "no." The answers for this quiz are given on the next page.

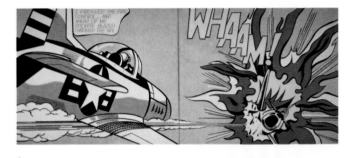

1

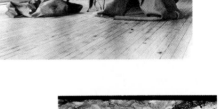

2

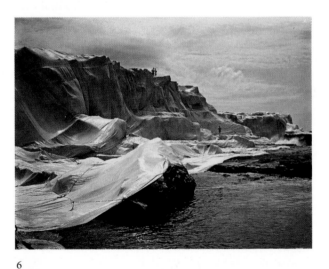

3

4

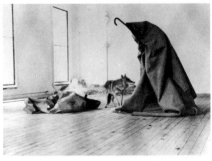

5

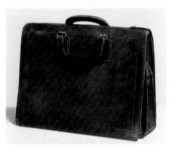

6

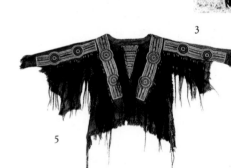

7

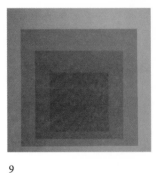

8

9

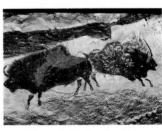

10

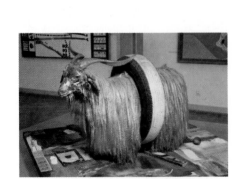

All the answers to the art quiz were "yes." (To score yourself, use the following scale: ten yes's = 100%, nine = 90%, eight = 80%, and so forth.)

In the following list, each of the works is identified by the kind of artwork it is, the name of the artist or the culture in which it was made, and its date.

1. Acrylic painting by Roy Lichtenstein, 1963.

2. Oil painting by Robert S. Duncanson, 1851.

3. Construction by Ron Anderson, 1984.

4. Ceramic sculpture by Marilyn Levine, 1985.

5. Buckskin shirt by an American Indian, early nineteenth century.

6. Environmental piece by Christo, 1969.

7. Performance piece by Joseph Beuys, 1974.

8. Painting on a cave wall by members of the Ice Age culture in western France, around 15,000–10,000 BC.

9. Lithograph by Joseph Albers, 1967.

10. Construction by Robert Rauschenberg, 1959.

Were you surprised that all of the answers were yes? If you answered no to some, you may have thought that artworks were mostly just pictures and statues. You probably did not think that they came in so many different forms and materials.

Probably you and everyone in your class answered yes to artwork 2, the painting of a landscape (fig. 1-1). It is very **traditional**. It has a familiar and recognizable form, style, and subject matter.

Most of you probably answered yes to artwork 8, the cave painting (fig. 1-2), even though this kind of art cannot be seen in a museum. Cave paintings were painted directly onto cave walls. However, reproductions of them are found in many art books. This ancient art was discovered about a century ago and then brought to our attention by art historians.

Probably fewer of you said yes to artwork 5, the Broulé Sioux Indian shirt (fig. 1-3). The shirt is not a painting or a sculpture. Yet objects like this—especially if they are from an old culture or a tribal culture—are found in many museums. In addition to items of clothing, masks, banners, water jugs, spoons, tools, and even weapons from older cultures are often looked upon as art.

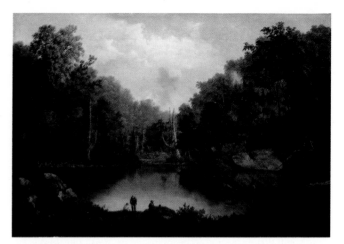

1-1 Robert S. Duncanson, *Blue Hole, Flood Waters, Little Miami River,* 1851. Oil on canvas, 29 ¼″ x 42 ¼″ (74 x 107 cm). Cincinnati Art Museum.

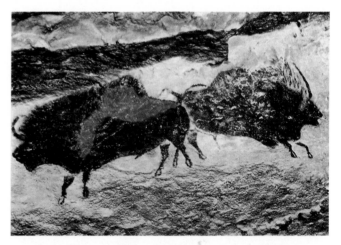

1-2 Painted in a cave near Lascaux, France around 17,000 years ago, these images of animals are the oldest paintings known to us. Although we have theories about this art and the people who made it, it is still a mystery. Chapter 18 will discuss some of those theories and the mystery. Cave painting, Lascaux, ca. 15,000 BC. Dordogne, France.

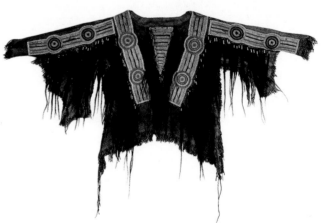

1-3 This is neither a painting nor a sculpture. Is it art? Shirt, Broulé Sioux, early nineteenth century. Buckskin with quillwork, beads and hair locks, 58″ (147 cm) arm spread. Courtesy of The National Museum of the American Indian/Smithsonian Institution.

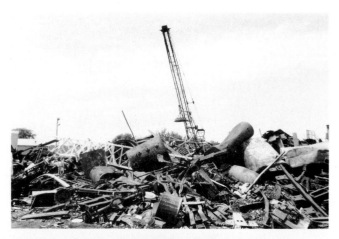

1–4 Might people in 3990 AD be interested in "junk" like this? Do you think they would put any of it in a museum?

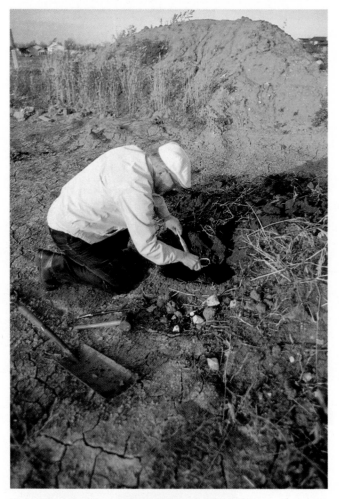

1–5 Archaeologists excavate to discover relics in places called "digs."

One hundred years ago you probably would not have found such objects in an art museum. At that time, people in this country and Europe had a very narrow idea of art. Only paintings, sculptures, and the styles of certain kinds of public buildings, called *architecture*, could be called art. Furthermore, in order to be considered an artwork, a painting, sculpture, or building had to be from the *Western civilization*. It had to be based on styles that developed in Europe and spread to the Americas.

Now the idea of art has become much broader. It can include many different kinds of objects. Objects can come from anywhere in the world, from any type of society, and from any time in history. In fact, almost any object has a good chance of being considered art if it is from a different culture or is very old or both.

Can you imagine some people from a society two thousand years from now digging in the rubble (fig. 1–4) and discovering objects from our present society? Suppose they found your radio. Would it be considered a work of art? Of course the answer depends on the abilities and interests of those future people. They might not recognize the object as a two-thousand-year-old radio. Even if they did, they might not find it interesting enough to save, much less call a work of art.

Try it Yourself

Look around you. Imagine that some of the objects you see will be discovered many years from now. Make a list of the things you think will survive and be valued. Discuss your list with your classmates. Imagine how these objects will look to someone who has never seen them before.

Objects from the past are often called *relics*. Scientists who explore ancient cities and villages to discover, identify, and catalog relics are called *archaeologists* (ark'kee ol'o jist).

Museum directors and art historians are especially interested in many of the things that archaeologists find (fig. 1–5). These people collect and study art of other times and places. They provide us with a great variety of things to see, wonder about, and enjoy.

Let us go back to the test to look at artworks 1, 3, 4, 6, 7, 9, and 10. These works are called **contemporary**

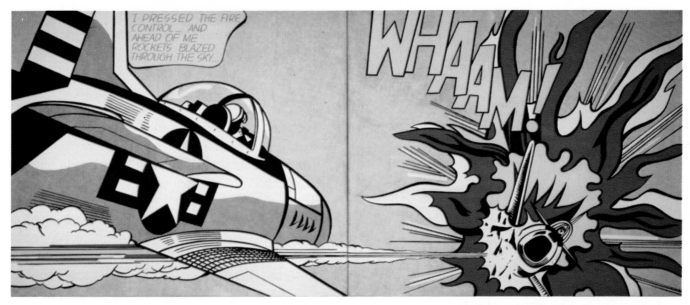

1–7 Is this art or a comic? Roy Lichtenstein, *Whaam!*, 1963. Acrylic on canvas, 68″ x 160″ (173 x 406 cm). Tate Gallery, London/Art Resource, NY.

because they were done in our own day and age. You probably identified artwork 9 (fig. 1–6) as an example of **abstract** art. Abstract art does not resemble things in real life. Artwork 2 (fig. 1–7) is not abstract and is not made from unusual materials. Because of its style, you may have thought it was a comic strip. Were you fooled by artwork 4, the ceramic sculpture (fig. 1–8)? Ceramic (se ram'ik) refers to baked clay, a material that has been used for thousands of years for making pottery. Until quite recently ceramic artists made only useful objects such as plates, bowls, jars, and vases. Now, many artists feel free to make anything out of

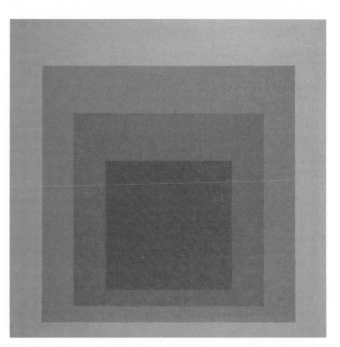

1–6 Josef Albers, *Homage to the Square: Glow,* 1966. Acrylic on fiberboard, 48″ x 48″ (122 x 122 cm). Hirshhorn Museum and Sculpture Garden, Smithsonian Institution, Gift of Joseph H. Hirshhorn, 1972.

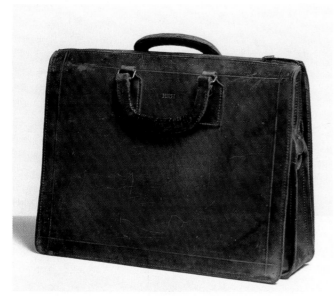

1–8 Marilyn Levine, *H. R. H. Briefcase,* 1985. Clay and mixed media, handbuilt (slab constructed), 16″ x 17 ½″ x 6 ¾″ (41 x 45 x 17 cm). O. K. Harris Works of Art.

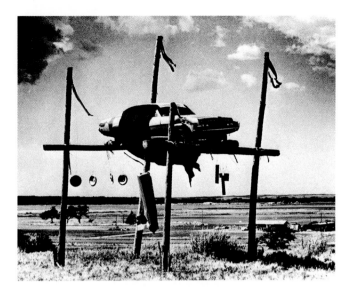

1-9 Ron Anderson, Photograph of *"Killing of a '69 XR–7"* by Bob Albright, from the August 12, 1984, issue of *The Daily Oklahoman.* ©1984, Oklahoma Publishing Company.

clay, even including fake briefcases. Artworks 3, 6, 7, and 10 may have misled you. Possibly you found it difficult to think of used cars on scaffolds (fig. 1–9), wrapped coastlines (fig. 1–10), stuffed goats (fig. 1–11), and performances (fig. 1–12) as art.

Years ago, people had a difficult time accepting even abstract paintings as art. Yet the abstract art by artists of the early twentieth century were paintings on canvas. The art could be framed and hung on a wall. Many of today's artists, however, do not feel limited by such restrictions. They are apt to make art out of almost any material and shape it into almost any form. They may even perform their art, as Joseph Beuys does. Not only that, new technologies have allowed some artists to experiment with neon lights, photography, film, video, and computers, to mention just a few materials. Some of this new art uses techniques that

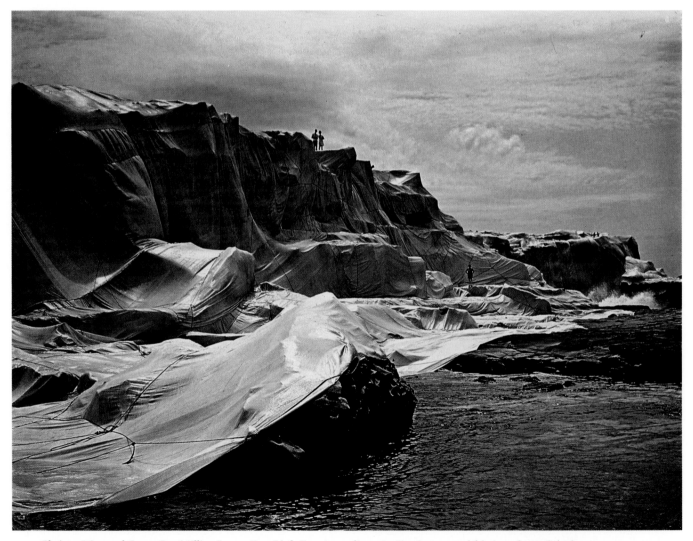

1-10 Christo, *Wrapped Coast, One Million Square Feet, Little Bay, Australia,* 1969. Erosion control fabric and 35 miles of rope. Photograph: Harry Shunk. ©Christo, 1969.

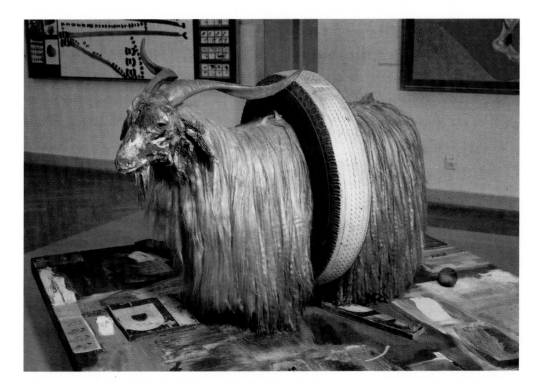

were not available even thirty years ago. Perhaps you are already filled with some wonder at the variety of art. This new freedom and technology, however, has raised some questions about the definition of art. These questions will be explored in the next chapter.

Summary

Usually, the word *art* makes people think of artworks, museums, and galleries. Art, however, is also people: artists, viewers, art historians, archaeologists, teachers, and students.

You have read just one chapter in this book. Yet you have already learned that today's art comes in an endless variety of forms. In the past, art objects included only paintings, sculpture, and public buildings found in Europe and the United States. Today the idea of what art is and can be has broadened. Common everyday objects from the past and from other cultures are now considered art.

One of the purposes of this book is to introduce you to some of the rich variety of today's art—a world of objects, places, and people for you to see, wonder about, and enjoy.

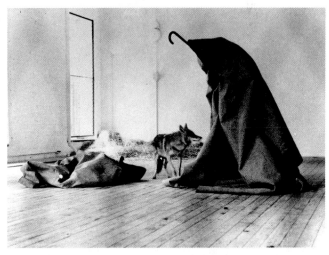

Chapter 2
When Is It Art?

Student Edition
Pages 10–17

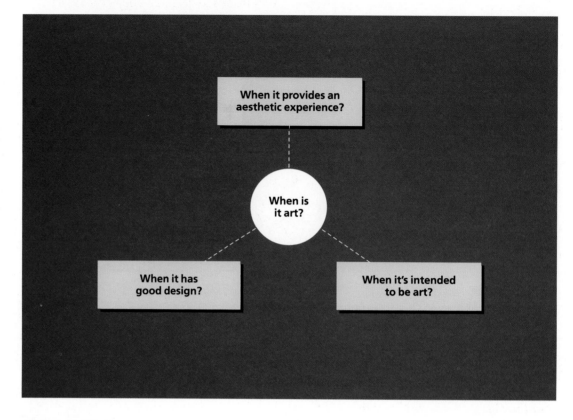

Overview

Chapter Objectives

Students should be able to:

EE 1   **1**   identify some conditions used to determine that an object is art

EE 1, 4

   2   identify objects that are designed well and prompt an aesthetic response, but are not art

EE 3, 4

   3   discuss some differences between artworks and well-designed utilitarian forms

Rationale

This chapter continues the aesthetic investigation started in the first chapter. Students are encouraged to explore and analyze various conditions under which an object can be considered a work of art. Among these are 1) characteristics (such as good design) that artworks have in common, 2) the aesthetic experience, and 3) human intention. Students discover that none of these conditions is completely sufficient as a definition of art. Indeed, many things that we do *not* think of as art can satisfy one or more of these conditions. Finally, the term *art world* is introduced as a useful concept to understand art in our time.

Essential Chapter Concepts

• *Philosophers of art* raise difficult questions about art and try to find answers to those questions, such as, What is art? How can art be evaluated?

• *Conditions* (requirements) for something to be called art may also apply to non-art forms.

• The *art world,* which is made up of artists, dealers, collectors, critics, museum directors and art teachers, also influences decisions about what is art.

• An *aesthetic response* occurs when an artwork, or any object, is seen and enjoyed for its own sake and not for its use.

• *Good design* is a logical and harmonious relationship among all the parts of an artwork.

Vocabulary

artworks	aesthetic response
harmony	conditions
traditional art	good design

Lesson Plan

2.1 Why Is It Art?

Page **T 12** Time: 1 period

Handouts

Some Conditions for an Artwork

Page **T 14**

Study Questions

Page **T 15**

Test Questions

Page **T 16**

Chapter Closure

Evaluation

1 *Criticism:* Can students apply some conditions to defend an object as an artwork? **R 5**

2 *Criticism:* Can students list five conditions that affect their judgment of objects as artwork? **R 5**

3 *Criticism:* Can students explain each of the conditions for an artwork they identified? **R 5**

4 *Aesthetic awareness:* Can students identify objects that may prompt an aesthetic response but that are not artworks? **R 5**

Notes

Why Is It Art?

Time: 1 period

Preparation

Rationale

This lesson asks students to defend an object as an artwork by using conditions introduced in the chapter. The experience, which is primarily aesthetic, encourages students to think about what art is and share their ideas with others.

Aesthetic Analysis Materials

A variety of art and non-art objects (for example: small vases, craft objects, posters, weaving, a painting, salt shaker, sea shell, water pitcher), Some Conditions for an Artwork (Handout)

Enrichment Materials

Slides:
• Basket, Ruanda, Africa, 31
• Mayan Vase, South American, 47
• Mycenaean Funeral Mask, 48

Overhead Transparencies:
• Oldenburg, *Floor Cake*, 15
• *Maria bowl*, 16

Large Reproductions:
• *Plate—Hunting Rams*, 7
• Prow ornament, Tlingit war canoe, 17
• Nubian Wall Painting, 5
• Stout, *Instructions and Provisions*, 2
• Kanaga, *Young Woman*, 18
• Glaser, Saratoga, 24

Teach the Lesson

Objectives

Students should be able to:

1   defend an object as an artwork using the conditions presented in Chapter 2.

EE 1, 4

Laser Discs:

della Porta, Este Cup, c 1550

Search Frame 2427

Sansovino, Doorknocker, c 1550

Search Frame 2423

Tubi, Cherubs Playing with Swan, c 1674

Search Frame 2462

Ernst, Capricorn, 1948/1975

Search Frame 2585

Calder, Untitled, 1976

Search Frame 2607

Calder, segment

Search 47447, Play To 49347

Vocabulary

Conditions are requirements that philosophers and critics of art generally agree an object must fulfill to be an artwork.

Good design refers to a logical and harmonious relationship among all the parts of an object.

Harmony occurs when the elements such as line, shape, color, texture, and space appear to fit well together.

Aesthetic response occurs when an object can be seen and enjoyed for its own sake. It does not have to be used in some way.

Philosophy of art refers to your beliefs about the reasons for, and the nature of, art.

Warm Up

Display two objects, for example, a ceramic vessel and a tea kettle. Divide the class in half. Assign one of the objects to each group. Select a note-taker for each group. Give students five minutes to list reasons for deciding whether the object is or is not an artwork. They may refer to Chapter 2 of the text for ideas. When the five minutes are up, ask the note-taker for each group to present their decision and their reasons supporting the decision.

Explore and Develop

1   Refer to Student Edition pages 10–11 for the concepts of *traditional materials, conditions,* and *good design*. Refer students to the Student Edition glossary for a definition of *harmony*. You may want to quickly list the art elements, each of which is discussed at length in subsequent chapters.

2   Attend to Student Edition pages 12–13 for the concept *aesthetic experience*.

3   See *intentions* on Student Edition page 14 and *expert opinion* on Student Edition page 16.

Begin Studio Experience 2.1

1   Provide the class with the handout Some Conditions for an Artwork, or display the list on the bulletin board. You may wish to add other conditions.

2   Divide the class into small groups. Provide each group with an art or non-art object. Based on time remaining in the period, give the groups 8–10 minutes to decide whether or not the object is an artwork. They must defend their decisions by determining if the object meets enough conditions to be called an artwork.

3   Ask each group to share their analysis with the class. Students should explain which conditions the object did or did not fulfill, and give their final decision. If a group is split on the decision, it might be helpful to include both sides in the discussion, with participation from the rest of the class.

Evaluate and Reflect

1   Can students explain why things they have responded to aesthetically are not art forms?

2   Do students understand how some, but not all, of the conditions for an artwork may apply to non-art objects?

3   Can students list some of the people who are influential in determining if something is a work of art?

Reteach

Pair students and have them role-play an interview. One student plays the art expert and the other plays a person with some object he or she wants to be classified as an artwork. Provide a list of the conditions for an artwork. Suggest they reverse the roles.

The study questions can be used to aid student understanding. You may want to have students compare their answers with those in the Teacher Edition.

Extend the Lesson

Beyond the Basics

Direct students' attention to the wrapped coast by Christo. Much has been written about the artist and his work. Suggest students find information to determine why Christo wrapped things. What was his intention? What was he trying to say? Look for information about other artists who produce similar works of art? Does this kind of information help in understanding the work?   **EE 1, 3, 4**   **R 4**   **R 5**

Cultural Connections

An additional condition for determining if something is art might be *Cultural Relevance*. Consideration might be given to the relationship of the work to the beliefs, values, or habits of a society—Recall the Indian shirt, fig. 2–12. Discuss slides Nos. 31, 47, 48, which represent African Ruandan, Mayan, and Mycenaean cultures.   **EE 3**   **R 4**

Suggest students look through art magazines such as *ARTnews* to find examples of contemporary work by artists from various cultures, preferably work that is non-traditional in materials and form. Using resource books, have students compare the contemporary work with past works from the same culture. Is there evidence of the artist's cultural heritage present in his/her work? If so, explain the relationship between past and present.   **EE 1, 3**   **R4**   **R 5**

Connecting with Other Subjects

Music   Contact the music teacher to determine what conditions are used to decide when sound is music. If possible talk to a dance teacher about the process of organizing movement into dance. In art the elements are organized according to the principles of design. What are the equivalent elements and principles used to create music and dance?   **R 5**

Some Conditions for an Artwork

Use the following conditions to determine whether an object is or is not an artwork.

1   Traditional materials and form. The object is made with materials traditionally associated with art forms, such as paint and canvas, wood, stone, clay, metal, gems, pencils, or pastels.

2   Good design. There is a logical and harmonious relationship among the object's parts.

3   Aesthetic response. The object is looked at for its own sake, or for its beauty and pleasurable qualities.

4   Intentions. Artists, museum and gallery directors, art collectors, and art critics intend the object to be art.

5   Expert Opinion. Artists, art critics, museum and gallery directors, teachers, and art historians judge the object to be a work of art.

Optional conditions:

6   Craftsmanship. The work demonstrates skill and care in the use of materials and procedures.

7   Cultural relevance. The work relates to the beliefs, values, and habits of a society. See, for example, the Indian shirt shown in Chapter 1, fig. 1–3.

8   Innovation. The work introduces something new and original.

Name: _____   Course: _____

Study Questions
Chapter 2–When Is It Art?

1 List/discuss conditions that can be used to determine when an object is art.

_____

_____

2 Even though philosophical questions may have many or no answers, how do they benefit us?

_____

_____

3 What are philosophers of art interested in?

_____

_____

4 Define good design.

_____

_____

5 How does an artwork provide the viewer with an aesthetic experience?

_____

6 Explain the principle of human intention in determining if something is considered art.

_____

7 Who makes the judgments in determining if something is a work of art?

_____

8 Where can *fine art* be found?

_____

9 What is considered *folk art*?

_____

10 What is considered *commercial art*?

_____

_____

Name: _____   Course: _____

Test Questions
Chapter 2–When Is It Art?

1 List four conditions that can help determine whether or not an object is an artwork.

_____

_____

_____

_____

2 An artwork with logical, harmonious relationships among its parts has

_____

_____

3 Watching a sunset, smelling a rose, or touching smooth, silky fabric can provide an

_____

_____

4 An artist who arranges and attaches three soda cans, a pair of sunglasses, and a skateboard onto a board intends for it to be

_____

_____

5 Artists, art critics, and museum directors are people in the art world who make _____ that often determine if something is a work of art.

6 _____ _____ is seen in art galleries, art museums, art magazines, and art books.

7 Art experienced daily in newspapers and on television is called _____ _____.

Study Answers
Chapter 2
When Is it Art?

1 Traditional materials and form, good design, aesthetic response, intentions, expert opinion.

2 By causing us to think in more creative ways.

3 What art is, how it can be evaluated, how people respond to it, how it relates to personal and social values.

4 Logical and harmonious relationships among parts of an artwork.

5 It is seen and enjoyed for its own sake; it does not have to be *used* in any way.

6 Someone, such as the artist or museum director, planned or intended something to be a work of art.

7 People including artists, dealers, collectors, art critics, museum directors, art teachers.

8 In art museums, galleries, art books, art magazines, homes, offices, public buildings.

9 Art produced by people who do not have formal art training.

10 Art that commonly appears in newspapers or on television.

Test Answers
Chapter 2
When Is it Art?

1 philosophy

2 good design

3 aesthetic experience

4 an artwork

5 judgment

6 fine art

7 commercial art

Chapter 2
When Is It Art?

In Chapter 1 we saw many things called art—from a stuffed goat to a ceramic briefcase. Today's art can be almost anything. It can even be a wrapped coast or an Indian shirt. However, the exciting variety of art in our time raises questions: Can anything be art? Are all stuffed goats and Indian shirts art?

These questions are part of the larger question, What is art? Long ago, this question was easy to answer. If something was a painting, a sculpture, or an architectural monument, it was art. But today, this question is difficult to answer. So many objects have been called art. If you saw an Indian shirt or stuffed goat in a store window, would you know whether or not it was art?

Think of some other ordinary things that may or may not be called art. For example, there are millions of photographs in the world. Some of them are art. They are shown in art galleries and discussed in art magazines. But many more are not art. Photographs in newspapers and magazines of events, people in the news, and products are not called art (fig. 2–1). They are called news photos or advertisements. Other photographs, called snapshots, are the kind you take at family gatherings or put in an album. If you saw a photograph in a store window, would you know whether or not it was art?

Perhaps a better question to ask is: *When* is it art? Under what **conditions** do things like used cars, stuffed goats, Indian shirts, and photographs become art? What is needed for something, *anything*, to be called an artwork?

Philosophy of Art

Asking serious, hard questions and then trying to answer them is called *philosophy*. Asking good questions is often more important than finding the answers. Philosophical questions often have many answers. Some cannot be answered at all, but can make people think in more creative ways.

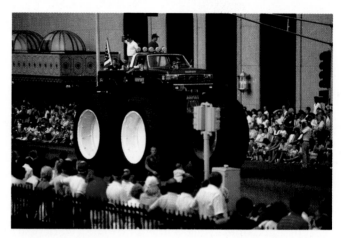

2–1 Photographs like this are printed in newspapers every day. They are not usually thought of as works of art. Other photographs hang in art museums, and are called works of art. What is the difference?

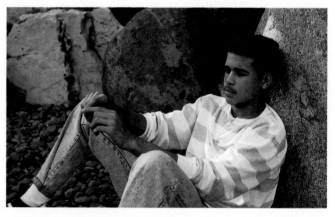

2–2 Photograph: Barbara Caldwell.

Try it Yourself

Are you a philosopher (fig. 2–2)? Do you have questions about astronomy, prehistoric life, geography, animals, or just life in general? List some questions that you wish you knew the answers to. List questions that you think are important about art. What does art mean to you?

The ***philosophy of art*** involves asking and answering all kinds of questions about art. Philosophers of art are interested in discovering more than just what art is. They want to know how art can be evaluated, how people respond to it, and how art relates to personal and social values.

Artworks as a Class of Objects: What Do They Have in Common?

A philosopher may try to answer questions about art by grouping them into a *class* of objects. That way, he or she can begin by asking what all these objects, as a class, have in common. Look back at the objects we saw in Chapter 1. They do not seem to have anything in common. Art can be made out of anything from cars to stuffed animals. Furthermore, some artworks, like Joseph Beuys's performance piece, are not even objects in the usual sense of the word. Clearly, the materials and form of an artwork are not what artworks have in common.

Good design may be an important trait to consider besides material and form. Good design can be defined as a logical and ***harmonious*** relationship among all the parts of an artwork. The opposite of good design is *chaos*.

Good design seems to be very important in evaluating art. Young people who are studying to become artists are taught the *principles of design*. Artists use these principles to make their art better. Knowing these principles can help you to appreciate art more. (The principles of design are covered in Chapter 10.)

Now, look again at some of the objects in Chapter 1. Do they all have good design? Is the relationship among the animals in the cave painting (fig. 2–3) logical and harmonious? The animals are placed haphazardly. Some animals are smaller than others for no reason. Some are not even finished. Furthermore, what is logical or harmonious about the combination of a tire and a stuffed goat (fig. 2–4)? Does a ceramic briefcase (fig. 2–5a) have a better design than a real briefcase (fig. 2–5b)?

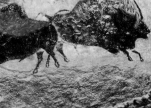

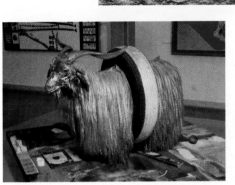

2–3

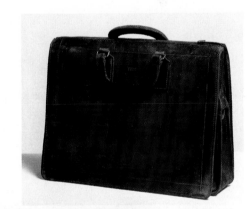

2–4 Is the relationship between the goat and the tire logical and harmonious? Is this construction a work of art? Are the animals in the cave painting arranged haphazardly? Is the painting a work of art?

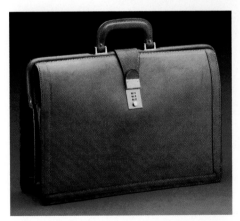

2–5a

2–5b Does a ceramic briefcase have a better design than a leather one? Is the leather briefcase a work of art? 2–5a Marilyn Levine, *H. R. H. Briefcase*, 1985. Clay and mixed media, handbuilt (slab constructed), 16″ x 17 ½″ x 6 ¾″ (41 x 45 x 17 cm). O. K. Harris Works of Art. 2–5b EC 28 Lawyer's Briefcase. Courtesy Hartmann Luggage Co.

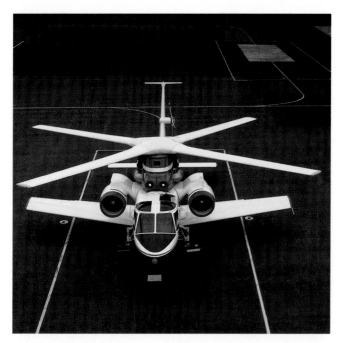

2-6 Can you identify some ways a Sikorsky X Wing plane demonstrates high standards of unity and balance? Is it a work of art? Photo courtesy United Technologies.

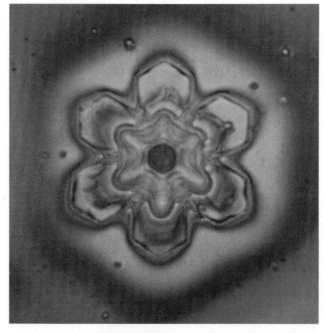

2-7 Compare the design of this snowflake to that of the *Mystic Circle* (fig. 2-8). Is the snowflake a work of art? Photomicrograph of a snowflake. ©Roger J. Cheng.

The example of the fake briefcase points out an important fact. Many things that are not artworks have good design. For example, we admire the design of products from real briefcases to Japanese cameras to military planes (fig. 2-6). In nature, we admire the design of trees, flowers, crystals, rocks, and snowflakes (fig. 2-7). The list seems endless. Many objects that are not art—whether manufactured or natural—have logical and harmonious relationships among their parts.

Even though good design may be important for many works of art, it is not found in all works of art. Many philosophers of art now say that there are probably no special traits that *all* artworks have in common. Therefore, you could not decide if an object was an artwork on the basis of its materials, form, or design.

The Aesthetic Experience

Suppose a philosopher of art has admitted that artworks as a group of objects have nothing in common. He or she may try to decide if an object is art by looking at the experience it gives a person. As a general rule, the purpose of an artwork is to provide viewers with an **aesthetic** (es the´tick) **experience**. Philosophers have struggled to define this concept for centuries. Most tend to agree that an aesthetic experience has to do with enjoying something for its own sake. Artworks are made to be seen and enjoyed for their own sake. They do not have to be useful. Some artworks, like pottery, jewelry, and weaving, are meant to be used *and* to provide aesthetic experiences. The Broulé Sioux Indian shirt, which was made to be worn as well as admired for its beauty, is a good example of this kind of art.

However, looking at an artwork is not the only way to have an aesthetic experience. For example, have you ever enjoyed watching a sunset (fig. 2-9), cheered at a parade, smelled roses, or blown seeds off a dandelion ball? When you do things like this, you are not trying to impress friends, earn money, or get a good grade. Instead, you do them for their own sake. In other words, you do them because you like the colors of an evening sky, the smell of roses, or the sight of dandelion seeds floating lazily on a gentle breeze.

You may also like to watch sports, especially when a team from your high school is involved (fig. 2-10). Suppose you did not care about the score and you watched the game for its own sake. Just by enjoying the movements of the players and the drama of competition (regardless of who won), you would have an aesthetic experience.

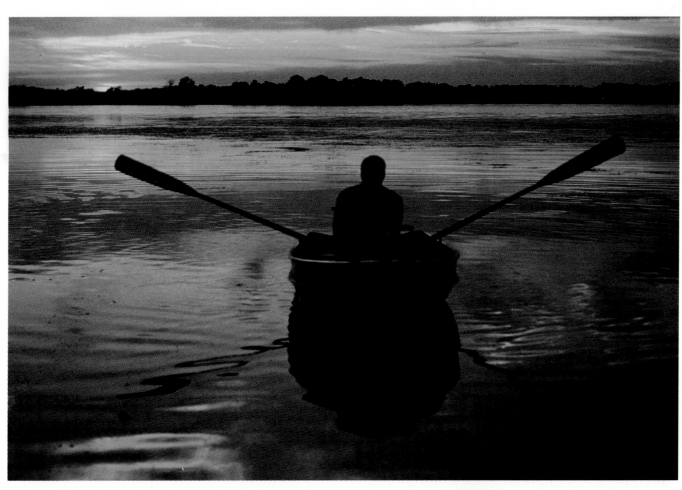

2–9 One of these scenes is quiet and contemplative; the other (fig. 2–10) is noisy and festive. Which do you prefer? Could you have an aesthetic experience in response to either? Skjold Photographs.

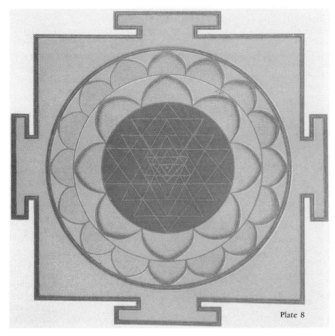

2–8 *Mystic Circle,* Sri Yantra, late eighteenth century, Rajasthan. Burnaby Gallery, British Columbia.

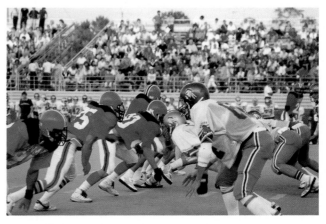

2–10 Which is more important—the drama of the action or the final score?

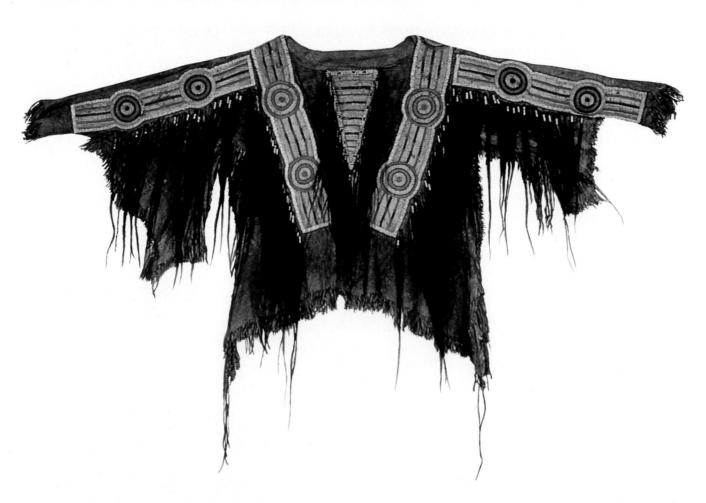

2–12 This Indian shirt was probably determined to be a work of art by the board of directors of a museum. Shirt, Broulé Sioux, early nineteenth century. Buckskin with quillwork, beads and hair locks, 58″ (147 cm) arm spread. Courtesy of The National Museum of the American Indian, Smithsonian Institution.

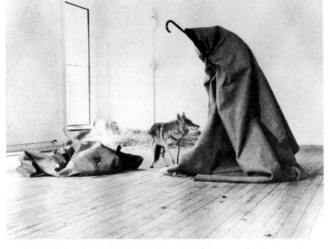

2–11 Would seeing a Beuys performance be an aesthetic experience for you? Why? Joseph Beuys, *Coyote—I Like America and America Likes Me*, 1974. ©1993 ARS, New York/VG Bild-Kunst, Bonn.

Try it Yourself

Think of some events you have been to, such as fairs, parades, festivals, and concerts. Also recall some things you have done with family or friends: celebrations, picnics, hiking, nature walks. Have you taken any trips recently? Have you been to the beach?

Which memories are the most vivid? Did you enjoy any of these events purely for their own sake? Make a list of the events that gave you an aesthetic experience. Describe one or two of them to a friend or classmate.

As you have discovered, many things besides looking at art can provide aesthetic experiences. Therefore, you will not be able to tell if something is an artwork just because it gives you an aesthetic experience.

On the other hand, would it be possible to tell if something is *not* an artwork because it does not give you an aesthetic experience? No. In reality, artworks do not always succeed in providing aesthetic experiences for everyone. Sometimes it is the *attitude* or *mood* of the person who sees the artwork that matters, not the quality of the artwork. We all have our personal feelings. Suppose you saw Joseph Beuys's performance piece, *I Like America and America Likes Me* (fig. 2–11), and were bored by it. This would not mean that others would not enjoy it. Indeed, on a different day, you might enjoy it yourself. The point is this: you cannot rely on your personal likes and dislikes on any given day to judge whether something is a work of art.

Intentions and Art

Today, many philosophers of art say that *human intention* is a necessary factor in determining whether or not something is art. People who make paintings, for example, "intend" them to be art. When Robert Rauschenberg attached an old tire to a stuffed goat, mounted them to a canvas, and smeared them with paint, he *intended* the whole thing to be a work of art. The museum director *intended* the Broulé Sioux Indian shirt (fig. 2–12) to be a work of art when he or she put it in the Museum of the American Indian even though the Broulé Sioux themselves may not have intended it to be art. If you saw a piece of driftwood on the beach (fig. 2–13), you probably would not call it art. But if you saw it mounted on a wall in someone's home, you probably would. The person who mounted the driftwood intended it to be seen as art.

The principle of human intention seems to be the answer to our question, When is it art? Perhaps this principle explains all of the examples presented in Chapter 1.

But does it answer all the questions? *Who* is to do the intending: just artists and museum directors? Can anyone—you, for example—intend something, *anything*, to be art? Suppose you wrapped your house with bed sheets. Would other people consider it a work of art—or a mess (fig. 2–14)? Would your neighbors appreciate it? Would your art teacher praise you for it? Suppose, like Joseph Beuys, you wrapped yourself in felt and walked around a room with a coyote. Would anyone take you seriously?

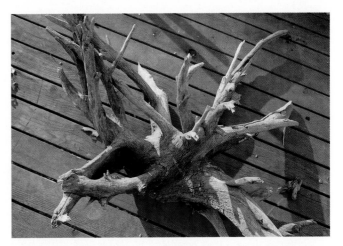

2–13 Under what conditions would this piece of driftwood be a work of art? Photograph: Barbara Caldwell.

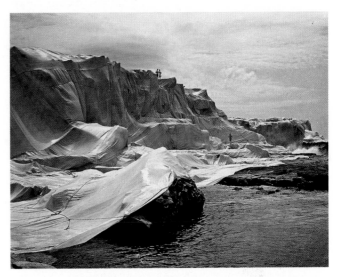

2–14 What do you think your dad would say if you wrapped your garage in "plastic-wrap"? Would he consider it a work of art? Christo, *Wrapped Coast, One Million Square Feet, Little Bay, Australia,* 1969. Erosion control fabric and 35 miles of rope. Photograph: Harry Shunk. ©Christo, 1969.

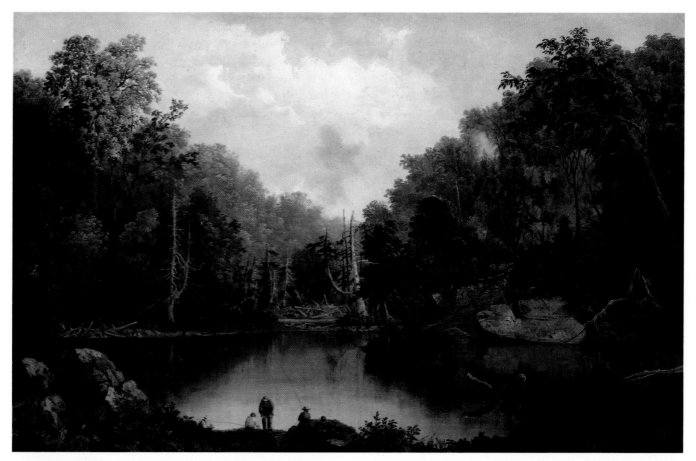

2–15 Objects like these, whether old or modern, are easily recognizable as art. Why are they so easy to recognize? These examples, along with those that are less traditional, including the Broulé Sioux shirt, the stuffed goat, the wrapped coast, and even the Beuys performance, belong to a world of things called *fine art*. Can all of these be found in museums or galleries? Where can we find pictures of these things? Robert S. Duncanson, *Blue Hole, Flood Waters, Little Miami River*, 1851. Oil on canvas, 29 ¼″ x 42 ¼″ (74 x 107 cm). Cincinnati Art Museum.

The Art World

Some art is ancient like the cave paintings. Some is traditional like Duncanson's (fig. 2–15). Some is modern like Albers' (fig. 2–16). Regardless of their styles, we have no trouble telling that these objects are art. It is other kinds of art that often raise questions. Useful objects from old or tribal cultures, like the Broulé Sioux Indian shirt, are not always easy to recognize as art. Experimental forms, like the ceramic briefcase, used car, wrapped coast, stuffed goat, and performance piece also raise questions.

In the final analysis, *there is no perfect method for determining when things like these are art.* Human intention is necessary. Good design and the aesthetic experience are important. But ultimately, determining when something is art seems to be a matter of judgment.

Who makes the judgments in these matters? It is people like artists, dealers, collectors, art critics, museum directors, and art teachers. All of them make up what is known as the *art world*—just as players, coaches, managers, umpires, and team owners make up the *sports world*. These people are involved not only in the production of art, but in selling it, collecting it, displaying it, writing about it, and teaching it. Their training, experience, and commitment gives them the authority to make judgments.

Do these people ever make bad judgments? Yes. Some objects should have stayed in history museums. Some examples of experimental art should have been forgotten. But there are also many traditional paintings and sculptures that were misjudged by experts in the past. Most of those works now are out of sight, gathering dust in museum basements.

The art that you see in art galleries and art museums is called *fine art*. It is fine art that is reproduced and written about in newspapers, art magazines, and art books like this one. Sometimes the term fine art is used to contrast it with *folk art* and *commercial art*.

Folk art is art produced by amateur or untrained artists. Commercial art is the kind of art that you see everyday in the newspapers or on television.

Summary

Philosophers of art ask difficult questions about art to try to define what art is. It is almost impossible to define art by looking for traits that all artworks have in common. Most works possess good design, but not all do. Furthermore, many things besides art have good design. Artworks should provide an aesthetic experience. They are meant to be appreciated for their own sake. But many things besides art can be experienced this way. Therefore, neither good design nor the aesthetic experience is a complete test of what makes something a work of art.

One thing that all art has in common is human intention. Traditional paintings, sculptures, ancient objects, experimental forms of art, and even pieces of mounted driftwood can be called artworks if someone intended them to be art. The art world decides what can be called *fine art*, the kind we see in art galleries and museums.

Aesthetic Analysis 2.1

Why Is It Art?

Select an object from home that you can defend as an artwork. Is it old or new? Why is it art? How does it meet the conditions listed in this chapter? Bring your object to school. Defend your object as art. What reasons would you give? Can you *prove* that something, anything, is art?

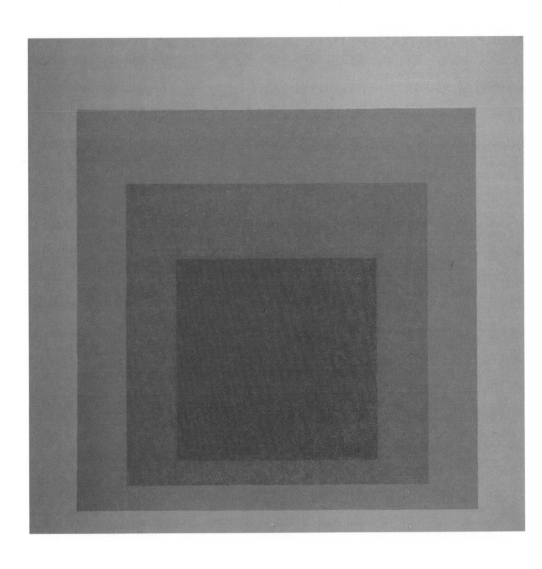

2–16 Josef Albers, *Homage to the Square: Glow*, 1966. Acrylic on fiberboard, 48″ x 48″ (122 x 122 cm). Hirshhorn Museum and Sculpture Garden, Smithsonian Institution, Gift of Joseph H. Hirshhorn, 1972.

Part II
What to Look For

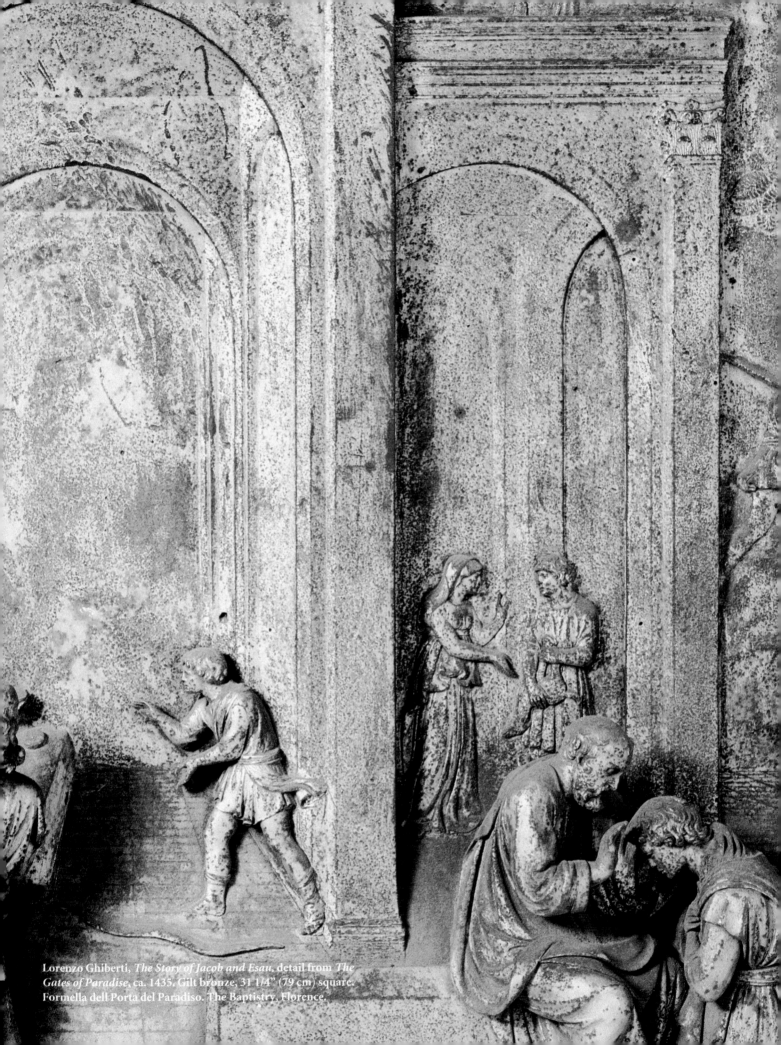

Lorenzo Ghiberti, *The Story of Jacob and Esau*, detail from *The Gates of Paradise*, ca. 1435. Gilt bronze, 31 1/4" (79 cm) square. Formella dell Porta del Paradiso. The Baptistry, Florence.

Chapter 3
Describing What You See

Student Edition
Pages 20–25

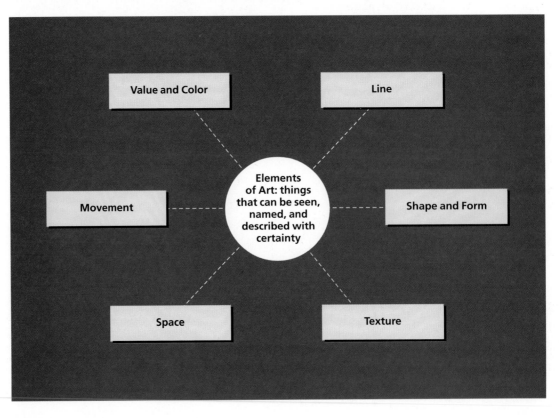

Overview

Chapter Objectives

Students should be able to:

EE 1, 3 **1** understand that describing artworks involves listing facts about the works and not opinions

EE 3 **2** learn how the process of describing will help them understand artworks

EE 1, 2, 3 **3** describe an artwork, noting facts about subject matter, art elements, and medium

Rationale

One way to understand and learn more about an artwork is to describe it. Unlike everyday pictures such as news photos, advertisements, and billboards, artworks require time and viewer involvement to be appreciated. Description is the first part of a four-stage criticism model, which also includes analysis, interpretation, and judgment.

Essential Chapter Concepts

• Describing an artwork involves listing the things that individuals can see in the work.

• Description should list only facts, not opinions.

• A good description provides a basis for the stages of analysis, interpretation, and judgment in art criticism.

Vocabulary

describe	fact
opinion	subject matter
shading	art elements

Meet the Artist

Pierre Auguste Renoir   Page 22

Lesson Plan

3.1   Describing an Artwork

Page **T 22**   Time: 1 period

Handouts

Guidelines for Describing an Artwork

Page **T 24**

Study Questions

Page **T 25**

Chapter Closure

Evaluation

1   *Criticism:* Can students differentiate between fact and opinion in the description process?   R 6

2   *Criticism:* Can students explain the two things required for a good description of an artwork?

3   *Aesthetic awareness:* Can students explain how describing an artwork helps them understand the work?

Notes

Describing an Artwork

Time: 1 period

Preparation

Rationale

In this chapter students learn what to look for when describing artworks. By describing artworks, they increase their understanding and enjoyment of artworks.

Criticism Materials

Study Questions, Guidelines for Describing an Artwork (Handout), writing paper, pencils

Enrichment Materials

Slides:
• Wood, *American Gothic,* 2

Overhead Transparencies:
• Wood, *American Gothic,* 17
• Renoir, *Luncheon of the Boating Party,* 18

Large Reproductions:
• Biggers, *Shotguns,* 3
• Matisse, *The Casbah Gate,* 8
• Carr, *Scorned as Timber,* 15
• Yan, *Brushfire with Animals Fleeing,* 16

Teach the Lesson

Objectives

Students should be able to:

1 describe Grant Wood's *American Gothic,* including things that can be seen and named   EE 3, 4

Vocabulary

A *description* of an artwork is a careful listing of those things that can be seen. It includes facts, not opinions.

Facts are real. They are things that really exist.

Opinions are personal beliefs and impressions which may be true for one individual but not for others.

Laser Discs:

Renoir, Girl with Watering Can, 1876
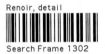
Search Frame 1300

Renoir, detail

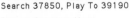
Search Frame 1302

Renoir, segment

Search 37850, Play To 39190

Renoir, Girl with Hoop, 1885

Search Frame 1320

Homer, Breezing Up, 1876

Search Frame 2032

Homer, detail
Search Frame 2034

Subject matter refers to things represented in the artwork, such as figures and objects, as well as details about them such as size, distance, and color.

Shading refers to variations in the dark and light of colors.

Art elements include line, shape, color, value, form, texture, space, and movement.

Warm Up

1 Display a slide or transparency of *Luncheon of the Boating Party.* Have students take two minutes to describe everything they see in the painting. Suggest that they look for other things besides people and objects. Allow students to share some of the things they described in the painting and list them on the board.

2 Compare their description with the one on page 20 in the Student Edition.

Explore and Develop

1 Be sure students can distinguish   R 6
between *facts* and *opinions.* Ask them to give some examples, or provide examples of both and ask students to differentiate.

2 Ask students to identify different kinds of *subject matter* in the Renoir, such as people and objects. Have students include details about them, such as size, near and far, and action.

3 Encourage them to look for things other than subject matter—the *art elements.* These elements will be developed in later chapters. However, students may be able to describe examples of form, line, color, texture, shades of color (value), and space in the Renoir.

Begin Studio Experience 3.1

1 Display *American Gothic* or have students look at Student Edition page 25.

W 2 **2** Distribute Guidelines for Describing an Artwork provided on Teacher Edition page T 24. Explain that the guidelines are very general and can be used to describe any artwork, even those that do not have recognizable subject matter. Students are to complete a factual description of Grant Wood's painting, *using those items in the guideline that apply easily to this painting.* They may think of things to add that are not in the guidelines.

W 2 **3** You may let students work on the description in small groups or individually. Point out that *label information* can be obtained from the reproduction on Student Edition page 25.

4 Share the descriptions. Some students may have seen this painting before. Did they see some new things in it?

Evaluate and Reflect

1 Did students deal with facts rather than opinions in their descriptions?

2 Are they including things in their descriptions that the majority of the group agree with?

3 Are they beginning to describe things in artworks that will contribute to their understanding of the work?

4 Are they including information in their descriptions that will provide a basis for the other stages of art criticism?

Reteach

W 2 Organize students into groups of four.
R 6 Display an artwork. Working individually, students should write a description of the artwork in five minutes. Give each group another five minutes to consolidate their descriptions. Stress that they should include facts rather than opinions.

Extend the Lesson
Beyond the Basics

Encourage students to find as much information about Grant Wood and his work as possible. Suggest they find at least three other paintings by the artist. Have them write descriptions of each. Suggest that it might be helpful to set up a chart or matrix showing all the details listed in their descriptions. What items or elements are found in all the artworks? What is unique or different in each of the works?

EE 1, 3

R 5
W 1

Cultural Connections

Divide the class into groups, and have each group look through the student text for an artwork from another culture to describe. Have them share their findings with the class.

EE 1, 3

W 2

American Gothic shows two people at a particular time and in a particular place. Direct students' attention to the definition of Gothic found in the back of their text. The Gothic style originated in a different time and place. Have students use art history resources to find examples of Gothic art or architecture. Have them write a description of the work and compare it to their descriptions of Wood's work. Is there a relationship between *American Gothic* and the European work created hundreds of years ago?

EE 1

R 3, 5
W 3

Connecting with Other Subjects

American History Grant Wood painted *American Gothic* in 1930. Suggest students search through a book of American history and make a list of events occurring during the same year. Who was president? What was happening in America? What was happening in the world? What was life like at that time? How might Wood's work have been influenced by these events and conditions?

EE 3

R 3, 5

3.1 **Handout**

Describing What You See

Guidelines for Describing an Artwork

When you describe an artwork, list only things that you can see. Report only facts. Don't worry about what the work means, or whether you like it or not. The guidelines below can be used to describe works with or without recognizable shapes. You may not use all of the items listed in the guidelines for a particular work.

1   Label information: Artist, title, and date of work. Medium (what is it made of). Processes used to make it. Size of artwork. Country where it was created.

2   Subject Matter:
a. Figures, animals, objects (trees, sun, clouds, grass, birds, machines, buildings, etc.). If there are no recognizable objects in the artwork, describe art elements: line, color, value, shape, texture, space, movement.

b. Describe what figures, animals and other things that move are doing. How many are there?

c. What is large/small, near/far, in front/behind?

3   Art Elements:
a. lines. Are they straight, curved, swirling, jagged, diagonal, vertical, horizontal, continuous, broken, heavy, thin, dark, light? Do they occur at edges where color, value or texture changes suddenly? Are there lines that direct your attention from one place to another?

b. colors. Are they warm, cool, bright, dull, opaque, transparent? Are they like colors you see in the real world, or different from real world colors? Is there a dominant color? Are there related colors?

c. values. Are the colors dark? light? both? Are there strong contrasts of dark/light? Are there soft contrasts of dark/light?

d. shapes. Are shapes realistic, unrealistic, or not representational? Do shapes appear flat or do they appear to have depth (roundness)? Are they geometric (squares, triangles, circles)? Are they organic (curved and irregular edges)?

e. textures. Are they visible in the artwork? Where? Don't confuse texture with patterns like checkerboard, stripes, and polka dot.

f. space. Does space appear deep? If so, is it due to: overlap; placement of small objects high in the picture and large ones low; making objects smaller as they get farther away; linear perspective (converging lines); colors that seem to advance and recede? Does space appear shallow? Why?

g. movement. If movement is suggested in the work, is it due to: alternating shapes; figures and other life forms doing something; repetition of one thing after another; elements that progress from large to small, small to large, dark to light?

Study Questions
Chapter 3–Describing What You See

1 What are the two parts of a description of an artwork?

_____

_____

_____

2 What is the difference between *fact* and *opinion* in describing an artwork? While looking at an artwork in your text, give an example of a fact and an opinion.

_____

_____

_____

3 Name two things that help describe a work of art.

_____

_____

_____

4 What is the easiest thing to talk about in a picture?

_____

_____

_____

5 List the art elements mentioned in this chapter.

_____

_____

_____

Study Answers
Chapter 3
Describing What You See

1 a) Looking, and,
b) telling or writing.

2 Facts include things people can see in the artwork, such as objects, people, shapes, colors; opinions are based on thoughts about the artwork. (Answers will vary for the second part.)

3 Knowing what to look for and using the right words to describe what you see.

4 Subject matter (people and objects).

5 Line, shape, form, space, color, texture, value, movement.

Teacher Lesson Notes

Describing What You See

T
27

Chapter 3
Describing What You See

One way to open ourselves to art is by taking the time to *look* at an artwork. Our world is full of images, such as advertisements, illustrations, billboards, and photographs. We get into the habit of glancing and not really looking. This is unfortunate, especially when good pictures are involved.

To make sure that we are looking, and not just glancing, at a picture, we should try once in awhile to *describe* it.

Description

According to the dictionary, **describe** means "to tell or write about, to give a detailed account of." If you were to describe a work of art, first you would *look* at it closely. Then you would *tell* or *write* about what you saw. This kind of telling or writing is called *description*.

When writing a description you must stick to the **facts**. Include things like the objects, people, shapes, and colors that you and others can see. Do not include **opinions**, such as: "The man is wearing a *stupid* hat,"

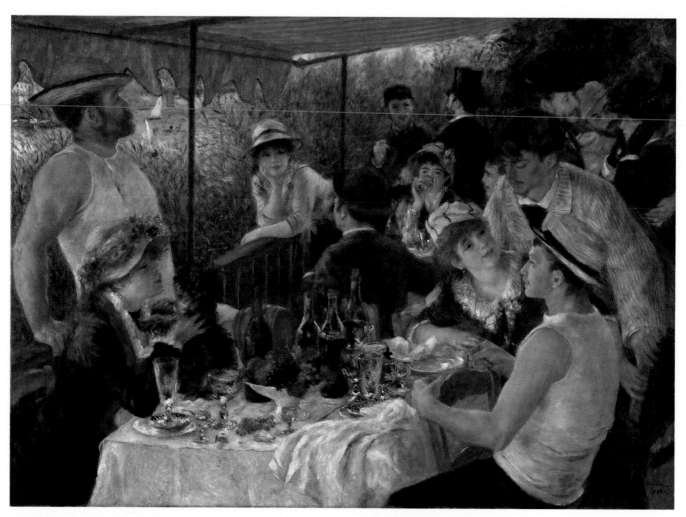

3–1 There are many things in this painting: people, objects, colors, and textures, even a puppy. Pierre Auguste Renoir, *Luncheon of the Boating Party*, 1881. Oil on canvas, 51″ x 68″ (130 x 173 cm). © The Phillips Collection, Washington, DC.

"That is a *pretty* color," or "This picture is about people having *a lot of fun*." These statements may be true for you but not for others. They are opinions, not facts.

How well can you describe a painting? Look carefully at and write about *Luncheon of the Boating Party* (fig. 3–1) by Renoir. To make the job somewhat more challenging, give yourself only fifteen minutes to write your description.

Do not continue reading until you have finished the description.

Did you feel that you needed more time to describe the picture? If you said yes, you are right.

Your description probably explained that there are a number of young men and women. They are gathered on what appears to be a deck. Some are sitting and some are standing. Several seem to be talking to one another. You probably also noted the table, the food and drink on the table, the young woman at the table holding a little dog, the railing behind the table, the people leaning on the railing, the awning overhead, and the leafy foliage beyond the deck. Did you have time to write about the people's clothes, their hats, or what they are doing? Did you notice the sailboats in the distance?

If you mentioned all those things, you did quite well, but that is only a *beginning*. A good description would have pointed out several more things about the people. For example, some are nearer to the viewer than others. Those on the left seem spread apart, while those on the right seem crowded together. Some are looking to the right, some to the left, some toward the viewer, and some away from the viewer.

Both the table and the railing are on the left side of the picture, but both lead your eye to the right. A good description would have called attention to this.

Meet the Artist

Pierre Auguste Renoir
1841–1919

Warm red and yellow colors fill a tranquil scene of carefree vacationers gathered at an afternoon meal. Bold brush strokes define faces and figures leisurely mingling in the summer sun. Pierre Auguste Renoir developed a reputation for his talent in portraying light-hearted scenes like *Luncheon of the Boating Party*.

As one of five children of a tailor from Limoges, France, Renoir had to save every penny he earned as a porcelain painter to attend the School of Fine Arts in 1862. There he became friends with other aspiring artists, including Claude Monet and Alfred Sisley. These men influenced each other's painting. They began to work in similar styles, using brilliantly colored dabs of paint and often painting outdoors. These techniques were considered unique and revolutionary. Later, this group of artists and friends became known as the Impressionists.

Renoir soon attained great status as a portrait painter. Underneath this success, however, he was often dissatisfied with his work. He was also self-conscious about being a member of the working class and not a part of the middle class group who were the subjects of his paintings. But the public adored him. In his lifetime Renoir was paid to paint over two thousand portraits of wealthy art lovers.

Why did he paint such joyous scenes when he was really unhappy? "There are enough ugly things in life for us not to add to them," he once said. The happy images Renoir painted contrasted with his emotions.

From delicate work on porcelain and drawing from models in an art class, Renoir learned the techniques necessary to paint on canvas. Using these skills, Renoir presented colorful scenes filled with happiness and untroubled ease, a world he created with paint and brush.

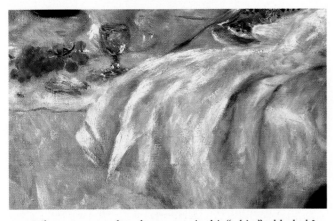

3-2 What are some colors that you see in this "white" tablecloth? Pierre Auguste Renoir, *Luncheon of the Boating Party* (detail), 1881. Oil on canvas, 51″ x 68″ (130 x 173 cm). ©The Phillips Collection, Washington, DC.

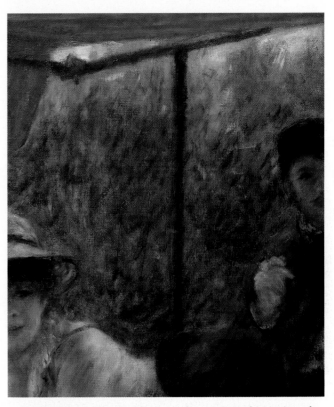

3-3 What other colors besides green do you see in this section of foliage? Pierre Auguste Renoir, *Luncheon of the Boating Party* (detail), 1881. Oil on canvas, 51″ x 68″ (130 x 173 cm). ©The Phillips Collection, Washington, DC.

If you said *all* of these things, you did *very well.* But even so, you would have described only the people and objects in the painting. Your description would have left out some of the most important things. The various lines, shapes, colors, and textures should have been described.

We hope you said something about color. But did you note that the white tablecloth (fig. 3–2) is not a single color of white, or that the foliage (fig. 3–3) is not a single color of green? Did you point out that some colors are lighter (or darker) and that some are brighter (or duller)?

As you can see, if you were to write a good description, you would need a great deal of paper and a lot of time. It is not something that can be done in fifteen minutes.

Even if you had been given one hundred minutes, you probably would have left out many important things. To describe a work of art, you need more than just enough time. You also need to *know what to look for* and to have the appropriate *vocabulary.* You need the right words to describe what you do see.

Knowing What to Look For

You may see as much as, and as clearly as, the average human being. But being able to see normally does *not* mean that you are going to see all of the things you should in a work of art. You first need some knowledge about what you are looking at. You also need some practice.

Compared to Renoir's painting, the Sunday comics (fig. 3–4), television cartoons, and other pictures that you see all the time are very simple. Leaves are usually one shade of green, skies are blue, and clouds are white and puffy shaped. Houses have

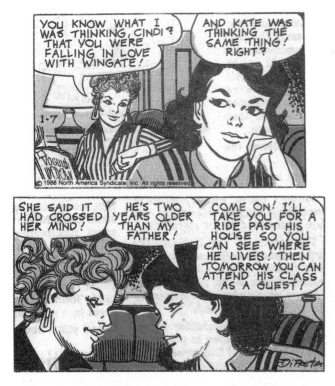

3-4 Comic strip art is obviously not very demanding of your ability to describe shapes and colors. *Rex Morgan, M.D.*, DiPreta, ©1988. King Features Syndicate. Reprinted with special permission of North America Syndicate.

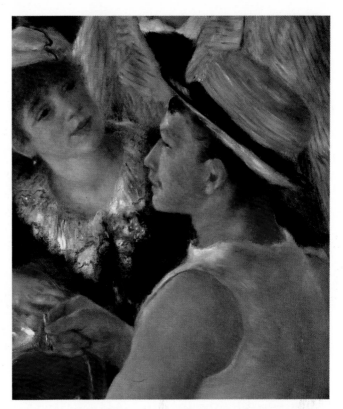

3-5 Can you name all the different colors in just this little section of Renoir's painting? Pierre Auguste Renoir, *Luncheon of the Boating Party* (detail), 1881. Oil on canvas, 51″ x 68″ (130 x 173 cm). © The Phillips Collection, Washington, DC.

pointed roofs and Santa Claus always has a round body and a red suit. Colors are plain and shapes are simple in this kind of everyday art.

As you can see, the shapes in *Luncheon of the Boating Party* are very complicated. The colors are even more so (fig. 3-5). For example, every item of clothing, whether it is a white shirt, a blue dress, or a brown suit, consists of different shades of white, blue, or brown. The leafy foliage consists of not only different shades of green, but also bits of yellow, blue, white, and brown. All of the colors in this painting come in different degrees of lightness and darkness. They vary in brightness and dullness. This quality is referred to as **shading**.

The complicated colors in *Luncheon of the Boating Party* are used to do more than just describe objects. The colors play an important role in providing unity and balance. They also add to the mood. The ways in which colors do this will be explained in later chapters. For now, when you look at pictures, pay more attention to colors. Look at line, shape, texture, and space.

Vocabulary

Probably the easiest thing for you to talk about in a picture is the *subject matter:* the people and objects. It may be more difficult for you to talk about colors and textures. You have not learned the right vocabulary for talking about art. For example, you may be able to recognize the color orange without knowing that it is a "secondary" color. You may not know how such a color relates to other colors. You may already be aware of the texture of a painting without having the words to describe it. On the other hand, you may not be aware of these things at all, until you first learn the words for them.

The Elements of Art

The *elements of art* are the beginning points for learning about art and art vocabulary. The elements of art are line, shape, form, value, color, space, texture, and movement.

In a particular work of art, some elements may be less important than others. For example, look back at the wrapped coastline pictured in the first two chapters. Here color probably plays a less important role than shape. But the element of color is still there. All of the elements are present in some degree in all works of visual art.

By learning the elements, you will see things that you may not have noticed before. You will also learn the words for those things.

Try it Yourself

Save your description of *Luncheon of the Boating Party*. You may want to add to it as you learn more about art in the next chapters.

Look at a picture for a few minutes. Then put the picture away and write a description of it from memory. After you have finished, look at the picture again. Compare your description with the picture.

Summary

Describing is telling about what you see. A description of an artwork should stick to the facts.

It is not easy to describe a painting like *Luncheon of the Boating Party*. There are many things to look for. There is the subject matter—the people and objects. There are the visual elements—lines, shapes, colors, textures, and space. The visual elements will be discussed in the next five chapters. Knowledge of these elements should help you see things in art that you did not see before. This knowledge will also provide you with words for those things.

Criticism Experience 3.1

Describing an Artwork

Describe Grant Wood's *American Gothic* (page 25). Your teacher will give you guidelines that will help you complete your description.

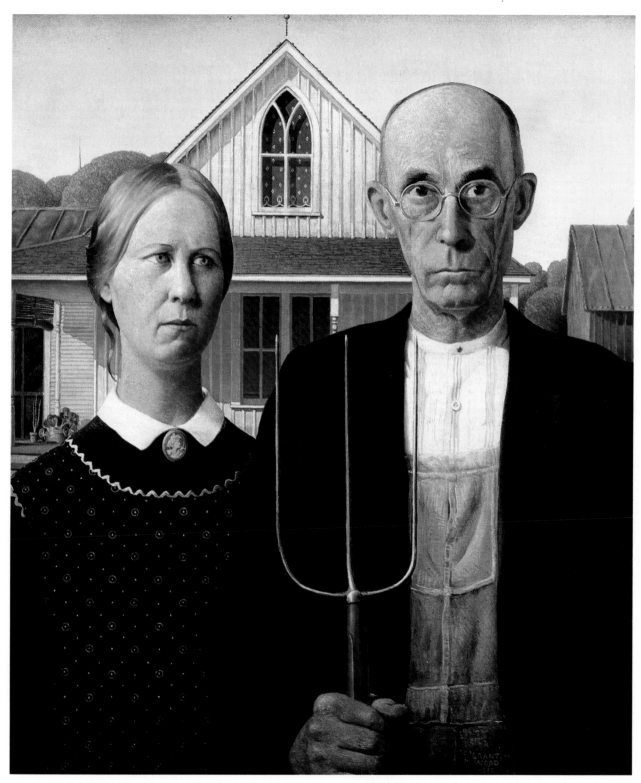

Grant Wood, *American Gothic*, 1930. Oil on beaver board, 30″ x 25″ (76 cm x 63 cm). The Art Institute of Chicago, Friends of American Art.

Chapter 4
Visual Elements: Line

Student Edition
Pages 26–39

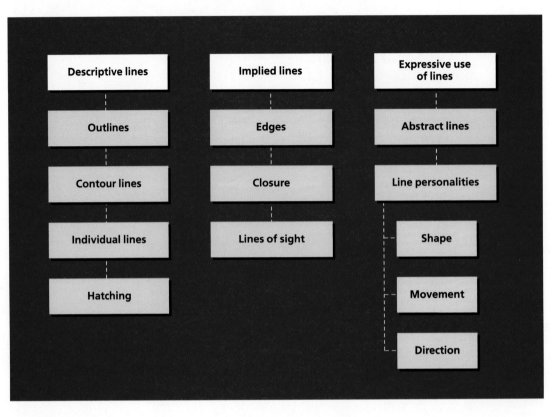

Overview

Chapter Objectives

Students should be able to:

EE 1 **1** identify descriptive and implied lines where they occur in the natural and built environment at edges, places of abrupt color, value or texture change, and where planes meet

EE 1, 3 **2** identify lines in artworks as descriptive, implied, abstract, outline, contour line, and hatching

EE 1, 2 **3** produce several different kinds of lines with each of several drawing tools

EE 3, 4 **4** associate some expressive qualities with different line techniques in drawing experiences, and when responding to artworks

Rationale

If students are to appreciate line as a sensory element they need to become aware of the variety of line in their natural and human-made environments and in art forms. Learning about line can increase students' ability to use line as a communicative element and help them perceive lines in artworks.

Essential Chapter Concepts

• *Descriptive lines* appear in artworks as outlines, contour lines, single lines and hatching.

• *Outlines* describe the outer edges of shapes that appear flat.

• *Contour lines* make figures and objects appear three-dimensional.

• *Implied lines* occur where textures, colors, and values change at edges of shapes in artworks.

• *Implied lines* also occur as a result of the perceptual tendency called *closure* and as a result of the tendency to follow a figure's *line of sight*.

• *Expressive lines* are associated with the artist's intent, or the qualities of the subject the artist wishes to communicate to the viewer.

• *Abstract lines* which are found in very abstract or nonobjective art are expressive lines meant to be seen mainly as line.

• *Descriptive lines* may also be expressive.

Vocabulary

line	hatching
contour line	closure
descriptive line	crosshatching
lines of sight	edge
outline	implied line
abstract lines	

Lesson Plans

4.1 Varieties of Line

Page **T 30** Time: 1 period

4.2 Expressive Line Drawings

Page **T 34** Time: 1 period

4.3 Contour Line

Page **T 36** Time: 1 period

4.4 Hatch and Crosshatch

Page **T 38** Time: 2 periods

4.5 Lines Express Feelings

Page **T 40** Time: 1 period

Handouts

Study Questions Page **T 42**

Test Questions Page **T 43**

Chapter Closure

Evaluation

1 *Production:* Did students produce varied lines with each of several drawing tools?

2 *Production:* Can students produce simple contour drawings that imply depth?

3 *Production:* Can students use hatching and crosshatching for shading in drawing?

4 *Criticism:* Can students differentiate between contour line and outline drawing in artworks?   R 1

5 *Criticism:* Can students identify descriptive, implied, abstract, and expressive line in works of art?   R 1

6 *Aesthetic awareness:* Can students identify real and implied line in the natural and human-made environment?   R 1

7 *Aesthetic awareness:* Can students discuss, at a beginning level, the expressive qualities of different kinds of line in works of art?

Varieties of Line

Time: 5 periods

Preparation

Rationale

Descriptive lines can vary in weight, character, direction, etc. Descriptive lines become expressive when the artist varies their character. Practice in producing lines that vary in character with each of several drawing tools will enable students to respond to a greater variety of line in artworks, and use a greater variety of line to express ideas in their own drawings.

Studio Materials

Drawing pencils, black felt-tip pens, steel drawing pens, black ballpoint pens, twigs and dry weed stems, pointed brushes, small bristle brushes, black ink, 12" x18" drawing paper, water containers, rulers

Enrichment Materials

Slides:

• Riley, *Current*, 25
• Cave painting, Lascaux, 72

Overhead Transparencies:

• Picasso, *Maternité;* Munch, *Sketch of the Model Posing,* 11
• Yuan, *Bare Willows and Distant Mountains,* 20

Large Reproductions:

• Catlett, *Sharecropper,* 12
• Yan, *Brushfire with Animals Fleeing,* 16
• Carr, *Scorned as Timber,* 15

Laser Discs:

Tiepolo, The Prison Visit, 1797-1804

Search Frame 2709

Bandinelli, Two Male Nudes, 1520

Search Frame 2639

Kollwitz, Self-Portrait, 1933

Search Frame 2754

Manet, The Races, 1864

Search Frame 3227

Kirchner, Lovers, 1915

Search Frame 3147

Toulouse-Lautrec, Jane Avril, 1892
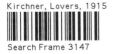
Search Frame 2936

Teach the Lesson

Objectives

Students should be able to:

1 discuss *line* as an element of art with variable characteristics based on how the medium is handled   **EE 1**

2 produce five lines with five different characteristics with each of five different drawing tools   **EE 1, 2**

Vocabulary

Line is an element of art used to define space, contours and outlines of shapes, and direction, or suggest mass and volume. It may be a mark made on a surface with a pointed tool or implied by the edges of shapes and forms.

Expressive lines are intended to express an idea, mood, or theme.

Warm Up

1 Give students one minute to create a pencil outline drawing of a simple shape, such as a purse, apple, tool, shoe, or bottle.

2 Discuss lines used by artists in figures   **W 2**
4–8, 9, and 10 on pages 28 and 29 in the Student Edition. Use one or two words to describe the characteristics (qualities) of lines used by the artists. Compare those line qualities with the quick outline drawings students did to introduce the concept of *expressive line.*

Explore and Develop

1 Write the definition of *line* on the chalkboard, and share with students.

2 Direct attention to the photographs on Student Edition pages 26 and 27 for lines that occur in our natural and humanmade environment. Where do lines suggest direction? Find shapes defined by line. Ask for one- or two-word descriptions of the lines in the photographs, such as *rhythmical, lacy, soft.*

3 Direct attention to different line qualities affected by different media: pencil drawing by Ingres, Studio Experience 4.3; brush drawing by Mokuan, figure 4–20; and pen by van Gogh, Studio Experience 4.5. You may want to use enrichment materials here as well.

4 Emphasize the many different drawing tools (media) artists use to achieve a variety of line qualities.

5 Have students look at Student Edition page 28 and examine the different lines produced by a student with different drawing media. Explain that the lines resulted from the student's inventiveness with each of the drawing tools.

Begin Studio Experience 4.1

1 Have students select five different drawing tools. Then give them brief guided practice with one of the drawing tools on scrap paper. Encourage students to associate descriptive words with their lines. **R 1**

2 Tell students to place a sheet of 12" x 18" paper horizontally and use a ruler to draw a border a ruler's width around the paper. Have students use a light pencil line to divide the rectangle into five equal sections.

3 Have students begin in the section at the left or right end of the rectangle, using the drawing tool just practiced with, and draw any kind of line from the top to the bottom edges of the rectangle. The line may be curvy, shaggy, textured, etc. Continue encouraging students to think of words like frantic, nervous, and graceful that describe the characteristic or quality of the various lines. To demonstrate different qualities that the tool can produce, students will create four more different lines running parallel to the first one, until they fill the first section with five lines. **R 1**

4 Students continue this practice with each of the five tools selected to produce a page with lines that vary in character and reflect qualities of the different media. Encourage practice with each tool before creating lines on the sampler page. Students may repeat the same line with different tools to compare the effects of each.

5 Tell students to print the name of the tool below the set of lines drawn with it.

Evaluate and Reflect

1 Did students achieve definite differences among the five lines produced with each medium?

2 Can students verbally describe the characteristics of some of their lines and those of their classmates?

3 Display overhead transparency 11, which includes Picasso's *Maternité* and Munch's *Sketch of the Model Posing*. Or, have students look at figures 4–8, 9 and 10 in the Student Edition. Can they begin to discuss the differences in linear techniques used by the different artists? Are students beginning to associate expressive qualities with the different line techniques, such as solid and bold, quiet and flowing, delicate and dainty, or energetic and restless?

Reteach

Students who have difficulty with this experience may need more practice using drawing tools. Provide a drawing book with examples of different kinds of line. Let students duplicate some of them, and then invent some of their own. Demonstrate with a medium, bringing several different lines part way down the page, and ask the student to continue them.

Extend the Lesson
Beyond the Basics

Illustrated children's books are wonderful sources of inspiration for artists working with line. Suggest students visit the children's section of a library or bookstore and spend some time just looking at the many ways illustrators use line. Students may have illustrated books at home. Suggest bringing them to share with the class.

EE 1

Show students a copy of *Brother Eagle, Sister Sky* illustrated by Susan Jeffers. The illustrations show a variety of lines used to draw scenes from nature. In addition the book is an excellent introduction/motivation for lessons concerning environmental issues and Native American history.

EE 1, 2

R 3

Line art usually photocopies well. Students may want to start a file of the different illustrative styles they find. Briefly discuss copyright laws and why it is okay to copy a section of a drawing for this purpose. Suggest magazine and newspaper advertisements as possible sources for their file.

EE 1

Cultural Connections

EE 1   Have students look through the text for examples of how artists from various cultures and ethnic groups have used line, such as Wu Chen, *Bamboo* (fig. 4–12), Mokuan, *The Four Sleepers* (fig. 4–20), Maqsud of Kashan, *The Ardabil Carpet* (fig. 17–6), and *Oni (King) of Ife* (fig. 17–11).

EE 2, 3   Suggest students find photographs showing art, clothing, architecture, fabric designs, jewelry, etc. from several different cultures . National Geographic and travel magazines are good sources. Direct students attention to the line studies shown on page 33 of their text. Have them do similar drawings by tracing from the photographs in order to study the lines used in the different cul-

R 5   tures. Have them analyze and discuss their findings.

EE 2, 3, 4   Have students listen to music from a variety of cultures. The music teacher may be able to make a composite cassette recording with the different sounds. Have students draw lines in response to the music. Have them display some of their drawings that they think look like the music sounded. Compare these drawings with the lines found in the artwork from different cultures. Is there a relationship?

Connecting with Other Subjects

Language Arts   Students might write a story incorporating 10 different meanings for the word *line* (see Student Edition page 26).   R 1

Any subject   Suggest students talk with other teachers regarding the term line as it applies to their subject. Hang a large sheet of paper on the wall. Start a list of different uses of the word line such as the bottom line, line of work, line of clothing, fishing line, parallel lines, linear equations, line graph, story line, timeline, etc. Have students add to the list as they think of other uses.   R 1

Expressive Line Drawings

Time: 1 period

Preparation

Rationale

This experience is a continuation of lesson plan 4.1. Here, students use lines to interpret the visual qualities of objects in the environment, such as textures and delicate, heavy and broken lines. Through practice with different drawing media, students develop descriptive drawing skills to express those perceived qualities.

Studio Materials

Same as those for lesson plan 4.1, plus displays of dry weeds embedded in balls of clay for small groups to work from, thin pieces of cardboard, wash dishes

Enrichment Materials

Overhead Transparencies:
• Ma Yuan, *Bare Willows*, 20
• Picasso, *Maternité*, 11
• Munch, *Sketch of the Model*, 11

Large Reproductions:
• Catlett, *Sharecropper*, 12
• Kanaga, *Young Woman*, 18
• Smith, *Snake Path*, 1

Teach the Lesson

Objectives

Students should be able to:

1 perceive and discuss qualities of line found in the natural environment   EE 1

2 associate expressive qualities with different line techniques in a drawing experience, and when responding to artworks   EE 1, 2, 3

3 apply the line techniques developed in lesson plan 4.1 to interpret line qualities and textures found in a dry weed display   EE 1, 2

Vocabulary

Descriptive lines appear in artworks as outlines, contour lines, and as hatching.

Expressive lines are associated with the artist's intent, or the qualities of the subject that he or she wishes to communicate to the viewer. When you become concerned with interpreting the aesthetic qualities of the object rather than copying it, you create expressive line.

Warm Up

1 Set up several displays of weeds. Divide students into small groups, one for each weed display. Give each group one minute to list five or six descriptive words for the kinds of line they see in their weed display. A spokesperson for each group can share their words with the class.

2 Let students dip the end of a frayed twig in a shallow puddle of ink and experiment with descriptive lines for some of the weed heads and seed clusters.

3 Discuss the spontaneity of *Bamboo* by Wu Chen (fig. 4–12). Have students practice the continuous pull-press-lift brush stroke to make long leaf shapes like those in the painting.

Explore and Develop

1 Students should determine which of their line-making techniques from lesson plan 4.1 might be used to render an expressive interpretation of the weed display. Have them use scrap paper to try different techniques.

2 Give guided practice with the continuous pen line to describe leaf, flower, and pod shapes. Demonstrate stippling with a bristle brush and the use of ink washes to obtain different values.

Laser Discs:

Picasso, Self-Portrait, c 1902

Search Frame 2957

Johns, Coat Hanger, 1960

Search Frame 3316

Feininger, Spire of Gelmeroda, c 1890/1955

Search Frame 2768

Heckel, Ruhende, 1912

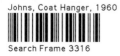

Search Frame 2758

O'Keeffe, Shell, c 1925

Search Frame 3009

Rubens, Pan Reclining, n. d.

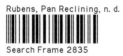

Search Frame 2835

3 To draw lines of stems and branches, students can try dipping the edge of a thin piece of cardboard in ink.

4 If you can, share a reproduction of Dürer's *Great Piece of Turf* with the class.

Begin Studio Experience 4.2

1 Encourage students to look for characteristics of the weeds that they can interpret with their line-making techniques. Direct them to van Gogh's *Grove of Cypresses* and da Vinci's *Study of a Tree* in Studio Experience 4.5 as examples of expressive drawings.

2 Students may use a very light pencil line to quickly lay out the structure of weeds in their displays on a vertical sheet of 12" x 18" paper.

3 Shallow containers with ink washes may be used in addition to ink at full strength.

4 When using sticks, stipple brushes, and the edge of cardboard, it helps to unload excess ink on scrap paper.

5 Instead of drawing the clay lump, students should try combinations of printed, stippled, and drawn line around the base of the display.

Evaluate and Reflect

1 If some students do not talk easily about their artwork, you may want to set the stage by talking with one student about his or her artwork while the group listens: How did you achieve this effect? What characteristics of the weeds were you most interested in? What quality was the most difficult to interpret?

2 Display the drawings. Can students identify certain line techniques that express sensory qualities such as textured, bristled, delicate, rhythmical, etc.?

3 Can students explain what they want others to see in their visual interpretation of the weeds?

4 What other environmental objects could these line techniques be used to interpret?

Reteach

Use cooperative groups with numbered individuals. Play "guess-my-line." Display artworks that include varieties of descriptive, implied, abstract, contour and expressive lines. Give the groups several minutes to list all the kinds of line they see in specific works. Call numbers for responses. Keep score.

Extend the Lesson
Beyond the Basics

Have students collect several different kinds of weeds. Ask them to look for weeds that are inviting to the touch and weeds that must be handled carefully because of thorns and bristles. Have them draw one of each kind of weed. Then have them analyze how the lines they used might be used to draw a fierce warrior, a graceful dancer, a haunted house, a peaceful cottage, a raging storm at sea or a sleeping child. **EE 1, 2**

Cultural Connections

Have students look at the work of Brazilian artist Aguilar on page 36. Suggest students look through resource books to find information about the country and its art. Look for other work by the same artist. Look for work by other contemporary Brazilian artists. How might the artists' work have been influenced by their history and culture? Is there evidence that the work may have been influenced by other artists and/or cultures? **EE 3** **R 3** **R 4** **R 5**

Connecting with Other Subjects

Science Have students plan a project they can do in connection with another subject. Students might collect and draw a sample of each kind of weed that grows in their area. The biology teacher might assist students in identification of the various kinds. Students might include observations of microscopic structures of each in their drawings.

Contour Line

Time: 1 period

Preparation

Rationale

The contour line is a descriptive line that, when properly used, makes figures and objects appear three-dimensional in artworks without shading. Practice in drawing the contour line will help students analyze it in the works of experts such as Ingres, Picasso, Gris, or Lachaise.

Studio Materials

12" x 18" white paper and black ball-point pen

Enrichment Materials

Overhead Transparencies:
• Picasso, *Maternité,* 11

Large Reproductions:
• Catlett, *Sharecropper,* 12

Teach the Lesson

Objectives

Students should be able to:

1   define the term contour line and identify it in artworks   **EE 1**

2   produce a drawing using contour lines that describe the three-dimensional characteristics of an object   **EE 1, 2**

Vocabulary

Contour lines describe the edges of forms and shapes within forms. Contour drawings make figures and objects appear three-dimensional.

Outlines describe the outer edges of shapes that appear flat.

Warm Up

1   Use an overhead projector to project a picture of a person against the chalkboard or a piece of wrapping paper. Have a student actually trace the contour lines.

2   One student might stand in front of the class, while the others sketch an outline of the student and lines such as clothing wrinkles, belts, sleeve edges, and so on.

Explore and Develop

1   Discuss figures 4–7, 8, and 9. Why do   **R 1** the cartoon shapes look almost flat? Why do the contour drawings appear to have depth? Have students look up the terms *two-dimensional* and *three-dimensional* in the Student Edition glossary.

2   In the drawing of a young man, Studio Experience 4.3, Ingres used lines to describe the outer edges of the form and surface changes within the form. Ask students to identify some of the lines that describe parts that would project outwards.

3   Which contour lines describe parts that appear rounded and closer to the viewer in *A Portly Courtier,* figure 4–8?

Begin Studio Experience 4.3

1   Ask students to place their paper horizontally and divide it in half with a light line. Have them place their non-drawing hand flat on one side of the paper, and trace around it to complete an outline drawing.

2   After looking at the drawing, have students place the hand over the outline, and produce a contour drawing on the other side of the paper without tracing the hand. They should begin drawing at one side of the hand where it joins the wrist and proceed around the fingers and thumb to the other side. Tell students to imagine that the pen is moving along the edges, ridges, and creases of the hand.

3   Encourage students to concentrate on looking at the form of the hand, allowing their eyes to move along the outer edges while the pen moves slowly on the paper. Explain that contour drawing makes them more perceptive.

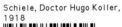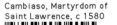

4 Students need not worry about realistic drawing, but should keep the pen moving and respond to all of the little curves and creases along the outer edges. On completion of the outer contours, have students make lines within one of the fingers that describe the joints, nail, and knuckle.

Evaluate and Reflect

1 Display the drawings. Did the process made students more perceptive in seeing details?

2 Do students understand why contour drawing looks more three-dimensional than an outline?

3 Can students name which dimension the contour line adds?

4 Describe the form in terms of contour lines?

Reteach

Display pictures on an overhead projector. Have students trace the contour lines of the images. Have students glue thin yarn on an object to show contour lines, then make a contour drawing of the object.

Extend the Lesson

Beyond the Basics

EE 1 Acquire plexiglass scraps from a local glass store and cut into rectangles slightly larger than your hand, one for each student. Have students observe the contours of their hand through the glass. Hooking one finger over the edge and bracing one edge against the abdomen or chest will allow students to trace the contours of many different poses on the glass while holding it firmly in place. Remind students to use water-based non-permanent markers only. Most markers will dry slowly and allow the drawing to be transferred onto paper for a record of the observations. If the marker dries too quickly simply place the glass over a light source and trace onto the paper. Window size sheets of plexiglass or using the windows of a ground floor classroom allow students to observe contours of the entire figure.

EE 1 Dress a model in striped clothing or drape with striped cloth to help students increase their perceptiveness. Observing figures or objects with projected stripes is also helpful. Cut strips of paper placed on an overhead projector work well and makes it easy to adjust the placement of the projected image.

Cultural Connections

Assign a small group to look through resource books for more drawings by the Spanish artists, Pablo Picasso and Juan Gris to share with the class.

EE 1, 4 Direct students' attention to Ingres' drawing on page 31. Ingres was a French painter. This drawing was produced about 1815. Have students find other works, preferably portraits, produced in the same year in other places. Suggest looking at the work of Goya in Spain. What American painter might students look for? Have students examine the contour lines found in the works.

Connecting with Other Subjects

EE 2 **Geography** Borrow contour maps from the drafting teacher or the county surveyor's office. Discuss the relationship between contour drawings by an artist and the making of contour maps. Suggest students approach a drawing of their face or hand as if they were making a contour map. Ask drafting students or a professional from the community to demonstrate contour mapping techniques for the class.

Line

Hatch and Crosshatch

Time: 2 periods

Preparation

Rationale

Experience with the techniques of hatching and crosshatching will contribute to students' understanding of how shading is used to describe depth and provide contrasts in artworks.

Studio Materials

white drawing paper, paper bags, lamps, and your choice of pencil, pen and ink, black ball-point pen

Enrichment Materials

Slides:
• Dürer, *The Riders on the Four Horses*, 38

Large Reproductions:
• Catlett, *Sharecropper*, 12

Laser Discs:

Bril, Heroic Landscape, c 1585

Search Frame 2783

Marcoussis, Portrait G. Apollonaire, c 1910/1940

Search Frame 2944

Piranesi, The Carceri: Gothic Arch, 1748-1750

Search Frame 3082

van Dyck, Portrait of a Man Standing, c 1620

Search Frame 2837

Campagnola, Landscape with Boy Fishing, c 1520

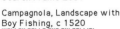
Search Frame 2633

Manzel, Heads of Man and Woman, 1899

Search Frame 2750

Teach the Lesson

Objectives

Students should be able to:

1 produce at least five value variations with hatching and crosshatching   EE 1, 2

2 use hatching and crosshatching to make objects appear three-dimensional   EE 1, 2

Vocabulary

Value is the degree of lightness and darkness in black pen or pencil drawings. Value also refers to the lightness of color in artworks.

Shading is the use of darks and lights to give a feeling of depth to forms.

Hatching is the technique of using closely spaced parallel lines to suggest light and shadow.

Crosshatching is the technique of using crossed parallel lines to suggest light and shadow.

Optical mixing occurs when looking at hatched and crosshatched lines on white paper. Because the lines are so close together, the eye blends them with the white of the paper and sees a variety of grays.

Warm Up

1 Ask students to briefly define *value*. How are values made when you are not using color?

2 Have students outline a small shape and then imagine that light is striking it from one side. Have students use lines to create values going from white to light to medium to dark across the shape. They may quickly rub in background tone around the shape to enhance the appearance of depth.

Explore and Develop

1 Turn to Studio Experience 4.4. Can students indicate which of the little drawings were produced with hatching? with crosshatching? Determine if some students used either technique in their practice drawings.

2 Can they explain how hatching is used to create light and dark values? Discuss the optical mixing of close, thin black lines with the white of the paper.

3 Discuss figure 4–13 by David Levine. Where are the darkest values? the lightest? the middle? Which values were produced with hatching? with crosshatching?

4 Describe some edges with value contrasts.

Begin Studio Experience 4.4

1 Direct attention to the hatched and crosshatched columns in Studio Experience 4.4. Have students outline two columns about 2 inches wide and 5 inches long, and then divide the columns into five spaces. Students will produce five value steps with hatched line in the first column, and five value steps with crosshatched lines in the second column. They should not leave space between the steps. Have students create edges resulting from value changes by making lines closer together, thicker, and heavier as they lower the value in each step.

2 Use the remaining time to let students build up little forms with rows of hatched lines as in Studio Experience 4.4. Tell students to imagine a light source, and use hatched and crosshatched lines to make a small shape look three-dimensional.

3 Place a paper bag or some other object in light directed from one side, positioned so students can see two outer surfaces and a little of the inside.

4 Have students make a light outline drawing of the bag about 6 or 7 inches high and use hatching and crosshatching to represent light and dark surfaces and shadows on the bag and the table.

Evaluate and Reflect

1 Can students use the terms *hatching, crosshatching, optical mixing,* and *shading* in discussing their work?

2 Can students explain how optical mixing occurs when using the hatching techniques on white paper?

3 Are edges resulting from value changes clearly visible in the students' hatched and crosshatched value scales and in their drawings of the paper bag?

4 How successful do students feel about making objects in drawings appear three-dimensional with the hatching techniques?

Reteach

Provide additional practice with a familiar tool, such as pencil or black ball-point pen to help students gain control over varied spacing of parallel lines. Obtain a book of Winslow Homer's engravings, which clearly demonstrate values produced with hatched and crosshatched lines. To help students analyze hatching, enlarge an image composed of hatched lines on the overhead projector. Some students might benefit from copying part of a work to further analyze

the placement of hatched lines to achieve value variations.

Extend the Lesson
Beyond the Basics

Using one of their contour drawings from lesson 4.3 and an imaginary light source have students shade the drawing with hatch and crosshatch. Suggest they experiment with various drawing materials such as pen and ink, markers, and pastels. Making several copies of the original contour drawing by tracing will allow students to experiment freely without risk of ruining their original drawing.   **EE 2**

Cultural Connections

Refer students to artists such as Honoré Daumier (French), who produced lithographs which include hatching, or the Dutch artist, Rembrandt, who used hatching and crosshatching in both drawings and etchings. African-American artist, Elizabeth Catlett (biography, Student Edition page 145) produces linocut prints in which hatched lines are also evident.   **EE 3**

Hatching and crosshatching are evident in many Japanese prints. Using resource books have students carefully examine techniques used in these prints. A magnifying glass may help students in analyzing the lines. Isolating and viewing only a small section through an opening cut in paper may also help students to see how the artist achieved the overall effect. Suggest students use the same approach to examine the work of Albrecht Dürer.   **EE 3**

Connections with Other Subjects

Language Arts Contact the language arts teacher about poems or stories which deal with moods that might be expressed with black and white, or possibly with a monochromatic color scheme. Discuss how terms associated with light and dark have been used in literature and theater as symbols representing concepts such as good/evil, enlightenment/ignorance, truth/lies, and birth/death.   **R 3 R 5**

Lines Express Feelings

Time: 1 period

Preparation

Rationale

In very abstract or nonobjective artworks, line is used primarily as an expressive visual element to suggest an idea, feeling, mood, or movement. Such lines are a major part of contemporary art that students should be able to respond to and enjoy. In this experience students create abstract drawings that use lines to communicate ideas or feelings.

Studio Materials

drawing pencils, black felt-tip pens, steel drawing pens, black ball-point pens, pointed and small bristle brushes, black ink, 12" x 18" drawing paper, water containers, shallow trays

Enrichment Materials

Slides:
• Mondrian, *Composition in White, Black and Red,* 17
• Pereira, *Oblique Progression,* 19

Overhead Transparencies:
• O'Keeffe, *Sky Above Clouds IV,* 4
• Evans, *Design Made at Airlie Garden,* 9

Large Reproductions:
• Carr, *Scorned as Timber,* 15
• Yan, *Brushfire with Animals Fleeing,* 16
• Chan, *Wild Thing,* 19

Teach the Lesson

Objectives

Students should be able to:

1 define abstract and nonobjective art **EE 4**

2 create abstract or nonobjective drawings in which lines are meant to communicate ideas, feelings, or emotions **EE 2**

3 describe expressive lines in artworks **EE 3, 4**

Laser Discs:

Motherwell, Automatism B, 1965-1966

Search Frame 3318

Kollwitz, Unemployment, 1909

Search Frame 2752

Picasso, Man with Guitar

Search Frame 3262

Noland, Another Time, 1973

Search Frame 2335

deKooning, Study for Woman Number One, 1952
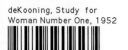
Search Frame 3025

Munch, The Scream, 1895

Search Frame 3333

Vocabulary

Abstract art stresses the form of its subject rather than its actual appearance. The subject is broken down into elements that do not necessarily resemble the subject itself.

Nonobjective art has no recognizable subject matter such as people, animals, or trees.

Abstract lines found in abstract art are not used to outline or describe objects or to suggest shading. They are expressive and meant to be seen only as line.

Warm Up

1 Ask students to think of a word that expresses a feeling, such as aggressive, awkward, explosive, graceful, nervous, or rhythmical. Then have students use a pencil to draw any kind of line that matches the feeling. Their lines may vary in direction, darkness/lightness, and thickness/thinness.

2 Have students write their names on the back of the paper, then collect the drawings. Pick several students at random to write their word on the chalkboard. Ask other students to pick a drawing out of the pile that they think matches the word. Display the drawings next to the words on the chalkboard.

Explore and Develop

1 Discuss how well the student drawings related to the ideas they were meant to express.

2 Use Student Edition pages 35–39 to analyze how artists use lines to express ideas and feelings.

3 Organize four groups. Assign to each group one of the artworks on Student Edition pages 36 and 37. Have each group work cooperatively to complete a description of the lines in the artwork. Tell students to focus on how line is used, the kinds of line, their directions, similarities, and differences. Each group should also describe the idea, feeling, or mood the artwork seems to express.

4 Have a student from each group present their description of line in the nonobjective artwork to the class, and the idea or feeling they think the work expresses.

Begin Studio Experience 4.5

R 4 **1** Discuss how van Gogh used line to communicate spiraling rhythm and energy in *Grove of Cypresses*, Studio Experience 4.5a. What kinds of emotions or ideas does da Vinci's drawing of a tree suggest? Describe different feelings suggested by the two drawings.

2 Have students look at the nonobjective line drawings in Studio Experience 4.5c and match them with the listed words. *(Answers: 1. graceful, 2. timid, 3. strong, 4. aggressive, 5. nervous)*

R 4 **3** What ideas do students associate with the abstract drawing 4.5d?

4 Ask the class to brainstorm a list of words that express feelings and list them on the chalkboard. Refer them to Student Edition page 36 for a starter list.

5 Ask students to divide a sheet of 12" x 18" paper into four parts. In one part, have students list three words that express feelings. Then tell students to draw in each of the other three parts an abstract or nonobjective sketch to express the words. Students may use any drawing tool or combination of media to make the lines.

6 Organize small discussion groups, and have students present their drawings and words to the group for matching.

Evaluate and Reflect

1 Can students discuss how line can be used expressively in abstract or nonobjective drawings?

2 Can students match drawings with words that express feelings?

3 Can students create drawings that communicate emotions and feelings with expressive line?

Reteach

Students who have difficulty working with very abstract or nonobjective line and shapes might focus on expressive line in representational drawings.

Extend the Lesson
Beyond the Basics

Suggest students study the lines of various facial expressions by looking in a mirror and tracing with a non-permanent water-based marker directly on the surface of the mirror. If done quickly the wet marker can be transferred onto a sheet o f paper. Certain colors in a set of markers will work better than others. If the ink beads up or dries too quickly just try a different color. Draw at least six different expressions. Sort the images according to line quality. Notice the kinds of lines of an angry or aggressive expression compared to a calm or smiling face.

EE 1, 2

Cultural Connections

Abstract and nonobjective art are terms that usually bring to mind artists like Jackson Pollock and Piet Mondrian; however abstract and nonobjective designs can be found throughout history and across cultures. Remind students of the definitions of these terms and have them use resource books to find examples of abstract and nonobjective art from several different cultures. Suggest students begin by looking at traditional American quilts.

EE 3

R 1

Connecting with Other Subjects

Science Direct students' attention to page 39. The title of the van Gogh work tells the viewer that the trees are cypresses. What kind of tree is shown in the drawing by Leonardo da Vinci? Have students look for trees in the work of other artists and use resource books to identify the type. The biology teacher might provide assistance.

Study Questions
Chapter 4–Visual Elements: Line

Line

1 Give two examples of line found in nature.

_____

2 Lines can also be found in the manufactured environment. Give two examples.

_____

3 Give two characteristics of, and draw an example of, each of the following kinds of descriptive lines:

Outline

_____

Contour line

_____

Hatching

_____

4 How does optical mixing occur when using thin black lines on white paper?

_____

_____

5 How can a form be drawn to make it seem more three-dimensional?

_____

_____

6 What are three ways that line can be implied? State one example of each.

_____

_____

7 Looking at artwork pictured in Chapter 4, give two examples of how artists have used line's expressive qualities. What expression is conveyed in each?

_____

_____

8 What are abstract lines?

_____

Test Questions
Chapter 4–Visual Elements: Line

Match the definitions on the right with the appropriate terms on the left:

_____ **1** Line of sight   **A**. Where one shape ends and another begins.

_____ **2** Expressive lines   **B**. Closely spaced thin black lines blend with white of the paper and appear to be gray.

_____ **3** Edge   **C**. Visually connecting marks to "see" lines where none exists.

_____ **4** Optical mixing   **D**. Implied lines along which figures in a painting look.

_____ **5** Horizontal lines   **E**. Lines that do not make recognizable images.

_____ **6** Closure   **F**. Give a feeling of calmness and stability.

_____ **7** Railroad tracks   **G**. Lines used to convey feeling.

_____ **8** Abstract lines   **H**. Lines found in manufactured environment.

_____ **9** Lines that are used to make recognizable pictures are called

_____   a. descriptive lines. c. expressive lines.
_____   b. abstract lines. d. none of the above.

_____ **10** The use of lighter and darker grays to make a drawn form seem more three-dimensional is known as

       a. blending.   c. shading.
       b. mixing.   d. suggesting.

_____ **11** This drawing includes descriptive and

       a. seen lines.   c. outlines.
       b. implied lines.   d. direct lines.

Test Questions (continued)
Chapter 4–Visual Elements: Line

_____ **12** Identify the following types of lines in the illustration below, by placing the appropriate letter in the space provided.

_____ **13**   a. Hatching

_____ **14**   b. Crosshatching

            c. Contour

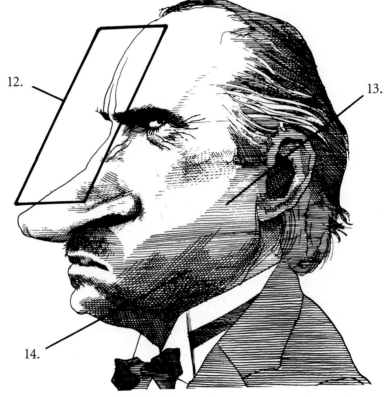

15 State one similarity of an outline drawing and a contour drawing. Give two differences between them.

_____

_____

_____

_____

Study Answers
Chapter 4
Visual Elements: Line

1 Possible answers include veins of a leaf, tree branches, spider webs, etc.

2 Possible answers include telephone lines, lines indicating highway lanes, etc.

3 Outline—A line joins itself to surround a shape; only outer edges are defined; usually same thickness throughout; shows little depth. Contour line—Defines edges, including edges of shapes within a form; shows depth; varies in thickness, darkness. Hatching—Closely spaced parallel lines. (Crosshatching—Hatched lines that cross.)

4 Closely spaced thin black lines blend with the white of the paper thus appearing to be gray. The mixing of the black and white happens in the eye.

5 By using a method called shading to develop lighter and darker grays.

6 By an edge. (Example: where one shape ends and another begins, which may be defined by a difference in color, texture, or value.) By closure. (Example: visually connecting marks to "see" lines where none actually exist.) By lines of sight. (Example: following a line of sight between two people.)

7 Answers may vary. Possible answers include: *A Portly Courtier* (text fig. 4–8): "relaxed" lines. *Mother and Child #2,* by Catlett (text fig. 4–15): "graceful" lines. *Grove of Cypresses,* by van Gogh (text Challenge 4–4a): "rhythmic" lines.

8 Lines limited to expression; they do not symbolize, outline or look like shading.

Test Answers
Chapter 4
Visual Elements: Line

1 D

2 I

3 A

4 B

5 G

6 C

7 J

8 E

9 A

10 C

11 B

12 C

13 A

14 B

15 Similarity: Differences:

Both define edges.   Outline—only outer edges are defined—line is same thickness throughout—shows little depth. Contour—also defines edges within a form—lines vary in thickness and darkness—shows depth

Chapter 4
Visual Elements: Line

The word *line* has many definitions in Webster's dictionary. You can *line* a ball in baseball, hit the *line* in football, memorize *lines* for a play, and avoid being last in *line* at the cafeteria. Even when the word is used to describe "long thin marks," there are many examples that fit this meaning.

Lines can be found in nature in such things as the veins of a leaf (fig. 4–1). The branches of trees in winter (fig. 4–2) and the wind-etched sands of a desert (fig. 4–3) have lines. Lines are everywhere in the world around you. On your way to school you probably saw telephone lines and electric power lines stretched between poles. If you looked down you probably saw the cracks of the sidewalk.

In fact, the printed letters and numbers you are reading right now are shapes made with lines. The letters *c* and *s* and the number *5* are made with single lines that are open at the ends. Some letters, like *f, t,* and *x,*

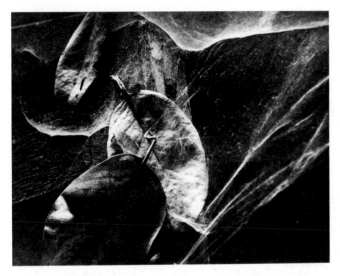

4–1 Wynn Bullock, *Leaves and Cobwebs,* 1968. Silverprint, 7 ½″ x 9 ¼″ (19 x 24 cm). © The Detroit Institute of Arts, Founders Society Purchase, Michigan State Council for the Arts Exhibition Fund.

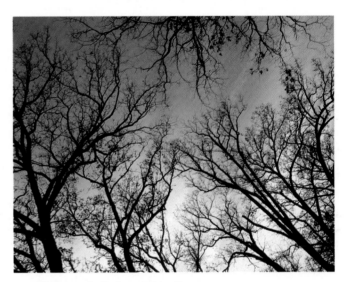

4–2 Photograph: Barbara Caldwell.

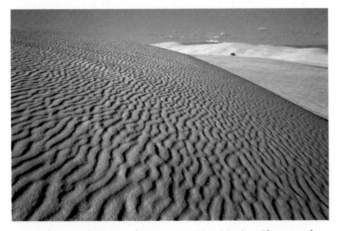

4–3 *White Sands National Monument,* New Mexico. Photograph courtesy U.S. Dept. of the Interior, Washington, DC.

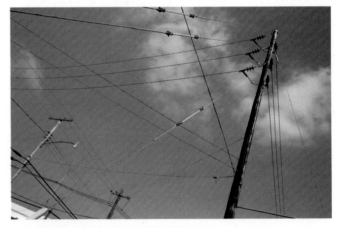

4–4 Photograph: Barbara Caldwell.

are made with lines that cross. Some, like *y* and *k*, are made with open lines that are connected in places. Many, like *a, b, e, 6,* and *9,* are made with lines that are partly open and partly closed. Of course, at least two—*0* and *8*—are made of single lines with no open ends. Isn't it amazing how many letters and numbers can be created by arranging or rearranging a few straight and curved lines (and dots to make *i* and *j*)?

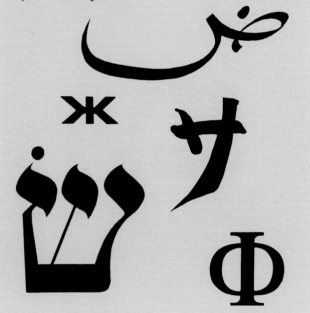

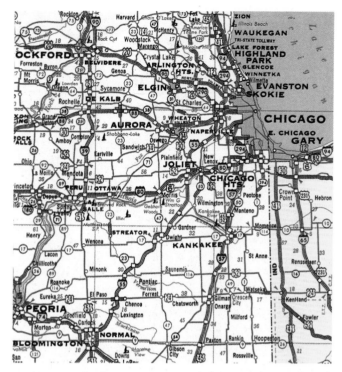

4–5 Courtesy ©Color-Art, Inc., St. Louis, Missouri.

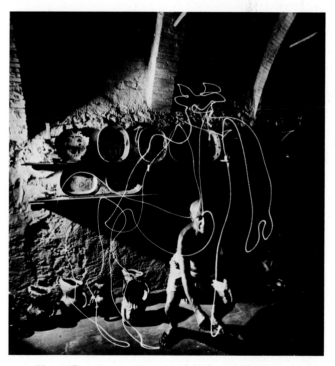

4–6 Gjon Mili, *A Centaur Drawn with Light—Pablo Picasso at the Madoura Pottery in Vallauris, France.* Photograph. ©1984. Sotheby Parke Bernet, Inc., New York.

A road map is another example of lines. Lines and shapes on a map are called *symbols.* They stand for other things. Figure 4–5 is a map of northern Illinois. The long lines stand for roads, highways, and rivers. On the roads and highways are dots (a little circle surrounded by a line) that stand for small towns. The little squares on Interstate Highways 80 and 39 stand for exits. The wandering blue line that runs beside Highway 6 is the Illinois River.

Art has as many kinds of lines as the lines you find in nature or in books and maps. Many lines in art are created by moving a tool such as a pencil, charcoal stick, pen, or brush. Did you know that some lines can even be made with light (fig. 4–6)?

Studio Experience 4.1

Varieties of Line

Select five different drawing media such as crayons, pencils, felt-tip pens, ball-point pens, drawing pens, sticks, and brushes. Make five different kinds of lines drawn from top to bottom of the page, with each medium. Record the medium under each set of lines.

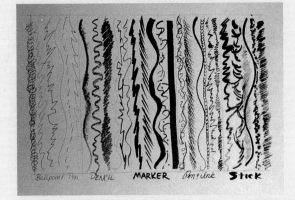

Studio Experience 4.2

Expressive Line Drawings

Use what you learned in Experience 4.1 to make an interpretive drawing of fall weeds.

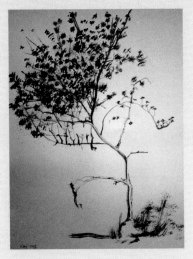

Kay Dye.

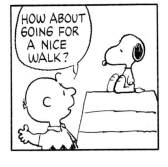
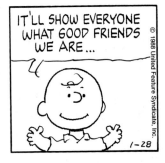
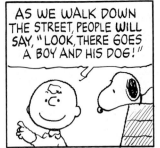
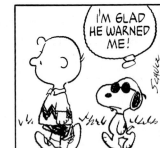

4–7 Charles M. Schulz, *Charlie Brown and Snoopy*, 1973. *Peanuts* reprinted by permission of UFS, Inc.

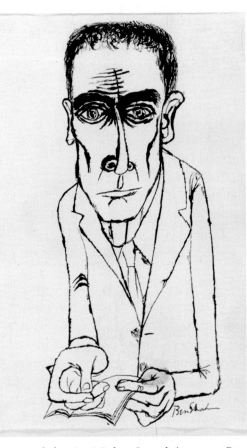

4–9 Ben Shahn, *Dr. J. Robert Oppenheimer*, 1954. Brush and ink, 19 ½″ x 12 ¼″ (50 x 31 cm). The Museum of Modern Art, New York. Purchase.

Descriptive Lines

You have been making lines since the first time you picked up a pencil. At first you probably made scribbles. Eventually your lines turned into recognizable pictures. This use of lines—whether by a child or an artist—is called *descriptive*. Descriptive lines come in many varieties.

Outlines

The most basic kind of descriptive line is an outline. An *outline* is a line that surrounds a shape. Alphabet letters and map symbols are examples of outlines. In school you use outlines to make letters. You also use them when you make pictures.

Like you, comic strip artists use outlines to create their characters, such as Charlie Brown and Snoopy (fig. 4–7). The lines of an outline drawing are usually the same thickness throughout. Also, only the outer edges of the shapes are defined. For these reasons, an outline drawing seems to have little depth. Charlie Brown and Snoopy are almost as flat as cutouts.

Contour Lines

Contour lines also define the outer edges of shapes. Unlike outlines, however, contour lines vary in thickness and darkness. They also define the edges of shapes within a form. They give a greater sense of depth to the object. Notice the contour lines in the Persian drawing *A Portly Courtier* (fig. 4–8). These lines smoothly trace the man's belly and even some of the folds in his clothes.

Contrast the Persian artist's "relaxed" lines with the intense, scratchy lines of Ben Shahn's *Dr. J. Robert Oppenheimer* (fig. 4–9). How do the dark thick lines add interest and help describe the subject?

Diego Rivera used ink and brush to create lines that describe an Indian mother carrying her child (fig. 4–10). Some lines are narrow and some are quite wide. Some, like the one that shows the underside of the mother's arm, are both narrow and wide. Compare Rivera's two people to Charlie Brown and Snoopy. Which pair seems to you to be the most solid, the most three-dimensional? Which picture has the most variety in its lines?

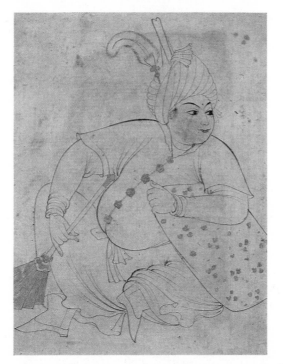

4–8 *A Portly Courtier*, Persia, Tabriz, ca. 1535. Ink and gold on paper, 5″ x 4″ (13.5 x 10 cm). Courtesy of The Arthur M. Sackler Museum, Harvard University Art Museums, Gift of Mr. Henry B. Cabot, Mr. Walter Cabot, Mr. Edward W. Forbes, Mr. Eric Schroeder and the Annie S. Coburn Fund.

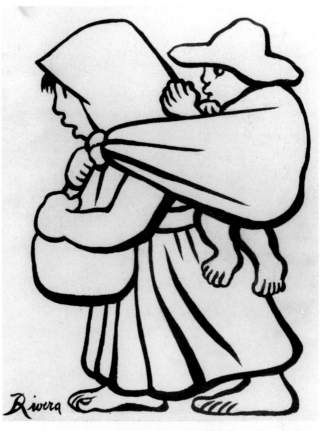

4–10 Diego Rivera, *Untitled (mother and child)*, 1936. Ink on paper, 12″ x 9 ¼″ (30 x 24 cm). San Francisco Museum of Modern Art, Albert M. Bender Collection, Gift of Albert M. Bender.

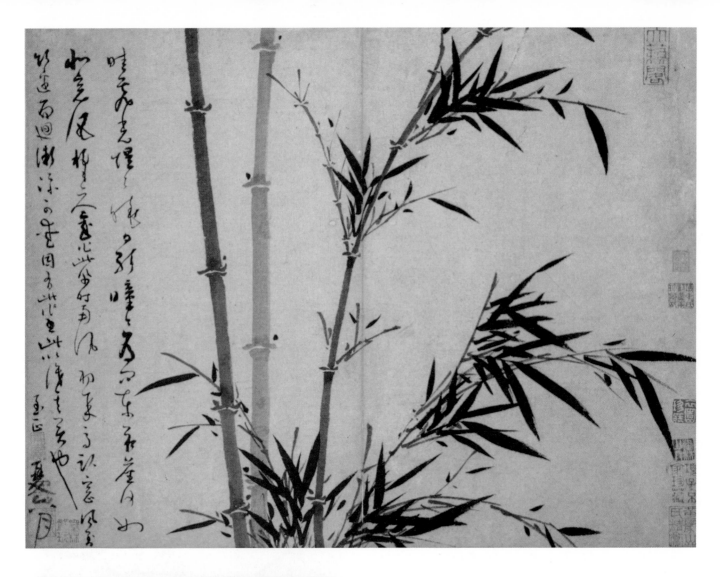

4–12 Wu Chen, *Bamboo*, Yuan dynasty, 1350 AD. Album leaf, ink on paper, 16″ x 21″ (41 x 53 cm). Collection of the National Palace Museum, Taipei, Taiwan, Republic of China.

Because of their variety, contour lines are more interesting and descriptive than outlines. Lines in drawings by professional artists are often called contour lines rather than outlines. When you draw, which kinds of lines do you use most often: outlines or contour lines?

Individual Lines

Just as a single line can represent the letter *S*, it can describe an individual strand of hair. Look at the close-up of a painting by Andrew Wyeth (fig. 4–11). Wu Chen used single strokes of an ink-loaded brush to describe the stalks and leaves of a bamboo plant (fig. 4–12). He also used individual strokes for each symbol of the Chinese writing on the left of the picture. This elegant writing is called *calligraphy*.

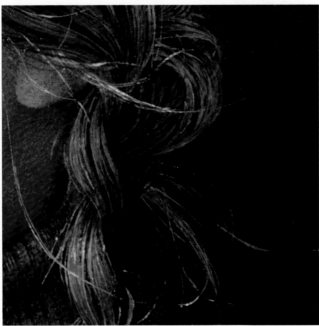

4–11 Andrew Wyeth, *Braids* (detail), tempera.

Contour Line

Produce a drawing using contour lines that describe the three-dimensional characteristics of an object.

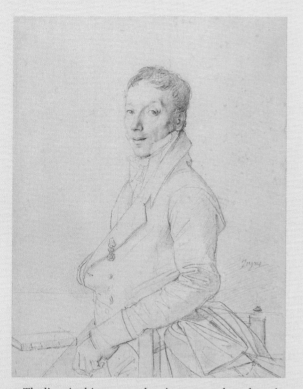

a. The lines in this contour drawing accurately and sensitively describe the edges of forms, and the details and folds of the coat found within the major forms. Jean Auguste Dominique Ingres, *Portrait of a Young Man*, ca. 1815. Pencil, 11″ x 8″ (29 x 20 cm). Museum Boymans-van Beuningen, Rotterdam.

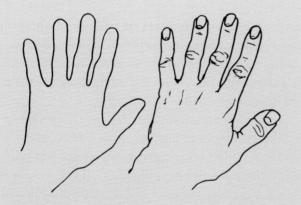

b. The outline of a hand is accurate, but appears flat and lacks information when compared with the contour drawing on the right.

Hatching

David Levine used contour lines to make a humorous drawing of a public person (fig. 4–13). But look closely at the lines in the face and coat. The artist used many thin, closely spaced, parallel lines called **hatching**. Hatching lines that cross, like those on the lower part of the head, are called **crosshatching**.

In hatching, the black lines are so thin and close together that they blend with the white of the paper. When this happens, they appear gray. This effect is called *optical mixing*. The mixing of black and white happens in the eye. When you look at Levine's picture, the black hatching lines are optically mixed in your vision. You see a variety of grays. These grays help to describe the nose, cheeks, chin, and jowls. The use of lighter and darker grays to make a form seem three-dimensional is known as *shading*. You will learn more about shading in the chapter on value and color.

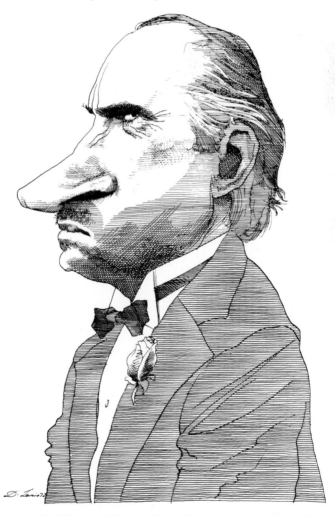

4–13 David Levine, *Nixon as The Godfather*, 1972. Reprinted with permission from *The New York Review of Books*. ©1963–73, Nyrev, Inc.

Hatch and Crosshatch

Use pen and ink, black ball-point pen, or pencils to practice hatching and crosshatching. Make several drawings. Try to achieve a wide range of lights and darks.

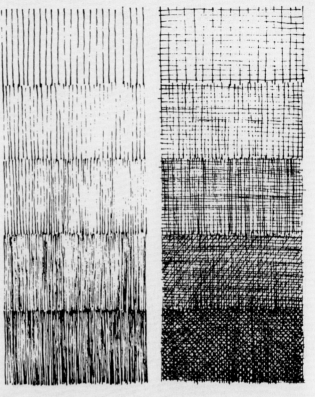

a. Hatch and crosshatch techniques.

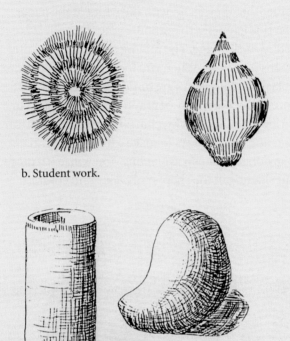

b. Student work.

c. Student work.

Implied Lines

The lines we have seen so far are just that: *seen* lines. They are visible. They have width and length. However, there are some lines that are not seen, at least not in the usual way. They are **implied**; that is, they are indicated indirectly. An actual line does not have to be present in order for a line to be suggested, or implied. Lines can be implied by *edges, closure,* and *lines of sight.*

Edges

Look at Renoir's painting of a boating party (fig. 4–14). Renoir did not use outlines or contour lines to set off one shape from another. Nevertheless, the lines are implied by **edges**. An edge exists where one shape ends and another begins. In Renoir's painting, an edge is

formed where an arm meets the railing and where the man's back on the right meets the chair. Another example of an edge is where the man's hand touches the railing. All these edges suggest the presence of lines. The lines are implied.

In a sculpture, an edge exists where the sculpture ends and the space around it begins. The edges of Elizabeth Catlett's carving of *Mother and Child #2* imply many graceful lines (fig. 4–15). If you were to draw her carving, the outside line would look almost like a rounded parallelogram. The curve of the mother's hand is repeated in the circle of the infant's head. What other curved lines and angles do you see in this sculpture?

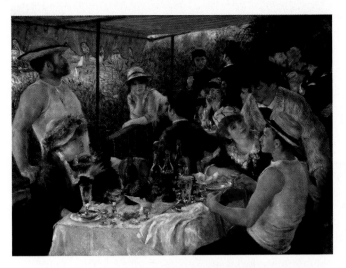

4-14 Pierre Auguste Renoir, *Luncheon of the Boating Party*, 1881. Oil on canvas, 51″ x 68″ (130 x 173 cm). ©The Phillips Collection, Washington, DC.

The outer edges of a building or the roofline can also suggest lines. But lines also are suggested by the edges around window and door openings, and the edges of overhangs, ledges, balconies, railings, posts, and trim. In the Japanese villa (fig. 4-16), most of the lines are horizontal. They emphasize the width of the building rather than its height. Horizontal lines suggest a sense of stability and restfulness. We associate these qualities with home. By contrast, most of the lines of the Sears Tower (fig. 4-17) are vertical. They emphasize the height of the building. Because we associate height with power, the vertical lines symbolize the strength of a powerful corporation.

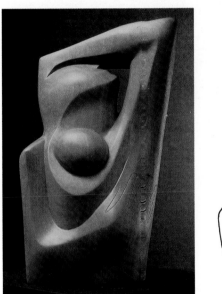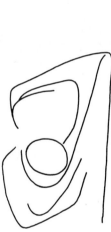

4-15 Elizabeth Catlett, *Mother and Child #2*, 1971. Walnut, 38″ (97 cm). Malcom Brown Gallery.

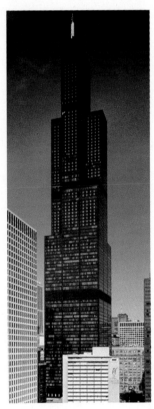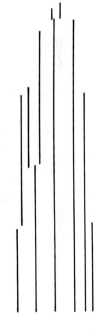

4-17 Skidmore, Owings and Merrill, Sears Tower, 1974. Chicago, Illinois. Rosenthal Art Slides, Inc., Chicago.

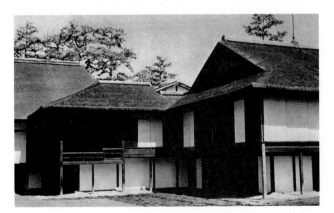

4-16 The Shoin, Katsura Imperial Villa.

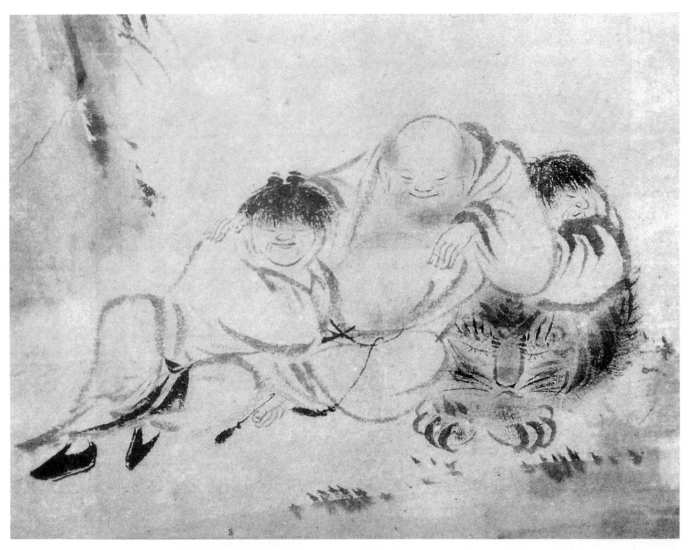

4-20 Mokuan, *The Four Sleepers* (detail). Muromachi (mid-fourteenth century). Ink on paper, 28″ x 14″ (71 x 36 cm). Maeda Ikutokukai Foundation, Tokyo.

Closure

Lines can even be implied by a simple arrangement of dots. For example, there are no lines in figure 4–18. Nevertheless, we see this arrangement of dots as a square rather than as four separate dots. We connect the dots in our "mind's eye" (fig. 4–19). Our tendency to connect marks this way, or to "see" lines where none exist, is called **closure**.

Closure is required to connect the loosely drawn and delicate lines in Mokuan's *The Four Sleepers* (fig. 4–20). Can you see the four sleepers? Would you agree that lack of clarity makes the picture more interesting and humorous? Why?

Closure is required even for viewing a photograph. The photograph in figure 4–21 provides limited "information." The student and the teacher are formed by just a few areas of black and white. The teacher's face has almost no outline or any other lines except a mouth.

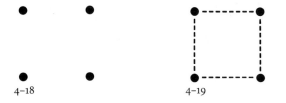

4-18

4-19

Lines of Sight

Have you ever looked up when someone else looked up? Looking in the same direction as another person is a natural tendency. The lines along which people look are called **lines of sight**. In Renoir's *Luncheon of the Boating Party*, the merrymakers are looking at each other. It is very natural for the viewer to also look along the same lines of sight. It is similar to the process of closure. Artists often use lines of sight to connect different parts of a picture. Which of the many lines of sight do you think are the most important in *Luncheon*?

Expressive Use of Lines

We have seen that artists use lines to describe shapes or forms. They also use lines to indicate shading. We have also seen how painters, cartoonists, sculptors, and architects use implied lines.

In addition to these uses, lines are also used by artists to express feelings and ideas. Some examples of the expressive qualities of lines have been mentioned already. Recall the "relaxed" lines of the Persian drawing (fig. 4–8) and the "intense, scratchy" lines of Shahn (fig. 4–9). The implied lines of the Catlett sculpture (fig. 4–15) can be described as "graceful." The lines of the Japanese villa suggest "restfulness and stability" (fig. 4–16), while the lines of the Sears Tower suggest "power and strength" (fig. 4–17). Lines—descriptive or implied—have their own "personalities."

Abstract Lines

Abstract lines are mainly found in abstract art. Abstract art can be nonrepresentational (also called *nonobjective*). There is little or no attempt to show a pictorial likeness or image. **Abstract lines** are not used to symbolize, to outline, or to look like shading. Abstract lines are expressive, not descriptive. As a viewer, you have little choice but to see abstract lines for what they are: lines.

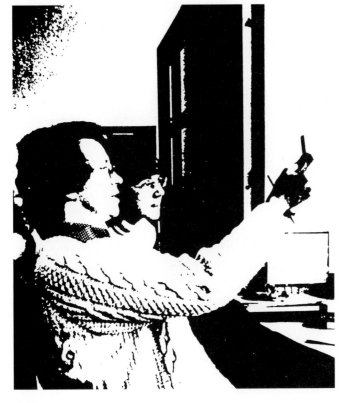

4–21

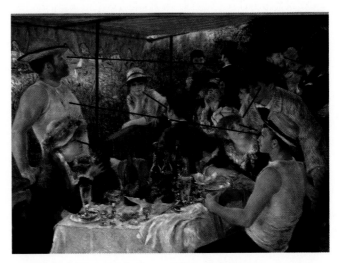

4–22 Which lines of sight do you think are the most important? Pierre Auguste Renoir, *Luncheon of the Boating Party,* 1881. Oil on canvas, 51″ x 68″ (130 x 173 cm). ©The Phillips Collection, Washington, DC.

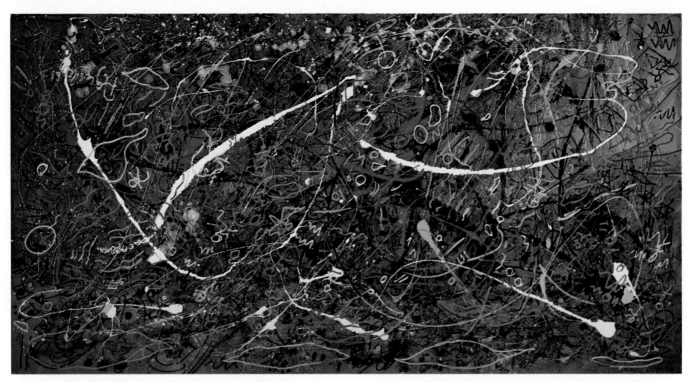

4–23 José Roberto Aguilar, *The Brazilian Myth (O Mito Brasileiro)*, 1981. Acrylic on canvas, 7´ x 13´ (2.4 x 4 m). Collection of Kim Esteve, São Paulo, Brazil.

Try it Yourself

Look at the examples of abstract art (figures 4–23, 4–24, 4–25, and 4–26). Come up with a word or two to describe the feeling that each work seems to express. You can use the words in the columns below or add your own words. Compare your set of words with your classmates' words. See if your choice of words agrees with theirs.

aggressive	delicate	soft
awkward	energetic	strong
balanced	explosive	swift
blunt	graceful	timid
bristling	nervous	unstable
brutal	powerful	weak
calm	restless	wild
chaotic	rhythmic	

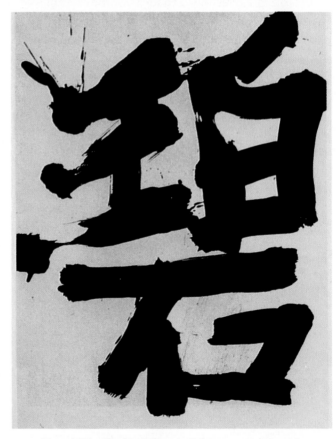

4–25 Kazuaki Tanahashi, *Heki*, 1965. Ink on paper, 36˝ x 28˝ (92 x 71 cm). East-West Center, Honolulu.

4–26 James Feltner, *Chien.*

4–24 Ibsen Espada, *El Yunque*, 1985. Oil and ink on paper applied to canvas. 53 ¼″ x 63″ (135 x 160 cm). McMurtrey Gallery, Houston.

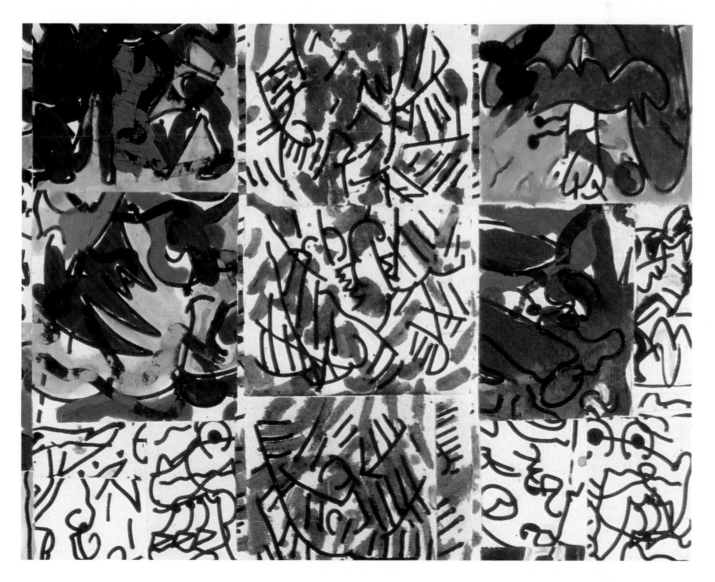

Line Personalities

If you did the Try it Yourself, you matched abstract lines with adjectives such as aggressive or calm. Could you match people you know with these adjectives?

How does a line acquire a personality? There is no single answer to this question. However, we tend to associate lines with other things in our experience. We associate certain feelings with a line's shape, movement, and direction.

Shape. Straight lines remind us of things like buildings that are strong or powerful. Curved lines remind us of people, animals, or plants that are soft, delicate, or graceful. Jagged lines suggest objects like broken glass, sawteeth, or lightning that are bristling, aggressive, or wild.

Movement. A line, as we explained, is often the record of real movement. We associate lines with the movements of animals, people, or even our own bodies. Straight lines may seem rigid or swift. Curved lines seem relaxed or graceful. Jagged lines seem nervous or awkward.

Direction. If a line has movement, it also has direction. Lines that move in vertical directions seem strong; horizontal lines seem calm or stable; and diagonal lines seem unstable (fig. 4–27).

These descriptions are *generalizations*. The personality of a particular line may be due to its shape, movement, and direction. But it can also be influenced by other elements in the artwork. For example, shapes, colors, textures, and even other lines in a work of art can affect the personality of a line. (The visual elements of shape, color, and texture are discussed in later chapters.)

Summary

There are many kinds of lines. We can see lines in nature and in our human-made environment. Letters and numbers on book pages are made up of lines. Lines appear on maps and even musical scores.

Lines in art also come in various forms. Lines can be *descriptive, implied,* and *abstract.* Descriptive lines are created with a variety of tools, and can be outlines, contour lines, single lines, or hatching. On the other hand, lines can be implied by the edges of forms in paintings, sculptures, and buildings. Lines can be implied by the process of closure and by lines of sight. Abstract lines, unlike descriptive lines, usually do not symbolize or represent anything except themselves.

All lines—whether descriptive, implied, or abstract—can express feelings and ideas. We can talk about lines as having personalities. We give personalities to lines by associating certain feelings with a line's shape, movement, and direction. The expressive qualities of lines are an important part of the aesthetic experience.

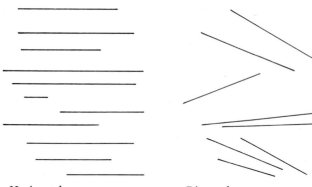

Horizontal   Diagonal

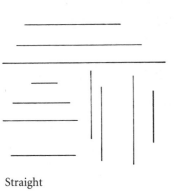

Straight

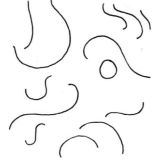

Curved

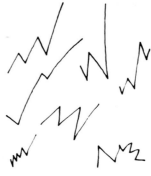

Jagged

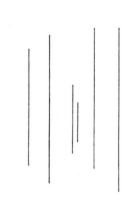

Vertical

4-27

Lines Express Feelings

Artists communicate ideas and feelings through lines. Van Gogh's drawing of cypress trees shows how lines can express spiraling rhythm and energy. Create an abstract or nonobjective drawing. Try to show a particular idea or feeling through the lines you use.

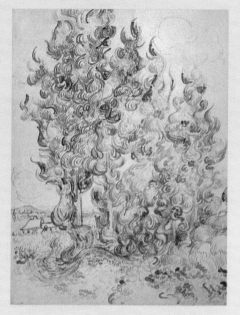

a. Vincent van Gogh, *Grove of Cypresses*, 1889. Pen and ink over pencil on paper, 24″ x 18″ (61 x 46 cm). The Art Institute of Chicago, Illinois (Gift of Robert Allerton).

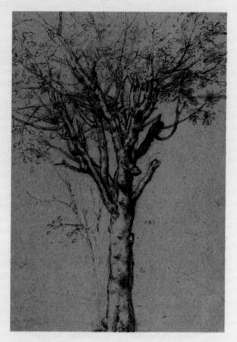

b. Leonardo da Vinci, *Study of a Tree*. The Royal Library, Windsor, England.

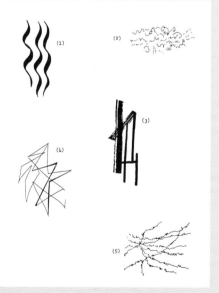

c. Match these words with the line drawings above. Timid, aggressive, strong, graceful, nervous.

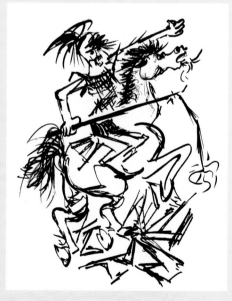

d. Create abstract drawings in which lines communicate ideas or feelings.

Chapter 5
Visual Elements: Shape and Form

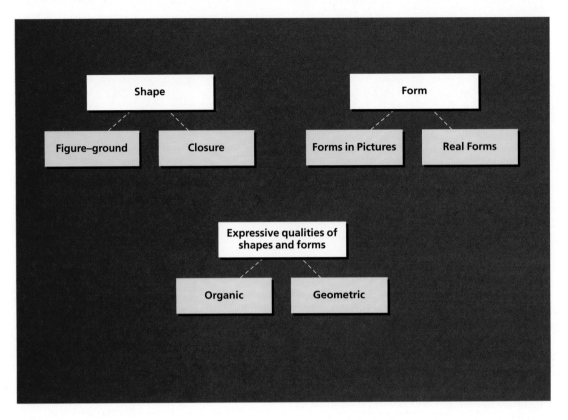

Overview

Chapter Objectives

Students should be able to:

EE 1   **1**   explain the figure-ground relationship in graphic artworks

EE 1   **2**   create compositions in which figure-ground relationships are stable or reversible

EE 1, 3   **3**   explain how foreshortening shape and form affects the apparent depth and viewing angles of objects and figures in artworks

EE 1, 2   **4**   produce foreshortened shapes using ellipses and trapezoids

EE 1, 4   **5**   explain how organic and geometric shapes and forms, and open and closed forms can relate to expressive qualities in artworks

Rationale

This chapter introduces several perceptual tendencies to see shapes and forms in certain ways, including figure-ground, closure, shape constancy, and size constancy. Knowledge of what affects the accuracy of visual perception will encourage students to look more carefully at their environment and artworks, rather than relying on what they *know* things look like. Awareness of these particular functions will contribute to their understanding of what artists do with shape and form in artworks.

Essential Chapter Concepts

• Shapes have height and width but no depth and are referred to as two-dimensional.

• Forms have height, width, and depth and are referred to as three-dimensional.

- Positive shapes are the figures in pictures.

- Negative shapes make up the ground in pictures.

- Figure-ground reversals may occur in two-dimensional patterns when shapes share the same contour line.

- Shape and size constancy influence what we see when looking at both real forms and pictures of forms.

- Foreshortening, the shortening of at least one dimension, is used to represent three-dimensional objects in a picture.

- Sculptors, ceramists, and architects deal with real three-dimensional forms.

- Organic shapes and forms are irregular and typical of forms found in nature.

- Geometric shapes and forms are very regular with straight or perfectly curved surfaces and edges.

Vocabulary

shape	foreshortening
positive shape	open form
pattern	ellipse
negative shape	organic shape
form	shape constancy
closure	geometric shape
figure-ground	size constancy
closed form	

Meet the Artist

Maurits C. Escher   Page 41

Mary Cassatt   Page 46

Lesson Plans

5.1   Reversible Drawings

  Page **T 48**   Time: 1 period

5.2   Reversible Patterns

  Page **T 50**   Time: 2 periods

5.3   Foreshortening

  Page **T 52**   Time: 1 period

5.4   Distance

  Page **T 56**   Time: 2 periods

5.5   Sculpting Without Seeing

  Page **T 58**   Time: 1 period

Handouts

Reversible Drawings   Page **T 60**

Foreshortening   Pages **T 61** to **T 63**

Study Questions   Page **T 64**

Test Questions   Page **T 65**

Chapter Closure
Evaluation

1   *Aesthetic Awareness:* Do students recognize that shape and form are elements that contribute to the aesthetic experience?

2   *Aesthetics/Criticism:* Are students able to explain figure-ground relationships and point them out in representational and abstract or nonobjective pictures?

R 1

3   *Aesthetics/Criticism:* Can students identify the dimensions of an object in a picture where foreshortening is used?

4   *Production:* Can students draw simple foreshortened shapes? Reversible patterns?

5   *Aesthetic Awareness:* Can students discuss artworks in terms of closure, size constancy, and shape constancy?

R 1

6   *Criticism:* Can students identify organic, geometric, open, and closed forms in artworks?

7   *Aesthetic Awareness:* Do students look for line, shape, and form when describing works of art?

Notes

Reversible Drawings

Shape and Form

Time: 1 period

Preparation

Rationale

When two figures share a common boundary line, they reverse, with first one appearing as figure, and then the other. Our eyes are accustomed to fixing on a specific figure, while everything around it is reduced to background. Reversible patterns can be found in advertising art, textile design, and optical paintings, such as those by Bridget Riley and Victor Vasarely, and in abstractions, such as Robert Motherwell's black lines on white.

Studio Materials

pencils or black pens, white paper, dark construction paper, scissors

Enrichment Materials

Slides:
• Riley, *Current,* 25
• Interior of Cordova Mosque (see pattern in arches), 62

Overhead Transparencies:
• Escher, *Circle Limit IV,* 3

Large Reproductions:
• Matisse, *The Casbah Gate,* 8
• Magritte, *The Plagiary,* 4
• Chan, *Wild Thing,* 19
• Glaser, *Saratoga,* 24

Teach the Lesson

Objectives

Students will be able to:

1 produce an outline drawing in which figure and ground are reversible (unstable)   EE 1, 2

2 understand that when two shapes share a common boundary line, they reverse the figure-ground relationship   EE 4

Vocabulary

Figures are shapes that seem to stand out from or appear to be on top of the ground.

Ground is the area that appears to be underneath or surrounding the figure.

Shape is a two-dimensional area with a boundary; it has only height and width and appears flat.

Warm Up

1 Ask students to draw several circles and squares about 3 inches wide. Have students draw an active line—one that makes some turns—in the middle of the first shape from top to bottom, dividing the shape approximately in half. Can they see the reversing figures? Which is figure and which is ground? You may want to demonstrate on the chalkboard.

2 Let students try different lines in their remaining shapes. Have them color one half of one of the drawings black to make the reversing illusion even stronger.

Explore and Develop

1 Can students explain what is different about the figure-ground relationship in their drawings and regular pictures? (They reverse.)

2 Use the Shape Quiz on Student Edition page 40 to explain these concepts:

a. Lines describe shapes.

b. The *figure* is the image the artist creates; it is placed on top of or surrounded by ground.

c. The *ground* is the area underneath or surrounding the figure.

d. In figure 5–4, the vase and the two faces share the same outline. We can't be sure which is the figure.

Laser Discs:

Motherwell, Reconciliation Elegy, 1978

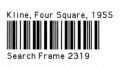

Search Frame 2337

Motherwell, detail

Search Frame 2339

Kline, Four Square, 1955

Search Frame 2319

Kelly, Colored Paper Image XI, 1976

Search Frame 3330

Matisse, Venus, 1952

Search Frame 2207

Soulages, 6 March 1955, 1955

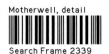

Search Frame 2217

e. When the artist uses the same outline or boundary for two shapes, a *reversible figure* is created because we can't see both shapes at the same time.

Begin Studio Experience 5.1

1 Have students lightly outline two rectangles about 5" x 7" on a sheet of white 9" x 12" paper.

Tell them to cut several 5" x 7" rectangles from a sheet of dark construction paper.

2 Students will fold one of the dark rectangles in half lengthwise. At this point, you may share the examples on page T 60.

3 Tell students to keep the fold to their left if they are right-handed, or to their right if they are left-handed. Students will draw an undulating line from the top to the bottom edge of the folded dark rectangle, dividing the space about equally.

4 Tell students to keep the paper folded and hold the folded side while cutting out the shape.

5 Have students unfold the dark shape and lay it in the pre-drawn rectangle on white paper. Do they have reversible figures? If students are not satisfied, have them try again.

6 To see the reverse work in a line drawing, have students lay their shape in one of their rectangles and trace around it with a good black line. Tell them to paste the dark paper figure in the other rectangle. Display the figures.

Evaluate and Reflect

1 Did students produce reversible figures?

2 Can students explain what makes a reversible figure-ground relationship?

3 Can students identify figure and ground in abstract or nonobjective works as well as representational ones?

Reteach

Provide pre-drawn 3" x 3" squares on white paper and pre-cut black rectangles. Have students cut the rectangles in half and alternate the shapes in neighboring squares on the white paper.

Extend the Lesson
Beyond the Basics

Explain to students that sometimes artists use the idea of reversible figures to create hidden images and optical illusions. Direct students' attention to the vase/faces on page 40. Ask them to consider what the image might look like if the details of the faces and the vase were filled in with shading techniques to create a realist effect. Suggest students trace their reversible figure onto a sheet of drawing paper and begin to fill in both spaces with shading techniques. Some students may want to make two tracings, one for experimentation and another for creating a finished drawing.

EE 1, 2

Cultural Connections

The Moors were past masters at filling floors and walls with patterns in which figures reversed. Assign a group of students to look for examples of Moorish art, particularly, the Alhambra in Spain. Have another group of students look for general information about the Moors. Use a map to see where the Moors lived and where the art is located. Identify dates and some events that took place at that time. What was happening locally and in other parts of the world?

EE 3

R 2

Connecting with Other Subjects

Science Ask students to look through science books and talk to the science teacher to find information about the workings of the human eye and how images are perceived. Some students may have difficulty seeing some image reversals. Why?

Reversible Patterns

Time: 2 periods

Preparation

Rationale

This experience builds on lesson plan 5.1. Here, students will create a reversible figure repeated across an entire surface, creating a reversible pattern similar to 13th century Moorish tile floors and walls or the prints of Maurits C. Escher. By completing this experience, students will be able to respond to artworks that present simultaneous views of space—reversing figure and ground.

Studio Materials

black 9" x 12" construction paper, light-weight white paper (for cutting shapes), glue, scissors, pencils, rulers, paper cutter, checkerboard (if you have one), 3" x 6" rectangles of white paper, 3" x 3" squares of black paper, 3" x 3" squares of white construction paper for patterns

Enrichment Materials

Overhead Transparencies:
• Escher, *Circle Limit IV,* 3

Large Reproductions:
• Nubian *Wall Painting,* 5
• Biggers, *Shotguns,* 3

Teach the Lesson

Objectives

Students should be able to:

1   create a pattern of reversible figures by alternating rows of white positive and negative shapes on a sheet of black construction paper   EE 1, 2

2   identify reversible figure patterns in both popular and fine arts   EE 3, 4

Vocabulary

Pattern is the repetition of elements or the combinations of elements in a readily recognized organization.

Organic shapes are found throughout nature and tend to have irregular edges that are never perfectly curved or straight.

Geometric shapes are very regular with edges that are perfectly straight or curved.

Warm Up

1   Give each student a 3" x 6" rectangle of white paper and a 3" x 3" square of black paper. Have them cut the black square into three equal strips and glue them down at equal intervals on the white rectangle. They should have created a very simple reversible pattern.

2   Ask students to define *pattern.* Establish the definition listed above. What is the organization of their striped patterns displayed vertically? horizontally? Display a checkerboard as an example of a reversible pattern.

Explore and Develop

1   Direct attention to Maurits C. Escher's biography and the accompanying print, *Circle Limit IV,* on Student Edition page 41. You may also want to display transparency 3. The print presents simultaneous views of angel and devil figures. The sphere appears three-dimensional because the figures become progressively smaller from the middle to the edges. Note that Escher's pattern is very complex and results from years of experimentation. The group will make simpler patterns.

2   Remind students that figure-ground reversals occur when two shapes share a common boundary line as shown in Studio Experience 5.1. The positive shapes they create may be *organic* or *geometric.*

Begin Studio Experience 5.2

1   Have students divide a sheet of 9" x 12" black construction paper into three rows

Laser Discs:

Matisse, Large Composition with Masks, 1953

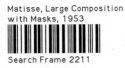

Search Frame 2211

Matisse, detail

Search Frame 2213

and four columns of 3-inch squares with ruler and pencil, keeping lines light. Students will place white shapes in these squares.

2 Point out the student example in Studio Experience 5.2. Negative and positive shapes were alternated in the rows, creating reversals horizontally and vertically.

3 Students should make a supply of 3" x 3" lightweight white paper squares. Tell students to fold *two* 3-inch squares in half and draw an undulating line on each square from the top edge to the bottom, dividing each folded square approximately in half. You may want to tell them to keep the fold to their left if they are right-handed.

4 Have students cut out the shape in each folded square. There will be two positive shapes and four negative. Tell students to position the two positive shapes in the first row of squares on the black paper. Students will place the negatives in back-to-back pairs in the two spaces below the positives.

5 If satisfied with the shapes, students will fold the positives and use them as patterns to draw the same line on at least four more folded 3-inch squares. Remind students to draw and cut with precision.

6 Students may find it easier to position the cutouts if they mark the middle of each outlined square on the black paper. They may try different arrangements, but should keep looking for the figure-ground reversal.

7 Have students use glue sticks to adhere the shapes to the black paper.

Evaluate and Reflect

1 Are figure-ground reversals readily visible in the students' works?

2 Can students describe the kinds of movement they sense in the reversible patterns?

3 Can students explain what causes figures to reverse?

Reteach

Have students divide a 9" x 12" sheet of white paper into 3-inch squares. Students will cut six 3-inch squares out of a sheet of colored paper and cut them all into the same *two simple* shapes (for example, from corner to corner of the square yields a triangle). Starting with the top row on the sheet of white paper, students will place half of the triangle in the left side of the first square, and the other half in the left side of the second square. Have students repeat until the page is full to produce a reversible pattern.

Extend the Lesson

Beyond the Basics

Encourage interested students to study Escher's work with reversible patterns. Have students work together in groups to discover other ways that shapes can be grouped to cause reversals. After studying Escher's prints, they might carve a linoleum block, and experiment with printing reversible images or patterns.

EE 1, 2

Cultural Connections

Direct students to Islamic art (page 225, fig.17–0) and the creation of patterns of reversible figures in floor and wall mosaics. There are reversible patterns in this small drawing.) Assign groups of students to find resource books showing similar designs from several other cultures such as African textiles and Navajo weaving. Have on hand current catalogs and advertisements showing home furnishings. Have students study the fabric designs and identify the source of inspiration for the contemporary fabrics.

EE 3

R 5

Connecting with Other Subjects

History Have students look at the works of Escher, Picasso, Calder, and Hopper (Chapter 5). Working together, have students lay out a timeline of historical events and several examples of each artist's work. Examine and discuss how each may have been influenced by the world in which he lived.

EE 1, 3

W 2

Shape and Form

Foreshortening

Time: 1 period

Preparation

Rationale

This activity increases students' understanding of foreshortening through application. Students create foreshortened shapes in drawings of geometric forms using ellipses and trapezoids with squares and rectangles cut from paper as patterns. (It is not a substitute for linear perspective, which will be presented in Chapter 7.)

Studio Materials

dark construction paper for patterns, pencils, 12" x 18" white drawing paper, scissors, glue sticks, duplicated trapezoid, square and rectangle shapes, carbon paper, rulers and heavy paper for patterns, duplicated sheets of trapezoid, square and rectangle shapes, visual examples on page T 61, T 62, and T 63.

Enrichment Materials

Slides:
• Raphael, *The School of Athens*, 91
• da Vinci, *The Last Supper*, 92

Large Reproductions:
• Swentzell, *The Emergence of the Clowns*, 22
• *Statue of Merti*, 6

Teach the Lesson

Objectives

Students should be able to:

1   draw foreshortened shapes that suggest depth in a picture, using ellipses, trapezoids, squares, and rectangles cut from heavy paper as patterns   EE 1, 2

2   identify and discuss foreshortening in two-dimensional artworks   EE 3

Vocabulary

Foreshortening makes a three-dimensional object represented in a picture appear at an angle by shortening one or two of the object's dimensions, such as width and depth.

A *trapezoid* is a shape with four angles and four sides, only two of which are parallel.

An *ellipse* is a somewhat flattened sphere—a curved shape that is short in the depth dimension.

Shape constancy is the tendency to see a shape as unchanging regardless of the viewing angle.

Laser Discs:

Toulouse-Lautrec, The Jockey, 1899

Search Frame 3237

Rubens, Saint Catherine of Alexandria, c 1600/1640

Search Frame 3164

Hopper, An American Landscape, 1920

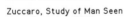

Search Frame 3310

Zuccaro, Study of Man Seen From Behind, c 1555

Search Frame 2649

Warm Up

1 Place one large can so the class sees the perfectly round bottom. Place another so they see across the bottom at an angle, and ask them to outline the two shapes.

2 Stand one shoe box on end so the class sees the rectangular bottom. Place another shoe box so they see across the bottom at an angle, and ask them to outline both shapes.

3 Ask students what they had to do to draw the can and box at an angle.

Explore and Develop

R 1 **1** Have students explain the terms *fore-shortening, ellipse,* and *trapezoid.* Ask the students to identify ellipses and trapezoids in the classroom. By swinging the class-room door from closed to open position, you can present a trapezoid. See if the students can perceive the distortion that occurs when a shape is viewed at an angle.

2 To explain *shape constancy,* compare the eye to a camera. The eye sees what the camera records, but shape constancy interferes with our ability to draw the "distorted" shape.

3 The photo images in figure A on page T 61 shows how the top of the shoe box photographed at an angle is actually shorter than the image taken from the top. The elliptical can lid in the angled picture is not as deep as it is wide. See also Student Edition pages 44 and 45.

4 Figure B on page T 61 shows how two ellipses can be placed one above the other and connected with lines to create a cylin-drical shape that appears to have a fore-shortened top.

5 Have students draw a vertical line about five inches long. Beginning at the top of the line, students will draw four or five ellipses of different lengths around the line.

6 Display figure C on page T 61. Show students how to connect the ellipses with lines to make three-dimensional drawings of vases, bottles, etc. Tell students to erase the back lines of all ellipses except the top one.

7 Attend to figures 5–20 and 5–22. The trailer in the truck drawing is a combina-tion of a square and a trapezoid. The wheels are ellipses. In the Bouts painting, the ceil-ing is a trapezoid and the back wall is a square.

Begin Studio Experience 5.3

1 Use the examples on pages T 62 and
T 63 to show how trapezoids, rectangles,
and squares can be combined to produce
foreshortened geometric forms. Give students duplicated sheets with trapezoids,
rectangles, and squares that have edges of
the same length (for example, two squares
with edges that match the height of the two
parallel edges of a trapezoid; two rectangles
with edges that match the height of the two
parallel edges of the trapezoid; a larger trapezoid with one height edge that matches a
height edge of the first trapezoid, etc.).

2 Have students use carbon paper to
trace the duplicated shapes on heavy paper.
Then let them cut the heavy paper shapes
out and use them as patterns.

3 Share the examples on pages T 62 and
T 63 with students. Demonstrate drawing
around combinations of the shapes to create foreshortened forms.

4 Encourage students to experiment with
combinations to draw clusters of buildings.
Trapezoids, squares, and rectangles can be
used for doors and windows too. Can they
make hallways and sidewalks? Where can
some ellipses be used? Tell them to try some
overlapping of shapes, erasing lines where
necessary to obtain an in-front-behind
appearance in the drawing.

Evaluate and Reflect

1 Discuss the results. Were students able
to use the given shapes to draw forms with
receding sides to suggest depth?

2 Ask students to identify shapes that
appear to recede. Which dimensions appear
shortened?

3 Can students explain foreshortening
and identify examples in pictures?

4 Can students explain shape constancy?

Reteach

Provide students with ellipses cut from construction paper. Show students how to glue
them in place, draw around them lightly,
connect them with lines, remove the shapes,
and erase the back lines of all but the top
ellipse. Provide pre-cut trapezoids, squares,
and rectangles. Assemble combinations to
suggest advancing-receding and foreshortened shapes.

Extend the Lesson

Beyond the Basics

EE 2 Establish a light source for the drawing, and add shading to the outlined forms to increase the appearance of depth.

EE 1 Explain to students that learning to see foreshortening is an important step toward drawing what one sees. Suggest that they look through magazines to find several interior and/or exterior scenes with an illusion of deep space. What the camera does in recording the image on a two-dimensional surface is similar to what artists do when they draw. Use a marker to outline the foreshortened shapes in the photo. Then ask students to take another look at their environment and identify shapes that they perceive as foreshortened.

Cultural Connections

EE 1 Ask students to look at Figure 17–0 on page 225. The work shows a very shallow space. The complicated patterns of the carpets and floor tiles are not foreshortened. Ask students to look carefully to find parts of the drawing where the artist has attempted to show depth. What kind of perspective has the artist used? Ask students to explain what the artist would need to do to make the drawing look more real.

Connection with Other Subjects

Math The connection between mathematics and the concepts studied in this chapter are very important. Work in each area may help in understanding the other. Suggest students review mathematical concepts related to the understanding of two and three-dimensional geometric figures and the division of space.

Distance

Shape and Form

Time: 2 periods

Preparation

Rationale

Size constancy is a tendency to see an object as unchanging in size regardless of its distance. To suggest an object is at a great distance in a representational drawing, the artist may drastically reduce its size in comparison to objects placed in the foreground of the picture. This experience lets the student compare the effect of distance on the size of an object with the student's knowledge of the size of the objects.

Studio Materials

black *water-soluble* markers with pointed nibs, 11" x 17" white paper, 12" x 18" paper frames, rulers, pencils, masking tape

Enrichment Materials

Slides:
• Raphael, *The School of Athens,* 91
• Indian, *Karibbe Attacks Iraj,* 52

Overhead Transparencies:
• Raphael, *The School of Athens,* 10

Large Reproductions:
• Biggers, *Shotguns,* 3
• Matisse, *The Casbah Gate,* 8
• Yan, *Brushfire with Animals Fleeing,* 16

Teach the Lesson

Objectives

Students should be able to:

1   demonstrate the effects of distance on the size of objects by tracing an outdoor scene on a windowpane to see how small the images are compared to what students know the size of the objects to be   **EE 1**

2   use diminishing size and foreshortening in a drawing to depict depth in the picture plane   **EE 1, 2**

3   analyze the use of diminishing size as a depth device when it occurs in artworks   **EE 1**

Vocabulary

Size constancy refers to the tendency to see objects as the size they actually are, or as a compromised size, rather than their apparent smaller size due to distance.

Warm Up

1   Have the students step into the hall with their pencils and a piece of paper. Ask them to write down their estimate of the size difference in height between the nearest and farthest room entrances or doors.

2   Then have them hold their pencils vertically, measuring the difference in height of the nearest and farthest doors, and write down their second difference estimate. Ask them to return to the room to share their estimates.

Explore and Develop

1   Show the slides of *The School of Athens* and *Karibbe Attacks Iraj.* Discuss the differences in depth, giving attention to the presence or lack of diminishing size to suggest distance.

Begin Studio Experience 5.4

1   Provide each student with the materials listed above. Have students stand at windows where they will see buildings, fences, sidewalks, and other objects. Tell students to tape the paper frame to the window so a scene is included in it. Make sure they don't include too much sky or large expanses of lawn.

2   Suggest that they brace an elbow against the window and rest their forehead on that hand to maintain a steady view. Students should concentrate on some central shape and trace it on the window. Tell them to

Laser Discs:

Bruegel, Rabbit Hunters, 1566

Search Frame 3158

Delacroix, Arabs Skirmishing in the Mountains, 1863

Search Frame 1130

Delacroix, detail

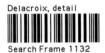

Search Frame 1132

Boudin, Ships and Sailing Boats Leaving, 1887

Search Frame 1204

Degas, Before the Ballet, 1888

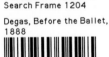

Search Frame 1352

Pissaro, Boulevard des Italiens, Morning, 1897

Search Frame 1480

keep that shape inside the traced outline while they complete the rest of the drawing.

3 Caution students not to change their position or viewing angle while drawing. They should not stop until the entire scene is outlined.

4 When the drawing is completed, ask them to step back and see the size of outlined objects as they were reflected on the retina of the eye versus the compromised size of the objects as they see them at a distance. Look for some converging lines and possibly ellipses.

5 If time permits, allow students to continue this experience by placing a sheet of white drawing paper over the window outline and tracing it with light pencil line. Tell them not to worry about crooked lines at this time.

6 Have students remove the paper frame and wipe the marker drawing from the window with a wet paper towel.

7 Let students use rulers and fine-point black markers to straighten lines and edges. Encourage students to use their knowledge of foreshortening and diminishing size to show distance.

Evaluate and Reflect

1 Can students describe how depth is shown in their drawings? Are there converging lines, large to small, and low to high objects in their drawings?

2 Display a reproduction of a representational scene. Can students locate depth devices in the artwork that are similar to what they used in their drawings?

Reteach

Occasionally students try to draw the scene on the window rather than trace it. They are looking at their drawing, rather than at the scene. Help them select a scene that will be easy to outline. Have them try again, concentrating on holding a steady position, closing one eye, bracing the head, and outlining shapes.

Extend the Lesson
Beyond the Basics

Some students may wish to take the drawing farther. To increase the illusion of depth, they might shade objects based on an imagined light source. Encourage students to make the connection between this system, isometric and linear perspective. **R 4**

Cultural Connections

Have students research the methods used to create the illusion of depth in two-dimensional art at different times in history and in different cultures: for example, position in space in Persian and Indian art or isometric perspective in Japanese paintings. Suggest students also look at the work of some of the primitive or untrained artists in early American history. Is there a relationship between their methods of showing depth and the other works prior to the Italian Renaissance? **EE 1, 3** **R 4** **R 5**

Connecting with Other Subjects

History One of the most significant events occurring during this period was the invention of a printing press with movable type in 1455. Gutenberg's invention, for the first time, made a wealth of information available to readers throughout Europe. In light of the tremendous growth and discovery occurring during the 15th century, ask students to consider how that growth may have been accelerated through this invention. **R 4**

Language Arts, History The discoveries of the Renaissance led to the "age of enlightenment." Explain to students how works by Masaccio and Donatello in the early 15th century were so real that viewers, having never seen anything like them before, were frightened and ran away. Ask students to consider the fear and superstition that was prevalent at the time, such as falling off the edge of a flat world, and the discoveries that began to shed new light on old beliefs. Suggest students work with the language arts and history teachers and write a paper exploring these ideas. **EE 3** **R 4** **R 5** **W 2** **W 3**

Sculpting Without Seeing

Time: 1 period

Preparation

Rationale

To experience forming a mental image on the basis of touch, students will form a clay sculpture with the clay concealed in a paper bag. The experience will help them appreciate the artist's need to visualize a form from all sides when creating a sculpture.

Studio Materials

modeling clay, large paper bags, wrapping paper for table tops, plastic bags (optional)

Enrichment Materials

Overhead Transparencies:
• Hepworth, *Pendour,* 2

Large Reproductions:
• Swentzell, *The Emergence of the Clowns,* 22
• Lucero, *Zoomorphic Dog Vessel,* 9

Teach the Lesson

Objectives

Students should be able to:

1 develop mental images of objects on the basis of touch by modeling a clay sculpture concealed in a bag   EE 1, 4

Vocabulary

Closed forms are solid and heavy and have few or no openings.

Open forms allow space to penetrate.

Warm Up

Ask students to pair off. Blindfold one student in each pair. Have the partner select a simple object and place it in the blindfolded student's hands. Using only the sense of touch, the blindfolded student will identify the object. Have the student verbally describe the object based on clues from touching it. Repeat for the second student.

Explore and Develop

1 Discuss the students' reactions to the Warm Up. Discuss the need for the sculptor to visualize or form a mental image of what a sculpture will look like since all sides of the work cannot be seen at once.

2 Discuss transparency 2, Hepworth's *Pendour,* as an open sculpture. Compare it with Noguchi's *Great Rock of Inner Seeking,* a closed form, in figure 5–34.

Begin Studio Experience 5.5

1 Explain how to model a three-dimensional clay form, which may be open or closed, with the clay concealed in a paper bag.

2 Have students cover tables with paper, lay a large bag on its side, place clay in the bag, and model a three-dimensional clay sculpture without seeing it. Students must use their powers of visualization and sense of touch to model a clay sculpture. Request that they turn the clay to model it from all sides.

3 Before taking the clay sculpture out of the bag, ask students to change places with their partner and use their sense of touch to visualize and describe what the other person's work looks like.

4 Were students able to create a reasonably accurate image of their partner's sculpture based on their sense of touch?

5 Have them return to their own sculptures, remove them from the bag, and compare what they had visualized with the real object.

Laser Discs:

Modigliani, Head of a woman, c 1910

Search Frame 2537

Arp, Mirr, 1936-1960

Search Frame 2549

Brancusi, Maiastra, c 1911

Search Frame 2561

Brancusi, Bird in Space, c 1911

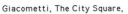

Search Frame 2563

Giacometti, The City Square, 1948-1949

Search Frame 2575

Brancusi, Agnes E. Meyer, 1929

Search Frame 2565

Evaluate and Reflect

1   What parts of the sculpture did or did not resemble what the student visualized?

2   What parts of the sculpture were easier to visualize? Can students explain why?

3   Did students create an open or closed form?

4   Were they more successful in visualizing their own sculpture than that of their partner?

5   Discuss how the sense of touch and visual perception can reinforce one another.

Extend the Lesson

Beyond the Basics

EE 1, 2   Some students may develop the clay pieces after discussing the expressive qualities of shapes and forms. Refer to text figures 5–32, 5–33, and 5–34, and the discussion of organic and geometric shapes and forms, and open and closed forms.

EE 1, 3

R 5   Georgia O'Keeffe was a painter who lived from 1887 to 1986. During the last years of her life, as her eyesight began to fail, she turned to sculpture. Have students find examples of her sculpture and compare them with her paintings. How are they alike or different? What mood or feeling do they think O'Keeffe was trying to communicate with her paintings? Do students feel that O'Keeffe's sculptures communicate successfully?

Cultural Connections

Have students look through their text for examples of sculpture by artists from other cultures, e. g. the Tlingit Indians of Southeast Alaska, fig. 17–26, the Ife and Benin cultures, Nigeria, 17–11 and 17–12, etc. They may note the emphasis on human figures and animals. Ask the students to think about what the sculptures mean to the various societies.

EE 3

R 5

Point out to students the psychological basis for how we perceive and interpret the meanings of open and closed forms. Ask them to consider the messages we perceive when we see a hand extended palm open as opposed to our perception of a closed fist, or open doors compared to closed doors. Have students look at figures 6.8 and 6.9. One figure is closed, the other is open. How did the artists achieve these effects? How does each figure make the viewer feel? Refer students to figures 18.11 and 18.50. Have students describe these figures and the effect of open and closed forms on the viewer. Do all cultures perceive these messages in the same way?

EE 1, 3

R 5

Connecting with Other Subjects

Language Arts Have students identify the style of the house in Hopper's painting on page 51. When was this style popular? When was the house probably built? Old buildings can be interesting subjects for artwork. Suggest students produce a series of drawings of old houses or other buildings in the community. Suggest they visit the historical society or public library to find information about interesting structures.

EE 2, 3

R 2

Reversible Drawings

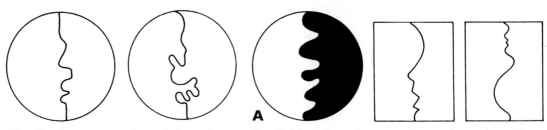

One line drawn across these circles and rectangles, dividing them about equally, results in reversible figures.

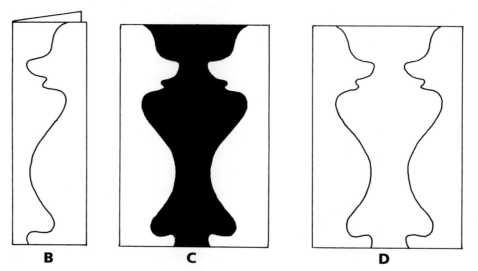

Animals should be drawn facing the fold. (**B**) Center the pattern in the 4" x 6" rectangle and trace around it. (**C**) The outlined drawing is a reversible figure. (**D**)

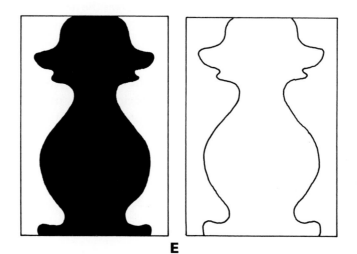

The paper pattern and the drawing do not reverse as effectively if the two profiles face outward. (**E**)

Foreshortening

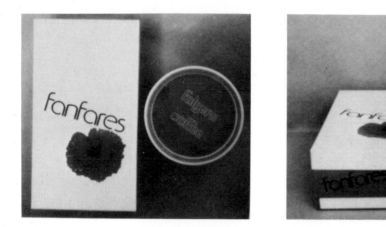

A Shoe box and coffee can viewed from above and at an angle.

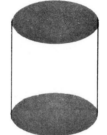

B Two ellipses can be placed one above the other and connected with side lines to create a cylindrical shape that appears to have a foreshortened top.

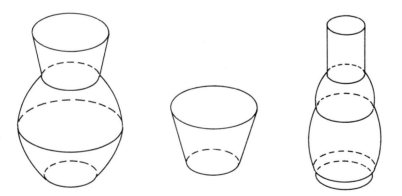

C Combine ellipses of different sizes, and connect them with lines to make objects that look three-dimensional.

Foreshortening (continued)

Make your own trapezoid patterns for each of these three-dimensional forms.

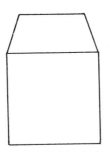

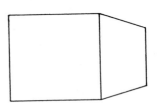

1. Trace a trapezoid with the long edge at the bottom. Add a square or rectangle to create a form with a receding top.

2. Use a trapezoid to create a receding side; add a square or rectangle to make the front.

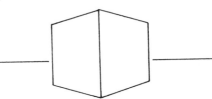

3. Join two trapezoids at the long edge to create a form with two receding sides. A ground line strengthens the appearance of depth.

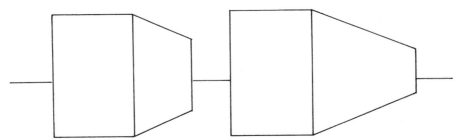

4. Make the trapezoid longer, and the form will appear to recede farther.

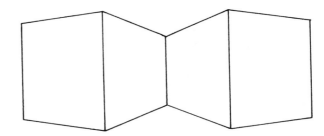

5. Four trapezoids joined at three corners seem to advance and recede. Could you add trapezoidal windows and doors?

Foreshortening (continued)

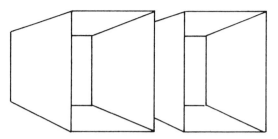

6. Here, rectangles and trapezoids were overlapped to produce an illusion of receding interior space. Two horizontal lines were added to suggest a shape at the back of the enclosure, which might be an opening or another surface. How would you shade the interior if you wanted the shape to appear as an opening?

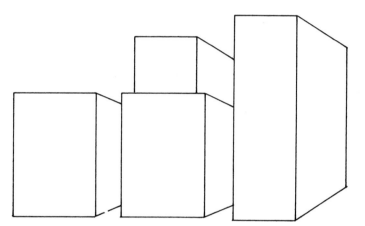

7. Overlapped rectangles and trapezoids of different sizes can be used to suggest the foreshortened shapes of buildings. Where could shading be used to further enhance the illusion of depth in the drawing?

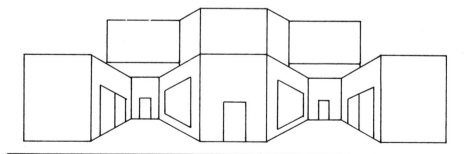

8. Try combining trapezoids with rectangles and squares to create forms that seem to recede in space.

Study Questions
Chapter 5–Visual Elements: Shape and Form

1 What is the difference between a shape and a form?

_____

2 What is the relationship between lines and shapes?

_____

3 Explain the term *figure and ground.*

_____

4 What are positive and negative shapes?

_____

5 Which artwork in the text is an example of figure-ground reversal?

_____

6 Give an example of *closure* found in this chapter.

_____

7 Define *shape constancy.*

_____

8 Define *foreshortening.*

_____

9 Define *size constancy.*

_____

10 What can be learned about a three-dimensional object using only the sense of touch?

_____

11 What is the difference between an organic shape and a geometric shape?

_____

12 Give one sculptural example of an open form and one of a closed form pictured in the chapter.

_____

_____

_____

Test Questions
Chapter 5–Visual Elements: Shape and Form

Circle the correct answer in each question.

1 An ellipse is to an ellipsoid as a

    a. circle is to a sphere.
    b. rectangle is to a cylinder.
    c. triangle is to a square.
    d. a and b.
    e. a, b, and c.

2 Shape constancy refers to the tendency to see

    a. all shapes the same no matter what the viewing angle.
    b. all objects the same size no matter how close or far away they are.
    c. foreshortened shapes.
    d. a and b.
    e. b and c.

3 This diagram illustrates

    a. a trapezoid.
    b. closure.
    c. a sphere.
    d. line of sight.

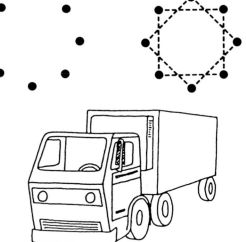

4 This drawing illustrates

    a. an aerial view.
    b. a two-dimensional object.
    c. size constancy.
    d. foreshortening.

5 How does viewing a three-dimensional artwork diffcr from viewing a two-dimensional artwork?

_____

_____

_____

Name: _____   Course: _____

Test Questions (continued)
Chapter 5–Visual Elements: Shape and Form

For questions 6 to 10 use the following list.

1. geometric/open   5. shaded
2. organic/open   6. hatched
3. positive shapes   7. three-dimensional
4. figure-ground reversal   8. two-dimensional

Answer the following questions while viewing the overhead transparency or text fig. 7–8 of the painted wood sculpture by Barbara Hepworth entitled *Pendour.*

6 This sculpture best illustrates _____ form.

7 Since this sculpture has height, width, and depth it is _____.

Answer the following questions while viewing the overhead transparency or text fig. 5–5 by M. C. Escher.

8 Sometimes the angels are the _____ and sometimes the devils are.

9 What term best describes this picture?

10 _____ lines are used to make patterns within shapes.

Study Answers
Chapter 5
Visual Elements:
Shape and Form

1 A shape is a two-dimensional area with a recognizable boundary; it has only height and width. A form is three-dimensional; it has height, width, and depth.

2 Lines can describe shapes; the edge of a shape implies a line.

3 A figure seems to stand out from a ground; the ground appears to be underneath and surrounding a figure.

4 Positive shape refers to the figure and negative shape to the ground.

5 *Circle Limit IV,* by M. C. Escher (text fig. 5–5).

6 Possible answers include: Visually connecting the dots to see a shape such as a circle or two squares as pictured in text figures 5–6 and 5–7; or visually connecting shapes to see an image such as a locomotive in text figure 5–8.

7 The tendency to see a shape as unchanging regardless of the viewing angle.

8 Making a three-dimensional object in a picture appear at an angle by shortening one or two of its dimensions.

9 The tendency to think that an object's size doesn't change no matter how far away it is.

10 Possible answers include: develops the ability to form a mental image without the use of sight; the sense of touch can make one more aware of an object's surfaces, edges, etc.

11 An organic shape is an irregular shape; a geometric shape is regular, having straight or perfectly curved edges.

12 Examples found in text may include: open form—*Untitled,* by Leeper (text figs. 5–28, 5–33, 5–35); or closed form—*Great Rock of Inner Seeking,* by Noguchi (text figs. 5–31, 5–32, 5–34).

Test Answers
Chapter 5
Visual Elements:
Shape and Form

1 A

2 A

3 B

4 D

5 A three-dimensional artwork has height, width and depth, therefore the viewer should move around the artwork to view it from more than one side. A two-dimensional artwork has only height and width, therefore it can be viewed only from one side.

6 2

7 7

8 3

9 4

10 6

Chapter 5
Visual Elements: Shape and Form

Shape

A **shape** is a two-dimensional area with a recognizable boundary. You can make a shape by drawing or painting lines on paper. You can make a shape by cutting something out of paper. The edge of the shape implies a line. As you can see, there is a relationship between lines and shapes.

Here is a quiz for you to test your knowledge about shape. Choose the response that identifies the following figures:

Shape Quiz I

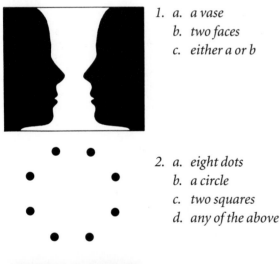

1. a. a vase
   b. two faces
   c. either a or b

2. a. eight dots
   b. a circle
   c. two squares
   d. any of the above

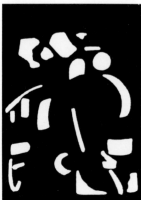

3. a. a black and white pattern
   b. a locomotive
   c. either a or b

Answers:
1. (c)
2. (d)
3. (c)

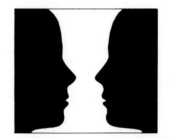 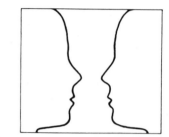

5-4 When you took the quiz, which did you see first: the vase or the faces? Did you see both? Can you see both at the same time? Does it matter whether the shapes are solid or outlined?

All of the shapes in the quiz can be seen in more than one way. Look again at the illustration for question 1 (fig. 5-4). It provides a good example of the tendency to see a **pattern** as two kinds of shapes: figure and ground. A **figure** appears to stand out, to be "on top of" a ground. A **ground**, on the other hand, appears to be underneath and surrounding a figure. The white shape in the illustration is the figure and the black shape around it is the ground *if you see the pattern as a vase.* However, the black shapes are figures and the white is the ground *if you see the pattern as two identical faces looking at each other.* Try to see it either way. Such a pattern can be "read" in two different ways, but not both ways at once. You can reverse the figure and ground. Artists use the term **positive shape** to refer to figure and **negative shape** to refer to ground.

Circle Limit IV by M. C. Escher (fig. 5-5) is an excellent example of figure-ground, or positive-negative, reversal in an artwork. Which is figure: black or white? Can you see it either way? Can you see it both ways simultaneously?

Maurits C. Escher

1898–1972

Devils link together and the spaces between them form angels. Or, do the spaces between the angels form devils? Maurits Cometis Escher experimented with many repeating patterns similar to the one in *Circle Limit IV*, in which the edges of one object help to form the shape of another.

Escher's fascination with the repetition of geometric shapes is just one aspect of his art. An accomplished printmaker, Escher first became interested in art in his high school in the Netherlands. There he learned to create designs by rolling ink on the textured surface of a carved linoleum plate, and imprinting this inked surface onto paper. This printmaking process could be repeated to make multiple copies of a single image.

Following formal training in graphic arts at college, Escher experimented with a range of subject matter for his prints. Early imagery included Escher's observations of the real world, especially scenes he recorded from visits to Italy and Spain. His interest in nature and reality gradually gave way to an obsession with invented landscapes— dreamy worlds filled with strange creatures and impossible perspectives.

Like the multiple patterns of devils and angels in *Circle Limit IV*, there are multiple levels on which to look at this artist: as a master printmaker, a master drawer, and as a man with a masterful sense of imagination and creativity.

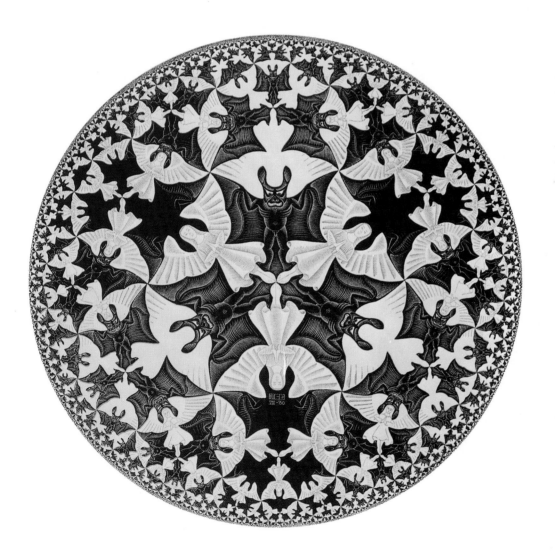

5–5 What are the reversible figures in this print by Escher? In what ways does the meaning change when the figures are reversed? M. C. Escher, *Circle Limit IV*, 1960. Woodcut in two colors, diameter 13 ½″ (34 cm). ©1960 M. C. Escher Foundation, Baarn, Holland.

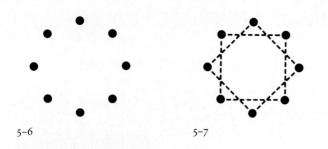

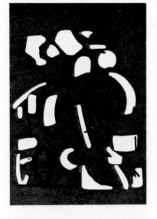

5-6   5-7

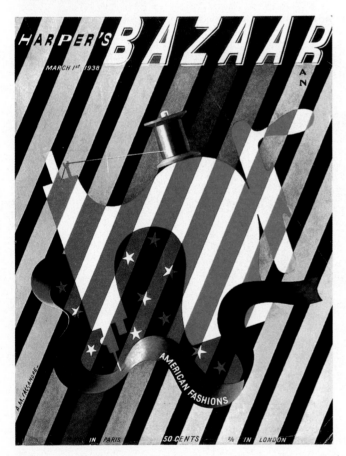

5-8 Did you see the locomotive when you took the quiz?

5-9 A. M. Cassandre, *Harper's Bazaar* magazine cover, March 1938, U.S.A. Courtesy *Harper's Bazaar*.

Return again to the quiz. Questions 2 and 3 involve **closure**. You learned about closure in the previous chapter. You probably saw the eight dots of question 2 as a circle (fig. 5–6). With some effort you could connect the dots to see them as forming two separate squares (fig. 5–7). It is much easier, however, to see a circle. The simplest shape is always the one that works best for closure.

Did you see question 3 as a random pattern of white shapes or as a locomotive (fig. 5–8)? At first you may not have seen the locomotive. But once your mind's eye connects the shapes, the locomotive stands out clearly.

At first glance, the cover of the 1938 issue of *Harper's Bazaar* (fig. 5–9) seems to be just some stripes that change color in the middle. A longer look reveals a few stars. The stars, together with the red and white stripes, remind us of the "stars and stripes," the American flag. Eventually, we see the image of a sewing machine. Because the sewing machine is not outlined, it is virtually a part of the black and lavender stripes. It is "embedded" in the background. It stands out from the background only because of a few changes in color and the addition of a spool of thread. The theme of the magazine is American fashion. In what ways does the cover express that theme? Do you think it is successful? Explain your answer.

The *Harper's* cover was influenced by early twentieth-century art, such as Picasso's *Three Musicians* (fig. 5–10). The painting can be read as an image of three musicians. Or it can be read as an abstract pattern of shapes. In fact, Picasso probably wanted you to appreciate the pattern more than the image, which is primarily humorous. The shapes of this painting are cleverly assembled. Although the shapes are not reversible, it is difficult to distinguish between figure and ground, or between positive and negative. Suppose this painting were an album cover. What kind of music would it be used for?

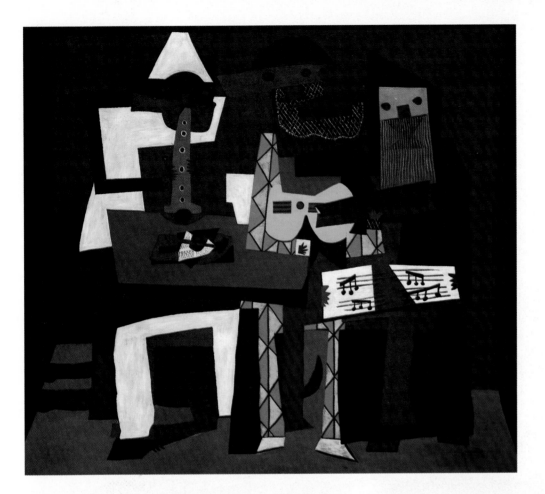

5–10 Pablo Picasso, *Three Musicians*, 1921. Oil on canvas, 6′ 7″ x 7′ 3 ¾″ (201 x 223 cm). The Museum of Modern Art, New York. Mrs. Simon Guggenheim Fund.

Studio Experience 5.1

Reversible Drawings

Produce an outline drawing in which figure and ground are reversible.

Studio Experience 5.2

Reversible Patterns

Create a reversible pattern. Cut an abstract figure out of construction paper. Then alternate the positive and negative shapes.

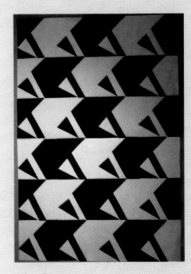

Kim Gass.

Form

Most of the things we use in everyday life are three-dimensional shapes, or ***forms***. A form has height, width, and depth. The chair you are sitting on and the desk you are working at are good examples of forms.

Forms in Pictures

In this section we will cover forms in pictures, that is, the *representation of three-dimensional objects on a two-dimensional surface.*

   Try this second quiz on shape. Answers to this quiz follow.

Shape Quiz II

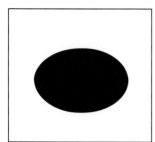

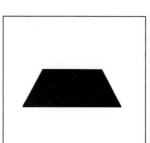

1. a. an ellipse
   b. a football
   c. a top of a pop can
   d. any of the above

2. a. a trapezoid
   b. a blade of a knife
   c. a side of a truck
   d. any of the above

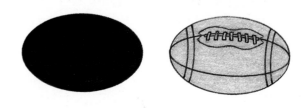

5–14

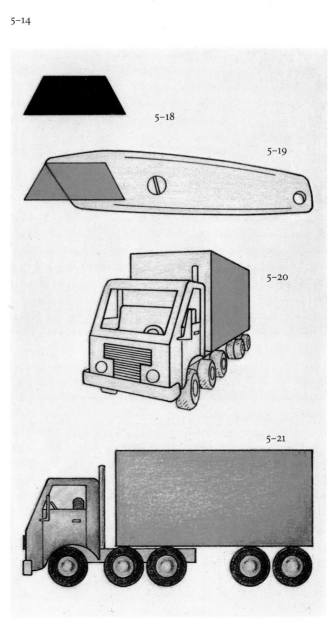

5–18

5–19

5–20

5–21

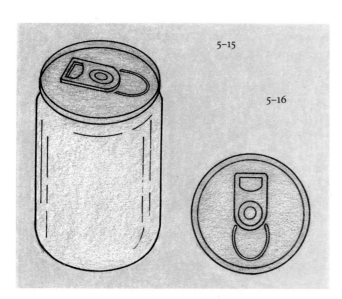

5–15

5–16

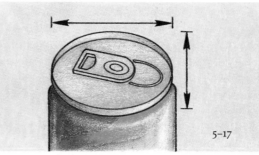

5–17

You probably guessed that the answer for both questions was (d), any of the above. Like the examples used in the first quiz, these illustrations can be seen in different ways.

The example in question 1 is an **ellipse** (fig. 5-13). An ellipse is a curved shape that is longer in one dimension than it is in another.

But, in a picture, an ellipse can also represent a three-dimensional *ellipsoid* (fig. 5-14). A football is an ellipsoid. (Did you ever kick an ellipsoid? Did it bounce like a round ball, or *sphere*?) An ellipse can show the top of a pop can as seen from an angle (fig. 5-15). But as you know, the true shape of a pop can top is a circle (fig. 5-16).

You may think of the pop can top as being shaped like a circle, even when you see the top from an angle. This is an example of **shape constancy**, or the tendency to see a shape as unchanging regardless of the angle at which you see it.

The artist who drew the ellipse wanted you to see it as a circle at an angle. He or she also wanted you to see the whole image as a three-dimensional *cylinder*. To make the pop can look as though it were on a table in front of you, the artist made the top look short in comparison with its width (fig. 5-17). The artist also curved the bottom edge of the can to match the curve of the ellipse at the top of the can. The object appears to be three-dimensional. Making a three-dimensional object in a picture appear to be seen at an angle by shortening one or two of its dimensions is called **foreshortening**.

Now look at the shape in question 2 of the quiz (fig. 5-18). It is a *trapezoid* with four straight sides. Two of its sides are parallel. A trapezoid can easily be used to represent the flat blade of a utility knife (fig. 5-19). It can also represent the side of an eighteen-wheel truck that is coming toward you (fig. 5-20). Compare the foreshortened view of the truck with its full view (fig. 5-21). Because of shape constancy, you think of it as being the same truck.

The use of foreshortening to make objects appear three-dimensional is very common in traditional paintings. Virtually every item in Dirk Bouts's *Polyptych of the Last Supper* (fig. 5-22) has been foreshortened. Identify as many items as you can. Some of these have been diagramed to show how they appear in the picture as it is, and how they would appear if not foreshortened (fig. 5-23).

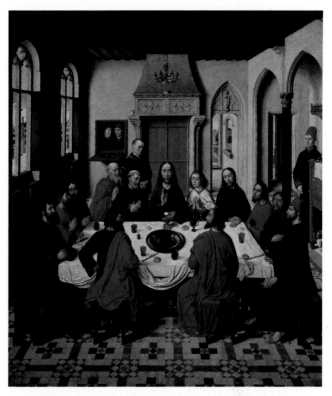

5-22 Dirk Bouts, *Polyptych of the Last Supper* (center panel), 1464-68. Oil on wood, 6′ x 5′ (183 x 153 cm). Louvain, Eglise de St. Pierre. Giraudon/Art Resource, NY.

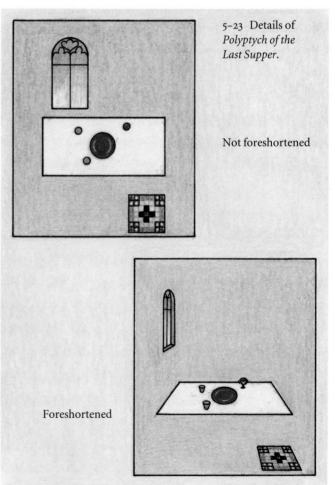

5-23 Details of *Polyptych of the Last Supper*.

Not foreshortened

Foreshortened

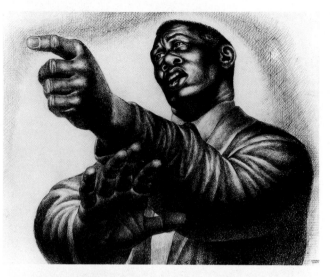

5-24 Charles White, *Preacher*, 1952. Ink on cardboard, 21 3/8″x 29 3/8″ (54 x 75 cm). Collection of The Whitney Museum of American Art (Purchase).

So far, we have seen examples of foreshortening in objects: pop cans, trucks, windows, and even floor tiles. Foreshortening can also be applied to people. Parts of Charles White's *Preacher* (fig. 5–24) are clearly foreshortened. Look at the lower part of his right arm, the upper part of his left arm, the palm and fingers of his right hand, and even his head. Notice how complicated the foreshortening is in both hands.

In Mary Cassatt's *The Bath* (fig. 5–25), both objects and people are foreshortened. This technique is readily seen in the forms of the basin and the pitcher. The effect of foreshortening is even more pronounced in the forms of mother and child. You may have noticed that their upper bodies, compared to their legs, are quite short. However, the most extreme effect of fore-shortening occurs in their faces. Look at how close together the eyes and the mouth are in both faces.

Meet the Artist

Mary Cassatt
1844–1926

Ignoring the objections of her parents, in 1861 Mary Cassatt boldly enrolled at the Pennsylvania Academy of Fine Arts. With a strong independent nature and financial support she was able to complete four years of work at this important art school at a time when art was frowned upon as an occupation for women. Rather than remain quietly at home, Mary preferred a life full of adventure and art.

Her keen desire to learn brought Mary to Paris, the center of the art world in 1865. There she was able to pursue her studies of the great masters of the past, while meeting and working with the new and influential Impressionist artists. Mary learned unfamiliar artistic techniques from her new friends, such as printmaking and the use of colorful pastels to create soft images. She also explored Europe, enjoying museums and attending gallery exhibitions of international art, from as nearby as Italy to as far away as Japan.

Inspired by what she saw, Mary began to create paintings and prints with renewed enthusiasm. Her explorations on the subject of mother and child were numerous. The gentle caress of the mother as she washes her child in *The Bath* is just one example of the hundreds of maternal images which Mary created during her lifetime.

Throughout her travels, her years living in Europe, and those when she returned to the United States, Mary remained an independent woman. She never chose to marry or have children. Rather, Mary Cassatt focused her life on the pursuit of technical expertise in painting and printmaking, and on achieving a beauty in her life and art which is uniquely her own.

5-25 Mary Cassatt, *The Bath*, ca. 1891–92. Oil on canvas, 39 1/2″x 26″ (100 x 66 cm). The Art Institute of Chicago, Robert A. Waller Fund.

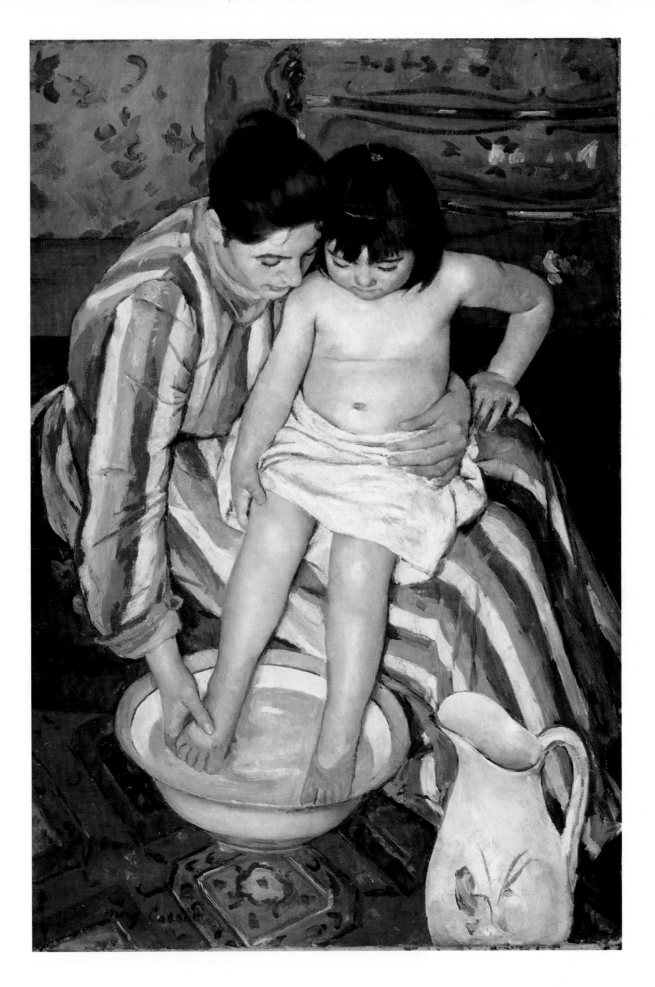

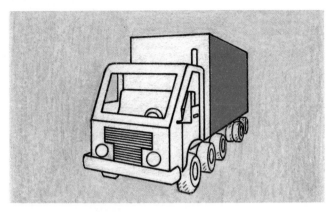

5–26

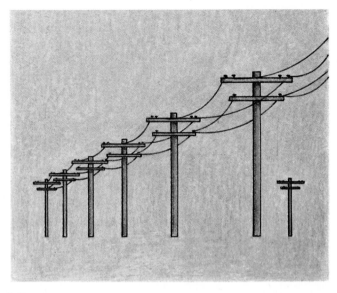

5–27

Look at the illustration of the foreshortened truck (fig. 5–26). Did you notice that the back of the truck is shorter than the front? This is because the back is farther away. To make something appear farther away in a picture, the artist makes it smaller. To show something close, the artist makes it larger. We tend to think of an object's size as unchanging no matter how close or far away it is. This tendency is called *size constancy*. An illustration of size constancy can be seen in a picture of utility posts (fig. 5–27). The artist drew the farthest away post twice—once on the left-hand side and again on the right-hand side beside the nearest post. Were you surprised to learn how small the image of the farthest away post is?

Studio Experience 5.3

Foreshortening

Create foreshortened shapes in drawings of geometric forms. Cut ellipses and trapezoids from paper to use as patterns.

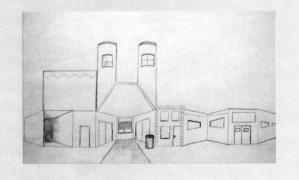

Studio Experience 5.4

Distance

Study how distance affects the size of objects. Trace an outdoor scene on a windowpane. Notice how small the images are compared to their actual size. Then trace the drawing. Use ruled lines and shading to enhance the illusion of depth.

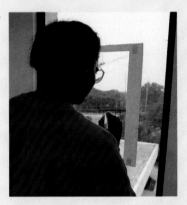

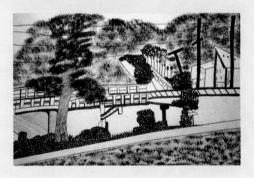

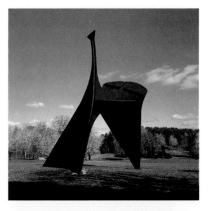

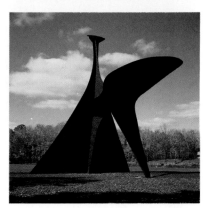

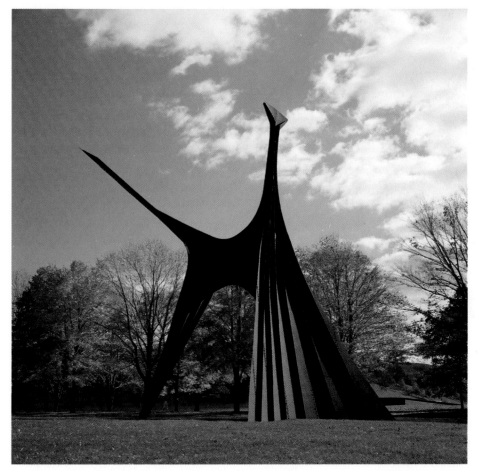

5–28 Alexander Calder, *The Arch* (three views), 1975. Steel painted black, 56′ high. Storm King Art Center, Mountainville, New York. Photographs by Jerry Thompson. Purchase and by exchange.

Real Forms

So far we have been talking about three-dimensional forms *in pictures*. Technically, all the pictures in this book, even the photographs, have only two dimensions—height and width—even though they may represent depth. However, you are surrounded by real forms. You, the other students and the teacher, as well as tables, cupboards, equipment, books, and the room itself have height, width, and depth.

Sculpture, pottery, metalwork, and architecture are a few examples of three-dimensional art. When a person makes a sculpture, he or she is making a *real* form, not the picture of a form. Suppose you wanted to make a sculpture of a truck. You would not foreshorten the side to make it *seem* long. You would make it long in reality.

When you look at a sculpture, you need to move around it in order to see its different sides (fig. 5–28). The many-sided form of a sculpture does not have to be viewed just by the eyes. You can also "view" it by moving your hands across its different surfaces, edges, and corners.

Sculpting Without Seeing

Model a clay sculpture while blindfolded. Or conceal the clay in a paper bag. Form a mental image of the sculpture and use your sense of touch to shape the clay.

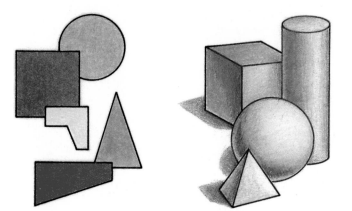

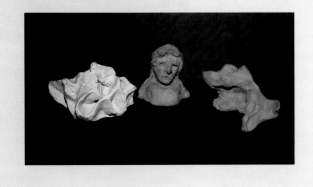

5-29 Organic Shapes and Forms.

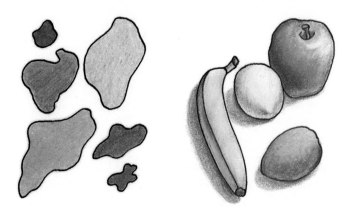

5-30 Geometric Shapes and Forms.

Expressive Qualities of Shapes and Forms

In Chapter 4 you learned about the expressive qualities of lines. For example, lines could be described as relaxed, excited, energetic, strong, or unstable. Shapes and forms also have expressive qualities. Artists typically classify shapes and forms as *organic* or *geometric* and *closed* or *open*.

Organic versus Geometric

Organic shapes and forms (fig. 5–29) are found throughout nature: earth, water, clouds, plants, animals, and people. Organic shapes tend to be irregular. Sometimes their edges are relatively straight, but never perfectly so. Sometimes their surfaces are relatively flat, but they are never perfect planes. Sometimes they are curved, but never perfectly round like a circle or a sphere.

Geometric shapes and forms (fig. 5–30) are typically found in things made by people, such as buildings, bridges, factories, and office machines. Unlike organic forms, geometric forms are very regular. Their edges and surfaces are straight or perfectly curved.

The forms of *The Mill* (fig. 5–31), a famous landscape painting by Rembrandt, are primarily organic. Even the few human-made objects, such as the mill and the rampart wall below the mill, show the effects of natural weathering and erosion. The edges of the forms are irregular.

Compare this painting to *House by the Railroad* (fig. 5–32) by Edward Hopper. The forms are primarily geometric. Except for the somewhat irregular lines of the roof and windows, the rest of the lines are fairly regular and straight. Note the vertical lines of the sides of the house. Horizontal lines are used for the eaves, the porch overhang, and the railroad track. Finally, notice the diagonal line of the shadow.

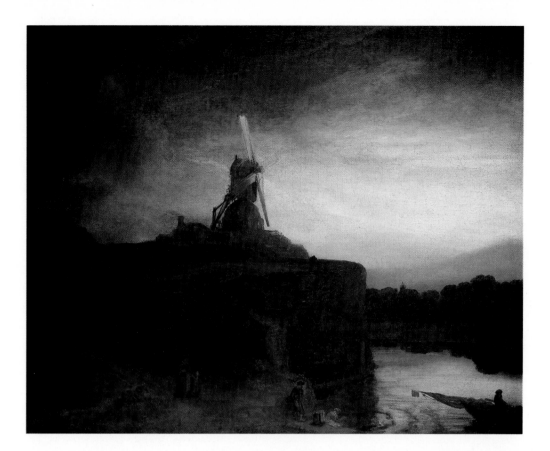

5–31 What do the geometric forms used in this painting seem to be expressing? Are the forms open or closed? Rembrandt van Rijn, *The Mill,* ca. 1650. Oil on canvas, 34 ½″ x 41 ⅝″ (0.88 x 1.06 m). ©1993 National Gallery of Art, Washington, Widener Collection.

5–32 As in the Rembrandt, can you tell what the geometric forms in this painting express? Are the forms open or closed? Edward Hopper, *House by the Railroad,* 1925. Oil on canvas, 24″ x 29″ (61 x 74 cm). Collection, The Museum of Modem Art, New York. Given anonymously.

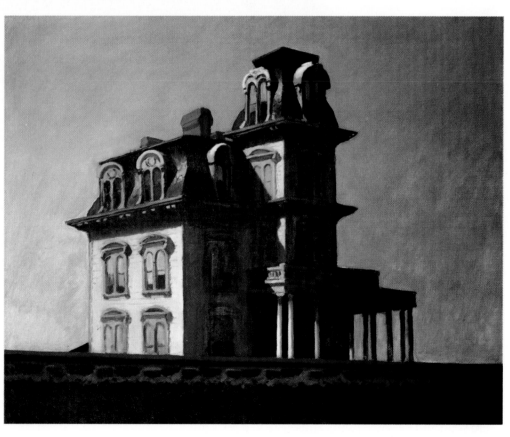

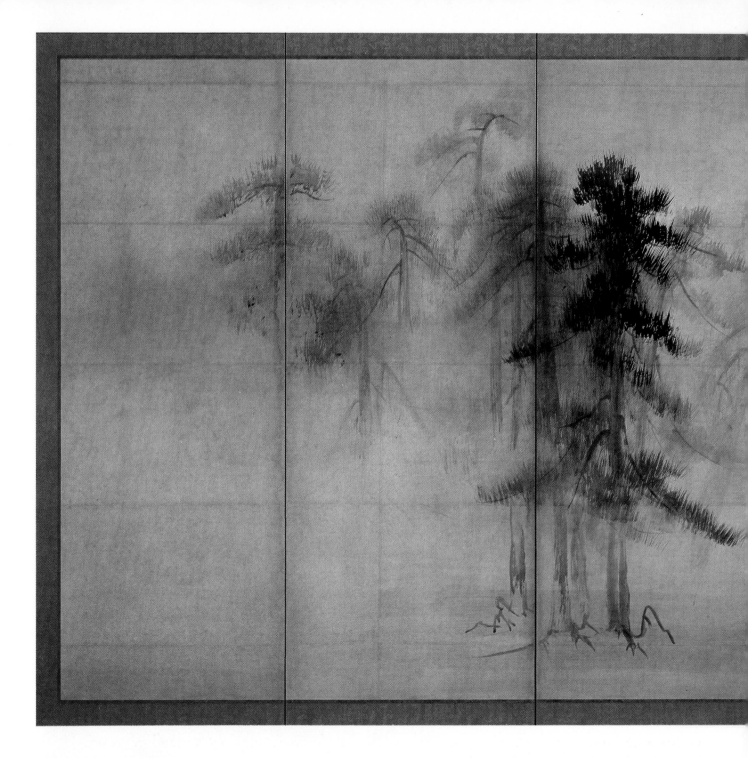

Closed versus Open

The scenes by Rembrandt and Hopper are similar. Both consist of single buildings set against the sky. Both express loneliness. The geometric forms in *House by the Railroad* make the loneliness seem even "starker." Furthermore, the forms in both paintings seem solid and heavy. The mill and the land it rests on seem massive. Even though the house by the tracks has a few windows, it looks heavy and dense. These are **closed forms** in both paintings. Nothing can penetrate them.

Open shapes and forms, on the other hand, allow space to penetrate. Notice the forms in the landscape *Pine Trees* (fig. 5–33) by Hasegawa Tohaku. Unlike the forms of Rembrandt and Hopper, the Tohaku trees are so open they almost float. Indeed, space penetrates the entire landscape. The pines are surrounded by acres of mist and light. How do the ideas and feelings expressed in the Tohaku compare with those in the Rembrandt? the Hopper?

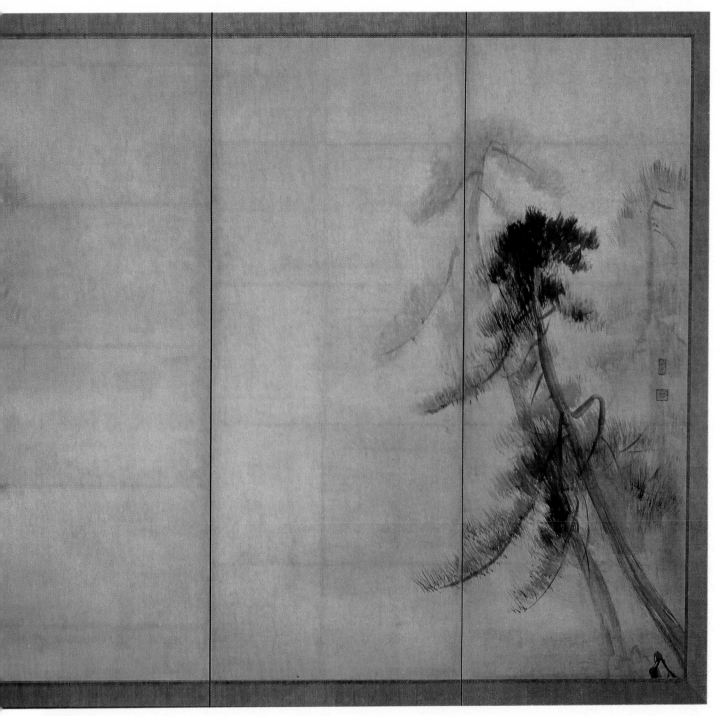

5-33 Hasegawa Tohaku, *Pine Trees*, Momoyama Period, Japan, 1539–1610. Ink on paper, 61″ (155 cm) high. Tokyo National Museum. (Photo courtesy the International Society for Educational Information, Inc.)

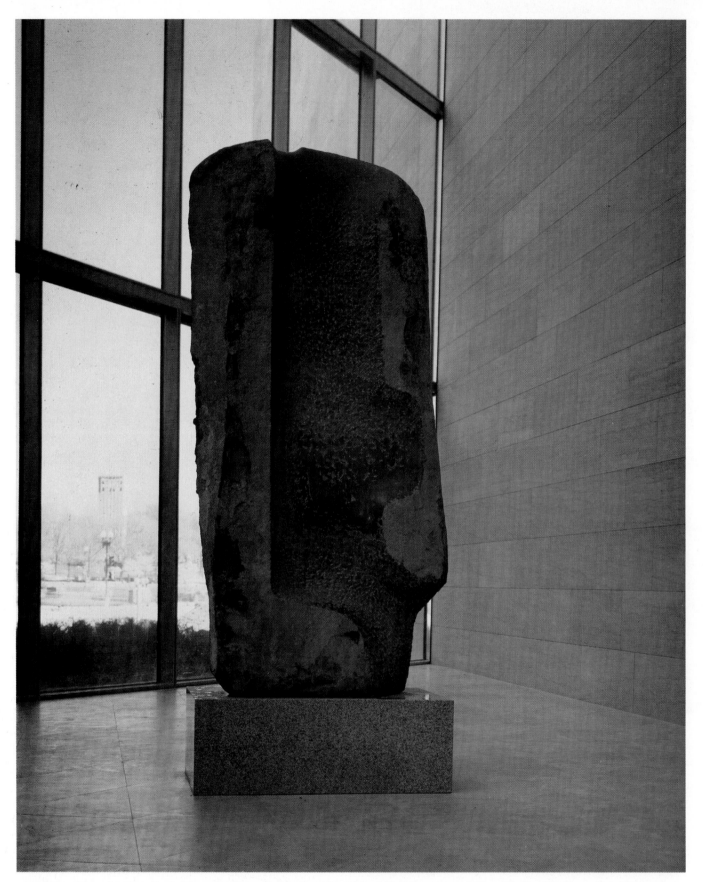

5–34 Isamu Noguchi, *Great Rock of Inner Seeking,* 1974. Basalt, 128″ x 63″ x 35″ (325 x 160 x 89 cm). ©1993 National Gallery of Art, Washington. Gift of Arthur M. Sackler, M.D. and Mortimer D. Sackler, M.D.

Forms in abstract art can also be described as organic or geometric and closed or open. The abstract sculpture in figure 5–34 by Isamu Noguchi is organic and closed. Abstract art does not represent things we see. However, it does express ideas. Noguchi's piece is called *Great Rock of Inner Seeking*. Do you think that it expresses the ideas suggested in the title? Explain your answer. Why did the artist use an organic form? a closed form?

Like the Noguchi piece, *Untitled* (fig. 5–35) by Doris Leeper is abstract. However, it is geometric and open. Even though it is open, does it seem as light as Tohaku's pines?

Try it Yourself

On a piece of paper, write a few sentences about the ideas and feelings that you think are expressed by Tohaku's *Pine Trees*, Noguchi's *Great Rock of Inner Seeking*, and Leeper's *Untitled*. Explain how the types of forms used in each work—organic or geometric, closed or open—affect the ideas and feelings that the work expresses.

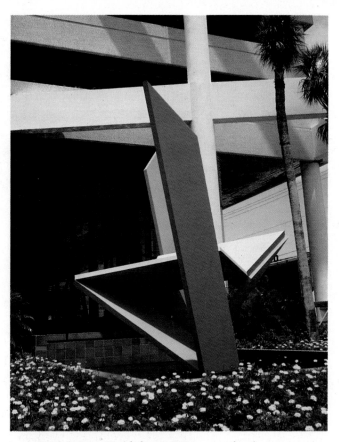

5–35 Doris Leeper, *Untitled*, 1984. Epoxy over aluminum, 15′ 3″ x 13′ 3″ x 12′ 9 ¼″. Barnett Centra, West Palm Beach, Florida. Photograph: David Zicki. Courtesy of the artist.

Summary

Shapes, like the letters and pictures in this book, have height and width but no depth. Forms, on the other hand, have height, width, and depth. Most of the things in this world, like ourselves, are forms.

This chapter discussed our tendencies to see shapes in certain ways. We see shapes in terms of figure-ground, closure, shape constancy, and size constancy. Figure-ground and closure often occur when we look at pictures or simple two-dimensional patterns. Shape and size constancy affect what we see when we look at both real forms and pictures of forms.

An artist often uses foreshortening to represent three-dimensional objects in a picture. Furthermore, an artist will make an object larger or smaller in a picture to make it appear to be closer or farther away.

Artists who make sculptures or pottery, and who design buildings or interiors, deal with real forms. To see a three-dimensional artwork such as a sculpture in its entirety, a viewer must see its many sides. A sculpture can also be appreciated through the sense of touch.

Finally, it is possible to classify shapes and forms as organic or geometric and as closed or open. Organic shapes and forms are typical of forms found in nature. With the exception of the planets and stars in the sky, and some crystals on the earth, geometric forms are almost always human-made. Closed forms tend to be dense or massive. Open forms are penetrated with negative shapes or space.

Try it Yourself

Now that you have learned more about shape, go back to your description of Renoir's *Luncheon of the Boating Party*. Can you see in the painting any examples of foreshortening? Are some of the forms of people larger than others? Why? Which forms are organic? Which, if any, are geometric? Which are closed? Which are open?

Chapter 6
Visual Elements: Value and Color

6 Visual Elements: Value and Color

Student Edition
Pages 57–73

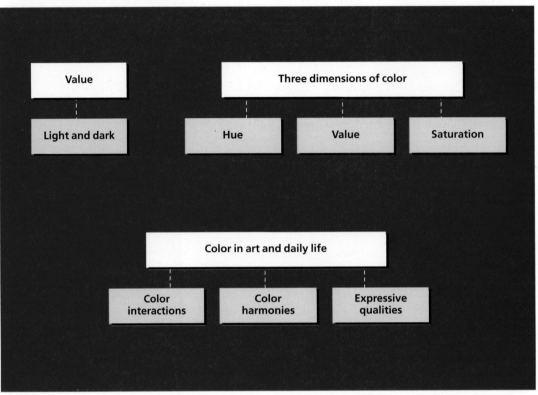

Overview

Chapter Objectives

Students should be able to:

EE 1 **1** explain the color qualities of hue, value, and intensity

EE 1 **2** identify hue, value, and intensity variations that are used to distinguish between forms, make objects appear three-dimensional, and contribute to the illusion of depth in artworks

EE 1, 3 **3** recognize and discuss artworks in which value and color communicate mood or emotion

EE 1 **4** define five basic color schemes: complementary, split complementary, triadic, analogous, and monochromatic, and recognize them in artworks

EE 1, 2 **5** mix at least five value and intensity variations of any color, and apply them in paintings

6 explain how color schemes, value, and intensity are used to create pictorial depth and three-dimensional forms EE 1

7 create value contrasts with drawing and painting media to indicate light sources and define forms EE 1, 2

8 use colors in drawing and painting to express moods EE 1, 2

Rationale

Color is one of the most powerful elements the artist uses for expression. It is also a powerful element for prompting aesthetic responses. This chapter introduces students to color as reflected light which the artist controls to create contrasts and values, moods, and expressive qualities.

Essential Chapter Concepts

• Environmental objects are visible only to the degree that they reflect light.

• Color is reflected light in the sense that a blue surface absorbs all the colors present in light except the blue rays, which are reflected. This is true for any color.

• Without light, there can be no color, and as light changes, so will colors.

• Objects in the environment appear solid and three-dimensional because of light and shadow.

• Light and dark values of color or of black and white are used in pictures to make objects look three-dimensional and to suggest depth in the picture plane.

• Color, value, and intensity (saturation) contrasts are used to express moods and emotions in artworks.

• Hue, value, and intensity (saturation) are affected by color interactions as demonstrated by several basic color schemes.

• Value is concerned with the *amount* and *intensity* is concerned with the *quality* of light reflected.

Vocabulary

color	intensity/saturation
primary colors	split complementary
hue	shading
secondary colors	triadic
value	chiaroscuro
intermediate colors	monochromatic
complementary colors	analogous

Meet the Artist

Vincent van Gogh   Page **71**

Lesson Plans

6.1   Value Contrasts

Page **T 70**   Time: 3 periods

6.2   Related Colors

Page **T 72**   Time: 3 periods

6.3   Monochromatic Colors   Notes

Page **T 74**   Time: 2 periods

6.4   Mixing Bright and Dull Colors

Page **T 78**   Time: 1 period

6.5   Matching Colors

Page **T 80**   Time: 3 periods

6.6   Warm and Cool Colors

Page **T 82**   Time: 3 periods

Handouts

Study Questions   Page **T 84**

Test Questions   Page **T 86**

Chapter Closure

Evaluation

1   *Aesthetic awareness:* Can students explain   R 3, 5
the importance of light in seeing color?

2   *Aesthetic awareness:* Can students   R 5
explain how secondary and intermediate
colors are mixed and relate to one another?

3   *Aesthetic awareness:* Can students   R 1
define the three properties of color and
identify hues resulting from value and
intensity variations in artworks?

4   *Aesthetic awareness:* Can students name
the hues included in five basic color
schemes and recognize them in artworks?

5   *Production:* Did students produce at
least five value and five saturation variations of any color and apply them to achieve
definition of shapes/forms and expressive
qualities in artworks?

6   *Production:* Did students produce
chiaroscuro effects resulting from a
directed light source in their artwork?

7   *Criticism:* Can students analyze the
effects of chiaroscuro in artworks?   R 4

8   *Criticism:* Can students apply color
vocabulary acquired in this chapter to   R 1
describe and analyze artworks?

Value Contrasts

Time: 3 periods

Preparation

Rationale

Artists use value to represent the effects of reflected light, to suggest depth, and to establish mood. Skill in manipulating value can help students understand how the artist achieves the desired effects, as well as help them learn to interpret meaning in artworks. In this experience, students create a black and white tempera still life painting, using value variations to suggest depth and mood.

Studio Materials

black and white tempera paint, assorted brushes, white paper, pencils, mixing trays, water containers, lamps, still life materials

Enrichment Materials

Overhead Transparencies:
• Adams, *Half Dome*, 12

Large Reproductions:
• Schwartz, *Untitled #16*, 11

Teach the Lesson

Objectives

Students should be able to:

1 create a black and white tempera painting of a still life   EE 2

2 use directed light to produce light, middle, and dark values   EE 1

3 produce at least five value variations to suggest depth, make forms appear three-dimensional, and suggest a mood   EE 1, 2

Vocabulary

Color is an element of design with three properties: hue, value, and intensity.

Hue refers to the color of a color—what distinguishes it from other colors.

Value is concerned with the degree of lightness and darkness of colors. Darker colors are lower in value; a shaded color is darker than a tinted one. Values without color are developed with only black and white.

Intensity is the strength or purity of a color. It is sometimes called saturation.

Warm Up

Conduct a short question/answer session. Where is the darkest place in the room? the lightest? Which surface is reflecting the most light? What does the term value mean in art?

Refer to figures 6–8 and 6–9, and ask which painting has the greatest range of values. Which has the strongest contrasts? How do the moods of the paintings differ because of the values used?

Explore and Develop

1 Display transparency 12 and ask students where the darkest, lightest, and middle values occur. What can they tell about the forms of the mountain because of the value contrasts? Based on the shadows, from which direction is the sunlight coming? What is the mood of the picture?

2 Display examples of chiaroscuro (see Beyond the Basics). Discuss how value contrasts are used to make forms look three-dimensional, suggest depth in the picture, and express a mood.

3 Focus on the nine-step value scale shown in figure 6–1. The scale demonstrates the range of lights and darks possible through mixing black and white paint: black, low dark, dark, high dark, middle value, low light, light, high light, white.

Laser Discs:

Rembrandt, A Girl with Broom, 1651

Search Frame 862

Harnett, My Gems, 1888
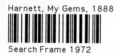
Search Frame 1972

Luks, The Miner, 1925
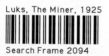
Search Frame 2094

Bellows, Both Members of This Club, 1909

Search Frame 2064

Bellows, detail

Search Frame 2066

Eakins, Baby at Play, 1876

Search Frame 2024

Begin Studio Experience 6.1

1 Refer to the student examples in Studio Experience 6.1. Ask where the light comes from in each painting. Where are edges defined by value contrasts? Where are some *high* (strong) contrasts? Where are some *low* contrasts? What devices besides darks and lights were used to suggest depth in these student works? Note that the still life objects are plain, but the value contrasts contribute excitement to the paintings. Do the different painting styles affect the mood of the two paintings?

2 Have students sketch a still life in light coming from one direction. Help them study the arrangement of values. Ask them to analyze where the very light, light, medium, dark, and very dark areas are.

3 Ask students to include a range of *at least* five values in their paintings, with some high and low contrasts.

4 Suggest that students place puddles of white on a mixing tray and add increasing drops of black to them to mix values.

5 Tell students to begin painting with middle values. Students should use high contrasts to establish a focal point and a range of values to make objects appear three-dimensional. Encourage students to form edges with value contrasts rather than outlining. Strong contrasts make forms appear to advance. Low (subtle) values make objects and background areas appear to recede.

Evaluate and Reflect

1 Can students identify five or more different values in paintings?

2 Can they determine where the light comes from in one another's paintings?

3 Did students use patterns of dark-light in their paintings that help direct the viewer's attention?

4 Do their painted forms appear three-dimensional as a result of value variations?

5 Can students describe the mood suggested in their painting?

6 Can students give some reasons why artists use value contrasts in artworks? What does chiaroscuro mean? Display a good example of chiaroscuro and ask students to analyze the composition.

Extend the Lesson

Beyond the Basics

Encourage interested students to look for the work of Rembrandt, Jan Vermeer, Caravaggio, Gentileschi and others who employed chiaroscuro in their work. Have them practice the technique in small pen and ink drawings with hatching, or ink washes.

EE 2, 3

Cultural Connections

In Western art light is often used to symbolize truth, hope, and new life. Dark is usually associated with evil, fear of the unknown, and death. Have students research non-Western art to determine what symbolic associations exist in the use of light and dark. What other approach might be used to express these concepts?

EE 1, 3

R 3, 4

Connecting with Other Subjects

Language Arts Have students look at *The Banjo Lesson* by Henry O. Tanner (fig. 6–5). His use of light and shadow is similar to the Baroque style in that he has created a dramatic effect through strong contrast in values. It is also similar in that Tanner has captured a moment in time. Perhaps the old man has just finished a demonstration and is waiting for the boy to repeat the movement. The boy seems poised and ready to play. Have students write a short story or poem about the people in this painting. Suggest the use of words associated with light, dark, and color to create mood.

EE 1, 3, 4

R 4
W 1

Related Colors

Value and Color

Time: 3 periods

Preparation

Rationale

Secondary and intermediate colors are often used to achieve more harmonious color relationships in artworks than can be achieved with primary colors. This experience, in which students use secondary and intermediate hues to produce color harmony in paintings, will help students recognize and analyze the use of these colors in artworks.

Studio Materials

tempera paint, assorted brushes, 12" x 18" or larger white paper, water containers, pencils, mixing trays, paper towels

Enrichment Materials

Overhead Transparencies:
• Raphael, *School of Athens,* 10
• Renoir, *Luncheon of the Boating Party,* 18

Large Reproductions:
• Chan, *Wild Thing,* 19
• Olbinski, *Private Fame,* 13

Teach the Lesson

Objectives

Students should be able to:

1   create a painting using predominantly secondary and intermediate colors   EE 1, 2

2   achieve unity through related colors   EE 1, 2

3   use color contrasts in a painting to define shape edges   EE 1, 2

Vocabulary

Secondary colors result from a mixture of two primary colors.

Intermediate colors result from mixing a primary color and the adjacent secondary color on the color wheel, e. g., yellow and green for yellow-green.

Warm Up

1   Have students mix a secondary color, such as green. Have students dampen the entire surface of a 9" x 12" piece of paper and place various amounts of yellow and green side by side. Students should tilt the paper and let the colors run together, creating new colors that fall between yellow and the intermediate yellow-green.

2   Have students repeat the exercise with blue and green. Remind students to keep the paper wet enough for colors to run and blend. Share the color variations.

Explore and Develop

1   Display examples of paintings done with predominantly secondary and intermediate colors, or refer to figure 6–25 and figure 19–20. Explain that artists often do not use pure primary colors in painting. Color schemes involving the secondary and intermediate hues often appear agreeable because of their shared colors.

2   Look at Frankenthaler's painting in figure 6–25. Ask what colors are shared by violet and orange; by violet and green; by green and orange.

3   Refer to the color wheel for names and locations of the secondary and intermediate hues. Ask students where colors darker or lighter in value are located on the wheel. Can students explain how to get a *high* (strong) value contrast between two shapes in a painting? (They must juxtapose colors that are high and low on the wheel.) How would they get *low* (subtle) contrasts?

Laser Discs:

Louis, Beta Kappa, c 1961

Search Frame 2323

Louis, 133, 1962

Search Frame 2325

Gorky, One Year the Milkweed, 1944
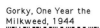
Search Frame 2311

Johns, Color Numeral Series: Figure 7, 1969

Search Frame 3324

Frankenthaler, Savage Breeze, 1974

Search Frame 3328

Derain, The Old Bridge, 1910

Search Frame 2151

Begin Studio Experience 6.2

1 Refer to the student works in Studio Experience 6.2. Ask students to identify the secondary and intermediate hues. Are there colors that seem to fall between the secondary and intermediate hues?

2 Explain that their paintings may be abstract or nonobjective. The main purpose is to explore color. To begin an abstract or nonobjective composition, have students use a pencil to *lightly* draw on a large sheet of paper. You may want to tell students to "take a walk with a line," letting it be straight, curvy, or crisscrossed. Encourage students to use their imagination. They may add to the original lines or delete some.

3 Remind them when mixing colors to start with the lightest hue and add the darker one. If you feel it is needed, put a mixing guide on the chalkboard:

1R + 1Y=O	2Y + 1R=YO	1Y + 2B=BG
1R + 1B=V	2Y + 1B=YG	1R + 2B=BV
1Y + 1B=G	1Y + 2R=RO	2R + 1B=RV

4 As the students develop their paintings, they may use one of the colors as a background, repeating it often enough so that it appears to be behind the other colors.

Evaluate and Reflect

1 Can students identify secondary and intermediate colors in the paintings? What in-between colors were produced?

2 Did students define edges of shapes by color/value contrasts?

3 Ask the students to discuss how unity is affected by related colors.

4 Ask the students to explain the role of light in seeing color.

5 Refer to the examples of Impressionism and Post Impressionism on Student Edition pages 284–286. Can students identify secondary and intermediate colors and variations? If possible, provide other examples of works by Cézanne, Monet, and Gauguin.

6 Ask students to describe the colors in an artwork of their selection that includes secondary and intermediate colors and variations. (See the Guidelines for Describing an Artwork in Lesson Plan 3.1.)

Reteach

Have students identify advertising art, package design and products that utilize secondary and intermediate colors. Why do they think those colors were used? Have students experiment with *color interaction* —how a color is affected when placed on top of or beside another color. For example, orange in a field of yellow-orange, or blue-green, etc.

Extend the Lesson
Beyond the Basics

Remind students that closely related colors produce a different effect than the use of contrasting colors. Have students draw a simple landscape or still life and trace to make a second copy of the same drawing. Have them paint one using an analogous color scheme and the other using a complementary color scheme. Discuss the differences in mood or feeling produced. Ask students to think about the kinds of ideas that each might be used to express.

EE 1, 2, 4

Connecting with Other Subjects

Language Arts, Science Have students read the National Geographic (Dec. 1989) article regarding restoration of the Sistine Chapel. Suggest that students investigate the scientific methods and equipment that made the restoration possible. The initial reaction when the first cleaned section was viewed by the public was that the artist's work may have been erased. Discuss how restorers were able to distinguish Michelangelo's work from previous attempts at restoration and the processes they developed to protect the original work.

EE 3

R 2

R 3

Monochromatic Colors

Time: 2 periods

Preparation

Rationale

A monochromatic scheme includes colors that go together most easily, resulting in extremely harmonious visual effects. The mood is generally quiet, restful, and, depending on the range of values, subtle. Using this scheme requires skill in tinting and shading to avoid the monotony of a single hue. Experience in creating a monochromatic painting will increase the students' awareness of the range of values possible for a given color. It will also sharpen their critical vocabulary concerning the use of value in space, form, and mood.

Studio Materials

tempera paint, assorted hair brushes, mixing trays, 12" x 18" white paper, water containers, paper towels, pencils

Enrichment Materials

Overhead Transparencies:
• Picasso, *Maternité,* 11

Large Reproductions:
• Magritte, *The Plagiary,* 4

Laser Discs:

Picasso, Le Gourmet, 1901

Search Frame 2267

Picasso, The Tragedy, 1903

Search Frame 2271

Picasso, Two Youths, 1905

Search Frame 2279

Cassatt, The Boating Party, 1893/1894

Search Frame 2016

Cassatt, detail

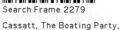

Search Frame 2018

Whistler, Wapping on Thames, 1860-1864

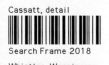

Search Frame 1984

Teach the Lesson

Objectives

Students should be able to:

1   create a monochromatic painting using one color, black, and white. The painting should include at least four values in addition to black and white.   EE 1, 2

2   define shapes in the painting through value contrasts, rather than outlining them   EE 1, 2

3   have knowledge of Picasso's Blue and Rose Periods and some of the primarily monochromatic paintings of these periods   EE 3

Vocabulary

Monochromatic means that one color is modified by changing the values and intensities of the hue through additions of black or white.

Intensity refers to the degree of purity or strength of a color.

Shading is the use of variations in value to suggest form, volume, and depth in artworks.

Tint is the value of a hue, which is made lighter generally by adding white to it.

Warm Up

1 Have students place two quarter-size puddles of white and two of black in a mixing tray. Ask them to select their favorite color, and mix one drop of it in the first white puddle, and two in the second. Have them add two and four drops of color to the two black puddles. Tell students to keep puddles separate, and mix each.

2 Ask them to paint a radial flower form with five or six petals on a small sheet of paper. Have students place the four contrasting values so that each petal is visible. Have students share what they learned and any problems they encountered.

3 Have them identify some paintings in which the petal forms are easily visible due to value contrasts, and some with very subtle contrasts.

Explore and Develop

1 Display examples of Picasso's monochromatic paintings. Be sure students recognize them as works by Picasso. Do students know what the scheme is called? Can they discuss concepts of tinting and shading in relationship to the painting being shown? Do they understand why forms appear three-dimensional and have depth?

2 Briefly explain what caused the onset of Picasso's Blue Period (death of a friend) and the Rose Period (making new friends and falling in love).

3 Provide titles for the Picasso paintings, and ask students what moods or emotions they feel are expressed in the paintings.

Begin Studio Experience 6.3

1 Focus on Student Edition page 64, which shows a value scale of red and examples of monochromatic paintings by students. What reactions do they have to the cool and warm colors used for the two student examples in Studio Experience 6.3? Note that any color can be used for a monochromatic scheme. Explain that they are to do a monochromatic painting based on a still life or a subject of their own choosing. The painting must include at least four values in addition to black and white.

2 Tell students to select a color they think will be most effective in expressing their subject and idea. Encourage them to premix their four distinct values to begin with.

3 Have students try to form the edges of shapes and forms in their paintings with value contrasts rather than outlines.

4 Foreground and background areas should also be completed with values of the chosen color.

Evaluate and Reflect

1 Can students distinguish at least four different values other than black and white in the painting?

2 Did students use value contrasts to define shapes and forms in their paintings?

3 How do students feel about their ability to use tinting and shading in a monochromatic work?

4 Ask students to discuss the mood or idea they wished to express in their painting.

5 Can students discuss the concepts of tinting and shading and strong and subtle value contrasts in relation to their paintings and other artworks?

6 Are they able to identify similarities and differences among their paintings and those by Picasso?

Reteach

Have students put three equal puddles of a color on a tray and add progressively increasing amounts of black to them. Do the same with white in three more puddles of the color. Use the six color values to paint a series of stripes or circles.

Extend the Lesson
Beyond the Basics

Ask students to look for examples of mono-chromatic paintings by artists other than Picasso. Students may prepare written explanations of how values are used in monochromatic paintings to deal with spatial relations like near/far, overlap, in front/behind.

EE 1, 3

W 2

Have students look again at *Homage to the Square* by Josef Albers on page 7 of the student text. From 1949 until his death in 1976 he focused all his work on color and color relationships. He influenced many artists during his life and his work continues to have a major impact. His approach is basic in the study of color theory for students throughout the world. Albers' early work inspired much of the research regarding the psychology of color. The psychological effect of color became important in planning the spaces in which people live and work. What are some of the things we know about color that might help a business to save money and increase productivity? What colors could help the healing process? What colors might stimulate learning? Have students research the psychology of color and its impact on the environments we create.

EE 3, 4

R 4

Cultural Connections

E 1, 3

Have students brainstorm a list of color association terms such as "feeling blue," "looking through rose colored glasses," and "seeing red." Why are these colors used to express a particular mood or feeling? Ask students to investigate how various cultures react to certain colors. Do all cultures make similar associations? Find out what colors are used in the ceremonies and celebrations of different cultures. Is wearing black to a funeral a universal concept? Is white the traditional color for brides in all cultures? What meanings or feelings are associated with each particular color?

Connecting with Other Subjects

Drama Coordinate with the drama teacher to design a set that uses monochromatic color to portray a mood in a school play.

Language Arts Connect with the language arts teacher to write a short story or poem that can be illustrated using monochromatic mood colors.

Language Arts When Picasso was twenty-one years old he began a series of paintings that became known later as his "Blue Period." Images from this period explored issues of loneliness, poverty, and suffering. Suggest students find information about Picasso's life prior to 1903 and the places where he lived and worked. What was the world like at that time? What events may have influenced Picasso's Blue Period?

Language Arts James Baldwin, a Black American and important writer, first published *Sonny's Blues* in 1957. The short story deals with a stormy relationship between two brothers and their lives in Harlem. The moods set by the author present an image dealing with loneliness, poverty, and suffering, the same themes seen in Picasso's blue paintings. Suggest that students read the story and design a book jacket using a monochromatic color scheme.

Music Ideas expressed by Blues musicians deal with the same issues of loneliness, poverty and suffering. Suggest students examine the content of several musical compositions labeled as "Blues" and write descriptions of each. Have them share their descriptions with the class. Suggest students also look for examples of common themes explored by visual, musical, and literary artists.

Value and Color

Mixing Bright and Dull Colors

Time: 1 period

Preparation

Rationale

In this experience, students mix a color with its complement to produce a nine-step saturation scale. Students concentrate on learning color concepts and skills rather than producing an immediate end product. The skills covered in this experience affect subsequent art studio and criticism experiences and aesthetic awareness.

Studio Materials

tempera paints, #12 hair brushes, mixing trays, water containers, 12" x 18" paper, scissors, 2" x 2" tag board pattern squares, glue, paint cups, color wheel display

Enrichment Materials

Slides:
• Matisse, *The Red Room*, 106

Large Reproductions:
• Matisse, *The Casbah Gate*, 8
• Chan, *Wild Thing*, 19
• Olbinski, *Private Fame*, 13
• Biggers, *Shotguns*, 3
• Glaser, *Saratoga*, 24

Teach the Lesson

Objectives

Students should be able to:

1 mix a color with its complement to produce a nine-step intensity scale, with a pure color at one end, three saturation changes, a neutral tone in the middle, three saturation changes, and the second color at the other end   EE 1, 2

2 incorporate the concepts of bright (high intensity) and dull (low intensity) colors into their critical vocabulary   EE 1

Vocabulary

Intensity is the degree of purity or strength of a color, and is determined by the quality of light reflected from it.

High intensity colors are bright. *Low intensity* colors are dull.

Complementary hues are colors directly opposite each other on the color wheel.

Warm Up

1 Display some color sample charts from the paint store. Mark some high intensity and low intensity colors. Ask students to pick some other colors that are of high and low intensity.

2 Provide students with a color and its complement in finger paint. Ask them to begin with the pure color, making concentric rings and adding gradually increasing amounts of the color's complement until a neutral tone (gray-brown) is reached in the middle. See who can make the most readily visible variations before reaching the neutral.

Explore and Develop

1 Ask students to identify the brightest and dullest colors in the finger paintings. Introduce the parallels, high intensity/bright, and low intensity/dull. Explain that in addition to shading and tinting colors, artists frequently mix a color with its complement to change the intensity of a color. Introduce the ideas that value affects the *quantity* of light a color reflects, and *intensity* affects the *quality* of light reflected.

2 Show examples of paintings with high intensity and low intensity colors. Ask students to identify them. Ask them to discuss differences in mood suggested by high and low intensity paintings.

Laser Discs:

Stella, Chyrow II, 1972

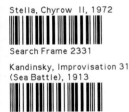

Search Frame 2331

Kandinsky, Improvisation 31 (Sea Battle), 1913

Search Frame 2247

Kandinsky, detail

Search Frame 2249

Miro, Flight of the Dragonfly before Sun, 1968

Search Frame 2265

Villon, From Wheat to Straw, 1946

Search Frame 2183

Klimt, Baby, 1917–1918

Search Frame 2245

3 Direct students to the intensity scales in figure 6–18 and Studio Experience 6.4. Discuss how on the intensity scale red loses intensity or brightness as green is mixed with it until a neutral tone is reached in the middle. Do students see that the same thing happens with the green as red is added to it? Note that many more intensity variations of either color can be produced than are shown on the scale.

Begin Studio Experience 6.4

1 Ask students to select a hue and use the color wheel to determine its complement. Plan on students painting at least nine (they may do more) circular swatches of color, each about 2.5 inches wide on a sheet of paper.

2 Tell students to paint a swatch of the first complementary color. Have them place four equal-sized puddles of the color on a mixing tray, then add gradually increasing amounts of the second color to each puddle and mix them well. The fourth puddle should be a half-and-half mixture of the two colors to produce a neutral gray-brown hue. Have students paint 2.5 inch swatches of each color, giving each an opaque coat.

3 Next, students will paint a swatch of the second complementary color. Have students place equal puddles of the second color on a mixing tray, then add gradually increasing amounts of the first color, mix them, and paint three swatches. Explain that there is no need to make another 50/50 mixture since it would be the same as the one already produced.

4 When the swatches are dry, tell students to use a pattern square to trace 2-inch squares on each of them. Have students cut out the squares of color and glue them on paper in sequential order, with the edges touching, to form a saturation scale. The arrangement should show pure hues at each end, and colors descending in intensity to a neutral tone in the middle. Edges of the squares should be visible due to intensity contrasts, and not because of white space between them.

Evaluate and Reflect

1 Did students produce at least three distinct intensity levels of each pure color descending to a neutral middle tone?

2 Can students correctly identify which colors are brighter and duller?

3 Can they explain what intensity means and how it differs from value of a color?

4 Can students identify bright and dull colors in the classroom and their clothing?

5 Can students analyze both intensity and value in Tanner's painting *The Banjo Lesson,* figure 6–5? Can they identify low intensity, light, and dark-valued colors?

Reteach

Repeat the mixing steps, taking students through it puddle by puddle.

Extend the Lesson

Beyond the Basics

Ask students to incorporate what they know about value and intensity in a simple landscape painting, e. g., large and small, high and low tree trunks, ground and sky. Use one color, its complement, black and white to create shapes in high and low intensities, light and dark values.   EE 1, 2

Cultural Connections

Organize the class into groups, and ask each group to research a culture's use of color. What do certain colors symbolize in the culture? For example, what is the importance of color in the Chinese New Year celebration? How was color used in Indian mask and costume decoration?   EE 3   R 2

Connecting with Other Subjects

Drama Based on advice from the drama teacher, make puppets or masks of plaster gauze or papier-mâché. Paint with colors selected to portray moods and personalities associated with a specific play.   EE 2   R 5

Matching Colors

Time: 3 periods

Preparation

Rationale

Students are asked to mix paints to match the colors of found materials. To complete the problem, they must utilize what they have learned about mixing colors in previous lessons.

Studio Materials

brushes, tempera paint, 9" x 12" white paper, pencils, glue, water containers, and assorted found materials

Enrichment Materials

Overhead Transparencies:
• Ernst, *Eye of Silence*, 1
• Picasso, *Still Life with Chair Caning*, 13

Teach the Lesson

Objectives

Students should be able to:

1 mix paint to match the colors of found materials such as fabric, colored papers, leaves, labels, photographs, wrappers, etc.   EE 2

2 explain what they had to do to make various colors   EE 1

Vocabulary

Triad harmonies include three equidistant hues on the color wheel, for example, the primaries, secondaries, or three intermediates.

Complementary colors are opposites on the wheel.

Split complementary schemes include one hue combined with hues on either side of its complement.

Analogous schemes consist of adjacent hues on the color wheel, for example, yellow, yellow-green, green and blue-green.

Warm Up

1 Ask students in advance to collect all kinds of materials with color: papers, wrappers, fabrics, leaves, feathers, bark, cardboard, wallpaper, wrapping paper, ribbon, burlap—anything that can be glued to paper. Provide a box of such materials in the classroom to supplement what is collected.

2 On the day of the lesson, have students tack a favorite colored scrap in one area on the bulletin board. Ask students to name some of the colors and discuss how they might go about mixing them.

Explore and Develop

1 Direct attention to the discussion of color harmonies on Student Edition pages 66–69. Ask students to explain what colors are involved in triadic, complementary, split complementary, and analogous color schemes. Ask students to use one of the schemes to guide their selection of materials for their collage.

Begin Studio Experience 6.5

1 Discuss selecting three or four items to arrange on the 9" x 12" paper. Students can cut or tear them into geometric or organic shapes of varying sizes. Explain that they will outline each of the shapes on the paper and glue the shapes next to these outlines. If there are three material shapes, there will be three outlined shapes.

2 Students should look for colors, not images. Caution students to avoid becoming involved in painting images and letters, and to instead concentrate on color.

3 Have students make the material shapes large enough so that they and the outlined shapes will fill the paper. Encourage students to think about composition when arranging the materials and their outlined shapes on the paper. They can touch or overlap. Material and outlined shapes may be alternated or set in columns side by side. A large shape and its outline might make a center of interest.

4 When they are satisfied with an arrangement, students should glue the shapes in place and begin mixing colors to match those of the materials as closely as possible. Tell them to paint the outlined shapes. If an object includes more than one color, students should lay in the lightest color first, let it dry, and paint in the darker color.

5 Give students the option of filling in background space with a neutral color if needed.

Evaluate and Reflect

1 How well did students mix colors to match those of selected objects?

2 Can students explain how they mixed some of the matching hues?

3 Ask them to identify secondaries, intermediates, complements, analogous colors, triads.

4 Which were the most difficult colors to match?

5 Was any tinting or shading involved?

6 Ask students to discuss their arrangements of material and painted shapes. Encourage them to look for alternation, dominance, similarities, differences, directional shapes, and effects of colors one on another.

Reteach

Mixing colors requires practice and patience. Have students read Student Edition pages 66–69, and answer Study Questions 9–23. Have them try to match colors in fig. 6–25 (Frankenthaler) using watercolor washes.

Extend the Lesson
Beyond the Basics

Encourage students to begin keeping a "color diary." Suggest they use a three ring binder and scraps of watercolor paper. Have students record each color as it comes directly from the container of paint. Suggest they mix values and intensities of each color. Label each sample as to manufacturer and name of color. Also note how the colors were mixed—the names and proportions used of each color. At this point students are ready to begin collecting colors for their "diary."

EE 1, 2

NOTE: Students should continue use of the color diary throughout their study of art. This approach is especially valuable to students interested in art related careers.

Cultural Connections

Using magazines, such as *National Geographic,* have students select several different cultures and analyze their use of color in clothing, decor, and art. Are there similarities or differences in their use of colors? Is there a relationship between the colors used and the color of the land? Is the use of color different within cultures that are technologically advanced as compared to cultures that are closer to nature?

EE 3, 4

R 2, 4

Connecting with Other Subjects

Social Studies Using maps and timelines have students identify where and when Isaac Newton lived. Have them identify artists who lived in the same place at the same time. Look at the artists' use of color before and after this period of time. Is there a relationship between Newton's color experiments and artists' use of color after that time. Have students write an explanation of how Newton's work may have influenced the work of others.

EE 3

R 2, 3, 4
W 2

Warm and Cool Colors

Time: 3 periods

Preparation

Rationale

The artist's choice of color contributes to the mood or expressive quality of an artwork. Considerable attention has been given to the effects of color on people, and their reactions to color. Artists divide colors into warm and cool categories. In general, warm colors suggest excitement, and cool colors have a quieting effect. This lesson provides the student a firsthand experience with the power of color.

Studio Materials

oil crayon sets which provide warm/cool colors, 9" x 12" construction paper in warm and cool colors

Enrichment Materials

Large Reproductions:
• Carr, *Scorned as Timber*, 15
• Nubian *Wall Painting*, 5

Teach the Lesson

Objectives

Students should be able to:

1   create two pictures of a scene, one in warm colors and the other in cool colors, with oil crayon on colored paper to demonstrate the expressive power of color   **EE 1, 2**

2   respond to the mood differences caused by warm and cool color schemes for the same scene   **EE 4**

Vocabulary

Warm colors are yellow, yellow-orange, orange, red-orange, red, red-violet.

Cool colors are yellow-green, green, blue-green, blue, blue-violet, violet.

Warm Up

1   Ask students to describe the hottest place they have ever experienced and think about their feelings. Have them write words or short statements to describe their feelings.   **W 2**

2   Ask students to concentrate on the coldest place they have ever experienced and think about their feelings. Again, have them write words or short statements to describe their feelings. Have students compare their feelings for hot and cold situations. How do they differ? What colors do they associate with the two experiences?   **W 2**

Explore and Develop

1   Direct attention to the expressive qualities of color, using Student Edition pages 69–71. Note that cool colors are located down the right side of the color wheel, beginning with yellow-green and ending with violet. Warm colors are on the left side, beginning with yellow and ending with red-violet.

2   If available, share examples of artworks with predominantly warm or cool colors. As examples are shown, encourage students to voice feelings and moods aroused by the colors. Ask them why the artist chose the colors used in the various artworks. Encourage both literal and expressive reasons.   **R 6**

3   Direct attention to van Gogh's paintings of his bedroom on Student Edition pages 70–71. Ask students to describe the hues, values, and intensities in the two paintings. What color schemes are evident? Which scene appears the most relaxed?

Laser Discs:

Picasso, The Lovers, 1923

Search Frame 2293

Frankenthaler, Wales, 1966

Search Frame 2327

Frankenthaler, detail
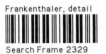
Search Frame 2329

Rothko, Orange and Tan, 1954

Search Frame 2317

Monet, The Houses of Parliament, Sunset, 1903

Search Frame 1406

Degas, Madame Camus, 1869/1870

Search Frame 1336

Begin Studio Experience 6.6

1 Direct attention to the student examples in Studio Experience 6.6. Explain that students are going to draw one scene in two color schemes, one cool and the other warm. They should create two moods with the one scene. Have them select colors that are best suited to the subject and the mood. Expressive differences should be due to color if everything else is held the same in the two drawings.

2 Have students use a warm hue of paper with the warm colors, and a cool hue with cool colors. The paper color may be used in the background.

3 Subject matter can be selected by the student: landscape, tree scape, a self-portrait, a still life, a building, a figure, etc.

4 You may want to have students make a light drawing of the scene on the first sheet of paper, trace it on tracing paper, and use carbon paper to transfer the drawing to the second sheet of paper.

5 Explain/demonstrate that oil crayons mix easily to produce secondary and intermediate colors, tints and shades, and intensity variations. Darker colors can be applied over lighter ones. Encourage students to use enough pressure on crayons to produce strong colors.

Evaluate and Reflect

1 Display the two drawings in pairs. Can students discuss the different moods resulting from the warm and cool color schemes in their drawings?

2 Are there differences and agreements about the moods of some pictures?

3 Can students explain how the warm or cool color scheme contributes to unity of the composition?

4 What were some individual reasons for selecting the colors they used in the warm or cool drawing?

5 What color schemes are identifiable in the various drawings?

6 Are the students beginning to apply descriptive and interpretive terms to their artworks?   W 2

Reteach

Ask students to think of a word-symbol combination, e. g., spicy and red pepper, cool and sunglasses. Use felt markers to draw the object, print the word, and fill in with appropriate colors to communicate the message.   R 1

Extend the Lesson
Beyond the Basics

Have students work in groups to describe the colors in paintings by artists such as van Gogh, Cezanne, Monet, Cassatt, Frankenthaler, and Bridget Riley. They should deal with hue, value and intensity in their reactions to the colors.   EE 1, 3

Cultural Connections

Display a group of artworks from a variety of cultures with similar themes or subjects, such as people working (*Detroit Industry,* figure 12–16) or family groups (*The Bath,* figure 5–25). Have students look at the works and determine the theme or subject of each. Ask students to discuss how the works are alike or different. What type of color relationships are used in each work? What mood or feeling is created? How would that feeling change if different colors were used?   EE 3, 4

Connecting with Other Subjects

Language Arts Write a short play developing characters that can be portrayed using warm/cool, complementary and monochromatic colors in face make-up, paper masks, costumes, and lighting.   EE 1

W 1, 3

Study Questions
Chapter 6—Visual Elements: Value and Color

Value and Color

1 Define value in art.

_____

_____

2 What are two reasons an artist uses chiaroscuro, or shading, in an artwork?

_____

3 Find two examples (other than those in chapter 6) that illustrate how light and dark are used to create a mood. Describe the mood you feel is portrayed. How did the artist create that mood?

_____

4 What did Isaac Newton discover about color?

_____

5 What is a spectrum?

_____

6 Why does an apple look red?

_____

7 What is the difference between mixing colored lights and mixing pigments?

_____

8 Name the primary colors.

_____

9 How are secondary colors made? Name the secondary colors.

_____

10 Name the intermediate colors. How are they made? Give an example.

_____

11 What is the color wheel?

_____

12 How are tints of a color made?

_____

Study Questions
Chapter 6–Visual Elements: Value and Color

13 What are shades of a color?

_____

14 Why are black, white and gray called neutrals?

_____

15 Where are complementary colors located on the color wheel? Name the complements of each of the primary colors.

_____

16 What happens when a color is mixed with its complement?

_____

17 Give an example (other than those given in the chapter) of each of the following color interactions: hue interaction, value interaction, and intensity interaction.

_____

18 Give an example of an analogous color scheme.

_____

19 What colors are in a monochromatic color scheme?

_____

20 What are considered the warm colors?

_____

21 What are considered the cool colors?

_____

22 Give one example of how the artist Vincent van Gogh used color to express his emotions.

_____

23 What color scheme did Helen Frankenthaler use in her painting *Cravat*? (Figure 6–25)

_____

Test Questions
Chapter 6–Visual Elements: Value and Color

Fill in the blanks:

1 An object is visible only to the extent that it _____ light.

    a. creates   c. effects

    b. alters   d. reflects

2 Using lighter and darker values to make something in a painting appear three-dimensional is known as _____.

    a. chiaroscuro   c. shading

    b. both a and c   d. tinting

3 When light is totally absorbed, the result is _____.

4 A _____ is any color with white added.

5 A _____ scheme is the use of one hue combined with hues on either side of its complement.

6 A rainbow is a large example of a _____.

7 _____ is the coloring matter in inks, crayons, and paints.

8 Blacks, whites and grays are called _____.

9 If a color is mixed with its _____ the resulting color will be a duller one.

10 Colors adjacent on the color wheel are _____.

11 Name two warm colors. _____ _____

12 Name two cool colors. _____ _____

Write the names of the primary, secondary, and intermediate colors in the correct places on the color wheel.

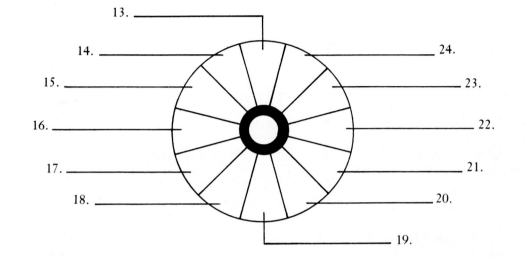

13. _____

14. _____

15. _____

16. _____

17. _____

18. _____

19. _____

20. _____

21. _____

22. _____

23. _____

24. _____

Write the complement for each color.

25 orange _____

26 red _____

27 yellow-orange _____

28 blue-green _____

Viewing the transparency of Georgia O'Keeffe's *Sky Above Clouds IV,* answer the following questions:

29 What color scheme is used?

30 What word best describes the shapes used?

31 How has the artist used color to make the cloud shapes seem to appear on top of the background color?

_____

32 What mood do you feel is portrayed in this painting?

Study Answers
Chapter 6
Value and Color

1 Range of light and dark in a picture.

2 To make something in a picture appear three-dimensional, to represent the effects of reflected light, to help establish a mood.

3 Answers will vary.

4 Color is a property of light.

5 The band of colors formed when a beam of white light is broken up by passing through a prism; consists of seven rays, each visible as a different color.

6 It absorbs every color except red, which it reflects.

7 Mixing colored lights is additive; when all colors are combined, the result is white (text fig. 6–13). Combining colored pigments is subtractive, and results in darker colors. A black surface absorbs all colors.

8 Red, yellow, and blue.

9 By mixing equal amounts of two primary colors. Green, orange, and violet.

10 Yellow-orange, red-orange, red-violet, blue-violet, blue-green, yellow-green. By mixing unequal amounts of two primary colors (e.g., two parts of red and one part blue produce red-violet).

11 A formal arrangement of the primary, secondary, and intermediate colors.

12 By adding white to a color.

13 Darker values of a color.

14 They have no identifiable hues.

15 Opposite each other. Red-green, yellow-violet, blue-orange.

16 The resulting color will be duller than either the original color or its complement.

17 Answers will vary. For example: Hue interaction—Violet will appear more blue next to red. Value interaction—A medium-gray circle will appear darker on top of a white square than on a black square. Intensity interaction—A medium yellow will appear more intense next to a neutral than it will on top of a bright yellow.

18 Blue-green, blue, blue-violet, violet.

19 Tints and shades of one hue.

20 Reds, yellows, oranges.

21 Greens, blues, violets.

22 Answers will vary.

23 A secondary color scheme, or a secondary triad.

Test Answers
Chapter 6
Value and Color

1 D

2 B

3 black

4 tint

5 split complementary

6 spectrum

7 Pigment

8 neutrals

9 complement

10 analogous

11 May include reds, yellows, oranges

12 May include blues, greens, violets

13 Yellow

14 Yellow-orange

15 Orange

16 Red-orange

17 Red

18 Red-violet

19 Violet

20 Blue-violet

21 Blue

22 Blue-green

23 Green

24 Yellow-green

25 Blue

26 Green

27 Blue-violet

28 Red-orange

29 Monochromatic

30 Organic

31 Answers will vary. Possible answer: The light blue cloud shapes seem to float on top of the darker blue background color.

32 Answers will vary. Possible answers: Peace, serenity, loneliness, etc.

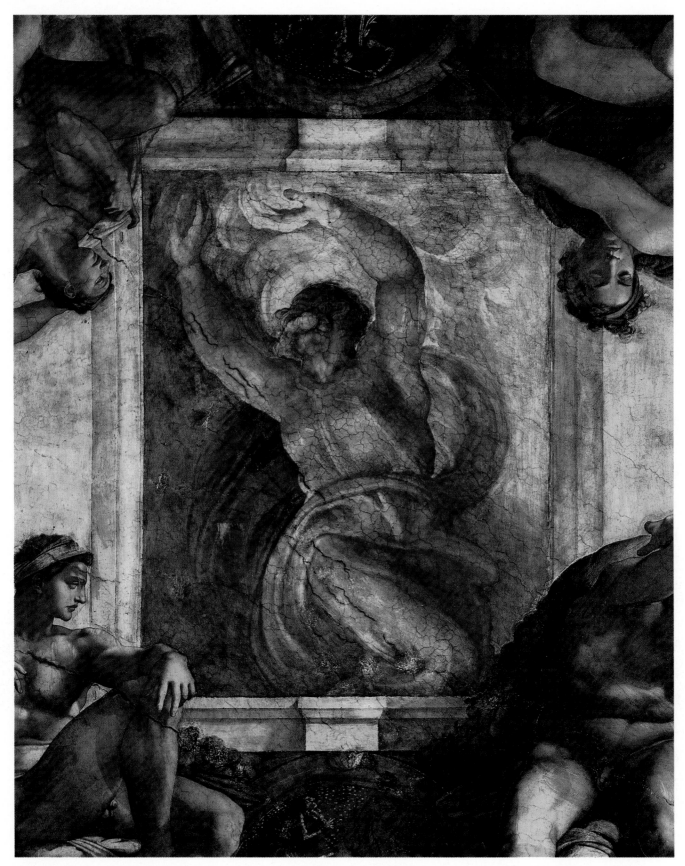

6–1 Michelangelo, *God Separating Light from Darkness.* The Sistine Chapel, The Vatican, Rome. Scala/Art Resource, NY.

Chapter 6
Visual Elements: Value and Color

Light and Dark

Without light we could not see lines, shapes, forms, or any objects. In fact, unless it is a source of light itself, an object is visible only to the extent that it *reflects* light.

Light, along with its opposite, dark, appears in the legends of most cultures. Among the episodes illustrated on the Sistine Chapel ceiling by Michelangelo is the separation of light and dark (fig. 6–1). Light is often used to symbolize truth, hope, and new life. On the other hand, dark is often associated with evil, the fear of the unknown, and death. Have you ever seen the sky just before a storm when light turns to dark (fig. 6–2)? Light and dark are also important in art.

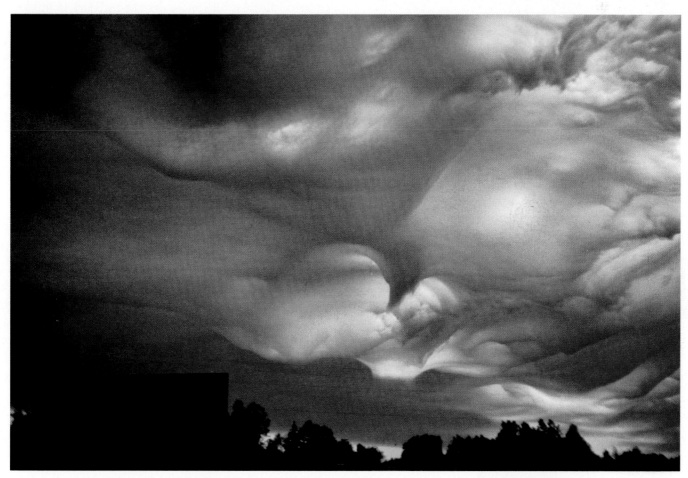

6–2 Light colors colliding with contrasting dark colors produce drama in a picture. Cynthia Stanton, *A Wild and Wicked Sky near Remus, Michigan,* August 16, 1988. Reprinted with permission of the Helen Dwight Reid Educational Foundation. Published by Heldref Publications, 1319 Eighteenth St., N.W., Washington, DC. 20036-1802. ©1988.

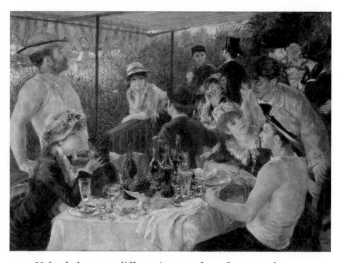

6–4 Value helps us to differentiate one form from another. Imagine what the world would be like if nothing had color. Pierre Auguste Renoir, *Luncheon of the Boating Party,* 1881. Oil on canvas, 51″ x 68″ (130 x 173 cm). ©The Phillips Collection, Washington, DC.

Value

Imagine the possible ranges of light and dark in this world. One extreme might be looking directly at the noonday sun. The other might be experiencing the blackness of a deep cave. But in daily life the range of light and dark is much less dramatic than that.

In artwork, the range of light and dark (seen under normal light conditions) is known as *value.* Typically, values are represented on a nine-step scale (fig. 6–3). White is at one extreme and black is at the other. In "black-and-white" reproductions (fig. 6–4) everything consists of different values on the gray value scale. You are able to distinguish different objects because of their different values.

The lightness or darkness of a particular value is *relative,* depending on its context. In other words it is light or dark in comparison to its surroundings. For example, the banjo face in Henry O. Tanner's *The Banjo Lesson* (fig. 6–5) appears light when compared to the shadows around it. But compared to the light values in the background, it appears rather dark.

6–5 Henry O. Tanner, *The Banjo Lesson,* 1893. Oil on canvas. 4′ ½″ x 3′ 11″ (123 x 119 cm). Hampton University Museum, Hampton, Virginia.

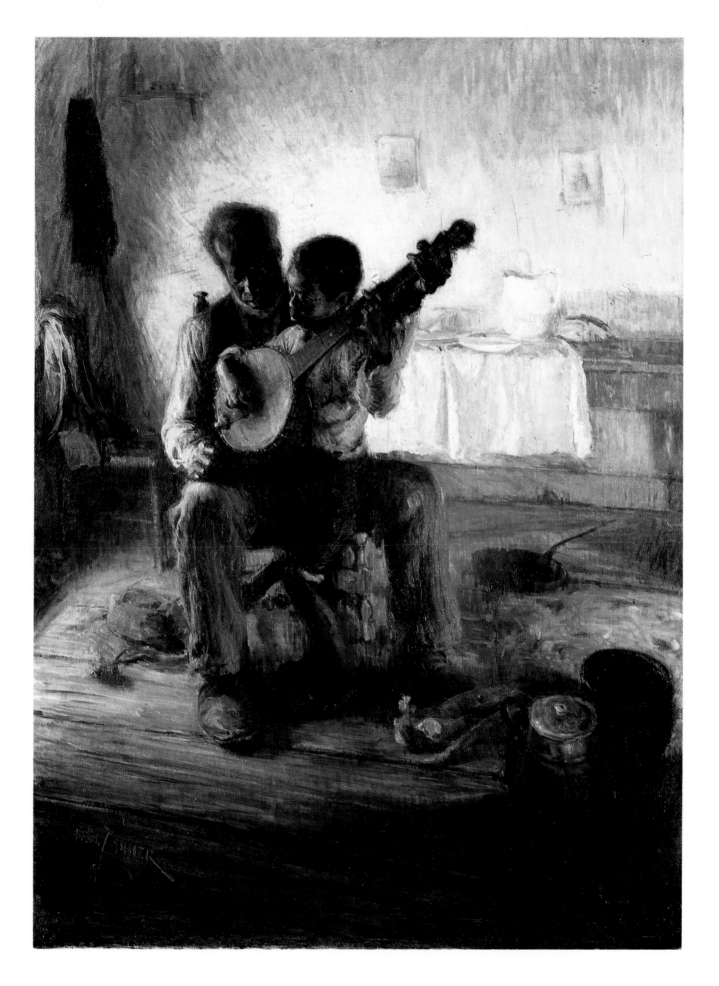

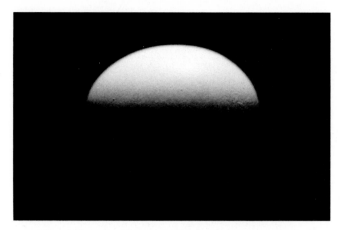

6–6 What is the color of the egg: white or dark gray?

The amount of reflected light can make the value of an object seem lighter or darker. You see the egg in figure 6–6 as being very light—either white or off-white. Now cover the upper half of the egg with your hand. You see that the lower half of the form is not very light (or white) at all. Reflected light causes the difference in value between the top and bottom halves of the egg. In this case, the reflection is stronger on the top.

Artists often take reflected light into account when they want to make a form look solid. The artist made the polyhedron (fig. 6–7) look three-dimensional by making some surfaces darker than others. Using lighter and darker values to make something look three-dimensional is called **shading**. The technical term is **chiaroscuro** *(kee-ah´-ro-skuh´-ro)*, an Italian word that literally means light-dark. Earlier, in Chapter 4, you saw an example of shading (fig. 4–13). Hatching and crosshatching was used to make the caricature of a celebrity look more three-dimensional.

Try it Yourself

Cut a ½" hole out of the middle of a piece of paper. Lay the paper over the drawing of the polyhedron. Move the paper around. Can you see that the values go from very light to very dark? Do the same with the picture of the egg.

Studio Experience 6.1

Value Contrasts

Create a black and white tempera painting of a still life. Shine a single light on the still life from one side. Use different values to suggest a mood and to make the objects appear three-dimensional.

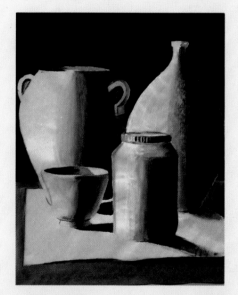

a. Kristy Skully.

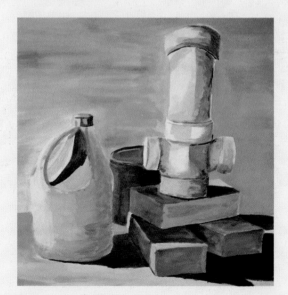

b. Maria Alvarez.

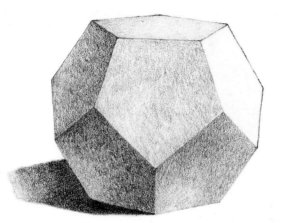

6–7 How many values did the artist use to make this polyhedron appear solid?

Value and Artistic Expression

Shading is a very effective way for an artist to create a mood. You may recall that light and dark often stand for good and evil. Artists will very often use value to express these moods. However, light and dark do not always stand for good and evil. Look back at two examples in Chapter 5. In Hopper's *House by the Railroad* (fig. 5–32), the light seems oppressive and depressing. In Rembrandt's *The Mill* (fig. 5–31), the darkness seems peaceful.

In *A Woman in White* (fig. 6–8), Picasso used mostly the middle range of the value scale. He kept the contrasts of light and dark to a minimum. The colors are neither very light nor very dark. The whole picture seems bathed in a bright, but soft light. This light gives a peaceful feeling. The woman herself looks peaceful and relaxed. In this painting, light seems to play a positive role. Do you think that the light was meant to symbolize something positive about womanhood? Why?

The artist used mostly the dark end of the value scale in *Mademoiselle Charlotte du Val d'Ognes* (fig. 6–9). However, very light values were used in places. A single source of light illuminates one side of the woman. The rest of the picture is left in relative darkness. The use of dark shading and strong contrast to create drama or establish a mood was very popular in the 1600s and 1700s. Like Picasso's woman, Mademoiselle Charlotte seems relaxed, though perhaps more solemn. Here, dark contributes to a somber mood, but not necessarily an evil one.

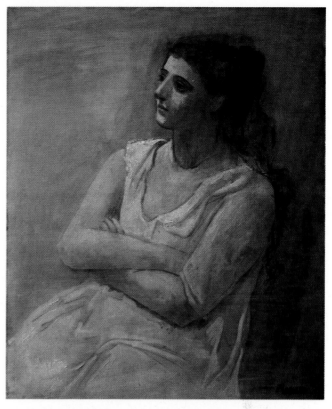

6–8 Pablo Picasso, *Woman in White*, 1923. Oil on canvas, 39″ x 31 ½″ (99 x 80 cm). The Metropolitan Museum of Art, Rogers Fund, 1951; from the Museum of Modern Art, Lizzie P. Bliss Collection.

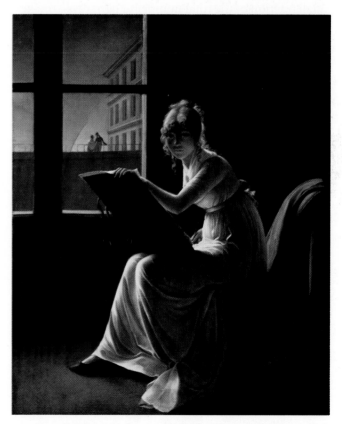

6–9 French Painter, Unknown, Portrait of a Young Woman, called *Mademoiselle Charlotte du Val d'Ognes*. Oil on canvas, 63 ½″ x 50 ⅝″ (161 x 129 cm). The Metropolitan Museum of Art, Bequest of Isaac D. Fletcher, 1917. Mr. and Mrs. Isaac D. Fletcher Collection.

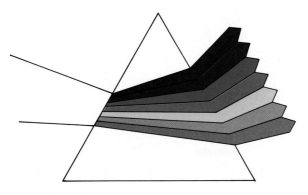

6–10 The visible spectrum.

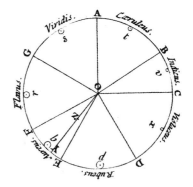

6–11 *Newton's Color Wheel*, from Isaac Newton, *Optice*, 1706. The British Library, London.

Color

Of all the visual elements, *color* is the most fascinating and puzzling. Because of its effects on people, color has been studied more than any of the other elements. To analyze color, we must return to the discussion of light.

In a famous experiment over three hundred years ago, Isaac Newton demonstrated that light is very complicated. He also showed that color is a property of light. When a beam of light passes through a glass object, called a prism, the light divides into the seven colors of the rainbow (fig. 6–10). Each of these colors represents a different ray of light. All seven rays—a small fraction of the total number of light rays—make up what is known as the *spectrum*. Newton demonstrated that white light includes all of the spectrum colors. Newton created a color circle to show the spectrum colors (fig. 6–11). Today we use a color wheel (fig. 6–15).

The average person thinks of color as belonging to objects. Strictly speaking, this is not true. There is a difference between light and *reflected* light. Light is the real source of color. Reflected light is the light given off by objects. When white light strikes a red apple, the apple looks red because it *absorbs* every color of light *except* red, which it reflects. A lemon absorbs all the colors except yellow (fig. 6–12). When light is totally absorbed by an object, the object appears black.

Color has three dimensions: hue, value, and saturation.

Hue

Hue identifies a color as blue, yellow, red, or green, and so on, as seen in the spectrum or the color wheel. In addition to the hues of the spectrum, an infinite number of hues can be created through intermixing.

At this point, however, a distinction must be made between colored light and pigment. Pigment is the col-

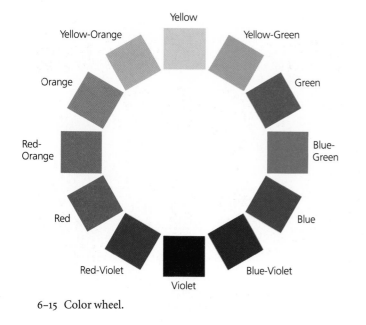

6–15 Color wheel.

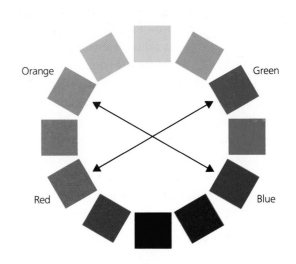

6–16 Complementary colors are opposite in hue and are also opposite each other on the color wheel.

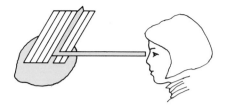

6–12 A lemon absorbs all the colors of light except yellow.

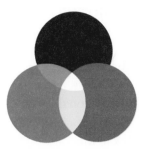

6–13 Primary and secondary hues in lights.

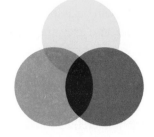

6–14 Primary and secondary hues in pigments.

oring matter found in such things as inks, crayons, paints, dyes, and glazes. Mixing colored lights is an *additive* process. When all colors are combined, the result is white (fig. 6–13). Mixing pigments, on the other hand, is *subtractive*. Pigments behave the same way as the surfaces of lemons or apples. They absorb all the colored rays except those we see.

Combining many different colors creates increasingly darker results—as you know if you've ever mixed paints. Theoretically if all three primaries are combined in the correct proportions, the final result would be black (fig. 6–14). A black surface absorbs all the spectrum colors. Since almost all artworks involve the use of pigments, the following discussion will focus on the behavior of pigment hues.

Red, yellow, and blue are called **primary colors**. Supposedly you can make any other hue with just these three, if you know how to mix them properly. Yellow and red make orange, yellow and blue make green, and red and blue make violet. Orange, green, and violet are

called **secondary colors**. Notice that on the color wheel (fig. 6–15), each secondary color is placed midway between the primary colors that produced it. Lying between the primaries and secondaries are the **intermediate colors**: yellow-orange, yellow-green, blue-green, blue-violet, red-violet, and red-orange. These are made by unequal mixing of primaries. For example, approximately two parts yellow mixed with one part red produces yellow-orange.

Hues directly opposite each other on the color wheel are called **complementaries**: red and green, orange and blue, yellow-orange and blue-violet, and so on (fig. 6–16). In addition to being opposite geographically, they are exactly opposite in hue. For example, yellow, a primary color, has nothing in common with its complement, violet, which is composed of red and blue. Complementaries play a role in both *saturation* and *color harmonies* (discussions follow).

Studio Experience 6.2

Related Colors

Mix red, yellow, and blue tempera paint to create a picture using only secondary and intermediate colors.

Next try making a hue that lies between a secondary and an intermediate hue, such as bluish green (between green and blue-green).

Can you think of some fancy names—turquoise, aqua—for these in-between hues? Can you invent some new colors?

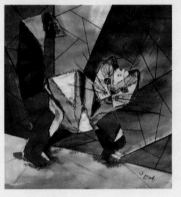

a. Ellen Zauke

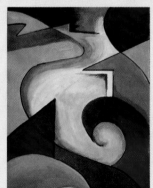

b. Christopher Green.

Value

You have already learned about the element of value. Value can be associated with shades of gray. Black, white, and gray are sometimes called neutral colors, or *neutrals.* These three colors have no hues.

However, value is an aspect of all colors. Every color has a normal value, which is shown on the wheel. The value, or the lightness and darkness of a color, can be changed by adding white or black to the color. Different values of red (fig. 6–17), for example, can be shown on a value scale. Lighter values of a color are called *tints.* Darker values are called *shades.*

Artists sometimes create paintings that use tints and shades of just one color. Such paintings are called **monochromatic**, meaning one color.

Saturation

Saturation describes the brightness and dullness of a color. It is sometimes called **intensity**. A color's saturation can be represented on a scale from bright to gray or dull (fig. 6–18). All of the hues on the color wheel are bright (or as bright as the printer was able to make them).

Yellow, blue, or red paint straight from the bottle will be bright. Mixing any two of the primaries, as you saw earlier, produces a new color. Secondary or intermediate hues on the color wheel are also bright. But if you mix a color with its *complement,* the resulting color will be a duller one, because each color subtracts from the other. If you mix complementaries in the right proportions, not necessarily in equal amounts, the result may be a neutral gray (fig. 6–19).

6–17 Value scale of red. What color should be added to make a tint of red?

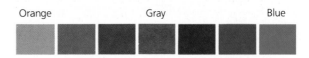

6–18 Saturation or intensity scales for orange and blue.

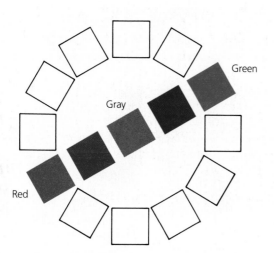

6–19 Mixing a color with its complement can produce a neutral gray.

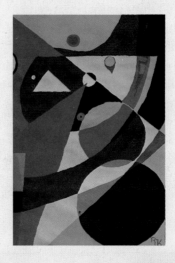

Studio Experience 6.3

Monochromatic Colors

Produce a monochromatic painting using a color and black and white. Use at least five values of the color you chose.

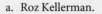

a. Roz Kellerman.

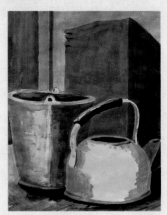

b. Mike Hernandez.

Colors of low saturation that have identifiable hues can be just as beautiful as bright colors. Most of the colors in nature are of this type: the olive greens and forest greens of spring and summer, and the golden yellows, burnt oranges, and brown-reds of fall (fig. 6–20).

The colors of clothes are not always bright. They may be dulled reds, greens, and blues, as well as browns. The colors of woodwork also tend to be of low saturation: mahogany (deep reddish brown), oak (brownish yellow), and maple (brownish yellow-orange).

Studio Experience 6.4

Mixing Bright and Dull Colors

Use tempera paint to mix a color with its complement to produce a nine-step saturation scale. You should have a pure color at one end, three saturation changes, gray in the middle, three saturation changes, and the second color at the other end.

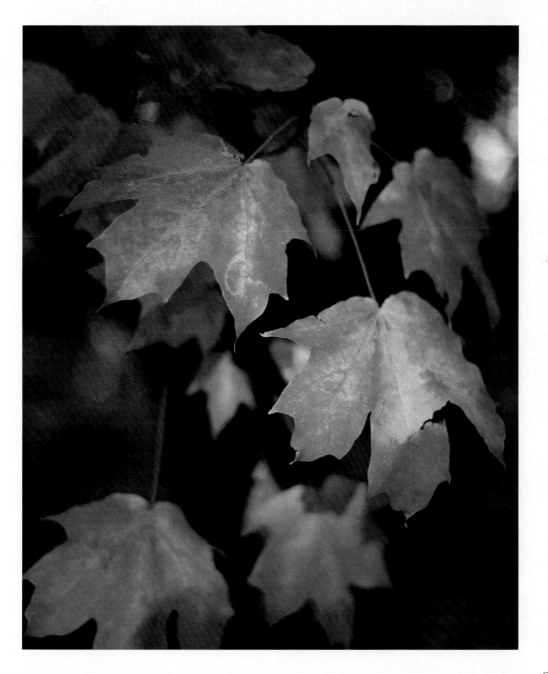

6–20 Which of the colors are saturated? Which are of low saturation? Photograph: Barbara Caldwell.

Matching Colors

Find some materials such as pieces of fabric, leaves, colored papers, labels, and wrappers. Mix paint to match their colors.

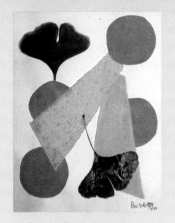
Judy Bertolotto.

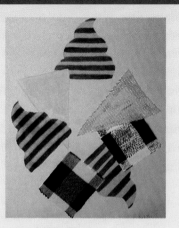
Kelly Strufert.

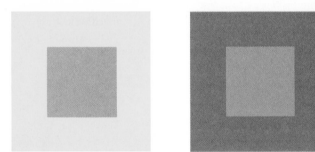

6–21 Which of the smaller squares appears more orange? Why?

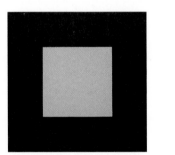

6–22 A tint appears much darker on which field of color?

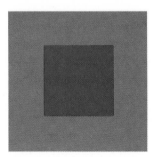
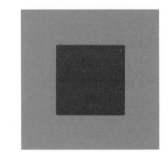

6–23 Which of the smaller squares appears to be of brighter intensity?

Color Interactions

Colors can be affected by other colors. A particular color can look different when placed side-by-side or on top of another color. Its hue, value, or saturation can be affected, depending on the combination. The following illustrations provide some examples.

Hue Interaction. A patch of yellow-orange appears more orange on top of a square of yellow. On top of a square of orange, it appears more yellow (fig. 6–21).

Value Interaction. A tint appears much darker on light color than it does on black (fig. 6–22).

Intensity Interaction. A medium bright blue will appear brighter on top of a neutral than it does on top of a bright blue (fig. 6–23).

Color Harmonies

Color harmonies are combinations of colors that are considered satisfying, or that produce certain effects. In the discussion of *hue,* you learned some color groups: secondaries, complementaries, and so on. These color combinations can also be thought of as types of color harmonies, or color *schemes.*

Triad harmonies consist of three equidistant hues on the color wheel. The triad harmony shown in figure 6–24 is made up of the three secondary colors. Other triad harmonies would be the primaries or three of the intermediates. Because of their mutual dissimilarity, a triad of the primary colors would be the most daring combination. Secondary or intermediate hues, on the

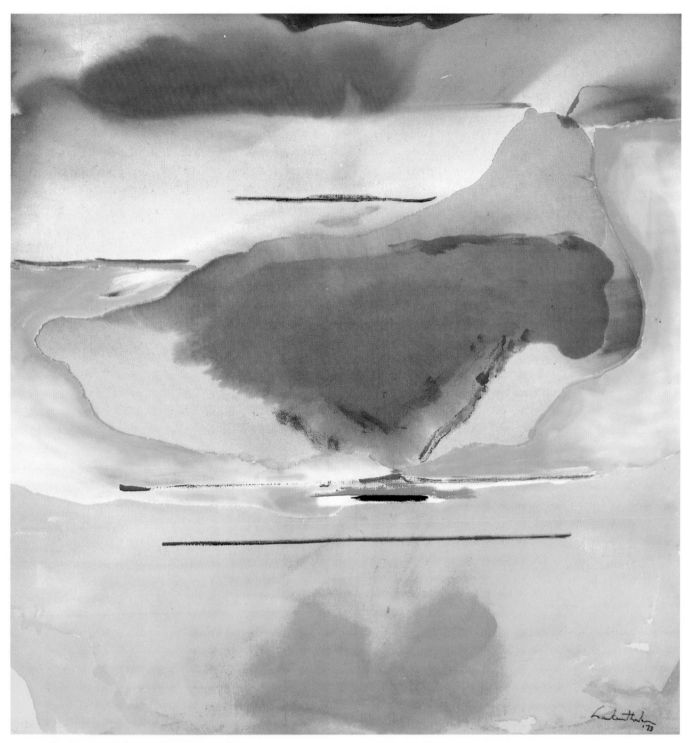

6–25 Helen Frankenthaler, *Cravat*, 1973. Acrylic on canvas.
62 ½″ x 58 ¾″ (159 x 149 cm). Courtesy of the artist.

other hand, are apt to be more agreeable because
of their shared colors. Perhaps that is why Helen
Frankenthaler chose a triad harmony of secondary
colors. She poured diluted colors of violet, green, and
orange onto a white canvas (fig. 6–25).

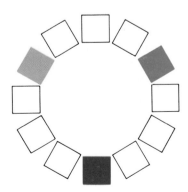

6–24 A triad scheme.

Complementary colors, as we have seen before, are opposite colors. Therefore, a *complementary combination* would provide the strongest contrast. There is a greater chance that the colors would "clash." For this reason, some designers prefer a **split complementary** scheme. They might choose one hue and combine it with hues on either side of its complement (fig. 6–26). This brings two of the colors closer together and tends to tone down the "violence" somewhat. The trim colors in Paris architect Jean Satosme's living room (fig.

6–27) consist of red against a variety of yellow-greens and blue-greens. These colors are split complementaries of red.

Analogous harmonies consist of adjacent hues on the color wheel, for example, yellow, yellow-green, green, and blue-green (fig. 6–28). Because of their strong "family resemblances," these kinds of hues are very agreeable. Yet they are different enough to provide interest. If necessary, contrast can be strengthened by varying the values. The inlaid colors decorating the

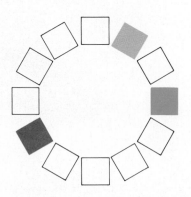

6–26 Split complementary scheme.

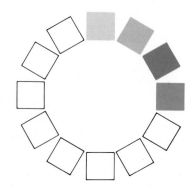

6–28 An analogous scheme.

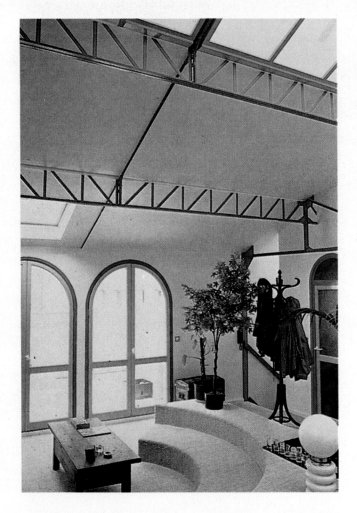

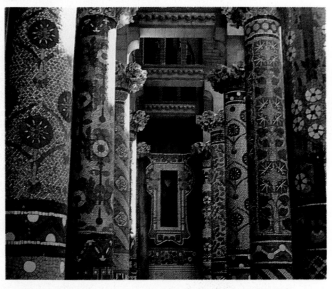

6–29 Llúis Domnèchi i Montaner, Balcony of the Palace of Catalan Music (Palau de la Musica Catalana), Barcelona. Art Resource, NY.

6–27 How do the neutral tones help soften the contrast in this interior?

balcony pillars of a music palace (fig. 6–29) range between red and blue-violet. The colors, along with the rich patterns, contribute significantly to the overall splendor.

Monochromatic combinations use tints and shades of one hue only (fig. 6–17). Because all the colors are the same hue, they go together very well. However, with the gain in harmony comes a loss of boldness. A monochromatic scheme risks being uninteresting because it is the least daring. However, Picasso's *The Old Guitarist* (fig. 6–30), which is mainly monochromatic, could not be called uninteresting. Because of the subject, the colors are very appropriate and contribute to the mood of sadness.

Expressive Qualities of Color

Why is blue appropriate for a picture with a sad mood? Imagine *The Old Guitarist* painted in tones of red, yellow, or orange. Given these alternatives, blue clearly seems to be the best choice. But this is not to say that blue always expresses sadness. In other contexts, blue can suggest such qualities as serenity, dignity, and elegance.

Color and its effects on people have been the subject of more research (and guesswork) than any other visual element. Red is said to raise blood pressure, while blue lowers it. Pink, a tint of red, has been shown to have a calming effect on violent children. In one experiment, factory workers thought that the building temperature had been raised after the colors of the walls were changed from blue and gray to red and brown. In fact, the temperature had remained at 70 degrees.

Artists are aware of the power of color. Artists divide colors into warm and cool categories. Reds, oranges, and yellows (the colors on the left side of the wheel) are considered *warm* colors. Blues, greens, and violets (the colors on the right) are considered *cool* colors (fig. 6–31). Reds and yellows make us think of such things as blood, fire, and the sun. Blues, greens, and violets remind us of sky, water, trees, grass, and shade. Whatever the reasons, the use of warm colors in a design is likely to excite us, while cool colors are likely to have a quieting effect.

Vincent van Gogh was one of the first artists to understand how color could be used for its own sake. He wrote about a painting in a letter to his brother, Theo: "I tried to express the terrible passions of humanity by means of red and green." Van Gogh often

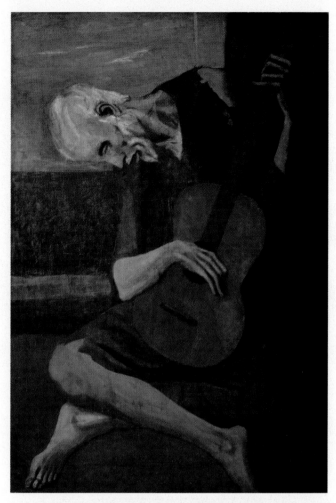

6–30 Pablo Picasso, *The Old Guitarist*, 1903. Oil on panel, 48″ x 32 ½″ (123 x 82 cm). The Art Institute of Chicago, Helen Birch Bartlett Memorial Collection.

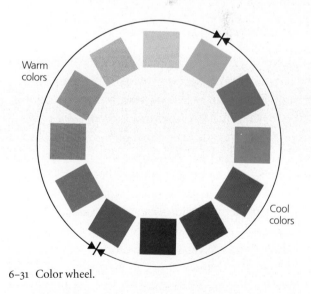

Warm colors

Cool colors

6–31 Color wheel.

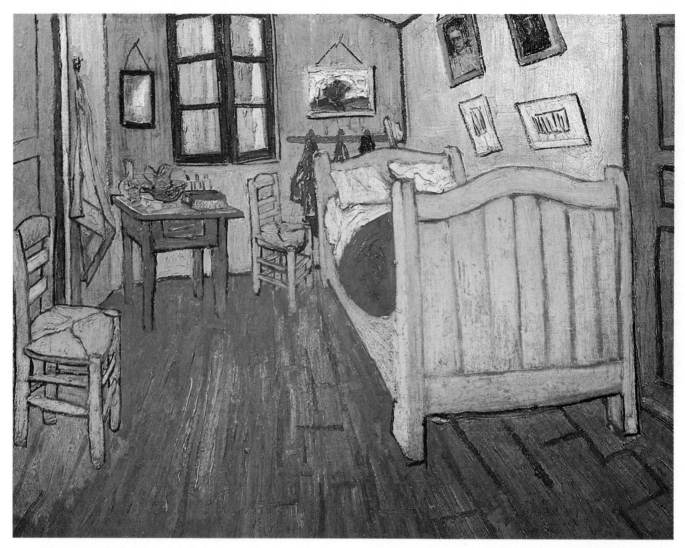

6–32 Vincent van Gogh, *The Artist's Bedroom at Arles,* 1889. Oil on canvas, 28″ x 36″ (72 x 91 cm). Stedelijk Museum, Amsterdam.

used color as a cry of pain and anguish, but he also used it in more peaceful ways. Two paintings of his bedroom are shown here. One uses mostly warm colors (fig. 6–32). The other uses mostly cool colors (fig. 6–33). Almost everything in these pictures is similar except their colors.

Color is something that you have lived with all your life. Are you surprised to learn that color is so complicated? Actually this discussion barely scratches the surface. Entire books have been written about color theory and the variables of color. Artists and designers deal with these issues all the time.

Why learn more about color? In some tribal cultures, color is not very important. The people in those cultures have normal vision, but they do not recognize many hues. In one culture, the people had words only

for light and dark and the color red. In effect, the people could not "see" yellows, oranges, pinks, blues, and so forth.

Think what you would be missing if the only hue you could distinguish were red! Knowing more about color enables you to *see* more of it. This will help you to enjoy the infinite variety and rich possibilities of color in art, and also in life (fig. 6–34).

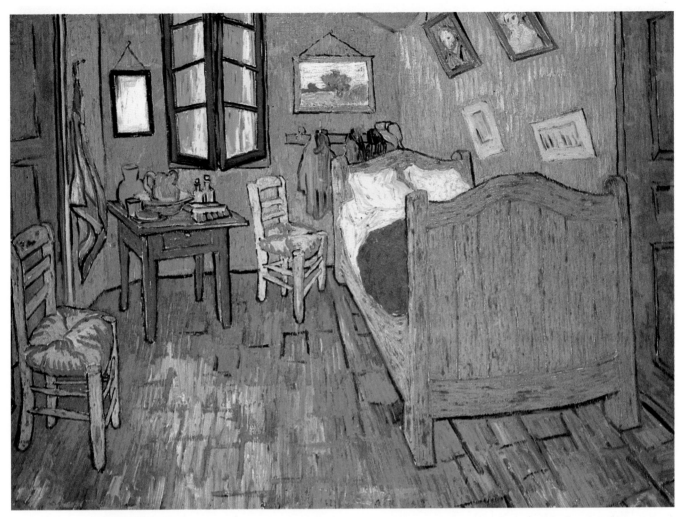

6–33 Vincent van Gogh, *The Bedroom*, 1888. Oil on canvas, 29˝ x 36˝ (74 x 92 cm). The Art Institute of Chicago, Helen Birch Bartlett Memorial Collection.

Meet the Artist

Vincent van Gogh

1853–1890

In 1988, Vincent van Gogh's colorful painting of irises sold for over fifty million dollars. But did you know that van Gogh died a penniless man? Van Gogh spent most of his life without money or possessions, choosing instead to devote his life to art.

Vincent was born in a small town in Holland near the border of Belgium. Throughout his life, Vincent maintained a strong relationship with his brother, Theo, who supported Vincent emotionally and financially throughout his career as an artist. There were times in Vincent's life when he was extremely depressed and experienced periods of mental illness. During these times, when he was staying at a hospital in St. Remy, France, and later when he moved to Auvers-sur-Oise, near Paris, Vincent was able to depend on Theo's love and assistance. Theo remained a source of support until the end of his brother's life, when Vincent committed suicide in 1890.

In a letter to his brother, Vincent once asked: "How…can I make myself useful, what end can I serve?" The answer to that question is in the bold brushstrokes, the brilliant colors, and the unique images which he portrayed in his paintings.

Describe the colors of both van Gogh paintings in terms of their hue, value, and saturation. Also describe your reactions to the colors of each. Which do you prefer, the warm or the cool painting? Why?

Imagine you are an interior decorator. What colors would you use to paint a hospital room? What colors would relax patients? cheer them up? Would your choice depend on the ages of the patients? Explain.

Imagine you are designing stage settings for a play. What colors would you use for a lively musical? a mystery set in England? a comedy?

Imagine you are a graphic designer. What colors would you use in a safety poster? an ecology poster? a travel poster?

Studio Experience 6.6

Warm and Cool Colors

To understand the expressive potential of color, create two pictures of one scene. Draw one picture in warm colors and one in cool colors. Use oil crayon on colored paper.

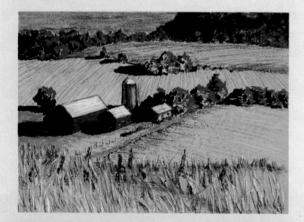

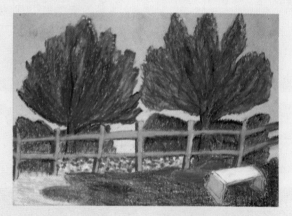

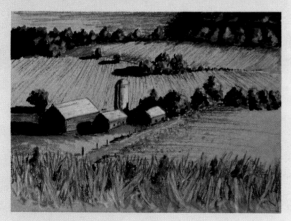

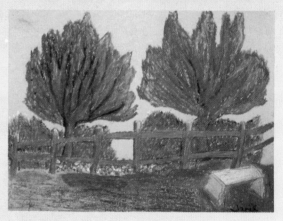

a. Mike Perrot.

b. Student work.

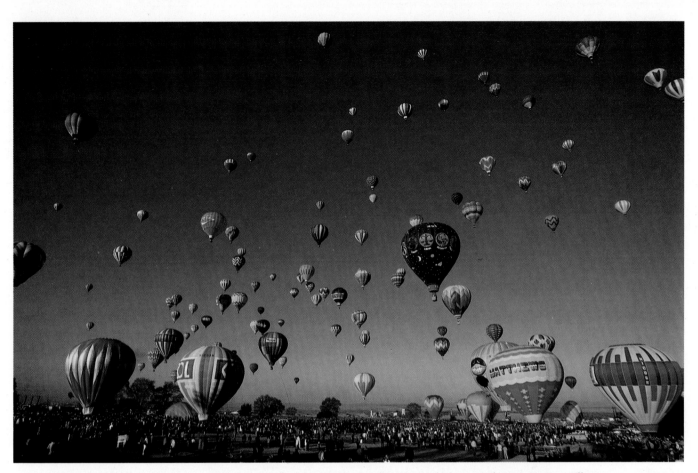

6–34 How do these colors contribute to the festive mood of the occasion? *Balloon Festival.* Photograph courtesy Ray Miller.

Summary

This chapter is about two related elements: value and color. The source of both value and color is light.

Value refers to the range of light and dark that can be seen in a work of art. This range can be represented in a value scale with white at one extreme and black at the other. An object's surfaces have lighter or darker values depending on the amount of light they reflect. Representing the surface light of an object is called shading or chiaroscuro.

Color, a powerful element in the hands of the artist, is a complicated subject. Usually, artists are involved with colors of pigments rather than colors of light. Pigments absorb light rays, reflecting only the colors not absorbed. Combining all pigments results in black, the absorption of all light rays.

Hue is the name of a color as seen in the spectrum or color wheel. Hues can be divided into groupings such as primary, secondary, and complementary.

Value applies to the lightness or darkness of a color on a scale from white to black.

Saturation describes the brightness or dullness of a color on a scale from bright to gray.

Hue, value, and saturation are affected by color interaction. Certain color combinations, or color schemes, are used often by artists and designers.

Color affects people. It is a powerful tool for expression and for prompting aesthetic responses. Artists divide hues into warm and cool categories, each with certain expressive and aesthetic potentials.

Try it Yourself

Now that you have learned more about color, go back to your description of Renoir's *Luncheon of the Boating Party.* Can you add anything new about the colors? For example, how would you identify the color of the stripes of the awning in terms of hue, value, and saturation? Would you describe the colors in this picture as being mostly light or mostly dark? mostly bright or mostly dull? mostly warm or mostly cool? Why?

Chapter 7
Visual Elements: Space

Student Edition
Pages 74–91

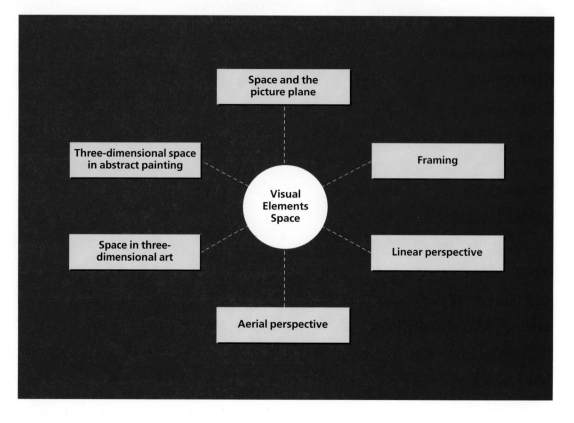

Overview

Chapter Objectives

Students should be able to:

EE 1 **1** identify and discuss devices used to suggest space and depth (foreshortening, diminishing size, overlapping, high and low placement, linear and aerial perspective) in artworks

EE 1, 2 **2** create the appearance of three-dimensional space in pictures

EE 1, 4 **3** demonstrate awareness of how three-dimensional space is created in sculptures and architectural interiors

EE 1, 4 **4** analyze a picture drawn in one- or two-point perspective by pointing out the eye-level line, vanishing point(s), converging lines, receding surfaces, and the height, width, and depth dimensions of forms

EE 1, 4 **5** explore effects and uses of space in artworks

Rationale

Space is a real part of our natural and humanmade environments and artworks. Not only do we see space in our immediate environment and in artworks, but we also feel it. Space is a *felt* presence that can contribute to our physical and mental comfort or discomfort. Space in art performs various functions. A basic knowledge of these functions and how they are implemented is important to the artist and the viewer.

Essential Chapter Concepts

• Space as an art element has numerous important functions, controlled by the way the artist manipulates the other art elements.

• We sense the form and size of space with our eyes, bodily movements, and our mind.

• Space exists as an illusion in the graphic arts and as a reality in the three-dimensional arts and architecture.

• Depth on a two-dimensional surface is represented by shading, foreshortening, making objects large or small, overlapping, high and low placement, linear perspective, and aerial perspective.

• The various devices for representing depth can be used in representational, abstract, or nonobjective artworks, depending on the artist's intentions.

• Framing, locating the borders of a picture, affects the space, point of view, and meaning of a work.

Vocabulary

space	one-point linear perspective
spatial	two-point linear perspective
volume	aerial perspective
framing	picture plane

Meet the Artist

Red Grooms   Page 79

Lesson Plans

7.1   Depth in Collage

Page **T 92**   Time: 2 periods

7.2   Identifying One-Point Perspective

Page **T 94**   Time: 1 period

7.3   Applying One-Point Perspective

Page **T 98**   Time: 2 periods

7.4   Identifying Two-Point Perspective

Page **T 100**   Time: 1 period

7.5   Applying Two-Point Perspective

Page **T 102**   Time: 2 periods

7.6   A Landscape with Aerial Perspective

Page **T 104**   Time: 3 periods

Handouts

Study Questions

Page Page **T 106**

Test Questions

Page Page **T 108**

Notes

Chapter Closure
Evaluation

1   *Production:* Can students create the appearance of depth in their own artworks using spatial devices presented in this chapter?

2   *Production:* Can students frame the height and width of a scene for an artwork?

3   *Criticism:* Ask students to explain how the various spatial devices contribute to the appearance of depth in artworks.   R 4, 5

4   *Criticism:* Can students point out and explain the height, width, and depth dimensions of forms drawn in one- and two-point perspective?   R 1

5   *Aesthetic awareness:* Can students discuss how space contributes to the organization and meaning of an artwork?   R 4

Space

Depth in Collage

Time: 2 periods

Preparation

Rationale

Most students can read some of the visual cues that indicate three-dimensional space in pictures but may overlook some of the obvious ones. Many have trouble making their own pictures appear to have depth. This collage activity provides experience in arranging cutout images to suggest depth through overlap, large to small shapes, and high and low placement.

Studio Materials

catalogs, magazines, newspapers, scissors, glue, 12" x 18" colored construction paper

Enrichment Materials

Slides:
• Bingham, *Fur Traders Descending the Missouri,* 18
• Pereira, *Oblique Progression,* 19
• Curry, *Baptism in Kansas,* 28

Large Reproductions:
• Olbinski, *Private Fame,* 13
• Biggers, *Shotguns,* 3
• Swentzell, *The Emergence of the Clowns,* 22
• *Nubian Wall Painting,* 5
• Tamayo, *Dos Hermanos,* 20
• Kanaga, *Young Woman,* 18

Teach the Lesson

Objectives

Students should be able to:

1 arrange images cut out of magazines, catalogs, and newspapers in a collage to suggest depth through overlap, large to small shapes, and low to high placement   EE 1, 2

2 identify and discuss the function of these depth devices in artworks   EE 1, 4

Vocabulary

Space is an element of art that indicates areas between, around, above, below, or inside something.

Picture plane is the flat surface that the artist uses as a frame of reference to create the illusion of forms in three-dimensional space through the use of perspective.

Collage is a composition made by gluing various materials to a firm surface. It was introduced by the Cubist artists Picasso and Braque.

Warm Up

Have students stand and look at the floor, then slowly lift their eyes to see things in front of them at gradually increasing distances. Direct attention to the Persian miniature in figure 17–0. Ask students to look at it in the same way, beginning with the lower figures and raising their eyes to see things higher in the painting. Ask them how depth is suggested in the picture. Guide answers to include low to high placement and overlap.

Explore and Develop

1 Ask what else the artist could have done with figures and shapes to strengthen the illusion of depth in the Persian miniature. (He could have diminished the size of distant figures.)

2 Show the slides by Bingham, Pereira, and Curry (or refer to figures 7–25, 7–29, and 10–6). Ask students to list the devices the artists used to indicate depth in the pictures. Guide discussion to include overlap, low to high placement of shapes, and large to small shapes.

Laser Discs:

Hartley, The Aero, c 1914

Search Frame 2098

Delauney, Political Drama, 1914

Search Frame 2145

Derain, The Old Bridge, 1910

Search Frame 2151

Derain, detail

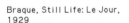
Search Frame 2153

Braque, Still Life: Le Jour, 1929

Search Frame 2173

Braque, detail

Search Frame 2175

Begin Studio Experience 7.1

1 Focus on the student examples in Studio Experience 7.1. Explain that students are going to create collages of images cut from magazines and catalogs. Colored construction paper will be used for backgrounds. Suggest they identify a subject for the collage, such as sports figures, fashion models, animals, people and pets, celebrations, etc.

2 Ask students to use all three strategies (overlap, large to small, and low to high placement of shapes) to suggest depth in the collage. Note that in the examples, larger shapes are placed lower on the paper and smaller shapes are placed higher. Some shapes overlap.

3 Encourage experimentation with placement of cutout shapes on the background paper. When the three depth devices are evident and the composition appears unified, tell students to glue the shapes down. Suggest they begin with the smallest shapes. Remind them to use all three of the space devices discussed in this lesson.

Evaluate and Reflect

1 Ask students to explain what they did to create an illusion of depth in their collages.

2 Do students feel their compositions appear unified? What gives their work unity? Do they associate overlapping with unity?

3 Discuss Seurat's *Bathing at Asnières* in figure 10–1. Can students identify where Seurat used three strategies to represent depth?

Reteach

• Film provides an illusion of movement in three-dimensional space. If you can obtain a film with figures and objects in outdoor scenes, run it without sound. Stop on frames where there are examples of forms overlapping, getting smaller with distance, and appearing higher in the picture. Prepare students to watch for cues that indicate what is near/far, large/small, in front/behind.

• Focus a slide of a scene that includes the three depth cues on a piece of white drawing paper. Have students trace around some near/far objects, some that overlap, and some that are higher in the picture plane. Have students remove the paper and color in a ground plane and the objects. Compare the slide image and the outlined image. Discuss the depth cues.

Extend the Lesson

Beyond the Basics

Have students look for examples of drawing and painting prior to the discovery of linear perspective. Suggest students look at overlapping in ancient Egyptian fresco paintings, vertical placement in East Indian and Persian paintings, and in Maya Indian murals, overlap and high/low placement in 13th and 14th century European art, etc. Suggest students set up a chart by listing the devices for creating depth in a vertical column and the works of art across the top of the page. Have them mark the perspective devices used in each work of art. Discuss the findings. **EE 3**

R 2, 5

Cultural Connections

Have students look for examples of artwork by various ethnic groups showing the use of positive and negative space or figure-ground relationships with shallow space. For example, Iroquois Indian bead work, Greek pottery, and pottery and textile designs from the ancient cultures of Mexico and South America. **EE 1, 3**

Connecting with Other Subjects

Science Have students talk with the science teacher and look through science books to find information about the ability to perceive depth. Suggest students study their environment to identify the visual clues that establish the distance from one object to another. Ask students to think of a situation they may have seen where it was difficult to establish how close or faraway an object may have been. Were certain visual clues missing or changed in some way? **EE 1**

R 3

Identifying One-Point Perspective

Time: 1 period

Preparation

Rationale

Of the many perspective devices for showing depth that artists have devised over the centuries, linear perspective is the most complex. It is also the most effective for creating a feeling of depth in pictures that include objects such as roads, buildings, cultivated fields, fence rows, arches, and columns. Students are introduced to the basic concepts of one-point linear perspective in this exercise.

Studio Materials

pencils, rulers, 12" x 18" white paper

Enrichment Materials

Slides:
• Raphael, *The School of Athens*, 91

Overhead Transparencies:
• Raphael, *The School of Athens*, 10

Large Reproductions:
• Matisse, *The Casbah Gate*, 8
• Carr, *Scorned as Timber*, 15

Teach the Lesson

Objectives

Students should be able to:

1 use one-point perspective to draw cubes that are above, overlapping, and below an eye-level line, with three of the cubes centered on the vanishing point, and three placed off to one side of the vanishing point   EE 1, 2

2 explain the concepts *eye-level line, converging lines,* and *vanishing point* as they apply in linear perspective   EE 1, 4

Vocabulary

One-point perspective is a way of representing three-dimensional objects on a two-dimensional surface, using a vanishing point and converging lines to represent forms.

Eye-level line is a horizontally drawn line that is even with the viewer's eye. In landscape scenes it can be the actual horizon line. It can be drawn in still life.

Vanishing point is a point on the eye-level line, toward which parallel lines are made to recede and meet in perspective drawing.

Converging lines are lines that represent the parallel edges of an object and meet at a vanishing point.

Laser Discs:

Canaletto, View in Venice, c 1740

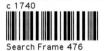

Search Frame 476

Piranesi, Prima Parte di Architetture Prospettiva, 1743

Search Frame 3080

van Eyck, The Annunciation, c 1425/1430

Search Frame 576

van Eyck, segment

Search 13715, Play To 15326

Botticelli, Adoration of the Magi, early 1480s

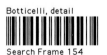

Search Frame 152

Botticelli, detail

Search Frame 154

Warm Up

Refer to *The Last Supper* by Bouts, figure 7–15, and the diagram of the painting on page 83. Discuss the converging lines and vanishing point shown in the diagram. Have students lay tracing paper over figure 7–15 and use a ruler to trace the converging lines for the sides of the table and top of the walls. Can they do one of the floor squares?

Explore and Develop

Note three important concepts:

a. Parallel lines appear to converge until they disappear at a vanishing point;

b. Objects that are far away appear smaller than those that are near;

c. The vanishing point falls on the eye-level line.

Begin Studio Experience 7.2

1   Focus on the first diagram in Studio Experience 7.2. Point out how the vertical and horizontal lines of the boxes are kept parallel with the vertical and horizontal edges of the paper.

2   Have students place a sheet of 12" x 18" paper horizontally on the desk and draw an eye-level line across the middle of the paper. Ask students to place a vanishing point on the center of the eye-level line.

3   Students should draw three squares in the center of the page, one straddling the eye-level line and surrounding the vanishing point, one above, and one below the line. Refer them to the diagram in Studio Experience 7.2.

4   Check to see that students are keeping horizontal and vertical lines parallel with edges of the paper. Refer to the vertical lines of the squares as *height lines* and the horizontal lines as *width lines*.

5   Have students extend converging lines from the bottom corners of the square above the eye-level line to the vanishing point. Next, students should extend converging lines from the top corners of the square below the eye-level line to the vanishing point. Note that no converging lines are needed for the middle square because it represents the front side of the box on the eye-level line.

6   Tell students to draw a third width line between the converging lines for the top and bottom boxes, keeping them parallel to the existing width lines. Explain that all of these shapes are drawn as if directly in front of the viewer. Ask students if they can see the bottom of one square and the top of another.

7   Have students complete the second set of boxes shown in Studio Experience 7.2. Tell students to draw an eye-level line across the middle of a sheet of paper and place a vanishing point on the left end of the line.

8 Next, students should draw three squares to the right side of the paper, one above, one straddling, and one below the eye-level line, as shown in Studio Experience 7.2. Caution students to keep horizontal and vertical lines parallel with the edges of the paper.

9 Have students draw converging lines from the corners of the squares to the vanishing point as shown in Studio Experience 7.2.

10 Have students add one height line to each of the squares. Note that the farther from the existing height line, the deeper the box will appear.

11 Next, have students add one width line to the top and bottom boxes. Note that it must connect with the two height lines they just added.

12 Ask students what surfaces they see in each drawing. Why do they see only two in the middle box?

Evaluate and Reflect

1 Can students identify the height, width, and depth dimensions of their drawings?

2 Ask a student to manipulate a real box in front of the class to explain what was done in the drawings.

3 Can students explain what happens to the parallel lines that describe the side of an object when the object is drawn in linear perspective? (They converge to a vanishing point).

4 Look at da Vinci's *The Last Supper* on Student Edition page 269. Have them identify height, width, and depth (converging) lines. Where is the vanishing point? About where is the eye-level line?

Reteach

• Provide students with photocopies of scenes in one-point perspective, and have them trace over the converging lines, extending them into the picture until they meet at a vanishing point. Help them plot the eye-level line in the picture.

• Have students manipulate a real box, placing it above and below eye level, and off to one side. Have them indicate the number of sides visible each time. Have them point to and feel what would be the height, width, and depth lines if they were to draw the box.

Extend the Lesson

Beyond the Basics

EE 1, 2 Place a real box below the eye level and off to one side, so students will see three sides. Have them draw it in one-point perspective. Have students draw the school hallway in one-point perspective. Project a slide of a scene with a road and other forms that appear in one-point perspective, and have students draw it.

EE 1 Use a video camera and monitor to observe scenes in the classroom and hallways. Use an overhead projector marker to trace the scene on the television screen. White paper held in front of the camera lens will allow the drawing to be seen easily. Concepts such as overlap, diminishing size, converging lines, vanishing point, and horizon line are easily illustrated and understood through this method. Understanding that perspective is the result of careful observation of reality is usually a tremendous help for students learning to draw.

Cultural Connections

EE 3 Have students examine the work of traditional Japanese artists who sometimes employed a device called reverse perspective. In this method parallel lines are made to converge as they approach the viewer. Reverse perspective produces a shallow space within the work and establishes a special relationship between the work and the viewer, a relationship in which the viewer is actively involved in the scene depicted. Have students examine traditional Japanese art to find examples of reverse perspective.

Connecting with Other Subjects

History In many European works produced during the 14th century disproportionate size was sometimes used to emphasize importance of a figure regardless of placement in the composition. Have students look for examples of work showing disproportionate size. Twentieth century artists sometimes use disproportionate size. Have students look for examples and then compare the contemporary with the earlier works. Did the contemporary artists use this device for the same reasons as the 14th century artist? Research these periods in history and write about the artworks in relation to the world in which they were produced.

EE 3

R 5

W 1, 2

Time: 2 periods

Studio Experience 7.3   Lesson Plan

Applying One-Point Perspective

Preparation

Rationale

This experience builds on lesson 7.2. Students locate the meeting place of converging lines in a photograph with one-point perspective. Students plot a vanishing point and an eye-level line. Then they apply the concepts from lesson 7.2 to produce a one-point perspective drawing based on the photograph.

Studio Materials

pencils, rulers, 12" x 18" paper, photographs (or photocopies) of covered walkways, hallways, room interiors, alleys, or bridges in one-point perspective

Teach the Lesson

Objectives

Students should be able to:

1   create a one-point perspective drawing based on a structure photographed in one-point perspective, plotting converging lines, a vanishing point, and an eye-level line   EE 1, 2

2   identify these components of one-point perspective in their drawings and in artworks   EE 1, 4

Vocabulary

One-point perspective is a way of representing three-dimensional objects on a two-dimensional surface, using a vanishing point and converging lines to represent forms.

Warm Up

1   Display slides of artworks in one-point perspective, and ask students to locate converging lines, vanishing point, and eye-level line.

2   Have students draw a rectangle or square on paper. Ask them to draw lines from corner to corner, making an X inside the square. Have students place a vanishing point at the intersection. Tell students to put two vertical height lines and two horizontal width lines between the converging lines about halfway between the square and the vanishing point to see an interior space.

Explore and Develop

Show and discuss slides of pictures done in one-point perspective. Have students use yardsticks to locate converging lines and the vanishing point on the projected image. Where would the eye-level line fall?

Begin Studio Experience 7.3

1   Refer to Studio Experience 7.3. The photographs were photocopied and enlarged so students could plot converging lines, a vanishing point, and eye-level line. Explain that students will copy a photograph to produce a drawing in one-point perspective. Note that shading and watercolor washes were used in the examples to increase the appearance of depth and solidity of the forms.

2   Provide students photocopies of a scene in one-point perspective. Have students lay rulers on the converging lines in the photocopy, draw them, and locate the vanishing point.

3   Tell students to lay a ruler horizontally across the photo, with the edge on the vanishing point. Students should keep the ruler parallel with the top and bottom edges of the photo, and draw an eye-level line to see how much of the scene is above and below the line. Have them place a vanishing point in the middle of the eye-level line.

Laser Discs:

Master of Barberini Panels, The Annunciation, c 1450

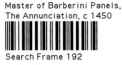

Search Frame 192

Corot, River Scene with Bridge, 1834

Search Frame 1138

Utrillo, Street at Corte, Cosica, 1913

Search Frame 2163

Grimmer, The Marketplace in Bergen op Zoom, 1597

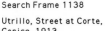

Search Frame 770

Henri, Snow in New York, 1902

Search Frame 2050

Sargent, Street in Venice, 1882

Search Frame 2040

4 Have students draw the left and right vertical sides (height lines) of the structure to the left and right of the vanishing point. Students should make them the same length *and parallel to the vertical edges of the paper*. Have them draw width lines between the two verticals.

5 Have students draw four converging lines from the top and bottom of the left and right height lines to the vanishing point. These represent edges in the photo such as where floors, walls, and ceilings meet.

6 Have students place a second set of height and width lines between the converging lines to suggest the distant corners of the structure. How far back they are placed depends on how deep the student wants the structure to appear.

7 Call attention to how shapes become shorter and closer together as they recede in the picture.

8 Have students keep adding height and width lines to designate shapes in the structure (windows, doors, columns, etc.).

9 Now, lay the photocopy aside, and develop the drawing with darks and lights to make forms appear more three-dimensional. Caution students to continue using the converging lines and vanishing point if they add anything.

Evaluate and Reflect

R 2 **1** Ask students to analyze their drawings. Did they draw parallel lines converging to a vanishing point?

R 5 **2** Can they identify the height, width, and depth dimensions in their drawings?

R 5 **3** Did they keep the horizontal and vertical lines of their drawings parallel with the top and bottom, and left and right edges of the paper?

R 5 **4** Can they explain how adding darks and lights made objects appear three-dimensional?

R 5 **5** Ask students to identify the height, width, and depth dimensions in an artwork with one-point perspective.

Reteach

Work with a small group, providing each student with a copy of the same one-point perspective photocopy. Ask them to follow your demonstration of each step in this experience.

Extend the Lesson
Beyond the Basics

EE 2 Students can experiment with a page full of forms in one-point perspective. Have students place a vanishing point at the center of a page filled with squares and rectangles. All converging lines should be drawn to the one vanishing point. Have students create openings in forms and create progressively smaller sequences of forms. Students can use shading or color to make the forms appear more three-dimensional.

Cultural Connections

EE 3 Direct students' attention to figure 7–27 on page 88 of the student text, a contemporary Navajo work. Suggest students look for examples of Navajo art from the past. Have R 3, 5 them research the Navajo culture. Discuss how Tsinahjinnie's work may have been influenced by Navajo history and culture. Is there evidence in his work of other influences? Examine the devices he used to create space. How did earlier Navajo artists create the illusion of depth?

Connecting with Other Subjects

Science Renaissance artists attempted to R 3, 5 master nature through scientific means of understanding optical effects. Artists today continue to study nature through modern technology, such as the microscope and computers. Have students research the technological advances from the Renaissance through present day that have helped artists to understand the world in which they live. How did these advances impact others? Report findings to the class.

Identifying Two-Point Perspective

Time: 1 period

Preparation

Rationale

In one-point perspective, only the depth dimension recedes. Students frequently draw objects from an angle where two sides of an object may be seen as receding, for example, width and depth, or height and depth. Two-point perspective is a system for representing two dimensions of an object as though they recede into space.

Studio Materials

pencils, rulers, 12" x 18" paper

Teach the Lesson

Objectives

Students should be able to:

1 draw two rectangular forms, one overlapping an eye-level line and another from above the eye-level, using two-point perspective   EE 1, 2

2 identify objects in artworks that are drawn in two-point perspective   EE 3, 4

Vocabulary

Two-point perspective is a way of representing three-dimensional objects on a two-dimensional surface, using two vanishing points and two sets of converging lines to represent forms with height, width and depth. Forms are seen from an angle and have two receding surfaces.

Warm Up

1 Ask students to compare the drawings for Studio Experiences 7.2 and 7.4. Note the three dimensions labeled in Studio Experience 7.2. Which one recedes? Have students look at Studio Experience 7.4. Identify the three dimensions. Which ones recede? Note that a corner is nearest the viewer rather than a side as in one-point perspective. Remind them that one form is above eye-level, while the other straddles the eye-level line.

Explore and Develop

Display Estes's *Drugstore*. Point out the near corner and the two receding sides. Have students lay yardsticks on the image to see how the converging lines meet at two vanishing points on the same eye-level.

Begin Studio Experience 7.4

1 Ask students to place a sheet of paper horizontally and draw an eye-level line a little below the middle of the paper. Have them place vanishing points on both ends of the line.

2 Refer to the example in Studio Experience 7.4. Tell students to draw two vertical lines, each about 3 inches long, one through the eye-level line and the other above it.

3 Have students draw converging lines from the top and bottom ends of each vertical line to both vanishing points.

Laser Discs:

Bril, Heroic Landscape, c 1585

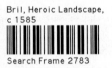

Search Frame 2783

Piranesi, The Carceri: The Gothic Arch, 1748-1750

Search Frame 3082

Rembrandt, Landscape with a Cottage and Barn, c 1650

Search Frame 2817

Sloan, The City from Greenwich Village, 1922

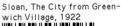

Search Frame 2090

Boudin, Bathing Time at Deauville, 1865

Search Frame 1186

Ostade, The Angler, c 1650

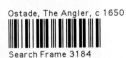

Search Frame 3184

4 Students should add two height lines to the left and right of the near corner vertical, keeping them parallel with one another and the edges of the paper. Explain that if they place one height line farther away from the corner than the other, it will be easier to determine which side(s) represents width and which is depth.

5 This completes a perspective image for the lower box. Students need to add two more converging lines to the form above the eye-level line to show the bottom surface.

6 Have students turn their drawings upside down to see a form below the eye-level line.

7 Allow students to develop their drawings. They may add a ground plane, shade the surfaces of the forms, or use value contrasts to set off the different surfaces.

Evaluate and Reflect

1 Ask students to analyze their drawings. Were they able to show two receding surfaces in the lower form and three in the upper one?

2 Can they identify the receding dimensions in each form?

3 Can they identify forms drawn in two-point perspective in artworks?

Reteach

Work with small groups. Use an overhead projector to show students step by step how to draw a form in two-point perspective that overlaps the eye-level line. Then guide them through drawing a form either above or below the eye-level line. Continue using the overhead projector, and lead them through adding a ground plane and openings to the forms.

Extend the Lesson

Beyond the Basics

Have students draw forms in both one- and two-point perspective on the same eye-level line. Let them experiment with adding doors and windows to develop the forms as buildings. Students may want to try sidewalks and parking lots. Suggest students add color and shading to enhance the illusion of depth. Use chalk or other blendable drawing media. Rub or blend the colors to soften edges and produce diminishing clarity as the objects recede into the distance. Suggest mixing colors to diminish intensity of objects in the distance. What other devices could be used to deepen the space?

EE 1, 2

Cultural Connections

Suggest students look through resource books to find examples of architecture as subject matter in the works of artists from a variety of cultures. What devices did the artists use to show depth? Was linear perspective used? Did the artists use one-point or two-point perspective? Arrange the works in order according to how real the work appears or how deep a space the artists have created. In which works does the illusion of depth appear to be most important?

EE 3

Connecting with Other Subjects

Geometry The basic shape of the buildings drawn in this lesson is the cube. Have students talk with the geometry teacher regarding the geometry of space division. Geometry allows easy division of a square by drawing diagonal lines from corner to corner. The intersection of these lines is the center of the square. The sides of a cube drawn in perspective can be divided in the same way. What other aids to drawing can be found in geometry? Have students use geometry to find the size and placement of windows, doors, blocks, walkways, etc. for their drawing.

Space

Applying Two-Point Perspective

Time: 2 periods

Preparation
Rationale

This lesson is a continuation of lesson 7.4. To reduce the complexity of the problem, students are given a starter picture on which to build a two-point perspective drawing. They are required to extend the picture beyond its boundaries by drawing additions in two-point perspective. They must use vanishing points and an eye-level line plotted from the original picture.

Studio Materials

pencils, rulers, pen, brush and ink, 12" x 18" drawing paper, photocopied pictures of buildings in two-point perspective

Teach the Lesson
Objectives

Students should be able to:

1 extend a picture of a building in two-point perspective beyond its original boundaries by drawing additions, using the vanishing points and eye-level line plotted for the original picture   EE 2

2 add forms of their own invention, with lines converging to the vanishing points   EE 2

Warm Up

1 Use an opaque projector to project a picture of a building on a large sheet of wrapping paper. Have students identify some converging lines in the building. Use a yardstick to extend those lines onto the paper. Once vanishing points are established, ask a student to locate the eye-level line.

2 Demonstrate adding something to the picture. Discuss using the vertical edges of the paper, the vanishing points, and existing converging lines as references. Ask students to suggest additions.

Explore and Develop

1 Refer to Studio Experience 7.5. Ask students to identify edges of shapes in the house that were used to establish the converging lines and vanishing points.

2 Note how the vertical lines of the house were kept parallel with the vertical edges of the paper.

3 Ask them where the photographer stood when taking the picture.

Begin Studio Experience 7.5

1 Have students place their rulers on the two vanishing points in the drawing for Studio Experience 7.5 so they can see where the eye-level line runs.

2 Tell students to cut out a photocopied picture of a building in two-point perspective. Have them cut along the building's edges and place the picture on a piece of 12" x 18" white paper. Have them use a ruler along the converging edges of shapes in the picture to estimate where the vanishing points will fall on the paper. Students should position the picture so both points can be placed on the paper. Have them glue the picture in place, keeping vertical edges parallel with the vertical edges of the paper.

3 Have students use a ruler and light pencil to extend lines from converging edges of upper and lower parts of the building onto the paper until the lines intersect. They should do this for both sides of the picture, using whatever linear edges are visible. Have them mark the vanishing points where the converging lines meet on both sides of the paper.

4 Tell students to locate the eye-level line by positioning the ruler on the vanishing points and drawing a horizontal line across the paper. The line should appear to pass behind the building.

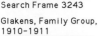

5 Students may add to the picture. For example, they may extend the building, using the converging lines that are already there, or put a second story on the building. Encourage them to draw in sidewalks, fences, street lamps, grass, and power poles, always making lines converge to the two vanishing points.

Evaluate and Reflect

1 Ask students to see if they can identify the original converging lines, vanishing points, and eye-level line in one another's drawings.

2 Are they satisfied with their additions to the original picture? Have them share additions that used converging lines plotted from the picture.

3 Were they able to add forms requiring new converging lines?

4 Can they explain why the vanishing points in two-point perspective are not always equal distances from the object?

Reteach

Provide students with photocopied pictures in which converging lines, vanishing points, and the eye-level line are plotted. Ask them to make some additions using those converging lines. Use the overhead projector to show them how to add a shape that is not on the eye-level line. Continue adding things to the drawing on the overhead projector while students copy. Then ask students to draw their own additions to the picture.

Extend the Lesson

Beyond the Basics

EE 2 Students can work from photographs of structures in perspective without a photocopy glued to the paper, to draw pictures in both one and two-point perspective. Have them explore using more than two vanishing points on the eye-level line to draw objects in perspective from different viewing angles.

EE 1,2 Take the class on a field trip to draw some real buildings and other forms in linear perspective. If possible visit the sites in advance and use a video camera and tripod to record about five minutes each of several different views of an interesting structure. Be sure to maintain a fixed viewpoint throughout taping. Prior to the field trip view the videotape with students and trace the structure on the screen using a projector marker. Review concepts of diminishing size, overlap, placement, and linear perspective.

Cultural Connections

EE 3 Have small groups research the various devices used by different people in different cultures and time periods to represent depth in two-dimensional artwork, and in R 5 sculptural relief such as Ghiberti's *Gates of Paradise*, Florence Baptistry .

EE 3 Suggest groups of students each choose a culture they find interesting and acquire a resource book containing a chronological history of the art of that culture. Examine R 5 the two-dimensional works and determine a date when artists first attempted to show an illusion of depth in their work. Did they find works showing two-point perspective? When was the work produced? Have students share their findings with the class. Have them work together to chart the devices used by various cultures to create the illusion of depth and the approximate dates each culture began using each device.

Connecting with Other Subjects

History Suggest students extend the R 3, 5 Cultural Connection lesson from this section by researching possible influences from other cultures. Have students compare the dates from the previous lesson with dates of journeys of trade and exploration that may have led to an exchange of ideas between artists from the various cultures. Suggest jotting down bits of information and dates on slips of paper to use with information charted in the previous lesson.

Space

Time: 3 periods

A Landscape with Aerial Perspective

Preparation

Rationale

Aerial perspective (sometimes called atmospheric perspective) is one of the older strategies for representing depth in paintings. It is used most frequently for outdoor scenes. The artist manipulates the medium to interpret the lighter, cooler, hazy colors that result from atmospheric effects when objects are far away. This lesson gives students the opportunity to use the medium to interpret the effects of atmospheric conditions on distant objects.

Studio Materials

black and white tempera, soft hair brushes, mixing trays, 12" x 18" white paper, pencils, water containers, paper towels

Enrichment Materials

Slides:
• Bingham, *Fur Traders Descending the Missouri*, 18
• Masaccio, *The Tribute Money*, 90
• Rembrandt, *The Mill*, 8

Overhead Transparencies:
• Ma Yuan, *Bare Willows*, 20

Large Reproductions:
• Yan, *Brushfire with Animals Fleeing*, 16
• Carr, *Scorned as Timber*, 15
• Schwartz, *Untitled #16*, 11

Laser Discs:

Turner, Dogana and Santa Maria della Salute, c 1843

Search Frame 1719

Gainsborough, Landscape with a Bridge, c 1785

Search Frame 1621

Gainsborough, detail

Search Frame 1623

Monet, Waterloo Bridge, Gray Day, 1903

Search Frame 1404

Monet, Bridge at Argenteuil on Gray Day, c 1876

Search Frame 1386

Tanner, The Seine, 1902

Search Frame 2056

Teach the Lesson

Objectives

Students should be able to:

1 create a landscape with black and white tempera paint, using aerial perspective to suggest depth

EE 2

2 use lighter values and less contrast to make background shapes seem farther away

EE 2

Vocabulary

Aerial perspective is the diminishing of color intensity to lighter and duller hues to give the illusion of distance in the picture plane.

Picture plane is the flat surface on which the artist creates the illusion of depth.

Warm Up

Ask students to look out of the window and compare the colors of near objects with colors of distant objects. Which are brighter? duller? Examine contrasts of color and value in foreground objects, and compare with those found in the background.

Explore and Develop

1 Discuss examples of artworks with aerial perspective. Focus on aerial perspective effects, but don't ignore other devices such as overlap and diminishing size. You may also refer to figures 7–25, 7–26, 5–31, and 18–46. Where do the edges of objects appear the sharpest and brightest? haziest and dullest? Where are the darkest values located? Ask students to point out places where forms are distinguished through value contrasts rather than outline.

2 Ask them to discuss the mood created by aerial perspective in the examples.

Begin Studio Experience 7.6

1 Emphasize that students are going to use only values of black and white to create atmospheric effects in their paintings. They should make objects that are close darker in value, with distinct edges resulting from dark/light contrasts.

2 Have students lightly outline a landscape with overlapping shapes to indicate foreground, middle, and background. List things that can be put in a landscape. (Refer to the enrichment materials for examples.) Encourage students to put something in the foreground, middle, and background.

3 If necessary, demonstrate working with tempera transparently and with opacity. Show how to make washes with the medium.

4 Suggest that students begin with puddles of white and add black to obtain different values. Water can be added to any of the values to produce transparent effects.

5 Since only light and dark values will be used to suggest depth in the picture, advise students to use the darkest values for shapes that are to appear the nearest. Values applied to distant shapes should become progressively lighter and less contrasting as the shapes are shown farther and farther away.

6 Students may incorporate the white of the paper during the painting process. Details should be placed in the foreground shapes and become less distinct in the middle ground.

Evaluate and Reflect

R 5 **1** Ask students how many values they included in their painting.

R 5 **2** Do their paintings include a progression of values from dark to light? Have them explain and show where they achieved less value.

R 5 **3** Did they achieve less value contrasts among the most distant objects?

R 5 **4** Can students identify artworks that include aerial perspective?

Reteach

If students have difficulty with the lesson, it may be because they didn't mix distinguishing values. Have students make a sampler of values with nine steps including black and white at either end.

Extend the Lesson
Beyond the Basics

Have students continue working with aerial perspective, but add two complementary colors so they can explore the use of bright and dull colors. EE 2

Suggest students look through the text and other resources to find examples of aerial perspective. Have them examine the works to determine how each artist achieved the desired effect. Suggest trying one of these techniques in their own work. EE 2, 5

Cultural Connections

Refer students' attention to Bingham's painting (figure 7–25) on page 86 of the student text. Color and detail are changed to create the appearance of distance. What mood or feeling has Bingham created? How would the mood differ if the colors and details were clear? Suggest students research this period in American history and the contributions made by the fur traders. Where did this scene take place? What was life like at this time and in this place? Have students look at other works by Bingham. Are there other examples of aerial perspective? What role does Bingham's work play in historical and cultural documentation? EE 3

R 3, 4, 5

Connecting with Other Subjects

Science Suggest students talk with the science teacher regarding the scientific reasons for aerial or atmospheric perspective. What is the viewer looking through that creates the effects of diminishing detail and changes in the properties of color? The video camera/monitor used in previous lessons is helpful in demonstrating the effects of aerial perspective. Try placing the camera near a window looking out over a field in which props have been set to illustrate each idea. EE 1

Study Questions
Chapter 7–Visual Elements: Space

1 How do we "see" space in our environment?

_____

2 What are two ways that the *spatial aspects* of a room can be determined?

_____

3 Give one spatial difference between the architecture of the central court of the East Building of the National Gallery of Art by I. M. Pei (text fig. 7–5) and the interior of the National Gallery's Rotunda by John Russell Pope (text fig. 7–6).

_____

_____

_____

_____

4 While looking at the photograph of the sculpture *Linear Construction* by Naum Gabo (text fig. 7–9), identify the positive and negative areas of the sculpture.

_____

_____

_____

5 Define *negative space* in a painting or drawing.

_____

_____

6 Draw an example of three overlapping shapes.

7 How do high and low placement of objects show spatial depth?

_____

_____

8 In a one-point perspective drawing of a simple subject, in what three directions do all lines go?

_____

9 What lines converge in linear perspective?

_____

10 Describe the directions of lines used in two-point perspective.

_____

_____

11 Define *eye level.*

_____

_____

12 Find an example of a painting (other than in the text) in which the artist uses aerial perspective.

_____

13 Find an example of a painting (other than in the text) in which an artist uses warm and cool colors to show depth.

_____

_____

14 What are two ways that *framing* can affect a painting?

_____

_____

15 What kind of linear perspective is primarily used in *The Country School* by Winslow Homer (text fig. 7–30)?

_____

_____

Test Questions
Chapter 7–Visual Elements: Space

Circle the correct answers:

1 T F   Space occurs only in three-dimensional artwork.

2 T F   Space is not always invisible.

3 T F   To an architect space isn't as important as shape/form.

4 T F   In a linear perspective drawing, parallel lines like railroad tracks and edges of the highway converge.

5 T F   In this woodcut, *The Prophet* by Emile Nolde, the negative space is white.

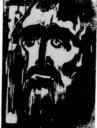

6 T F   An artist using aerial perspective in a painting tries to make everything in the background as distinct as objects in the foreground.

7 T F   Changing the borders of a picture affects the space, point of view, and meaning of a picture.

8 T F   An object higher on the picture plane appears closer than something that is placed lower.

9 T F   Overlapping, or making something appear to be in front of something else, implies depth.

10 T F   Warm colors tend to advance and cool colors tend to recede.

11–15   Identify the correct information on the illustration by placing the correct number on the corresponding line.

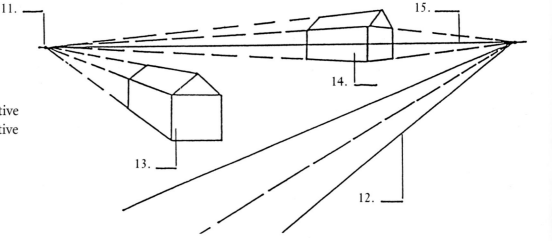

1 Vanishing point
2 Eye level
3 One-point perspective
4 Two-point perspective
5 Converging lines

For questions 16 through 20, use the following list.

1	positive space	6	informal
2	negative space	7	formal
3	mobile	8	one-point perspective
4	organic/open	9	two-point perspective
5	geometric/open		

While viewing the overhead transparency or text fig. 7–5 of The Central Court of the East Building of the National Gallery of Art, Washington, DC, answer the following questions.

16 What word describes the type of architectural design used by I. M. Pei? _____.

17 Alexander Calder's sculpture is a _____.

While viewing the transparency or text fig. 7–8 of *Pendour* by Barbara Hepworth, answer the following questions.

18 The carved holes in the sculpture are _____.

19 This sculpture is a(n) _____ form.

While viewing the transparency or text fig. 18–47 of *The School of Athens,* by Raphael, answer the following questions.

20 The linear perspective used in this painting is primarily _____.

While viewing the overhead transparency of Georgia O'Keeffe's *Sky Above Clouds IV,* answer the following questions.

21 What kind of *shape* does O'Keeffe use in this painting?

_____

22 How does she use the size of shapes to show depth?

_____

_____

23 Which do you think are the *positive* and *negative areas* in this painting?

_____

_____

Study Answers
Chapter 7
Visual Elements: Space

1 By seeing its boundaries (floor, ceiling, walls of an interior; buildings, trees of the exterior).

2 a. By walking around it, and, b. by staying in one place and looking around with your eyes.

3 The East Building's spaces vary in size, form, and level; the design is *informal*. The Rotunda has less variety, repeated columns, and a central focus— a large fountain/sculpture; the design is *formal*.

4 Positive—areas occupied by the plastic and plastic threads; negative—all areas in between the plastic shapes/forms.

5 The areas around objects in a picture, the background, or the ground in a figure-ground relationship.

6 Drawings should show one object or shape partially in front of another.

7 Something lower in a picture appears closer than something higher.

8 Vertical, horizontal, or toward the vanishing point.

9 Lines that describe the edges of receding shapes.

10 Vertical lines and (two sets of) converging lines.

11 The height of the viewer's eyes relative to the ground or floor.

12 Examples will vary. Should have features including: objects farther away are lighter, softer, cooler, duller, having less contrast; outlines and detail are less distinct.

13 Examples will vary. Should show warm colors advancing and cool colors receding.

14 Framing can change: a. the space, b. the point of view, and, c. the meaning of the scene.

15 One-point perspective.

Test Answers
Chapter 7
Visual Elements: Space

1 F

2 T

3 F

4 T

5 F

6 F

7 T

8 F

9 T

10 T

11 (1.) Vanishing point

12 (5.) Converging line

13 (3.) One-point perspective

14 (4.) Two-point perspective

15 (2.) Eye level

16 (6.) Informal

17 (3.) mobile

18 (2.) negative space

19 (4.) organic/open

20 (8.) one-point perspective

21 Organic

22 Larger shapes are lower on the picture plane and smaller shapes are higher.

23 Answers may vary, but the most likely answer will be: clouds take up the positive space and the sky beneath occupies the negative space.

Teacher Lesson Notes

Chapter 7
Visual Elements: Space

Answer these true–false questions before reading about space.

Space Quiz

1. Space is empty. (T–F)
2. Space is always invisible. (T–F)
3. Unlike shape or form, space cannot be measured. (T–F)
4. The experience of space can be related to the sense of movement. (T–F)
5. Spatial is the adjective form of the word space. (T–F)

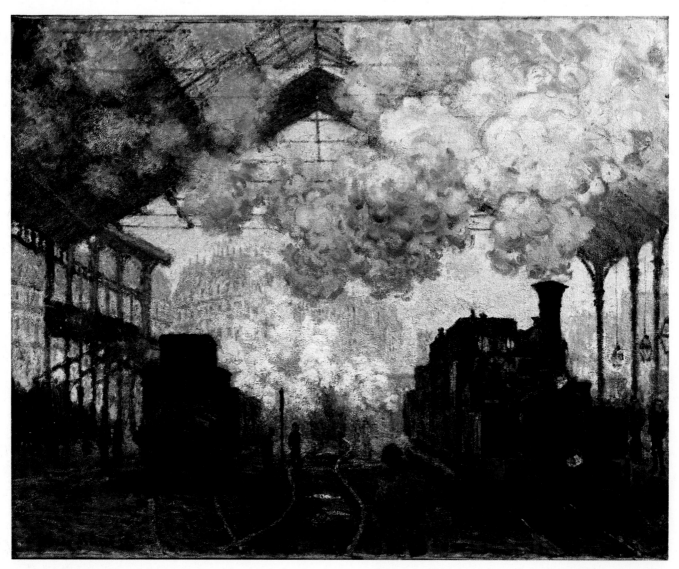

7–1 Claude Monet, *La Gare St. Lazare, Paris,* 1877. Oil on canvas, 32 ½″ x 39 ¾″ (83 x 101 cm). Fogg Art Museum, Cambridge, Massachusetts (Maurice Wertheim Collection).

Space in Our Environment

We often think of *space* as the emptiness that surrounds objects, or the emptiness inside of hollow shapes such as boxes or buildings. Also, we think of space as being invisible. So, why is it considered one of the visual elements? There are at least two answers to that question.

First, space on this earth is not really empty. It is filled with oxygen and other gases we call air. And as you know, air is not always clean and clear. Sometimes it is full of smoke, dust, or *pollution* (fig. 7–1) that can be seen. Sometimes it is full of particles of water and dust that we call *clouds* (fig. 7–2) or *fog,* which can also be seen. So, space is not always invisible.

Second, we "see" space by seeing its *boundaries.* The space inside a room has size and form. For example, the ceiling, floor, and walls of a room (fig. 7–3) determine the size and form of a space. Interior space in a room is often called **volume.** Outdoors, the size and form of a space is determined by buildings, plants, reflecting pools, and other objects (fig. 7–4). We could say that space is "empty form."

You can sense, or experience, space around you through movement. While sitting at your desk, you can sense the space under the desk simply by moving your legs and feet. You can sense the size and volume of your classroom, or its **spatial** aspects, by walking around in it. (You can also sense the spatial aspects by just looking around the room.)

How did you do on the quiz? The correct answers are:

1.F,   2.F,   3.F,   4.T,   5.T.

Try it Yourself

How well do you know the location of things in your room at home? Stand in the center of the room. Then, with your eyes closed, try to find the middle drawer of your dresser. Can you sense the correct direction, distance, and height of the drawer (or other object)?

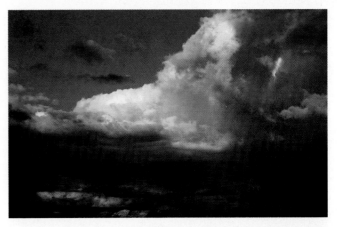

7–2 Photograph: Barbara Caldwell.

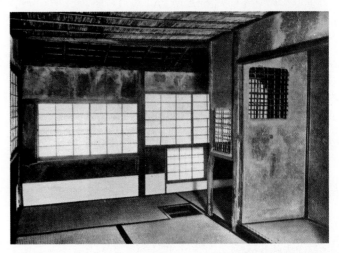

7–3 The Hasso-no-seki tea room, Konchi-in temple, Kyoto.

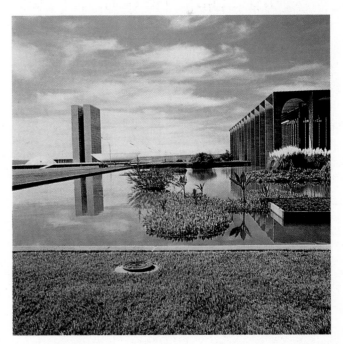

7–4 Foreign Office Building, Brasilia.

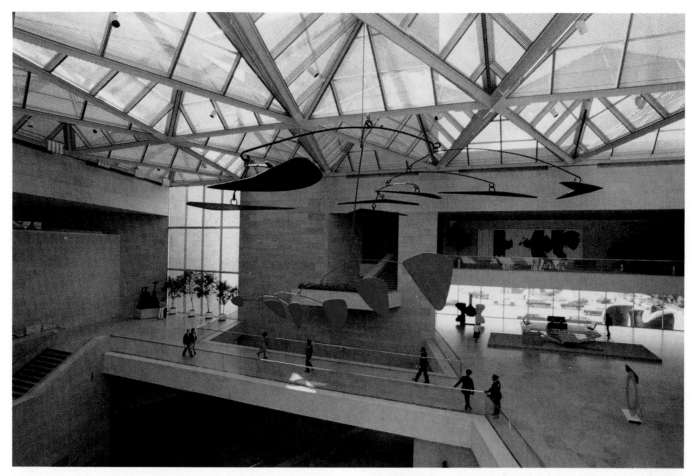

7–5 *East Building of the National Gallery of Art, Washington.*
©1993 National Gallery of Art, Washington, opened 1978,
I. M. Pei, architect.

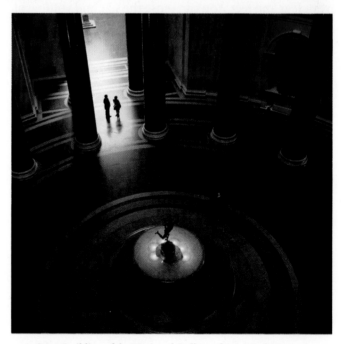

7–6 *West Building of the National Gallery of Art, Washington.*
©1993 National Gallery of Art, Washington, opened 1941,
John Russell Pope, architect.

Space in Three-Dimensional Art

To the architect, space is probably the most important visual element. An architect must design pleasing and interesting spaces in which people live, work, or play. The architect I. M. Pei did just that in 1978 when he designed the central court of the East Building of the National Gallery of Art (fig. 7–5). The spaces in the central court vary in size, form, and even level. These spaces provide an exciting environment for strolling and viewing art.

The interior of the National Gallery's rotunda (fig. 7–6) is very different. The rotunda was designed by John Russell Pope and completed in 1941. The rotunda is a large, circular area defined by huge columns. It does not have the same variety of Pei's central court.

Yet the rotunda is as dramatic as the newer interior. Pope's design is formal. It follows the traditional rules of architecture. Pei's design is modern and informal.

The courtyard of a library (fig. 7–7) in San Juan Capistrano, California, is rather formal even though it is quite new. The courtyard was designed by Michael Graves in 1983. The rectangular space of the courtyard is *symmetrical,* or identical on both sides. It is less dramatic than either of the interiors at the National Gallery, but it is no less beautiful. And it is very appropriate for the peace and quiet of a library. Which of the three spaces do you prefer? Why?

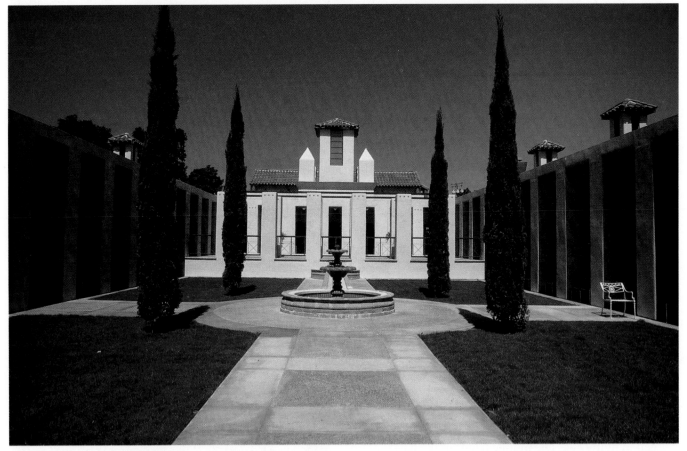

7–7 San Juan Capistrano Regional Library; SJC, California. Michael Graves, architect. Photograph ©1986 by Bruce Iverson.

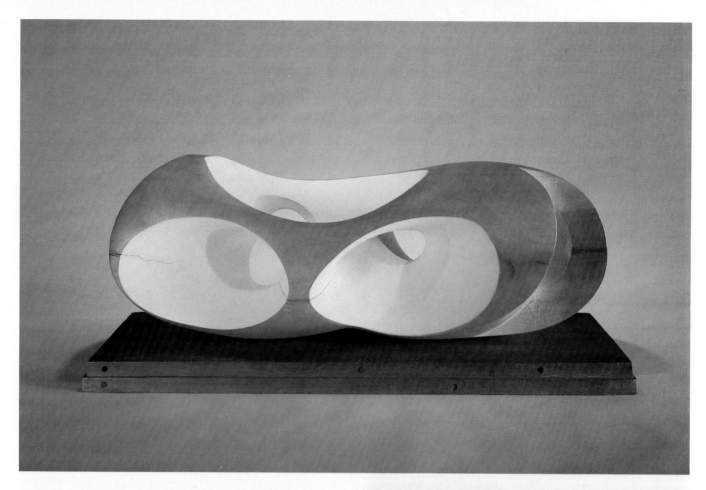

7-8 Barbara Hepworth, *Pendour*, 1947. Painted wood, 12 1/8" x 28 3/8" x 9 3/8" (31 x 72 x 24 cm). Hirshhorn Museum and Sculpture Garden, Smithsonian Institution, Gift of Joseph H. Hirshhorn, 1966.

Space is also important to the sculptor. Modern sculptors often work with open forms, as Doris Leeper did in her sculpture *Untitled* (fig. 5–35). Barbara Hepworth's *Pendour* (fig. 7–8) is carved wood. The artist intentionally carved openings in it to create a unique relationship between form and space, or positive and negative.

A more extreme example of open form is *Linear Construction* (fig. 7–9) by Naum Gabo. Made of a plastic frame and nylon strings, it is more like a harp than a traditional sculpture. On a much larger scale is Alexander Calder's huge *mobile.* Part of this mobile can be seen in figure 7–5. The mobile hangs in the East Building of the National Gallery.

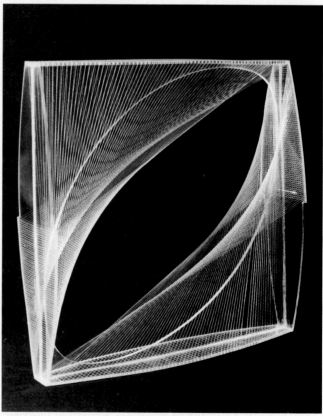

7-9 Naum Gabo, *Linear Construction*, 1942–43. Plastic with plastic threads, 14" x 13 5/8" x 3 1/2" (36 x 35 x 9 cm). The Tate Gallery, London/Art Resource, NY.

Red Grooms

1937–

Beneath layers of plastic, acrylic and brilliantly colored paint hides a wire armature, or skeleton base, draped with canvas and burlap. These materials, molded into bucking horses, high-riding cowgirls and cowboys, and gymnastic clowns, fill a fifty-foot long space.

Red Grooms decided to create *Ruckus* Rodeo after visiting a state fair in Fort Worth, Texas. In this sculptured environment, the artist has re-created certain events which you might see at a rodeo, but has exaggerated and distorted the details. A green horse with a yellow mane throws his rider in the air. A sixteen-foot-tall yellow bull sports six-foot-long horns. Cowboys wrestle steers and ride bareback broncos while fans cheer and hats are enthusiastically waved in the air. The sizes, colors, and actions of the people and animals in *Ruckus* Rodeo are unrealistic and imaginary.

This life-size walk-in sculpture of a western rodeo has been termed a **sculpto-pictorama,** and its artist, Charles Rogers Grooms, has been nicknamed "Red." Red has created other sculpto-pictoramas including *City of Chicago* and *Ruckus Manhattan*, which memorialize major cities in the United States.

Born in Nashville, Tennessee, in 1937, Red Grooms was encouraged by his parents to pursue his early talent and interest in art. Influenced by visits to the Tennessee State Fair and the Ringling Brothers and Barnum and Bailey Circus, Red began to create unique versions of imaginary circuses in his backyard. From performing original skits for his classmates to working at a local art gallery after school, Red was committed to a career as an artist. In fact, by the age of eighteen he had already exhibited his paintings at a gallery in his hometown.

Red has spent most of his career in New York City. There he has worked collaboratively with other artists since 1957 to create skit-like performances known as "happenings," and sculpto-pictoramas like the dramatic and colorful *Ruckus Rodeo*. With this colorful city and its inhabitants as his subjects, Red Grooms has devoted his life to pursuing an art filled with humor and activity, teeming with excitement and life.

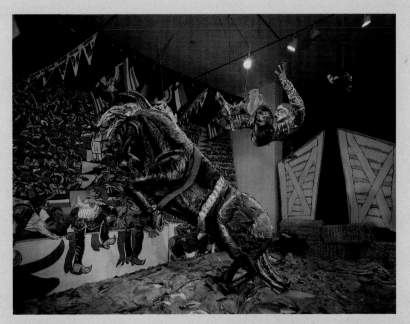

Red Grooms, *Ruckus Rodeo*, 1975–1976. Sculpture wire, celastic, acrylic, canvas and burlap, 174″ x 606″ x 294″ (442 x 1539 x 747 cm). Commissioned by the Modern Art Museum of Fort Worth. Museum purchase with funds from the National Endowment for the Arts and the Benjamin J. Tillar Memorial Trust.

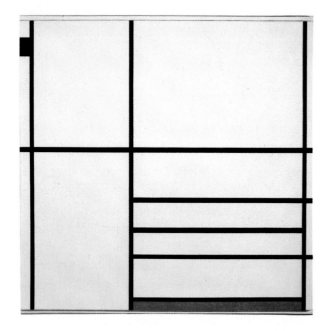

7-10 Piet Mondrian, *Composition in Black, White and Red*, 1936. Oil on canvas, 40 ¼″ x 41″ (102 x 104 cm). The Museum of Modern Art, New York. Gift of the Advisory Committee.

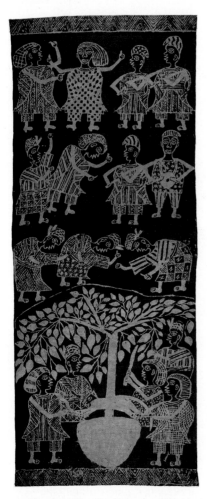

7-11 Senabu Oloyede, Oshogbo, Nigeria. Wall hanging, starch resist on cotton. 33 ¼″ x 75″ (85 x 191 cm). Gift to Field Museum of Natural History from Robert Plant Armstrong.

Space and the Picture Plane

So far in this chapter, the word *space* has been used to mean a three-dimensional area. Some artists, however, use the term to refer to the flat, two-dimensional surface of a painting. The flat surface of a painting or drawing is sometimes called the **picture plane.** Modern artists, especially those who paint abstract pictures, take great care in deciding where to place shapes on the picture plane. For example, they may place shapes high or low, or to the left or the right on the picture plane.

Piet Mondrian was a very skilled abstract artist. He took great care in arranging each line, shape, and color on the picture plane. The space in his *Composition in Black, White and Red* (fig. 7–10) is very balanced.

Artists sometimes define space as being the unfilled areas of the picture plane. They also use space to refer to the "background" of the painting or to the ground of a figure–ground relationship. (A "figure" stands out on top of a ground. A "ground" appears to be underneath and surrounding a figure.) These areas are sometimes called *negative space*. In the Mondrian painting, negative space would be the white areas. In the wall hanging by Senabu Oloyede (fig. 7–11), it would be the black areas.

Representing Three-Dimensional Space in Two-Dimensional Art

Many pictures, especially those we call "realistic," appear to have the three dimensions of height, width, and depth. Of course, these pictures do not have actual depth. In Chapter 5, you learned that depth can be created by shading and foreshortening (figures 7–12, 7–13). These methods make an object seem solid and three-dimensional. Depth can also be created by changing the size of an object to make it appear closer or farther away (fig. 7–14).

In this chapter, you will learn four more ways to create a sense of depth: *overlapping, high and low placement, linear perspective,* and *aerial perspective.* Bouts's *Polyptych of the Last Supper* (fig. 7–15) will be used to illustrate the first three methods.

Overlapping

A simple way to suggest depth in a picture is by having things overlap. An object is placed in front of and partially covering something else (fig. 7–16). In the Bouts

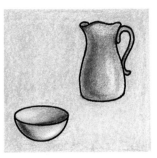

7–12 Shading.

7–13 Foreshortening.

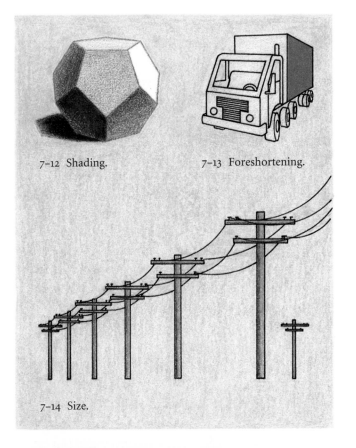

7–14 Size.

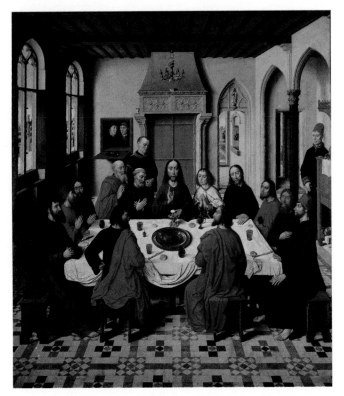

7–15 Dirk Bouts, *Polyptych of the Last Supper* (center panel), 1464–68. Oil on wood, 6′ x 5′ (183 x 153 cm). Louvain, Eglise de St. Pierre. Giraudon/Art Resource, NY.

painting, the two men that overlap the table appear to be closer to us than the table itself. The table is closer to us than the central figure of Jesus.

High and Low Placement

Usually, something that is lower in a picture appears closer to us than something that is higher (fig. 7–17). The two men on "our" side of the table are lower in the picture than Jesus. Therefore, they are closer to us than Jesus is. Their cups are lower than Jesus' cup and therefore closer.

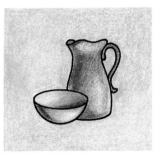

7–16 Overlapping forms.

7–17 Which of these objects (higher or lower) appears to be closer to us?

Try it Yourself

Take a blank sheet of paper. Think of the surface of the paper as "space." In the middle of this space, place a cutout of a house or tree. This image becomes a "frame of reference." Now take a cutout of an animal or person and place it below the frame of reference. Does it appear small? When placed above the frame of reference, it should appear large (fig. 7–18). What causes this "magical" effect? (For an answer, reread page 48 on size constancy in Chapter 5.)

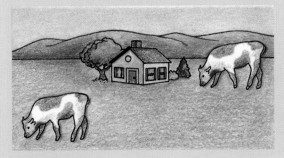

7–18 Which of these forms appears larger?

Depth in Collage

Cut out images from magazines, catalogs, and newspapers. Arrange them in a collage to suggest depth. Use overlap, large and small shapes, and low or high placement in the picture.

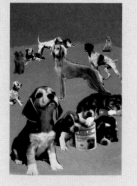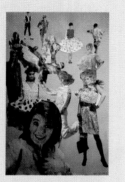

a. Corinna Carey.   b. Mark Gardener.

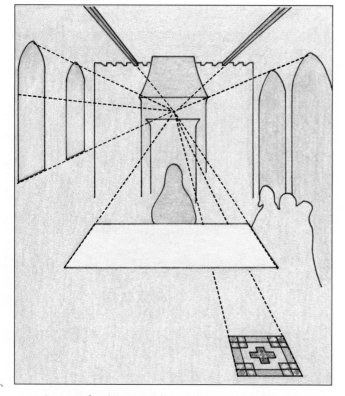

7–20 In artwork using one-point perspective, many lines converge at a single vanishing point that appears to be in the distance.

Linear Perspective

Linear perspective is the most complicated method for showing depth. Look at the drawing of a basketball court (fig. 7–19). Vertical lines are used for the posts supporting the backboards. Horizontal lines are used for the sidelines. The center and end lines appear to be parallel in the drawing (as they are in real life). But in fact, they are not. They *converge,* or come together, at a point in the distance. This is called the *vanishing point.* When all these lines are extended by dotted lines they meet at the point. This type of perspective is called **one-point perspective.**

Polyptych of the Last Supper also has one-point perspective. Look at the diagram in figure 7–20. Many lines are vertical or horizontal. Many more lines converge: the ends of the table, most of the lines in the floor pattern, and most of the beams in the ceiling.

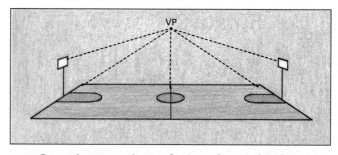

7–19 One-point perspective uses horizontal, vertical, and converging lines.

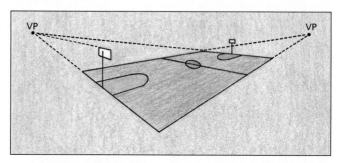

7–21 Two-point perspective uses vertical lines and two sets of converging lines, but no horizontal lines. Therefore, there are two vanishing points.

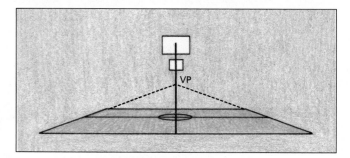

7–22 One-point perspective with the vanishing point located above eye level.

Look at the men sitting at each end of the table, as well as the tops and bottoms of the two windows. Dotted lines from the men and the windows converge.

Two-point linear perspective is used in the second drawing of a basketball court (fig. 7–21). There are vertical lines and *two* sets of converging lines. There are no horizontal lines. The converging lines of the center line, end lines, and edges of the backboards go to the left vanishing point. The sidelines, which are the other set of converging lines, go to the right point.

Compare the drawing of the basketball court in figure 7–22 with figures 7–19 and 7–21. Figure 7–22 has one-point perspective. However, the viewer seems to be standing on the floor. In the first and second drawings, the viewer seems to be sitting in the bleachers. The *eye level* is different. Eye level refers to the height of the viewer's eyes relative to the ground. In the third picture, the eye level is below the height of the backboards. In the first two pictures, the eye level is above. Usually the vanishing point (or points) is on the eye level.

Where is the eye level in relationship to the men in *Polyptych of the Last Supper*? Would the viewer be sitting, standing on the floor, or standing on a stepladder?

Try it Yourself

Choose a photograph or picture. Lay a ruler along any of the lines of the picture. Try to find the vanishing point or points. (See the example in figure 7–23.) WARNING: One or both of the points may be out of the picture. If so, glue the picture to a large piece of paper if you need to draw lines outside of the picture.

Try to find the vanishing point and eye level of *The Country School* (fig. 7–30). (TIP: Lay your ruler along the lines formed by the benches on either side of the room, the top edge of the window on the left, and the top edge of the wall on the right.)

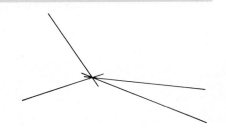

Studio Experience 7.2

Identifying One-Point Perspective

Draw three cubes in one-point perspective. Place one cube above the eye level, one overlapping the eye level, and one below the eye level. Place the vanishing point in the center. Then draw three cubes that are off to one side of the vanishing point.

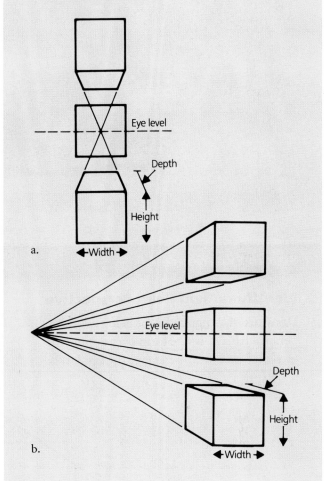

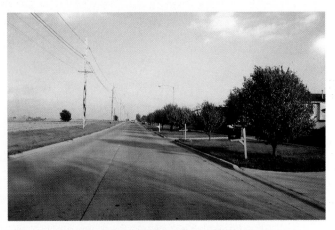

7–23 Can you locate the vanishing point of this picture?

Applying One-Point Perspective

Find a photograph of a structure with one-point perspective. Create a drawing of it. Show converging lines, a vanishing point, and eye level.

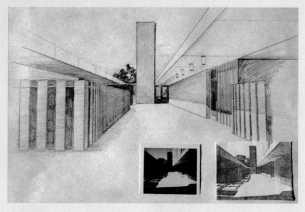

a. Sarah Johnson.

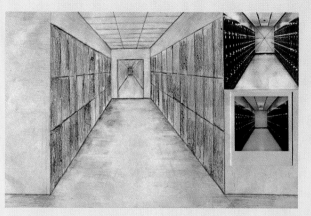

b. Malcolm Ferguson.

Identifying Two-Point Perspective

Draw two rectangular forms using two-point perspective. Draw one form overlapping the eye-level, and the other above the eye-level.

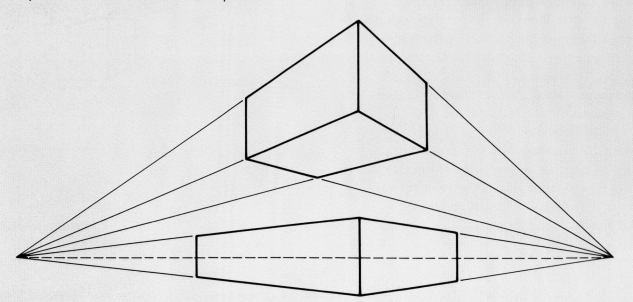

Applying Two-Point Perspective

Photocopy a photograph of a building that has two-point perspective. Glue the copy onto a piece of drawing paper. Extend the picture beyond its original boundaries by drawing your own additions. Locate the vanishing points by extending the lines that appear in the photograph.

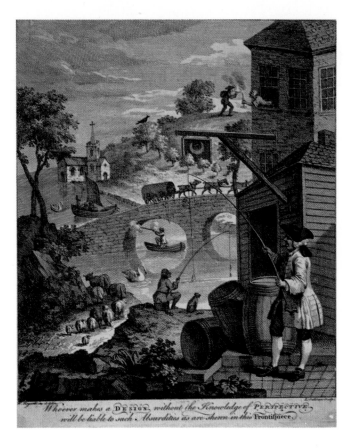

Try it Yourself

Study the picture *Frontispiece to "Kirby's Perspective"* (fig. 7–24) by William Hogarth. This picture does not represent depth using the methods discussed in this chapter. How many violations or inconsistencies of size, overlapping, high–low placement, and linear perspectives can you see? Make a list. Compare your list with a classmate's.

7–24 William Hogarth, *Frontispiece to "Kirby's Perspective"* (Joshua Kirby's edition of Dr. Brook Taylor's *Method of Perspective*), 1753. Engraving, 8 ¼" x 6 ¾" (21 x 17 cm). Reproduced Courtesy of the Trustees of the British Museum.

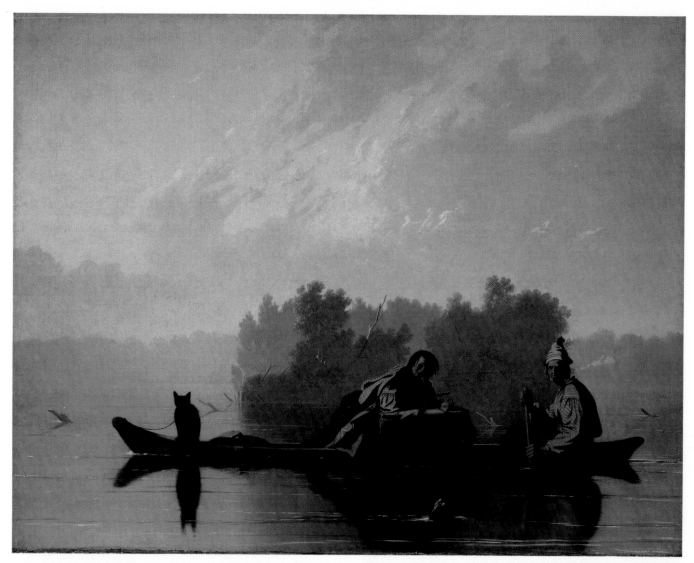

7-25 George Caleb Bingham, *Fur Traders Descending the Missouri.* Oil on canvas, 1845. 29″ x 36 ½″ (74 x 93 cm). The Metropolitan Museum of Art, Morris K. Jesup Fund, 1933.

Aerial Perspective

Recall that air is often filled with fog, smog, or air pollution. When the air is filled with particles, objects become less visible. Notice how indistinct the buildings in the distance are in Claude Monet's *La Gare St. Lazare* (fig. 7–1).

But even in the country, and on clear days, moisture in the air can affect the appearance and color of things in the distance. When an object is far away, its colors become lighter, cooler, and duller. The colors lack hue or value contrast. The object's outlines and details become less distinct. In a picture, this effect is known as *aerial perspective.* Notice how George Caleb Bingham used colors to create aerial perspective in *Fur Traders Descending the Missouri* (fig. 7–25). The colors create four layers in the scene. Each layer appears at a

greater distance. Notice the boat, a hazy island behind the boat, a hazier island beyond it, and the still hazier riverbank in the background.

In traditional Chinese ink painting, aerial perspective is used to create glowing mountain scenes. In *Bare Willows and Distant Mountains* (fig. 7–26), the artist was able to suggest various degrees of distance. Although the ink technique is monochromatic (Chapter 4), the Chinese artist controlled the values and clarity of details. The trees in the lower right are relatively dark and distinct. The trees and houses across the river are hazy and shrouded in mist. The mountains in the background almost disappear.

A Landscape with Aerial Perspective

Create a simple landscape that has aerial perspective. Use values of black and white tempera paint to create this effect. Use lighter values and contrasts to make shapes seem farther away.

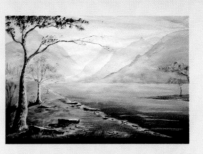

Mick Carreras.

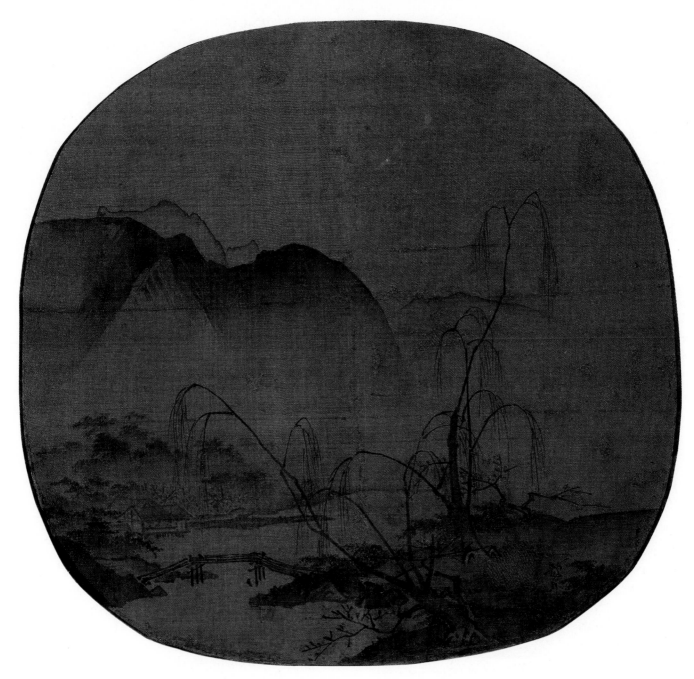

7–26 Ma Yuan, *Bare Willows and Distant Mountains*, China, Southern Song dynasty, about 1200. Round album leaf; ink and colors on silk, 9″ x 8″ (24 x 21 cm). Chinese and Japanese Special Fund. Courtesy, Museum of Fine Arts, Boston.

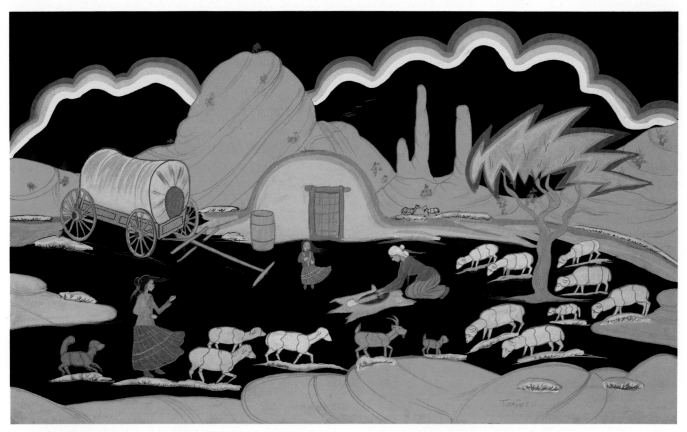

7-27   Andrew Tsinahjinnie, *Pastoral Scene*, Navajo. Tempura, 20 ½″ x 32″ R. O. Cline Land Co., Inc.

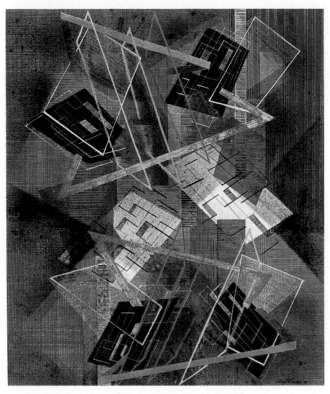

7-29   I. Rice Pereira, *Oblique Progression*, 1948. Oil on canvas, 50″ x 40″ (127 x 102 cm). Collection of Whitney Museum of American Art, New York. (Purchase).

Three-Dimensional Space in Abstract Painting

People tend to think that abstract art does not have spatial depth. But this is not true. Painters of abstract works are concerned with more than just the two-dimensional space of the picture plane. For some abstract painters, the suggestion of three-dimensional space is also important.

Look at the depth in Andrew Tsinahjinnie's stylized and semiabstract picture of a Navajo settlement, *Pastoral Scene* (fig. 7–27). Depth is conveyed through variations of size, overlapping, high–low placement, and even some foreshortening.

Hans Hofmann used some overlapping in *Flowering Swamp* (fig. 7–28). He created depth, however, mainly through *color variation*. Notice how the warm colors tend to come toward the viewer. The cool colors tend to go back.

Foreshortening, overlapping, size variation, and color variation create depth in Irene Rice Pereira's abstract *Oblique Progression* (fig. 7–29). The sense of movement through and around lines and shapes in space is quite vivid.

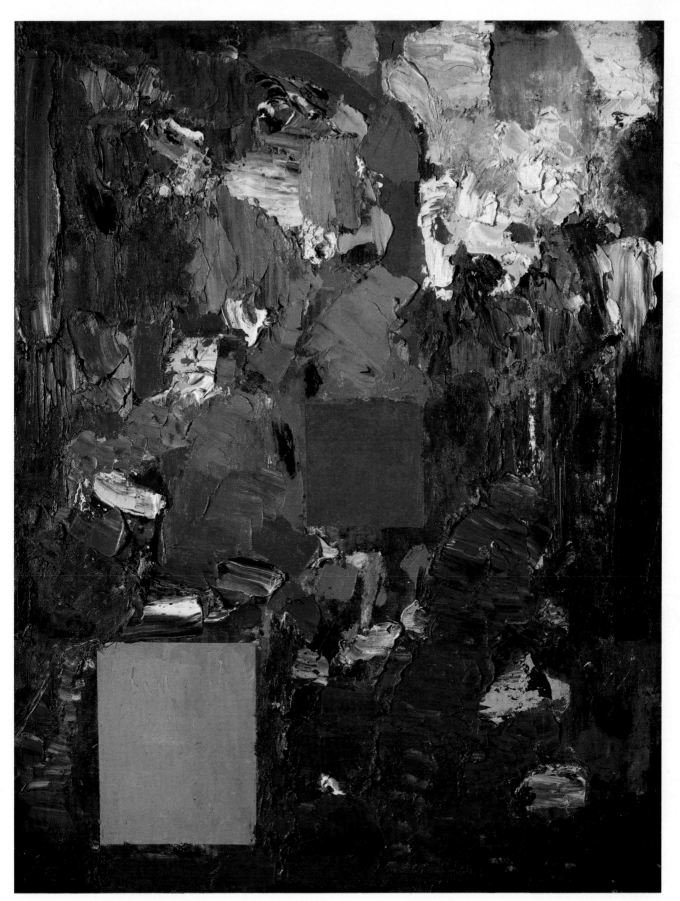

7-28 Hans Hofmann, *Flowering Swamp*, 1957. Oil on wood, 48″ x 36″ (122 x 91 cm). Hirshhorn Museum and Sculpture Garden, Smithsonian Institution, Gift of the Joseph H. Hirshhorn Foundation, 1966.

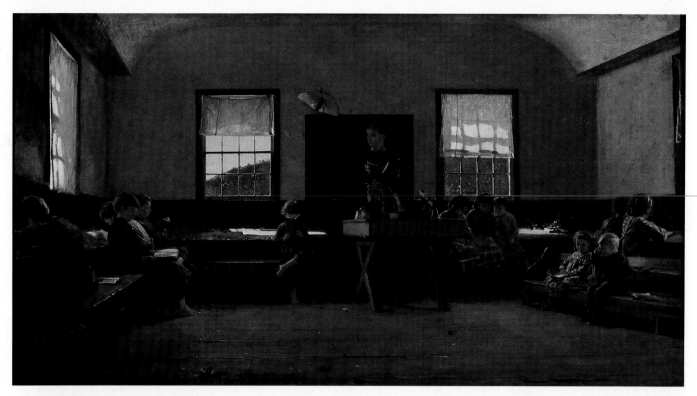

7–30 Winslow Homer, *The Country School,* 1871. Oil on canvas, 21 ³⁄₈˝ x 38 ³⁄₈˝ (54 x 98 cm). The Saint Louis Art Museum (Purchase).

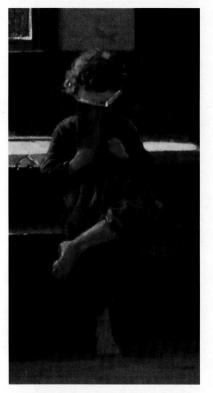

7–31 Creating a close-up is one result of changing the frame of a picture. Winslow Homer, *The Country School* (detail).

Framing

Framing establishes the limits of what is seen in a picture. Winslow Homer framed *The Country School* (fig. 7–30) so that we see almost the entire one-room school. Because of the teacher's size and location, she is the most important person in the picture. But she, along with the students, is relatively small in comparison to the size of the painting. Therefore, she appears to be relatively far away.

Framing can affect the point of view and the meaning of a scene. Look at the single boy sitting to the left of the teacher. He is one of the farthest-away people. Suppose that we reframe the picture so that we see only him. In the new frame (fig. 7–31), he is much larger in comparison to the size of the picture. Therefore, he appears to be very close. Pictures like this that are framed very close to the central image are sometimes called *close-ups.*

In the new picture, the focus is just on the boy and what he is doing. In the original, he was merely a small part of a large scene. In what ways to you think the story has been changed? Is the new story more interesting or less interesting than the original?

Cut out two "L" shapes (at least five inches for one leg and three inches for the other). Use the L's to make an adjustable frame (a). Move the frame across a picture. Stop when you come to an interesting part. Adjust the size of the frame by sliding the two L's as needed to create a close-up (b). See how many new pictures with different stories you can make out of the original. If possible, use a photocopying machine to enlarge each of your new pictures.

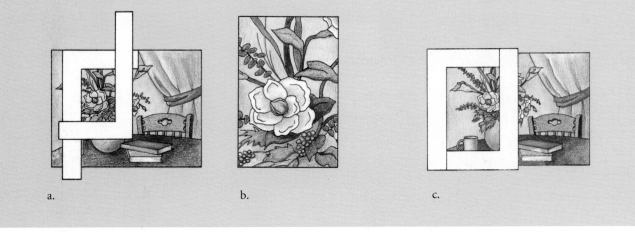

a.   b.   c.

Summary

The size and form of a space can be determined by its boundaries and the objects it touches. The interior spaces of hollow objects and buildings are referred to as volume.

We sense the form and size of a space not only with our eyes but also by our bodily movements.

Space is very important to artists who deal with three-dimensional artworks. Architects, especially, have to consider space when they design buildings and interiors. Modern sculptors often include holes in their works to create added space. They may make open sculptures out of strong lightweight materials.

Artists who make paintings and drawings often use the word *space* to refer to the two-dimensional area of the picture plane.

Artists who make realistic pictures are representing depth on a two-dimensional surface. They create the illusion of three-dimensional objects and people surrounded by three-dimensional space. Depth is created by shading, foreshortening, and making objects large or small. These methods were explained in Chapter 5. Depth can also be created by overlapping, high and low placement, linear perspective, and aerial perspective. Color variation is also used in abstract art to create depth.

Framing means deciding the borders of a picture. Framing affects the space shown in the picture. It can also determine the point of view and meaning of a picture.

Now that you have learned about space, go back to your description of Renoir's *Luncheon of the Boating Party.* Can you recognize examples of high and low placement or overlapping? Can you locate the vanishing point and eye level? Is the eye level high, low, or average with respect to a standing person?

The framing of *Luncheon* allows us to see the whole party on the deck. Try changing the space and the scene by reframing the painting.

Chapter 8
Visual Elements: Texture and Movement

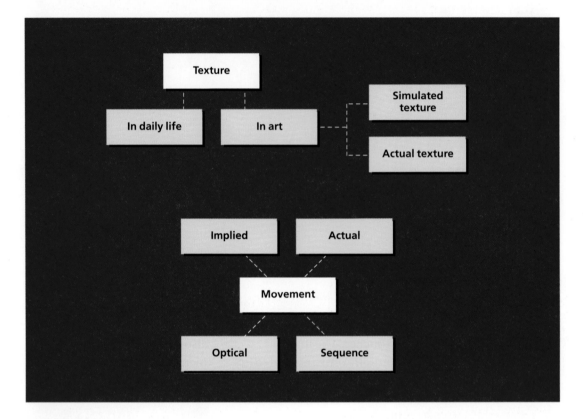

Overview

Chapter Objectives

Students should be able to:

EE 1, 3 **1** identify textures in artworks and their environment

EE 1 **2** respond to some tactile differences between various textures

EE 1, 3 **3** distinguish between simulated and real textures in artworks

EE 1, 2 **4** create artworks that include simulated or real textures as expressive elements

EE 1 **5** explain how movement is implied in static artworks

EE 1 **6** discuss the role of actual movement in mobiles and other kinds of kinetic art

7 demonstrate awareness of camera position, camera movement, shots, and sequences in films   EE 2

8 create artworks with movement, using strategies discussed in this chapter   EE 1,2

Rationale

Texture and movement are important elements in art. Texture plays a greater role in life than students realize. Movement may be experienced in artworks in several ways. Learning about texture and movement will help students understand how these elements function in both art and daily life. Knowing more about the role of sequence and movement will help students become more critically aware of popular arts such as comics and movies.

Essential Chapter Concepts

• Texture refers to the surface quality of objects.

• Texture is related to the sense of touch (tactile sense).

• In photographs and realistic paintings, the simulated textures are usually the most important.

• In craft objects and richly textured paintings, the actual textures are usually the most important.

• Paintings and sculptures contain various degrees of implied movement.

• Some artworks, such as mobiles and kinetic art, actually move, while others suggest optical movement.

• A comic strip suggests movement through time through sequence of images.

• An episode in a film is a sequence of action divided into a series of camera shots.

Vocabulary

texture	implied movement
sequence	simulated texture
optical movement	track
glossy	tactile
kinetic art	pan
shot	zoom

Meet the Artist

Claes Oldenburg   Page 101

Lesson Plans

8.1   Simulated Textures

Page **T 114**   Time: 2 periods

8.2   Textures in Clay

Page **T 116**   Time: 2 periods

8.3   Suggesting Movement in Clay

Page **T 118**   Time: 2 periods

8.4   Movement in a Comic Strip

Page **T 120**   Time: 2 periods

8.5   Making a Storyboard

Page **T 122**   Time: 2 periods

Handouts

Study Questions   Page **T 124**

Test Questions   Page **T 126**

Chapter Closure
Evaluation

1   *Production:* Display the collages. Can students identify the simulated textures taken out of their original contexts? Can they discuss how these textures function in their collage contexts?

2   *Production:* Can students create a variety of interesting textures in clay tiles?

3   *Production:* Can students create sculptures in which movement is suggested by the directions of lines and forms?

4   *Criticism:* Can students identify and describe actual and simulated textures in an artwork?

5   *Production/Criticism:* Display the cartoons and storyboards. Can students explain how the content is sequenced in the series of frames?

6   *Criticism:* Ask students to identify the positions and movement of the camera as well as the different shots used in a film sequence.

7   *Aesthetic awareness:* Are students more aware of the role of texture in art and their environment? Do they talk about artworks, clothes, furnishings, and so on in terms of texture?

8   *Aesthetic awareness:* Are students more aware of the structure of a film or video? Do they notice such things as position, point of view, and movement of the camera as well as the action of the story?

Notes

R 1

Simulated Textures

Time: 2 periods

Preparation

Rationale

Artists frequently simulate texture to suggest the surface quality of an object. Simulated textures are present in artworks, photographs, and all forms of popular art in our world today. Textures play an important role in communicating the message of an artwork or an advertisement. In this experience, students use simulated textures to help describe imaginative figures and objects.

Studio Materials

magazines, catalogs, scissors, 12" x 18" construction paper, manila paper, pencils, glue sticks

Enrichment Materials

Slides:
• Dali, *The Persistence of Memory,* 112
• Chagall, *I and the Village,* 109

Overhead Transparencies:
• Ernst, *The Eye of Silence,* 1
• Dali, *The Persistence of Memory,* 5

Large Reproductions:
• Biggers, *Shotguns,* 3
• Magritte, *The Plagiary,* 4
• Mackie, *Self-Portrait,* 14
• Olbinski, *Private Fame,* 13

Teach the Lesson

Objectives

Students should be able to:

1   assemble simulated textures taken from magazine pictures into new contexts   EE 1, 2

2   create a collage of imaginative objects and figures that emphasize the unexpected and fantastic   EE 2

Vocabulary

Texture refers to the surface quality of an artwork. It is usually perceived through the sense of touch.

Simulated texture is implied texture. It can be seen but not felt.

Surrealism is a 20th century style of painting in which artists combine normally unrelated objects and situations. Scenes are often dreamlike or set in unnatural surroundings.

Warm Up

1   Ask students to share one of the wildest dreams they ever had.

2   Ask students to imagine the fantastic. For example, what would Earth look like through alien eyes? What will the first space travelers see on Mars?

3   Discuss examples of Surrealism by Dali, Ernst, de Chirico, Chagall, Tchelitchew, Miró, Tanguy, Masson, and Klee.

Explore and Develop

The Dali and Ernst transparencies are excellent examples of the combination of normally unrelated objects and situations in Surrealistic artworks. Discuss how the artists portray a fantasy world based on imagination, dreams, and the subconscious mind.

Begin Studio Experience 8.1

1   Direct attention to the student works in Studio Experience 8.1, in which students used simulated textures from magazine pictures to create collages.

2   Discuss creating a surrealistic collage using the expressive qualities of simulated textures found in magazines. Students will take simulated textures out of their original

Laser Discs:

Klee, The White House, 1923
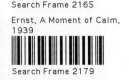
Search Frame 2165

Ernst, A Moment of Calm, 1939

Search Frame 2179

Miro, Head of a Catalan Peasant, 1924

Search Frame 2261

Miro, detail
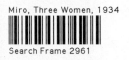
Search Frame 2263

Miro, Three Women, 1934
Search Frame 2961

Hamilton, Fashion Plate, 1969

Search Frame 3287

contexts and use them for new purposes. For example, grass may become hair, tree foliage may become a creature's coat, carpet may become a roadway, an automobile grill may become part of a face.

3 Students should select a dominant shape such as a robot, a human figure, a mask, a portrait, an animal, or an imaginary hybrid figure. Tell students to construct the shape with textures. As they collect their simulated textures, stress that they *should not* use whole pictures.

4 Some students may find it easier to make an outline drawing of the dominant object on manila paper. They can use the drawing as a pattern for cutting out the texture shapes that they will assemble on the colored construction paper.

5 Encourage students to select colored construction paper that goes with their idea. Have students use a glue stick to assemble the parts on the colored paper. Remind them to position parts that will be overlapped first.

6 The background should be surrealistic too. Suggest that it have depth, a weird flying object, something repeated three times, and color provided by a sheet of construction paper.

Evaluate and Reflect

1 Did the students take textures out of their original contexts and put them in new ones? Ask them to discuss how the textures help express their idea.

2 Have students describe the tactile sensations suggested by some of the textures in their collages. What contrasts of textures do they see?

3 Why did they select certain textures? Are the textures different from those they would normally associate with the object represented?

4 Have them address how they achieved unity in their collages. Consider repetition, dominance, and similarities.

Reteach

Have students work cooperatively in small groups. Tell the groups to bring examples of simulated textures to class. Have students categorize and mount the examples. Ask the groups to write short descriptions of the various textures. You may also want to have students who had trouble with the collage try another on 9" x 12" paper, creating only a dominant figure and a ground plane.

W 2

Extend the Lesson
Beyond the Basics

Although Surrealism formally began early this century and continues in the work of artists today, its roots can be traced back to the work of Hieronymous Bosch, late 15th century, and works produced by Francisco Goya during the last years of his life, early 19th century. Suggest students examine the work of these artists in addition to the Surrealists.

EE 3

Cultural Connections

Suggest students study the works of several Surrealist artists from different nations. Have them examine the subject matter and content of each. Have students read about the place where each artist lived and what was happening in his/her world at the time. What events may have influenced the work? What other artists may have influenced the work? Suggest students review the definition of Surrealism and write a brief statement about each of these works explaining why they are considered Surrealistic.

EE 3

R 1, 5
W 4

Connecting with Other Subjects

Psychology Since the work of Sigmund Freud was a major influence in the work of Surrealist artists, suggest students research and write a paper about the connections between Freud's work and the Surrealist movement.

R 5
W 2

Literature/Arts The Surrealist movement was not limited to the work of visual artists. Surrealism appears in music, dance, film, theater, and literature. Suggest students talk with other teachers to find examples of Surrealism in these areas. Discuss findings with the class.

R 5

Textures in Clay

Time: 2 periods

Preparation

Rationale

Texture is an important surface element in art and may be used to enhance a surface decoratively or expressively. Texture is related to touch (the tactile sense) and can be responded to visually. In this experience students explore and create real textures.

Studio Materials

clay, rolling pins, canvas or heavy wrapping paper, laths, clay boards, modeling tools, plastic bags, colored slips, clear glaze, examples of clay pottery, tiles, or sculpture that show extensive use of texture for surface enhancement

Teach the Lesson

Objectives

Students should be able to:

1   produce at least five different textures on a clay tile using three of four methods: pushing and pinching with fingers, pressing clay on clay, incising, and impressing   EE 2

2   organize the textures on the tile so that the design appears unified   EE 2

Vocabulary

Tactile means of or relating to the sense of touch.

Incising is a way to make lines and figures by cutting into the clay with a sharp tool.

Impressing is a method of making figures and shapes by stamping or pressing an object into the clay.

Laser Discs:

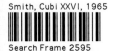
Noguchi, Great Rock of Inner Seeking, 1974

Search Frame 2605

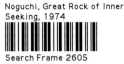
Smith, Cubi XXVI, 1965

Search Frame 2595

Rodin, The Evil Spirits, 1899

Search Frame 2526

Verrocchio, Guiliano de' Medici, c 1475

Search Frame 2378

Giacometti, Kneeling Woman, 1956

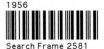
Search Frame 2581

Segal, Girl Putting on an Earring, 1967

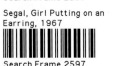
Search Frame 2597

Warm Up

Demonstrate how to roll out a clay slab and one or two ways to use a tool to impress textures. Have students roll out a small slab of clay and experiment with one tool, impressing rows of as many different textures as they can invent in three minutes. Encourage students to use the tool every way they can think of. Group the tiles and discuss the results. Let students share how some textures were made.

Explore and Develop

1   Show examples of clay work that demonstrate surface enhancement with textures. Identify the procedure used.

2   Remind students that real textures can be seen and felt. Things we can feel appeal to our tactile sense. Identify some real textures in the classroom. Don't overlook clothing.

3   List four methods of producing textures   R 1
in clay and define each. Then demonstrate them, referring to the definitions as you use each method.

Begin Studio Experience 8.2

1   Have each student knead a lump of clay about the size of a softball on a canvas-covered surface (wrapping paper will work for one class period). Tell students to roll it into a slab about 7" x 10" and lay the slab on a clay board for easy movement later.

2   Encourage students to experiment with the various procedures on small pieces of clay before proceeding to the tile. Keep clay not being used in plastic bags.

3   Students can create exciting surfaces of four or five different textures. Note that the textures can be interwoven; they do not have to be placed in horizontal rows. Ask students to think about ways to give the tile an organized appearance. For example, a dominant texture can be placed centrally, with others arranged around it. The tile can be divided into four or five sections like a puzzle, each to be filled with different textures.

4 Tell students to put a hole in the tile to hang it from later.

5 The use of colored slips is optional. Glaze will usually enhance the clay body and will help to keep the pieces clean. When the tiles are dry, have students fire the pieces.

6 Explain the effects of light and shadow on the relief tiles. You may want to hang finished tiles on a wall.

Evaluate and Reflect

1 Were students able to create four or five textures? Ask students to identify and name the different procedures used on their tiles.

2 Which of the textures are they especially pleased with?

3 Are students satisfied with the unity of the tiles?

4 Have them display the pieces vertically and discuss the contrasts of light and shadow caused by the relief textures.

Reteach

Students who have trouble with this project may simply need more practice.

Extend the Lesson

Beyond the Basics

EE 2 Clay cylinder pots can be made by covering a cardboard tube with newspapers left loose enough that the tube can be pulled out. Form a slab of clay around the cylinder. Cut and attach a bottom. Apply the various methods to fill the surface of the cylinder with decorative textures. Be sure to remove the cardboard tube when the clay is dry enough to support itself. Waiting too long will result in the clay shrinking and cracking if the tube is not removed.

EE 2 Have students gather a variety of objects, both human-made and natural, that could be used to impress designs into the surface of their clay pots. Suggest students work together to make a clay sampler of various textures. Roll a slab of clay and cut into two inch square tiles. Fill each tile with a different texture. After firing, assemble the tiles into an interesting arrangement and install on the classroom wall or in the hall. Have students design and create a teaching handout or display showing the technique and "tool" for making each texture.

Cultural Connections

Clay pottery and sculptures have been produced by cultures around the world from ancient to modern times. Although the material is the same, the pottery is unique in that it reflects the diversity of each culture. Assign groups of students to research the pottery of several different cultures. Encourage them to look for examples of ancient works as well as contemporary works. Suggest students examine the works to determine where the artists got their ideas. What similarities and differences exist among the different cultures? Is the work of the contemporary artists similar to the techniques and surface decoration found in the ancient works? Is there evidence of outside influence? Identify at least one characteristic that distinguishes the work of each culture. — EE 3 / R 5

Connecting with Other Subjects

Science/History Have students gather resource materials regarding the work of archaeologists. Have them research how the remains of pottery have helped in the understanding of ancient civilizations. Determining uses of various containers and analyzing remains of contents often provide important pieces to puzzles of the past. Do any of the surface designs provide information regarding the pottery's use. Suggest students talk with the science teacher to find additional information and resources. Suggest talking with the history teacher to explore the same ideas from a different viewpoint. — R 5

Suggesting Movement in Clay

Time: 2 periods

Preparation

Rationale

Movement is implied in paintings and sculptures, and real in kinetic artworks. Because implied movement contributes to the unity of static artworks, it is an important element. Learning about movement will help students understand and criticize artworks.

Studio Materials

clay, clay tools, clay boards, water containers, plastic bags, table coverings

Enrichment Materials

Slides:
• Boccioni, *Unique Forms of Continuity*, 23

Overhead Transparencies:
• Hepworth, *Pendour*, 2

Large Reproductions:
• Lucero, *Zoomorphic Dog Vessel*, 9
• Swentzell, *The Emergence of the Clowns*, 22

Teach the Lesson

Objectives

Students should be able to:

1 create an abstract clay sculpture in which movement is suggested by the shape and placement of forms   EE 2

2 use textures for surface contrasts and to complement implied movement   EE 1, 2

Vocabulary

Implied movement is the look (and feeling) of movement in a static artwork. It results from the artist's use of elements such as subject matter, line, shape, progressions, and repetitions.

Warm Up

Display Boccioni's *Unique Forms of Continuity in Space.* Have students take the position of the sculpture. Ask them to compare the position to the sculpture. Discuss

how the figure (subject matter), lines, and forms of the sculpture suggest movement. Note the diagonal forms that indicate motion. The polished, light-reflecting surfaces also contribute to the feeling of movement. Ask students to describe how their eyes move over the forms of the sculpture.

Explore and Develop

1 Explain that the look and feeling of movement in the sculpture is called *implied movement.* Display Hepworth's *Pendour* and have students describe the kinds of movement implied by the lines and surfaces of the form. Note repeated shapes and movement into, as well as around, the forms of the sculpture. *Sevillanas* by Voulkous or stabiles by Alexander Calder can also be used to explain implied movement.

2 Ask students to list the various directions that movement can take in a sculpture: vertical, diagonal, curving, radial, spiral, around and through, horizontal.

Begin Studio Experience 8.3

1 Focus on Studio Experience 8.3 for examples of clay sculpture in which movement is suggested by the shape and placement of forms. Textures were used for surface contrasts.

2 Have students wedge softball-size lumps of clay. They can begin shaping the main form on a clay board while thinking about the various directions that movement can take.

3 Students can pinch and pull parts out of the main form, making the parts seem to move in a common direction. They can make parts and add them onto the main form. The parts can be similar in shape but vary in size. Have students work the sculpture from all sides. Have them experiment with the use of wood scraps to shape forms and create surface textures.

Laser Discs:

Archipenko, Woman Combing Her Hair, 1915
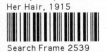
Search Frame 2539

Caro, National Gallery Ledge Piece, 1978
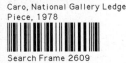
Search Frame 2609

Smith, Voltri VII, 1962

Search Frame 2593

Giacometti, The City Square, 1948-1949

Search Frame 2575

Calder, Untitled, 1976

Search Frame 2607

Smith, Circle I, Circle II, Circle III, 1962

Search Frame 2589

4 Encourage students to use procedures they learned in Studio Experience 8.2 to incise, press, impress, and pinch textures into clay surfaces. Ask them to think about placing textures so they contribute to the implied movement of forms in their sculpture.

5 You may select a student's work to discuss during the forming process while the group listens. Provide ideas that all can use as they continue to work with their sculptures.

6 If the pieces are to be fired, they may need to be hollowed out to reduce the thickness of walls.

7 If more than one period is required to finish, wrap the pieces in plastic. Fire when dry.

Evaluate and Reflect

W 2 **1** Ask students to talk about dominant movement in their sculptures. How does it contribute to unity of the sculpture?

W 2 **2** Have them discuss how the parts were organized to contribute to the movement.

R 2 **3** Discuss how textures were used to provide contrasts that contribute to the visual interest of the sculpture. How do the textures contribute to implied movement in the form?

4 Do they feel their sculptures are interesting to look at from all sides?

5 Have them give titles to their sculptures that reflect what they were trying to do.

Reteach

W 3 Ask students to list the different kinds of movement discussed in Chapter 8 and locate artworks in the text that demonstrate each kind of movement in the list.

Have students lay acetate over an art reproduction and draw lines on the acetate to identify the movement they see in the artwork.

Extend the Lesson
Beyond the Basics

Certain kinds of lines and shapes imply movement better that others. Suggest students analyze implied movement by examining still photos, drawings, paintings, and sculptures of figures in action. Have them take tracings of basic lines and shapes found in figures that appear to be moving and figures that are standing or sitting still. Compare the lines and shapes in each. **EE 1, 3**

Cultural Connections

Texture is a prevalent element in artworks around the world. Have students research the use of texture in artworks from various cultures to determine: 1) how materials used by various cultures affect the textural appearance of their artworks, 2) how various cultures use texture as a decorative element. For example, some African masks are made from roughly carved wood. The Benin people of North-west Africa include textures in their bronze castings for decorative and symbolic purposes. **EE 3** **W 2,4**

Connecting with Other Subjects

Music/Dance Movement is an element in art, music, and dance. Students may listen to music and create lines and shapes that emphasize the movement of the music. Have them observe a dance group or a videotape of dancers, and interpret their movements in gesture drawings with chalk or charcoal. **EE 2**

Language Arts Direct students' attention to the painting by George Bellows on page 99 of the student text. Bellows did many paintings of boxers. Suggest interested students look for other examples of his work and examine them to determine how he created movement. Have students answer questions such as: When was the work created? Where did the event take place? Who were the fighters shown in each painting? Interested students may want to read a biography about one of the famous fighters and write a report or share with the class. **R 4, 5** **W 2**

Movement in a Comic Strip

Time: 2 periods

Preparation

Rationale

This experience takes advantage of students' interest in comics as a means of introducing them to sequence and implied movement. Students can apply these concepts to art criticism and aesthetic appreciation.

Studio Materials

pencils, white drawing paper, fine-point felt pens, erasers, examples of comic strips

Enrichment Materials

Large Reproductions:
• Swentzell, *The Emergence of the Clowns,* 22
• *Nubian Wall Painting,* 5

Teach the Lesson

Objectives

Students should be able to:

1 draw a four-panel cartoon based on a joke, event or story, using visual cues and sequences of frames to suggest movement   EE 2

Vocabulary

Sequence refers to the following of one thing after another in logical order. In the case of comic strips, a sequence of pictures is used to suggest movement.

Frame refers to each individual drawing or scene in the sequence.

Close-ups in comic strips are drawings in which figures and objects are made large to appear close to the viewer. For example, a figure's head may fill the whole frame.

Warm Up

Ask students to describe some of their favorite cartoon characters and comic strips. Ask them to explain how movement is shown in the strips. Use the opaque projector to display a comic strip.

Explore and Develop

1 Call attention to the sequence of draw-   R 2
ings, called frames, in the comic strip. The sequence suggests movement in time and space. Be sure the students appreciate the logical sequence of episodes that must occur for a comic strip to work.

2 Display a list of devices that can be used in individual frames to show movement.

a. The position and stance of figures communicate attitude and movement.

b. Depth is suggested through overlap, diminishing size, low and high position on the page, and shading.

c. Characters and props are positioned to direct the viewer's eye in each drawing and from one frame to another.

d. Multiple contour lines, breeze lines, and little dust clouds imply movement.

e. For extreme speed or action, characters or objects lift off the ground.

f. Movement is implied through shifts in viewing angles from frame to frame, and through close-ups and long views.

3 Continue looking at a comic strip, and ask students to identify some of the above devices.

Begin Studio Experience 8–4

1 Write the terms *situation, setup,* and   R 1
punch line on the chalkboard. Focus on Studio Experience 8.4. Explain that frame 1 establishes the situation. Frames 2, 3, and 4 show the setup. Frame 5 shows the punch line, which is a reversal of people saying, "Monkey see, monkey do."

2 Have the students create a four- or five-frame comic strip based on a joke, story, school event, episode from history, or TV comedy. Encourage them to incorporate the sequence of situation, setup, and punch line.

3 Have them draw all the frames the same size and lightly outline each drawing with pencil so they can make changes easily. Remind students to plan for the placement of word balloons if they are needed but to keep words to a minimum.

4 Tell students to complete the drawings with a black felt-tip pen and erase the pencil lines.

Evaluate and Reflect

1 Display the cartoon strips. Ask students to discuss how the drawings communicate the idea, joke, or story with a minimum of words.

2 How did students imply movement within and between frames of the cartoon strip? What movement devices did they use?

3 Are they satisfied with the sequence of the episodes that make up their cartoon strips?

4 Can viewers quickly recognize what is happening and where (the location)?

Reteach

Allow students who have difficulty inventing their own character to use a character from their favorite comic strip. Encourage them to create a strip involving at least three frames. (This will allow them to deal with a situation, setup and punchline.)

Extend the Lesson

Beyond the Basics

R 4, 5
W 2
Have students find resource books showing the history of comics. Have them choose a few favorites to analyze. Some artists intended to simply entertain by using humorous characters and situations while others used their work as platforms for social and political commentary. Have students examine the works to determine the purpose of the work and how sequence and movement was used to convey the idea.

Cultural Connections

Comics are popular throughout the world. Talk to language teachers for suggestions on how to acquire comics from other cultures.

EE 2

The visual language is universal. Pictures can be used to communicate with others regardless of the language they speak. Suggest students plan a series of drawings to teach someone how to do something, such as how to tie a shoe, how to cook something, or get from one place to another. The information must be communicated entirely with visual images, no words. Sequence and implied movement are critical elements if directions are to be easily understood.

Connecting with Other Subjects

Science The invention of the camera has led to viewers being able to see things normally invisible. Single frame photographs taken by strobe light flashing sixty times a second have recorded movements never before seen. Suggest students look for examples of photography showing a record of actual movement.

Science Direct students attention to the series of photographs by Eadweard Muybridge (figure 8–19) in the student text. In 1869 Muybridge invented a shutter for his camera that allowed him to capture, for the first time, an accurate image of a horse in motion. In 1877 Muybridge photographed a running horse at a race track. He used twelve cameras with strings attached and stretched across the track to trigger the shutters. Prior to this event people argued about whether or not all four of the horse's feet were ever off the ground at the same time. Muybridge's photos showed that all four feet left the ground at one point during the gallop; however, they were all tucked up under the belly instead of stretched to the front and rear as previously shown in traditional paintings.

Making a Storyboard

Time: 2 periods

Preparation

Rationale

Watching television accounts for a major portion of most people's time. This lesson will provide students with insight into the planning that goes into the shots and sequences that affect the programs they watch.

Studio Materials

storyboard tablets, video camera, cassette player and TV, drawing tools

Enrichment Materials

video of a program or commercial

Teach the Lesson

Objectives

Students should be able to:

1   draw a storyboard that explains the sequence of events in a short (3–4 minute) video production   **EE 2**

Vocabulary

A *storyboard* is a large tablet with pages on which artists make sketches of shot sequences. The sequences are drawn in rows of picture frames and caption boxes.

A *shot* is an unbroken segment of a scene or action in a video or film.

A *sequence* is a series of shots in a video or film.

Warm Up

Prior to this lesson, assign students to watch a TV commercial. Ask them to list the sequence of activities and make rough drawings of them. If you have storyboard tablets, give each student a page to use for the assignment. Have students share the storyboard sequences in class when beginning this lesson.   **W 2**

Explore and Develop

1   Run a video for a few minutes and help   **W 2** students identify some shots that might be illustrated on a storyboard. Explain how shot sequences are planned on a storyboard. Action is described sequentially with pictures and captions. The frames are filled with drawings that describe the characters' movements. Positions related to the story's sequence are recorded in the caption boxes.

2   Explain that the storyboard is used by a production director while working with the crew and actors to tape the episode.

Begin Studio Experience 8.5

1   You may want to organize the class into   **W 2** small groups of three. Have students list ideas, stories, an episode in history or literature, a local news event, or a commercial that they think would be fun to plan as a short video production.

2   If the students are going to plan TV   **R 1** productions, their sketches should include   **W 1** notes to show the various camera shots that   **W 2** can be used: close-ups (CU), extreme close-ups (ECU), long shots (LS), wide shots (WS), cut (quick change of scenes), fade (diminishing sound and brightness to black).

3   The storyboard can also show when the camera should move toward or away from the subject (zoom), follow action (track), move right and left from a stationary position (pan), or move up and down from a stationary position (tilt). Students should also note when one picture fades out and another fades in (dissolve).

4   When the groups have completed their storyboards, have them do a walk-through of the action sequence, using the storyboard as a guide. Students may want to look through the camera viewfinder and try some of the camera positions.

5 If time permits, videotape the productions. Or, have the class vote on one to produce, and make it a class effort.

Evaluate and Reflect

1 Ask students to determine if their storyboards were planned well enough to guide taping of a TV production or to direct the actors in a live production of the episode.

2 Can students explain the various camera shots that can be used in a video or film production?

3 Can students identify the camera movements that may be required during a video production?

4 Run a short videotaped episode and ask students to use a checklist to indicate camera shots and camera movements they see.

Reteach

Prepare a checklist of camera shots and camera movements. Provide copies for each student. Run part of a video and stop it each time one of the shots or movements is evident. Have students check it off. Run another part of the video and ask students to check off shots and camera movements on their own. Evaluate their efforts as a group.

Extend the Lesson

Beyond the Basics

Local television stations and advertising agencies frequently use storyboards in planning programs and commercials. Arrange a field trip or invite an artist from the community to visit the class. Storyboards are also used in planning stage productions and other activities where it is important to visualize a sequence of events. EE 3 R 5

Remind students of earlier lessons using the video camera to teach drawing concepts. Suggest students plan and produce a series of video lessons, for use in the district's elementary art programs, that illustrate the elements of art and the principles of design. Suggest students watch children's educational television programs for ideas and techniques. Assign someone to visit and talk with the elementary art teacher. After researching and gathering resources students should begin work on the storyboard. Groups of students could work with other elementary teachers in planning video lessons addressing other subjects. EE 2 R 5 W 2

Cultural Connections

Plan a short video lesson to teach elementary children about other cultures. Suggest students select a theme, such as family life or games children play, emphasizing how we are alike rather than different. Develop a storyboard for each idea. EE 2

Connecting with Other Subjects

Health/Language Arts/Drama Suggest groups of students work with other high school teachers in creating a video lesson to illustrate concepts connected to their subjects. Students may use live actors or animation. Possible ideas might include using claymation to address the issue of drinking and driving, a collage with movable parts to illustrate a poem or short story, or live actors demonstrating a technique. Make a storyboard showing the sequence of the lesson. R 5 W 2

Study Questions
Chapter 8–Visual Elements: Texture and Movement

1 Define *texture*.

_____

2 What two senses are used in relationship to texture?

_____

3 Name two characteristics of each: glossy surface, matte surface. Give three examples of objects having each type of surface.

_____

_____

4 Define *tactile*.

_____

5 Define *simulated texture*. Give an example of *simulated texture* and a*ctual texture*.

_____

_____

6 What are four ways texture can be developed on a clay surface?

_____

_____

7 What is a *collage*?

_____

_____

8 Describe *viewer movement*.

_____

_____

_____

9 How does the scene from the movie, *North by Northwest* (text fig. 8–13), illustrate *implied movement*?

_____

_____

_____

10 Find a photograph in a newspaper or magazine that shows *implied movement.*

11 Name two artworks pictured in your text that illustrate o*ptical movement.*

_____

12 Define *kinetic art.*

_____

_____

13 Whose sculpture pictured in chapter 7 is an example of kinetic art?

_____

14 Who were the Futurists?

_____

_____

15 Describe one way in which comic strips and films are similar and two ways in which they differ.

_____

_____

_____

16 What is a *storyboard?*

_____

_____

_____

17 Give an example of how sound can add to the feeling of movement on film.

_____

_____

_____

Test Questions
Chapter 8–Visual Elements: Texture and Movement

Circle the correct answer(s).

1 Texture involves our sense(s) of

a. sight
b. touch.
c. sound.

d. a, b and c.
e. a and b.

2 An artist who paints a picture of a tree so that it looks like the leaves are real has

a. used the actual texture.
b. simulated a texture.

c. created a tactile texture.
d. invented a texture.

3 A composition developed by gluing colored paper, photographs, magazine pictures, fabric, and other two-dimensional materials onto a flat surface is

a. an assemblage.
b. a painting.

c. a collage.
d. a montage.

4 A group of Italian artists who create artworks that express the speed and motion of modern society is called

a. Surrealists.
b. Cubists.

c. Futurists.
d. Precisionists.

5 A _____ is made to help a director visualize a sequence of shots prior to the actual shooting of a movie.

a. cartoon
b. video

c. diagram
d. storyboard

6 The textures on the surface of a ceramic form, a handblown glass form, or a marble sculpture are

a. actual.
b. imitated.

c. simulated.
d. kinetic.

7 A marble sculpture that captures a dancer in mid-pose

a. has preserved a moment in time.
b. is a static work of art.
c. implies movement.

d. a and b.
e. all of the above.

8 The pictures drawn in a comic strip are called

a. captions.
b. balloons.

c. outlines.
d. frames.

9 State one of the major differences of the sequencing of a comic strip and the sequencing of a movie.

For questions 10 through 14 use the following list to fill in the blanks.

1	warm and cool	7	tactile
2	analogous	8	static
3	primary	9	electricity
4	kinetic	10	wind
5	implied	11	air currents
6	optical	12	simulated

While viewing the transparency (#7) or text fig. 8–16 of *Edetta* by Victor Vasarely, answer the following questions.

10 This work illustrates _____ movement.

11 The artist used _____ colors.

While viewing text fig. 9–1 of the mobile by Alexander Calder, complete the following statements.

12 This mobile is a _____ sculpture.

13 It is powered by _____.

Look carefully at the overhead transparency of *The Eye of Silence*, a surrealist painting by Max Ernst.

14 This work illustrates a/an _____ texture.

Study Answers
Chapter 8
Texture and Movement

1 Surface quality of an object, especially in regard to how it feels.

2 Touch and sight.

3 Glossy surface—smooth, slippery, shine (examples: glass, mirror, car, chrome, etc.). Matte surface—smooth, non-slippery, no shine (examples: chalkboard, napkins, banana peel, etc.).

4 Perceptible to the sense of touch.

5 Texture represented in a photograph, realistic picture, or realistic sculpture. Examples will vary.

6 Impressing objects into the clay surface, incising with pointed instruments, pinching with fingers, and adding pieces of clay onto the surface.

7 A composition made by gluing various kinds of papers and other flat materials onto a flat surface.

8 Involvement of the person looking at the artwork, either by walking around it or by scanning it with his/her eyes.

9 Answers may vary. Possible answers may be: the position of the man's body indicates he is running; the tilted position of the plane indicates it is in flight rather than on the ground.

10 Examples will vary.

11 *Untitled,* by Leeper (text fig. 5–35), *Current* by Bridget Riley (text fig. 8–17).

12 Artworks that actually move by electric motors, wind, air currents, etc.

13 Alexander Calder's mobile.

14 A group of Italian artists whose aim was to express the speed and motion of modern society.

15 Similarity:

Both rely on sequence to tell a story.

Differences:

comic strip—The viewer has control over movement and sequence;

film—The viewer has no control over direction, speed, or sequence;

comic strip—Sequence appears in a series of pictures called "frames";

film—Sequence is a series of "shots" (like a comic strip frame, but containing action).

16 Series of pictures used by the director and camera person to visualize a sequence before actual shooting begins.

17 Answers will vary. The volume, speed, or type of sound can enhance a mood or expression desired by the director. For example, a very fast-paced musical background can make fast movement on screen seem even faster.

Test Answers
Chapter 8
Texture and Movement

1 E

2 B

3 C

4 C

5 D

6 A

7 E

8 D

9 Differences:

comic strip—The viewer has control over movement and sequence.

movie—The viewer has no control over direction, speech or sequence.

comic strip—Sequence appears in a series of pictures called "frames."

movie—Sequence is a series of "shots" (like a comic strip but containing action).

10 (6.) optical

11 (1.) warm and cool

12 (4.) kinetic

13 (11.) air currents

14 (12.) simulated

Chapter 8
Visual Elements:
Texture and Movement

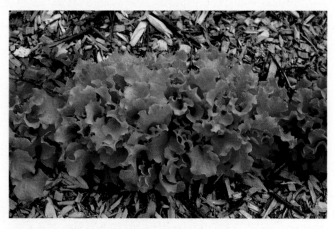

8-1

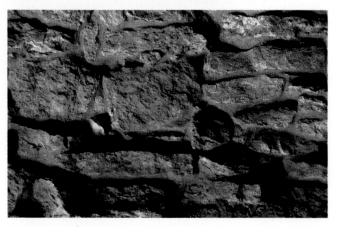

8-3

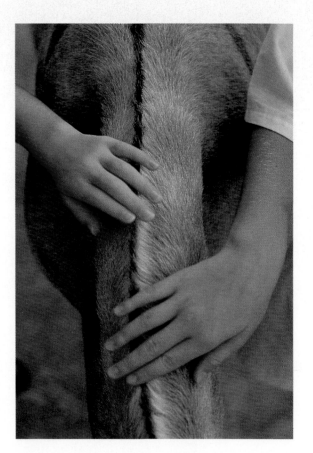

8-2

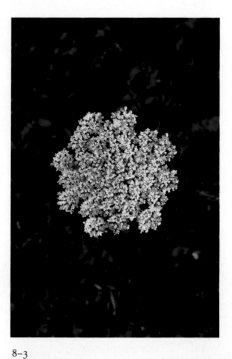

8-4   Photographs: Barbara Caldwell.

Texture

Texture refers to how the *surface* of something feels to the touch: rough, smooth, hard, soft, gritty, slick, and so forth. Texture is everywhere (figures 8–1, 8–2, 8–3, 8–4). In art, texture is described as *glossy* and *matte*. *Glossy* means slippery, like the surface of a newly waxed floor. *Matte* means smooth but nonslippery, like the surface of a chalkboard.

Although texture is related to touch, we do not always have to touch something to sense its texture. At times we can feel texture just by looking at it.

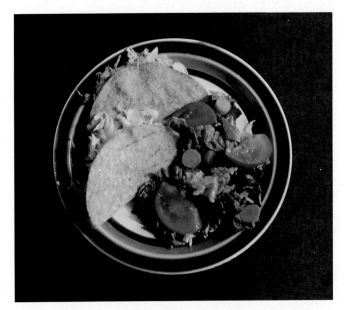

8–5

Try it Yourself

List some things in the classroom, such as the chalkboard, woodwork, a countertop, or the ceiling.

Describe the texture of each item in a few words. Then touch some of these items. Did you discover additional qualities about their textures? If so, change or add to your descriptions. Can you sense the texture of the ceiling by just looking at it and "touching" it in your imagination?

Texture in our daily lives is very important. It is more important than we often realize. Take eating out, for example. The atmosphere of a restaurant depends a great deal on the textures. Examples of glossy textures include plates, cups, silverware, glasses, countertops, coffee machines, and mirrors. Matte textures include napkins, place mats, tablecloths, carpeting, and drapes. Rough textures may be found in such things as unvarnished paneling and brick planters.

What about the food (fig. 8–5)? Flavor is important. But so is the texture of the food, or the way it feels in the mouth. You would be very disappointed in a hamburger bun that was not "fresh." It should have the correct balance between softness and firmness, and between moistness and dryness. The same, of course, is true for everything inside the bun.

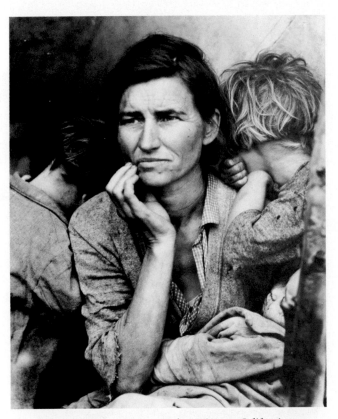

8–6 Dorothea Lange, *Migrant Mother, Nipomo, California,* 1936. Photograph: Dorothea Lange Collection, The Oakland Museum.

Texture in Art

All art objects have texture. In a photograph, it is not the glossy texture of the photograph itself that is important. It is the texture we see in the picture. In *Migrant Mother* (fig. 8–6), a photograph by Dorothea Lange, we see the textures of the lined face of the mother, her hair, the hair of her children, and the material of their tattered clothes. Such textures are called **simulated textures.** They relate to the images in the photograph and not its surface. You cannot touch them, but they are nevertheless vivid. The textures in *Migrant Mother* play an important role in telling a story about the sad conditions of migrant families in the 1930s.

Like photographs, realistic paintings have simulated textures. For example, look at the painting of a longhorn steer (fig. 8–7). Don Nice captured the colors of the animal's hide as well as its texture—right down to the little bristles of hair.

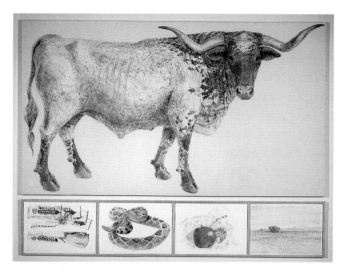

8–7 Don Nice, *Longhorn Steer, Western Series, American Predella #6,* 1975. Acrylic on canvas and watercolor on paper, 91˝ x 120˝ (231 x 305 cm). Delaware Art Museum, Wilmington.

8–8 Jean Dubuffet, *The Cow with the Subtile Nose,* 1954. From the Cows, Grass, Foliage series. Oil and enamel on canvas, 35˝ x 45 ¾˝ (89 x 116 cm). The Museum of Modern Art, New York. Benjamin Scharps and David Scharps Fund.

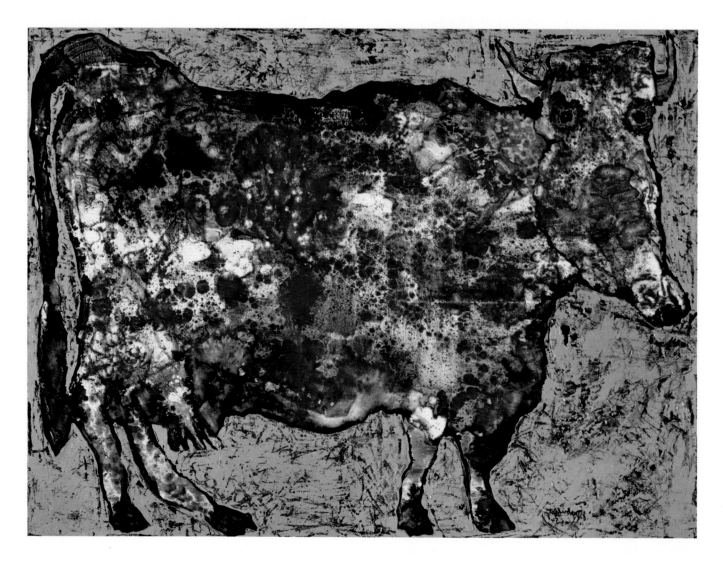

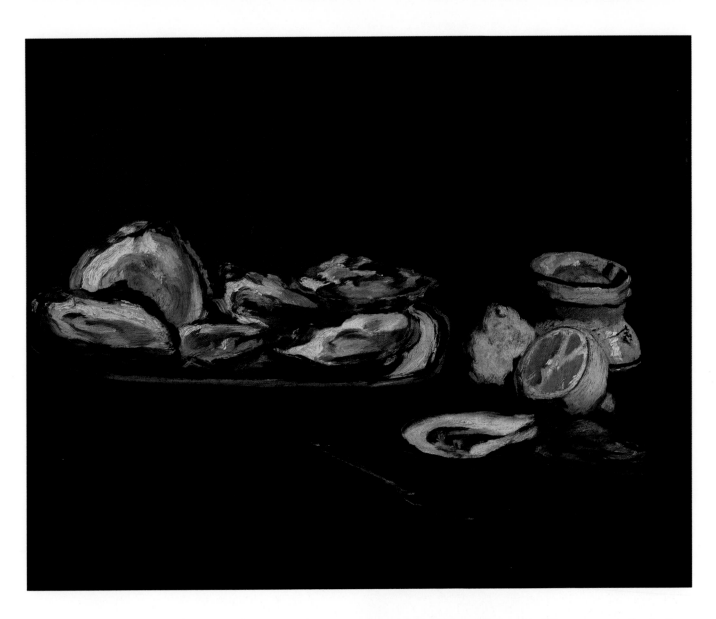

8–9 Edouard Manet, *Oysters,* 1862. Oil on canvas, 15 ⅜″ x 18 ⅜″ (41 x 48 cm). ©1993 National Gallery, Washington, Gift of the Adele R. Levy Fund, Inc.

Simulated texture is either nonexistent or unimportant in abstract or semiabstract painting. The texture seen in *The Cow with the Subtile Nose* (fig. 8–8) was not intended to resemble cowhide. The artist, Jean Dubuffet, wanted you to sense the texture of the paint itself. He mixed oil and enamel paints, applied them thickly, and worked them to create a spotted effect. If you saw this work in the Museum of Modern Art, you might be tempted to feel the bumps and ridges—the actual texture—of its paint.

In some paintings, like Edouard Manet's *Oysters* (fig. 8–9), both kinds of textures play roles. The textures of the oysters, along with the lemons, are perhaps realistic enough to make you hungry. The texture of the thick strokes of paint used to create the oysters is also visible. This painting gives you the best of both "worlds": simulated and actual textures. It appeals not only to your sense of sight and touch, but also to your imagination of food.

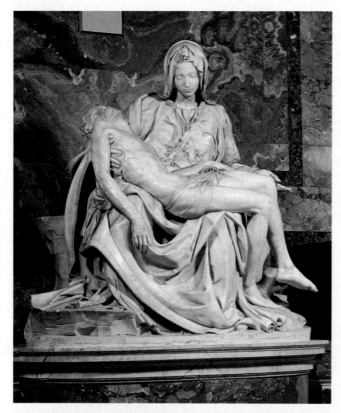

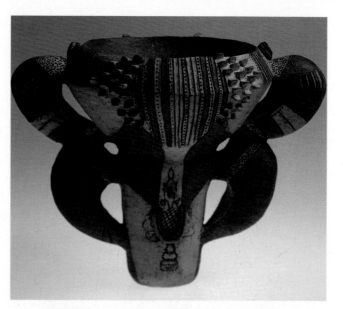

8–12 Viola M. Wood, *Festival Form*, 1975. Ceramic, 12″ x 8″ x 4″ (30 x 20 x 10 cm). Collection of the artist.

8–10 Michelangelo, *Pietà*, 1498–1500. Marble, 5′ 9″ (2 m) high. St. Peter's, Vatican State. Erich Lessing/Art Resource, NY.

8–11 Marilyn Levine, *Trent's Jacket*, 1976. Ceramic, wood and metal hooks, 35″ x 18″ x 8″ (89 x 46 cm x 20 cm). Private Collection. O. K. Harris Works of Art.

Look at Michelangelo's famous sculpture of the Pietà (Italian for *pity*) in figure 8–10. It is made out of polished marble. The actual texture is smooth and hard. But, like Manet's painting, the sculpture lets you experience the simulated textures of the flesh and clothing of Jesus and Mary. The gown clings to Mary in some places and gathers in heavy folds in other places. Yet you never lose sight of the fact that it is stone.

Can you tell what material Marilyn Levine used to make *Trent's Jacket* (fig. 8–11)? Even if you saw the piece in the gallery you would probably not guess. The "jacket" is not leather but *ceramic* (the material of which bricks are made). Levine succeeded so well in making a hard material resemble a soft material that she has fooled the viewer. Works like this are sometimes called "fool-the-eye" art. However, do you think *Trent's Jacket* could fool your *touch*?

There are no simulated textures in the ceramic vase by Viola M. Wood (fig. 8–12). The only important textures are the actual ones. The artist varied the texture by scratching the clay and adding pieces of clay. Note how the rough surfaces are contrasted with the smooth surfaces. Everything about this piece—its textures, its colors, even its weight—appeals to the senses. It invites us to pick it up and hold it.

Try it Yourself

At home look at some of your favorite objects, such as clothing, jewelry, a watch; or old toys, dolls, teddy bears, games. Do you like these things because of their textures? Is the texture of a teddy bear actual or simulated, or both?

Find a natural object from outdoors and a human-made object, such as a brick, a weathered board, or a rusty nail. Bring them to class. Describe the texture of each object.

Studio Experience 8.1

Simulated Textures

Use magazine photographs with simulated textures to create a Surrealistic paper collage of imaginative objects and figures.

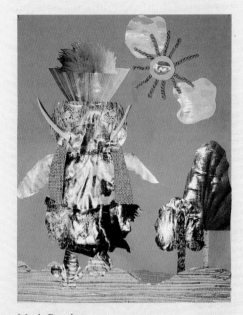

Marie Ramirez.

Studio Experience 8.2

Textures in Clay

Produce five different textures on a clay tile. Use three of these methods: pushing and pinching with fingers, pressing clay on clay, incising and impressing with a tool.

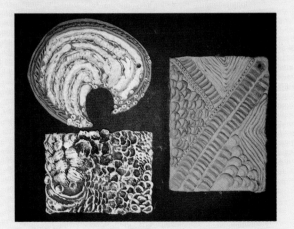

Tim Ziegler.

Movement

Space, as you saw in Chapter 7, involves movement. To experience a famous building or sculpture you must move in it or around it. You can best appreciate craft objects like Wood's vase (fig. 8–12) by rotating them in your hands. Even two-dimensional art involves movement. When you studied the textures in *Oysters* (fig. 8–9), your eyes probably moved from one object to the next.

Each of these instances could be considered examples of viewer movement. The viewer, not the art object, moved. Viewer movement, even if it involves only the eyes, is a necessary part of experiencing art. This alone is a good reason to call movement a visual element. But there are other relationships between visual art and movement. They are: *implied movement, optical movement, actual movement,* and *sequence.*

Implied Movement

An image, whether a picture or a sculpture, captures a moment in time. By stopping time, it implies a relationship to time, and also to movement. The subject may be as motionless as the oysters in Manet's still life. Or the subject can be frozen in action. In the scene from the movie *North by Northwest* (fig. 8–13), the airplane is frozen in midair. The man is clearly running. The photograph implies a great deal of movement. In this case it is implied by the subject matter. Whether you have ever seen the movie or not, you immediately know that the man is in danger. You have a basic knowledge of aircraft. You know that this one—even if it is a slow crop duster—is too close for comfort. Indeed, with some imagination, you can hear its propeller and feel the pounding heart of the man.

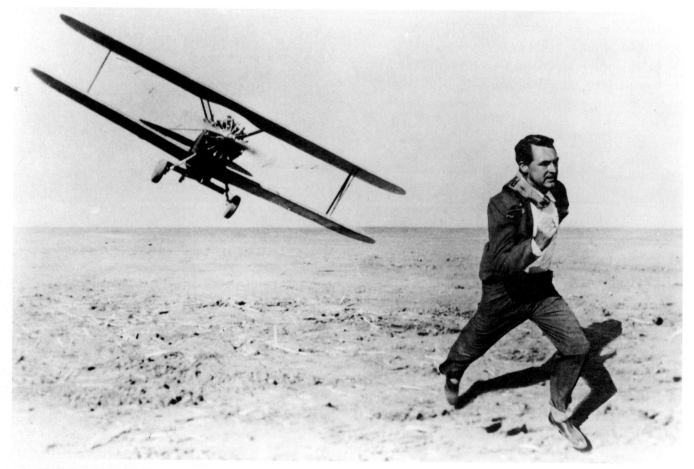

8–13 Cary Grant in a scene from *North by Northwest*, directed by Alfred Hitchcock. ©1959 Loew's Inc. Ren. 1987 Turner Entertainment Co.

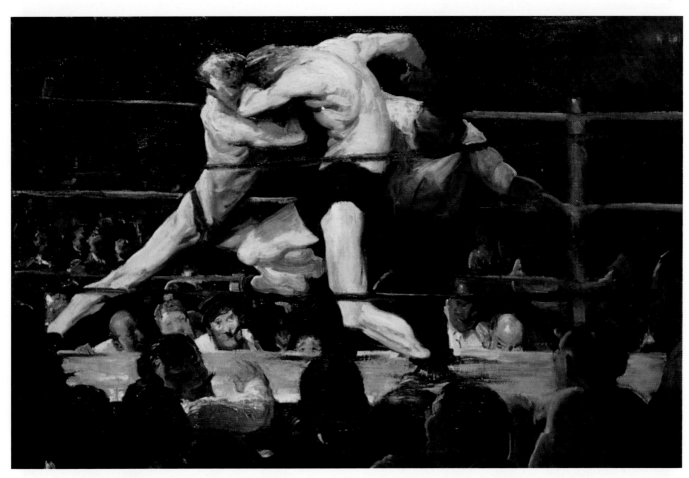

8–14 George Bellows, *Stag at Sharkey's,* 1909. Oil on canvas, 36 ¼″ x 48 ¼″ (92 cm x 123 cm). ©The Cleveland Museum of Art, Hinman B. Hurlbut Collection.

In *Stag at Sharkey's* (fig. 8–14) by George Bellows, movement is implied by the subject of boxing and by Bellows' style of painting. Bellows used diagonals in the men's bodies, exaggerated postures, and lively brushwork to imply movement. Two boxers are flailing away at each other at close range. The one on the right is ready to deliver a punch with his free arm. Although the next moment is not shown, you can easily imagine the punch landing and the sweat flying.

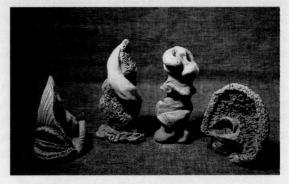

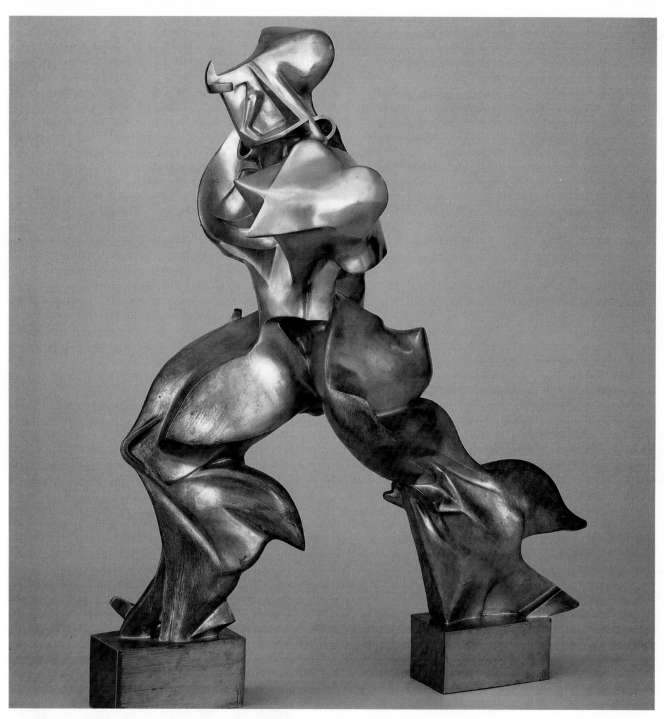

8–15 Umberto Boccioni, *Unique Forms of Continuity in Space*, 1913. Bronze (cast 1931), 43 ⅞″ x 34 ⅞″ x 15 ¾″
(111 x 89 x 40 cm). The Museum of Modern Art, New York. Acquired through the Lillie P. Bliss Bequest.

The title of Umberto Boccioni's *Unique Forms of Continuity in Space* (fig. 8–15) suggests movement, and for good reason. The artist was a member of the *Futurists.* The aim of this group in Italy was to express the speed and motion of modern society. Boccioni's sculpture is abstract. However, we can clearly tell that it is a figure walking with determination. The figure is striding to the left. The forward tilt of the trunk, the bend of the forward leg, and the extension of the rear leg resemble the movements of a walker. Even the swollen thighs suggest vigorous striding. But in some places the forms are disrupted and broken up. In other places they seem to sprout fins. These suggest that the figure is striding through a wind tunnel. Boccioni's sculpture is more than just an illustration of a walking person. It is a symbol of dynamic movement.

Claes Oldenburg

1929–

You've seen it a hundred times: someone dumping french fries out of a little paper sack. But Claes Oldenburg has frozen the act in time and space, and *Shoestring Potatoes Spilling From a Bag* becomes a gravity-defying performance, a large-scale example of implied movement.

Many of Oldenburg's works are large sculptures of commonplace household objects. In works such as *Shoestring Potatoes Spilling From a Bag* or the artist's 1988 work, *Spoon Bridge and Cherry* (the bridge-sized spoon that spans a body of water in Minneapolis), the sheer size of the sculpture shows us movement we might not have noticed in the object itself. In all his art, Oldenburg challenges the viewer to look at ordinary things—a typewriter, a slice of pie—in an extraordinary manner.

Claes Thure Oldenburg was born in Stockholm, Sweden, in 1929. His father was a member of the Swedish foreign service and the family traveled a great deal between Sweden, Norway, and the United States before settling in Chicago in 1936. By the time he was seven years old, Oldenburg had lived in three different countries and experienced many unique environments. Beginning in his childhood and continuing throughout his life, Oldenburg has recorded his daily experiences in these different places in both drawings and notes. These notations have become source books for ideas for some of his artwork.

Though Oldenburg has expressed his ideas with many different art media, including film, printmaking, drawing and painting, he is best known for his oversized sculptures which monumentalize American life. In each medium explored, Oldenburg has attempted to communicate something about art and about life by examining the everyday, ordinary aspects of our lives in new and exciting ways. "I am for an art that takes its form from the lines of life itself, that twists and extends and accumulates and spits and drips, and is heavy and coarse and blunt and sweet and stupid as life itself."

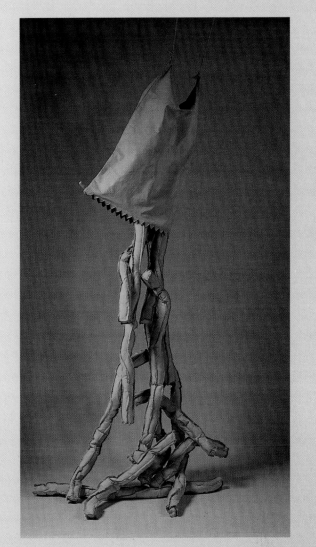

Claes Oldenburg, *Shoestring Potatoes Spilling From a Bag*, 1966. Canvas, kapok, glue, acrylic, 108″ x 46″ x 42″ (274 x 117 x 107 cm). Collection Walker Art Center, Minneapolis, Gift of the T. B. Walker Foundation, 1966.

Optical Movement

So far, movement has only been implied in the examples. The works have been static and motionless. They imply movement because of their subject matters, their forms, or a combination of the two. Some static works known as *Op Art* (or Optical Art) seem, almost

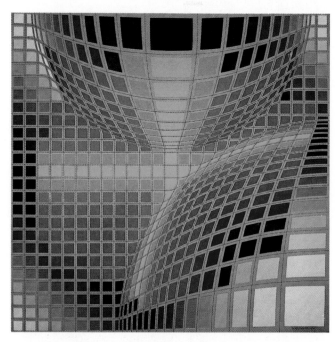

8–16 Victor Vasarely, *Edetta*, 1984. Acrylic on canvas, 39 ¾″ x 39 ¾″ (101 x 101 cm). Courtesy Circle Fine Art Corporation, Chicago, Illinois.

miraculously, to move. *Optical movement* is an illusion, a response by the eyes to lines, shapes, and colors arranged in certain ways. The viewer may feel dizzy after staring at the art. Stare for a few seconds at *Edetta* (fig. 8–16) by Victor Vasarely. Does the pattern of shapes shift between being a checkerboard and a network of diagonals? Does it tend to swell and contract almost as if it were inhaling and exhaling? Did you have different sensations? How would you describe them?

The compact pattern in *Current* (fig. 8–17) by Bridget Riley is even more interesting, or disturbing. The monotony of the bending lines seems infinite. There are no places for the eye to stop and focus. Notice that the lines, especially those along the narrow valleys where the bending of the lines is tightest, seem actually to vibrate.

Actual Movement

Although the lines and shapes created by Vasarely and Riley seem to move, their works are static. Some works, called **kinetic art**, actually move. Some kinetic works are connected by pulleys and chains to electric motors. Some are installed outdoors and are set in motion by the wind. Still others, called *mobiles*, hang from ceilings and slowly move with the currents of air

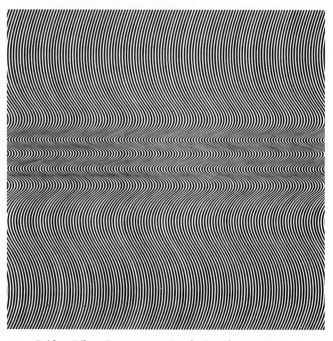

8–17 Bridget Riley, *Current,* 1964. Synthetic polymer paint on composition board, 58 ⅜ ″ x 58 ⅞″ (148 x 150 cm). The Museum of Modern Art, New York, Philip Johnson Fund.

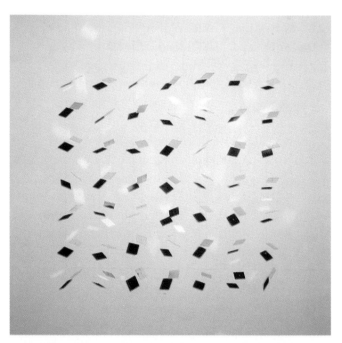

8–18 Julio Le Parc, *Continual Mobile, Continual Light,* 1963. Steel and nylon, 63″ (160 cm) high. The Tate Gallery, London/Art Resource, NY.

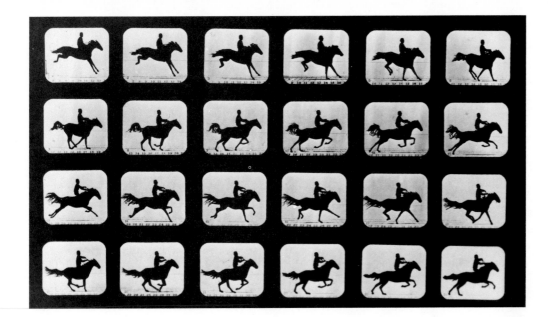

8–19 Eadweard Muybridge, *Attitudes of Animals in Motion.* Courtesy of Sotheby's Inc., 1987.

8–20 Milton Caniff, *Terry and the Pirates,* 1943. Reprinted by permission: Tribune Media Services.

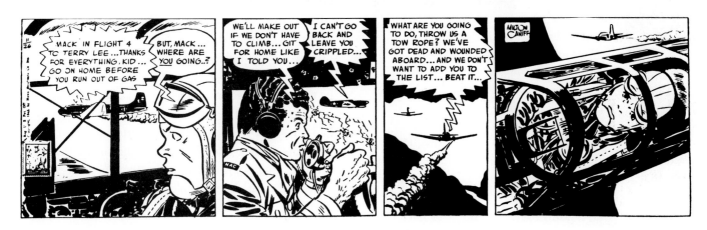

in a room. Recall Alexander Calder's huge mobile in the East Building of the National Gallery (fig. 7–5).

Julio Le Parc's *Continual Mobile, Continual Light* (fig. 8–18) consists of nothing more than pieces of polished metal hung on nylon threads. Because of their light weight, the metal pieces move rather freely. But the main movement is due to their reflections that dance off walls and ceiling. The motions of *Continual Mobile, Continual Light* are random. They have no particular order. This is true of most kinetic art.

Sequence

Comics and movies involve **sequence.** One thing follows after another in logical order. For example, the words on this page are arranged in a certain sequence for you to read.

Using a number of cameras, Eadweard Muybridge produced a sequence of still pictures. The sequence illustrates the positions of a horse and rider as they

leap over a hurdle (fig. 8–19). In fact, the series is "read" like a page in a book, from left to right and from top to bottom. Each scene shows a slightly different position. Because of the many repeated scenes, the suggestion of actual movement is very strong.

Like a series by Muybridge, a comic strip also uses a sequence of pictures called *frames.* However, a comic strip is not intended to be a study of movement. It is intended to tell a story, like the sequence of *Terry and the Pirates* (fig. 8–20) by Milton Caniff. One frame follows another, each showing a scene or slice of action representing a new stage in the story. Conversation, or *dialogue,* is printed in "balloons" above the characters' heads. Because comic strips mix dialogue with pictures while telling stories, they are sometimes referred to as *narrative* art.

The character Terry was a pilot of a fighter plane during World War II. The *Terry and the Pirates* sequence shown here is a very short part, or *episode,* of a long story about Terry's adventures. The dialogue takes place on the radio between Terry and the pilot of a war-damaged cargo plane. Notice how both the drawing and dialogue contribute to the story. To make the sequence as dramatic as possible, Caniff used a variety of framing and points of view. The first frame is a close-up of the inside of Terry's cockpit. It shows the action from the young hero's point of view. The second shows it from the cargo pilot's point of view. The third frame is a distant view of both planes flying over mountains. The final frame, a close-up of Terry's plane at an odd angle, ends the episode.

Try it Yourself

Continue the story of *Terry and the Pirates*. Does the damaged cargo plane make it over the mountain? Does Terry radio for help? Does he return to base? Does either plane encounter enemy fighter planes?

Like a comic strip, a movie, or *film,* relies on sequence to tell its story. But unlike a comic strip, a film is a picture that actually *moves.* The viewer has no control over its movement or speed. He or she cannot look ahead to see what is going to happen nor look back to see what was missed (unless, of course, the viewer is watching it on a VCR).

A sequence in a film is a series of shots. A *shot* is like a frame of a comic strip, except it contains action. If the *Terry and the Pirates* episode were on film, the first shot would be of Terry in his cockpit, the second of his friend in the cargo plane, and so forth. Each shot would last perhaps five seconds. In the viewing of a film, a shot is an unbroken segment of a scene or action. Direct connections between shots are called *cuts.*

Like comic strip frames, film shots can show distant views or close-ups, as well as different points of view and angles. A camera can *tilt* (pivot up and down from a stationary position), *pan* (pivot sideways from a stationary position), *track* (move to follow an action), and *zoom* (make an image appear nearer or farther by means of a zoom lens). Finally, a camera can remain in a fixed position, with movement coming entirely from the action of the scene.

In the opening scenes of *Star Wars,* Princess Leia's starship is captured by a spaceship of the evil Galactic Empire. Following the capture, empire troops blow up the main bulkhead of Leia's ship and attack the defending rebel troops. The battle sequence, which takes less than fifty-nine seconds of viewing time, requires thirty-two shots. (The average length of a shot is less than 1.9 seconds.) Eight of those shots are described here. Almost all were filmed with cameras in stationary positions at chest height.

Studio Experience 8.4

Movement in a Comic Strip

Draw a comic strip with four or five panels. You can base the comic strip on a joke or story. Use a sequence of frames and visual cues to suggest movement.

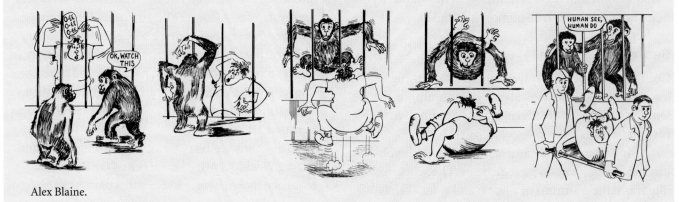

Alex Blaine.

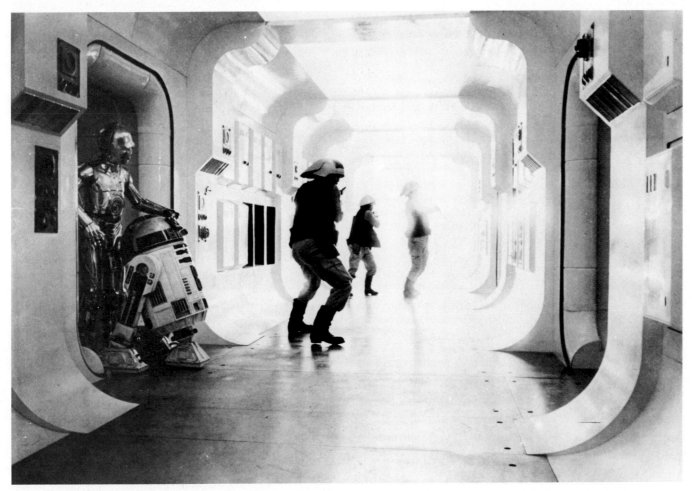

8–21 Artoo-Detoo and See-Threepio helplessly watch rebel troops defend the rebel blockade runner in the film *Star Wars*. ™ & © Lucasfilm Ltd. (LFL) 1977. All Rights Reserved. Courtesy of Lucasfilm Ltd.

Shot	Length of shot/ Camera position	Shot	Length of shot/ Camera position
Rebel soldiers retreat to corridor where Artoo-Detoo and See-Threepio are hiding.	3 seconds/Fixed camera at chest level	*cut to:*	
		Close-up of See-Threepio.	1 second
cut to:		*cut to:*	
The robots watch help-lessly as rebel troops are fired on (fig. 8–21).	1 second	Rebel troops killing and being killed.	1 second/Waist level
cut to:		*cut to:*	
Close-up of See-Threepio.	1 second	Robots move to other side of corridor, followed by explosion.	4–5 seconds/Camera pans to follow robots.
cut to:		*cut to:*	
Empire troops killing and being killed.	1 second	Smoke. Rebel troops in full retreat.	1 second

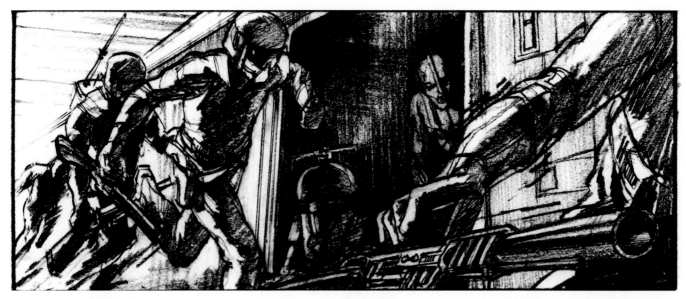

8–22   Artists are often called upon to make storyboards for movies like *Star Wars*. This illustration represents one shot of a sequence. ™ & © Lucasfilm Ltd. (LFL) 1977. All Rights Reserved. Courtesy of Lucasfilm Ltd.

The battle sequence ends with Darth Vader surveying the battle results. (The camera is at waist level to emphasize the evil commander's size.) Because of the shortness of the shots and the confusion of a pitched battle, odd angles of view were not used. A panning camera was used only once. Otherwise, the sequence would have been too hard to follow.

Movies like *Star Wars* contain complicated action. For these movies, artists are hired to make *storyboards*. A storyboard looks much like a comic strip. Each frame (fig. 8–22) represents a shot. A storyboard helps the director and the camera people to visualize a sequence before the actual shooting begins. The storyboard picture in figure 8–22 corresponds to the first shot in the listed description. Notice that the eye level in the picture is very low (about at the knees), while the position of the camera in the film is chest level.

Sound

Sound is an important element in film. In battle sequences the sounds of explosions and zapping weapons add to the realism. Music is often used to establish mood. In this case, it is used to increase the feeling of tension during the moments before the bulkhead is attacked. In *Star Wars*, as in *Terry and the Pirates*, dialogue is very important to clarify the action. In the scenes before the battle, See-Threepio explains to Artoo-Detoo that the pursuing ship knocked out their ship's main reactor. Seconds later, he says, "We're doomed! There'll be no escape for the Princess this time." What would film be like without sound? You have probably seen "silent" movies. You may recall that the action had to be interrupted every so often to show printed dialogues on the screen.

Try it Yourself

Add a sequence of your own to **Star Wars.** Make two columns. Explain the action in the left column. Indicate the point of view and position of the camera in the right-hand column. Tell whether the camera is stationary, tilting, panning, tracking, or zooming.

Closely observe a movie, either in a theater or on a VCR at home. See how an idea is developed by a sequence of shots. Take notes on what you see and hear.

Take notes on a commercial. What kinds of shots are used to make the product look appealing?

REMEMBER: With a VCR, you can reverse the tape and replay a sequence.

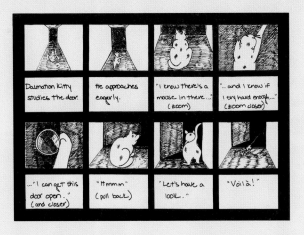
Summary

Texture refers to how the surface of something feels to the touch. All artworks, like all objects, have actual textures. Photographs, realistic paintings, and realistic sculptures also have textures that can be seen but not felt. This kind of texture is called simulated texture. In artworks that do not have simulated textures, such as crafts or abstract paintings and sculptures, the only important textures are the actual ones.

All art involves movement. At the very least, a viewer must move his or her eyes to appreciate an artwork. An artwork can capture a subject in a moment in time. In such cases, the movement is implied. Optical movement is the illusion of movement. The patterns of lines and colors typically found in Op Art appear to move when the viewer stares at them. Actual movement is found in kinetic art. Parts of a kinetic artwork can be set in motion by a motor or by wind or air. Kinetic art is not static.

Comics and movies rely on sequence. In a comic, the sequence of viewing is from left to right (and also from top to bottom in the Sunday comics), but the viewer is free to skip around and move his or her eyes at any speed. In a film, the movement is actual. Both the movement and the sequence are determined by the film, not the viewer. A sequence is made up of a series of shots. Each shot consists of an unbroken view of a scene of action.

Part III

How Is It Organized?

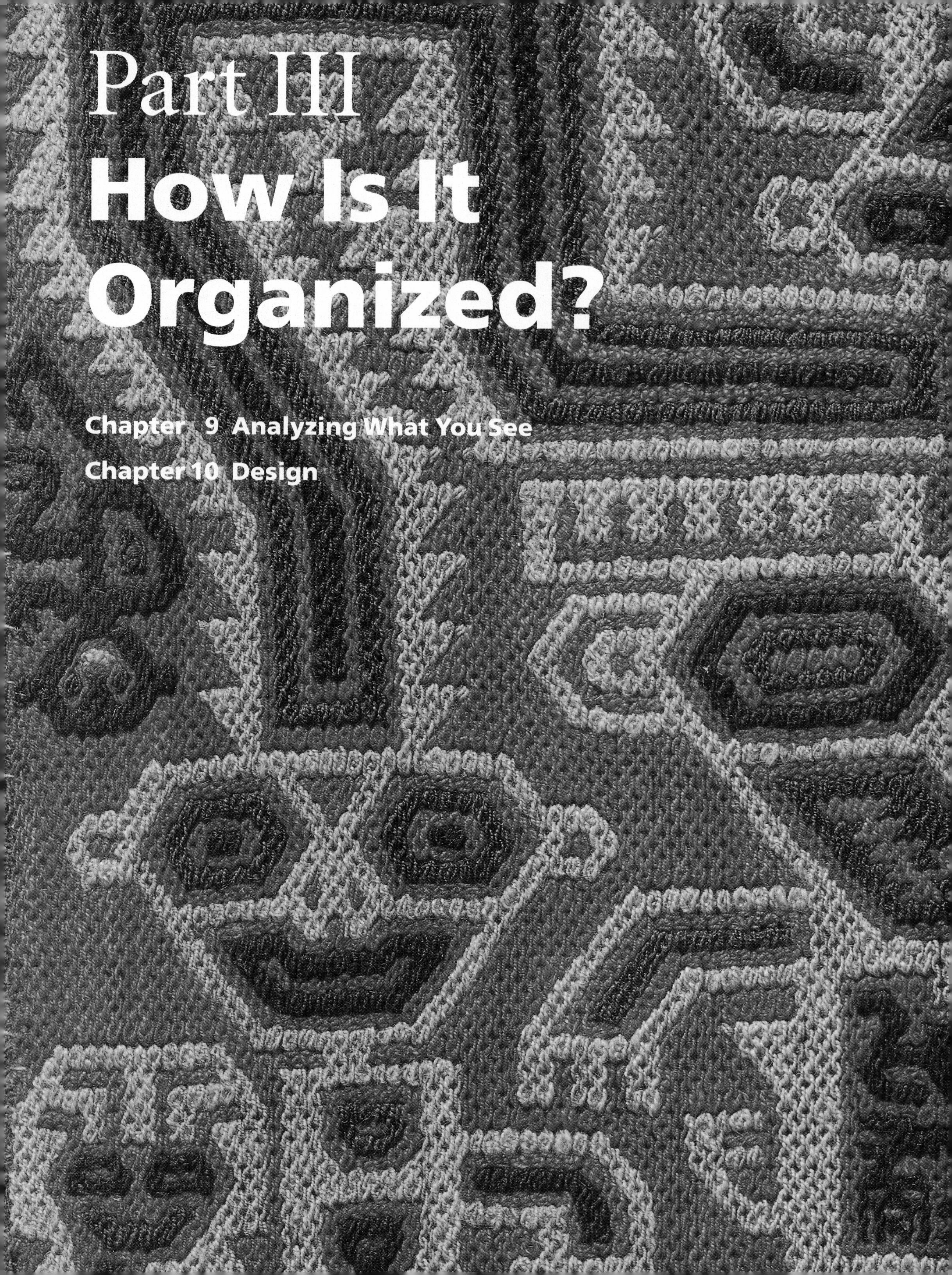

Mantle, Detail three figures. Wool, embroidered with colored wools, Peru, pre-Inca period, Early Nazca, ca. 600. The Metropolitan Museum of Art, Gift of George D. Pratt, 1932.

Chapter 9
Analyzing What You See

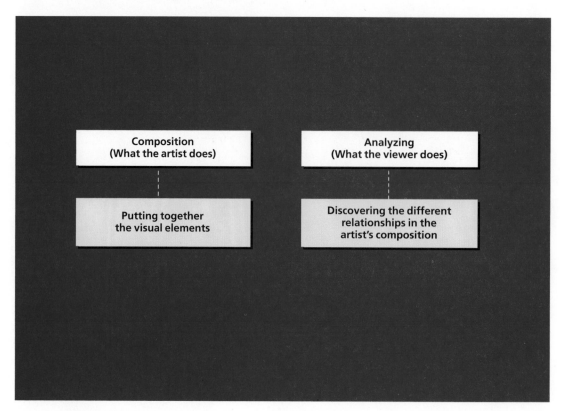

Overview

Chapter Objectives

Students should be able to:

EE 1   **1**   explain the concept of composition and how an artwork is composed

EE 3, 4   **2**   differentiate between *describing* and *analyzing* an artwork

EE 1, 3   **3**   analyze the relationships among elements in an artwork

Rationale

Analyzing a work of art involves identifying relationships among the elements in the work. In preceding chapters, students were introduced to the relationships among art elements through reading, studio experiences, and discussions. Now that the groundwork has been laid, students are introduced to the process of analysis, the second part of the four-stage criticism model presented in the text.

Essential Chapter Concepts

• Analyzing is what the viewer (or critic) does when he or she determines how the work was composed.

• Description involves relating facts about an artwork, while analysis involves identifying how the work is organized.

• Composing refers to the act of organizing the elements of an artwork into a harmoniously unified whole.

• Composition refers to the way the art elements are interrelated.

Vocabulary

composing   analyzing

Meet the Artist

Grant Wood   Page 115

Lesson Plan

9.1   Criticism Experience: Analyzing American Gothic

Page **T 132**   Time: 1 period

Handouts

Guidelines for Analyzing an Artwork

Page **T 134**

Examples of Responses for Analysis of American Gothic

Page **T 135**

Study Questions

Page **T 136**

Test Questions

Page **T 137**

Chapter Closure

Evaluation

1   *Aesthetic awareness:* Can students explain how an artwork is composed?   R 2

2   *Art history:* Can students give some facts about Grant Wood?   R 2

3   *Criticism:* Can students explain the difference between describing and analyzing an artwork?   R 1

4   *Criticism:* Can students complete an analysis of an artwork using guidelines provided in Experience 9.1?   W 2, 4

Notes

Analyzing *American Gothic*

Time: 1 period

Preparation

Rationale

In preceding chapters, students have been reading about, describing, and discussing the art elements. Students have been composing these elements in studio experiences. They are now ready to learn a system for analyzing the relationships among the elements in an artwork. Chapter 9 introduces guidelines for analyzing artworks, which will increase students' understanding of art criticism.

Analysis Materials

Guidelines for Analyzing an Artwork (Handout)

Examples of Responses for Analysis of *American Gothic* (Handout)

Enrichment Materials

Slides:
• Wood, *American Gothic,* 2

Overhead Transparencies:
• Wood, *American Gothic,* 17

Teach the Lesson

Objectives

Students should be able to:

1   analyze the relationships among elements in an artwork   EE 1, 3

2   determine how the parts of the artwork contribute to the composition as a whole   EE 1

Vocabulary

Analyzing involves finding relationships in a composition.

Composing is the process the artist uses to organize the art elements.

Warm Up

Refer to Student Edition page 111. Have students match the statements with the pictures. Discuss the analysis statements of the four artworks. Ask students how they would describe the artworks. Compare their descriptions with the analyses. Can students see how they differ?   W 2   R 5

Explore and Develop

1   Go over the material on Student Edition page 112. You may want to have students work in small groups to answer the following questions:

   a. What is the difference between analyzing and describing an artwork?   W 1

   b. What does the artist do when he or she composes an artwork?   R 2

   c. What should you look for when you analyze an artwork?   R 5

   d. Name two kinds of relationships given on Student Edition page 112.

2   Have students look at the descriptions they wrote of *American Gothic.*

Begin Criticism Experience 9.1

1　Give students the Guidelines for Analyzing an Artwork or have them use Student Edition page 114.

2　Students can work individually or in small groups. Point out that they have only 15 to 20 minutes to complete their analysis.

3　Have students share their responses.

Evaluate and Reflect

R 5　**1**　Did students explain how the art elements contributed to the composition?

R 5　**2**　Did students focus on the relationships among the art elements?

R 5　**3**　Did students demonstrate the difference between analyzing an artwork and describing it?

4　Ask students to discuss the new things they discovered about this artwork as a result of their analysis.

Reteach

Go over the sample responses to *American Gothic*. Ask students to compare the kinds of statements they made in their description of this artwork with those they made in their analysis. Focus on the differences between analysis and description.

Extend the Lesson
Beyond the Basics

Have students research the architectural style of the house in *American Gothic.* The style is called Carpenter Gothic.　EE 3

Grant Wood was part of a group of artists known as the Regionalists. The name was derived from the fact that they painted scenes and subjects typical of the region in which they lived. Wood studied in Europe and the Gothic period became a major influence in his work. Who were the other Regionalist artists? Have students find examples of works by the other Regionalists and examine to determine what may have influenced their work. Describe and analyze a work by one of the other artists. How are these works similar or different than Wood's work?　EE 3, 4　R 5　W 2

Cultural Connections

Grant Wood painted scenes and subjects found in Iowa. Another Regionalist, Thomas Hart Benton, painted Missouri. Have students examine the work of both artists. Suggest they write a description of each artist's work and then try to describe what life in each place may have been like based on the information shown in their paintings. How were the cultures of Iowa and Missouri similar or different? Suggest students read to learn as much about each state as possible, such as climate, landscape, politics, how most people earned their living, recreation, and social/economic conditions.　EE 3　R 5　W 2

Connecting with Other Subjects

History *American Gothic* was painted in 1930. Have students research this period in history outside of the United States. What world events may have affected people in Iowa? What major works of art were created in other countries in 1930? Identify other individuals, such as scientists, writers, and musicians who were doing important work in 1930. Ask students to write a brief essay explaining how and why all of these individuals and events are connected.　R 4　W 2

Guidelines for Analyzing an Artwork

Analyzing involves identifying relationships among elements in an artwork. It means looking at how the artist organized subject matter and elements including line, shape, form, texture, colors, and space so that they interrelate as a composition. The guidelines below can be used to analyze an artwork. You may not need all of the items. You may want to add relationships that are not listed here.

1   Similarities

   a.   Are things similar in shape, form, value, color, pattern, size, or texture?

   b.   Are some lines or edges similar in direction: horizontal, vertical, diagonal, circular?

2   Contrasts

   a.   Are there contrasts of dark/light, cool/warm, large/small, curved/angled, hard/soft, rough/smooth? (Contrasts can occur in line, color, value, texture, shape, or form.)

3   Repeated Elements (Rhythm)

   a.   Is anything repeated over and over?

   b.   Is there a repeated alternation of elements?

   c.   Are there progressions from large to small, warm to cool, light to dark and so on?

4   Movement

   a.   Are there elements that direct your vision?

   b.   Are there continuous lines, edges, arrangement of shapes and forms?

   c.   Are there lines of sight?

5   Dominance

   a.   Is there an area, element, or arrangement that dominates the rest of the work? Is it due to size, central location, complexity, isolation, contrast of some kind, or convergence?

   b.   Does one element dominate the whole work? Is there one color or texture, or a pattern that covers the whole work?

6   Balance

   a.   What arrangements or relationships of elements contribute to the balance in the composition?

   b.   Is balance symmetrical, asymmetrical, approximately symmetrical, radial?

7   Relationships Between Subject and Medium

   a. What are relationships between the subject and the art elements?

   b. What are relationships between the subject and the medium used to produce it?

Examples of Responses for Analysis of *American Gothic*

1   Similarities among elements
- The pattern of the woman's apron and the curtain.
- The shapes of the figures' heads and the trees.
- The blue in the man's overalls and the sky.
- The pitchfork shape is repeated in the man's overalls, shirt, his face, and the windows.
- Vertical lines in the figures, pitchfork, the man's clothing, the house and barn siding.
- Curved lines in the pitchfork, the woman's apron top, collar and chin, the man's overall pocket, collar and chin. Circles in her apron, figures' faces, his glasses.

2   Contrasts of elements
- Light and dark blue in clothing; warm and cool colors in the house.
- Curved and oval shapes in the figures contrast with angles, straight lines, and edges in the house.
- Size of the man with size of the woman; size of the figures with size of the house, barn, and trees.

3   Repeated elements
- Curved lines in the figures' clothing and chins.
- Vertical lines in the house siding and the man's clothing, pitchfork, and figures.

4   Elements that direct vision
- Vertical lines in figures, figures' clothing, pitchfork, and house establish upward movement.
- Curved lines in fork, clothing, and chins suggest rhythmical upward movement.
- The diagonal roof lines and the horizontal porch roof direct vision to the figures' heads.

5   Dominant element
- The figure of the man dominates due to size and he overlaps everything.

6   Balance
- The large, heavy form of the man is balanced by the smaller figure of the woman and the house, which is placed off center to the left.

7   Relationship between subject and medium
- The figures are outside, so natural colors were used for sky, flesh, clothing, and so forth. Colors range from light at the top to dark at the bottom of the painting, making the figures feel heavy and important. The artist used paint to represent meticulous detail in the figures and objects. The arrangement is very formal, with solemn expressions, many vertical lines, angles and hard edges along forms.

Name: _____   Course: _____

Study Questions
Chapter 9—Analyzing What You See

1 What is the difference between *describing* and *analyzing* an artwork?

_____

_____

_____

2 Define *composition*.

_____

_____

_____

3 Who composes works of art?

_____

_____

_____

4 Define *dominance*.

_____

_____

_____

5 Give two examples of relationships that can be found in an artwork.

_____

_____

_____

_____

Test Questions
Chapter 9–Analyzing What You See

Fill in the blanks.

1 _____ an artwork points out facts about the lines, shapes, and colors used.

2 _____ an artwork points out the relationships between and among the elements.

3 _____ refers to how the lines, shapes, colors, etc., have been put together.

4 An artist _____ an artwork.

You may have viewed overhead transparencies of several artworks in the previous chapters and studied them in reference to a particular element, such as line, shape, texture. While viewing the overhead transparencies now, pay close attention to the *relationship* of the elements.

While viewing *The Persistence of Memory,* by Dali (text fig. 19–36), answer the following question.

5 What are two similar sets of shapes in this painting?

While viewing *Sky Above Clouds IV,* by O'Keeffe (transparency #4), answer the following questions by circling T (true) or F (false).

6 T F This painting has a definite area of dominance.

7 T F This painting has many color and shape variations.

While viewing *Circle Limit IV,* by Escher, (text fig. 5–5) answer the following questions by circling T (true) or F (false).

8 T F This woodcut repeats similar shapes and patterns.

9 T F Sizes of the shapes representing the angels remain the same throughout the picture plane.

While viewing *Edetta,* by Vasarely (text fig. 8–16), answer the following questions by circling T (true) or F (false).

10 T F This work consists of a number of similar shapes of different sizes.

11 T F The colors in this work are all of the same value.

Study Answers
Chapter 9
Analyzing What You See

1 Describing an artwork points out facts about the lines, shapes, and colors. Analyzing an artwork points out the relationship between those elements.

2 Composition is the way lines, shapes, colors, etc., are put together.

3 The artist.

4 An area that seems most important; a focal point.

5 Answers will vary.

Test Answers
Chapter 9
Analyzing What You See

1 Describing

2 Analyzing

3 Composition

4 composes

5 Rectangles, circles, organic shapes.

6 F

7 F

8 T

9 F

10 T

11 F

Teacher Lesson Notes

Chapter 9
Analyzing What You See

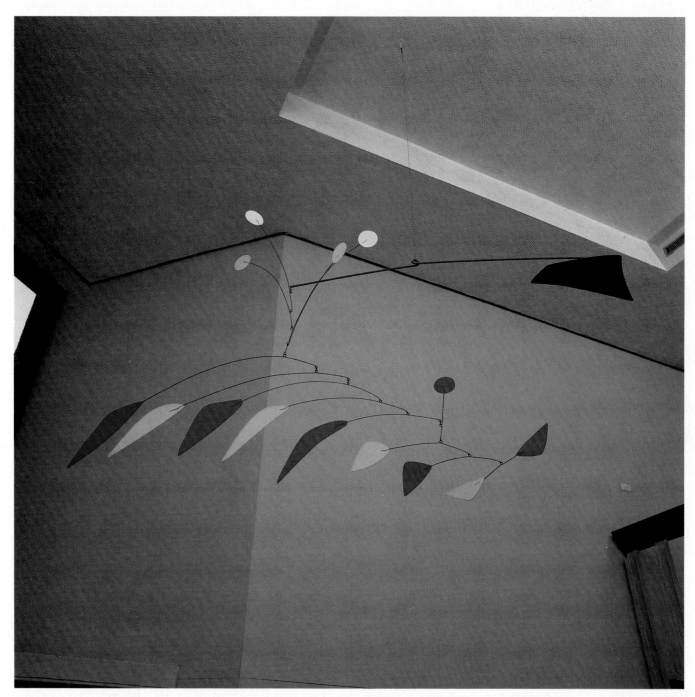

9–1 Alexander Calder, *Spring Blossoms*, 1965. The Pennsylvania State University.

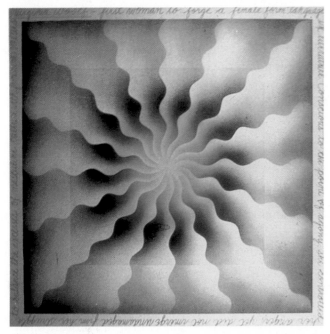

9–2 Judy Chicago, *Virginia Woolf,* 1973. Sprayed acrylic on canvas, 5′ x 5′ (153 x 153 cm). Courtesy of the artist.

Now that you have completed Part II you should be able to identify and describe many things in an artwork. The purpose of this chapter is to teach you how to *analyze* a work of art. Analyzing is somewhat different from describing. But before going further, look at the following four statements. Each is a short *analysis* of one of the four artworks shown (figs. 9–1, 9–2, 9–3, 9–4). See if you can match the right statement with the right picture.

A. Although they differ in size and color, most of the shapes are similar in being rectilinear. The dominant feature is the post in the center.

B. Because it consists of a series of identical boxlike shapes separated by equal spaces, this artwork lacks not only variety but dominance.

C. A series of wavy lines, which are identical in size and shape, provide rhythm but little variety for this artwork. The dominant feature seems to be the center from which the lines radiate.

D. This work consists of a number of similar shapes of different sizes that form a rhythmic pattern.

9–3 Donald Judd, *Untitled,* 1985. ½″ aluminum and ⅛″ blue plexiglass over ⅛″ black plexiglass, 6 units each ½ x 1 x ½ meters, overall 4 ½ x 1 x ½ meters. Courtesy Leo Castelli Gallery, New York.

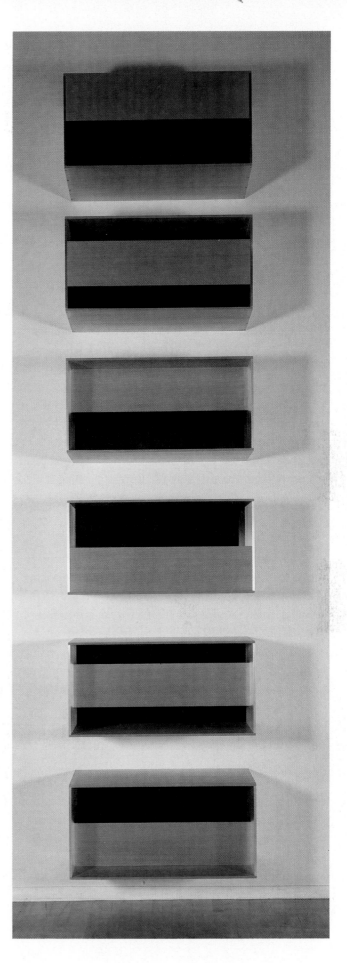

(Answers: A = fig. 9–4, B = fig. 9–3, C = fig. 9–2, D = fig. 9–1)

How well did you do in the matching exercise? Were you confused by terms such as "rhythm" and "dominance"? Perhaps certain descriptive words, like "wavy lines" and "boxlike shapes," gave you enough clues to match the statement with the correct work. These short statements show how words, if used well, can both *describe* and *analyze* an artwork. Describing has to do with pointing out facts about the lines, shapes, and colors. Analyzing has to do with pointing out the *relationships* among these things.

Composition

The chapters of Part II covered each of the visual elements separately. In Chapters 9 and 10, we will see how the elements work together to make a complete work of art.

Composition refers to the way that lines, shapes, and colors have been put together. The artist, of course, is the person who has to put these things together. This task is called **composing.** The final result of composing a painting or a sculpture is called a composition.

Analyzing the Composition

Even though you, the viewer, do not do the composing, it sometimes helps if you know *how* a work of art was composed. In order to see how it was organized, to see what makes it tick, you have to break it down or "*decompose*" it. This is called **analyzing,** or *analysis.*

Analyzing an artwork means finding relationships in the composition. Two or more things in a work may have something in common. They can be related to each other.

Consider people, for example. Usually, when we talk about being related to somebody, we think of families. You are related to your uncle even though you may have nothing else in common with him. But there are other kinds of relationships besides family relationships. You are related to your classmates because you are all in the same classroom and being taught by the same teacher. You can be related to others because you are a fan of the Dallas Cowboys, like to ride horses, have brown eyes, and so on.

When you stop to think about it, everybody is related to everybody in some ways; everybody also is different from everybody in some ways. Often an analysis points out both differences and relationships. For example, Jenny likes indoor activities and Susie likes outdoor activities. Yet both are members of 4-H.

Try it Yourself

Think of one or two of your friends. List the things you have in common. You can list likes and dislikes, as well as appearance. Also list things that are different about the two (or three) of you.

Like people, colors and shapes in an artwork are often related in some ways and different in some ways. Look at Statements A and D on page 111. These statements point out both differences and relationships within an artwork. Statement A, in analyzing the composition of the painting in figure 9–4, says, "Although they differ in size and color, most of the shapes are similar in being rectilinear." Statement D, which is about the mobile (fig. 9–1), says, "This work consists of a number of similar shapes of different sizes."

Another kind of relationship has to do with one thing being more important than another thing. For example, a leader is more important than a follower. In a group that has a leader, all group members are related to each other. But also each follower is related to the leader in a special way and vice versa. Have you ever been a leader? Have you ever been a follower?

This kind of relationship in art is pointed out in the second sentence of statement A: "The dominant feature is the post in the center." The second sentence of statement C (about the abstract painting in figure 9–2) also speaks of dominance: "The dominant feature seems to be the center from which the lines radiate." You will learn about dominance in the next chapter.

In fact, Chapter 10 will discuss in detail several visual relationships. By being able to recognize these relationships and by learning the vocabulary for them, you will be able to analyze an artwork.

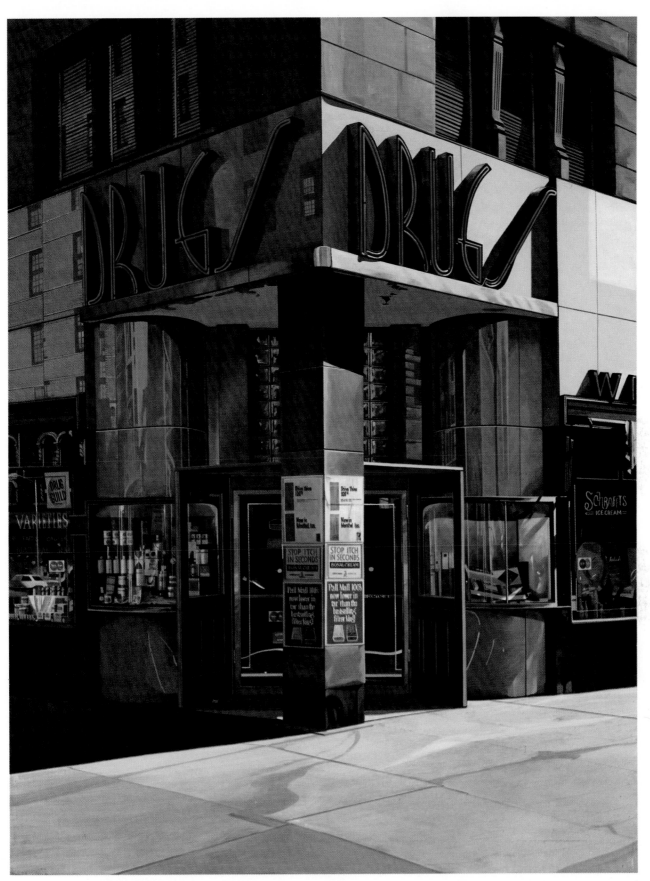

9-4 Richard Estes, *Drugstore*, 1970. Oil on canvas, 60″ x 44″ (152 x 113 cm). The Art Institute of Chicago, Restricted gift of Edgar Kaufmann.

Analyzing *American Gothic*

Analyze *American Gothic* by Grant Wood using the following guidelines, or more detailed guidelines provided by your teacher.

Procedure: In Chapter 3, you described *American Gothic*. However, you only included facts, the things about the painting that could be named and described with certainty. *Analyzing* involves identifying the relationship between things in the painting. How did the artist organize subject matter and elements including line, shape, texture, colors, and space so they interrelate as a composition? Take fifteen or twenty minutes to answer the following questions about *American Gothic*.

1. What similarities can you find among elements such as shape, colors, lines, patterns, size, direction of lines, and shapes?

2. Are there contrasts of elements such as color, shapes, forms, texture, direction, or size?

3. Are there elements in the picture that are repeated in some systematic way?

4. Are there elements that lead your eye through the composition?

5. Is there some element or area in the painting that is dominant or that seems most important?

6. What makes the painting seem to be balanced?

7. Can you describe a relationship between the subject and the way the artist used the medium (oil paint)?

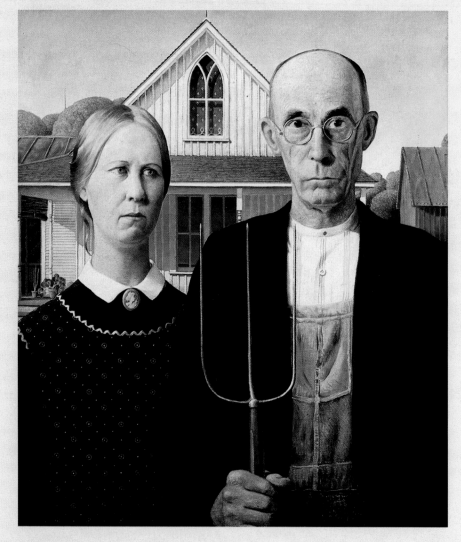

Grant Wood, *American Gothic*, 1930. Oil on beaver board, 30″ x 25″ (76 x 63 cm). The Art Institute of Chicago, Friends of American Art Collection.

Grant Wood

1891–1942

Few paintings have achieved as powerful a hold on the imagination of an entire country as Grant Wood's *American Gothic*. A spinsterish woman wearing proper clothing and a serious expression is posed beside a stern man, gripping a pitchfork and staring intently at the viewer. A few strands of hair escape from the woman's tidy bun and fall down her neck emphasizing her otherwise immaculate appearance; the dark jacket suggests that this stoic farmer is dressed to attend church.

The posed figures standing before a white building, with their stiff posture, reserved manner, stony faces and unblinking eyes, have become symbols of the American family. *American Gothic* has come to symbolize farm life and traditional work values in the midwest United States.

Grant Wood was born in 1891 on a small farm in rural Iowa. There he lived a quiet childhood for the first ten years of his life, without telephones, radios, televisions or cars. He was educated in a one-room schoolhouse, and spent his free time drawing on scraps of cardboard from cracker boxes which his mother saved for him. In 1901, Grant's father died suddenly; the Wood family sold their farm and moved to the nearby city of Cedar Rapids to be close to relatives. During the next forty-one years of his life, Grant traveled and spent time in Europe, but always returned to live and paint in this Iowa city.

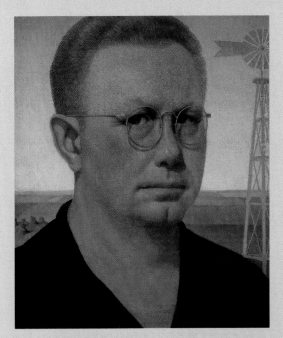

Grant Wood, *Self-Portrait*, 1932–41. Oil on masonite 14 ¾″ x 12 ⅜″ (38 x 31 cm). Davenport Museum of Art.

Though the time he spent on the family farm was brief, strong memories of his early experiences became the subjects of his paintings. From hayrides in the fields to the midday meal, Grant painted the types of people and the landscapes which he recalled from his childhood. During the prime of his career in the 1930s, he painted very little of the life he observed from the window of his Cedar Rapids home. Grant Wood chose instead to paint a romanticized version of rural Iowa as he remembered it from his youth.

Summary

Composing is what the artist does when he or she puts all the elements together to make a work of art.

Analyzing means figuring out how the work was composed. An analysis points out the relationships between and among the elements in a composition.

Chapter 10 will cover more about composing an artwork. It will also discuss what kinds of relationships to look for in a composition.

Chapter 10
Design

Student Edition
Pages 116–127

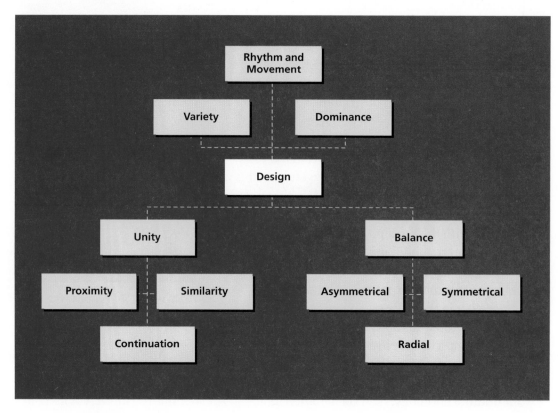

Overview

Chapter Objectives

Students should be able to:

1 explain the concept of unity in artworks   EE 1

2 describe how proximity, similarity, and continuation contribute to unity   EE 1

3 define each of the principles of design (unity, variety, dominance, rhythm and movement, and balance)   EE 1

4 explain three ways to achieve rhythmical movement   EE 1

5 explain three ways to achieve balance   EE 1

6 use the design principles to analyze relationships among elements in artworks   EE 1, 3

7 use the design principles as general guidelines for analysis   EE 1, 3, 4

Rationale

Most artworks, with the exception of some contemporary artworks, can be analyzed in terms of the design principles. In this chapter, students learn to analyze artworks in terms of composition, or the way the design principles are used to organize the art elements.

Essential Chapter Concepts

• The whole of an artwork is more important than any single part.

• The artist uses a plan (design) to organize all of the elements that make up an artwork.

• The process of design involves thinking about and organizing the visual elements to create visual order.

• The organization of an artwork can be analyzed in terms of design principles: unity, variety, dominance, rhythm and movement, and balance.

• Most artworks can be analyzed in terms of design principles.

Vocabulary

unity	continuation	rhythm
design	proximity	variety
movement	design principles	similarity
dominance	balance	

Meet the Artist

Faith Ringgold   Page 118

Lesson Plans

10.1 Movement and Unity in Sculpture

Page **T 142**   Time: 4 periods

10.2 Dominance in a Low-Relief

Page **T 144**   Time: 3 periods

10.3 Drawing with Balance

Page **T 146**

Time: 1 period

10.4   Criticism Experience: Analyzing an Advertisement

Page **T 148**   Time: 1 period

Handouts

Study Questions

Page **T 150**

Test Questions

Page **T 152**

Chapter Closure

Evaluation

1   *Criticism/Aesthetic awareness:* Can students define each of the design principles?   R 1

2   *Criticism:* Can students analyze artworks using the design principles?   R 5

3   *Criticism:* Can students analyze the composition of their own artwork in terms of the design principles?   R 5

4   *Production:* Did students create artworks that satisfy design principles of unity, variety, balance, rhythm, movement, and dominance?

Movement and Unity in Sculpture

Time: 4 periods

Preparation

Rationale

In this experience, students construct a three-dimensional sculpture of wood scraps selected and organized to affect visual movement and unity throughout the form. Manipulating small wooden forms in a construction is a direct and fairly easy way for students to explore ways to control visual movement and unity in a three-dimensional artwork.

Studio Materials

wood scraps of varied sizes and shapes, hand tools, glue, dowels, nails, clamps, rubber bands, linseed oil, stain

Enrichment Materials

Slides:

• Nevelson, *Sky Cathedral*, 44

Large Reproductions:

• Stout, *Instructions and Provisions*, 2
• Prow ornament, Tlingit war canoe, 17
• *Statue of Mitry*, 6

Teach the Lesson

Objectives

Students should be able to:

1   construct a three-dimensional sculpture of wood scraps selected and organized to create visual movement and unity throughout the form   EE 1, 2

Vocabulary

Unity refers to the sense of wholeness in an artwork. The parts relate successfully.

Proximity refers to the placement of elements near to each other to make them look related.

Similarity refers to making components of an artwork similar in shape, color, texture, or form.

Continuation occurs when the viewer's vision is directed by lines, edges of shapes, or arrangement of objects.

Warm Up

Have a good supply of interesting wood shapes. Ask students to experiment with grouping or stacking six to eight pieces that go well together. Ask them why they selected those particular shapes. Tell students to look for similarities in forms, continuity of edges, and forms that suggest movement.

Explore and Develop

1   Direct attention to Student Edition pages 116–117. Discuss how unity is directly affected by proximity, similarity, and continuation.

2   Ask students to lay their collection of shapes out so that they demonstrate each of these principles. Ask them to describe movement affected by continuation in the grouping of shapes.

Ask students to explain why unity is so important in an artwork. (Unity makes the viewer aware of the whole work rather than parts.)

3   Display Nevelson's *Sky Cathedral*. Have students point out things that are similar. What affects proximity and similarity? What are some reasons for painting the whole sculpture black?

4   Focus on the explanation of variety on Student Edition page 119, and ask students to indicate variety in Nevelson's sculpture.

Laser Discs:

Pollock, Number I (Lavender Mist), 1950

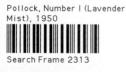

Search Frame 2313

Pollock, detail

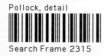

Search Frame 2315

Pollock, segment

Search 43450, Play To 44905

Gorky, Organization, c 1936

Search Frame 2307

Gorky, detail

Search Frame 2309

Puni, Suprematist Construction, 1915–1916

Search Frame 2541

5 Show other examples of artists' constructions. Have students analyze how the artists interrelate forms, lines, and space to achieve unity. Are there edges, surfaces, or shapes that direct eye movements? What is repeated? Is something dominant? What elements did these artists interrelate?

Begin Studio Experience 10.1

1 Have students collect wood shapes that are similar and others that are dissimilar in shape, size, and color. Let students group them to see which pieces go well together.

2 Students may modify shapes with hand tools. Surfaces can be carved, scored with a saw, sanded, stained, oiled, or painted. **Caution students to use woodworking tools with extreme care and to wear protective glasses if necessary.**

3 Parts can be attached with glue, nails, or wooden dowels in holes made with a drill. When students glue, remind them to make contact with two flat surfaces. Hold the pieces in place with rubber bands or clamps. *Do not* let students attach pieces at sharp corners or edges; they won't hold.

4 Have students arrange shapes so that edges and surfaces help direct attention from part to part. Students may use repetition, alternation, or progression to direct the viewer's eye.

5 Stains and oil can bring out beautiful grains in wood. Tell students to use paint colors sparingly, so that they help with unity and movement.

Evaluate and Reflect

1 Can students show how visual movement is directed through their construction?

2 Have students talk about proximity, similarity, and continuation in their sculptures.

3 Can students explain how visual movement is affected in a classmate's sculpture?

4 Ask students to explain what they did to achieve unity with variety in their constructions.

5 Do they feel their constructions are interesting from all sides?

6 Display some of the artists' constructions again, and ask students to talk about things they see now that they didn't see before creating their constructions.

Reteach

Display two artworks, one an obvious example of visual organization and the other a poorly organized composition. Use the Chapter 10 study questions, asking students to concentrate on one design principle and one art element at a time. For example, ask students to analyze the relationship of proximity and shape; similarity and shape; or balance and color in both displayed examples.   R 5

Extend the Lesson

Beyond the Basics

Assign some students to research the development of constructions as an art form. Note the different materials made available by modern industry and technology. Identify artists who are noted for their constructions. Ask them to look for historical connections such as Dada and Constructivism.   R 5

Connecting with Other Subjects

Social Studies Suggest students try to find additional information about Nevelson and her family history. They immigrated to America from Russia in 1905. Other well-known American artists were also immigrants. Have students research this period in American history. What other artists immigrated to America? What other immigrants from this period went on to make significant contributions in other fields such as science and industry? Students may want to work in groups each researching a different area.   R 5 W 4

Dominance in Low-Relief

Time: 3 periods

Preparation

Rationale

There are two general ways in which dominance may be used in an artwork. The artist may make one element or area more important than others, or a single element may dominate the entire work. In this lesson, students use a dominant form in an artwork so that they can explore the relationships with other elements in the work.

Studio Materials

heavy cardboard, carbon paper, oak tag, tablet backs, shirt boxes, mat board scraps, drawing paper, textured fabrics, string, doilies, glue, heavy duty aluminum foil, burnishing tools, scissors, X-acto knives, black permanent markers, steel wool

Enrichment Materials

Slides:
• Curry, *Baptism in Kansas,* 28
• Hokusai, *The Wave,* 104

Large Reproductions:
• Tamayo, *Dos Hermanos,* 20
• *Plate—Hunting Rams,* 7

Teach the Lesson

Objectives

Students should be able to:

1 use aluminum foil to make a low-relief in which textures, shapes, and lines are organized around a dominant form **EE 1, 2**

2 use patina to accentuate the relief **EE 2**

Vocabulary

Dominance is a principle of design that stresses the importance of one element, or a combination of elements, over everything else in the composition to make it attract the viewer's attention first.

Design is the plan the artist uses to organize the art elements to achieve unity in an artwork.

Balance is a feeling of equilibrium among all the parts of a composition. Balance may be symmetrical, asymmetrical, or radial.

Low relief means that shapes project slightly from the surface they are attached to.

Warm Up

Show the slides listed above or refer to figures 10–5, 10–6, and 19–22. Ask students what attracts their attention first in each one. Can they explain why? Develop the definition of dominance.

Explore and Develop

1 Note that dominance of an element can be achieved through contrasts of size; contrasts of shapes where one element is different from the rest; central location; and lines of sight.

2 Point out that the artist must develop a design to show how elements will be organized if one element (figure, shape, object) is to be made dominant.

3 Focus briefly on the explanations of balance on Student Edition pages 124–125. Be sure students understand the idea of equal distribution of the parts of a composition.

Begin Studio Experience 10.2

1 Direct attention to Studio Experience 10.2. Define *low relief,* then explain how to create a foil relief. Students will stretch aluminum foil over shapes cut from lightweight cardboard and mounted on a heavy cardboard surface. Point out that the aluminum foil will tear if the relief is too high.

2 Have students cut a piece of heavy cardboard about 9" x 12". Have them trace around the cardboard base on drawing

Laser Discs:

Gaughin, Haystacks in Brittany, 1890

Search Frame 1540

daVinci, detail

Search Frame 1542

Gaughin, Self-Portrait, 1889

Search Frame 1536

Redon, Evocation of Roussel, c 1912

Search Frame 1512

Cezanne, Le Chateau Noir, 1900/1904

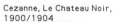

Search Frame 1456

Cezanne, detail

Search Frame 1458

paper and plan (design) the composition with a dominant form and supporting elements.

3 Have students use the drawing and carbon paper to trace various parts of the picture on heavy paper and cardboard. To make shapes, students can tear the cardboard or cut it carefully with an X-acto knife. Textured fabrics can be cut to shapes as well. Students may want to perforate or score the cardboard. Explain that the foil will pick up these details. Have them glue shapes onto one another to produce varied levels of relief.

4 Tell students to trail white glue from the dispenser and allow it to harden to produce lines, or lay string in trailed glue.

5 As students glue the shapes to the base, remind them to keep analyzing the composition for dominance and balance. Encourage proximity of parts since large empty spaces will be very noticeable under a foil cover.

6 Students should cut a piece of heavy-duty aluminum foil about one inch larger on all sides than the base board and then brush a coat of white glue over *all surfaces,* including edges of shapes, and crevices. Keeping water in the brush will make spreading the glue easier.

7 Tell students to lay foil over the composition and rub gently, working from the center outward. They should force the foil into depressions before sealing it to raised surfaces. Pencil erasers, wood burnishers, and fingers can be used to work the foil around edges and down into crevices and textures.

8 When they have burnished the entire surface, students should fold the extra foil behind the base board and glue it to the back. They can color (patina) the foil surface with a black permanent marker or black India ink. Tell them to buff the raised surfaces with steel wool and tissue to produce contrasts between polished raised surfaces and dark depressions.

Evaluate and Reflect

1 Can students identify a dominant element in their compositions? R 2

2 Have students explain how they organized their composition to make an element dominant. R 2

3 Ask them to discuss how they maintained balance in the composition. R 2

4 Did they use contrasts of dark and light to emphasize the relief of shapes? R 2

5 Can students explain how repetition and placement of elements contribute to unity in their compositions? R 2

6 Ask students to explain why unity is so important in artworks. R 2

Reteach

Have students experiment with cut-paper shapes. Have them arrange cut or torn paper shapes to achieve dominance of a shape or group of shapes. Encourage students to practice with different strategies: central location, size, complexity of a shape or group of shapes, contrasts of size or shape.

Extend the Lesson

Beyond the Basics

Have students find examples of relief sculpture on the facades of buildings in their community. They might make sketches, or take pictures of these examples and accompany them with brief written explanations: the name and location of the building, the date of building's construction, what they think the relief is for. EE 1

W 1

Cultural Connections

Study examples of relief artwork from other cultures, noting the period of time when they were made, the purpose of the reliefs, the subjects or symbols used, and what they were made of. EE 3

Drawing with Balance

Time: 1 period

Preparation

Rationale

An understanding of how the parts of a composition are arranged so that no one element or part overpowers the rest of the work is important in critical analysis as well as production of artworks. Students generally understand the physical concept of balance, but are not familiar with the different ways it can be achieved in artworks. This lesson introduces them to the basics of symmetrical, asymmetrical, and radial balance.

Studio Materials

drawing paper, drawing pencils, objects for still life arrangements

Enrichment Materials

Overhead Transparencies:
• Renoir, *Luncheon of the Boating Party,* 18
• Evans, *Design Made at Airlie Garden,* 9
• Escher, *Circle Limit IV,* 3

Large Reproductions:
• Schwartz, *Untitled #16,* 11
• Biggers, *Shotguns,* 3
• Olbinski, *Private Fame,* 13

Teach the Lesson

Objectives

Students should be able to:

1   make three contour drawings of five or six objects arranged in symmetrical, asymmetrical, and radial balance, with one object dominant in each drawing   EE 1, 2

Laser Discs:

Renoir, Madame Monet and Her Son, 1874

Search Frame 1292

Degas, Four Dancers, c 1899

Search Frame 1356

Degas, detail

Search Frame 1358

van Gogh, Flower Beds in Holland, c 1883

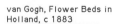

Search Frame 1516

Stella, Star of Persia II, 1967

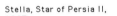

Search Frame 3322

Escher, Drawing Hands, 1948

Search Frame 3192

Vocabulary

Balance is the arrangement of elements to create a feeling of equal distribution of visual weight throughout the composition. The composition does not feel heavy to the left, right, top or bottom.

Asymmetrical balance is attained when the elements on either side of a vertical axis are different, but are placed in the composition to create a feeling of equally distributed weights.

Symmetrical balance occurs when identical elements are equally distributed on either side of a central axis. Both sides look the same.

Radial balance results from repeating identical or very similar elements around a central point like a bicycle wheel or a target.

Dominance occurs when one element or shape is made more important than anything else in the composition.

Warm Up

1   Group five or six objects, one of which is larger than the others, in an unbalanced grouping. Ask for volunteers to arrange the objects so they feel balanced.

2   Direct attention to figures 10–9a and 10–9b. Which version of the picture seems to cause the least tension or to be the most comfortable? What is the difference between them? What principle of design is involved?

Explore and Develop

1   Display examples of artworks that demonstrate three kinds of balance. Ask students to identify and define the kind of balance used for each artwork. Refer students to the discussion of balance on Student Edition pages 124–126, and look at the examples.

R 1

Begin Studio Experience 10.3

1 Have students look at Studio Experience 10.3. Explain that they will do three contour drawings of the same objects. Each drawing will demonstrate one of the three kinds of balance. There will always be a dominant object. Have available objects that are easy to draw for still life arrangements. One should be larger and the others should be similar in size and shape. If cylindrical objects are provided, recall Studio Experience 5.3, which showed how to use ellipses organized around a vertical to draw such objects.

2 Divide the time period in three equal parts, and have students make and draw the first arrangement. Ask them to maintain the same viewing angle for the second and third arrangements.

3 Remind them that they are working with dominance and balance. As they make arrangements, ask them which object will be central in the symmetrical arrangement. Which will be central in the radial arrangement? How will they offset the weight of the dominant form in the asymmetrical arrangement?

Evaluate and Reflect

1 Display the finished drawings. Can students explain how balance relates to the dominant form in a composition?

2 Can students identify the kind of balance used in one another's drawings?

3 Which of the three drawings is the most interesting, and why? Which do they find least interesting?

4 Have students make an arrangement that does not balance.

Reteach

Have students study the examples in their text. Refer to the study questions dealing with balance and dominance and ask them to provide answers. Have them experiment with arrangements of cut paper shapes.

Extend the Lesson
Beyond the Basics

This lesson is an exercise meant to introduce the concepts of balance. The expectation is that students will incorporate the balance concepts into their critical vocabulary, and use them in future art production experiences.

Have students study balance in both natural and human-made objects. Suggest students look for examples of each kind of balance and sketch their findings in a sketchbook. Which kind of balance, if any, seems to dominate in the natural world? In the human-made environment? Why?

Cultural Connections

Study examples of artwork from other cultures, looking specifically for works that demonstrate the different kinds of balance. Find examples of symmetrically balanced designs like the Peruvian mantle (Student Edition fig. 10–10). Can students find examples of radial design similar to that used in the Pomo Indian basket (Student Edition fig. 10–13). Have students examine the works to determine if one kind of balance seems to be preferred over another in any of the cultures.

EE 1, 3

Connecting with Other Subjects

Social Studies Direct students' attention to Curry's painting, page 120 of student text. *Baptism in Kansas* was painted in 1928 and provides a great deal of information about life in Kansas during that time. Suggest students research a favorite period in history and select a number of artworks that illustrate the way people lived. What did people wear, or drive, or do for entertainment? Prepare a report using visual images created by artists to enhance the presentation. Students may want to give their reports in both history class and in art.

EE 3

W 1, 4

Analyzing an Advertisement

Design

Time: 1 period

Preparation

Rationale

Commercials and advertisements are part of students' everyday world. These images can be analyzed according to the same design principles and procedures used to analyze artworks.

Criticism Materials

examples of advertising art from magazines, newspapers, and posters, Guidelines for Analyzing an Artwork (Handout 9.1)

Enrichment Materials

Large Reproductions:
• Glaser, *Saratoga*, 24

Teach the Lesson

Objectives

Students should be able to:

1   analyze an advertising artwork using the Guidelines for Analyzing an Artwork (Handout 9.1)   EE 1, 3, 4

Vocabulary

Dominance is a principle of design that stresses the importance of one element, or a combination of elements, over everything else in the composition to make it attract the viewer's attention first.

Similarities of elements (color, texture, shape, form, line) establish relationships that contribute to unity.

Continuation occurs when lines, edges of forms and shapes, or arrangements of objects and figures direct the viewer's attention.

Warm Up

Ask students to name the last thing they bought as the result of an advertisement. What was it about the visual elements of the advertisement that appealed to them? Can they recall the dominant element in the advertisement?

Explore and Develop

1   Display advertisements from magazines, newspapers, catalogs, and brochures. Which ones attract student attention first? Why?

2   Review the principles of design.

3   Have students look at the advertisement in Studio Experience 10.4. Discuss how it was designed to attract and hold attention.

a. The carrot shapes are the dominant form. There are similarities between the carrot shapes and the negative spaces between them and in the vertical columns of text.

b. The carrot shapes and the vertical columns direct attention down to the small pan and the vitamin container. The handle directs attention to the left. The vertical sides of the vitamin container and columns of text direct attention up to the bold captions.

c. Variety results from contrasts between the bright color of the carrots and the black of the text, the texture and value of the text against the white ground, and the size of the carrots compared to the other objects.

d. Balance results from the carrots in the upper right, the diagonal thrust of two carrots toward the vitamin bottle in the lower left, and the heavy letters of the caption in the upper left.

e. Alternation of the positive carrot shapes and the space in between them causes a rhythmical movement left toward the bold caption, which also contributes to balance.

Begin Criticism Experience 10.4

1 Organize the class into four or five groups, and have the groups analyze an advertisement. Have students use the Guidelines for Analyzing an Artwork (see Handout 9.1) to analyze the composition.

2 Have students share their advertisements and analyses.

Evaluate and Reflect

R 5 **1** Did students analyze the composition of an advertisement in terms of the design principles?

R 5 **2** Can students identify and discuss the principles of design in a commercial artwork?

3 Do students agree with each other's analysis?

R 6 **4** Which of the displayed advertisements does the class feel is the best composition? Ask them to explain why.

Reteach

Organize the class into small groups. Have each group select an advertisement from the board display that they feel needs improvement. Use construction paper and felt markers to redesign the ad. Have the groups analyze their ads using the Guidelines for Analysis from Experience 9.1.

Extend the Lesson

Beyond the Basics

E 1, 4 Ask students to make two collections of advertisements: one of advertisements that appeal strongly, and the other of advertisements that lack appeal. Have them analyze the two groups of advertisements to see if there is a relationship between design and appeal of the advertisements.

EE 1, 2, 4 Suggest students visit a discount store or grocery that carries many different brands of each product. Have them select a product that has the least interesting package and purchase it. Begin by describing and analyzing the package. Then brainstorm the ways the package could be improved. Design a new package and create a magazine advertisement to sell the product. Describe and analyze the new designs.

Cultural Connections

EE 1, 3 Many familiar products have been around for decades and are marketed throughout the world. Suggest students select one of these products and research the history of the package design and advertising. Also look for examples of the packaging and advertisement used to sell the product in other parts of the world. Suggest contacting a company directly. They may have historic information available in brochures or displays. Inquire about getting samples of packaging and advertisements used in other countries. How have the designs changed over the years? What changes were made to appeal to customers in other cultures?

Connecting with Other Subjects

EE 3 **Social Studies** Have students look at Lawrence's painting, *Going Home*, on page 123. This is one of many "social protests" produced by Lawrence over a period of more than thirty years. His paintings speak of the conditions and despair of African Americans living in the ghettos of New York. Examine the figures in the painting very carefully. What mood or feeling is conveyed by the poses of the figures? Describe what is happening in the painting. Do the people in the painting seem excited about their journey? Where are they going? Where is "home"? Suggest students find other examples of works by Jacob Lawrence. Examine the works and then talk with the social studies teacher regarding the issues and ideas expressed in Lawrence's work.

Name: _____   Course: _____

Study Questions
Chapter 10–Design

1 Why is unity so important in a successful work of art?

_____

_____

_____

2 Name and describe three ways that unity can be achieved in a work of art.

_____

_____

_____

3 Define variety.

_____

_____

4 Select an artwork (other than in the text). List five examples of the artist's use of variety. Look for variety of colors, shapes, textures, lines, sizes, etc.

_____

_____

_____

5 Define *dominance.*

_____

_____

6 Select an example of an artwork (other than in the text) that has a strong area of dominance. Give two reasons why you feel the area is dominant.

_____

_____

_____

7 Find an example of an artwork (other than in the text) that does not have a dominant area. Explain why.

_____

_____

8 Define *radial balance*.

_____

_____

9 Define *rhythm*.

_____

_____

10 What are the three basic methods of rhythm?

_____

_____

11 Find an example of each of the three different methods of rhythm that can be seen in your daily environment.

_____

_____

_____

12 What affects *visual weight* in a painting?

_____

_____

13 What is the difference between symmetrical balance and asymmetrical balance?

_____

_____

14 The painting called *Mae West* by Salvador Dali (text fig. 10–12) is an example of approximate symmetry. List four differences between the two sides.

_____

_____

_____

15 Study the symmetrically balanced design of the Peruvian textile (text fig. 10–10) and the radial balance achieved in the Pomo Indian basket (text fig. 10–13). Using your own symbols, shapes, and lines, create a symmetrically or radially balanced design.

Test Questions
Chapter 10–Design

Design

Match the correct terms on the right with the definitions on the left.

1 _____ A "felt" balance

2 _____ Several different objects of several different sizes

3 _____ Andy Warhol's *Soup Cans*

4 _____ Elements arranged around a central object

5 _____ Two red shapes, three orange shapes, two red shapes, three orange shapes, etc. across the picture plane

6 _____ Exactly the same on both sides

7 _____ Similar colors, textures, shapes

8 _____ Focal point in a composition

9 _____ *The Scream* by Edvard Munch

10 _____ Equal distribution of eye attraction on either side of the composition's center

a. Dominance

b. Variety

c. Asymmetrical

d. Alternating rhythm

e Symmetrical balance

f. Progressive rhythm

g. Symmetrical balance

h. Repetition, alternation

i. Helps achieve unity

j. Radial design

Circle the correct answers.

11 The plan an artist uses to organize the composition of an artwork is referred to as

a. design. c. a set of rules.
b. an element. d. none of the above.

12 If the viewer of an artwork is aware of the entire work before looking at the individual parts, the composition has

a. dominance. c. monotony.
b. radial balance. d. unity.

13 An artist who places a row of trees extending from the lower left side to the upper right in a painting helps to achieve unity by

a. variety. c. continuation.
b. proximity. d. similarity.

For questions 14 through 19, use the following list to fill in the blanks.

1. Asymmetrical
2. Symmetrical
3. Approximately symmetrical
4. Rhythm

5. Dominance
6. Variety
7. Unity
8. Continuation

Answer the following questions while viewing the overhead transparency of *Oni (King) of Ife.*

14 Lines are repeated, which shows _____.

15 The sculpture is an example of _____ balance.

16 Besides horizontal lines, the sculpture has vertical and crossed diagonal lines which provide _____.

While viewing the overhead transparency of *Design Made at Airlie Garden,* an oil and mixed media on canvas by folk artist Minnie Eva Jones Evans, answer the following questions.

17 This painting is an example of _____ balance.

18 There is not one definite area of _____ in this painting.

19 Since the viewer's eye is directed throughout the painting and all working parts work together, _____ is achieved.

20 Explain how the artist used color and shape to create a feeling of rhythm and movement throughout the painting.

_____

_____

_____

_____

_____

_____

_____

Study Answers
Chapter 10
Design

1 Unity results from parts that work together, making the viewer aware of the total work of art rather than individual parts.

2 Proximity—placing objects close together; similarity—making things similar in color, texture, shape, or form; continuation—directing viewer's vision by lines, edges of shapes, or arrangement of objects.

3 Difference in use of materials and objects, contrasts of values, textures, colors, etc.

4 Examples and answers will vary.

5 Occurs when one element appears to be more important, or attracts more attention than anything else in the composition.

6 Examples and answers will vary.

7 Examples and answers will vary.

8 The repetitive placement of similar elements around a centrally dominant object.

9 Sense of movement resulting from controlled repetition.

10 a) repetition of the same elements with little or no variation; b) repetition of two or more elements on an alternating basis; c) progressive repetition of an element from large to small, dark to light, etc.

11 Possible answers include: a) repetition of identical items hanging on a rack in a clothing store, or canned goods on grocery shelves; b) arrangement of bushes in front of a home or business that uses alternating kinds of plants; c) repeated architectural details, such as windows, dormers, balconies.

12 Relative size, brightness of color, contrasts of value or texture, complexity of shape, and distance from the center of the composition.

13 Symmetrical balance—identical balance on both sides of a vertical axis. Asymmetrical balance—"felt" equalization of visual weight.

14 Answers will vary.

15 Answers will vary.

Test Answers
Chapter 10
Design

1 C

2 B

3 H or E

4 J

5 D

6 E

7 I

8 A

9 F

10 G

11 A

12 D

13 C

14 (4.) Rhythm

15 (2.) Symmetrical

16 (6.) Variety

17 (3.) Approximately symmetrical

18 (5.) Dominance

19 (7.) Unity

20 Answers will vary. For example, the colors blue and green have been used throughout the painting. An example of movement through the painting begins with the alternating blue and green shapes in the lower left corner moving in a semi-circular pattern toward the middle of the painting. The alternating blue and green shapes reverse the curve, then reverse again, continuing close to the right edge of the painting. Other comments may refer to the use of warm colors or point out that all shapes have similar curves.

Chapter 10
Design

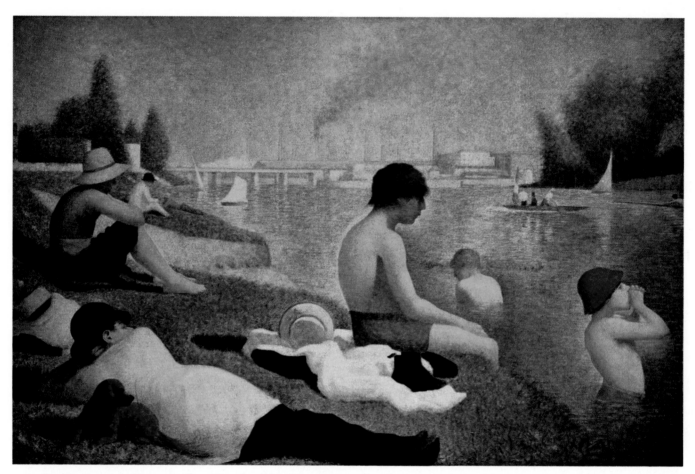

10–1 Georges Seurat, *Bathing at Asnières*, 1883–1884. Oil on canvas, 6′ 7″ x 9′ 11″ (201 x 302 cm). Reproduced by courtesy of the Trustees, The National Gallery, London.

In Chapter 9, you learned that artists compose elements to create a work of art. The final result is called a composition. The artist follows a plan, or ***design,*** to organize the composition. In the final composition, the different elements should all work together.

There are no exact rules for achieving good composition in works of art. However, there are some principles of design that can be followed. The principles of *unity, variety, dominance, rhythm and movement,* and *balance* can be helpful in seeing how the various elements are organized and how they work together.

Unity

Unity in art can be compared with teamwork in sports. A basketball team needs five players. But to be successful, the coach must make the five members play as a unit. Likewise, if an artwork is to be successful, the artist must make the elements work together as a unit. If a work of art does not have unity, it will appear to be a collection of individual parts. If the composition is successful, you are aware of the whole work of art before looking at individual parts. The main purpose of the artist's plan is unity.

Several aspects of design contribute to unity. They can be demonstrated by examining Georges Seurat's painting, *Bathing at Asnières* (fig. 10–1).

Proximity

One way to make separate objects look unified is to place them close together, or in **proximity.** In Seurat's painting there are groups of people and objects. There are the three boys on the right. A pile of clothing is by the large boy. The man and dog form a group of two. There are groupings of trees and buildings in the distance. Notice how the individual figures and objects along the riverbank are tied together by their proximity. Your eye moves from one to another.

Similarity

A second way to achieve unity is to make things **similar** in color, texture, shape, or form. Several objects in the painting, even those that are distant from each other, are connected by their similarity in color. Red-orange, for example, appears in the dog, the hat of the boy in the water, and his shorts. Can you identify some other items with red-orange? What other colors are repeated in Seurat's painting?

Several objects in the painting have similar shapes. For example, the dome shape occurs in the hats, the heads of the two hatless bathers, and even in some of the trees. There are many triangle shapes. For example, look at the bent legs of the persons sitting on the bank. The arms of the boy holding his hands to his mouth are bent in a triangle. Look for a triangle in the back of the reclining man, and in the shadow behind the large boy's arm. The boat sails are also triangular. Can you identify some other repeated shapes in the painting?

Continuation

When you view an artwork, your eye often follows a certain path. The flow of vision can be caused by a line, edges of shapes, or the arrangement of objects. This is called **continuation.** The edge of the riverbank in Seurat's painting is a good example of a line that directs the flow of vision. The riverbank continues from the lower right corner to the upper left side. Another is the line of the bridge and buildings.

Continuation is often reinforced by the similarity and placement of the forms. For example, your vision tends to move from the large figures in front to the small ones at the far end of the riverbank. Then you look along the buildings, past the boat sail reflected in the water, and back down to the boy with cupped hands. The continuation in *Bathing at Asnières* is shown in figure 10–2.

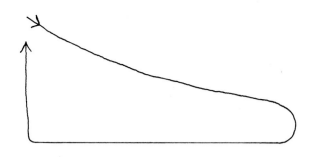

10–2 Diagram of continuation in Seurat's *Bathing.*

Studio Experience 10.1

Movement and Unity in Sculpture

Construct a three-dimensional sculpture. Choose wood scraps and organize them to create visual movement and unity throughout the form.

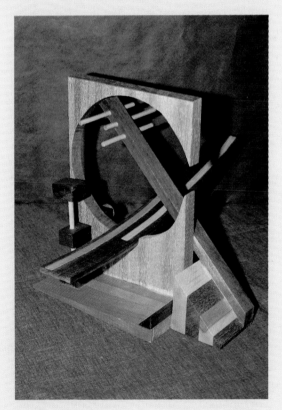

Kay Dye.

Faith Ringgold

1930–

As a child, Faith Ringgold suffered from asthma. She spent many days at home with her mother, Willi Posey Jones, who was a fashion designer and dressmaker. To keep Faith entertained while she was ill, she would give her fabrics, thread, crayons, and watercolors to play with. Without knowing it, Willi was helping her daughter to become an artist.

Faith Ringgold grew up in Harlem, New York, during the Great Depression. This was a difficult time when many people were unemployed and struggling to provide food and clothing for their families. Faith remembers that time as a very important part of her life which influenced her later artwork: "Mostly, I remember people. Faces of people. Everything about people. And...early on, I got involved with the souls of people."

Faith studied art education in college and taught in the New York City Public Schools. Together, she and her students explored African heritage and culture through art. From this experience Faith developed a sense of pride in being a black American.

1972 was a year of change for Faith. While teaching African crafts at a New York college, she had a retrospective exhibition of her paintings of the previous ten years. One of her students expressed disappointment in Faith's artwork: "I didn't see any of the techniques you teach us... beading, tie-dyeing. Why aren't you using the techniques of African women?" Faith could not answer her student's question. She began to realize that fabric and beads had been part of her life since childhood; perhaps she should use these materials and techniques in her artwork. Faith's childhood experiences, her youth in the Harlem community, and her interest in African culture could be combined to form a new type of art.

Faith began using cloth, beads, rope, thread, and ribbon to create unusual sculptures of people. Some of these sculptures were of people she remembered from growing up in Harlem. Others were of famous people like Wilt Chamberlain and Martin Luther King, Jr. Some of her sculptures are small, while others are larger than life. A small sculpture, *Lena*, requires that you look closely to learn about this little person who lives on the street, while *Martin Luther King* is larger than life-size, emphasizing Dr. King's importance to Faith and to all people.

Today Faith continues to work with a variety of traditionally African materials in her art, using them in sculptures of unique individuals, quilts which tell stories of people, and even performances which involve singing and dancing. Faith Ringgold's artwork portrays both her passion for people and her understanding of the struggles of modern life.

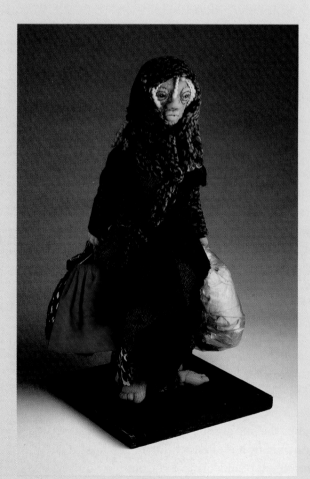

Faith Ringgold, *Lena*, 1978. Mixed Media. ©Faith Ringgold.

Variety

A composition can be so unified that it is uninteresting. A good example is the pattern in a tile floor. All of the tiles are the same color, in close proximity, and constantly repeated. The floor is very unified, but not very exciting.

Variety refers to differences. Variety may involve different materials and objects, and different forms of the same thing. Contrasts of values, textures, and colors also provide variety. Seurat's *Bathing* has a lot of variety. People of varied sizes, who are dressed differently, are doing different things. There are sailboats, buildings, trees, a dog, a river and a riverbank. There is also a variety of colors, lines, textures, and shapes.

Even with all of this variety, *Bathing* is a peaceful and relaxed scene. Seurat used related colors (yellow-greens and blues). The figures are posed in relaxed positions. Variety contributes interest to a picture, or to anything in life. Too much variety, however, can be disorderly and confusing. Therefore, variety in *Bathing* has been brought under control by unity.

Once in a while, an artist may use unrelieved repetition on purpose. In *100 Cans* (fig. 10–3) Andy Warhol repeated the same soup can one hundred times. Perhaps the work is a critical comment on the monotony of repeated commercial images that are forced upon us every day. By comparison, Joseph Cornell's *Object ("Roses des vents")* has a great deal of variety (fig. 10–4). It includes many different objects: maps, charts, rocks, compasses, a spring, seeds, and pictures. Cornell has pushed variety to the limit in this sculptural work. Perhaps the work is a comment on our tendency to gather and keep collections of odds and ends.

Dominance

When one element appears to be more important or attracts the most attention, we say it is **dominant**. The dominant element or form is usually a focal point in a composition. We tend to look at it first. In Seurat's painting, the large boy sitting on the bank by the pile of clothing dominates the picture. The boy is a focal point to which our eyes keep returning. Why does he dominate? One reason is his size. He is the second largest figure in the painting. Another reason is his location, which is near the center. The warm colors in his hair, flesh, and shorts contrast with the cool color of the water.

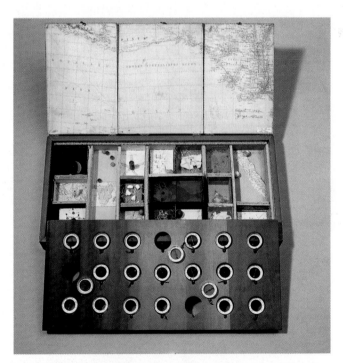

10–3 Andy Warhol, *100 Cans*, 1962. Oil on canvas, 72″ x 52″ (183 x 132 cm). Albright-Knox Art Gallery, Buffalo, New York, Gift of Seymour H. Knox, 1963.

10–4 Joseph Cornell, *Object ("Roses des vents")*, 1942–1953. Wooden box with twenty-one compasses set into a wooden tray resting on plexiglass-topped and partitioned section, divided into seventeen compartments containing small, miscellaneous objects and three-part hinged lid covered inside with parts of maps of New Guinea and Australia, 2 5/8″ x 21 1/4″ x 10 3/8″ (7 x 54 x 26 cm). The Museum of Modern Art, New York. Mr. and Mrs. Gerald Murphy Fund.

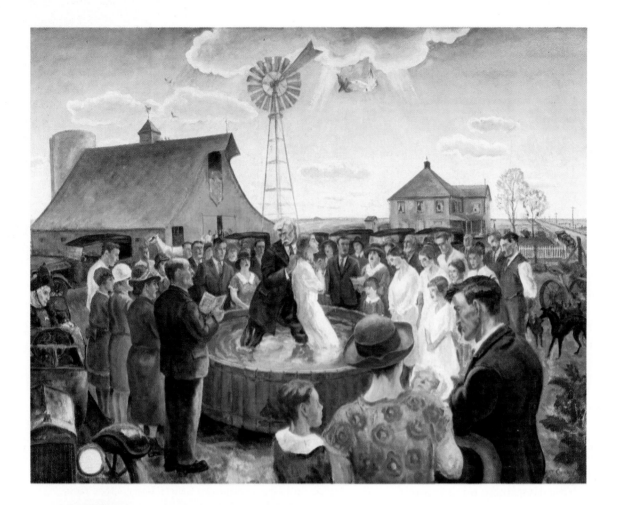

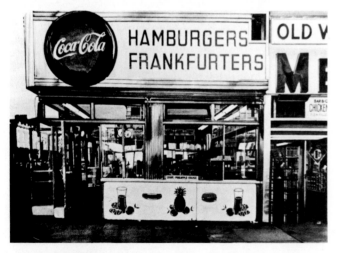

10-5 Richard Estes, *Nedick's*, 1969–1970. Oil, 48″ x 66″ (122 x 168 cm). Private collection.

10-6 John Steuart Curry, *Baptism in Kansas*, 1928. Oil on canvas, 40″ x 50″ (102 x 127 cm). Collection of Whitney Museum of American Art. Gift of Gertrude Vanderbilt Whitney.

An element does not have to be large or in the center of the artwork in order to dominate. An element may dominate because it is different from everything else. For example, the Coca-Cola sign in the painting by Richard Estes (fig. 10-5) stands out because it is the only major circular shape. The composition is filled with mostly rectangular shapes.

The preacher and the young woman are the dominant figures in John Steuart Curry's *Baptism in Kansas* (fig. 10-6). The two figures are centrally located at the hub of two circles. One circle is formed by the water trough. The other circle is formed by the ring of onlookers. This kind of composition is called *radial design*. Most of the people are looking at the central pair of figures. This fact is especially important to this radial design. They draw our attention to the pair. (This kind of direction, called *lines of sight,* was defined in Chapter 4.) Have you often looked where other people are looking or pointing?

Dominance in Low-Relief

Arrange lightweight cardboard shapes around a heavy dominant form on a piece of cardboard. Glue in place. Stretch aluminum foil over the work to make a low-relief sculpture.

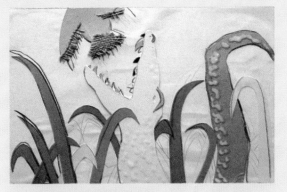

Cardboard shapes glued in place.

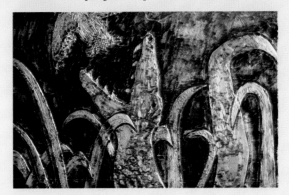

Finished work by Nick Capodice.

Rhythm and Movement

When you think of rhythm, you may think of the beat in music or the movements of a dancer. A painting also has **rhythm** and **movement.** Controlled repetition of shapes and lines, or the alternation of light and dark areas, creates a sense of movement. This is called rhythm. Although continuation contributes to visual movement, rhythm is a more powerful way to create movement.

There are three methods for creating rhythm. First, rhythm can be created by repeating the *same* element, such as a shape or a figure, with little or no variation. Secondly, it can be created by repeating two or more elements on an *alternating* basis, such as circle-square, circle-square. Thirdly, it can be created by

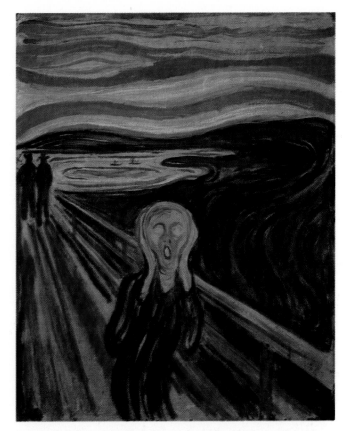

10–7 Edvard Munch, *The Scream*, 1893. Oil on canvas, 36″ x 29″ (91 x 74 cm). ©Munch Museum, Oslo 1993.

progressive repetition, in which an element changes gradually from large to small, dark to light, and so on.

Most artworks include more than one kind of rhythm. Andy Warhol's *100 Cans* (fig. 10–3) shows unvarying repetition in the vertical rows of cans. In the horizontal rows, rhythm comes from the alternation of red and white on the label.

The Scream by Edvard Munch (fig. 10–7) involves a rhythm of curved shapes and lines that become progressively larger from the upper left to the lower right. Our eyes follow their movement toward the main figure. Then the converging lines of the bridge provide a progression of shapes from large to small. These lines direct us back into the left part of the picture. Do you experience a movement in and out of the painting that suggests the echoing of a scream?

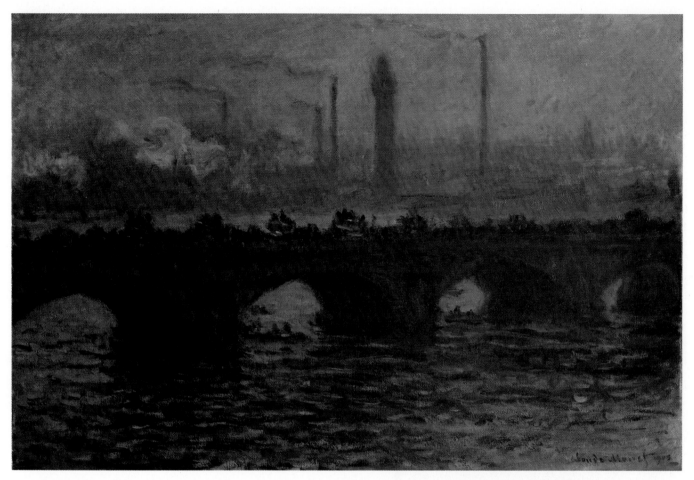

10-8 Claude Monet, *Waterloo Bridge,* 1903. Oil on canvas, 25 ¾″ x 36 ⅝″ (65 x 93 cm). Worcester Art Museum, Massachusetts.

You can see all three types of rhythm in Claude Monet's painting, *Waterloo Bridge* (fig. 10–8). The negative spaces beneath the arches *alternate* with the positive forms of the arches, creating a rhythmical movement diagonally across the picture. The arches become *progressively* smaller from left to right, reinforcing the visual movement across the painting. Monet also created a progression of colors from light and bright in the foreground water, to the dark of the bridge, to the grayed or dull colors in the background. *Repeated* white and light green brush strokes on a dark color suggest waves and reflections in the water.

You can find rhythm in Seurat's *Bathing*, but it is more subtle. The curved line along the head, neck, and back is repeated in all of the seated figures, and in the boy in the water with cupped hands. The edge of the riverbank provides a continuous flow of line that brings our eyes to progressively smaller forms. Look closely at the reflections in the water for rhythmic light and dark alternations. The light is coming from the right of the painting. It causes an alternation of light and dark values on all of the figures and objects. Can you identify more examples of alternation and repetition in the background?

Balance

Look at the two examples of the painting *Going Home* by Jacob Lawrence (fig. 10–9A, B). Which one do you like better? Most people choose example (A) as more satisfying than (B). Before reading further, can you explain what was affected by removing the seated figure in the striped pants and the reclining figure from the left front of the picture? Why?

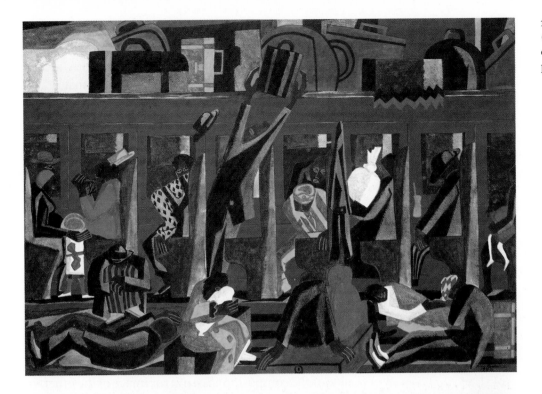

10-9A Jacob Lawrence, *Going Home*, 1946. Gouache on board. Collection IBM Corporation, Armonk, New York.

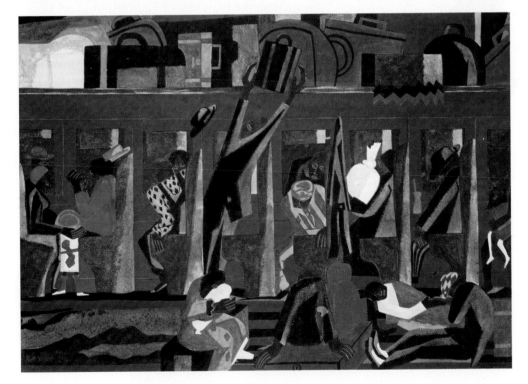

10-9B This version of Jacob Lawrence's painting has been photographically altered. Which do you think is better balanced?

Removing the figures in Jacob Lawrence's painting made the right side of the picture appear heavier than the left. It affected the balance of the composition. **Balance** in a composition refers to an equal distribution of *visual weight* on either side of a composition's center. The visual weight of images and objects in a painting depends on their relative size, brightness of color, contrasts of value or texture, complexity of shapes, and distance from the center of the composition.

The unchanged reproduction of *Going Home* (A) is *asymmetrically* balanced because the artist achieved a feeling of equally distributed visual weights with figures and objects that are different. The figure that is putting the bag on the shelf creates a forceful diagonal thrust to the right. This thrust and the weight of the figures in the lower right foreground are balanced by the weight of the figures that are in the lower left foreground of the picture. Lawrence carefully positioned all of the figures and objects in *Going Home* to create a "felt" equalization of visual weights.

Symmetrical balance is simpler to achieve and easier to analyze. The decorative symbols woven into the seventh century Peruvian mantle (fig. 10–10) are arranged in symmetrical balance. Identical elements are equally distributed on either side of a vertical axis in the center of the composition. Robert Indiana's *The X-5* (fig. 10–11) is a contemporary example of pure symmetrical balance. In this very precise painting, one side of the composition is a mirror image of the other.

Sometimes the two sides of a composition are similar enough to imply a vertical central axis, and varied just enough to challenge you to identify the differences. This kind of balance is called *approximate symmetry*. You can see it in the painting called *Mae West* by Salvador Dali (fig. 10–12). At first glance, this appears to be a purely symmetrical painting. But look closely and you will discover a number of differences between the two sides. Do you think the painting looks like a portrait, a room interior, or both?

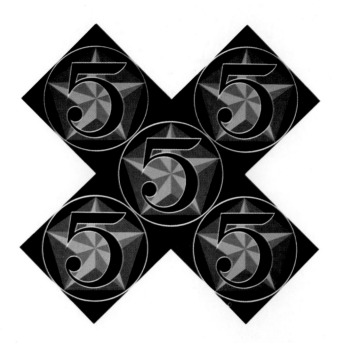

10–11 Robert Indiana, *The X-5*, 1963. Oil on canvas, 108″ x 108″ (274 x 274 cm). Each of five panels is 36″ x 36″ (91 x 91 cm). Collection of Whitney Museum of American Art. Purchase.

10–10 Mantle. Detail: three figures. Wool, embroidered with colored wools. Peru, pre-Inca period, Early Nazca, ca. 600. The Metropolitan Museum of Art, Gift of George D. Pratt, 1932.

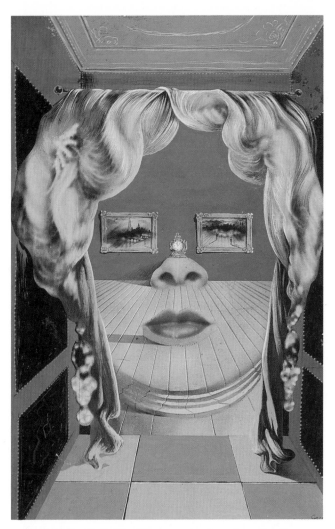

10–12 Salvador Dali, *Mae West*, ca. 1934. Gouache, 11″ x 7″ (28 x 18 cm). The Art Institute of Chicago, Gift of Gilbert W. Chapman in memory of Charles B. Goodspeed, 1949.

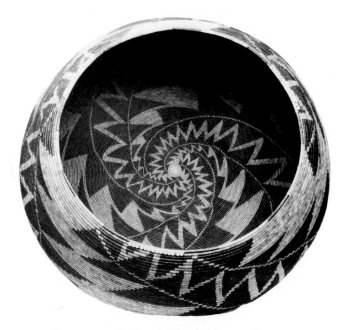

10–13 Pomo storage basket. California. Nineteenth century. Coiled basketry, 13 ½″ x 21″ (34 x 53 cm). Courtesy of The National Museum of the American Indian/Smithsonian Institution. (1332g).

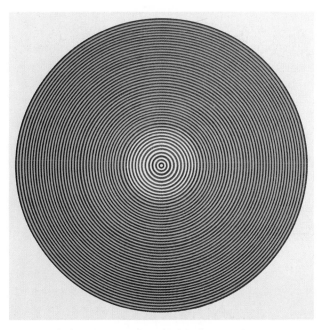

10–14 Tadasky, *A-101*, 1964. Synthetic polymer paint on canvas, 52″ x 52″ (132 x 132 cm). The Museum of Modern Art. New York. Larry Aldrich Foundation Fund.

Radial balance results from the repetitive placement of two or more identical or very similar elements around a central point. The Pomo Indians of northern California wove into their baskets geometric designs that radiate outward from a central point (fig. 10–13). The radial balance causes a spiraling movement over inner and outer surfaces of the basket. *A-101* (fig. 10–14) by Tadasky is a radially balanced optical painting. The painting is designed to create the illusion of movement. Try staring at the center of the concentric circles until the black lines begin to whirl.

John Curry's *Baptism in Kansas* demonstrates a more subtle use of radial balance (fig. 10–6). The figures of the preacher and young woman are a central point. Around them are circles of people and automobiles. Even the placement of the house and barn suggests a larger circle that goes off the page.

Look again at Seurat's *Bathing at Asnières* (fig. 10–1) to analyze how it is balanced. You will have no trouble recognizing that it is asymmetrical and well balanced. When you begin to analyze the distribution of visual weights, however, you discover that most of the people are on the left. Even the man lying down, who is the largest figure of all, is on the left. The large man, the placement of the figures, and the diagonal thrust of the riverbank direct attention to the upper left. But on further analysis, you discover that this left-ward tilt is counterbalanced by several things: the right-of-center placement of the large boy, the warm-cool color contrasts between the blue water and the orange hair, shorts, and hat of the boys on the right, and the fact that almost everyone is looking to the right.

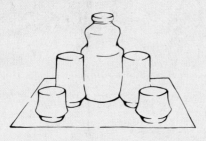

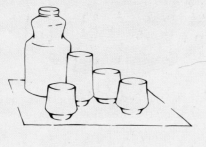

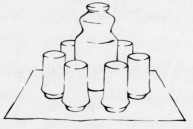

Seurat was very concerned about such things as unity and balance. His *Bathing at Asnières* demonstrates all of the design principles. However, some of the other examples included in this chapter do not. Andy Warhol's *100 Cans* (fig. 10–3) has unity, but very little variety and no dominance. Cornell's work of art (fig. 10–4) has variety in the objects. It also has some unity because of a network of horizontal and vertical lines on the upper maps, the compartments in the box, and the rows and columns of compasses. However, it lacks dominance and rhythmical movement. Both Robert Indiana's *The X-5* (fig. 10–11) and Tadasky's *A-101* (fig. 10–14) have little variety.

Some works of art seem to defy all of the principles of design. *Black Painting* by Ad Reinhardt (fig. 10–15) appears to be simply a large black square. If you look at it long and hard, you may see the shape of a cross. Even if you do see the shape, however, there is little variety, no focal point, no rhythm, and no visual movement. Since there are no visual weights, there is nothing on which to base decisions about balance. Black dominates the painting.

The **principles of design** are based on the fundamentals of vision—on how we see everything in our environment. (Recall the discussions on perception of color and shape, object size, figure and ground, and space in Chapters 4, 5, 6, and 7.) They are apparent in most artworks. They give us a way to analyze a composition. The principles of design also help us understand how parts of an artwork are organized.

Summary

The artist is always aware that a whole work of art is more important than any single part. Therefore, he or she must have a plan for organizing all of the elements that make up an art form. This plan, or design, can be analyzed in terms of certain principles: *unity, variety, dominance, rhythm and movement,* and *balance.*

Unity is described as a sense of wholeness or oneness that is present when all parts of an art form work together. When a composition is unified, you find your vision moving easily over the objects, shapes, and elements. Your concern is for the total form rather than individual parts. Although unity is dependent upon all of the design principles, it is especially enhanced by *proximity, similarity,* and *continuation.*

Too much unity can result in monotony. Therefore, the artist includes some *variety.* Contrasts of colors, different shapes, and variations of lines or

10–15 In some nonrepresentational works, one element is totally dominant. Black dominates this painting and the viewer's perception of it. What meanings are suggested by a large black square? Ad Reinhardt, *Black Painting*, 1960. Oil on canvas, 60″ x 60″ (152 x 152 cm). Photograph courtesy of The Pace Gallery.

textures can create some interest and excitement. Look for examples of unity with variety in your environment, such as the design of a building, a shopping mall, or a landscaped park.

Sometimes an element or area of an artwork appears to be *dominant*. It attracts your immediate attention. Other parts of the composition may be emphasized in varying degrees. These contrasts help to direct visual movement from an initial focal point to other parts of the artwork.

Rhythm and movement result from the organized repetition of an element or elements in a work of art. Three methods of creating rhythm are repetition, alternation, and progression.

Balance is a feeling of equilibrium among all the parts of a composition. Balance in an artwork may be symmetrical, approximately symmetrical, asymmetrical, or radial.

The principles of design are very interdependent. Artists use them all, and in many different ways. These principles will help you to analyze and appreciate a variety of art forms. You may also find them helpful in creating your own works of art.

Criticism Experience 10.4

Analyzing an Advertisement

Use the analysis guidelines in Chapter 9 and Experience 9.1 to analyze an advertisement. Cover the principles of design in your analysis.

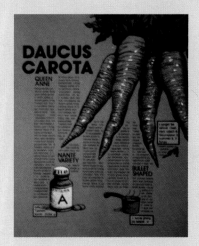

Lauri Lazar.

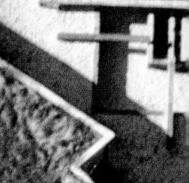

Part IV
What Is It Made Of?

Mary Miss, Field Rotation, 1981. Wood, gravel, concrete, steel, earth and water. Structure, 7' x 56' x 56' (2 m x 17 m x 17 m), centered in 4 1/2 acre site. Governors State University, Park Forest South, Illinois.

Chapter 11
Introduction to Media

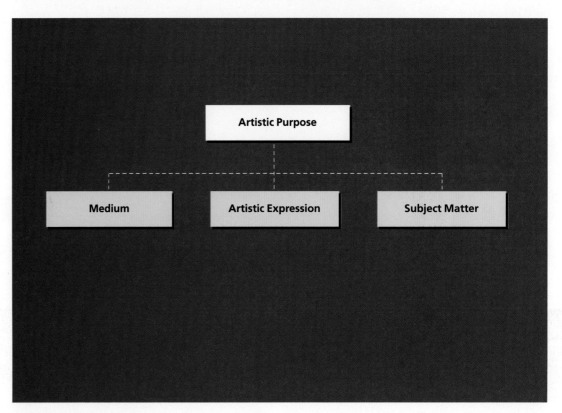

Overview

Chapter Objectives

Students should be able to:

1 explain what an art medium is and list several two- and three-dimensional media   EE 1, 2

2 discuss the relationships among art media, subject matter, and what is expressed in the artwork   EE 1, 2

Rationale

This chapter introduces Chapters 12 and 13, which are concerned with two- and three-dimensional media respectively. It is important for students, whether engaged in looking at, criticizing, or making art, to have a basic understanding of art media. Years of experience underlie the artist's sensitivity to media and the ability to inter-relate the medium, subject matter, and content in a work of art.

Essential Chapter Concepts

• Medium is the material used for making an artwork. Media is the plural form.

• The choices of medium and subject matter are interrelated.

• When analyzing a work of art, we look for good relationships among the medium, subject matter, and expressive purpose.

Vocabulary

medium

subject matter

two-dimensional

three-dimensional

Lesson Plan

11.1 Introduction to Media

Page **T 158**   Time: 1 period

Handouts

Study Questions

Page **T 160**

Test Questions

Page **T 161**

Chapter Closure

Evaluation

1   *Criticism:* Can students define the term art medium and name several two- and three-dimensional media?   R 1

2   *Criticism/Aesthetic awareness:* Are students able to talk at a beginning level about the interrelationship of medium to subject matter and to the artist's purpose?   R 5

Notes

Introduction to Media

Time: 1 period

Preparation

Rationale

Students are introduced to the concept of medium, and the importance of interrelating medium, subject matter, and expressive intent. The material serves as an introduction to Chapters 12 and 13, which deal with two- and three-dimensional media.

Discussion Materials

Chapter 11 Study Questions, Test Questions

Enrichment Materials

Slides:
• Bingham, *Fur Traders*, 18
• Boccioni, *Unique Forms*, 23
• Greenough, *George Washington*, 32
• Giacometti, *Man Pointing*, 33
• Daumier, *Connoisseurs*, 120

Overhead Transparencies:
• Ernst, *Eye of Silence*, 1
• Hepworth, *Pendour*, 2
• Pei, *East Building*, 6
• Vasarely, *Edetta*, 7
• *Oni*, 8
• Adams, *Half Dome*, 12
• Picasso, *Still Life*, 13
• Oldenburg, *Floor Cake*, 15

Large Reproductions:
• Stout, *Instructions and Provisions*, 2
• Smith, *Snake Path*, 1
• Mackie, *Self-Portrait*, 14
• Lucero, *Zoomorphic Dog Vessel*, 9
• Prow ornament, Tlingit war canoe, 17
• Schwartz, *Untitled #16*, 11

Laser Discs:

Matisse, Jazz, The Funeral of Pierrot, 1947

Search Frame 3247

Munch, Two Women on the Shore, 1900–1910

Search Frame 3337

Rembrandt, Woman Bathing her Feet in a Brook, 1658

Search Frame 3180

Rembrandt, Woman Bathing her Feet in a Brook, 1658

Search Frame 3182

Manet, The Man in the Tall Hat, 1859

Search Frame 2924

Stella, Jarama II, 1982

Search Frame 2333

Teach the Lesson

Objectives

Students should be able to:

1   explain what an art medium is and list several two- and three-dimensional media   EE 2

2   understand the relationship among the medium, subject matter, and purpose of the work   EE 1, 2

Vocabulary

Medium is the material(s) used to create an artwork, such as watercolor, pencil, pastels.

Subject matter refers to what is represented in an artwork.

Two-dimensional artworks have height and width, and are done on a flat surface.

Three-dimensional artworks have height, width, and depth, such as sculpture.

Warm Up

To introduce how the medium, subject matter, and expression of ideas are interrelated, use examples from dance, music, and drama, in which the relationships are evident. Write the columns below on the chalkboard. Ask students to match the art form with the statement.

1. Dance—Ballet
2. Music—Jazz
3. Music—Flute
4. Music—Trumpet
5. Drama—Comedy
6. Drama—Tragedy

a) serious dialogue expressing ideas about world hunger

b) loud, forceful sounds expressing rapid marching movement of people

c) expression of a deer leaping and bounding through a meadow

d) expression of a big city's fast-paced nightlife

e) soft, piercing sounds expressing movement of a bird in flight

f) humorous dialogue expressing an obsessive interest in a sport

Answers: 1–c, 2–d, 3–e, 4–b, 5–f, 6–a

Explore and Develop

1 Use the study questions to focus on the chapter content. Depending on class size, you might divide the class into four groups and give each group two study questions to answer, or have students work individually to complete all the questions.

2 Discuss answers to the study questions.

3 Have students visualize and discuss how R 4 effective Charles Peale's portrait of Washington (figure 11–1) would be if done in pencil or pen and ink rather than oil paint. Ask them why Greenough chose marble for his sculpture of Washington (figure 11–2). Would the sculpture be as effective in wood or concrete?

Evaluate and Reflect

1 Can students distinguish between art medium, subject matter, and expressive intent?

2 Ask students to look at an artwork such as Bellows's *Stag at Sharkey's* (figure 8–14) or Hopper's *House by the Railroad* (figure 5–32) and discuss the relationships among medium, subject matter, and the artist's expressive intent. Ask them to consider the artist's purpose based on how the medium was used, the choice of subject matter, and the way the subject is portrayed.

Reteach

Have students identify the medium and subject matter of *American Gothic*. Ask students what they think the artist's purpose was. Have them consider the capabilities of the medium; how the medium was used; the subject matter and objects included in the painting; the way the artist portrayed the subject matter.

Introduction to Media

Study Questions
Chapter 11–Introduction to Media

1   Define *medium* (as used in this chapter).

_____

_____

2   Name three media that can be used for painting.

_____

3   Name three media that can be used for sculpture.

_____

4   What are two capacities of a medium that an artist should understand?

_____

_____

5   Give an example of how the artist's choice of medium and the subject matter can be interrelated.

_____

_____

6   How does the relationship to the environment in the painting *George Washington at the Battle of Princeton* by Charles Wilson Peale differ from that of the sculpture *George Washington* by Horatio Greenough (text figures 11–1 and 11–2).

_____

_____

7   Give an example from the chapter of how the medium selected by the artist helps to express an idea.

_____

_____

8   When analyzing a work of art, a good relationship of what three things should be looked for?

_____

_____

Test Questions
Chapter 11–Introduction to Media

1 Fill in the blank. The _____ is the material used to make an artwork.

2 Painting, a two-dimensional art, can be done with several different media. Name three.

_____

_____

_____

3 Sculpture, a three-dimensional art, can be done using several different media. Name three.

_____

_____

_____

Match the description in the left-hand column with the media in the right-hand column.

_____ **4** Landscape.

_____ **5** Describes environment.

_____ **6** Becomes part of the environment.

_____ **7** Provides tactile and visual information.

_____ **8** Information gained mainly by visual perception.

_____ **9** Appropriate for portraits.

A. Oil painting

B. Sculpture

10 Give one example from the chapter explaining how an artist interrelates the medium and the expression of ideas.

_____

_____

_____

_____

Study Answers
Chapter 11
Introduction to Media

1 The material used for making an artwork.

2 Answers may include oils, watercolor, acrylic, casein, gouache, tempera.

3 Answers may include welded steel, bronze casting, wood, stone, plaster and plastic.

4 What can be done with the material, and how far it can be taken to support the artist's purpose.

5 Answers may include oil paints—landscape; marble—larger-than-life, three-dimensional portrait.

6 The painting *describes* an environmental setting; the sculpture *becomes a part of* the setting.

7 In text figure 11–2, Greenough used marble to express his ideas about George Washington as a great, powerful, and heroic leader (massive, solid sculpture suggests strength). In text figure 11–3, Giacometti used cast bronze to express man's frailty (spindly, tall figure seems lost in space).

8 Good relationships among the medium, subject matter, and expression of ideas.

Test Answers
Chapter 11
Introduction to Media

1 medium

2 Answers may include oil color, watercolor, tempera, acrylic, casein, and gouache.

3 Answers may include welded steel, bronze casting, wood, stone, plaster, and plastic.

4 A

5 A

6 B

7 B

8 A

9 A and B

10 Possible answers: A marble sculpture can express an artist's ideas about strength and leadership; a bronze sculpture can express an artist's ideas about man's frailty.

Teacher Lesson Notes

Chapter 11
Introduction to Media

The word *medium* is the singular form of media. It has two meanings that apply to art. Medium can refer to the material used for making an artwork. It can also refer to the liquid ingredient of a paint, such as water, linseed oil or egg yolk, in which pigment is suspended. For this discussion, we are interested in the first use of the term.

The following chapters will introduce you to a variety of two- and three-dimensional art forms, and the media associated with each of them. For example, painting is a *two-dimensional* art form. The media used for painting include oil, watercolor, acrylic, and tempera. Media for sculpture, a *three-dimensional* art form, include welded and cast metal, wood, stone, plaster, and plastic. As you will see, the various media are used to make different kinds of art. They are also used for different expressive purposes.

A medium is not always a material that does just what the artist wishes. Think of the artist's work with the medium as a contest. The artist wants to use the medium for a certain purpose. The medium, however, may not have the capabilities to support the purpose. Each medium has special capabilities and limitations. The artist learns through trial and error what the material can do. The artist then uses that information to achieve his or her purpose. The more an artist knows about a medium, the greater his or her mastery of the medium will be.

The artist's choice of medium is often related to the *subject matter,* what is represented in the work. For example, carved stone would not be a very good medium for expressing the qualities of a landscape. Oil paint, on the other hand, is excellent for representing colors, tones, sky, clouds, hills, and trees in a landscape.

Both the sculptor and the painter can do portraits, however. For example, Charles Peale portrayed George Washington in an oil painting as a victorious Revolutionary War general (fig. 11–1). Horatio Greenough used marble to produce a larger-than-life sculpture of Washington that looks like a Roman emperor seated on a throne (fig. 11–2).

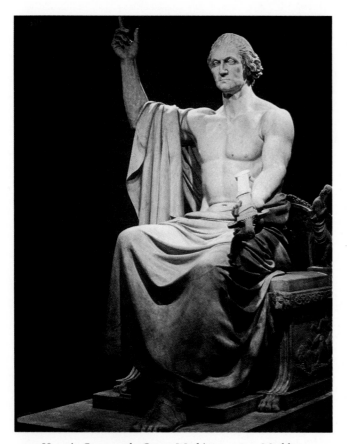

11–2 Horatio Greenough, *George Washington,* 1840. Marble, approx. 11´4˝ (347 cm) high. National Museum of American Art, Washington, DC, USA/Art Resource, NY.

11–1 This portrait of George Washington expresses the American feeling of the nationalism and confidence which sustained the country during the Revolutionary War. Charles Wilson Peale, *George Washington at the Battle of Princeton,* 1780–1781. Oil on canvas. Yale University Art Gallery (Gift of the Associated in Fine Arts and Mrs. Henry B. Loomis, in memory of Henry Bradford Loomis, B.A. 1875).

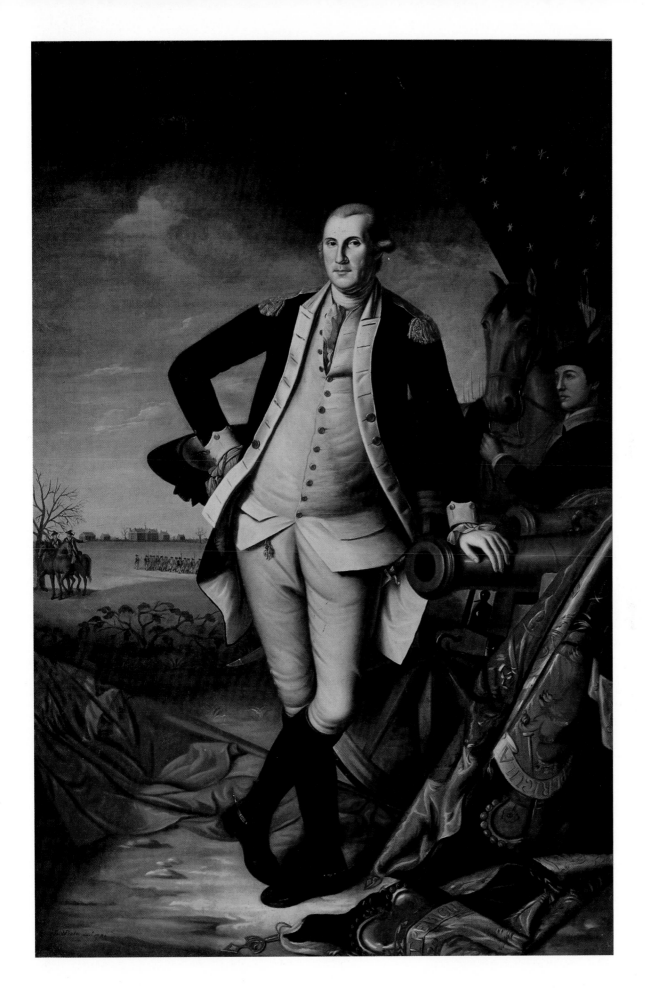

Each portrait of Washington contains its own information. Peale's painting gives the illusion of depth. The figure, cannon, and other objects look three-dimensional. An apparently confident General Washington, wearing a Continental Army uniform, leans against a cannon. Behind him are the American battle flag and his waiting horse. The banners of the defeated British troops (Hessian mercenaries) are at his feet. In the background, American soldiers take British prisoners away. The figures and objects, colors and textures are placed in an environmental setting, which contributes to the meaning of the artwork. Do you think the painting expresses the confidence of a general, or the confidence of a young republic capable of winning and defending its freedom?

In contrast to the painting, Greenough's sculpture of Washington has real depth and textures. You can both see *and* feel the rounded three-dimensional forms and the different textures. The viewer can move around the sculpture and see it from different angles to get more information. Greenough's sculpture was originally created for the Capitol rotunda in Washington, DC. However, the American public demanded that it be removed. Americans objected to seeing a former president portrayed as a partially nude Roman emperor.

The medium is also the artist's means of expressing ideas. For example, Greenough designed and carved the marble sculpture to express his ideas about George Washington as a great, powerful, and heroic leader of our country. By comparison, the form that Alberto Giacometti gave the sculpture called *Man Pointing* (fig. 11–3) would not be practical for carving in marble. Nor would stone be as effective for expressing his ideas about the human condition. Giacometti used bronze casting to produce this spindly, seven-foot-tall figure that does not appear heroic or powerful. Greenough's massive sculpture of Washington displaces space and suggests great strength. *Man Pointing* is so slender that the figure seems lost in space—perhaps even threatened by the surrounding emptiness. The bronze casting medium seems well suited to expressing ideas such as man's frailty.

More often than not, the artist already has a form or idea in mind before he or she selects a medium. Then the artist chooses the medium that will best express that idea or form. When analyzing a work of art, we look for good relationships among the medium, subject matter, and expression. In Chapters 12 and 13, you will learn about many artworks in many different media. Studying the examples and working with your own art materials will help you understand the interaction between the medium and expression of ideas.

Analysis Experience 11.1

Choosing Media

Look at Greenough's sculpture of Washington (fig. 11–2). Write down as many reasons as you can think of for making the sculpture in marble, rather than in wood, concrete or papier-mâché.

Try it Yourself

How do you think the public would react if, say, Jimmy Carter or George Bush were portrayed as a Greek god or Roman emperor? How would you react? If you don't think that kind of sculpture would be appropriate, what kind of symbolism would you suggest for a portrait of a modern president?

11–3 Alberto Giacometti, *Man Pointing*, 1947. Bronze, 70 ½″ (179 cm) high, at base 12″ x 13 ¼″ (30 x 34 cm). The Museum of Modern Art, New York. Gift of Mrs. John D. Rockefeller, III.

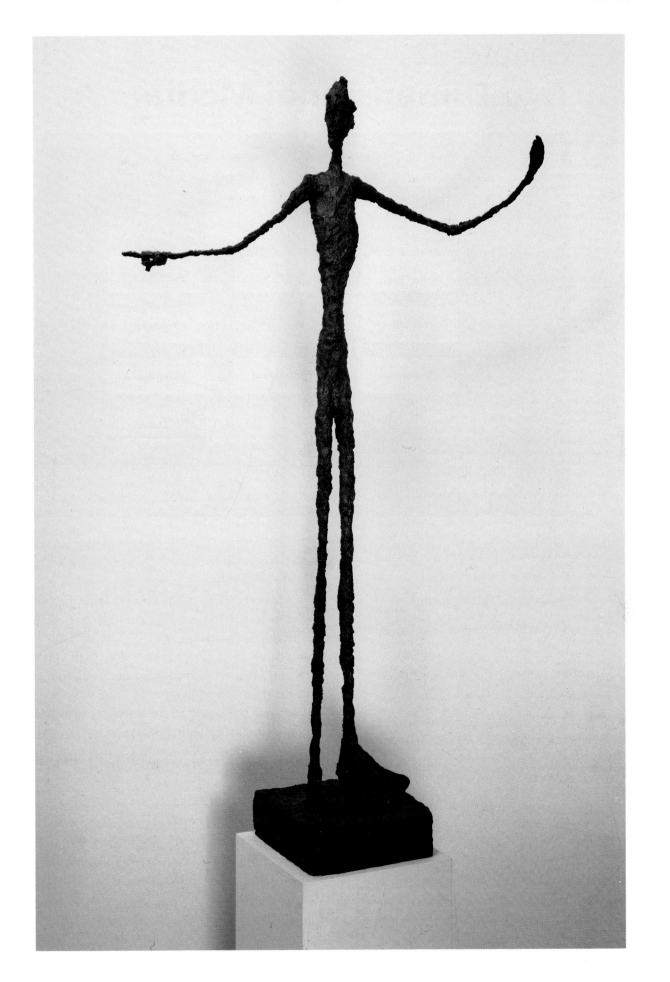

Chapter 12
Two-Dimensional Media

Student Edition
Pages 134–157

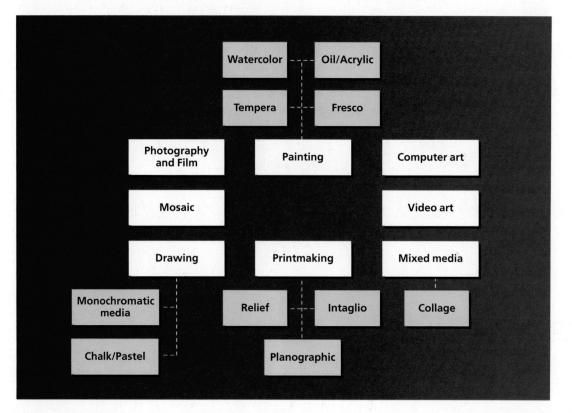

Overview

Chapter Objectives

Students should be able to:

1   list major categories of two-dimensional media   **EE 2**

2   list examples of media under each category   **EE 1, 2**

3   explain the expressive possibilities, origins, and histories of these examples   **EE 1, 2**

4   understand that the domain of two-dimensional media is extensive and complex   **EE 1, 2**

5   identify the medium of an artwork   **EE 1, 2**

6   produce two-dimensional artworks that show relationships among the medium, subject, and expressive intent   **EE 1, 2**

Rationale

Chapters 12 and 13 introduce the major categories of two- and three-dimensional media. In many ways, these chapters elaborate on the notion introduced in Chapters 1 and 2 that art media today can take almost any form. To understand art, students should be knowledgeable about the expressive characteristics of media and their advantages and disadvantages. Knowing something about the medium of a particular work is often necessary to fully describe and analyze the artwork. Chapter 12 focuses on two-dimensional media: drawing, painting, mosaic, printmaking, photography and film, video art, computer art, and mixed media.

Essential Concepts

• All painting media include pigments, vehicle (and sometimes a thinner), and a support.

• Mosaic consists of designs or pictures generally composed of tesserae, or glazed ceramic tiles.

• Prints are usually produced on paper. Several prints of one image can be made from a single plate.

• Like printmaking, photography produces identical copies (also called prints) from a single negative.

• A film camera contains exposed and unexposed reels of film. The film is fed through the camera in a rapid stop-and-go motion like that of the movie projector.

• Video, like photography and film, transforms light into images, but by electronic means rather than chemical.

• Computer art, like video, is electronic, but produces imagery by converting digital data into a pixel (a specific location on a video screen). Pixels can be manipulated to form patterns or images.

• Mixed media consists of combining two or more media. The most familiar and popular classification of mixed media in the two-dimensional realm is collage.

• Photographs, photocopies, audiotape, videotape, and so on are used to document art in which the emphasis is on an idea rather than an object.

Vocabulary

chiaroscuro	relief print	wash
mixed wash	screen print	collage
chalk	intaglio	graded wash
opaque	serigraph	

Meet the Artist

Elizabeth Catlett   Page 145

Lesson Plans

12.1   Contrasts in Chalk Drawing

Page **T 166**   Time: 2 periods

12.2   Watercolor Washes

Page **T 168**   Time: 1 period

12.3   A Tempera Painting

Page **T 170**   Time: 2 periods

12.4   A Linoleum Block Print

Page **T 172**   Time: 5 periods

12.5   A One-color Screen Print

Page **T 174**   Time: 3 periods

12.6   A Unified Collage

Page **T 176**   Time: 2 periods

Chapter Closure

Evaluation

1   *Production:* Can students successfully manipulate variations of line and value?

2   *Production:* Can students successfully manipulate the medium to create washes as well as opaque lines?

3   *Production:* Can students control figure-ground relationships and color registers in a three-color linoleum reduction block print?

4   *Production:* Can students express an idea with a paper stencil in a one-color screen process?

5   *Criticism:* Display the collages. Did students use collage materials to express a theme of their own? Can students identify themes in the work of their classmates?

6   *Criticism:* Can students identify the medium of an artwork? Can students explain how the choice of medium affected the content of that work?

7   *Aesthetic awareness:* Can students discuss the expressive possibilities and the limitations of various traditional media?

Contrasts in Chalk Drawing

Time: 2 periods

Preparation

Rationale

In this lesson, students use black and white and one or two colors of chalk to produce dramatic contrasts of dark and light value and descriptive line work. They practice with the medium to transform a line drawing into an image that looks three-dimensional.

Studio Materials

colored chalks or pastels, black and white chalks, gray paper, tissue or felt blenders, fixative

Safety note: Use fixative only if an outdoor spray area is available.

Enrichment Materials

Slides:
• Michelangelo, *Creation of the Sun and the Moon*, 95

Overhead Transparencies:
• Picasso, *Maternité*, 11

Large Reproductions:
• Olbinski, *Private Fame*, 13
• Yan, *Brushfire with Animals Fleeing*, 16
• Magritte, *The Plagiary*, 4

Teach the Lesson

Objectives

Students should be able to:

1 use one color and black and white chalk to create implied movement and depth with contrasts of value and line   EE 2

2 describe and analyze their compositions, giving attention to movement and depth implied by strong value contrasts and line   EE 4

Vocabulary

Chiaroscuro is the use of value contrasts to represent dramatic effects of light and shadow.

Chalk is a stick of color including a binder, preservative, chalk, and pigment that have been mixed with water, formed into sticks, and dried.

Warm Up

Give students pieces of gray paper and have them use white chalk to produce light values, as well as white. Students can continue to practice drawing with black, white, and colored chalks. They can make a range of shades and tints going down and up from the value of the paper, draw black and white lines over chalk-toned areas, and juxtapose strong value contrasts to suggest implied movement. Note that chalks blend easily, produce a variety of lines, and can be worked in a controlled or spontaneous manner.

Explore and Develop

1 Display the slide of Michelangelo's work and discuss how he modeled form. Note the interplay of light and shadow he used to show a twisted torso and bulging muscles. Picasso's *Maternité* (Overhead Transparency 11) demonstrates movement implied by value contrasts and line. Display and discuss artworks with chiaroscuro, such as works by Caravaggio, Rembrandt, Gentileschi and de la Tour. Discuss how light and shadow were used to show folds in drapery, and make forms look three-dimensional. Attend to how the dramatic value contrasts suggest movement and mood in the works.

Laser Discs:

Rubens, A Lion, c 1614

Search Frame 2831

Peale, Dr. John Warren, c 1806

Search Frame 2983

Prud'hon, Venus, 1810

Search Frame 2908

Prud'hon, Adonis, 1810

Search Frame 2910

Rubens, Pan Reclining, c 1600/1640

Search Frame 2835

Boucher, Tete-a-tete, 1764

Search Frame 2888

Begin Studio Experience 12.1

1 Hang a jacket, sweater, or shirt on a chair back or wall hook and focus light on it to produce strong lights and darks. Study how light "strokes" curving surfaces, gradually progressing from high light values to low dark values and black in the folds. Have students point out some dramatic contrasts of dark and light that give life to the object.

2 Discuss where they might use the gray of their paper to represent middle or low light values; where straight white or black could be used; where they might apply some descriptive line.

3 Advise including any shadow on the wall to help anchor the jacket shape to the page.

4 Have students do a sketch with light white lines on the gray paper to determine how the space will be filled. Suggest that students use chalks to produce bold broad strokes as well as sharp lines and perhaps some hatching.

5 Tell students to use low dark values for the concave folds and shadows caused by overlap.

White can be used for highlights and accent lines. Have students shade and tint the colored chalk to describe tonal effects in between light and dark areas.

6 Encourage students to step about 6 feet back from their drawing once in a while to see if there are enough value contrasts, especially the dark ones. Are they getting a full range of values?

Evaluate and Reflect

1 Are students satisfied with the range of values they included in their drawings? Where are strong contrasts? Are there soft contrasts? Is there a dominant value or tone?

2 Do they feel the value contrasts are descriptive of those that occurred in the jacket?

3 Have them explain how they used line descriptively. What kinds of line did they use? Do lines and edges direct the viewer's attention?

4 Can students analyze the relationships of values, lines, tints, and shades of color in their drawings? What gives the composition a feeling of unity? Are there similarities of shapes, values, color, lines, or edges?

Reteach

Have students work with black and white only. Provide a simple object to draw, and emphasize using a range of values across the surface of the object to make it look three-dimensional.

Extend the Lesson

Beyond the Basics

Have students try the same approach on white paper, using the paper to represent the lightest values. Have them provide accents and strong contrasts with dark values. Suggest that students use a different medium such as ebony pencils.　　EE 2

Cultural Connections

If possible find articles of clothing from different cultures for students to draw. Borrowing from a theatrical costume department or thrift shop purchases may provide interesting selections. Suggest students produce a series of drawings showing the clothing worn in a variety of cultures or over a period of time.　　EE 2, 3

Connecting with Other Subjects

Social Studies Käthe Kollwitz lived from 1867–1945 in Germany. Her artwork showed the suffering and devastation that resulted from war and poverty. Have students research her life, work and events happening in Germany during her lifetime. Have them look for as many works by Kollwitz as they can find. Arrange the works chronologically. Using history books have students compare events in Germany with the artwork created by Kollwitz.　　R 3, 5

Watercolor Washes

Time: 1 period

Preparation

Rationale

The four exercises in this lesson will help students develop skills with watercolor. Experience with the procedures should provide students with some basic concepts that will be useful in responding to and analyzing watercolor paintings.

Studio Materials

box watercolors, #7 and #12 pointed hair brushes, 9" x 12" heavy white paper, water containers, paper towels, drawing boards

Enrichment Materials

Large Reproductions:
• Yan, *Brushfire with Animals Fleeing,* 16

Teach the Lesson

Objectives

Students should be able to:

1 create watercolor washes that are flat, graded, and mixed   **EE 2, 3**

2 cover a wash with opaque lines   **EE 2**

Vocabulary

Wash is a thin, transparent layer of paint, or a thinned mixture of paint and the solvent that carries pigments in suspension in a paint.

Flat wash is an area of thin paint that is uniform throughout when dry.

Graded wash is an area of thin paint that is graded from dark to light, or light to dark.

Mixed or *mingled wash* is an area onto which washes of different colors are dropped from a brush and allowed to flow together.

Warm Up

Direct attention to Student Edition pages 137–138 and the three stages of a watercolor painting by Dong Kingman. Note the overlapping washes used in parts of the painting. Can the students define *watercolor wash*? Show examples of other watercolor paintings.

Explore and Develop

1 Demonstrate mixing a wash in the lid of a watercolor box. Have the students do the same.

Begin Studio Experience 12.2

1 To make a flat wash, have students divide a 9" x 12" sheet of paper in half with a light pencil line. Have students brush clear water over one half of the paper and blot it to leave it damp. Students should lay the paper on a board and tilt the surface just enough so that the wash will flow but not run down the paper.

2 Have students load a #12 brush with the wash, shake out excess liquid on a towel, and stroke a band of wash from one side to the other across the top of the rectangle. Remind students to keep the area wet.

3 Students should reload, shake out excess liquid, set the tip of the brush just over the bottom edge of the first wash, and stroke across the rectangle again. This picks up excess paint puddled along the bottom of the first band as the second band of wash is laid in.

4 Have students continue this process rapidly down the page while the paper is damp to avoid lines. After the last band of wash, students should dry the brush and use it to pick up excess paint along the bottom edge. Ask them to try it on their own on the other half of the paper.

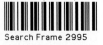

5 Next have students make graded washes. Graded washes run from light to dark, dark to light, or alternate. Have students mix four puddles of a color wash, making them progressively darker. Have students again dampen half of a 9" x 12" paper and lay in a band of the lightest wash.

6 Students should load with the next darkest wash, place the tip of the brush just over the bottom edge of the first wash, and lay the second band in, continuing until all grades are laid in. Repeat on the other half of the page.

7 Mixed washes can include a variety of hues, values, and intensities. Ask students to wet the paper and blot it, then use a wet brush to pick up a load of color and drop the color onto the paper.

8 Have students repeat with a second color and let them flow into one another. Tell students to vary the intensity of the color with more or less water. Some paper whites may be saved within the wash area.

9 To lay opaque lines and colors over areas of wash, have students try using a #7 brush to make lines of varying width and intensity over one of the wash experiments.

10 Encourage students to try some wash lines over the existing wash to see the effects. Some overlays result in muddy colors. Others produce desirable effects.

Evaluate and Reflect

1 Can students explain some expressive purposes the different washes can be used for?

2 Did students produce flat, graded, and mixed washes?

3 Do students feel confident that they can produce transparencies and opacities with the medium?

4 Display a watercolor. Ask students to describe the different washes and opacities.

Reteach

Have students who are not satisfied with their washes repeat the series of exercises. Explain that this medium requires practice.

Extend the Lesson
Beyond the Basics

Have students use at least two kinds of washes in a watercolor painting. Have them include varying intensities of color, including some opacities. **EE 2**

After students have completed the exercises in this lesson, suggest they browse through books of watercolor paintings to find examples where these techniques have been used. Suggest they select an artist whose work appeals to them and study the works carefully to determine: what they like about the work, what color relationships have been used, how is the work organized, and what mood or feeling has the artist created. Have students produce a watercolor painting in a similar style. **EE 2, 4** **W 1**

Cultural Connections

When looking through art history books one usually finds oil paintings. Prior to the mid-19th century watercolor was used primarily for preliminary work or sketches. Although Andrew Wyeth's watercolor paintings are appreciated as finished works, most of them were studies for tempera paintings. Winslow Homer was one of the first artists to use watercolor in finished works. Suggest students look for examples of watercolor from different cultures. **EE 3**

Connecting with Other Subjects

Science Suggest interested students research the chemical compositions of the various pigments used in paint. In addition to how the paint appears and handles, artists are concerned about permanence, drying time, and toxicity. Many traditional pigments have been replaced with synthetic products because of toxicity or expense. Originally they were made from many different materials such as earth, plant leaves, semi-precious stones, lead, sulfates, zinc and even the urine of cows which had been fed mango leaves. **R 5**

A Tempera Painting

Time: 3 periods

Preparation

Rationale

Students are asked to produce a tempera painting based on an artwork that portrays a situation for which they can imagine an outcome. Students paint what they imagine will happen next in the original painting. Emphasis is placed on experimenting with the medium to produce expressive effects that communicate the subject and idea.

Studio Materials

tempera paint, hair and bristle brushes, heavy white paper, pencils, mixing trays, water containers, paper towels

Enrichment Materials

Slides:
• Munch, *The Scream*, 29

Large Reproductions:
• Yan, *Brushfire with Animals Fleeing*, 16
• Biggers, *Shotguns*, 3
• Smith, *Snake Path*, 1
• *Nubian Wall Painting*, 5
• Swentzell, *The Emergence of the Clowns*, 22

Laser Discs:

West, Battle of La Hogue, 1778

Search Frame 1730

West, detail

Search Frame 1732

Bellows, Club Night, 1907

Search Frame 2058

Raphael, Saint George and the Dragon, 1504/1506

Search Frame 204

Raphael, detail

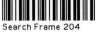

Search Frame 206

Homer, Hound and Hunter, 1892

Search Frame 2036

Teach the Lesson

Objectives

Students should be able to:

1   describe and analyze a painting that portrays a situation, and create a painting that shows what might happen next   EE 2, 4

2   use the medium to produce expressive effects similar to those of the original painting   EE 2

Vocabulary

Opaque paint is not transparent; it does not let light pass through.

Warm Up

Ask students if they have ever missed the end of an exciting TV program or begun a good magazine story only to find it is continued in the next issue. Have they ever wished they could give a movie a different ending? Have students briefly describe these situations. Explain that they are going to have the opportunity to create their own ending to a story or situation.

Explore and Develop

1   Introduce artworks that tell stories, such as those listed under Enrichment Materials. Have students brainstorm outcomes or endings for the situation shown in one or two paintings.

2   Discuss how artists use color, lines, and shapes to create moods such as excitement, danger, calmness, and loneliness. How did the artists use design principles of movement, dominance, directional lines, and shapes to convey an idea and to tell what is happening?

Begin Studio Experience 12.3

W 4 **1** Have students select a painting. Several students may share the same work. Have them prepare short written descriptions and analyses. Students should include subject matter, line, shape, color, and space in their descriptions. Have students look for relationships between the medium and subject. Are there opaque and transparent colors, different kinds of brush work, contrasting or related colors?

2 Have students lightly sketch their idea for an outcome to the situation in their chosen painting.

3 Suggest that students begin with light colors, then the medium, and finally the darker colors to build up forms and areas in the painting. Demonstrate how to make washes, stippling, and textured brush strokes with hair and bristle brushes. A piece of sponge can provide texture.

4 Depending on effects needed, students can work wet in wet or let one color dry before placing another over it. Mixed colors can be held for the next period if trays are covered with plastic.

Evaluate and Reflect

1 Can students describe and analyze paintings?

2 Ask students to discuss how they used the medium and elements to communicate their ideas about the subject.

3 Can students explain similarities and differences between their use of the medium and the way the artist used the medium?

Reteach

Review the guidelines in Chapters 3 and 9 to help students describe and analyze paintings. If they had difficulty with tempera, they might try another color medium such as oil crayon or chalks.

Extend the Lesson
Beyond the Basics

Students might use the same subject and idea in an abstract or nonobjective painting and explore the way in which art elements are used to relate to the subject or the work. EE 2

Tempera paint purchased for use in schools is not the same as the tempera used by artists today and in the past. Have students research traditional tempera paint, how it is made and techniques for its use. Suggest students purchase artist-grade dry pigments and make "real" tempera to use in their paintings. Suggest using a traditional support for the painting also. R 3

Cultural Connections

Have students look for examples of artworks that tell stories about ancient myths and legends from several different cultures. Have them describe and analyze the works. Many of the myths and legends were created to explain natural phenomena. Suggest students select a phenomena they find interesting and make up a story to explain how and why it happens. Then have them produce a tempera painting illustrating their story. EE 2, 3

W 1

Connecting with Other Subjects

Language Arts Compile a list of words and write each word on a slip of paper, enough for each student to have several words. Put them in a container and have each student take several. Have students invent or modify type styles that look like the objects or actions indicated by the words. Have students brainstorm ideas. Ask them to think about what "sleeping" letters might look like, or melting, exploding, climbing, eating, and dancing. How would words like tower, zebra, spider, bridge, or electricity look? Books and catalogs of existing type styles might be helpful. EE 2

A Linoleum Block Print

Time: 5 periods

Preparation

Rationale

The woodcut was used by Albrecht Dürer as a major medium. Relief printing methods continue to be used as art media today. Elizabeth Catlett and Pablo Picasso have used linoleum to produce single and multiple color reiief prints. This experience acquaints students with the lino cut process using three colors.

Studio Materials

linoleum mounted on upsom board, cutting tools, registry frames, water-based inks, brayers, inking plates, print paper, carbon paper, bench hooks, electric irons

Enrichment Materials

Large Reproductions:
• Catlett, *Sharecropper,* 12

Teach the Lesson

Objectives

Students should be able to:

1   produce a three-color print using the linoleum reduction block procedure   **EE 2**

2   analyze the composition of the print   **EE 4**

Vocabulary

Relief print is a print in which the image on the plate is in relief; the raised surfaces print.

Intaglio is the reverse of relief printing. The image to be printed is engraved, scratched, or etched into a surface.

Warm Up

Demonstrate the reduction block process with a small square of heavy cardboard on which you have rubber cemented 3 pieces of tablet backing. Trace around the square on a piece of paper. Mark which is the top

edge of the plate on the back. Select one light, one medium, and one dark color. Place a small amount of the light color on the inking plate, roll it out, and apply to the shapes on the cardboard plate. Place the plate, inked side down, inside the square drawn on the sheet of paper. Turn the plate and paper over and rub the back side of the paper. Remove the plate and pull the shape off the block that is to remain the lightest color in the print. Continue the procedure for the two remaining colors.

Explore and Develop

1   Have students outline their piece of linoleum several times and plan their composition. Let students use felt-tip markers to indicate where the colors will go. Have them prepare their linoleum pieces by gluing them to a backing material. Tell them to put their names on the backside and stack and weight the blocks while glue dries.

Begin Studio Experience 12.4

1   Depending on the time available, you may want students to plan either a one- or three-color composition. As another option, have students trace the composition on tracing paper to allow them to reverse the drawing when transferring it to the linoleum. Otherwise, the image will be reversed when printed.

2   Have students transfer their drawing to the linoleum by laying carbon paper on the block, then the traced drawing (drawing-side down). Have students remove the carbon paper and use a ball-point pen to *firmly* outline the drawing on the block.

3   If paper color is being incorporated, have students use the fine V-gouge to outline the area to remain paper color and use the large U-gouge to remove that area.

Safety Precaution: Demonstrate use of the gouges. Advise directing the cutters away from the hand and using a bench

Laser Discs:

Gaughin, The Universe is Created, c 1894

Search Frame 3239

Munch, Two Women on the Shore, 1910s

Search Frame 3339

Picasso, Woman's Head, 1906

Search Frame 3260

Nolde, Fischdampfer, 1910

Search Frame 3143

Wechtlin, The Skull, c 1512

Search Frame 3131

hook to hold the block. Using a warm iron will soften the linoleum and make cutting easier.

4 Have students make a registry frame by nailing two strips of material the same thickness as the lino block with backing. The strips can be 1 inch wide and must make a right angle equal to the length and width of the block. Students should glue and tack tabs of cardboard to the outsides of the right angle.

5 Have students cut all the paper needed to print an edition, plus a couple of extras. If the block is 5" x 7" and the registry strips are 1 inch wide, the paper should be 7" x 9".

6 Have students ink the block with the lightest color to be printed and place it in the registry frame ink side up. Tell students to print the whole edition with the first color. Have students write their names on a registry frame and keep using it.

7 Have students clean and dry the block. Students should cut the area(s) that represent the lightest color out of the block, outlining first with the fine V-gouge, then scooping out with the large U-gouge. Make sure students keep referring to the color plan in the drawing to avoid cutting out the wrong areas.

8 Tell students to print the second color over the first one; the second color should be darker. Remind them to always use the same registry frame and place the block in the same position every time. Students should continue to reduce the block and print succeeding colors. Because the block is eventually destroyed, be sure students print enough copies the first time. They should allow colors to dry before printing another over them.

Evaluate and Reflect

1 Ask students to evaluate the accuracy of their registry for each color.

2 Were students able to follow their plan?

3 Is the image printed with flat colors and not over- or under-inked?

4 Can students analyze the prints? Is the composition unified? Does it have variety and rhythm? Is there a relationship between the subject and the art elements?

Reteach

Have students answer the study questions directed to printmaking. Ask them to read the text sections on printmaking and describe the differences between the procedures.

Extend the Lesson

Beyond the Basics

If students did a one-color print this time, have them try the reduction process at a later date.   EE 2

Cultural Connections

Have students research the influence of Japanese printmakers on the European Impressionists. How did they come to know about the Japanese prints? What did they admire about the work that influenced their own work? Have students study Japanese prints and the paintings of the European Impressionists. What characteristics found in the Impressionist paintings may have resulted from the influence of Japanese printmakers?   R 5

Connecting with Other Subjects

Previously students learned about Jacob Lawrence's paintings that depicted the poverty and despair of the black people. Elizabeth Catlett was dedicated to the civil rights movement both in her life and work. Have students examine the people in both artists' works. They are different people presented from different points of view; however, the content of the messages, regarding this important social issue, is very similar. Lawrence's paintings and Catlett's prints both speak out against things that are wrong.   EE 3

Two-Dimensional Media

A One-color Screen Print

Time: 3 periods

Preparation

Rationale

Screen printing is probably the most versatile printing process used today. Screen printing inks provide unparalleled color and texture versatility. The image does not reverse, it does not involve transfer by extreme pressure as other processes do, and it can be applied to almost any surface—paper, fabric, wood, metal, glass, plastic, and of course T-shirts, wallpaper, and bumper stickers. Students are surrounded by screen-printed images. This lesson introduces them to some of the basic skills involved in the process.

Studio Materials

wooden frames (may be hinged to baseboards), polyester screen fabric, squeegees, stencil paper, one-inch masking tape, water-based screen inks, X-acto knives, cutting boards, gun stapler, paper

Enrichment Materials

Large Reproductions:
• Chan, *Wild Thing*, 19

Teach the Lesson

Objectives

Students should be able to:

1   design and print a stencil for a one-color screen print   EE 2

2   arrange positive and negative shapes in the stencil to create an image that expresses an idea   EE 1, 2

Vocabulary

Screen print is a technique of printmaking in which stencils are used on porous fabrics such as nylon and polyester. Ink is forced over the screen and passes through the openings in the stencil. The process was originally referred to as silk screen because silk was the first fabric used.

Serigraphy refers to the screen printing process when done by an artist, rather than commercially. It means "drawing on silk."

Warm Up

Display some popular examples of screen printing, such as T-shirts, jerseys, or helmets. Call attention to any screen-printed shirts students are wearing. See figure 14–7 for a T-shirt logo. Show examples by Warhol and Vasarely.

Explore and Develop

1   Demonstrate how to build a frame and cut and stretch the fabric over the grooved frame surface.

2   Show how to use wide masking tape to seal the frame and interior edges where the frame and fabric meet. If a permanent seal is desired, use water tape rather than masking, and seal it with two coats of shellac or urethane varnish.

3   To help students grasp the screen process quickly, have them make a few openings in a piece of lightweight drawing paper cut about half an inch smaller on all margins than the screen opening. No cuts should be made closer than one-half inch of the paper margin. Students should put print paper in place, tack the stencil to the bottom of the screen with two small pieces of masking tape, and pull ink across the screen. The paper stencil will be held to the screen by the ink.

Begin Studio Experience 12.5

1   Have students plan an image on a piece of paper a bit smaller than the screen opening. Advise them to stay at least half an inch away from the edges of the paper. Remind students that what they see in the drawing is what they will get in the print.

Laser Discs:

Rauschenberg, For Dante's 700th Birthday, 1965

Search Frame 3029

Rauschenberg, Booster, 1967

Search Frame 3320

Rauschenberg, Hoarfrost Editions: Preview, 1974

Search Frame 3326

2 Have students tape the drawing to a cutting surface and cut out the positive areas with an X-acto knife. **Tell students to use X-acto knives with extreme caution.**

3 Tell students to tack the stencil to the underside of the screen with masking tape. Loose inside pieces can be held in place with a little rubber cement.

4 Students should attach the screen to the baseboard hinges, put pre-cut printing paper in place, and lower the screen. When they are satisfied with the position of the image on the print paper, have them use masking tape to make registry tabs on the baseboard along three edges of the paper.

5 With the screen lowered on a piece of print paper, have students hold the squeegee about 15 to 20 degrees off vertical and pull the ink across the stencil to the bottom of the screen. Students should remove the print and put another sheet of paper in place, using the registry tabs for position. Have them add ink as necessary and keep printing.

Evaluate and Reflect

1 Were students able to print clear images without ink bleeding under the stencil?

2 Does the printed image dominate the space on the paper or are more shapes needed?

3 Were they able to control the positive and negative shapes in the stencil so that the subject or idea is clearly communicated?

4 Have students discuss the print stroke process.

5 Ask students how they could introduce a second color into the screen print.

Reteach

Have students practice with simple pre-cut paper stencils until they achieve a clear print without bleeds. They may also be given a source book such as *Screen Printing: Contemporary Methods and Materials* by Frances and Norman Lassiter.

Extend the Lesson
Beyond the Basics

Have students explore ways of introducing several colors into a stencil screen. They might explore block outs, cutting more than one stencil for different colors in an image. Assign students to research other screen print procedures that could be used in the classroom: hand cut, block out, tusche resist, and photographic.

Throughout history and across cultures artists have used their work to speak out either for or against things they feel strongly about. Kollwitz, Catlett, Lawrence, Kirchner, and Dürer all had something important to say. The visual images they produced spoke eloquently about many different issues. Students often make arbitrary decisions when selecting subject matter for their artwork. Suggest they use their artwork to "speak" about things they think are important. Suggest brainstorming a list of issues and discuss how they might incorporate the ideas into this lesson.

EE 2

Cultural Connections

EE 3

Prior to the invention of the camera, artists' renderings of foreign lands were printed in books, newspapers and journals. Although many artists represented what they saw accurately, often an artist's stylized interpretation, distortions resulting from lack of skill, or the artist working from descriptions rather than observation caused the viewers to develop many misconceptions about other people and places. Photography changed the way we view the world. Suggest interested students look for examples of these early works, such as Albrecht Dürer's *Rhinoceros*. Had Dürer actually seen a rhinoceros? Or was he working from an eyewitness account or the work of another artist? Compare these early images of various cultures and places with modern photographic essays. Suggest that our view of the world still may not be accurate since we are seeing what the photographer chooses to show us. Discuss.

Two-Dimensional Media

A Unified Collage

Time: 2 periods

Preparation

Rationale

Artists associated with Dadaism and Cubism utilized real materials in collages as a means of objecting to social situations and to formality in art. Picasso and Braque were concerned with textures and associative content that might be obtained from ready-made materials. This lesson gives students experience in using real materials for their associative content.

Studio Materials

heavy paper or poster board, white glue, scissors, drawing and painting media, various papers, magazines, photos, fabrics, package parts

Enrichment Materials

Overhead Transparencies:
• Picasso, *Still Life with Chair Caning,* 13

Large Reproductions:
• Tamayo, *Dos Hermanos,* 20
• Chan, *Wild Thing,* 19

Teach the Lesson

Objectives

Students should be able to:

1   create a collage using a combination of found and drawn or painted elements   EE 1, 2

2   use found materials for their associative content to help express an idea   EE 1

Vocabulary

Collage is a composition with various materials such as paper, fabric, yarn, oil cloth, wallpaper, and leaves glued on a flat surface.

Laser Discs:

Matisse, Beasts of Sea, 1950

Search Frame 2203

Hamilton, Fashion Plate, 1969

Search Frame 3287

Gris, Fantomas, 1915

Search Frame 2257

Lipchitz, Bas Relief I, 1918

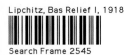

Search Frame 2545

Picasso, Guitar, c 1926

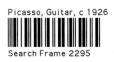

Search Frame 2295

Warm Up

1   Display examples of collages. Explain that some artists added real materials to their paintings for various reasons. Picasso and Braque did so in their search for a new kind of pictorial reality. The use of actual materials provided rich surface textures and reality that did not depend on realistic subject matter. Ernst and Schwitters used materials from trash cans in their collages to object to the formality of realistic art and for social commentary.

2   Ask students to brainstorm ideas they could build a collage around, such as life in America, school life, the seasons, a creature's environment, a time and place, a polluted environment, a plastic society, beauty aids, physical fitness.

Explore and Develop

1   Explain that the collage may be non-representational or contain recognizable images. In either case, students should use drawing or painting media to reinforce the subject and idea and help with unity of the composition.

2   Materials should be selected for their associative qualities. They should prompt viewers to connect ideas or think of things the materials remind them of. The materials help to form connections with the idea the work expresses.

3   Materials should also increase the visual and tactile sensations of the collage. Encourage students to think about how the materials can be organized in a unified composition that expresses an idea.

Begin Studio Experience 12.6

1 Areas of the support surface can be painted or covered with something before students attach other materials. Students can use symbols and images from magazines and photographs; they can also alter these images. Students may draw or paint creatures, objects, and things on various materials to be cut out and placed in the collage.

2 Have students arrange found objects and anything they drew. When they are satisfied with the composition, they should glue everything in place. Drawing and painting may be used to unite the materials and strengthen the communicative qualities of the collage.

Evaluate and Reflect

R 1 **1** Ask students to describe the idea of their collage in a few words. Write the words on the chalkboard and display the collages. Ask students to match the words with the collages.

2 Have students explain how the found materials in their collages are associated with the idea they wished to express.

3 Have students discuss what they did to interrelate the found materials and drawing or painting.

Reteach

Have students read the chapter and answer study questions. Use a cooperative group approach to review the questions. Demonstrate how to make a collage to help students understand the concepts and skills involved.

Extend the Lesson
Beyond the Basics

Assign individuals to report on the different kinds of collages created by the Cubists, Picasso and Braque. Have others report on forms of collage created by Dada artist Kurt Schwitters and contemporary artists like Richard Hamilton, Andy Warhol or Romare Bearden. **EE 3** **R 3, 5** **W 2, 4**

Many individuals save mementos from special occasions, important events, vacations, and relationships. Often they are stored in a box on a shelf and viewed only on rare occasions. Suggest students create a collage that tells a story about themselves or an important event in their lives. Have students photocopy things they may not want to actually glue down in their collage, such as family photos or valuable keepsakes. **EE 1, 2**

Cultural Connections

Pop Art originated in England during the fifties and became important in the United States and Japan during the sixties. Have students examine the work of Pop artists in all three countries. Since Pop Art reflects the popular culture much can be learned by studying these works. English artist Richard Hamilton's collage, *Just What is it that Makes Today's Homes so Different, so Appealing?*, would be a good place to start. **EE 3**

Connecting with Other Subjects

Any subject Assign groups of students to collaborate with teachers from the various disciplines within the school to create artwork that could be used in course description catalogs or yearbooks. Have students research the assigned subject and then create a collage of images that visually explain what the course of study involves. Students will probably want to create images that photocopy well since most schools do not use color printing in their publications. **EE 2**

Two-Dimensional Media

Study Questions
Chapter 12–Two-Dimensional Media

1 Why does it help to know the capabilities and limitations of a medium when creating an artwork?

_____

_____

2 Name three two-dimensional media.

_____

3 Name five tools that can be used to make monochromatic drawings.

_____

4 Name two ways by which values are controlled in pencil drawing.

_____

5 Name two ways of achieving different values with ink.

_____

6 What are sticks of colored chalk made of?

_____

7 When were pastels introduced, and by whom were they used?

_____

8 Name two ways of preserving a pastel drawing.

_____

9 What are three things that all painting media have in common?

_____

10 When and where was the use of watercolor first promoted as an art medium in its own right?

_____

11 What are the three stages of developing a composition that watercolorist Dong Kingman uses?

_____

_____

12 State two ways in which watercolor differs from tempera.

_____

13 In the history of art, when did the use of tempera reach its peak?

_____

14 Give two characteristics of tempera.

_____

15 Name a contemporary American artist who uses tempera.

_____

16 When and how was oil paint first used?

_____

_____

17 When did canvas replace wood as a principal painting surface? What is the major advantage of painting on canvas?

_____

_____

18 Give two characteristics of oil paint.

_____

19 What is acrylic made of?

_____

20 Give two examples of acrylic's versatility.

_____

_____

21 Explain the process of creating a fresco.

_____

_____

22 Define _mosaic._

_____

23 What effect is characteristic of an Early Christian mosaic? Why?

_____

24 How is a print different from a drawing?

_____

_____

25 How is a relief print prepared?

_____

_____

26 How does the intaglio process differ from the relief process?

_____

27 Describe two kinds of intaglio processes.

_____

_____

28 What simple principle is lithography based on?

_____

29 How does Käthe Kollwitz's lithograph _Death Seizing a Woman_ resemble her charcoal drawing _Self-Portrait with a Pencil?_

_____

30 What method is serigraphy (screen printing) based on?

_____

31 Define the following photography terms: Negative, Focal length and Zoom lens.

_____

32 How do you feel when looking at Ansel Adam's black and white photograph, _HalfDome, Merced River, Winter Yosemite Valley?_

_____

33 Why is editing considered a very creative part of filmmaking?

_____

34 Define _collage._

_____

35 Who invented the collage and when was it invented?

_____

36 What is conceptual art?

_____

37 What is the purpose of documenting a "temporary" artwork?

_____

Test Questions
Chapter 12–Two-Dimensional Media

Circle the correct answers.

1 T   F   Hunter-artists drew on the walls of caves in prehistoric times, possibly with crude forms of colored chalks and charcoal.

2 T   F   Pastels are quite durable and do not need any special treatment.

3 T   F   *Drypoint* refers to scratching lines directly into the bare copper plate.

4 T   F   Canvas is the most common support for oil and acrylic paintings.

5 T   F   *Pulling a print* refers to turning the handle on an intaglio press.

6 T   F   It is recommended to apply oil paints directly to raw canvas.

7 India ink taken directly from the bottle is

a. semi-transparent.
b. translucent.
c. transparent.
d. opaque.

8 Early Christians pieced together thousands of small bits of tesserae and set them in cement, creating designs on walls, ceilings, and floors called

a. frescoes.
b. mosaics.
c. papyrus.
d. seccoes.

9 A collage

a. is a two-dimensional artwork.
b. was invented by Picasso and Braque.
c. can be viewed from all sides.
d. can include many materials.
e. a and b.
f. a, b and d.

10 When drawing with a pencil, the darkness can be controlled by

a. the direction of the pencil strokes.
b. the amount of pressure applied by the artist.
c. using different pencils with varying amounts of graphite.
d. a, b and c.
e. b and c.

Use the following list to answer questions 11 through 22 about various painting media.

1. Oil paint   4. Watercolor
2. Acrylic   5. Tempera
3. Fresco

11 _____ Used primarily to add color to drawings until potential was developed by English artists for landscape painting in the 1800s.

12 _____ Synthetic medium, pigments are mixed with polymer, water-soluble.

13 _____ Andrew Wyeth, a contemporary artist, finds that the characteristics of this medium work well for fine detail.

14 _____ Pigments are mixed with linseed oil.

15 _____ A transparent color medium which is used for washes as well as fine detail.

16 _____ Consists of pigment and an emulsion such as eggyolk, casein, or gum arabic.

17 _____ Dries slowly, colors blend easily, can be opaque or translucent.

18 _____ Pigments that have been mixed in water and applied onto an area of wet plaster.

19 _____ Pigments are bound in gum arabic, available in small tubes or in small cakes.

20 _____ Helen Frankenthaler uses this medium in a process on canvas known as staining.

21 _____ First used as colored glazes to give a tempera underpainting more luster.

22 _____ Used by fourteenth, fifteenth, and sixteenth century muralists.

Use the following list to answer questions 23 through 30 about printmaking processes.

1. Relief   3. Lithograph
2. Intaglio   4. Serigraph (screen print)

23 _____ Prints what is below the surface of the plate

24 _____ Resembles a drawing made with crayon or charcoal

25 _____ Prints the raised areas

26 _____ Etching

27 _____ Based on the principle that oil and water don't mix

28 _____ Stencil method

29 _____ Engraving

30 _____ Woodcut

Match the following photography and film terms with the most appropriate definition.

31 _____ Moviola

32 _____ Negative

33 _____ Film speed

34 _____ Zoom lens

35 _____ Movie

36 _____ Developing

37 _____ Focal length

38 _____ Editing

a. Cutting and splicing segments of film

b. Process involving immersing the film in special chemicals

c. Distance between lens and plane of film in the back of the camera

d. Machine that runs film at various speeds

e. Semi-transparent image in which lights and darks are reversed

f. Relative sensitivity to light

g. Still pictures on a long strip of film moving in succession and projected on a screen

h. Lens with changeable focal length

39 Name one way that ink washes and watercolor are similar.

_____

40 State one similarity of, and one difference between, a drawing and a print.

_____

_____

41 What is not considered a necessary part of conceptual art?

_____

42 State two methods of documenting a temporary artwork. Do you feel documenting classifies a temporary artwork as a two-dimensional artwork? Why or why not?

_____

_____

_____

43 While looking at overhead transparencies of these works, answer these questions: _The Eye of Silence_ by Max Ernst and _The Persistence of Memory_ by Salvador Dali are both oil paintings. How have the two artists used the same medium to create different effects? Describe each artist's use of the medium.

_____

_____

_____

Use this list to answer questions 44 through 50.

        1. Drawing using charcoal and colored chalk
        2. Oil painting which shows very little blending of colors
        3. Blended colors of a pastel drawing
        4. Mixed media
        5. Photograph with strong value contrast
        6. Serigraph (screen print)
        7. Fresco

44 _____ (View overhead transparency, *The School of Athens*)

45 _____ (View overhead transparency, *Still Life with Chair Caning*)

46 _____ (View overhead transparency, *Sky Above Clouds IV*)

47 _____ (View overhead transparency, *Half Dome, Merced River, Winter Yosemite Valley*)

48 _____ (View overhead transparency, *Edetta*)

49 _____ (View overhead transparency, *Maternité*)

50 _____ (View overhead transparency, *Sketch of the Model Posing*)

Study Answers
Chapter 12
Two-Dimensional Media

1 So an artist has some idea of what can and cannot be achieved with the medium.

2 Answers may include drawing, painting, mosaic, printmaking, photography, film, video art, computer art, mixed media.

3 Charcoal, pen and ink, pencil, crayon, felt marker.

4 By pressure and by the proportion of graphite in the pencil.

5 Hatching and ink washes.

6 Precipitated chalk, pigment, and powdered gum.

7 In the 1700s; used mostly by portrait painters.

8 By spraying with a fixative or framing under glass.

9 Pigments, vehicle, and support.

10 Early 1800s in England.

11 First, laying in the lighter washes; then adding and overlapping more light washes; and lastly applying darker washes, bright colors, and opaque strokes.

12 Answers may include: Watercolors are thin and transparent; tempera is creamy and opaque; when using watercolors, an area is lightened by adding more water; when using tempera, white is added to lighten.

13 Late Middle Ages (between 1100 and 1500).

14 Answers may include: Opaque; can be painted over; dries rapidly; colors change while drying.

15 Andrew Wyeth.

16 In the 1400s: first used for colored glazes—thin films of transparent varnish—brushed over tempera paintings to give them a luster.

17 Mid-sixteenth century. It is very lightweight compared to wood.

18 Flexible—can be transparent or translucent, thick or thin; dries slowly—allows artist to blend colors and create a wide variety of effects.

19 Pigments and liquid polymer.

20 Answers may include: It can imitate effects of watercolor and oil. When thinned with water, it acts like watercolor; when extended with liquid polymer, its colors can be used as glazes. Modeling paste or gel medium can be added to make glazes. Modeling paste or gel medium can be added to make it thicker. It is fast-drying, which can be slowed down by adding retarders. It is water soluble; tools and brushes can be cleaned with water rather than turpentine. It can be applied directly to canvas without causing the canvas to rot.

21 Pigments are mixed in water, an area of a wall or ceiling is spread with wet plaster, colors are applied to the plaster before it dries.

22 A design or picture composed of many pieces of stone or glass—called tesserae—set in cement.

23 A glittering effect. Since glass reflects and tesserae do not lie on a uniformly flat plane, they reflect in all directions.

24 A print can be reproduced several times; a drawing is one of a kind.

25 An artist draws on a block of wood or linoleum and cuts away areas that are to remain white. When block printing ink is rolled across the plate, it clings to the raised areas. When paper is pressed against the plate, the ink is transferred to the paper, making the finished print.

26 The relief image is above the surface on the plate; the intaglio image is below the surface.

27 In engraving, lines are cut into the plate with a burin. Ink is rubbed into the lines, which are transferred to a sheet of paper under extreme pressure by using an intaglio press. For an etching, the artist covers the plate with a "ground" and draws into the layer with a needle. When the plate is placed in acid, the exposed lines are eaten by the acid. Inking the plate and pulling a print are the same as those for engraving.

28 Water and oil repel each other.

29 Brisk, spontaneous strokes are similar in the print and the drawing.

30 Stencil method.

31 Negative—a semi-transparent image of a scene with the lights and darks reversed. Focal length—the distance between the lens and the plane of the film in the back of the camera. Zoom lens—a lens with changeable focal lengths.

32 Possible answers include: threatened, scared, comforted, knowing the storm will pass.

33 Cut and spliced segments of film can be composed into a final product.

34 Fragments of things—photographs, various papers, etc.—pasted onto a flat surface.

35 Pablo Picasso and Georges Braque, around 1912.

36 Art reduced to its idea or concept; art without object.

37 To provide evidence of its existence.

Test Answers
Chapter 12
Two-Dimensional Media

1	T
2	F
3	T
4	T
5	F
6	F
7	D
8	B
9	F
10	E
11	4
12	2
13	5
14	1
15	4
16	5
17	1
18	3
19	4
20	2
21	1
22	3
23	2
24	3
25	1
26	2
27	3
28	4
29	2

30 1

31 D

32 F

33 G

34 1

35 H

36 B

37 C

38 A

39 When thinned with water, they both become translucent.

40 Both can be produced on paper; a print can be reproduced several times, whereas a drawing is one of a kind.

41 It is not necessary that something is actually made.

42 Answers may include two of the following: writing, xerox copies, photographs, film, audio tape, videotape, photographs. Answers will vary.

43 Answers will vary.

44 7

45 4

46 2

47 5

48 6

49 1

50 3

Chapter 12
Two-Dimensional Media

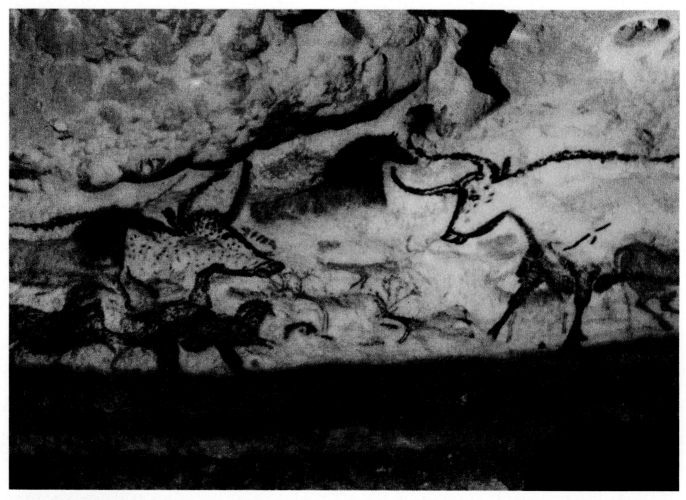

12–1 *Hall of Bulls,* left wall, Lascaux, ca. 15,000–13,000 BC. Dordogne, France. Courtesy of Scala/Art Resource, NY.

Chapter 11 suggested that working with a medium is like a contest. When you play tennis, it helps if you know something about your opponent. In the same way, it helps if you know the capabilities and limitations of your medium when making a picture. Also, in order to appreciate an artwork, it helps to know what a medium is and something about it. This chapter describes various two-dimensional media: drawing, painting, mosaic, printmaking, photography and film, video arts, computer art, and mixed media.

Drawing

Monochromatic Drawing Media

When you draw, you make controlled marks on paper with a tool such as charcoal, pen and ink, pencil, crayon, or felt marker. These tools are drawing media. Some of these tools date back thousands of years. During the Ice Age (around 12,000 BC), hunter-artists used pieces of charcoal on cave walls to outline shapes of animals (fig. 12–1). As early as 2500 BC, Egyptian scribes used ink on sheets of *papyrus,* made from a plant that still grows along the Nile. In the 1400s, European artists began using pencils.

You have been using some of these tools since you were a child. However, that does not mean that drawing is necessarily easy. Sometimes drawing media require more skill than other kinds of media to produce good results. Usually, the artist has only two colors to work with—the color of the tool and the color of the paper.

You learned about values and shading in Chapter 6. You can often get different values in a drawing just by changing the amount of pressure on the pencil or drawing tool. If you rub a stick of charcoal hard, it makes very dark tones. The marks conceal the white of the paper. If you rub the stick lightly, it makes lighter tones. The marks allow tiny bits of white paper to show through and mix optically with the black grains of the charcoal. Observe how Käthe Kollwitz varied the pressure on the charcoal tool to create her self-portrait (fig. 12–2). In some places, like the extended arm, the strokes are broad and dark. In others, like the face and head, they are quite delicate.

Variety like this also can be produced by certain kinds of pencils. The pencil contains a combination of clay and graphite rather than lead. The amount of graphite in the pencil determines the type of line it can make. A hard pencil produces thin, light lines (fig. 12–3). A soft pencil produces thicker, darker lines (fig. 12–4). (Pencils used in school are usually 2B, or medium soft.) With just a few pencil strokes, Felix Klee, Paul's son, captured the quality of a sleeping kitten (fig. 12–5). Did he press harder in some places than others, use more than one type of pencil, or both?

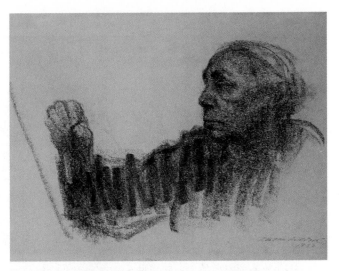

12–2 Käthe Kollwitz, *Self-Portrait, Drawing*, 1933. Charcoal on brown laid Ingres paper, 18 ¾″ x 24 ⅞″ (48 x 63 cm). ©1993 National Gallery of Art, Washington, Rosenwald Collection.

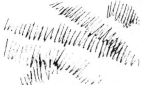

12–3 Hard pencils, such as 2H, produce thin and light lines.

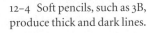

12–4 Soft pencils, such as 3B, produce thick and dark lines.

Try it Yourself

Try to obtain pencils with different grades, like 2H (medium hard), 5H (very hard), and 5B (very soft). Discover the different kinds of lines they make.

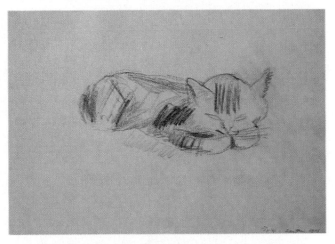

12–5 Notice how the thicker lines create darker values than the thin lines. Felix Klee, *Fritzi*, 1919. Pencil, 7 ⅝″ x 10 ⅝″ (19 x 27 cm). Collection, The Museum of Modern Art, New York. Gift of Mrs. Donald B. Straus.

Different values can also be obtained from India ink. Ink poured directly from the bottle is *opaque,* that is, not transparent. When applied to paper, it completely masks the color of the paper. The pen and ink drawing (fig. 12–6) uses shading to show details and rounded forms. The different values were made by hatching (Chapter 4). Notice how bold the strokes are and how they go in different directions.

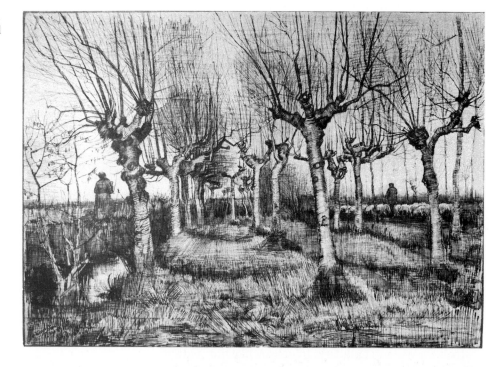

12–6 The different values apparent in this pen and ink drawing were obtained by various hatching techniques. Vincent van Gogh, *Pollarded Birches,* 1884. Pencil, ink and paint on wove paper, 16″ x 22″ (40 x 55 cm). Rijksmuseum, Amsterdam.

Japanese artist Shin'cihi used ink in a different way to create shaded effects and depth. In his work (fig. 12–7), the artist used *ink washes,* which are films of water-thinned ink spread with a brush. An ink wash is semitransparent, or *translucent.* It allows the white of the paper to show through and produce gray. To control the values, Shin'cihi controlled the amount of the water in the mixture and overlapped some of the washes. Notice how the thinnest washes were used for the lighter parts of the scene (where the sun shines in the morning mist). The white of the paper itself represents the lightest part of all.

Colored Chalk or Pastel

Colored *chalks* lie somewhere between drawing and painting media. Like charcoal sticks or pencils, sticks of colored chalk can be applied directly to paper. But unlike most drawing media, colored chalks are multi-colored. Hunter-artists may have used an early form of colored chalk. They mixed clay with iron oxide, a pigment that produces brownish reds and yellows.

Pastels are a high-quality form of chalk with a wide range of hues. They were introduced in the 1700s. At that time they were especially popular with portrait painters. Pastels allow the artist to use a variety of colors without needing to mix paints or prepare canvas. However, they are quite fragile. The surface of a picture made with chalk or pastel can be easily smeared or dusted away. Pastel drawings must be sprayed with shellac mixed with alcohol or framed under glass.

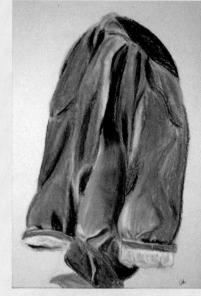

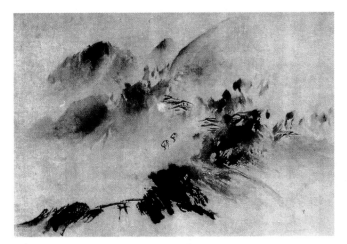

12-7 Shin'cihi, *Hisamatsu,* 1971.

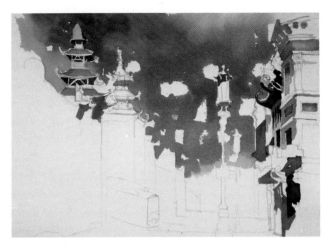

12-8 The first stages of a watercolor painting by Dong Kingman. *Chinatown, San Francisco.* Watercolor, 18″ x 22″ (46 x 56 cm). Collection of Rocky Aoki.

Painting

Mention the word art, and most people think of painting. All painting media consist of colored powders called *pigments* and a liquid in which the pigments are mixed. This liquid is called the *vehicle.* The paint is applied to a surface, such as a wall, board, paper or canvas, called the *support.*

Watercolor

Watercolors consist of pigments mixed with water. They are applied with a brush to white paper. Like ink, watercolors have been around for centuries. At first they were used only to add a little color to drawings. In the early 1800s watercolors came into their own. At that time, their potentials were discovered and developed by English watercolorists. Since then, this medium has been very popular, especially for colorful, lively outdoor scenes.

The methods of working with watercolors are similar to those used for ink washes. In developing a composition, watercolorist Dong Kingman works in stages. He first lays in the lighter washes, then adds and overlaps more light washes. Finally, he applies darker washes, bright colors, and opaque strokes (figures 12–8, 12–9, 12–10). Among other procedures, Kingman also first wets the paper and stretches it. Then he blocks out the whites (sometimes with rubber cement, which is later removed).

Despite his years of experience, Kingman plans carefully before touching brush to paper. But in the end, Kingman's pictures, like all good watercolors, are fresh and spontaneous looking. They catch the spirit of the subject with an ease that comes from long practice.

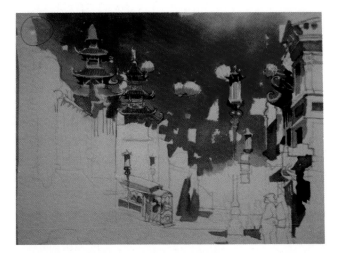

12-9 Second stage.

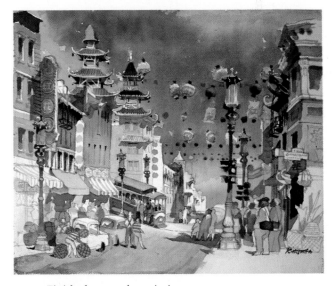

12-10 Finished watercolor painting.

Watercolor Washes

Produce watercolor washes that are *flat* (uniform, unchanging), *graded* (light to dark), and *mixed* (varied hues and intensities). Then paint opaque lines over the washes.

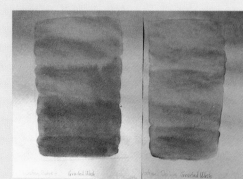

a. Flat washes.

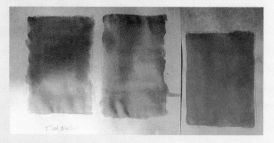

b. Graded washes.

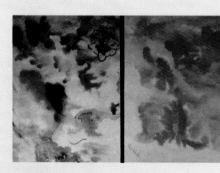

c. Mixed washes.

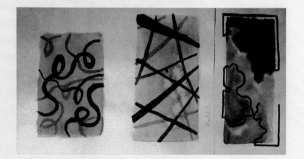

d. Opaque lines over washes.

Tempera

Tempera is applied to paper, wood, or canvas. The medium of tempera consists of pigments mixed with an *emulsion.* An emulsion is a watery liquid with droplets of oil suspended in it. Egg yolk, a natural emulsion, has been the traditional emulsion used in tempera. Today there are many different emulsions. They can be based on casein (a milk product), gum arabic, plastic, and wax.

Unlike watercolors, which are thin and relatively transparent, tempera is creamy and opaque. To make an area white, the artist may use white paint or the paper. To lighten a color, the artist adds white paint, not water. Water is used as a thinner to make the paint flow better or to make it transparent. It is also used to clean brushes.

Tempera was used by the Greeks and Romans. It reached its peak in the late Middle Ages, between 1100 and 1500. During this period, tempera was the favorite medium for paintings on wooden panels, like *The Adoration of the Magi* (fig. 12–11) by Gentile da Fabriano. Tempera dries quickly with a soft matte finish and lends itself to fine detail. Because it is opaque, tempera allows the artist to paint over previously painted areas. The artist can continually improve effects of shading or texture. (This method does not work very well with watercolors.)

The *Adoration* has a greeting-card charm that is due to the medium of tempera. Note the delicate colors in the painting. In many places the colors are enhanced with gold foil. Note also the detail of the many figures and animals, especially the decoration of the Magi's crowns and splendid costumes.

The advantages of tempera for some kinds of painting, however, are disadvantages for other kinds. Rapid drying prevents the easy blending of colors. Tempera produces delicate effects instead of lively, spontaneous-looking effects. Furthermore, tempera colors tend to change while drying, making it difficult to predict the final results. Tempera gave way to oil in the 1400s and 1500s as the most popular medium. Still, some artists, notably Andrew Wyeth, use it to this day. When painting subjects like *Braids* (fig. 12–12), Wyeth finds the characteristics of tempera to be ideal for his purposes.

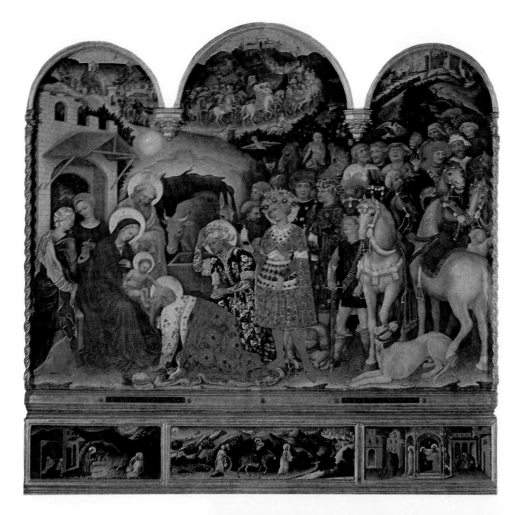

12–11 Gentile da Fabriano, *The Adoration of the Magi*, 1423. Tempera on wood panel, approx. 9´ 11˝ x 9´ 3˝ (302 x 282 cm). Galleria degli Uffizi, Florence.

12–12 Andrew Wyeth, *Braids*. Tempera.

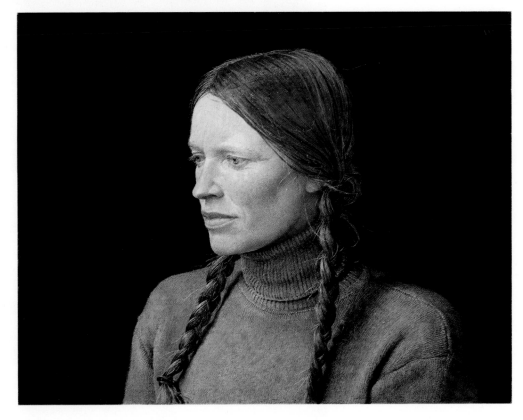

A Tempera Painting

Create a tempera painting based on an artwork that portrays a situation. In *your* painting, show what happens next.

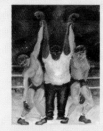

a. Darrell Wu.

b. Sue Musselman.

12–13 Emilio Cruz, *Past Pastures,* 1983. Oil on canvas, 72″ x 48″ (183 x 122 cm). Collection of the artist. Photograph: John Majjiotto.

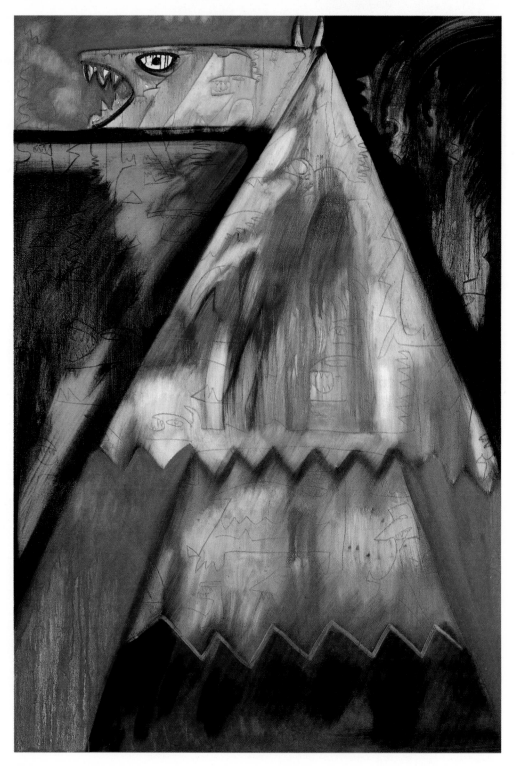

Oil

Oil is the star attraction, not just of paint, but of all media. It is made up of pigments mixed with linseed oil. Turpentine is the thinner or solvent. The popularity of oil dates back to the 1400s. It was first used for colored *glazes,* which are thin films of transparent varnish. Glazes were brushed over tempera paintings to give them more luster. Somewhat later, at about the time of Leonardo da Vinci, artists began using oil paint from start to finish. Later still, in the middle of the 1500s, canvas replaced wood as the principal type of support. To this day, *oil on canvas* is perhaps the most popular medium of all.

Oil is much more flexible than tempera. It can be opaque or translucent, as thick as plaster or as thin as watercolor. Most importantly, it dries slowly. It allows an artist more freedom to blend colors and create a great variety of effects. You have seen some of that variety in the paintings in this book. How does the dry brushwork of Hopper's *House by the Railroad* (fig. 5–32) differ from the fluid brushwork of Bellows's *Stag at Sharkey's* (fig. 8–14)?

For more examples of oil paint's variety, compare and contrast the styles of Rembrandt (fig. 5–31), the unknown painter of *Mademoiselle Charlotte du Val d'Ognes* (fig. 6–9), Renoir (fig. 3–1), and Mondrian (fig. 7–10). The works of contemporary painter Emilio Cruz are especially representative of the medium. The word *exuberance* (full of life and high spirits) is often used to describe his paintings. Look at Cruz's *Past Pastures* (fig. 12–13). Exuberance is obviously expressed in the subject matter, especially in the terrifying head. But it is also expressed in the rich creamy paint and the iridescent colors. Cruz transformed paint into explosive energy.

Canvas is the most common support for oil paintings. It has several advantages for the artist. For one thing, it is very light. A large oil painting can be carried by one person. If thoroughly dry, a painting can even be removed from its thin wooden frame *(stretchers),* rolled, and shipped in a mailing tube. The same size painting on wood would be heavy and very awkward to handle or ship. It may surprise you to know, however, that oil rots fabric, including canvas fabric. To prevent canvases from rotting, artists have had to coat them with a layer or two of a special glue or gesso (a plaster-like substance) before applying paints. Today synthetic products are available for preparing canvases.

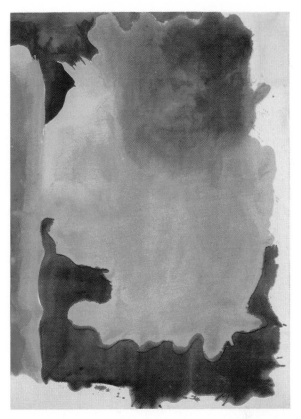

12–14 Helen Frankenthaler, *Canal,* 1963. Acrylic on canvas, 81″ x 57 ½″ (206 x 146 cm). Purchased with the aid of funds from the National Endowment for the Arts in Washington, DC, a Federal Agency; Matching gift, Evelyn Sharp. Photograph: David Heald © The Solomon R. Guggenheim Foundation, New York.

Acrylic

Acrylic is a synthetic medium that came into use after World War II. Acrylic paints are made from plastic material suspended in a water-soluble liquid, or polymer. Acrylic can be applied to anything, including canvas. Acrylic is the most versatile medium we've covered so far. When thinned with water, it acts like watercolors. When its colors are extended with liquid polymer, they can be used as glazes. Special materials can be added to acrylic to make it thicker than oils. Normally fast drying, it can be made to dry slowly by the addition of "retarders." Most importantly, it can be applied directly to canvas without rotting it.

Helen Frankenthaler has taken advantage of this capability by pouring water-thinned acrylics onto raw canvas. This is a new approach to painting called *stained canvas.* The results of colors spreading, mixing, and sinking into the canvas are visible in *Canal* (fig. 12–14). Sometimes the canvas is warped or tilted in different directions during the process.

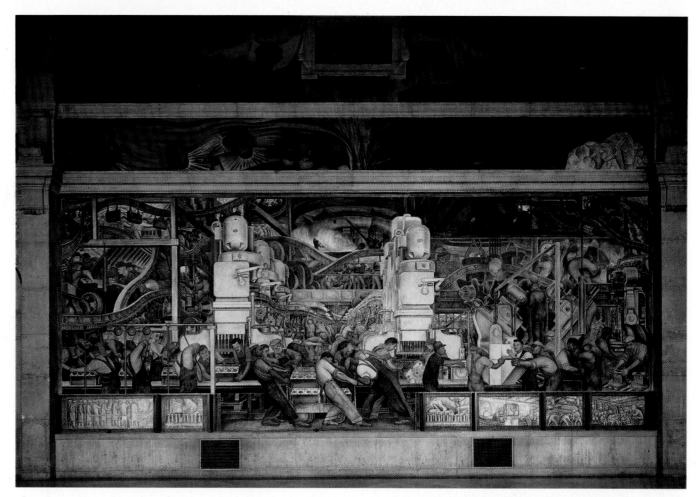

12–15 Diego Rivera, *Detroit Industry*, 1932–1933. Fresco, mural. ©The Detroit Institute of Arts, Founders Society Purchase, Edsel B. Ford Fund and Gift of Edsel B. Ford.

Fresco

If acrylic is the newest paint medium, fresco is one of the oldest. It is used to make paintings, or murals, on walls. Fresco painting consists of mixing pigments in water, spreading wet plaster onto a wall or ceiling, and applying the colors to the plaster before it dries. (Many cultures painted on a wall or ceiling after the plaster had dried, a method called secco.)

The first people to use fresco were probably the Minoans. Their seafaring culture flourished on the island of Crete around 1500 BC. The most famous examples of fresco were made by Italian artists from the early 1300s to the mid-1500s.

As you know, plaster dries quickly. Therefore the artist must plan ahead when spreading plaster. The artist must be able to paint the area within a few hours. A large mural, such as Diego Rivera's *Detroit Industry* (fig. 12–15), had to be painted in sections. To avoid leaving a water mark, Rivera probably ended each section at the edge of a figure or object, rather than in the middle. Possibly Rivera could do only a few of the

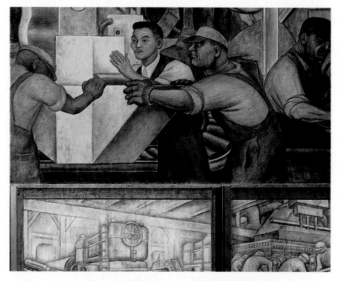

12–16 Diego Rivera, *Detroit Industry* (detail), 1932–1933. Fresco, mural. The Detroit Institute of Arts, Founders Society Purchase, Edsel B. Ford Fund and Gift of Edsel B. Ford.

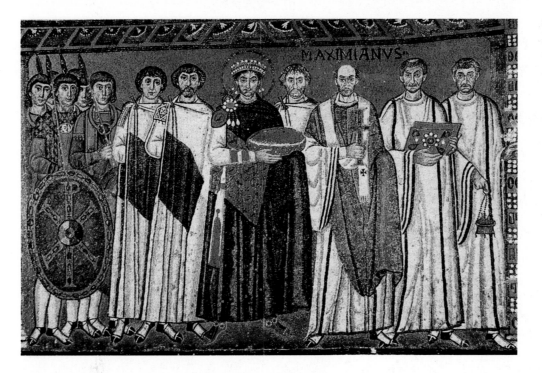

laborers or one machine at a time in *Detroit Industry* (fig. 12–16). Because of the difficulties of working with the fresco method, the artist cannot easily make in-process changes or add fussy details. Perhaps this is why Rivera made the forms in his mural so bold.

Fresco does have two advantages: durability and permanence. It is *in* the plaster, not a film of paint *on* the plaster. Fresco can better withstand the effects of air pollution and wear and tear in general. A fresco is part of a wall or ceiling, and will survive as long as that wall or ceiling does.

Mosaic

A mosaic is a design or picture made from many pieces of stone or glass. These pieces, called *tesserae,* are set in cement. Mosaics are typically used to decorate a wall, ceiling, or floor. An artist must piece together thousands of individual bits of tesserae to complete a mosaic. In some ways a mosaic is more like a crossword puzzle than a drawing or painting. A mosaic has been called a "painting in stone." Mosaic is colorful, durable, and part of a wall or ceiling. In these ways it is similar to fresco.

Mosaics have not been very popular since the 1300s, but they were once more popular than frescos. The Romans, who embedded mosaic designs in floors and walls, used tesserae made of stone cubes. The Early Christians covered the walls and ceilings of their churches with mosaics made from pieces of glass.

Because glass reflects, and because tesserae do not lie on a uniformly flat plane, the mosaics reflect in all directions. Imagine the glittering effect inside a church filled with mosaics like *Emperor Justinian and Attendants* (fig. 12–17). Note the simplicity of both the composition and the individual figures. Even more than fresco, the medium of mosaic forces the artist to think in terms of large bold images. But the severity of the design is tempered by the sparkle of its surface.

Printmaking

Like drawings, prints are produced on paper, but with an important difference. A print can be *re*produced several times. The major techniques of printmaking involve the use of ink, paper, and a *plate*. A plate is the surface on which the picture or design is made. A plate is often a piece of wood or copper. To produce a print, a piece of paper is pressed against an inked plate. This process can be repeated many times to make many prints of one image.

Relief Prints

A *relief print* is so called because the image on the plate is in *relief,* that is, it projects or sticks up from the surface of the plate (fig. 12–18). The *woodcut* was devel-

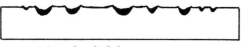

12–18 A cross section of a relief plate.

oped in the 1300s to produce large quantities of religious pictures. The woodcut is still the most common kind of relief printing. (Linoleum is also used.) The artist draws on a block of wood, then cuts away the areas that are to remain white. The parts that will be printed are raised from the background. Black ink is rolled across the plate and clings to those parts that are in relief. When paper is pressed against the plate, the black ink is transferred to the paper, making the finished print.

Albrecht Dürer was a skilled sixteenth-century German artist. Study his *The Riders on the Four Horses from the Apocalypse* (fig. 12–19). Every black line that

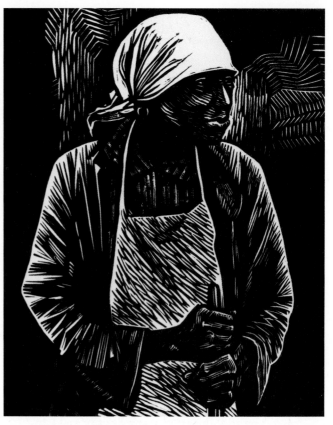

12–20 Elizabeth Catlett, *The Survivor,* 1983. Linocut, 11˝ x 10˝ (28 x 26 cm). Courtesy Malcolm Brown Gallery, Cleveland, Ohio.

describes shape or detail is exact. Dürer had to cut around each of these lines when carving the wooden block. It is hard to believe that this complex image is a woodcut.

Elizabeth Catlett has a different approach. In her *The Survivor* (fig. 12–20), the marks of the cutting tool are much more evident. Like many other twentieth-century artists, Catlett believes that the qualities of a medium should be visible, even celebrated, in every work of art.

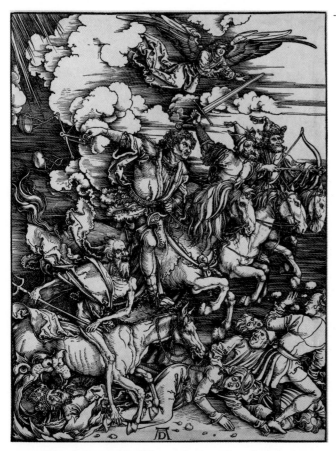

12–19 Albrecht Dürer, *The Riders on the Four Horses from the Apocalypse,* ca. 1496. Woodcut, 15¼˝ x 11˝ (39 x 28 cm). The Metropolitan Museum of Art, New York, Gift of Junius S. Morgan, 1919. (19.73.209)

Try it Yourself

Do you prefer Dürer's type of woodcut or Catlett's? People who like traditional art appreciate the great skill as shown by Dürer's approach. People who like modern art prefer works like Catlett's. Catlett's woodcuts may seem somewhat primitive, but they bring out the qualities of the medium. Are you a traditionalist or a modernist? Perhaps you appreciate both approaches, realizing that different standards must be applied to each. In any case, explain your position.

Elizabeth Catlett

1919–

African American painter and sculptor Elizabeth Catlett has focused her life and her art on civil rights. "I have always wanted my art to service Black people—to reflect us, to relate to us, to stimulate us, to make us aware of our potential." (Samella S. Lewis, *Art: African American.* New York: Harcourt Brace Jovanovich, 1978, p. 125).

Catlett's first experience with discrimination occurred when she was rejected from an art college which had never before accepted a black student. Bitter but determined, she entered Howard University, a predominantly black school, and pursued her studies with several famous black art professors.

In 1938, following in her father's footsteps, Catlett became an art teacher. Her first job in North Carolina paid only $59 each month, half the salary paid to white teachers. Recognizing the injustice in this system, Catlett helped campaign for equal wages for both black and white teachers.

Catlett went on to receive a master's degree in sculpture, to direct the art department at a university in New Orleans, and to teach at two schools in New York. Her dedication to the civil rights movement continued, reflecting itself in her politically active life and her emotionally vibrant artwork. During her first visit to Mexico in 1946 at the age of 27, Catlett decided to stay in this country to work on her linoleum prints with other printmakers; she remained there to marry, raise three children, and pursue her career as an artist. She became a naturalized citizen of Mexico in 1962.

Elizabeth Catlett's devotion to black people and to the citizens of Mexico remains an important aspect of her work today. This dedication is apparent in the intensity of the characters in her prints and sculptures. Strong-willed, determined and proud, these figures, like the artist who created them, illustrate the powerful impact of a life dedicated to art.

A Linoleum Block Print

Produce a three-color print using the linoleum reduction block procedure.

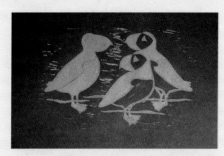

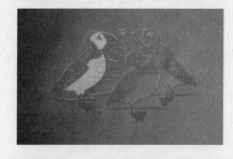

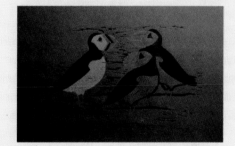

Chris Listello.

Intaglio Prints

Intaglio (in TAH lee-oh; Italian for "to cut in") is the opposite of relief printing. Rather than being above the surface, an intaglio image is below it (fig. 12–21). The lines, unlike relief printing, do not project. The artist cuts the lines that are to print *into* the plate. An intaglio plate is usually a sheet of copper or zinc. Sheet plastic is sometimes used.

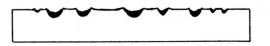

12–21 A cross section of an intaglio plate.

Three kinds of intaglio are *engraving, etching,* and *aquatint.* To do engraving, the artist cuts lines into the plate using a special gouge called a *burin.* To do etching, the artist first covers the plate with a layer of wax, called a *ground.* Then the artist draws in the wax with a needle. When the plate is placed in acid, the exposed lines are eaten by the acid. To do aquatint, the artist bonds particles of resin to the plate, then blocks out those areas that are not to be eaten by the acid with a coat of shellac. When placed in acid, only the very small spaces between the resin particles are eaten.

All three intaglio methods use the same printing technique. Black ink is rubbed into the etched lines or areas. These inked areas are transferred to a piece of paper under the extreme pressure of an intaglio press. Engraved lines look hard and brittle. Etched lines appear softer. Aquatint produces gritty-textured areas of gray.

To make *Todd* (fig. 12–22) Xiaowen Chen used etching and aquatint. Some of the thinner, lighter lines on Todd's desk have been etched once or twice. The darker lines were made by drawing and "biting" the lines with acid several times. The gray areas on this side of the desk are the result of aquatint. The dark shadows around Todd and especially behind his left shoulder are the result of a combination of aquatint and densely hatched etched lines. Chen's print shows how the medium can be used to achieve variety in tone and texture.

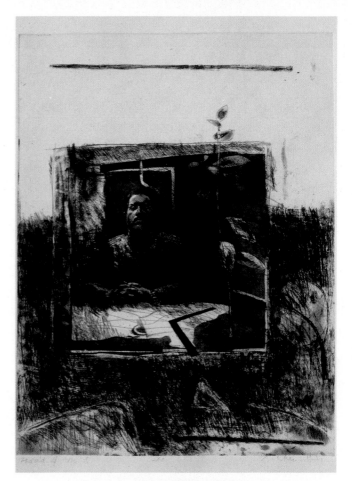

12–22 Xiaowen Chen, *Todd.* Etching and aquatint.

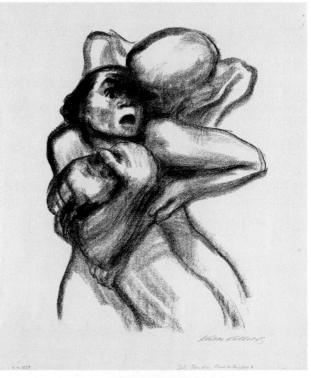

12–24 Käthe Kollwitz, *Death Seizing a Woman,* 1934, Plate IV from the series *Death,* 1934–1936. Lithograph, 20˝ x 14˝ (51 x 36 cm). Collection, The Museum of Modern Art, New York. Purchase Fund.

Planographic Prints

In planographic printing, the image is *on* the surface of the plate (fig. 12–23). *Lithography* is one of the most widely used of all printmaking methods. It is based on the principle that oil and water do not mix. The artist draws on the flat surface of a block of limestone with a grease crayon. Then the surface is dampened with water. Of course, the grease lines do not absorb the water. When the artist rolls oily ink onto the plate, the damp part of the surface repels the ink. The ink is received by the crayon lines. These lines are then transferred to the paper.

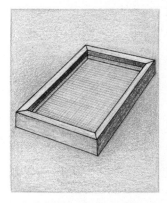

12–23 A cross section of a planographic plate.

A lithograph tends to look like a drawing made with crayon or charcoal. Compare Kollwitz's lithograph *Death Seizing a Woman* (fig. 12–24) with her charcoal self-portrait (fig. 12–2). The brisk lines in the lithograph seem as spontaneous and direct as those done in charcoal.

Screen Prints

Screen printing is the newest printmaking medium. It is a stenciling process. The stencil is placed on a screen made of nylon or polyester, stretched tightly over a frame (fig. 12–25). The stencil can be made of paper or other blockout or resist materials. Ink is forced through the open areas with a squeegee. A separate screen is needed for each color printed. Screen prints do not reverse the image. They do not need heavy pressure, and can be printed on most surfaces.

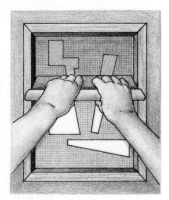

12–25 Silk screen.

12–26 Pulling a squeegee across the silk screen.

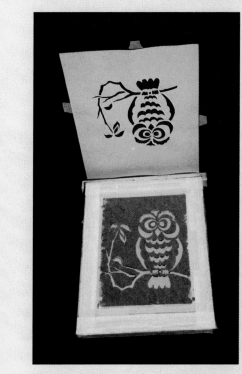
Photography and Film
Photography

Photography has become the modern *folk* medium, or art of the common people. Probably you and your friends have all used cameras at some time. However, you may not know much about the technology of photography.

Like printmaking, identical copies, called prints, can be produced by photography. A photographer captures a scene from life onto light-sensitive film with a camera. A camera is simply a dark box with a *lens* that lets in light when the photographer trips its *shutter,* which opens and closes rapidly. To make the image of the scene visible, the film must be *developed.* This involves immersing it in special chemicals. At this stage the film has become a *negative.* A negative is a semi-transparent image of the scene in which the lights and darks are reversed. In a black-and-white film negative, the whites are opaque and blacks are clear. Light grays are barely translucent and dark grays are semitransparent (fig. 12–27).

To make a print of the image, the photographer passes light through the film negative onto light-sensitized paper, which is then developed. This becomes the final product. The print is a positive image of the original scene (fig. 12–28).

So far we have discussed the basics. The photographer can control some things such as lighting, time of day, point of view, and distance. The photographer can also control film speed, width of the lens opening, focus, shutter speed, and flash. The time and temperature of the chemical bath and length of exposure on the contact paper can also affect the final photograph.

Using available light is very important. For example, suppose a subject is very dark and the photographer does not have a flash. He or she would need to use fast film (which is the most sensitive to light), a wide lens opening to let in as much light as possible, and a slow shutter speed.

A most interesting variable is the *focal length* of the lens. This is the distance between the lens and the plane of the film in the back of the camera. By changing the focal length, the photographer can control the composition of the subject within the frame. The longer the focal length, the larger the subject appears to be and the more it fills the frame (fig. 12–29). Lenses with short focal lengths are sometimes called *wide-angle* lenses. They are good for indoor scenes or situations where the photographer is close to the subject and wants to make it appear farther away (fig. 12–30). *Telephoto* lenses have long focal lengths. They are good for enlarging subjects that are in the distance (fig. 12–31). Expensive cameras come with interchangeable lenses. Some lenses have fixed focal lengths. Some have changeable focal lengths called *zoom* lenses.

Consider the decisions that Ansel Adams made when he photographed *Half Dome, Merced River, Winter, Yosemite Valley* (fig. 12–32). Did he journey some distance to locate the subject? Did he search for the spot from which to shoot it? Did he try different lenses to compose the scene within the frame? Did he wait long for the light and the cloud formations to appear before shooting? Did he take a number of shots? Could you have achieved the same results with this subject with your camera?

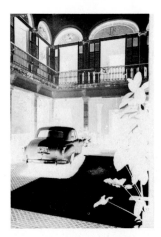

12–27 Black and white film negative.

12–28 The positive image print.

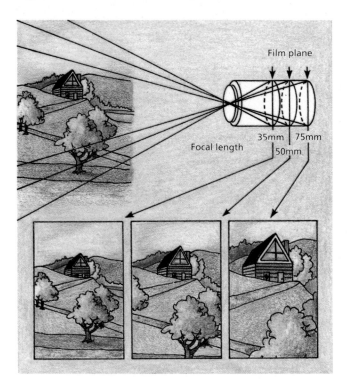

12–29 Focal length.

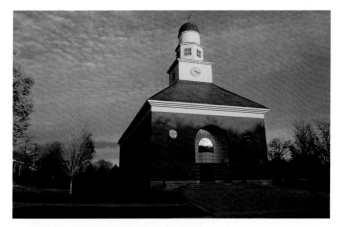

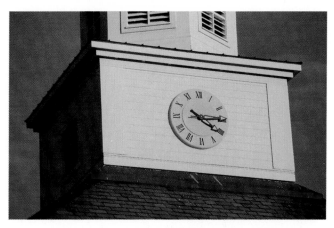

12–30 Wide-angle lens. Photographs: Barbara Caldwell.

12–31 Telephoto lens.

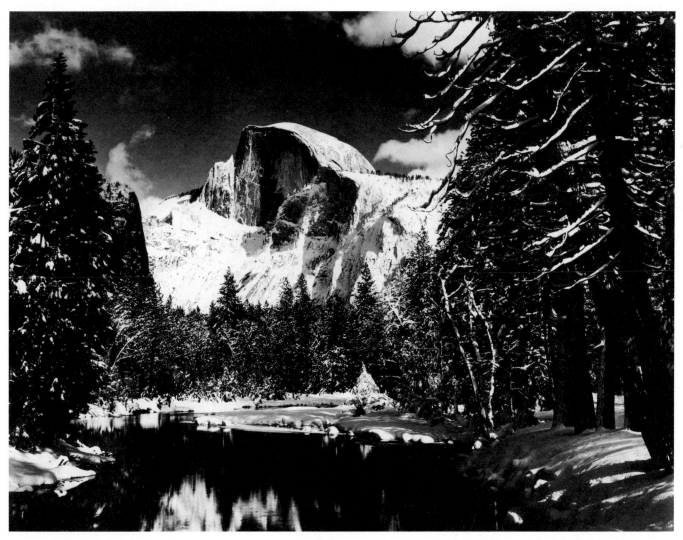

12–32 Ansel Adams, *Half Dome, Merced River, Winter, Yosemite Valley*, 1971. Silverprint, 15″ x 19″ (38 x 49 cm). © The Detroit Institute of Arts.

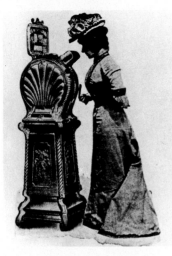

12–33 The mutoscope.

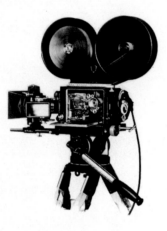

12–34 The 35mm Mitchell NC.

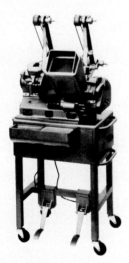

12–35 The moviola.

Film

People have always been fascinated by moving pictures. The "peep show" (fig. 12–33) created the illusion of motion. The viewer turned a crank to move a series of photographs. Each photograph showed a slightly different motion. If the viewer turned the crank rapidly, the images appeared to be moving. If the viewer turned the crank too slowly, the viewer saw only the individual still pictures. The illusion of motion disappeared. Today's movie projector is based on the same principle of still pictures moving in rapid succession. Of course, the pictures are printed on long strips of film and projected onto a screen for all to see.

The film camera, like a still-photography camera, is an enclosed box (fig. 12–34). The film is contained in large reels called film *magazines*. The film has holes on both sides; sprockets on the camera hold the film in place. The film is fed through the camera in a rapid stop-and-go motion. A single frame of film is pulled into position behind the shutter, the film stops, the shutter opens, and a single image is exposed. This is repeated twenty-four times a second. This is the standard rate of speed for sound film.

Like the photographer, the filmmaker must consider lighting and the placement of people and objects within a frame. In addition, the filmmaker must also consider the movement of people and objects, as well as the movement of the camera. Recall what you learned about film shots and sequence in Chapter 8.

After the film has been shot, the scenes are cut and put together into the final product. This stage of filmmaking is called editing. The editor does not use all the film that was taken. The one-minute battle sequence in *Star Wars* described in Chapter 8 may have been edited from several minutes of film. When first developed, the shots of rebel troops were much longer than one second each. They were probably not in the same order as they appeared in the final sequence. To identify segments and rearrange their sequence, the editor uses a *moviola* (fig. 12–35). A moviola is a machine that runs the film at various speeds.

Commercial films like *Star Wars* are the creation of a *director* who supervises an army of people: writers, artists, musicians, carpenters, camera operators, sound technicians, editors, stunt men and women, not to mention actors and actresses. Think of it. All of these people are involved in the making of an *illusion*.

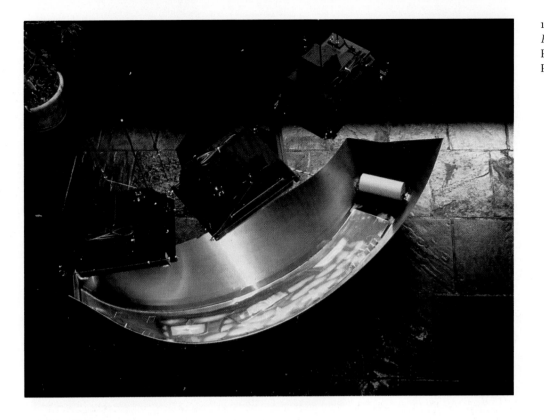

12–36 Shigeko Kubota,
River, 1979–1981.
Photograph ©1983
Peter Moore.

Video Art

Video refers to the picture portion of television. The images seen on television are created by electronic signals. (The images seen on film are created by chemical means.) A video camera is a tube with a lens and a photosensitive electronic plate in the back. The image on the plate is converted to electric signals by a scanner. The scanner reads the image from left to right and line by line from top to bottom in one-thirtieth of a second. The signals are transmitted through the air or carried by cable to a television. There, the signals are converted back to the original image by a "gun" that fires them at the screen. These signals are exactly the same as those read by the scanner. Television signals can also be stored on magnetic tape that can be played back at any time.

Because of recent breakthroughs in technology, many artists now use video instead of film. They use *camcorders*. Camcorders are hand-held units that combine the functions of camera and recorder. Camcorders are small, easy to operate, and relatively inexpensive. They also produce high-quality images. Thus for the individual artist, video has distinct advantages over film. Video tape is cheaper than film. The artist can play it back immediately on a camcorder instead of waiting for a film to be processed in a labo-

ratory, threaded through a projector, and viewed in a darkened room.

Nam June Paik was one of the pioneers of video art. He began making works for galleries and public television as early as the late 1950s, long before camcorders hit the market. He manipulated images electronically to create moving geometric patterns. Some have jokingly called these patterns "moving wallpaper." He also used television sets to make novel sculptures.

A good example of a mixed media art is *River* (fig. 12–36) by Paik's wife, Shigeko Kubota. (Mixed media is discussed later in this chapter.) *River* consists of three television sets suspended from the ceiling. The images on the television sets are reflected in a stainless steel trough containing water and a motorized wave machine. Gallery-goers can see the images on the sets, the reflections of the images in the moving water, or the reflections of their reflections bouncing up into space. Critic Brooks Adams compared Kubota's *River* to "a fountain, an indoor garden, a reflecting pool."

Computer Art

Like video, computer art is electronic. The technology for computer art is developing rapidly. Presently, two-dimensional images in color can be produced with personal computers. Three-dimensional images and animated art can be produced on large systems that only government, industries, and universities can afford.

The brain of the computer, the central processing unit (CPU), basically is a board with electrical circuits and transistors. The smallest unit of information for the CPU is a *bit*, or *binary* digit. Binary refers to two numbers: 1 and 0. Think of a bit as an electrical switch: 1 is on, 0 is off. A string of binary numbers, that is, a pattern of on–off switches, makes up a *pixel*. A pixel can be translated into a dot in a specific location on the video screen. Of course, dots can be extended into lines, and lines can form images.

Most people type on a keyboard when they use computers. But an artist-operator draws his or her lines with a *light pen* on a *digitizing* tablet (fig. 12–37). If the computer and video monitor have color capability, the artist can make lines in color. British painter David Hockney was invited to create an "electronic painting" soon after this technology was invented. His *Untitled* (fig. 12–38) is the delightful result.

To create three-dimensional art, the artist uses foreshortening, perspective, aerial perspective, shading, texture, cast shadows, and reflections. Special programs are required to create these effects on a

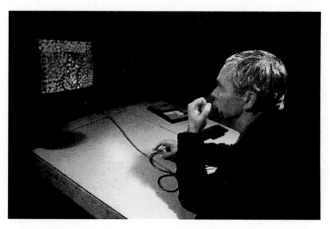

12–37 Artists working with computers can access thousands of colors in a split second. Courtesy Invision.

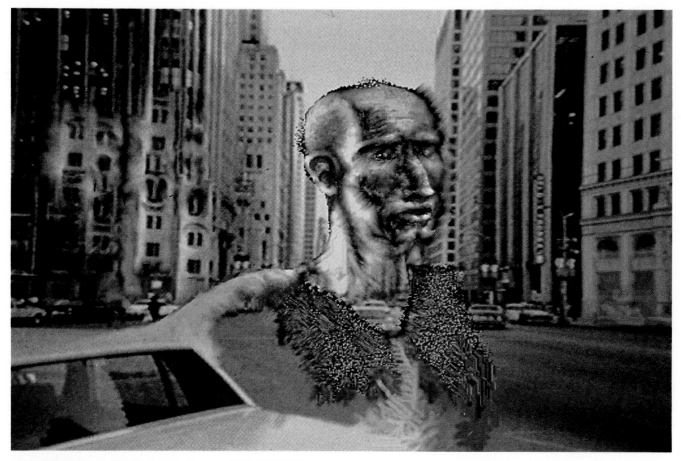

12–39 Hiromi Ono, *City Faces*, 1987. Courtesy SIGGRAPH '88.

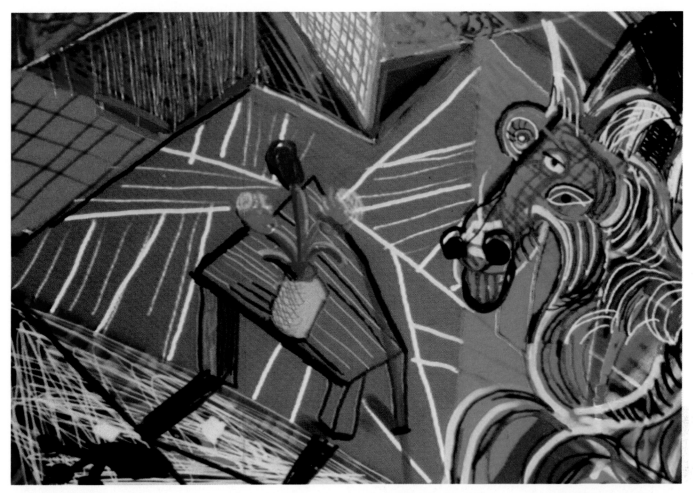

12–38 David Hockney, *Untitled* from Painting with Light Series. The artist spent eight hours straight on a sophisticated computer to create such images. Courtesy Invision.

computer. *Programs* are sets of instructions for a computer to perform. And each of these programs contains long columns of mathematical calculations. Even longer programs are required to create animation, the illusion of objects moving through space. Television commercials often use computer-generated animation. For example, you have probably seen three-dimensional images of company trademarks rotating and zooming through space in commercials. Such an animation, even if it lasted only ten seconds, would require the efforts of a team of designers and engineers working with a powerful computer.

Hiromi Ono, a computer artist, uses computer graphics programs to create original art. Ono worked with digitized video images to produce a ghostly interpretation of the urban landscape in *City Faces* (fig. 12–39).

Try it Yourself

Look for examples of computer-generated art on television. Take notes on both their three-dimensional and animated effects. Create a design of your own for computer art or a commercial. Try making your initials appear three-dimensional. Create a storyboard to describe them rotating and moving through space.

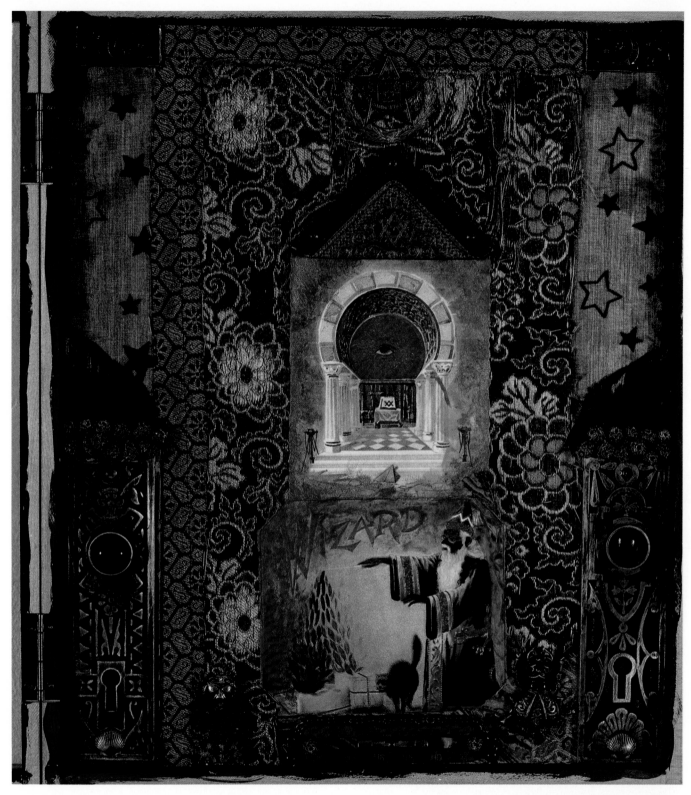

12–40 Many times, artists combine several media to arrive at a single image. Betye Saar, *Wizard*, 1972. Assemblage box and mixed media, 13 ½″ x 11″ x 1″ (34 x 28 x 2.5 cm). Collection of the artist.

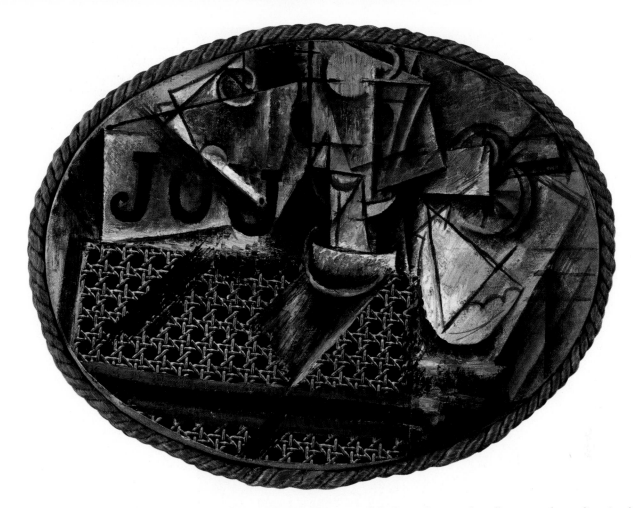

12–41 One specific category of mixed media is collage. Pablo Picasso was one of the first artists to make collage a popular medium in which to work. Pablo Picasso, *Still Life with Chair Caning*, 1911. Oil and pasted oilcloth simulating chair caning, oval 10 ⅝″ x 13 ¾″ (27 x 35 cm). ©1993 ARS, New York/SPADEM, Paris.

Mixed Media

So far, we have covered everything from mosaics to computer art in this chapter. Since the nineteenth century, new media like acrylics, silk screen, photography, film, video, and computer art have been developed. No doubt the list of two-dimensional art will continue to grow in the twenty-first century.

Many artists no longer adopt the pure approach of keeping the media separate. Some artists mix two or more together, or add "foreign" materials. Recall, for example, the stuffed goat attached to a painting in Chapter 1 (fig. 1–11). The artist of that work, Robert Rauschenberg, has made a career out of what he calls "combine paintings." Some of these works often are not paintings at all. Betye Saar combined assorted fabrics, brass hardware, jewelry, knickknacks, and pictorial elements in *Wizard* (fig. 12–40). Like Rauschenberg's goat, Saar's mixed media work is difficult to

interpret. Because it tends to mix two-dimensional and three-dimensional approaches, Saar's work is also difficult to classify.

Collage

A *collage* consists of fragments of things that are pasted on a flat surface. The artist may use photographs, colored paper, pieces of material, news clippings, and other odds and ends. In addition, strokes of paint, charcoal smears, or anything, as long as it is basically flat, may be combined with the collage materials. This type of two-dimensional art was invented around 1912 by Pablo Picasso and Georges Braque. Collages have become very popular in recent years.

Still Life with Chair Caning (fig. 12–41) is an early collage by Picasso. Picasso combined painting with a piece of oilcloth that looks like the woven material of a chair. What was Picasso trying to express? Probably

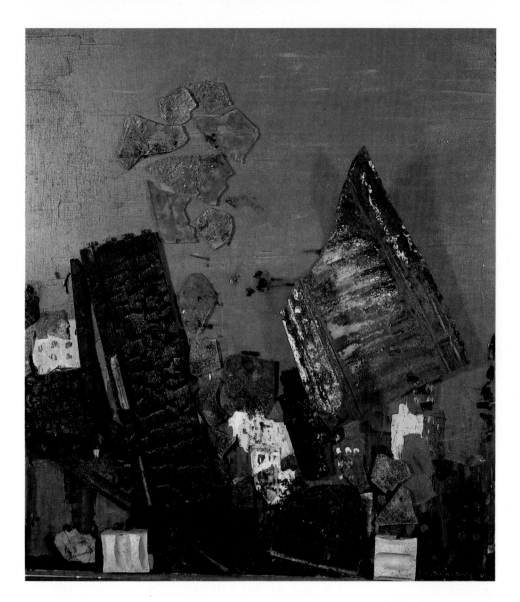

nothing. More likely he simply wanted to experiment, to pioneer a new kind of medium that others could use for expressive purposes. A half century after Picasso's experiment, Yvonne Parks Catchings expressed the pain of social crisis in a collage titled *The Detroit Riot* (fig. 12–42). The red symbolizes the heat and violence of the riot itself. The scraps of wood and broken glass symbolize the destruction.

Documented Art

During the late 1960s and early 1970s some artists began to create a new kind of art that mixed art with the life around it. Their works engaged the viewer in ways very different from that of traditional media. Examples of this new art include the wrapped coastline and the performance piece with a coyote you learned about in Chapter 1. (You will learn more about this art form, called "environmental art," in the next chapter.)

Studio Experience 12.6

A Unified Collage

Make a collage with a combination of found materials and drawn or painted elements. Select materials that have special meaning for you.

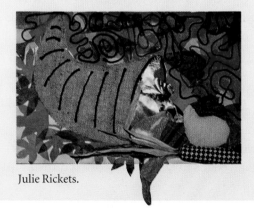

Julie Rickets.

"One of several proposals to rid my life of accumulated art. With this project I will have all of my accumulated paintings cremated by a mortuary. The container of ashes will be interred inside a wall of the Jewish Museum. For the length of the show, there will be a commemorative plaque on the wall behind which the ashes are located. It is a reductive, recycling piece. I consider all these paintings a body of work in the real sense of the word. Will I save my life by losing it? Will a Phoenix arise from the ashes? Will the paintings having become dust become art materials again? I don't know, but I feel better."

12-43 Conceptual art pieces are usually temporary events. Therefore, many of these events were documented either by filming, photographing or writing in order to keep a record of the actions that took place. John Baldessari, *Cremation Piece*, 1969. As shown at The Jewish Museum in the exhibition *Software*, 1970.

Other artists began a trend going in the opposite direction. They reduced their art to just its idea or concept. Some of these artists have argued that it is possible to create art without objects. This type of art is sometimes called *concept* art.

One thing that both developments had in common was the use of *documentation*. Because the works were temporary, a record of them had to be made. Works were documented in the form of writing, photocopies, photographs, film, audiotape, or videotape. The wrapped coast and the performance piece were documented with photographs (figures 1–10 and 1–12). John Baldessari's *Cremation Piece* is documented in a printed statement (fig. 12–43). The statement describes the idea, as well as some of the actions that Baldessari took to carry out his idea back in 1969.

Try it Yourself

Recall the comparisons made between Dürer's traditional approach to printmaking and Catlett's modern approach.

Examples of concept art, like the one by Baldessari (fig. 12–43), could be described as *post-modern*. Do you think this post-modern approach may lead to new possibilities in the future? Explain.

Summary

This chapter on two-dimensional media has indeed been complex. It organized two-dimensional media under the topics of drawing, painting, mosaic, printmaking, photography and film, video art, computer art, and mixed media.

Charcoal, pencil, and ink are examples of drawing media. They are monochromatic. They involve only the color of a single tool mixed with that of the paper. Colored chalks and pastels are multicolored, and resemble painting. However, like other drawing media, they have a fragile surface.

Painting includes watercolor, tempera, oil, acrylic, and fresco. Most painting media have ancient origins. Oil on canvas was not fully developed until the sixteenth century, however, and acrylic was developed in this century.

Mosaic is created from pieces of stone or glass that are set in walls, floors, or ceilings. Because of its unique materials and working process, mosaic differs from fresco and all the painting media.

Printmaking includes relief, intaglio, and planographic processes. The oldest of these media is the woodcut, a relief process. Engraving and etching, both intaglio methods, date back to around 1500 when they replaced the woodcut. The planographic methods are relatively new. Lithography was developed in the 1800s. Silk screen was developed in this century.

Photography and film involve photochemical processes. Video art and computer art, which involve electronic processes, use even more modern technologies.

Mixed media reflects new ideas about art. Many twentieth-century artists have experimented with using media, both new and old, in novel ways. They have mixed the media, as in collages. They have combined media with life itself. Other artists have attempted to eliminate the medium altogether and keep just the idea.

Chapter 13
Three-Dimensional Media

Student Edition
Pages 158–185

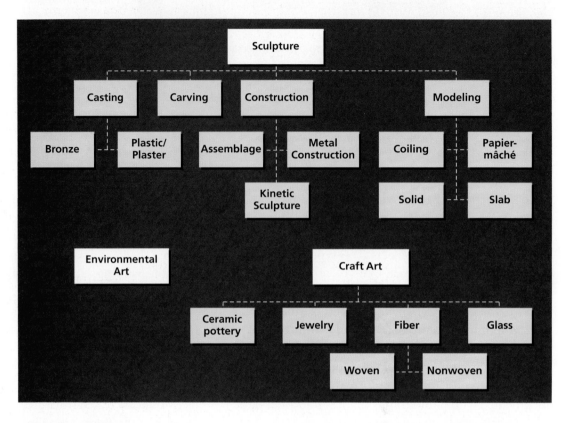

Overview

Chapter Objectives

Students should be able to:

1 describe six major areas of three-dimensional art   EE 1, 2

2 describe the characteristics of each area of three-dimensional art

3 list and explain the procedures for at least six different media used for sculpture

4 identify artists who work with the different media for sculpture

5 identify the media and procedures used in examples of three-dimensional artworks

6 demonstrate at least beginning levels of skill in the use of several three-dimensional media

7 analyze the relationships among medium, subject matter, and meaning in three-dimensional artworks

8 be open-minded toward new or unfamiliar media and procedures used for three-dimensional artworks

Rationale

Chapter 13 introduces students to six major categories of three-dimensional art: sculpture, environmental art, ceramic pottery, jewelry, fibers, and glass. Sculpture is divided into carving, casting, modeling, construction, assemblages, metalwork, and kinetic art. Media and procedural subdivisions are also included under pottery and modeling. Knowledge of media and procedures, their characteristics, and history contributes to the student's understanding of art and is also helpful in the critical analysis process.

Essential Chapter Concepts

• The third dimension is real in three-dimensional works rather than implied as in two-dimensional artworks.

• Sculpture that is created to be seen from all sides is called sculpture in the round.

• Sculpture that is attached to a surface is called low or high relief, depending on how far the shapes project from the surface.

• Movement may be implied in sculpture through positive and negative forms, or it may be real as in kinetic artworks.

• Lost-wax casting developed over 6,000 years ago. The process makes it possible to produce sculptures that are very large or small, and very complex or simple.

• Coil, slab, and pinch are three methods for hand-building pottery.

• Constructions and assemblages are 20th century forms of sculpture that may involve forms shaped by the artist and ready-made materials.

• Environmental artworks may involve the viewer in the artwork, or make the work a part of the environment.

• Metalworking includes jewelry, sculpture in the round, and relief.

• Fibers and fabrics are now used to produce three-dimensional sculpture.

Vocabulary

relief sculpture	sculpture in the round
lost-wax casting	convex
armature	environmental art
constructions	relief
mold	cast
assemblages	harmony
kinetic	cloisonné
concave	

Meet the Artist

Marisol   Page 171

Chapter Closure

Evaluation

1   *Aesthetic awareness:* Can students list and describe the characteristics of six major areas of three-dimensional art?   R 1

2   *Aesthetic awareness:* Can students discuss media and procedures used for several forms of sculpture and modeling?   R 2

3   *Aesthetic awareness:* Can students identify artists who work with these media?

4   *Aesthetic awareness:* Do students examine and discuss three-dimensional artworks created with unfamiliar materials and methods?

5   *Criticism:* Do students discuss media and procedures when analyzing a three-dimensional artwork?

6   *Production:* Have students demonstrated beginning levels of skill in producing some three-dimensional artworks?

Three-Dimensional Media

A Sculpture with Movement

Time: 5 periods

Preparation

Rationale

The carving process is the most difficult of the sculpture procedures appropriate for the school art program. The artist must visualize and plan how the form will look from all sides. Students will experience planning, visualizing, and carving a small three-dimensional form with dominant movement.

Studio Materials

molding plaster, quart milk cartons, carving knives, rasps, chisels, sandpaper, plastic mixing buckets, vermiculite (optional); clay, clay boards or banding wheels, clay carving tools, finishing tools, desk covers

Enrichment Materials

Overhead Transparencies:
• Hepworth, *Pendour,* 2

Large Reproductions:
• Statue of Mitry, 6
• Swentzell, *The Emergence of the Clowns,* 22
• Lucero, *Zoomorphic Dog Vessel,* 9
• Stout, *Instructions and Provisions,* 2

Teach the Lesson

Objectives

Students should be able to:

1 carve an abstract plaster or clay sculpture that has a dominant movement which makes it interesting from all sides   EE 1, 2

2 analyze how movement is implied throughout the form   EE 1, 4

Vocabulary

Concave refers to surfaces that are hollow or curve inward.

Convex refers to surfaces that curve outward.

Abstract art portrays subject matter in an unrealistic manner.

Nonobjective art has no recognizable subject matter. Subject matter may be the art elements.

Warm Up

If using plaster, have students mix and pour the forms in quart cartons. Adding vermiculite will make it softer and add texture. It will take 10 to 15 minutes to set up if poured thick. If using clay (which should not be too wet), have students wedge and form up blocks about 4" x 8". Place on boards or banding wheels and don't cover.

Laser Discs:

Brancusi, Bird in Space, 1925

Search Frame 2563

Arp, Mirr, 1936–1960

Search Frame 2549

Noguchi, Great Rock of Inner Seeking, 1974

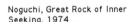

Search Frame 2605

Moore, Two Piece Mirror Knife Edge (model), 1976

Search Frame 2601

Moore, Knife Edge Mirror Two Piece, 1977–1978

Search Frame 2603

Moore, Three Motives Against Wall, I, 1958–1959

Search Frame 2599

Explore and Develop

1 Recall Studio Experience 5.5, in which students relied on visualization and sense of touch to model clay forms.

2 Display examples of sculptures. Ask students to describe the concave and convex surfaces of the sculptures. Explain abstract and nonobjective.

3 Have students explain how movement is implied in these forms. What similarities occur in each? What contrasts do they see? Note the lack of thin, extended appendages; how the parts are interrelated to suggest movement and unity around the form.

4 List ways that movement can be implied in sculpture: curved forms; alternating contrasts like concaves and convexes, solids and voids, textures and nontextures; progression of planes or shapes from large to small; edges or lines that lead one into another.

5 Briefly demonstrate the use of tools appropriate for the medium. Emphasize the carving process if using clay. **Caution: Have students use proper care when using carving knives and chisels.**

Begin Studio Experience 13.1

1 Tell students to outline their blocks on paper several times and use the side of crayon or chalk to explore an abstract form with surfaces that imply movement. Then have students outline the form on all sides of the block.

2 For plaster, put several layers of newspaper on the table. Students should use a dull knife, chisels, and rasps to block out the big shapes in the sculpture. Have them periodically throw away the chips. They should do the blocking out while the plaster is damp. Insist that the students keep turning the form around to work all sides.

For clay, students should use dull knives and wire loops to block out the big shapes. Placing clay on a board or banding wheel permits rotation of the piece so it can be seen and worked from all sides. Students should cover clay forms at the end of the period so they will not harden too much until carving is completed.

3 Negative forms may be hollowed out or taken clear through the block. Once the whole sculpture is blocked out, students should refine the larger forms, leaving the small parts and details for last. **Caution them to avoid breathing plaster dust. Be sure the area is well ventilated. Wear dust masks if necessary.** Plaster forms can be smoothed with rasps, scraped with the edge of a knife, and sandpapered when dry. Have students dampen the plaster form before resuming work to hold down some dust.

Dull knives and rubber and wooden scrapers can be used to smooth and refine clay surfaces. Blocks of wood can be used to lightly beat areas into shape or leave textured surfaces. Leather-hard surfaces can be sponged to smooth them. Solid clay forms need to be hollowed out to prevent cracking in drying or explosions in the kiln. Students should do this before the clay is too dry. Dry clay surfaces can also be sanded.

Evaluate and Reflect

1 Have students analyze movement and unity of their sculptures. Can they identify similarities? contrasts? continuations? Are there any progressions, such as large to small, small to large?

R 5

2 Discuss how implied movement contributes to the expressiveness of the sculpture.

3 Are students satisfied that their sculptures are interesting from all sides?

W 3 ### Reteach

Have students write a short paragraph about the carving process in sculpture. What materials are used? Have them identify artists who work with carving materials. What kinds of sculpture do they produce? Have them answer study questions 1 to 7.

Extend the Lesson
Beyond the Basics

Some of the oldest art forms are sculpted. Ask students to research pre-historic sculpture to determine materials used, primary subject matter, and why these subjects might have been used for sculpture.

EE 3

R 3

Have students look at *The Kiss* by Constantin Brancusi, a work which reflects his interest in primitive sculpture. *The Kiss* was created in 1908 as a monument for a cemetery in Paris. A smaller version of the work is located in The Philadelphia Museum of Art. Suggest students look for other examples of Brancusi's artwork which were influenced by primitive sculpture. Point out to students that his style changed around 1910. Have students research to determine the ideas behind this new approach.

EE 3

W 2

Students may not be familiar with the work of women sculptors like Barbara Hepworth. Have them look through resource books for other women artists who create sculpture. Describe the media they use, and the kinds of sculpture they create.

EE 3

Cultural Connections

R 4 Many contemporary sculptors, such as Henry Moore, were influenced by the prehistoric monument, Stonehenge, in Great Britain. The mystery of Stonehenge has produced many theories as to its purpose. Astronomers believe it was created by ancient man to track the movement of the sun across the sky in order to predict the beginning of the new year and to determine the day of the summer solstice. Why might knowledge of these events be of critical importance to ancient people? Peruvian Inca Indians used a similar device to chart the movement of the sun.

R 4
W 1 Suggest students research Stonehenge and similar structures found in different parts of the world. Have students look at works by Henry Moore and David Smith. Their styles are very different but both artists created sculptures that are monumental in scale. Have students develop theories regarding the purposes of the modern sculptures from the viewpoint of someone in the future.

Connecting with Other Subjects

Language Arts Many of the abstract sculptors knew each other or at least were familiar with the works of other artists working with similar ideas. Abstract sculpture was inspired by Cubism and particularly the collages and constructions of Picasso. Assign groups of students to find information about the abstract sculptors. Make a card for each sculptor including dates, names and places connected to his/her work. Suggest making reduced photocopies of works found in books to serve as visual reminders of the artists, styles and techniques. Attach photocopies to the cards. As research is completed begin setting up a working display by laying out all of cards and looking for relationships and connections.   **EE 3** **R 3** **W 2**

History Have other groups of students look for connections outside of the world of art. Have them research the period in history, the places where the artists lived and worked, and the important events of the time that may have influenced these artists. Suggest students follow interesting "leads" that will help them track sources of ideas outside of this time period, such as Henry Moore's work as it relates to Stonehenge and Brancusi's interest in primitive sculpture.   **EE 3** **R 3**

Sculpture on the Wild Side

Time: 5 periods

Preparation

Rationale

Commemorative sculpture permeates the history of art, from Myron's *Discobolus* to Michelangelo's *David* to Oldenburg's *Falling Shoestring Potatoes.* Equestrian sculptures that remind us of the deeds of past heroes adorn city squares and courthouse lawns. And once in a while, art students ought to do something for the humor of it.

Studio Materials

plaster gauze or papier-mâché paste, newspapers, armature materials (small boxes, tubes, cardboard, sticks, containers), water pans, masking tape, white glue, tempera paint

Enrichment Materials

Slides:
• Myron, *Discobolus,* 75
• Greenough, *George Washington,* 32
• Oldenburg, *Giant Soft Fan,* 49

Large Reproductions:
• Lucero, *Zoomorphic Dog Vessel,* 9
• Stout, *Instructions and Provisions,* 2
• Swentzell, *The Emergence of the Clowns,* 22
• Statue of Mitry, 6

Teach the Lesson

Objectives

Students should be able to:

1 create a somewhat bizarre commemorative sculpture that communicates the idea to viewers with a minimal title **EE1, 2**

2 exercise craftsmanship in using materials so that they contribute to the final appearance of the sculpture **EE 4**

Vocabulary

Commemorative means "in remembrance of something."

Armature is a framework used to support material being modeled in sculpture.

Warm Up

Ask students to think of the most memorable ideas or events they can remember. List them on the chalkboard.

Explore and Develop

1 Show examples of commemorative art. **R 1** Define commemorative art; it may be two- or three-dimensional. Have students tell what they think some of the sculptures commemorate. What do they think of the recent ones by Oldenburg, Grooms, and Ukeles?

2 Focus on the student examples in Studio Experience 13.2. These were made of papier mâché or plaster gauze. Explain the use of found materials for an armature. Masking tape and string can be used to hold parts temporarily. Newspaper can be wadded, shaped, and held with tape or string.

Begin Studio Experience 13.2

1 Using papier mâché or plaster cloth, demonstrate how to shape paper with tape and how to apply the medium.

2 Demonstrate how to model details with the medium by modeling and covering some parts separately, then adding them to the main form. Both materials can be cut with heavy scissors or utility knives. **Advise caution when using the mat knife.**

3 Have students collect materials for decorative and communicative effects. Have them use white glue to hold materials on either medium.

Laser Discs:

Desjardins, Louis XIV on Horseback, 1698–1699

Search Frame 2464

Houdon, Voltaire, 1778

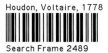

Search Frame 2489

Messionier, A Horseman in a Storm, c 1880

Search Frame 2520

Manship, Diana and her Hound, 1925

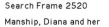

Search Frame 2559

Smith, Sentinel I, 1956

Search Frame 2587

Segal, Girl Putting on an Earring, 1967

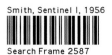

Search Frame 2597

4 Students can use acrylic or tempera paint on either medium. Adding a little white glue to the liquid tempera makes it more permanent. Have students print a title as an optional addition to the finished work.

Evaluate and Reflect

1 Do students feel they were successful in using the materials to communicate their idea to others?

2 Can other students grasp the idea or meaning of the sculpture?

3 How do students feel about the craftsmanship or final appearance of their artwork?

4 Did students exercise imagination and some humor in their sculptures?

Reteach

Direct students to study questions relevant to the modeling or build-up process: 10, 12, 13, 14, 18, 19, 20. Ask them to look up and share answers in a small group.

Extend the Lesson

Beyond the Basics

EE 1 Have students look for commemorative sculpture in the community. Record the title, location, medium, and purpose of the sculpture. Share with the class.

EE 3, 4 Assign groups of students to research national commemorative sculptures such as Mount Rushmore, the Lincoln
R 3 Memorial, or the Vietnam Veterans
W 1, 2 Memorial and report to the class. Include information about the individuals or events commemorated, the artist(s) who designed it, and information about its construction. Have them look for biographies and related literature about the individuals or the events. Suggest students begin by describing and analyzing the artwork. Suggest contacting the National Parks Service for additional resource material.

Cultural Connections

The totems and painted relief carvings pro- EE 3
duced by the Northwest Coast tribes—for example, the Tlingit tribe—will interest students. They can determine their pur- R 5
pose, the meanings of symbols used, and the beliefs underlying their development.

Many traditional American quilts were EE 2, 3
commemorative works of art. Scraps of fabric saved from clothing and household items represented the family history and each piece usually had a story behind it. Quilts produced to celebrate special events were rich with symbolism. Most of the early quilts were intended to be used for warmth, but some elaborate and purely decorative designs began to develop. The use of trapunto, produced by over-stuffing an area, created a type of low relief. The soft sculpture techniques shown in figures 13–52 and 13–53 are derived from trapunto tecniques used in quilting. Suggest students produce a commemorative soft sculpture.

Connecting with Other Subjects

Social Studies Suggest students make a list R 3
of the wars and conflicts in which America W 2
has been involved. Have them look for an example of commemorative sculpture for as many events as possible. The National Parks Service may provide helpful information. Suggest working with the history teacher and prepare a presentation to be shared in both classes.

Language Arts Suggest students read *The* R 3
Quilters (1956), by Norma Bradley Allen and Patricia Cooper, a play showing the joys and hardships from a woman's point of view during pioneer days. The pieces of the quilt tell the story.

A Wood Relief

Time: 3 periods

Preparation

Rationale

Relief sculptures have been used throughout history to tell stories, record events, and decorate architecture. For example, the frieze around the Parthenon depicts a procession of young men paying tribute to Athena. Reliefs continue to adorn public buildings today. This activity, in which students construct a relief of wood shapes, introduces them to some of the challenges involved in designing and producing relief sculpture.

Studio Materials

assorted wood scraps, dowels, base panels, hand tools, white glue, nails, sandpaper, paints, stains

Enrichment Materials

Slides:
• N. America, Onandaga, Broken Nose Mask, 3
• Africa, Double Face Mask, 66

Large Reproductions:
• *Plate—Hunting Rams,* 7

Teach the Lesson

Objectives

Students should be able to:

1   construct a relief of wood shapes that demonstrates compositional organization through similarity of shapes, proximity of shapes, and continuation of edges from shape to shape   **EE 2**

Vocabulary

Low relief sculpture projects slightly from the surface to which it is attached.

High relief sculpture stands out boldly from the surface to which it is attached.

Warm Up

Ask students to explain what relief sculpture is and give examples they have seen. Direct attention to the example in Studio Experience 13.3. It suggests what can be done with wooden scraps from the industrial arts shop.

Explore and Develop

1   Discuss assemblage, which includes   **R 1**
relief sculpture. Nevelson's *Sky Cathedral* can be used as an example of high relief. Ask students what gives Nevelson's sculpture unity. See also Stella's *Katsura* in figure 13–30 and discuss what gives it unity. Show examples of relief sculpture to make the historical connection.

Begin Studio Experience 13.3

1   Provide students with plywood or masonite to build the relief on. Have them select a group of shapes that go well together visually. Have them experiment with grouping the shapes on the base board. Encourage some similarities in shape, color, grain, and size. Pieces may be layered or stair-stepped.

2   Encourage students to think of an idea or descriptive phrase that the relief might represent.

3   The pieces may be used as found, or they may be modified with hand tools. (Reliefs can be completed in two periods if shapes are used as found.) **Caution students to exercise proper care when using hand tools.** If any sanding or staining is needed, students should do it before attaching the pieces to the base. Shapes may be attached with white glue and elevated with finish nails or dowels. Holes should be drilled for dowel attachments.

4 Linseed oil, stains, acrylics, and enamels may be used to enhance the wood and help with unity, contrast, and dominance.

Evaluate and Reflect

1 Ask students to analyze their compositions. Do the pieces of the relief interrelate so that the viewer is aware of the whole form rather than parts? Can students identify similarities and continuities? Is there a dominant area or element?

2 Is there an idea or thematic purpose underlying the selection and arrangement of shapes?

3 Are students satisfied with their craftsmanship and final appearance of their reliefs?

Reteach

Students who had trouble selecting and organizing shapes into an interesting composition can experiment with geometric cardboard shapes produced on the paper cutter. Have them work with a "family" of shapes, placing them carefully to obtain proximity and continuity. Cardboard can be layered to obtain variations in relief. Ask students to analyze the composition before gluing it down.

Extend the Lesson

Beyond the Basics

EE 3   Organize students in two groups. One can research examples of low relief, and the other can review high relief. The first group
R 3   might study Egyptian, Sumerian and
W 4   Assyrian structures. The other groups might research high relief on the walls of European cathedrals constructed in the Middle Ages and the Renaissance. Bring the groups together for discussion and comparison of findings.

E 1, 2   Have students look for buildings in the community, either public or private, with exterior views that give little indication of
W 1, 2   the building's purpose or usage and/or buildings that would provide interesting locations for relief sculptures. Have students research and possibly interview building occupants. Have them design a relief sculpture for the building. Suggest they approach the problem as if the sculpture were going to be installed. Willing occupants might work with students in an artist-client relationship. Finished work should include a proposal, artist renderings of the work from several viewpoints, a set of working drawings (ask drafting teacher for help or collaborate with a drafting student), cost estimates, and a model of the sculpture.

A similar approach could be taken for designing relief sculptures to be installed in various areas of the school.

Cultural Connections

Have students browse through resource   EE 1, 3
material to find examples of contemporary relief sculpture in buildings in other parts of the world. *National Geographic* may be a good place to start. Examine the works to determine if they tell stories, record events, or simply decorate the building. Compare with relief sculptures found in local or nearby communities. Discuss similarities and differences.

Connecting with Other Subjects

Science Have students research how some   R 5
of the ancient reliefs were made. Compare early processes with methods of construction used today. Identify the tools used and their purposes. Talk with the technology teacher to find out what new tools are used for the same purpose.

Language Arts Suggest students select a   R 4
favorite relief sculpture that tells a story. Identify the story from the credit line or by examining the content. Find the written form of the same story and read it. If titles are not available show the sculpture to the language arts teacher for suggestions.

A Hand-Built Coil Pot

Time: 2 periods

Preparation

Rationale

Hand-building procedures for making pottery were used by prehistoric peoples and are still employed by contemporary ceramists. Coil building was developed into a fine art by Native American artists such as Maria Martinez. The coils of clay may be used as the dominant decorative element on the exterior of a vessel. In this lesson, students construct a cylindrical pot inside a clay field tile, thereby preserving the outer coil surface, while permitting rapid construction within the supportive tile walls.

Studio Materials

clay, 12" x 6" clay drainage tiles, clay boards, clay tools, plastic bags, table covering, engobes, clear glaze (optional)

Enrichment Materials

Overhead Transparencies:
• Maria bowl, 16

Large Reproductions:
• Lucero, *Zoomorphic Dog Vessel*, 9
• Swentzell, *The Emergence of the Clowns*, 22

Teach the Lesson

Objectives

Students should be able to:

1 construct coil pots, using clay drainage tiles as molds, to explore the decorative and expressive potentials of the coils   EE 2

2 experiment with decorative shapes that can be made with coils and the addition of lumps, balls, and small slabs of clay   EE 4

Warm Up

Have students tell about the clay hand-building procedures they have used. Direct attention to the student examples in Studio Experience 13.4. If possible, prepare about 6 inches of coil building in a tile to show students how the process works.

Explore and Develop

1 Explain that building a coil pot inside a clay drainage tile lets them use the supporting walls of the tile to explore the decorative potentials of coiling. Students do not have to wait for the bottom coils to become firm before building the top. In fact, the whole pot can be built in one session. The supporting walls permit things to be done with coils, lumps, small slabs, and openings that would not be possible in construction of a freestanding pot.

2 Be sure the inside edges of the tile openings are free of burrs. They may be quickly removed with a file. To begin, have students roll a slab of clay a bit larger than the tile opening and press an open end of the tile against the clay. Have them cut along the inner edge of the impressed circle, making a bottom the tile will slide over.

3 Tell students to lay the bottom piece on a clay board and attach the first three inches of coils *before* sliding the tile over them. They should keep checking to be sure the tile will fit over the coils. Students should join the coils firmly on the inside but should *not* smooth the coils on the outside.

4 Have students set the tile over the first 3 inches of coils and continue building. Encourage students to try forming loops, spirals, and zigzags of coils to set into the walls. Slip can help join coils. Students should push them gently against the tile wall and smooth them together on the inside only.

5 Coils and slabs can be pressed against textured surfaces before being added to the pot. Students should place the textured surface against the tile wall. As building progresses, they should smooth clay over the inner coil surface to strengthen attachments.

6   Do not let students flair the top out beyond the tile opening, as the tile must be lifted off the clay pot. Tell them to drape the tile with plastic when not working on the pot. When building is completed, students should let the clay dry overnight to shrink away from the tile wall. Students should lift the tile off after shrinkage has taken place. Make sure students do *not* lift the pot by the rim or upper half, because it can be pulled apart. Have students complete any trimming or additional decorative procedures while the clay is damp. Engobes can be added when the piece is leather hard. Proceed with drying and firing.

Evaluate and Reflect

1   Have students discuss how the coils and shapes contribute to the visual organization of their pots.

2   What similarities and contrasts do they see?

3   Discuss the rhythmical movement of line over the pot's surface.

4   How do they feel about their craftsmanship in constructing their pots? Did their pots hold together when they removed the tile?

5   Did students explore alternatives in creating different kinds of coils and coil shapes?

Reteach

Assign study questions dealing with ceramics: 14, 15, 16, 17, 23, 24, 25.

Extend the Lesson
Beyond the Basics

This procedure is not mastered in one trial. If time permits, have students use what they have learned to build additional pots. Try new things with the coils: leave openings, vary coils in size, alternate coils with some other shape, impress images in slab shapes worked in among the coils. Enhance the coil pattern with color.   **EE 2**

Suggest students use one of the handbuilt pottery techniques shown in this chapter to produce an abstract sculpture. Suggest they begin by drawing an object from nature, such as flowers, cabbage leaves, a seashell or the human figure. Have them distill their drawing to reduce it to its simplest form. Use this drawing as a guide for making the sculpture. Ask students to consider what texture or surface treatment would be appropriate for their sculptures.   **EE 2**

Cultural Connections

Have students read the biography of Maria Martinez, Student Edition page 240. Every early culture developed pottery forms, techniques for decorating them, and kilns to fire them in. Have students select early cultures and research the characteristics of their pottery forms. How were they made, decorated and fired? What were they used for?   **EE 3**   **R 3**

Connecting with Other Subjects

Science   Have students research to find information about the firing process that changes clay into ceramics. Suggest talking with the chemistry teacher to explore the same ideas from a scientific viewpoint. Examine the chemical composition of various glazes and determine why they produce certain effects. Share information with the class.   **R 3**

A Harmonious Stained Glass Panel

Time: 4 periods

Preparation

Rationale

The Gothic style of architecture made it possible to include many windows in churches and cathedrals. This development opened the way for a form of expression that emphasized a new element—light. Windows of stained glass create a special excitement when the light in a room is transformed by the colors of the glass.

Studio Materials

scraps of stained glass, 8" x 10" or 9" x 12" picture frame with plate glass (supplied by students), Duco cement, glass cutters, cutting oil, tablet backs or pieces of backing board, flat-nose pliers, paper, watercolors, brushes, felt-tip pens, black or gray window glazing putty, glass cleaner, safety goggles

Enrichment Materials

Slides:
• French Stained Glass Window, 51

Large Reproductions:
• Glaser, *Saratoga*, 24

Teach the Lesson

Objectives

Students should be able to:

1 use stained glass remnants to construct a small panel of harmonious colors and shapes   EE 1, 2

Vocabulary

Harmony is a condition in which the elements of an artwork appear to fit well together.

Warm Up

Provide scraps of colored glass. Have students tape different colors of glass on the window. Have them place some related colors side by side and contrasting colors together. How do the colors affect one another? Do students have preferences? Could both contrasting and related colors be used in the same composition? **Instruct students in safe handling of glass and glass cutting and breaking tools. Provide safety glasses for all students.**

Explore and Develop

1 Show examples of stained glass windows and panels. Discuss the harmony of colors. Note how lead came lines become a part of the composition. They provide a pattern that contributes to unity, which is especially apparent when clear glass is used, as in figure 13–64. The black lines in the examples for Studio Experience 13.5 were made with black putty, which fills in the spaces between pieces of glass. What contributes to unity in the student examples?

Begin Studio Experience 13.5

1 Have students use a pointed marker to trace a line on the glass around the inner edge of the picture frame. Have students carefully remove the glass from their picture frames and trace around the glass on paper two or three times.

2 With available glass colors in mind, have the students explore some compositional ideas with watercolor in outlined shapes. Colors will not match the glass but give a general idea of what will go where. Panels may be abstract or nonobjective. Encourage them to think about colors that harmonize. If symbols are to be included, students may have to use the glass cutter and pliers to shape some pieces. Implied movement, organizing around a central shape, converging lines, rhythmical alternations, and repetition of a motif can contribute to dominance and unity.

3 Have each student place the watercolor sketch under the glass on a drawing board. *The black line on the glass should be against the sketch.* Ask them to select and put pieces of stained glass in shallow Styrofoam or aluminum containers to take to their work area.

4 Have students begin arranging glass pieces on the glass plate using the sketch as a general guide. *All glass shapes should be placed inside the black line,* which leaves about ¼ inch open so the plate will drop back into the frame when finished. Students can shape pieces of glass by holding them firmly and nibbling small bits off over a waste container. If large enough, students can score them with a glass cutter, and while gripping one side with the thumb and finger, pull the other side off with pliers. **Caution students to avoid glass cuts and eye injuries from particles formed by breaking glass.**

5 The pieces of glass are assembled on the plate somewhat like a mosaic. They do not have to fit snugly. Spaces will be filled in with putty. On the other hand, very large spaces filled with putty are unattractive. Have students run a bead of Duco cement all the way around the bottom edge of each piece and set in place. The bead of cement keeps putty from leaking under the piece of stained glass.

6 When all pieces are in place, tell students to check for excessively large spaces and put glass in them. They should *push* small amounts of putty into the spaces and not pull their fingers along the spaces. Gentle downward pressure does the job nicely. Putty should be level with, or just under, the surface of the glass shapes. The putty will dry overnight. Tell students to use a single-edge razor blade to scrape dry putty off glass.

7 Have students put screw eyes in the top of the frame, make a nylon cord loop, glue the glass plate in the frame, with the stained glass side to the front, and hang the panel in a window.

Evaluate and Reflect

1 Do students feel the colors they selected work well together? If not, how could they improve the composition?

2 Are they satisfied with the interrelatedness of the glass pieces and shapes?

3 Ask them to analyze dominance in the stained glass panels.

4 Are students satisfied with the craftsmanship in their stained glass panels?

Reteach

See lesson 13–6.

Extend the Lesson

Beyond the Basics

Churches built before the Gothic cathedrals had solid walls and very few windows. Artists were called upon to decorate the walls. With the introduction of Gothic architecture artists were no longer needed for this purpose. Why? How did artists respond to this change? Ask students to think about more recent innovations that may have produced significant change in today's world. How may those changes have affected artists?

EE 3

R 4

Connecting with Other Subjects

History Ask students to think about what it means to "shed a little light on a subject." Light is associated with knowledge and understanding; however, the associations are often more than symbolic. The "dark ages" were actually dark. The architecture was heavy, massive, and windows were very small. Gothic architecture opened spaces up and filled them with light. Discuss these ideas. How might actual light have contributed to the growth of knowledge over the next four hundred years?

R 4

A Window Panel with Paper

Three-Dimensional Media

Time: 2 periods

Preparation

Rationale

The art of stained glass has an interesting history with beginnings in Egypt sometime prior to 1500 BC. From the 11th to the 16th century it was reserved for religious use. It was nearly lost in the 17th and 18th centuries. The art nouveau movement and glass makers like La Farge and Tiffany revived the art in the 20th century. Today, stained glass is a popular art practiced by professionals and amateurs.

Studio Materials

colored cellophane or tissue paper, black construction paper, glue sticks, X-acto knives, newsprint, chalk, pencils

Enrichment Materials

Large Reproductions:
• Glaser, *Saratoga*, 24

Teach the Lesson

Objectives

Students should be able to:

1   design a simulated stained glass panel from black construction paper and colored cellophane or tissue   EE 1, 2

Vocabulary

Harmony is a condition in which the elements of an artwork appear to fit well together.

Warm Up

Give each student a 3" x 6" strip of black paper. Have them fold it in half and use chalk to draw a geometric shape that fills most of the square. Have students cut the shape out through both layers of paper at once. Tell students to unfold the paper with the chalk line side up and glue cellophane or tissue over the opening on one side. They should place glue around the outer edges of the other side and fold the paper shut, sandwiching the tissue inside. Display all the squares, in a group and touching one another, on a window so colors can be seen with light passing through.

Explore and Develop

1   Display examples of stained glass windows or panels. Ask students where they have seen examples of stained glass. Do they know how the pieces of glass are held in place? Point out the lead came in the examples. Direct attention to Student Edition page 184. Discuss how colored light is emphasized in stained glass art. Point out how the lead came makes a pattern of line in a stained glass work.

Begin Studio Experience 13.6

1   Give students 18" x 24" sheets of newsprint and black construction paper, sheets of cardboard, pencils, a piece of white chalk, X-acto knives, and glue.

2   Students should fold the newsprint in half, then fold it again to make a center crease, which makes it easier to work out a symmetrical composition. If this is a first experience, encourage students to work with nonrepresentational shapes or simplified symbols. Explain that they should leaves strips of paper about half an inch wide between shapes they cut out. Remind them of the lead came which becomes a part of the design in a stained glass window.

3 When they have worked out a satisfactory pattern on newsprint, have students lay it on a sheet of cardboard and cut the openings out with an X-acto knife (or scissors). **Advise students to exercise care when using the knives.**

4 Tell students to lay the newsprint pattern on a folded sheet of black construction paper, trace the openings with white chalk, and cut out the openings.

5 Students should unfold the construction paper, with the chalked side up, and glue colors of cellophane or tissue paper over the openings on one side of the paper. Have them refold the paper and determine if any more openings need to be cut. If not, they should open the paper up, run glue around the openings on the other side of the paper, and fold it closed, sandwiching the colors in between.

6 Display the finished work against a lighted window to appreciate the colored light.

Evaluate and Reflect

1 Are students satisfied with their selections of colors? Do they seem to work together?

2 Are they satisfied with the appearance of their work? If not, what could they do differently?

3 Discuss how the compositions are balanced.

4 Do the black lines provide a pattern that helps to unify the work?

Reteach

Students may prefer to work with two separate sheets of construction paper. Repeat shapes on one piece of paper, leaving 2" strips between shapes when cutting them out. Trace open shapes on second paper, and glue tissue over openings. Sandwich construction paper pieces together.

Extend the Lesson
Beyond the Basics

If this is a first experience, or some students finish quickly, challenge them to try another panel, using symbols to communicate an idea—that was a primary purpose of stained glass windows in the Gothic period. Students might experiment with overlapping colors to create new hues. Black paper shapes can be glued to the tissue or cellophane placed in openings.   **EE 2**

The influence of Medieval stained glass can be found in other art forms. Before the invention of the printing press all books were made by hand and many of them included painted illustrations or illuminations. Compare early illuminations with those produced during the 13th and 14th centuries to see the influence of Medieval stained glass. The same influence can be seen in the work of 20th century artist Georges Rouault. Describe and analyze one of Rouault's paintings.   **EE 3, 4**

R 4
W 2

Cultural Connections

Direct students' attention to the jewelry designs on pages 178 and 179 of the student text. Have students use library resources to find examples of how people in different cultures have adorned themselves. Include examples from their own culture. Prepare a display or presentation to share with the class.   **EE 3**

R 3, 4
W 2

Connecting with Other Subjects

Science Have students research the history of glass and the techniques used to produce it. Investigate the ingredients used to make glass and the chemical changes that occur during the process . Compare ancient techniques with methods used by contemporary artists and manufacturers. If possible visit a museum or gallery that has a collection of ancient and contemporary glass.   **R 3**
W 2

Name: _____   Course: _____

Study Questions
Chapter 13–Three-Dimensional Media

Three-Dimensional Media

1 What is the main difference between low relief and high relief sculpture?

_____

_____

2 Define *sculpture in the round.*

_____

_____

3 For what purpose did Egyptians place life-size sculptures in the tombs of their rulers?

_____

4 Two common materials used for carving are _____ and _____.

5 What does a sculptor usually make before beginning to carve a sculpture?

_____

6 What are two ways that the surface of a wood or stone sculpture can be treated?

_____

7 How does the treatment of the surface of Henry Moore's *Reclining Figure* (text fig. 13–8) relate to the form?

_____

8 Describe the *casting* process.

_____

_____

9 What is the process that is used for casting hollow metal sculptures?

_____

10 What is an armature?

_____

11 Describe the process of casting with polyester resin that Duane Hanson uses to create his very life-like sculptures.

_____

_____

12 How did George Segal make the plaster figure in the environmental sculpture *The Parking Garage* (text fig. 13–18)?

_____

13 Define *modeling.*

_____

_____

14 What four stages are necessary to produce a sculpture or pottery from clay?

_____

15 How are forms constructed from coils of clay?

_____

16 What are two ways that slabs of clay can be formed?

_____

17 Name one ceramic sculpture illustrated in the chapter that was made using the coil process; the slab process.

_____

18 What are constructions?

_____

_____

19 What is an assemblage?

_____

_____

20 Name two artists who use the assemblage procedure.

_____

21 Name three sources of energy that an artist may use for kinetic sculpture.

_____

22 Environmental artists like to (a) involve the spectator in the artwork, or (b) make the work a part of the environment around it. Give one example of each that is described in the chapter.

_____

23 Name three things that prehistoric people used for containers before the discovery of clay.

_____

24 How were the first pots and clay figures fired?

_____

25 Name the three methods of hand-building with clay.

_____

26 Give three reasons why gold has been a desirable metal for jewelry-making for over 6,000 years.

_____

_____

27 Describe the _repoussé_ process.

_____

_____

28 Describe the _enameling_ process. Give one example of this method.

_____

_____

29 Name four materials other than metal used to make jewelry.

_____

30 Describe the process of weaving.

_____

_____

31 For what kind of sculpture are Claes Oldenburg, Susan Anton, and Barbara Johansen Newman known? What sculpture medium do they use?

_____

32 Who first discovered how to make glass; and when?

_____

33 Name two ways that glass can be formed into three-dimensional objects.

_____

_____

34 How are individual pieces of glass in a stained glass construction held together?

_____

35 What effect has technology had on contemporary three-dimensional artists?

_____

_____

_____

Test Questions
Chapter 13–Three-Dimensional Media

Fill in the blanks or circle the correct answers below.

1 Name the four categories of sculpture that are discussed in this chapter. _____,

_____, _____, and _____.

2 Sculpture that is part of, or attached to, a surface

    a. is called a relief.
    b. can project slightly or a great deal.
    c. is a twentieth century innovation.
    d. all of the above.
    e. a and b.

3 Sculpture in the round

    a. can be seen from all sides.
    b. is always circular.
    c. is always placed on a base.
    d. all of the above.

4 The glass blow pipe was invented between

    a. 2500 and 2000 BC.   c. 500 and 300 BC.
    b. 1,000 and 800 BC.   d. 200 and 100 BC.

5 Pressing a hand into wet sand and filling the impression with plaster is a simple example of

    a. the lost-wax process.
    b. a one-piece mold.
    c. using an investment.

6 Prehistoric pots and clay figures were fired in

    a. underground caves.
    b. brick kilns.
    c. shallow pits.

7 Clay forms that are hardened and finished by firing in a kiln are called

    a. ceramic sculpture.
    b. repoussé.
    c. cloisonné.

8 Slab, coil, and pinch are handbuilding processes used for working in

    a. bronze.   c. clay.
    b. glass.   d. fibers.

9 Casting, annealing, soldering, cutting, piercing, and engraving are all procedures used for making

    a. metal jewelry.
    b. handblown glass forms.
    c. repoussé forms.

10 The process of raising lines and shapes in relief on thin metal is called

    a. tooling   c. annealing.
    b. repoussé.   d. burnishing.

11 T F Egyptians placed life-size figures of wood and stone in their tombs to provide homes for the spirits of their rulers.

12 T F Lead came is most often used to join stained glass pieces in three-dimensional forms.

13 T F Christo's *Wrapped Islands* is an example of environmental art.

14 T F In weaving, the *weft* threads are woven through the *warp* threads.

15 T F To be considered a sculpture, a form must be at least a foot in height.

16 T F Gold has been a favorite metal for jewelry-making because of its malleability.

For questions 17 through 22 use the following list of words.

    1. texture
    2. happening
    3. armature
    4. assemblage
    5. carved sculpture
    6. environmental

17 A sculptor wanting to make a large, cast bronze form will first make a clay sculpture over a framework of metal rods and plaster called a/an _____.

18 When the artist Ernst Barlach carved the wood sculpture, *The Vision*, he left the marks of the carving tool, emphasizing the _____.

19 A sculpture which contains several materials such as wood, plaster life masks, paint, photographs, fabric, and other found objects is called a/an _____.

20 Creating a/an _____ sculpture may involve a construction crew and earth moving equipment.

21 A _____ is an art experience that involves the artist in person, and sometimes viewers, as active participants.

22 *The Presidents,* by George Borglum and his son, at Mount Rushmore National Park is a gigantic

    _____.

For questions 23 through 30, use the following list of words.

    1. soft sculpture   4. pottery

    2. kinetic sculpture   5. lost-wax casting

    3. painted metal   6. painted wood

While viewing overhead transparencies, answer the following questions:

23 The sculpture created by Nancy Graves was most likely made of _____.

24 The mobile made by Alexander Calder is only one type of _____.

25 Artists, like Claes Oldenburg, who make sculpture out of stuffed fabric, create _____.

(Overhead Transparency # 2)

26 Barbara Hepworth used _____ to make this smooth, organic-shaped sculpture.

(Overhead Transparency # 8)

27 This sculpture made of copper alloy shows that the Ife tribe in Africa have used the _____ process for a long time.

(Overhead Transparency # 16)

28 The form shown in this transparency is a clay form called _____.

Study Answers
Chapter 13
Three-Dimensional Media

1 Low relief—Shapes project slightly. High relief—Shapes project a great deal.

2 Sculpture that is created to be walked around and seen from all sides.

3 To provide homes for the spirits of the deceased.

4 Wood and stone.

5 Drawings or small clay models of the sculpture.

6 The surface can be highly polished, left textured, or be given a combination of polished and textured areas.

7 Moore sanded the surface, emphasizing the wood grain, which contributes to the flow of the sculptural form.

8 A liquid substance such as molten metal, plaster, or plastic is poured into a mold, where it is held until hardened.

9 Lost-wax casting.

10 A framework used to support material being modeled.

11 Hanson applies plaster gauze strips directly to sections of the body of a person whose skin and hair have been heavily greased. Flesh colored polyester resin is painted into the molds and laminated with layers of glass cloth. The hardened casts are assembled to create figures.

12 George Segal makes molds by forming plaster gauze over fully clothed living models. The molds, which are made in sections, are removed and reassembled to become the sculpture. The surface of the sculptures are rough because he does not smooth the molded texture of the plaster.

13 An additive process in which a sculpture is built up in a pliable material like clay, wax, or plaster.

14 Preparation, shaping, decorating, and firing.

15 Coils of clay are placed one on top of another. Joints are smoothed together.

16 By beating flat with the hand or paddle, or spread with a rolling pin.

17 Coil—*Cavalryman with Horse* Qin dynasty (text fig. 13–21); *Zwartman* by VandenBerge (text fig. 13–22); Slab—*Leaning Man III* by Frey (text fig. 13–23).

18 Sculptures built from parts which may be of the same or different materials.

19 Sculptures constructed from a variety of found objects and materials, which in their original states were not necessarily meant to be used in art forms.

20 Louise Nevelson and Marisol Escobar.

21 Answers may include wind and air current, falling water, temperature changes, springs, motors, magnets, etc.

22 (a) *Ruckus Rodeo* by Grooms (text fig. 13–33) and *The Diner* by Segal (text fig. 13–37), and (b) *Spiral Jetty* by Smithson (text fig. 13–34) and *Wrapped Coast* (text fig. 1–10) or *Surrounded Islands* (text fig. 13–36) by Christo.

23 Animal skins, shells, gourds, and woven baskets, etc.

24 In shallow pits lined and covered with twigs and dry wood.

25 Pinch, coil, and slab.

26 Because it has great beauty and value, it never tarnishes, it is easy to stretch.

27 Hammering or pressing sheet metal from one side to raise shapes, or patterns on the other side.

28 Ground glass, colored by metal oxides, are fused to metal by heating them in a kiln. Cloisonné is one example.

29 Answers may include plastic, wood, leather, fabric, fibers.

30 One thread, called the weft, crosses over and under alternate warp threads, which are stretched on the loom.

31 Soft sculpture. Fabric.

32 Egyptians, about 3000 BC.

33 By casting or blowing.

34 By lead strips called "came," which are soldered together at joints; or by copper-foil tape, which is soldered together along the foiled edges.

35 Answers may include: has provided limitless new materials for sculptural creation; has provided the possibility for combining many materials, etc.

Test Answers
Chapter 13
Three-Dimensional Media

1 Carving, casting, modeling, and construction.

2 E.

3 A.

4 D.

5 B.

6 C.

7 A.

8 C.

9 A.

10 B.

11 T

12 F

13 T

14 T

15 F

16 T

17 (3.) armature

18 (1.) texture

19 (4.) assemblage

20 (6.) environmental

21 (2.) happening

22 (5.) carved sculpture

23 (3.) painted metal

24 (2.) kinetic sculpture

25 (1.) soft sculpture

26 (6.) painted wood

27 (5.) lost-wax casting

28 (4.) pottery

Chapter 13
Three-Dimensional Media

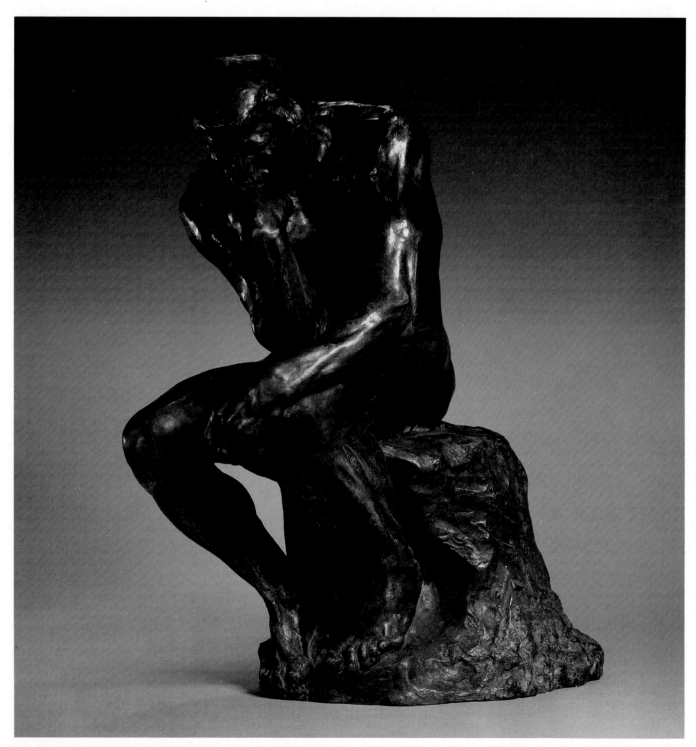

13–1 Auguste Rodin, *The Thinker*, 1880. Bronze, 28 ⅛″ x 14 ⅜″ x 23 ½″ (72 x 36 x 60 cm). ©1993 National Gallery of Art, Washington. Gift of Mrs. John W. Simpson.

In Chapter 12, you learned about the media that artists use for two-dimensional art. Artists use many other media to create three-dimensional art. In fact, there are few materials that are not used in the creation of art. If you were asked to list some examples of media used for sculptures, you would probably think of wood, stone, and metal, or pottery made from clay. You might also think of media you have used in school such as papier-mâché and plaster. Would you be surprised to learn that three-dimensional forms can be produced with crocheted fiber (fig. 13–2)?

Sculpture

We will begin this chapter with a discussion of four categories of sculpture: carving, casting, modeling, and construction. Each type of sculpture uses different media. Sculpture that is part of, or attached to, a surface is called **relief.** In a *low relief,* the shapes project slightly. The section of a carved sandstone wall made in the twelfth century for the Bayon Temple at Angkor Thom, Cambodia (fig. 13–3) is an example of low relief sculpture. *High relief* figures project a great deal, as in the cast bronze panel by Lorenzo Ghiberti (fig. 13–4). Sculpture that is created to be walked around and seen from all sides, like *The Thinker* by Auguste Rodin (fig. 13–1), is called sculpture in the round. Both reliefs and sculptures in the round can be cast, carved, or constructed in a variety of materials.

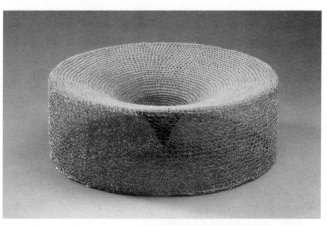

13–2 Norma Minkowitz, *Passage to Nowhere,* 1985. Fiber, acrylic, pencil, shellac, 7 ½″ x 9 ¾″ (19 x 25 cm) diameter. Bellas Artes, Santa Fe.

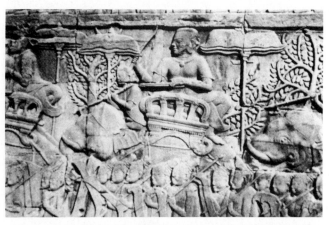

13–3 Processional Scene from the Bayon Temple, Angkor Thom, late twelfth century, Cambodia. Sandstone.

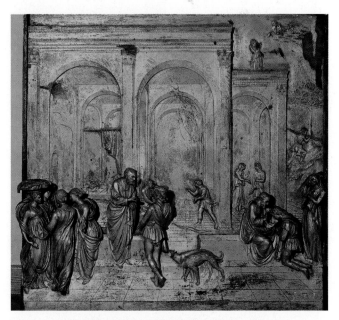

13–4 Lorenzo Ghiberti, *The Story of Jacob and Esau,* detail from *The Gates of Paradise,* ca. 1435. Gilt bronze, 31 ¼″ (79 cm) square. Formella dell Porta del Paradiso. The Baptistry, Florence. Scala/Art Resource, NY.

Try it Yourself

Look for relief sculptures in your community. What kind are they? What are they made of? Where are they located? Do the reliefs record or symbolize events or beliefs? Is their purpose simply decorative?

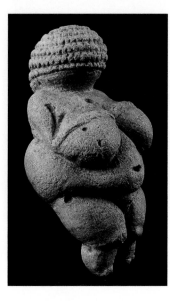

13–5 *Venus of Willendorf,* original ca. 15,000–10,000 BC. Stone, 4 ³⁄₈″ (11 cm) high. Naturhistorisches Museum, Vienna, Austria. Erich Lessing/Art Resource, NY.

13–6 *Pair Statue of King Mycerinus and Queen Kah-merer,* Fourth Dynasty. Greywacke, 54 ½″ (138 cm) high. Museum Expeditions. Courtesy, Museum of Fine Arts, Boston.

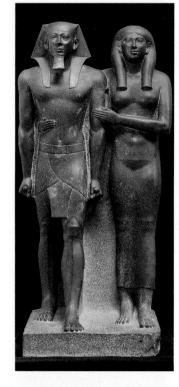

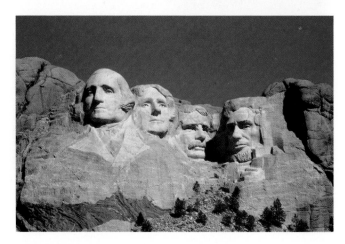

Carving

We know that humans have carved forms since the Stone Age. They used materials such as bones, horn, antlers, wood, and stone. Approximately 15,000 years ago, an Ice Age carver created the little figure known as the *Venus of Willendorf* (fig. 13–5). Imagine carving this statuette from stone with crude and clumsy tools made of stone. Over 4,500 years ago, Egyptian artists produced life-size figures in both wood and stone, using tools made of bronze (fig. 13–6).

The basic tools for sculpture in stone include metal hammers and a variety of chisels and files. The sculptor also uses sanding, grinding, and polishing equipment. Basic tools for wood include wooden mallets, gouges with different shaped cutting edges, rasps, scrapers, and sanding and polishing materials. Power sanders, band saws and chain saws are also used by some wood sculptors.

Stone sculptures can be small enough to hold in the hand, like the *Venus of Willendorf,* or large enough to fill a mountainside, like the portraits of four presidents on Mount Rushmore (fig. 13–7). This gigantic relief carving required the use of pneumatic hammers and chisels driven by compressed air. The size of carved wood sculpture is limited to the size of wood pieces that can be obtained from the largest trees.

Sculpting in stone or wood is very demanding. The sculptor usually makes drawings and small clay models to show what the sculpture will look like from all sides. In the first phase of carving, the sculptor chisels or gouges out the general forms on the surfaces of the wood or stone. The sculptor is interested in making all the forms on the surface interrelate. The viewer's eye should move from one part to the other.

As the carving continues, the forms are refined. The sculptor decides where to place positive and negative areas. Positive areas may be solid and/or **convex** (curving outward). Negative areas may be openings and/or **concave** (curving inward). These forms provide contrasts. They also contribute to eye movement around and across the sculpture. Positive turns to negative as the eye moves smoothly from solid forms to openings in Henry Moore's *Reclining Figure* (fig. 13–8). Ernst Barlach created contrasting convex and concave areas that direct eye movement around the forms of *The Vision* (fig. 13–9).

13–7 George Borglum and Son, *The Presidents,* 1927–1941. Carved granite. Mount Rushmore National Monument. Courtesy United States Department of the Interior, National Park Service.

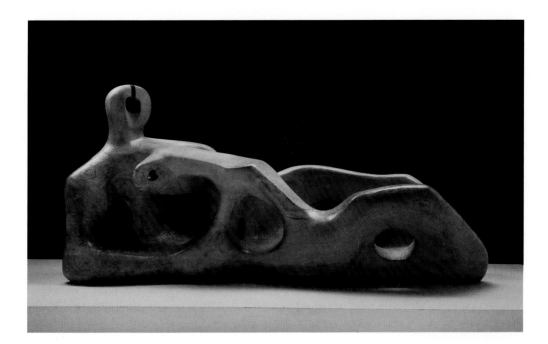

The finished stone or wood sculpture can be highly polished or textured. The sculpture may have both polished and textured surfaces. Moore sanded the surface of Reclining Figure to emphasize the wood grain. The smooth surface contributes to the flow of the sculptural forms. Barlach blended the characteristic marks of the gouge and the wood grain in *The Vision*. Do the textures add meaning to the two sculptures? How do the textures affect the feelings that you get from each sculpture?

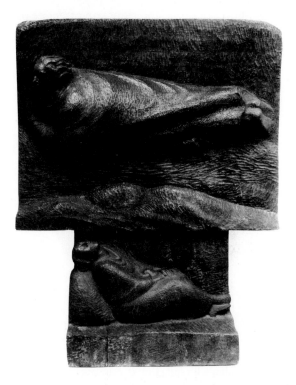

13-9 Ernst Barlach, *The Vision*, 1912. Relief (oak). Staatliche Museen zu Berlin, PreuBischer Kulturbesitz, Nationalgalerie.

Studio Experience 13.1

A Sculpture with Movement

Carve an abstract or nonrepresentational sculpture from plaster. Create forms that cause the viewer's eye to move from one part to another.

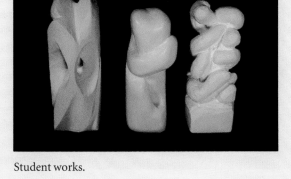

Student works.

Casting

So far we have discussed sculpting in wood and stone. The sculptor works directly on these materials. Sculptors use a method called *casting* when they work with metals, plastic, or plaster. The liquid material is poured into a hollow shape called a *mold.* The material hardens into the sculpture itself. This is the simplest casting procedure. For example, you can press your hand in wet sand to make a mold, and fill it with plaster to make a cast. The most complex casting procedure is the lost-wax process.

Lost-Wax Bronze Casting. The first *lost-wax castings* were of small solid objects like the statuette in figure 13–10. Obviously, solid metal figures could not be made very large because of the weight and expense of the metal. In order to make large figures, ancient cultures developed the method of hollow bronze casting. The cast metal figures of horse and rider you often see in

parks, plazas, and around state buildings are made with this process.

Today, the procedure for casting a metal sculpture is called lost-wax (from the French term *cire-perdue*). Keith Knoblock used this procedure to create a bronze sculpture of Abraham Lincoln (fig. 13–11). First, he used a nonhardening, oil-based clay to model a life-sized figure. The clay was modeled over an *armature.* An armature is a framework of metal rods and plaster. Next, he made a mold by applying plaster to the clay model in sections. Thin metal shims were placed between mold sections so they could be easily separated later (fig. 13–12). When the plaster was hard, he removed the mold in sections from the clay model.

The sculptor now had a mold of Lincoln made of plaster. His next step was to line each section of the mold with wax to make a wax casting. Knoblock brushed a 3/16-inch coating of melted wax onto each piece of the plaster mold (fig. 13–13). He removed the

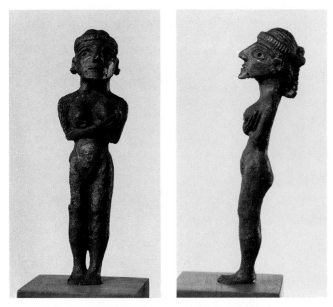

13–10 Tell al-Judaidah female statuette, Phase G, about 3000–2700 BC. Copper-base alloy with sufficient tin content to be called bronze, overall height, 5 ¾″ (14.6 cm). Courtesy of The Oriental Institute of the University of Chicago.

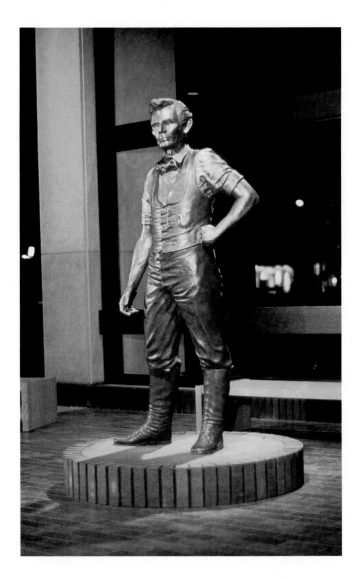

13–11 Keith Knoblock, *Lincoln,* 1977. Cast bronze, 6′ 4 ¾″ (195 cm). McLean County Law and Justice Center, Bloomington, Illinois.

wax castings from the plaster molds and reassembled them into seven sections of the figure (fig. 13–14). Notice the wax rods and cup shapes attached to each wax cast. Long steel nails, which don't show here, were pushed through the wax so they protruded inside and outside of the wax cast. Each wax section was suspended in a cylinder made of black asphalt roofing felt with a wire mesh insert (shown raised here) that became part of, and reinforced, the mold (fig. 13–15). A liquid mixture of heat-resistant materials called the *investment* was poured outside and inside of the hollow wax casting to form the outer mold and the mold core. The tops of the cup shapes attached to the wax rods were left uncovered. When the mold material was hardened, the asphalt cylinders were removed. The wire mesh was now embedded in the outer mold. The molds were placed in a kiln (a high temperature oven) and baked at 1150°F for several days until the wax melted and ran out through the channels left by the

wax rods shown in figure 13–14. The nails, mentioned above, were now embedded in both the outer mold and the mold core. They held the core in place, preserving the empty space where the wax had been. Molten bronze was poured through the channels to fill the ³/16-inch voids that were the shape of the sculpture parts (fig. 13–16). When the metal cooled, the molds were chipped and dug away from the cast, and the sections were ground and cleaned with a variety of hand and power tools. The seven casts were welded together and the surface was treated chemically to give it a brownish color. The sculpture was completed by attaching it to a base of concrete in which the skatelike forms on the feet (fig. 13–14) were submerged to help steady the figure.

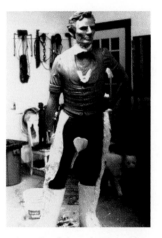

13–12 Applying plaster to the clay model.

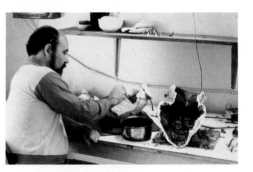

13–13 Coating the sections of the plaster mold with melted wax.

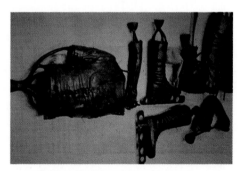

13–14 The wax castings.

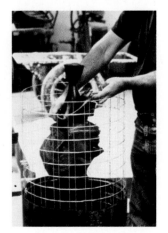

13–15 Reinforcing the mold with wire mesh and roofing felt.

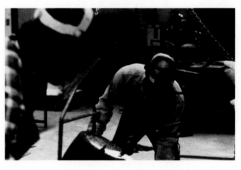

13–16 Pouring bronze into the mold.

Plastic and Plaster Casting. Without the caption, you would think that figure 13–17 is a photograph of a football player. Yet the life-size football player is a sculpture. It was cast in a plastic reinforced with fiberglass. Duane Hanson applies plaster gauze strips directly to the body of a person to make a mold. The person's skin and hair is heavily greased so the plaster will not stick. Molds are made in sections and then painted with fleshcolored plastic. The plastic is coated, or laminated, with several layers of glass cloth. When assembled, the hardened sculptures are sometimes mistaken for real people.

George Segal forms molds of plaster gauze around living models who are fully clothed. The molds, which are made in sections for various parts of the body, are reassembled to become the sculpture (fig. 13–18). Segal does not smooth away the texture of the plaster. You can see and feel the rough surface of his sculptures.

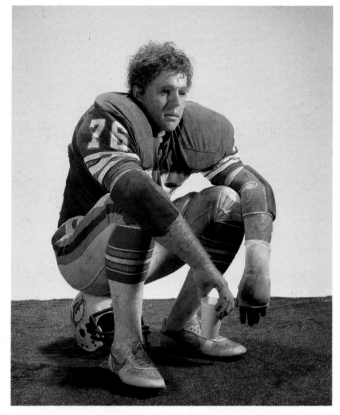

13–17 Duane Hanson, *Football Player,* 1981. Polyvinyl, polychromed in oil with accessories, 43 ¼″ x 30″ x 31 ½″ (110 x 76 x 80 cm). The Lowe Art Museum, University of Miami, Museum purchase through funds from the Friends of Art and public subscription, 82.0024.

Studio Experience 13.2

Sculpture on the Wild Side

Use plaster gauze or papier-mâché over an armature of cardboard, tubes and small cartons to create a trophy or commemorative sculpture that's a bit bizarre. It might be for a sport, dancing, eating, a pet, a hobby, contest, etc.

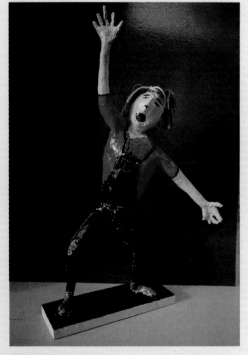

Rod Lemke.

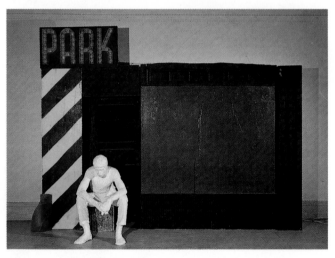

13–18 George Segal, *The Parking Garage,* 1968. Plaster, wood, metal, electrical parts and light bulbs, 10′ x 12′ 8″ x 4′ (3 x 4 x 1.3 cm). Collection of The Newark Museum. Purchase 1968 with funds from the National Council on the Arts and Trustee contributions.

Modeling

Modeling is a method that produces a sculpture made from a pliable material like clay, papier-mâché, wax, or plaster. In this section, we will consider *ceramic* sculpture made from clay and papier-mâché.

Clay is taken through four stages to produce either sculpture or pottery: preparation, shaping, decorating, and firing. *Preparation* involves mixing water with the clay. The clay is aged for several weeks until it becomes workable. Air bubbles must be forced out. *Shaping* the clay is done by hand-building methods or on a potter's wheel. *Decorating* the form can be done with techniques such as those shown in figure 13–19. *Firing* the clay form is done twice—once to harden it, and a second time to add a *glaze,* a transparent or colored glassy coating, to the work.

Solid Modeling. Perhaps you have made a solid sculpture from a lump of clay. Parts can be shaped from or added to the lump. Textures and patterns such as those shown in figure 13–19 can be added to the surface. Any parts of a solid clay sculpture that are thicker than one inch should be hollowed out to prevent the work from exploding when fired. When the clay is dry enough to support itself, but not completely dry, the form can be hollowed out from the bottom with a wire loop tool.

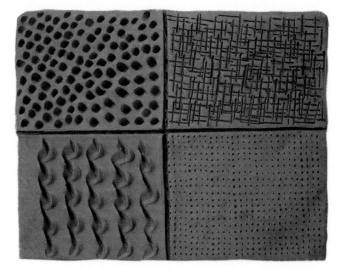

13–19   Texture pressed in clay.

13–20 Although this sculpture is bronze, it was first modeled in clay. It shows the expressive qualities of solid clay modeling. David Aronson, *Virtuoso.* Courtesy of Pucker Gallery, Boston, MA. ©1993 Photograph by David N. Israel.

Coiling. The coiling procedure was used by the Chinese over 2,000 years ago. The life-size figures of the warrior and horse shown in figure 13–21 were created from clay coils. (Thousands of figures like this were found during excavations at the tomb of the first emperor of Ch'in. No two of the ceramic warriors have the same face.) Coils are made by rolling ropes of clay to a desired thickness on a canvas-covered surface. The coils are placed on top of each other and pressed together. Coils can be made longer or shorter as needed. The artist smooths the inside and outside with vertical wiping movements. He or she finishes the surface by scraping or by beating it with a paddle.

Peter VandenBerge used coils to build his sculpture (fig. 13–22). Then he modeled clay on its surface to create three-dimensional features. The hat was made from slabs. The artist decorated the figure with colored clay *slips*, clay mixed with water to a creamy consistency, with coloring agents added.

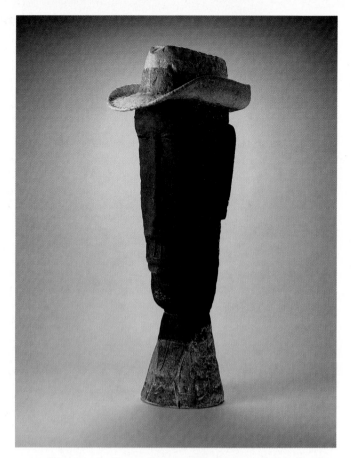

13–21 *Cavalryman with Horse,* Qin dynasty (221–206 BC), terra cotta. Cavalryman is 5′ 10 ½″ (180 cm) high and saddle horse is 5′ 7 ½″ (172 cm) high and 6′ 7 ¾″ (203 cm) long. Courtesy of Cultural Relics Bureau, Beijing and The Metropolitan Museum of Art, New York.

13–22 Peter VandenBerge, *Zwartman,* 1986. Clay and slips, hand-built (coiled), 45″ x 14″ x 17″ (114 x 36 x 43 cm). Collection of the artist. Photograph courtesy George Erml.

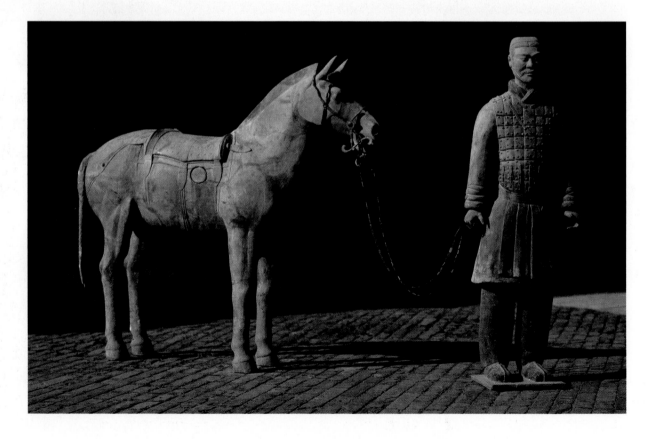

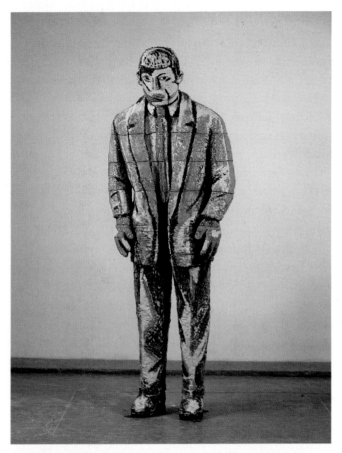

13–23 Viola Frey, *Leaning Man III*, 1985. Clay and glazes, hand-built, 102 ½″ x 35″ x 18″ (260 x 89 x 46 cm). Rena Bransten Gallery, San Francisco.

Slab Building. Slabs are sheets of clay that are beaten out with the hand or spread with a rolling pin. Sculptures made from slabs are supported by various materials until the clay dries. Materials such as crumpled newspaper, foam rubber, and dacron are used as supports. Slabs can be used to construct smaller sculpture. The slabs are rolled and folded. When they are dried but not completely hard, the slabs are joined together with clay slip.

Viola Frey makes very large ceramic sculptures with slabs and coils. She forms and fires them in sections. The sections are stacked upon each other when finished to complete the sculpture. Frey's *Leaning Man III* (fig. 13–23) is over eight feet (2.5 m) tall. Imagine having a sculpture that large in your home.

Papier-Mâché. Papier-mâché is an ancient modeling medium. Chinese soldiers used it to make armor before the Bronze Age. Papier-mâché, which is lightweight and strong, is made from wet paper and glue. The paper is soaked in water overnight. Then it is mashed in a strainer to remove the water. White glue is added as a binder.

This clay-like medium can be modeled into all kinds of shapes. It can be formed into molds or placed over armatures of wood, rods, and wires. When dry, forms made from papier-mâché can be carved, bored, sanded, and painted. The Linares family in Mexico create fantastic papier-mâché animal sculptures (fig. 13–24.)

Strips of newspaper that have been soaked in wheat paste can be placed over cardboard, tubes, and boxes. The form shown in figure 13–25 was created this way. This process requires several days for drying. The plaster gauze used by Duane Hanson and George Segal (figures 13–17 and 18) has replaced papier-mâché because it dries quickly. However, it does not have the smoothness and detail of papier-mâché.

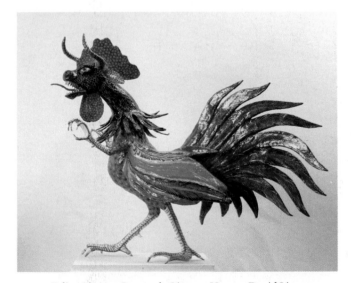

13–24 Felipe Linares, Leonardo Linares-Vargas, David Linares-Vargas, *Alebrijes*, 1989. Papier-mâché. Photograph courtesy Musée national d'art moderne, Centre Georges Pompidou, Paris.

13–25 Pierre Richard *Move Move Mann*, 1987. Papier-mâché, 27″ x 12″ (69 x 31 cm). Collection of Julian Davis Wade.

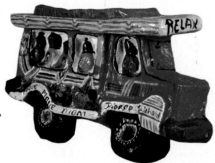

Construction

Constructions are sculptures that may be built from more than one material. They may be built from traditional materials, such as wood or metal, that are used in new ways. Constructions are a development of the twentieth century. They are a result of modern technology, as well as modern ideas about the nature of the art object.

George Sugarman glues together layers of wood that have been cut into shapes with a band saw. Then he paints the forms to hide the wood grain and to help direct visual movement over the surfaces (fig. 13–26).

Richard Lippold combines thin metal rods and wires to create constructions that radiate from a center as in *Number 7: Full Moon* (fig. 13–27). The central cluster of wires reflects light, and the metal rods create open three-dimensional forms. *Number 7: Full Moon* had to be carefully designed before it was constructed.

Assemblage. Sculptures constructed from a variety of found objects and materials are called ***assemblages.*** These materials, in their original states, were not necessarily meant to be used in art forms. The sculptor may select objects because of their similarities or their contrasts. The objects may suggest certain meanings. Assemblages may or may not meet the principles of composition, depending on the artist's intent. How an

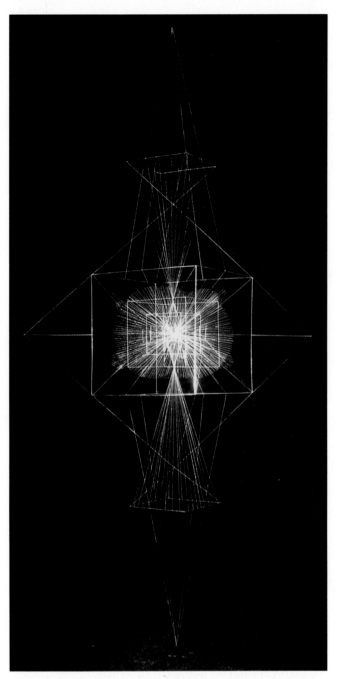

13–27 Richard Lippold, Variation *Number 7: Full Moon,* 1949–50. Brass rods, nickel-chromium and stainless steel wire, 10′ x 6′ x 6′ (305 x 183 x 183 cm). The Museum of Modern Art, New York. Simon Guggenheim Fund.

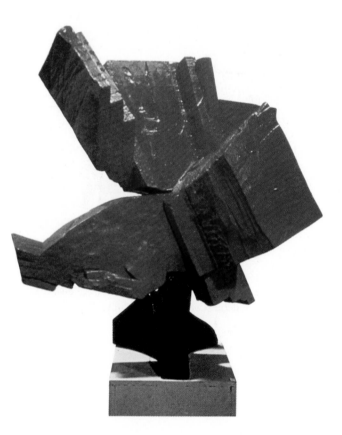

13–26 George Sugarman, *Freya,* 1964. Laminated, polychromed wood. 30 ¾″ (78 cm) high. Private collection.

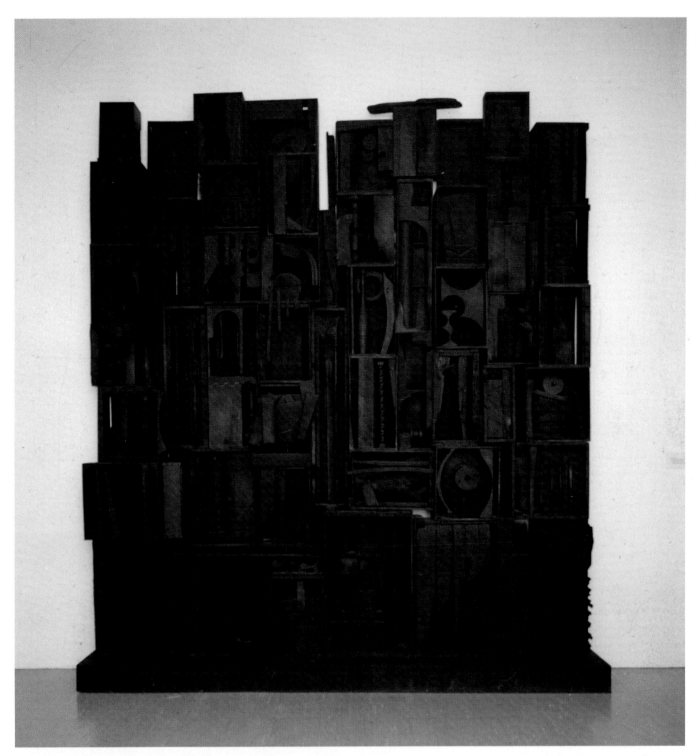

13–28 Louise Nevelson, *Sky Cathedral*, 1958. Assemblage: wood construction painted black, 11′ 3 ½″ x 10′ ¼″ x 18″ (344 x 305 x 46 cm). The Museum of Modern Art, New York. Gift of Mr. and Mrs. Ben Mildwoff.

assemblage is constructed depends on the materials used. Louise Nevelson nailed, glued, and pegged together discarded wood forms (fig. 13–28). Her assemblage is made up of dozens of boxes filled with carefully arranged wooden objects.

Assemblages allow artists great freedom in choosing materials that express their ideas. Marisol's life-size

Try it Yourself

List some materials to use in a construction that are more incongruous (not harmonious, not related) than those in Rauschenberg's stuffed goat assemblage (fig. 1-11).

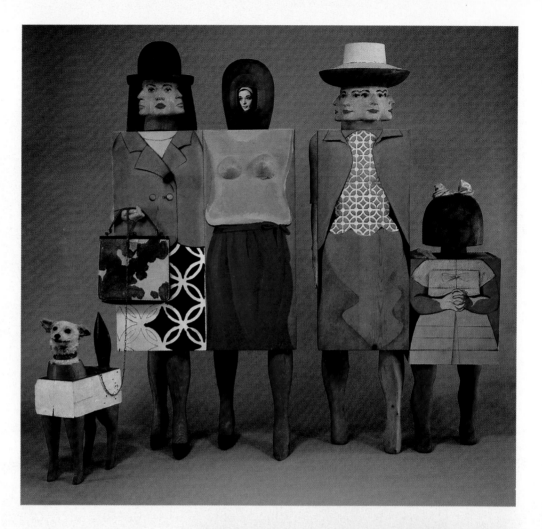

13-29 Marisol, *Women and Dog*, 1964. Wood, plaster, synthetic polymer and miscellaneous items. 6′5″ x 7′7″ (196 x 231 cm). Collection of Whitney Museum of American Art. Purchase, with funds from the Friends of the Whitney Museum of American Art.

boxlike figures (fig. 13–29) may include wood, plaster life masks, paint, photographs, fabric, and more. Her constructions are caricatures. They are exaggerated descriptions of contemporary personalities, their manners and characteristics.

Assemblages and constructions include works that may be classified as reliefs, as well as those that are sculpture in the round. *Kastūra* (fig. 13–30) by Frank Stella is a construction that projects about two feet from the wall. Stella cut the parts out of sheet aluminum and painted them with a range of wild colors. The composition is given unity by repetition of shapes based on drafting tools.

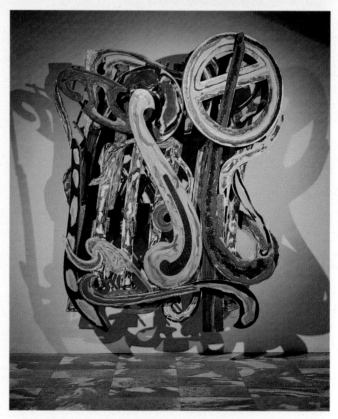

13-30 Frank Stella, *Kastūra*, 1979. Oil and epoxy on aluminum and wire mesh. 9′7″ x 7′8″ x 30″ (292 x 234 x 76 cm). The Museum of Modern Art, New York. Acquired through the Mr. and Mrs. Victor Ganz, Mr. and Mrs. Donald H. Peters, and Mr. and Mrs. Charles Zadok Funds.

Marisol

1930–

Carved wooden boxes, plaster casts of faces and hands, and bits of fabric are uniquely combined and assembled to form a three-dimensional composition. "Found" objects, or discarded items collected and reused by the artist, are embellished with hand-crafted materials. Carefully drawn and painted details adorn the sides of figures sculpted from rough pieces of lumber. This arrangement of contrasting elements might be complemented with a background, creating a "tableau," or an arranged scene. The sculpted figures in these unusual works of art, known as assemblages, may wear three or more faces cast from plaster—all the single face of the artist, Marisol.

Born in 1930 in Paris, Marisol Escobar spent the early years of her life traveling from one glittering world capital to another with her wealthy Venezuelan parents. Her mother died when Marisol was eleven years old, and Marisol looked to her father for support. With his stability and encouragement, Marisol was able to become an adventurous artist and an independent and creative individual.

Her travels brought her from Europe to New York in 1950 where she studied art and developed friendships with other artists in Manhattan. At this time, Marisol explored a variety of different art media, searching for her own artistic style. During this quest for originality and independence, she discarded her last name; since that time she has been known simply as Marisol.

In New York, Marisol discovered a unique means of expression in sculpture, combining unusual materials in new ways. Using carpenter's tools—power saws, axes, electrical devices—in combination with traditional art supplies, she began creating the unique sculptures for which she is now famous.

A Wood Relief

Construct a relief of wood shapes, observing the principles of composition. Express an idea or theme in your construction.

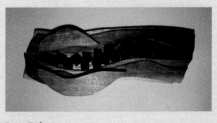

Pete Belzer.

Metal Construction. There are many techniques for constructing metal sculpture. In general, metal can be cut with hand or power saws, hand or power shears, tin snips, and welding torches. Holes can be drilled in metal. Pieces can be joined with the use of metal screws, nuts and bolts, riveting, crimping edges together, soldering, and welding.

Richard Stankiewicz created a construction by welding industrial scrap and old machine parts (fig. 13–31). What do you think about the artist's comment on modern society's endless waste of objects and materials?

13–31 Richard Stankiewicz, *Our Lady of All Protections*, 1958. Iron and steel, 51″ x 31″ x 32″ (130 x 79 x 81 cm). Albright-Knox Art Gallery, Buffalo, New York. Gift of Seymour H. Knox, 1959.

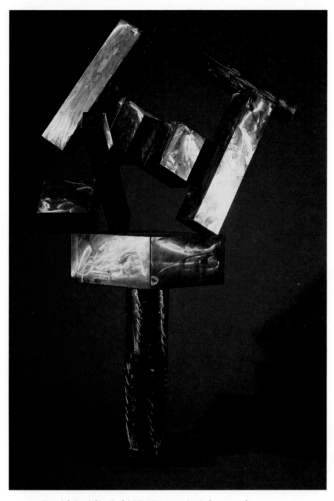

13-32 David Smith, *Cubi XVII*, 1963. Stainless steel, 107¾″ x 64⅜″ (274 x 165 cm). Dallas Museum of Art. Eugene and Margaret McDermott Fund.

Sheets of stainless steel are welded together by David Smith to create combinations of cubes and cylinders (fig. 13–32). These constructions of cubes look like they should fall. Smith's sculptures are often placed outdoors. The highly polished mirrorlike surfaces reflect everything around them.

Kinetic Sculpture. You were introduced to *kinetic* sculpture in Chapter 8. These constructions move or have moving parts, and may also use light and sound. In previous centuries, machines and robotlike figures had been designed for entertainment. But, like today's cuckoo clocks, those automated constructions could only repeat their actions. The movements of modern kinetic sculptures are generally random. The sources of energy for kinetic sculpture include wind and air currents, falling water, temperature changes, springs, motors of all kinds, air pumps, pull strings, thin rods and wires that vibrate, pendulums, magnets, and electromagnets.

Environmental Art

Environmental art began in the 1960s. Mixed media and different procedures are used to create these forms. The basic idea is to involve the spectator in the artwork, or to make the work a part of the environment surrounding it. Environmental artists have taken several different directions over the past twenty years, as the following examples show.

Red Grooms constructs huge enclosed environments that people can walk through. *Ruckus Rodeo* includes fourteen cowboys and cowgirls, a rodeo queen on horseback, a sixteen-foot Brahma bull, and more (fig. 13–33). The floor is covered with painted burlap, and the rodeo audience is painted on canvas that wraps around the walls. What would it be like to enter the make-believe world of *Ruckus Rodeo*? Imagine walking among Grooms's larger-than-life figures frozen in a moment of action.

Another kind of environmental sculpture involves making changes in a natural setting. These works are called *land* or *earth art.* The artist may need the help of construction crews and earth-moving equipment, as in the case of *Spiral Jetty* (fig. 13–34). Robert Smithson created a 1,500-foot-long earth and rock spiral that extends into Utah's Great Salt Lake. According to a legend, the lake was once connected to the Pacific Ocean by an underground waterway. The waterway supposedly caused whirlpools to form at the lake's center. Perhaps Smithson's choice of the spiral form was inspired by this legend.

Mary Miss takes another approach in her constructions. She combines wood, steel, and concrete with earth and sometimes water in environmental works like *Field Rotation* (fig. 13–35). Miss enclosed a sunken area with a wall constructed of wood. She mounded earth up against the outsides of the wall. Eight rows of wooden posts extend from the central construction out over a four-and-one-half-acre area that makes up the whole artwork. Viewed from the air, this environmental sculpture resembles a giant pinwheel.

Many environmental works like those of Smithson and Miss are placed in out-of-the-way locations where you might not have a chance to see them. And, of course, most of them are temporary. Photographs like these are the only records of them.

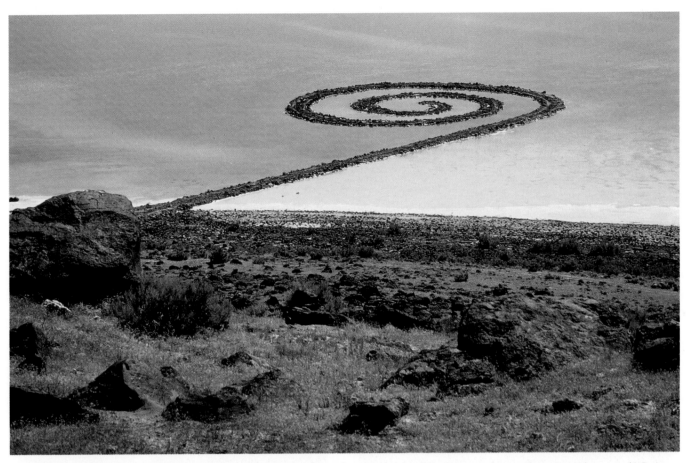

13–34 Robert Smithson, *Spiral Jetty*, 1970. Black rock, salt crystals, earth and red water (algae) composing a coil 1500′ x 15′ (457 x 5 m). Great Salt Lake, Utah. Photograph Gianfranco Gorgoni. Courtesy Contact Press Images Inc., New York.

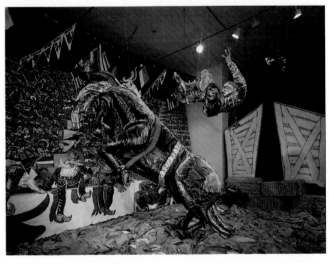

13–33 Red Grooms, *Ruckus Rodeo*, 1975–1976. Sculpture wire, celastic, acrylic, canvas and burlap, 174″ x 606″ x 294″ (442 x 1539 x 747 cm). Commissioned by the Modern Art Museum of Fort Worth. Museum purchase with funds from the National Endowment for the Arts and the Benjamin J. Tillar Memorial Trust. See page 79.

13–35 Mary Miss, *Field Rotation*, 1981. Wood, gravel, concrete, steel, earth and water. Structure, 7′ x 56′ x 56′ (2 x 17 x 17 m), centered in 4 ½ acre site. Governors State University, Illinois.

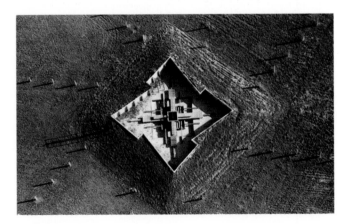

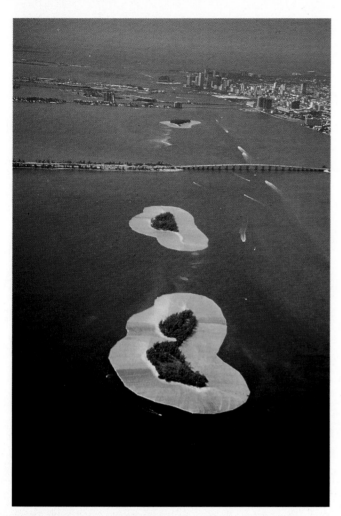

13–36 Christo, *Surrounded Islands, Biscayne Bay, Greater Miami, Florida*, 1980–1983. ©Christo 1983. Photograph: Wolfgang Volz.

The largest environmental projects have been created by Javacheff Christo. His *Wrapped Coast* is shown in Chapter 1. In 1983, he finished surrounding eleven islands in Biscayne Bay with 6,500,000 square feet of pink plastic that floated on the water. The plastic extended 200 feet from the shore of each island (fig. 13–36). Can you picture what the project looked like from an airplane? Picture eleven pink-skirted islands covered with lush vegetation, surrounded by blue-green water, and basking in a bright sun.

On a smaller scale, George Segal creates environments based on events from everyday life. They include life-size plaster figures and real objects. The counter, stools, coffee maker, and other objects in *The Diner* came from a real restaurant (fig. 13–37). You can become a part of this little environment by moving around and viewing it from different angles. Perhaps you can imagine what the two lonely figures are thinking about.

And finally, there are the performance works like Joseph Beuys's *I Like America and America Likes Me* that was presented in Chapter 1 (fig. 1-12). These productions, sometimes called *happenings,* usually involve the artist in person and some props. Sometimes, the viewers are invited to participate.

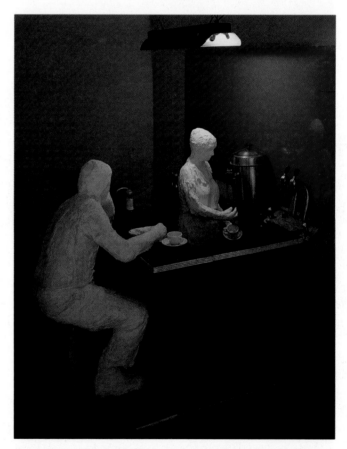

13–37 George Segal, *The Diner,* 1964–1966. Plaster, wood, chrome, laminated plastic, Masonite, fluorescent lamp, 93 ¾″ x 144 ¼″ x 96″ (238 x 366 x 244 cm). Collection Walker Art Center, Minneapolis. Gift of the T. B. Walker Foundation, 1966.

Ceramic Pottery, Jewelry, Fibers, and Glass

Before the Industrial Revolution in the 1800s brought the mass production of goods, items such as dishes, metalware, and clothing were hand-crafted. Today, artists who work with ceramics, jewelry, fibers, and glass sometimes provide designs for industrial mass production. However, mainly they make one-of-a-kind creations that are expressive, personal, and valued for their unique qualities.

Ceramic Pottery

Imagine life without containers to eat and drink from or to store things in. Prehistoric people used animal skins, shells, gourds, and woven baskets as containers. The baskets were sometimes coated on the inside with clay to seal them. Pottery making may have been discovered by the accidental burning of such a basket, which resulted in hardening the clay lining. The first pots and clay figures were fired in shallow pits lined and covered with twigs and dry wood.

Try it Yourself

Every early culture developed its own style of pottery. Research a culture and write a short report on its pottery. How was it made, decorated, and fired? What was the pottery used for?

Hand-Building Procedures. It is easy to make pottery by hand. Clay is easy to handle. The methods for making pottery by hand are similar to those used for ceramic sculpture. The methods of *pinch, coil,* and *slab* building can be used to hand build pottery.

Pinch pots are made by pushing the thumb down in the center of a fist-sized ball of clay, leaving enough clay for the bottom. The walls are formed by squeezing the clay up and out between the thumb on the inside and the fingers on the outside, while rotating the pot in the other hand. The procedure is repeated until the wall of the pot is as thin as desired. A coil may be added to the bottom for stability, and designs can be incised or pressed on the surface (fig. 13–38).

A *coil pot* can be made in almost any shape. The first coil is attached to a base made from a slab of clay. The form can be curved outward by making the coils progressively wider in circumference. The process is reversed to make the form curve inward.

The jar shown in figure 13–39 was made by people who lived on the island of Crete over 3,000 years ago. It is four feet high. Its thick coils were thinned and shaped by beating the outside with a paddle while a rounded form was held inside.

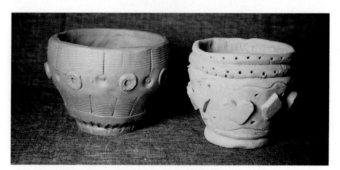

13–38 *Left:* Pinch pot with foot. *Right:* Coil built pot with some coils partially exposed as part of the surface decoration. Earthenware.

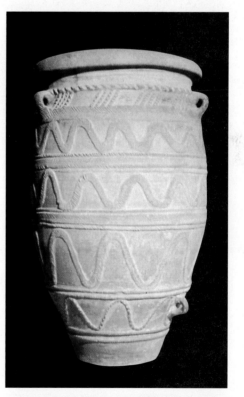

13–39 Pithos, Knossos, Crete, ca. 1450–1400 BC. Earthenware storage jar with applied rope decoration, height 4´ (122 cm). Reproduced by Courtesy of the Trustees of the British Museum, London.

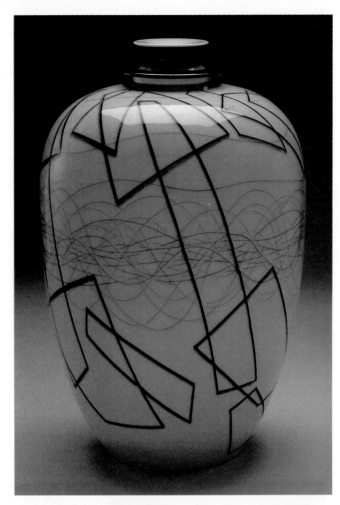

13–40 Michael Remsen, *M. S. 2,* 1991. High-fired porcelain with transparent Chun glaze, 24″ (61 cm) high.

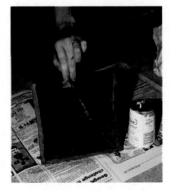

13–41 Joining edges.

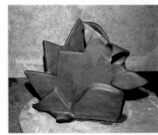

13–42 Slab-built sculpture.

Slabs, or sheets, of clay are rolled out with a rolling pin or pounded out with a paddle. Containers may be formed by draping slabs over convex forms like a volleyball. Slabs can also be pressed into concave forms such as a dish. The edges of slabs can be joined with slip to build geometric containers (fig. 13–41). The surfaces can be decorated with textures.

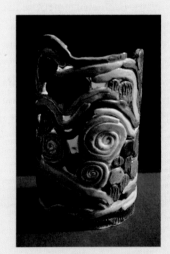
Throwing on the Wheel. *Throwing* is the term used to describe forming clay on the potter's wheel. The production of small wheel-thrown pots began about 3000 BC. The wheel lets a person make rounded symmetrical forms in much less time than by coiling.

The potter centers a ball of clay on a rapidly turning wheel. He or she raises the clay into a cylinder or rounded form. It takes great technical skill and a keen sensitivity for good form to create a beautiful jar. Michael Remsen made the vessel shown (fig. 13–40) of porcelain clay. He threw the jar and the lid separately. He decorated the ceramic ware by slicing the surface and filling the depressions with colored slip. This method is known as *mishima,* a decorative art that originated in Korea. To finish the piece, the artist covered the jar and lid with a transparent glaze.

Jewelry

Prehistoric people made jewelry from materials such as bone, wood, seeds, stones, shells, and hair. Once metalworking procedures were developed, metal became the most common material for jewelry and ceremonial objects. For over 6,000 years, gold has been the most sought after metal. Gold is not only beautiful, but it also never tarnishes. It is easy to stretch. One ounce of gold can be hammered into a sheet of one hundred square feet! This ability of gold (or any metal) to be extended or shaped by hammering is called malleability. Because gold is so malleable, ancient metalworkers used it to create paper-thin objects. They used a process called *repoussé*. The sheet metal is hammered on one side to create shapes and patterns on the other

side. The features of the mask (fig. 13–43) were raised in relief by pushing the lines and shapes out from the inside with modeling tools.

In addition to repoussé, other metalworking procedures developed over 2,500 years ago. These procedures include casting, annealing (heating metal to make it easier to form), soldering, bending metal over

13–43 Funeral mask, about 1500 BC. Beaten gold, about 12″ (30 cm) high. Royal tombs, Mycenae. National Archeological Museum, Athens.

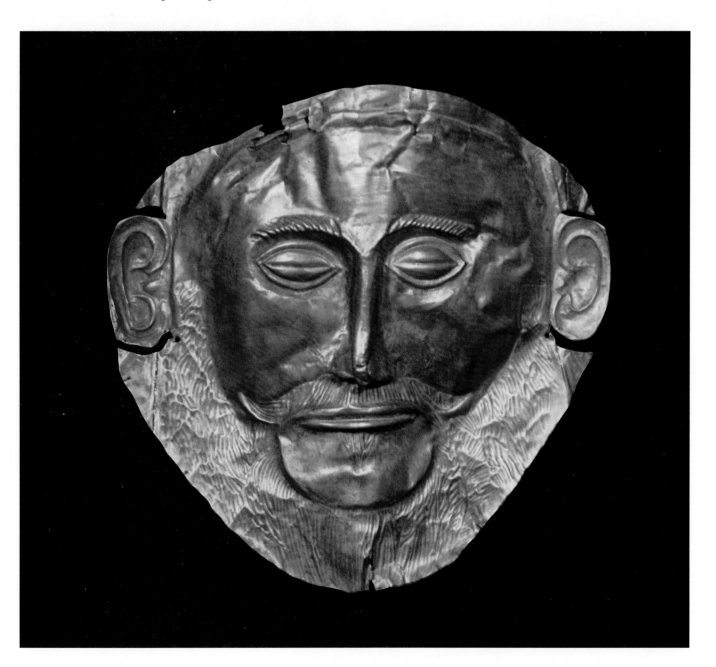

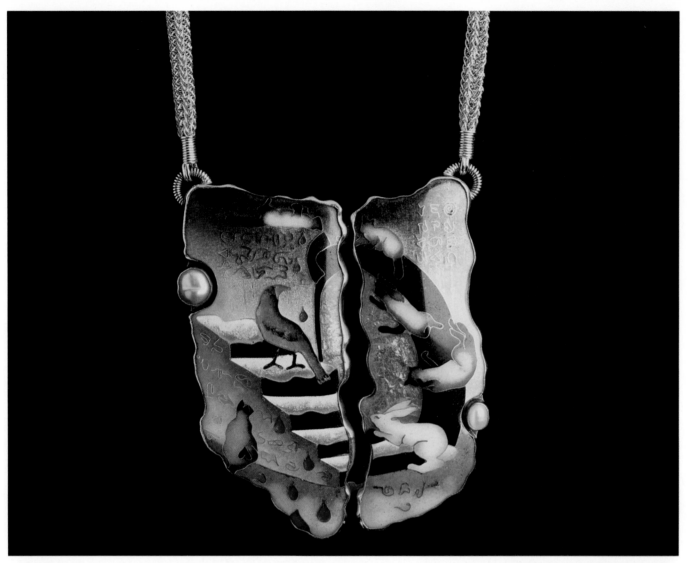

13-45 Colette, *Pectoral #6*, 1985. Sterling silver, fine silver, 24k and 14k gold, bronze, cloisonne, enameled, fabricated. 9 ¼″ x 3 ⅛″ x ¼″ (24 x 8 x .6 cm). ©American Craft Museum. Photograph: George Erml.

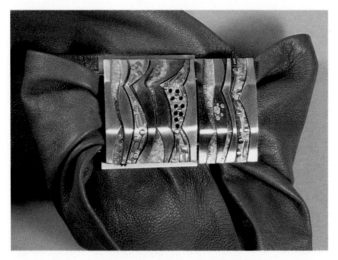

13-44 Mary Ann Scherr, *Waist Watcher Monitor Belt Buckle.* This buckle buzzes if the wearer's posture sags. Sterling silver and NU-Gold (bronze), electronics and leather. Courtesy of the artist.

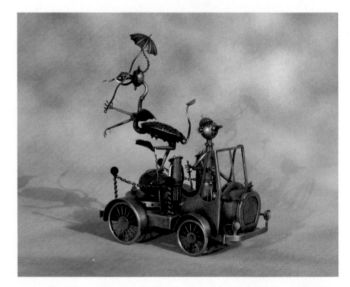

13-47 Earl Krentzin, *Truck.* Silver, 18k gold, semiprecious stones. Courtesy of the artist.

steel stakes or into depressions, cutting, piercing, and engraving. Look closely at the belt buckle (fig. 13–44). Notice how the metal was pierced. Some parts were cut with a saw and soldered on the larger silver form. The metal was bent slightly, and the line designs were engraved in the recessed areas.

Enamels are made from ground glass and metal oxides for color. They can be fused to metal by heating them to about 1,450°F in a kiln. Over the centuries, several different methods have been developed to make enameled jewelry. One of these is **cloisonné.** The pendant shown in figure 13–45 is an example.

Today, some artists use the materials, tools, and procedures needed to make jewelry to produce small sculptures (fig 13–47). Can you tell which parts were sawed, pierced, bent and shaped by hammering and cast, before being soldered together? Krentzin may be a jeweler, a sculptor, or both. He produces carefully crafted art forms that challenge your imagination.

Woven Fiber Forms

Weaving is the most common method of working with fibers. Weaving can be done on a complex loom or a simple wooden frame (fig. 13–48). In plain weaving, one thread, called the *weft,* crosses alternately over and under *warp* threads. The warp threads are stretched on the loom. Weaving was once just a two-dimensional art. Today, it is used in three-dimensional pieces. In figure 13–49, layers of fibers were woven together. Then the layers were gathered to create depth. Other woven works may be stuffed with materials such as dacron or foam rubber to make them three-dimensional.

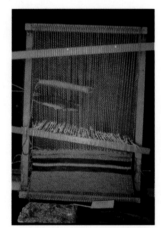

13–48 Simple frame.

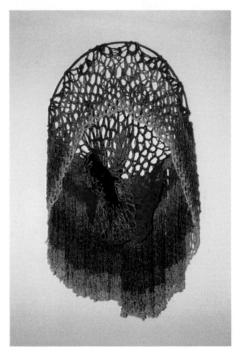

13–49 Barbara Bohnett, *Joy Inside My Tears*, 1978. Woven fiber, 42″ x 22″ (107 x 56 cm). Collection, The Universtiy Museum, Illinois State University, Normal, Illinois.

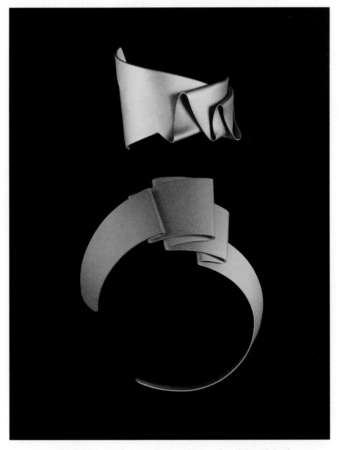

13–46 Gerhardt C. Herbst, *Collar and Bracelet*, 1985. This aluminum collar and bracelet was colored by anodizing, a process of depositing an oxide film electronically on the metal's surface so it will absorb dye colors. Aluminum, sandblasted, anodized. Collar: 6″ diam. x 1″ (15 x 3 cm). Bracelet: 3″ x 2 ½″ x ¾″ (8 x 6 x 2 cm). ©American Craft Museum. Photograph: George Erml.

Nonwoven Fiber Forms

Three-dimensional forms can be made from fibers with nonweaving procedures. *Macramé* is done by tying fibers in a series of knots such as the square knot and the clove hitch. Sometimes knots are combined with weaving to give the work more support. The three forms that make up *Implications* (fig 13–50) by Jane Sauer have knotted inner cores. Strands of the fiber were pulled from the cores to give the forms a hairy texture.

Claire Zeistler constructed *Tri-Color Arch* (fig 13–51) by wrapping one fiber around a core of other fibers. For tall pieces like this one (about six feet), the artist may wrap the fiber around a wire armature.

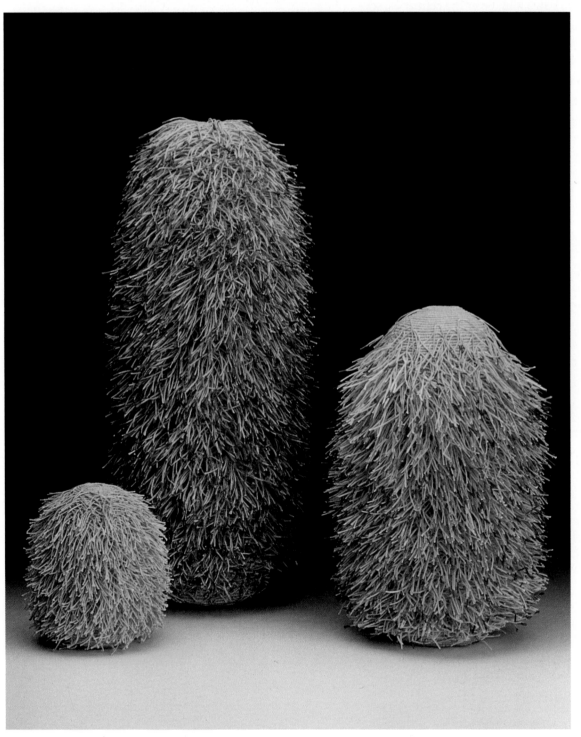

13–50 Jane Sauer, *Implications*, 1985. Waxed linen, paint, knotted, 14″ x 6″ (36 x 15 cm) diam.; 8 ½″ x 5″ (22 x 13 cm) diam.; 3 ½″ x 3 ½″ (9 x 9 cm) diam. Courtesy of the artist.

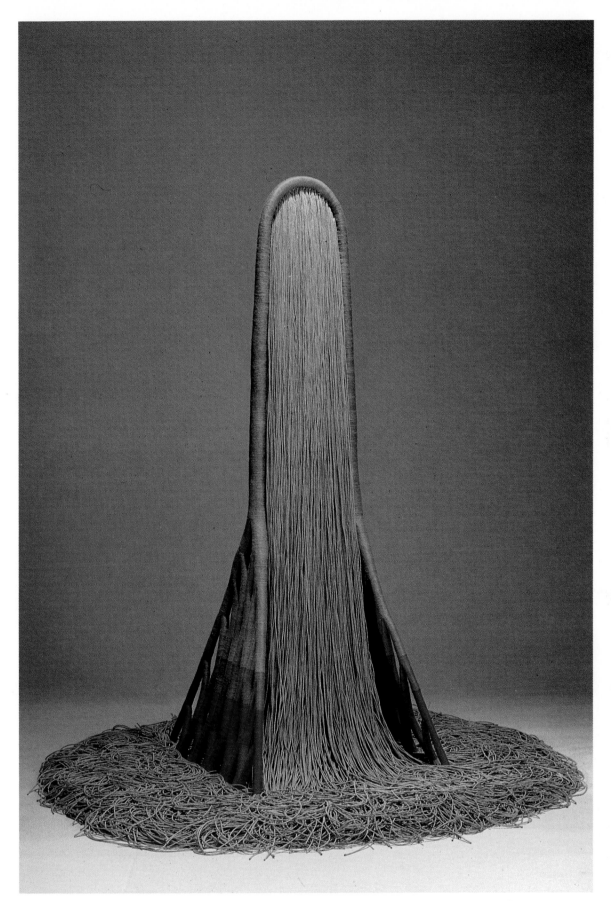

13-51 Claire Zeistler, *Tri-Color Arch*, 1983–1984. Hemp, synthetic fiber knotted, wrapped, 74″ x 11″ (188 x 28 cm); spill 66″ x 44″ (168 x 112 cm). Courtesy Rhona Hoffman Gallery, Chicago.

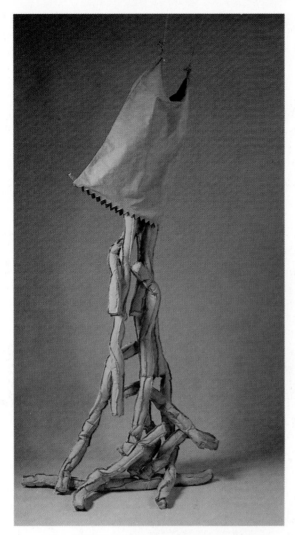

13–52 Claes Oldenburg, *Shoestring Potatoes Spilling from a Bag,* 1966. Canvas, kapok, glue, acrylic, 108″ x 46″ x 42″ (274 x 117 x 107 cm). Collection Walker Art Center, Minneapolis. Gift of the T. B. Walker Foundation, 1966.

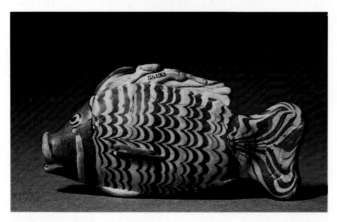

13–54 Glass bottle shaped like a fish, ca. 1370 BC Egyptian, from el Amarna. Glass, 5 ½″ (14 cm). Reproduced by Courtesy of the Trustees of the British Museum.

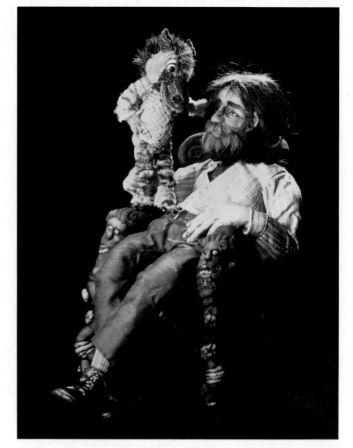

13–53 Jo Ellen Trilling, *Portrait.* Fabric, wire, fur and paint, 27″ x 20″ (69 x 51 cm).

Soft Sculpture

Claes Oldenburg was one of the first persons to create soft sculpture out of stuffed fabrics (fig. 13–52). His innovative use of fabrics inspired other artists. Soft sculpture artists began to experiment with a combination of materials to create three-dimensional forms. Jo Ellen Trilling combined fabric, wire, fur, and paint in *Portrait* (fig. 13–53).

If you look at commercial stuffed animals, you can get some ideas about how soft sculpture is constructed. However, the artist must adapt construction procedures to the individual project and to the materials being used. Almost any fabric, whether printed or plain, textured, furry, coarse, or shiny, can be used for soft sculpture.

Glass

Glass is also a beautiful art medium with a very long history. The Egyptians discovered how to make glass about 3000 BC. The first glass objects were beads and solid shapes. Sometime between 1500 and 1350 BC, the Egyptians produced glass vessels, such as the fish-shaped bottle in figure 13–54.

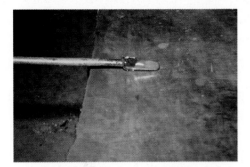

13–55 Rolling the gather on the marver.

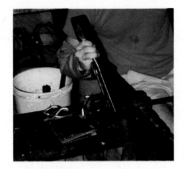

13–56 Indenting a groove using jacks.

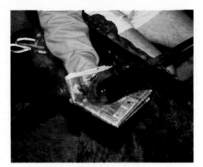

13–57 Using wet newspaper to form the hot glass.

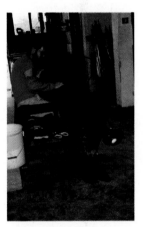

13–58 Blowing the glass form.

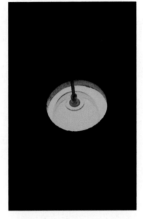

13–59 Reheating the form in the glory hole.

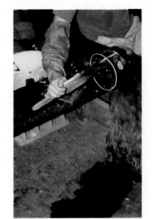

13–60 Shaping the glass attached to a pontil.

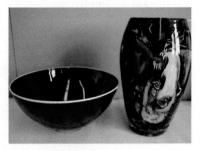

13–61 Steve Ramsey, freeblown glass vessels.

The invention of the blowpipe between 200 and 100 BC was to glassmaking what the potter's wheel was to ceramics. The blowpipe made it possible to produce hollow glass forms rapidly. Glass can be cast flat or into a mold. It can be *freeblown,* or formed on the blowpipe in the open air. It can also be blown into a mold. While hot, glass can be bent, twisted, and pulled into shapes. Glass can even be welded to glass.

When glass is freeblown, the heated tip of a blowpipe is barely dipped in molten glass. Then the blowpipe is rotated to wind the glass into a *gather* on the end of the pipe. The artist rolls the gather on a flat metal surface called the *marver.* This allows the glass to chill. The artist is also able to center the gather on the blowpipe (fig. 13–55). Next, the artist aims the blowpipe toward the floor and blows a small bubble.

Working at the glassblower's bench, the artist rolls the pipe back and forth on the bench arms. Spring steel legs connected at the bend, called *jacks,* are used to indent a shallow groove on the glass just in front of the blowpipe (fig. 13–56). While constantly rotating the pipe on the bench arms, the artist forms the hot glass. The artist may use tools such as concave wooden

blocks, paddles, the jacks, cutting shears, and even a wet pad of newspaper to form the glass (fig. 13–57).

Each time it is blown in this forming stage, the vessel increases in size (fig. 13–58). To keep the glass in a workable stage, the artist periodically reheats it. The artist inserts the vessel into the furnace opening, called the *glory hole* (fig. 13–59). The vessel is transferred from the blowpipe to a *pontil.* A pontil is an iron pipe to which the glass is attached for final shaping. The hot glass may be opened up by using a paddle on the inside of the rotating form (fig. 13–60). Eventually, the vessel is removed from the pontil and cooled slowly in an oven.

The artist may etch or engrave the glass form. Further enhancing can be done by sandblasting, cutting, grinding, and polishing the glass. Steve Ramsey used colored transparent glass to create these freeblown vessels (fig. 13–61). In these pieces, glass interacts with the light that passes through it.

Stained Glass. Windows of stained glass cause a special excitement when the light in a room is transformed by the colors of the glass. In the window shown in figure 13–63, the artist carefully selected colors so that they relate to the theme of the work and balance one another. He also planned the organization of the lead lines that run through the panel. The lines not only hold the glass together and provide structural strength. They also create an attractive composition of lines and shapes. When a panel is completely made up of colorless glass, (fig. 13–64), the composition of the lead lines is an important factor in your enjoyment of the panel.

Before constructing a stained glass form, the artist makes a full-size drawing of a design on pattern paper. The pattern shapes are cut out and used to guide the cutting of each glass shape. Individual pieces of glass can be held in place with channeled lead strips called *came*. These strips are soldered together at joints where they meet.

A work may include many intricate and curved shapes, or be three-dimensional like a container or lamp. The edges of each piece of glass can be wrapped with copper foil tape, leaving about $1/32$ inch overlap on both sides. The pieces of glass are soldered together along the foiled edges. The foil technique was used to construct the Baroque style lamp in figure 13–62. The glass contains streaks and swirls that give it movement when lit from behind, softening and diffusing the bulb light.

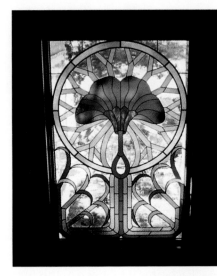

13–63 Terry Garby.

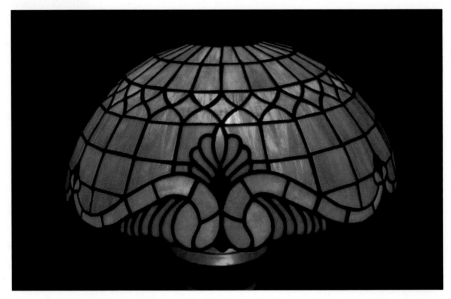

13–62 Terry Garby.

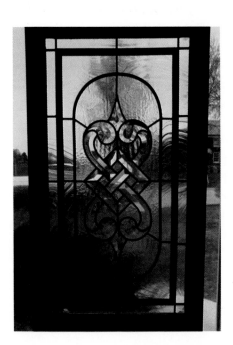

13–64 Terry Garby.

A Harmonious Stained Glass Panel

Use stained glass pieces to construct a panel. Arrange the pieces to create harmonious colors and shapes. **WARNING: Use extreme caution when you handle pieces with jagged edges.**

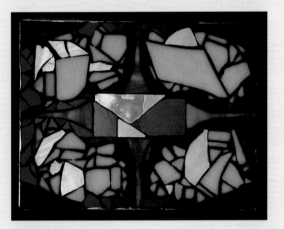

Lila Marks.

A Window Panel with Paper

Use tissue paper or cellophane shapes sandwiched between two sheets of construction paper to make a window panel. Openings in the construction paper will reveal the colored tissue.

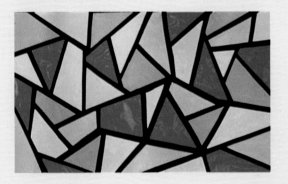

Myra Schwartz.

Summary

Three-dimensional art forms can be created with almost anything. As you have seen, artists are not limited to traditional materials such as wood, stone, or metal for sculpture. If a material is safe to work with, it may be used to create artworks.

Some three-dimensional forms are made to be seen from all sides. These works may be freestanding, located indoors or outside, or suspended from ceilings. Other three-dimensional works, called reliefs, project out from a surface. Reliefs are viewed mainly from the front.

Sculpture can be divided into categories based on the kinds of materials and procedures used to make it. *Carving,* most commonly done in wood or stone, requires the artist to cut material away to produce a form. *Casting* may be done in metal, plastic, or plaster. Casting involves making a mold from a model. *Modeling* is a building-up process, usually done with clay to produce sculpture. The sculpture is made permanent by firing it in a kiln. *Construction* is a twentieth-century development. Constructions can be reliefs or sculpture in the round. Anything that can be glued, nailed, crimped, welded, bolted, wired, melted, soldered, or otherwise joined may be used for constructions.

In the 1960s some artists began creating environmental artworks that capture and transform space. They frequently involve the spectator. There are several categories of environmental art. Some works may be an area enclosed with some material such as canvas, and filled with constructed forms, special lighting, and sound effects. Other works may be outdoor projects that involve the real environment of land, sky, and water.

Other three-dimensional art include pottery, jewelry, fibers, and glass. All of these arts have histories of development extending over several thousand years. Every early culture developed pottery and methods of decorating and firing it. There are many materials used to make jewelry. The procedures were developed by ancient cultures; some have been borrowed from modern industrial technology. Even fibers, originally used for weaving and the production of fabrics, are now used to create three-dimensional art. Glass can be blown, cast, molded, and laminated to produce three-dimensional art. Stained glass, once reserved mainly for church windows, is now used to create both two- and three-dimensional artworks such as windows, lamps, containers, and constructions.

The growth of modern technology has lead to discoveries of new art media. Given the artist's exploratory nature, the list of art media will continue to grow. The forms that art may take will probably become even more diverse.

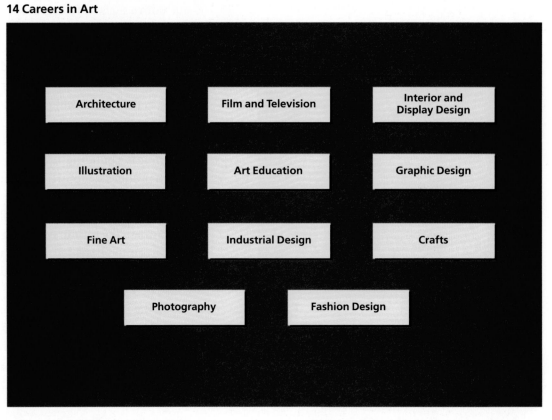

Chapter 14
Careers in Art

Architecture

Film and Television

Interior and Display Design

Illustration

Art Education

Graphic Design

Fine Art

Industrial Design

Crafts

Photography

Fashion Design

Overview

Chapter Objectives

Students should be able to:

1   learn about art careers through shared class reports   EE 2

2   name ten areas in which art careers are possible   EE 2

3   be familiar with some of the skills and responsibilities associated with art careers   EE 2, 3

4   demonstrate greater understanding of commercial and industrial art   EE 2, 3

Rationale

Students encounter art and design in a variety of forms every day. They may become more critically aware of the art that is a part of their lives if they know something about the responsibilities and skills required of the people who design these forms. Information about various jobs in art may help students decide if they want to pursue an art career.

Essential Chapter Concepts

• Architecture is the art of designing and constructing buildings and environmental areas.

• Interior design includes planning interior space and furnishings.

• Graphic design is concerned with visual communication through two-dimensional images.

• Industrial design includes conceiving and designing objects that meet the needs of people.

• Fashion design involves the creation and production of apparel.

• Illustration entails drawing with every medium to clarify ideas through visual images.

• Film and television graphics include the design and production of films and tapes.

• Art educators provide programs in art production, art history, aesthetics, and art criticism for students in the public schools. They need a working knowledge of media for all of the visual arts.

• Fine artists are skilled in the use of art media and techniques. They create compositional arrangements that demonstrate uniqueness of interpretation and individuality of technique.

• Photography is the art of making photographs for fine art or commercial purposes.

Vocabulary

architect   interior designer

graphic designer   fashion design

illustrator   film-television graphics

art educator   fine artist

photographer

Lesson Plan

14.1 Exploring a Career in Art

    Page **T 214**   Time: Variable

Handouts

Career Report Outline

Page **T 216**

Study Questions

Page **T 217**

Test Questions

Page **T 219**

Chapter Closure
Evaluation

1   Can students identify the major art careers?   **R 2**

2   Are students familiar with the training and responsibilities associated with various careers in art?

3   Can students discuss the contributions to daily living made by people in visual arts careers?

4   Did students complete informative art career reports?   **W 3**

Exploring a Career in Art

Time: Variable

Preparation

Rationale

Researching and reporting on responsibilities and training required for the various art and art-related jobs may help students decide if they are interested in art careers.

Report Materials

Career Report Outline (Handout), bibliography

Enrichment Materials

Large Reproductions
• Glaser, *Saratoga*, 24

Teach the Lesson

Objectives

Students should be able to:

1 prepare a report on a career in art to share with their classmates   EE 2, 3

2 research the training, responsibilities, and earnings for various art jobs   EE 3

Warm Up

Invite an artist, designer, ceramist, or architect to speak to the class. Or have the school counselor visit the class and suggest how students can find out more about art schools and training in art careers.

Explore and Develop

1 Refer to Chapter 1 and make a list of   R 2
occupations in art.

2 Let students volunteer for occupations that interest them. You may want to assign different careers to the other students to cover as many careers as possible.

3 Provide the Career Report Outline on   R 3
page T 216 and the bibliography.

4 When students do their research,   W 4
encourage them to find pictures that relate to the occupation.

5 When students have completed their reports, have them share them with the class.

Evaluate and Reflect

1 Ask students to indicate occupations in art that they did not know about before this activity.

2 Ask students to list some of the art forms they encounter every day produced by people in the art occupations reported on.

3 Have them discuss any changes in attitude toward specific art forms that resulted from this information.

Reteach

1 Assign an occupation to students. Ask them to produce a drawing that represents the specific occupation. Have them make a caption card. Display the drawings and caption cards.

2 Assign an art occupation to students, and ask them to bring in a picture that represents that occupation. Have students use the text information to prepare a summary card for the occupation. Make a bulletin board arrangement of the pictures and summary cards.

Extend the Lesson

Beyond the Basics

EE 1 Students might contribute to a display of various art forms (toy, furniture, cars, advertisements, etc.) that demonstrate the work of designers.

EE 3 Ask students to search for a historical photo sequence of some product that shows changes in the design of the product over

R 5 time, such as the telephone, automobile, airplane, or a kitchen appliance. Most of the jobs listed in credits at the end of a film are art-related. Have students copy the job titles from a film credit and find out what each one involves. What training is needed to prepare for one of these jobs?

The U.S. Department of Labor publishes a series of occupational and career information guides that may be helpful to students. Suggest looking for these materials at libraries and state employment offices.

Cultural Connections

EE 3 Have students do some research to identify fashions in different countries. They might compare architectural styles used to build

R 5 homes in different countries.

EE 3 The clothes popular with high school students throughout the United States are designed by individuals from many different places in the world. Examine labels in your own clothing or in stores to determine the designer and his/her country. Is there evidence of his/her cultural heritage in the products designed? Students may want to use resource materials to review traditional clothing styles from each of the cultures.

Connecting with Other Subjects

Language Arts There are many art-related careers within other areas that are not labeled as such. Suggest students research to find art-related jobs within other subject areas. For example, hiring practices in the engineering field during the 1950s involved giving candidates art materials and telling them to create something. What might an employer learn by doing this? How might art be important to a hairdresser, a chef, or a salesperson in a department store? Examine the role of art in the successes of top people in several different career fields? Is there a connection? Brainstorm and discuss.

EE 1, 3

R 5

W 3, 4

Career Report Outline

Use this outline to prepare a report on a career in art. The report should include information about the training, responsibilities, rewards, and positives and negatives of the occupation. You may acquire information through library resources and interviews with persons in the occupation.

I.   **Job Title**

II.   **Employment prospects**

    A.   places that employ people with this specialty

    B.   chances of obtaining a position in this occupation

III.   **Training required for this occupation**

    A.   apprenticeship—where, how long

    B.   art school—how long

    C.   college degree—undergraduate, graduate

IV.   **Skills required to succeed in this occupation**

V.   **Job responsibilities**

VI.   **Personal characteristics required to succeed in this occupation**

    A.   social skills, the ability to interact with people

    B.   knowledge of certain materials, procedures, equipment, technology, etc.

    C.   imagination and creativity

    D.   ability to work independently

    E.   highly technical skills

VII.   **Salary range**

    A.   How many hours per day, and days per week do people in this occupation work?

VIII. **Job future**

IX.   **Examples**

    A.   locations where people in this career work

    B.   names and pictures, if possible, of people interviewed for this report

X.   **Your Conclusions**

    A.   Give some reasons why you would or would not choose this career.

Study Questions
Chapter 14–Careers in Art

1 Name three things that an architect needs to consider when designing a building.

_____

2 What are the responsibilities of a landscape designer?

_____

3 Imagine you are an interior designer. Find a pleasing example in a magazine of the interior of a home or office. Describe the color scheme, furniture, fabrics, floor coverings, and lighting fixtures.

_____

_____

_____

4 Name three possible clients who use the services of exhibit designers.

_____

_____

5 What do graphic designers do with clients' ideas?

_____

_____

6 Name at least four items that a graphic designer may design.

_____

_____

7 Name five occupations in which someone interested in graphic design could specialize.

_____

_____

8 Describe the six steps involved in designing a new product.

_____

_____

_____

9 What are three qualities that a successful cartoonist must have?

_____

_____

10 Describe three responsibilities of a film art director.

_____

_____

11 What is the job of an animation artist?

_____

_____

12 Name three opportunities available for someone interested in art education.

_____

13 What training do public school art teachers need?

_____

14 Where do the majority of the fine artists today obtain their training?

_____

_____

15 Explain the relationship between an art gallery and an artist.

_____

_____

16 What are some requirements for the job of a photojournalist?

_____

_____

17 Name three other careers involving photography.

_____

18 Select one of the photography careers. Name three things that a photographer may have to know besides just "pointing and shooting."

_____

_____

_____

Test Questions
Chapter 14—Careers in Art

Match the descriptions in the left-hand column with the careers in the right-hand column. Write the correct letter in the blanks at the left.

_____	**1**	Translates ideas into visual images
_____	**2**	Plans visually appealing grounds around buildings
_____	**3**	Does sketches of clothing for newspapers, magazines
_____	**4**	Designs products that are used every day
_____	**5**	Designs and constructs buildings
_____	**6**	Works with color schemes, furniture, floor coverings
_____	**7**	Supervises corporation art or design department
_____	**8**	Composes pictorial stories for magazines and newspapers
_____	**9**	Arranges a group of mannequins in a department store
_____	**10**	Helps young people understand and appreciate art
_____	**11**	May create in a studio and exhibit work in an art gallery
_____	**12**	Draws characters for films
_____	**13**	Needs a great imagination to make humorous drawings
_____	**14**	May teach Greek and Roman Art in a university
_____	**15**	Makes photographs to be used in place of drawings for commercial publications

a. Art Historian

b. Interior designer

c. Graphic designer

d. Photojournalist

e. Art Director

f. Landscape architect

g. Fashion illustrator

h. Architect

i. Art teacher

j. Display designer

k. Sculptor

l. Illustration photographer

m. Cartoonist

n. Industrial designer

o. Animation artist

Circle the correct answer.

16 T F It is not necessary for package designers to understand the product the package holds.

17 T F It takes twenty-four drawings for each second of an animated film.

18 T F A film director uses storyboards as an outline of the characters' actions in a film.

19 T F The main requirement for public school art teachers is a background in drawing and painting.

20 T F Computer graphics technology has eliminated the need for training in design.

Study Answers
Chapter 14
Careers in Art

1 Possible answers include a client's needs, cost, building codes, space limitations, construction materials, foundation, supporting structure, exterior appearance, etc.

2 To plan outdoor areas that provide usable and visually appealing grounds around buildings and residences.

3 Answers will vary.

4 Answers may include department stores, museums, art galleries, manufacturers, convention centers.

5 Translate them into visual images that the public understands.

6 Answers may include album covers, brochures, packages, magazine covers, posters, billboards, etc.

7 Answers may include corporate art director, ad agency art director, graphic designer, computer graphics, silk screen printing, record jackets, signage, and outdoor advertising.

8 1) Sketches are made.
2) Sketches are developed into a prototype.
3) After a design direction is approved, detailed drawings are made from the model.
4) Using the detailed drawings, engineers make a full-scale production or working model.
5) If the production model is approved, working drawings are made to use in tooling up for production.

9 Drawing ability, rich imagination, ability to generate ideas continually, a distinctive drawing style, ability to write gags.

10 Answers may include being responsible for the authenticity of sets, costumes, props and locations; knowing how to analyze a script; having mastery of mood development and set construction; knowing how to obtain materials and equipment.

11 They draw and develop characters for animated films.

12 Answers may include elementary and secondary art teachers, college and university art teachers, art history teachers, art educators in teacher education programs, studio art teachers.

13 College degrees and knowledge of art history, aesthetic analysis, and varied art media.

14 At universities or art schools.

15 An art gallery may choose to show, advertise, and sell an artist's work. The gallery usually is certain that the public is interested and that the artist can consistently supply new work. The gallery retains a set percentage of the selling price for any work.

16 To make stories with pictures rather than words; be able to use all kinds of cameras and lenses; know darkroom and printing procedures; be able to travel.

17 Fashion, illustration, advertising, or portrait photography.

18 Answers will vary. A sample answer: Fashion photographer—has to be able to direct the model's movements during photo sessions, to control and create special lighting effects on location and in a studio, to create a specific mood in a picture.

Test Answers
Chapter 14
Careers in Art

1 C

2 F

3 G

4 N

5 H

6 B

7 E

8 D

9 J

10 I

11 K

12 O

13 M

14 A

15 L

16 F

17 T

18 T

19 F

20 F

Teacher Lesson Notes

Chapter 14
Careers in Art

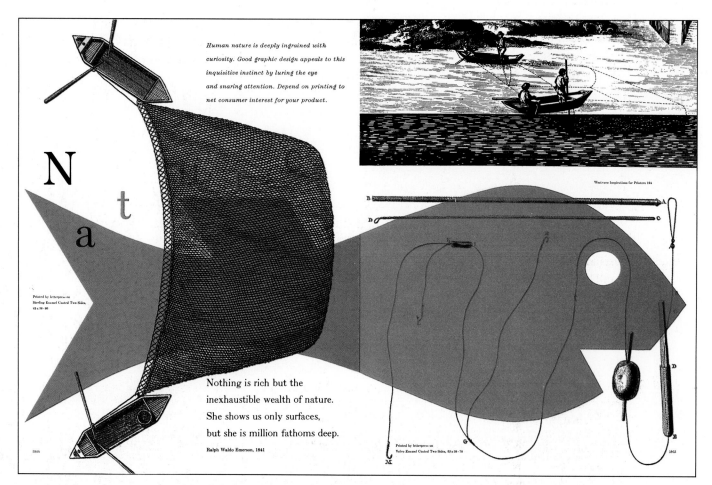

14–1 An eighteenth century engraving printed over a fish becomes modern graphic design, perhaps influenced by an earlier design. Bradbury Thompson, *Nature*, 1953. Courtesy Westvaco.

Throughout this book, you are invited to look at and read about the work of fine artists. They have produced an incredible variety of two- and three-dimensional art. However, their work makes up only a small percentage of the art we experience every day. Did you know that this book was made by artists? A designer selected the type style and decided on the size of the pages and the page layouts. A designer created the cover, and graphic artists provided drawings and charts.

Whenever you open a book, magazine or newspaper, turn on the TV, or go to a movie or a play, you encounter the work of artists. An artist's work is visible when you walk through a shopping center or grocery store, drive down a highway or a city street, or select some item of wearing apparel. Artists' designs determine the appearance of things all around us—advertisements, furniture, automobiles, toys, and your school building, to name a few. Some of the hundreds of art careers will be described in this chapter.

Architecture

Architects design buildings from private homes to manufacturing plants and skyscrapers that meet specific functions and satisfy a client's needs. Architecture is often referred to as the art of space. The architect must use space wisely and without waste to provide beauty and comfort in functional and flexible environments.

Architects estimate costs, follow local building codes, and provide detailed construction plans. He or she plans for everything that goes into a building, including construction materials, heating and plumbing, ventilation, stairways, and lighting to name a few. Construction methods for the foundation and supporting structure must be explained. The exterior appearance of a building is also the architect's responsibility. New structures should fit into their surroundings. They should be made with materials and in a style compatible with what is already there.

Architects must be able to draw, build models (fig. 14–2), have a good background in mathematics, know construction materials and procedures, and be knowledgeable of the history of architecture. They need a good sense of design and plenty of imagination.

Architectural Renderers. An architectural renderer creates drawings and paintings of the proposed building so that everyone involved can see what it will look like. The drawings may include trees, automobiles, people and surrounding structures. These elements suggest scale and show how the building will look in the selected environment (fig. 14–3). Construction materials such as brick, wood, aluminum, and stone must be easily identified. Architectural renderers can be employed by architectural firms or work free-lance. Architectural renderers need skill and imagination in working with watercolor, acrylics, pen and ink, and pencil.

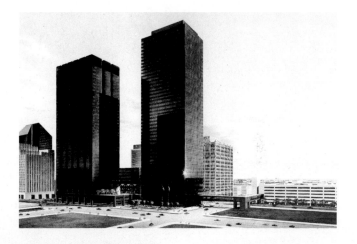

14–3 Rendering of proposed new office towers for downtown Houston. Courtesy Houston Chamber of Commerce.

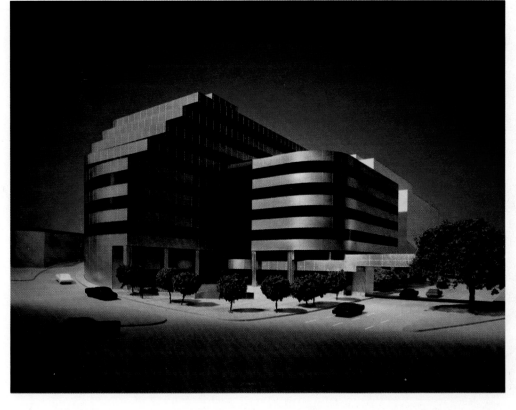

14–2 Model of Selegie Road Commercial Center, Singapore, 1986. Emery, Roth and Sons.

Landscape Architects. Some architects specialize in planning outdoor areas. They design usable and visually pleasing grounds around buildings and residences. They plan for drainage, land contours, and the planting of trees, flowers and shrubs. Landscape architects advise architects on how best to relate buildings to the land on which they are located. Landscape architects plan outdoor areas for private homes, commercial sites, school grounds, housing projects, highway beautification, and recreational grounds. They are knowledgeable about art, architecture, mechanical drawing, botany, and ecology. They generally have attended architectural schools that have an emphasis in landscape architecture.

Interior and Display Design

Interior designers plan and design interior space for everything from homes to giant industrial plants, from automobiles to airplanes (fig. 14–4). They advise on color schemes, furniture, fabrics, floor coverings, and lighting fixtures. They make drawings, paintings, and models of interiors. Plans may be drawn for the interior of one room or an entire department store. They are trained in art schools that specialize in interior design. Interior designers are skilled in architectural drawing, color, and design. They are employed by manufacturers of furniture, automobiles, airplanes, and buses. Interior designers plan the environments in which people live, work, study and play. Any company with interior space that is used by people, such as restaurant chains and hotels, uses the services of interior designers.

Exhibit and display designers work for agencies that sell some item or service such as department stores, museums, and art galleries. Manufacturers that exhibit products at convention centers employ these designers to plan and construct exhibits and displays. Exhibit and display designers design and build display cases and lighted boxes, organize props, and arrange lighting for the displays. They often make sketches and scale

14–5 Milton Glaser, Grand Union Supermarket.

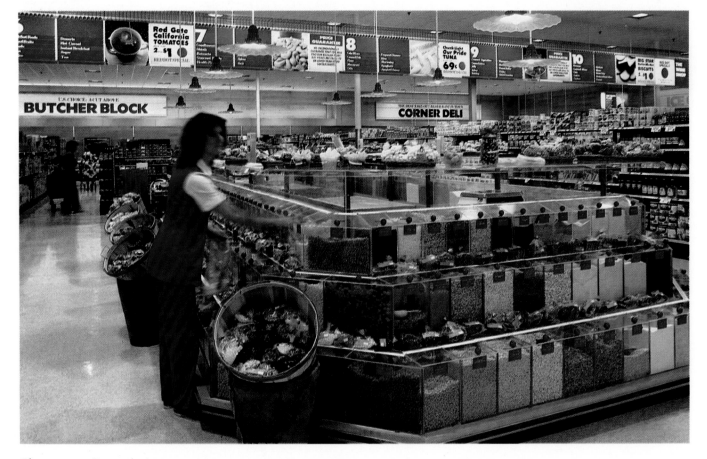

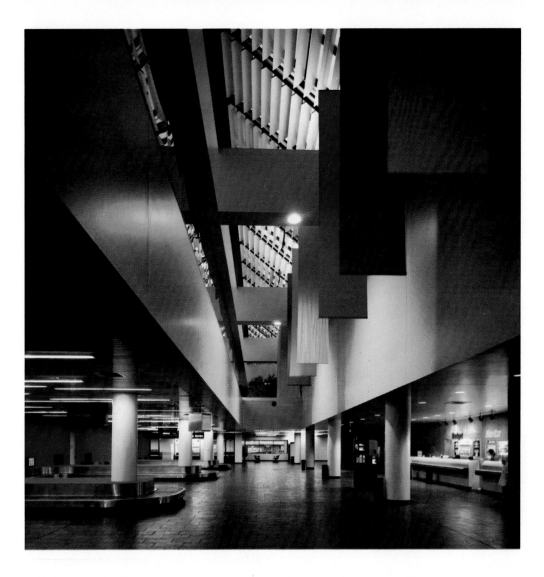

14-4 Skylit Solar Court, Albany County Airport, Colonie, N.Y. Norman McGrath, photographer. Photograph: courtesy Einhorn Yaffee Prescott, P.C.

models for clients. They need a knowledge of graphic design, type, color, display, theatrical lighting, and carpentry. In addition, they need skill in drawing and model building.

Department store display designers specialize in interior and window displays for department stores. Large department stores may employ display designers, but these designers frequently freelance for several different stores and shops. Individuals who specialize in department store displays need skills in design, color, lighting, lettering, illustration, and carpentry.

Graphic Design

You see the work of graphic designers every day. Advertisements on TV and in magazines and newspapers, signs and billboards, posters, brochures, record jackets, clothing logos, package design, and much more are done by graphic designers. Graphic designers

translate the ideas of clients into visual images that the public will find appealing and difficult to ignore.

Corporate art directors supervise people in art or design departments. The art staff create visual materials that project a positive image of the company and the product. They produce magazine and newspaper advertisements, promotional packages, audio-visual materials, TV ads, brochures, and public relations materials. Corporate art directors are knowledgeable in all areas of graphic design. They must be good administrators since they work with sales people, production workers, and management personnel, as well as the staff in the art department.

Advertising agency art directors also head teams of artists who produce all kinds of advertising materials for clients. Agency art directors consult with clients to determine how to best promote a product. The agency team studies the market that will buy the product, then

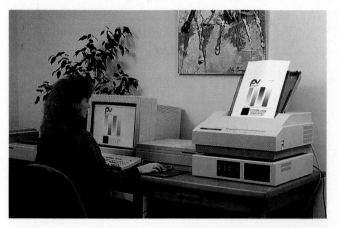

14-6 Courtesy Input-Output Computer Imaging Center, Normal, Illinois.

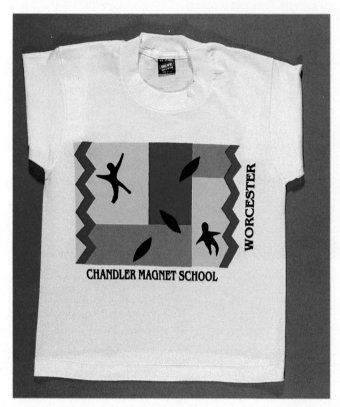

14-7 Logo design for T-shirts. Design by Erika Wade. Courtesy Chandler Magnet School.

develops a marketing plan. The plan includes ideas for advertising and promotional displays. The director prepares sketches and layouts of each piece of advertising. The layouts show text and typeface, color, illustrations, and photographs. If the client approves the plan, specialists on the agency team prepare newspaper and magazine advertisements, radio and television commercials, posters, and brochures. Agency directors must know advertising, have a good design background, and be able to visualize and develop ideas.

Graphic designers plan visual presentations for such things as record jackets, advertisements, brochures, package designs, magazine covers, filmstrips, posters, and billboards. Graphic designers work out sketches called roughs. The roughs offer clients and art directors alternatives to choose from. Approved roughs are then worked up in detailed drawings called comprehensives (in color if required). Everything is arranged to exact size, including blocks of text, the type of lettering, sketches of all artwork, and photos. When the comprehensives are approved, the designer works with computer artists, illustrators, typographers, and photographers to make finished pieces. These pieces are turned over to paste-up artists who prepare the materials for photocopying.

Computer graphic designers. Instead of pens, brushes and rulers, the computer graphics designer uses a digitizing pad or a mouse. Using special software and color printers, the computer graphic designer can put together text, type, images, and layout to create full-color or black-and-white graphics. Images can also be put on videotapes or slides. Three-dimensional images can be put into the computer and rotated in any direction to see all sides. The computer graphics designer must have a good sense of composition and a good foundation in graphic design.

Screen printers use their skills to reproduce images on T-shirts, uniforms, sports clothes, jackets, hats, posters, signs, greeting cards, calendars, and illuminated panels on pinball machines and mirrors (fig. 14-7). Screen prints can be produced on almost any surface including paper, fabric, glass, plastic, metal, rubber, wood, leather, and fur. The screen printer must know about different screen procedures and inks and paints that are suitable for various surfaces.

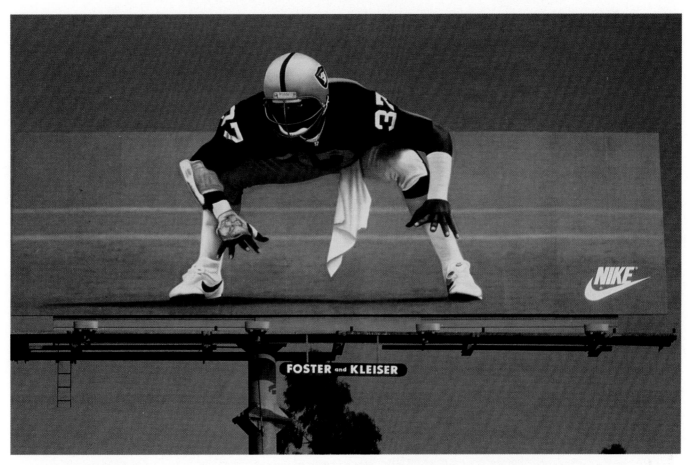

14–8 Courtesy NIKE, Inc.

Record jacket designers. On an album or CD cover, a designer tries to produce an image that communicates the mood or message of the music, the performance style of the recording artist, or the personalities of the group. The designer sketches several ideas for a cover. A comprehensive drawing of the accepted sketch is made to show color, images, and lettering. Photographers, illustrators, typographers, and printers produce a finished jacket.

Signage. Effective signs result from careful attention to design, lettering, and color. Commercial artists and graphic designers create both illuminated and non-illuminated signs. Examples include carved and sandblasted signs, truck lettering, wall murals, banners, and show cards. Signage also includes signs that are developed according to a "systems" approach. For example, all of the signs in a hospital or a corporate office building have a similar design format. This type of signage is called architectural sign systems or environmental graphics.

Outdoor advertising. Outdoor advertising is another form of commercial advertising. Poster panels or an eight-sheet poster for a billboard are often part of a multimedia campaign. In preparing outdoor advertising media, the designer must consider cost, size, method of reproduction, and location. Billboards have become a popular art form offering creative compositions of shapes and colors. They sometimes involve three-dimensional form, moving parts, and lighting effects (fig. 14–8). Outdoor advertising designers need skills in photography, painting, illustration, and type design. A knowledge of advertising psychology also helps.

Industrial Design

Industrial designers work to improve the appearance and quality of products. Products can be as simple as a soft drink can or as complex as a space shuttle. Designers are responsible for the form and appearance of all the objects that are part of your daily life, from automobiles and calculators to your skateboard and bicycle. Industrial designers must understand production processes, the characteristics of the materials used in those processes, and the function of every product they work on.

Product designers are employed by manufacturers that make consumer products. They must have a keen sense of design, understand consumer needs, and know style trends. The product must perform well, be attractive to consumers, and economical to manufacture. When planning a product such as a new vacuum

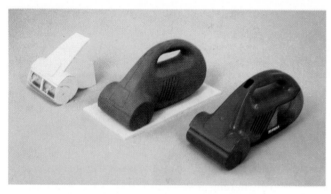

14-9 Preliminary prototypes of paper, clay and wood. Courtesy Eureka Vacuum Company.

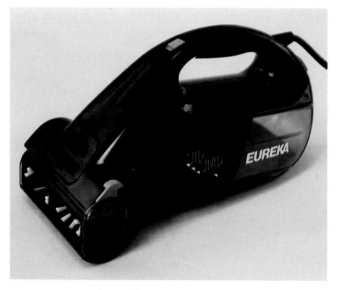

14-10 Marco Ferrari and Sam Hohulin, *Step Saver Vacuum.* Courtesy Eureka Vacuum Company.

cleaner, the designer works from sketches to develop a model, called a prototype. The model may be made from paper, clay, or wood (fig. 14-9). Once a design is approved, the designer makes detailed drawings and works with engineers to produce a full-scale working model (fig. 14-10). If the working model is approved, detailed working drawings are developed for the engineers to use in producing the new product.

Package designers design containers that will attract consumers, inform them about the product, and make them feel confident about the product's quality. Once sketches for a new package are approved, a prototype box is made. Designers may use a foam core, colored paper, transfer letters, and marker and pencil illustrations (fig. 14-11).

Furniture designers create all kinds of new furnishings that are constructed from wood, metal, plastic, and fabric. They work closely with manufacturing engineers to design furniture that is durable, attractive, and that can be produced cost-effectively with available technology. Suppose a furniture manufacturer asks a designer to create a plastic table. The designer works up ideas in drawings. If the manufacturer likes one, the designer builds a model. If the model is approved, the designer makes precise drawings, which are used to make a production model.

Toy designers are employed by manufacturers of games and toys. Most toy designers have backgrounds in industrial design. They know what kinds of materials are safe, durable, and easy to maintain. They must like to work in miniature. Like other industrial designers, they take the development of a toy or game

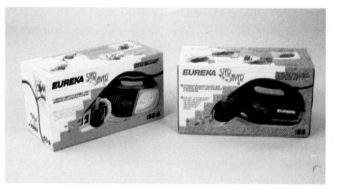

14-11 (left) Prototype box, and (right) final production box. Courtesy Eureka Vacuum Company.

through the steps of research, sketching, designing, model building, and production. A knowledge of children's interests and development is necessary.

Fashion Design

Fashion designers create clothing for every kind of activity, from athletic events to formal occasions. Fashion designers must be creative with colors, textures, and fabrics. They must be able to sketch their ideas with flair and style in various media. Because their drawings are used for the production of new garments, they must understand how garments are assembled. A knowledge of the history of clothing design and contemporary trends is necessary.

Fashion illustrators draw clothing and models for newspapers, magazines, department store catalogs, and brochures. They must be able to illustrate the texture and special qualities of the fabrics. For example, some fabrics cling to the body, others fall straight or in folds. They also have to illustrate jewelry and hair styles. Along with a knowledge of painting media, a knowledge of the history of fashion and contemporary fashion is helpful.

Illustration

Editorial illustrators are employed by magazines, newspapers, television stations, and book publishers. Editorial illustrators need to make drawings and paintings that complement the written text. The style of an artist usually determines the type of illustrations he or she creates. Some illustrators specialize in certain media such as pen and ink, watercolor, or collage. An art director may hire them for jobs which require that specialty. Illustrators may also specialize in subjects, such as sports activities, automobiles, animals, or landscapes.

Medical illustrators create extremely accurate pictures, transparencies, and overlays for medical schools, medical supply companies, publishers of medical journals and books, and advertising agencies. In addition to drawings for the public and medical profession, they also prepare charts, graphs, and diagrams for medical researchers. Their work requires patience, attention to detail, a knowledge of anatomy, and excellent drawing skills.

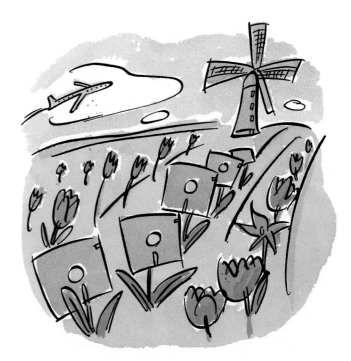

14–12 Diane Bigda created this watercolor and pen and ink illustration for a magazine article about a meeting of computer software producers that was to be held in Holland, 1993.

Cartoonists produce drawings for advertisements and stories, comic strips and comic books, editorial cartoons, greeting cards, and animated cartoons for TV or movies. Comic strips are meant to entertain. Editorial cartoons aim to influence public opinion, and advertising cartoons are meant to sell products. Most cartoonists do their work with brush, pen and ink, wash, and Zip-a-Tone (commercially printed stick-down patterns of dots or lines). They may be employed by newspaper chains and magazines. Some cartoonists work on a free-lance basis and sell their work to publishers. Cartoonists must have rich imaginations and be able to generate ideas continually. The ability to draw well and rapidly in a distinctive style that people recognize is essential for success. Comic strip cartoonists must be able to write stories or one-liners to accompany their work.

Technical illustrators produce drawings for assembly of everything from bicycles to the installation of instrument panels in airplanes. For a good example of their work, look at an automobile repair manual. Technical illustrators are employed by every kind of industry. Their drawings aid in the construction and maintenance of complex machinery and industrial products.

Film and Television

Art directors coordinate the efforts of artists, graphic and costume designers, and scene builders involved in making a film or television production. They work with film directors and producers to develop appropriate environments for their production. Art directors are responsible for the authenticity of sets, costumes, props, and locations. The director must be able to create set constructions for a scene that establish a mood. An art director must understand the production from beginning to end.

Storyboard illustrators are employed by advertising agencies and the film and television industries. They develop storyboards based on a story for a film or the action for a TV commercial. A storyboard may contain fifty or sixty sequenced sketches that illustrate the progress of action. The dialogue is printed under each drawing. The number of storyboards needed depends on the length of the production and may range from three to thirty. The comic-strip-like boards are used by the film director as an outline of the characters' actions in a film or the progress of an animated commercial. Storyboard artists must be able to produce descriptive drawings very rapidly.

Television graphic artists are employed by television studios to produce advertising and promotional materials. They create visuals for newscasts, art for commercials, and sets for shows. They also design logos for the station. They must quickly provide finished products that will be impressive on the screen.

Animation artists also use storyboards to draw and develop the characters for animated films. They listen to recordings of the voices for the characters as they develop them in drawings. It takes twenty-four drawings for each second of film. The animation artist must be able to draw well and rapidly, and have the patience to work on a project for a long time. Some feature length films take several years to complete.

Art Education

Elementary and secondary art teachers work with children and adolescents from kindergarten through high school. They are certified to teach art and hold degrees from colleges and universities. School art teachers need a background in art history, critical aesthetic analysis, and a working knowledge of many different art media. They must be able to help students use these media to express their ideas and feelings. The art experiences can give children and adolescents a lifelong enjoyment of the visual arts. Art teachers plan programs that give students basic art skills and knowledge. Secondary art teachers must provide experiences for students who wish to specialize in one area of art production. They can also advise talented individuals who might pursue an art career.

College and university art teachers are often *studio art instructors* who majored in a studio area during their college training. They instruct courses in their area of specialization (drawing, painting, printmaking, ceramics, etc.). They generally have a Master of Fine Arts degree. In addition to teaching, most university art teachers produce art for exhibition and sale. Some achieve regional and national recognition for their artwork. Participation in selective and competitive exhibitions is expected of studio art instructors.

Art historians are employed by colleges and universities to teach art history. They must have completed graduate programs with emphasis in an area of art history, such as Modern Art, Greek and Roman Art, or Baroque and Rococo. Art historians conduct research, write papers and books, and sometimes give lectures to community groups.

Art educators are employed by colleges and universities that have teacher education programs. They usually have a Master's or Doctoral degree and experience as public school art teachers. They instruct courses to prepare people to teach art in elementary and secondary schools, or at the university level. They may also prepare people to work in art administration or as city art supervisors.

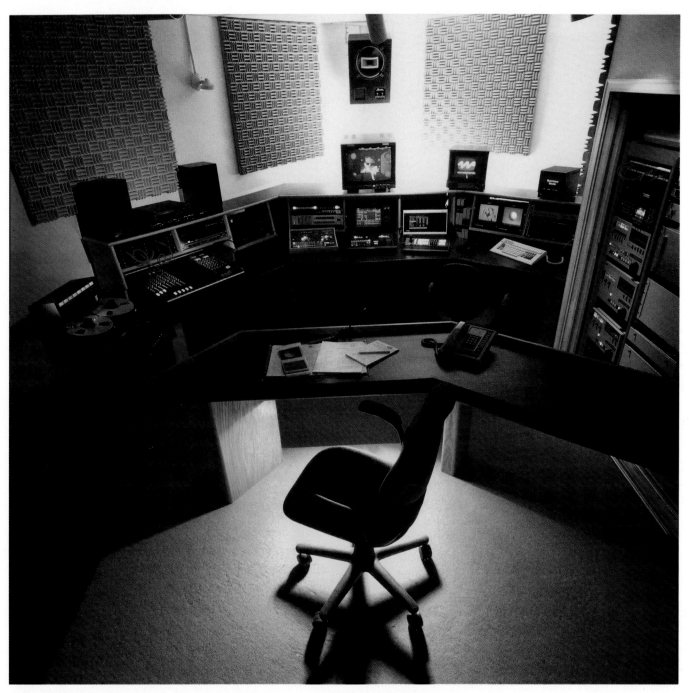

14-13 Courtesy Wave Inc., Worcester, Massachusetts. Photographer: Jonathan Kannair.

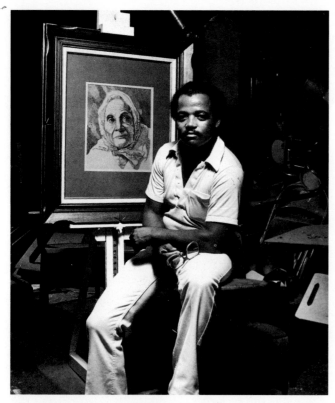

14–14 John Joiner. Photograph courtesy The Arizona Bank.

Crafts

Crafts can be defined as works in wood, clay, fiber, metal, glass, and plastic that have some use or are related in form to useful objects. For example, wheel-thrown pottery is a craft, although not all wheel-thrown pots can be used to hold food or liquid.

Like fine artists, craftspeople often find it difficult to make a comfortable living from the sale of their works. Many teach their craft or supplement their income with a second job. Some craft studios specialize in one medium such as ceramics or stained glass. They employ craftspeople to produce work from the designs of others, rather than original works of their own.

In recent years, the differences between crafted objects and fine art have become less obvious. Wooden chairs have taken on the look of fine sculpture. Woven clothing is often hung on walls as decoration. The distinctive styles of a few craftspeople have even placed them on a par with fine artists. There is great demand for their work.

Fine Art

Fine artists create two- and three-dimensional works of art to sell. A fine artist must have the self-discipline to work several hours a day to produce his or her art. Most fine artists work alone, motivating themselves to start and finish their projects. In order to become known by the art-buying public, fine artists must establish a connection with a gallery. The gallery "represents" artists. The gallery agrees to show, advertise, and sell their work. It charges each artist a percentage of the final selling price in exchange for its services.

Because it may take years for an artist to establish a reputation, find a suitable gallery and produce enough artwork to sell, many must hold a second job to supplement their income. Most artists need a studio or workshop to work in. And while some are self-taught, many artists have university or art school degrees. The life of a fine artist may seem attractive and simple, yet it is a life of constant challenge.

Photography

Photojournalists take the pictures you see in magazines and newspapers. They make pictorial stories with their cameras. Photojournalists must be expert in the use of many different cameras and lenses. They must be able to handle them with speed and accuracy under all kinds of conditions. They also know darkroom and printing procedures. They travel to many different locations to photograph people and events, such as scenes of human tragedy, war, celebrations, and affairs of state. Because it takes so many years to develop a reputation as a photojournalist, many of them start out as freelancers. They may take pictures on assignment from editors or try to sell their work to a publisher.

Fashion photographers create pictures for newspapers, department store catalogs, and magazines. They work with models in a studio or on location at such places as a beach, a shopping mall, or an airport. They are skilled in creating special lighting effects on location and in the studio. Photographing models in action at fashion shows requires planned lighting and rapid camera work during the presentation. Fashion photographers create moods in pictures. They direct the movements of the models, from natural to dramatic poses to flamboyant action.

Illustration photographers provide photos for books and magazines, record jackets, travel brochures, corporation annual reports, and advertisements. Photographs are frequently used in place of drawings and paintings for commercial publications. Illustration photographers work closely with agency and corporate art directors. They use models, props, backgrounds, and sets to make an idea come alive. An illustration photographer must be able to produce photos that are vital and stimulating.

Advertising photographers specialize in taking pictures of products for advertisements. The photographer may work with an ad agency art director to fulfill the needs of an ad layout. They take pictures of products ranging from jewelry to refrigerators. The finished photos must attract the public's attention, make the product appealing, and hold the viewer's attention long enough for communication about the product. Ad photographers take photos of many different surfaces (foods, fabrics, fur, glass, diamonds, wood, plastic, metal, and so on). They must have skill and experience in arranging backgrounds and lighting effects.

Portrait photographers make photo studies of their subjects. They generally have a studio, but will go to locations for special events such as graduations, weddings, birthdays, and award ceremonies. Portrait photographers are expert at posing subjects and arranging complementary lighting for children, men, and women of all ages. They know how to use a variety of cameras, film, and development processes. They can produce photographs that resemble painted portraits.

There are many other art-related careers that were not discussed in this chapter. For more information about careers in art, you may want to consult your art teacher or school guidance counselor. You can also write to college and university art departments and professional art schools.

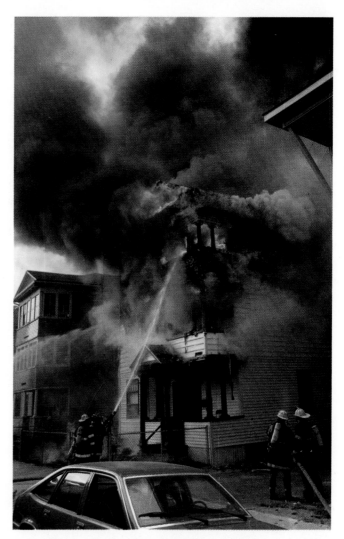

14–15 Courtesy The Worcester Telegram and Gazette.

Research Experience 14.1

Exploring a Career in Art

Research a career in art that interests you. Consider the training, responsibilities, and rewards of the job. Write down reasons why you feel you would like this job.

Part V
What Is It Saying?

Henri Matisse, *The Red Room*, (detail) 1908–1909. Oil on canvas, 71″ x 97″ (180 x 246 cm). The Hermitage Museum, Leningrad.

Chapter 15
Interpretation: There Is More to It Than Meets the Eye

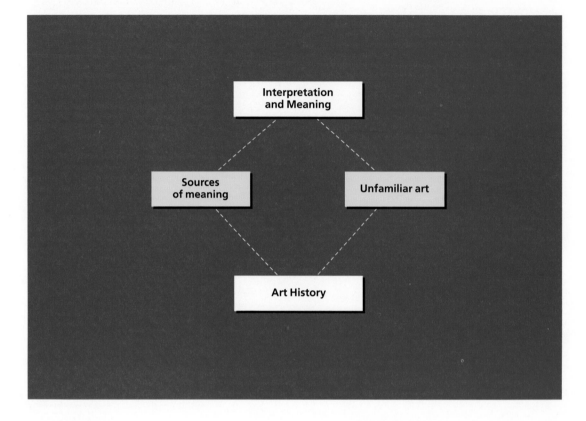

Overview

Chapter Objectives

Students should be able to:

1 interpret artworks by explaining their meaning or content   **EE 3, 4**

2 understand that interpretation of an artwork often involves more than just the visible aspects of the work   **EE 3, 4**

3 interpret an artwork on the basis of description and analysis, their own experience, and background knowledge of the work and artist   **EE 3, 4**

4 refer to art history when possible to complete interpretations of artworks   **EE 3, 4**

Rationale

This chapter is an introduction to interpretation, the third part of the critical analysis model. Interpretation is the most creative and rewarding part of criticism. Interpretation not only calls for the student to synthesize information from the description and analysis phases. It also brings into play the student's personal storehouse of experience and knowledge. For interpreting familiar works with familiar themes, the application of this storehouse is almost unconscious. For unfamiliar works, especially those from unfamiliar times and places, this storehouse is inadequate, requiring the student to do some research. The main source for such research is art history. Thus, Chapter 15 prepares the student for the art history chapters that follow.

Essential Concepts

• To interpret a work is to explain the meaning of it.

• Interpretation, the third step of the art criticism model, requires a viewer to synthesize information from description and analysis along with knowledge relevant to the work. Thus, interpretation is based on both what is seen and *not* seen in the work.

• Art history is the study of art, especially with regard to the ways it has existed through time. It provides information about periods of history, periods of art, the social contexts of art, and the evolution of styles.

• Art history can provide some of the knowledge needed to interpret works from both Western and non-Western cultures.

Vocabulary

historical context　　　　social context

Meet the Artist

Sokari Douglas Camp　Page 203

Lesson Plans

15.1　Criticism Experience:
Interpreting American Gothic

　　　Page **T 226**　Time:　1 period

Handouts

Interpretation Guidelines

Page **T 228**

Examples of Responses for Interpretation of *American Gothic*

Page **T 229**

Chapter Closure

Evaluation

1　*Criticism:* Do students understand that to interpret a work is to explain its meaning?　R 5

2　*Criticism:* Do students understand that interpretation is based on a synthesis of description, analysis, and knowledge?　R 5

3　*Criticism:* Can students interpret an artwork using information obtained from description, analysis, and knowledge from their own experiences?　W 2　R 5

4　*Criticism/Art history:* Do students appreciate the importance of art history in helping them to access works from distant times and places? Do they voluntarily use art history references to interpret unfamiliar artworks?　R 3　R 5

Notes

Interpreting *American Gothic*

Time: 1 period

Preparation

Rationale

This lesson introduces interpretation, the third part of the four-step criticism model. Students will learn to synthesize information from the description and analysis phases. The interpretation process helps students determine the meaning of an artwork.

Interpretation Materials

Interpretation Guidelines (Handout), Examples of Responses for Interpretation of *American Gothic* (Optional Handout)

Enrichment Materials

Slides:
• Wood, *American Gothic,* 2

Overhead Transparencies:
• Wood, *American Gothic,* 17

Teach the Lesson

Objectives

Students should be able to:

1   interpret *American Gothic*, using information from their earlier descriptions and analyses, and relevant knowledge from their own experiences   EE 3, 4

Vocabulary

Historical context refers to the historical circumstances of an artwork. It explains the period in which the work was created and prevalent art and art styles of that time.

Social context refers to the environment a work was created in. It explains how the art was experienced by people of that time and place and what their aesthetic preferences were.

Warm Up

Find an interesting picture in a popular magazine or the school yearbook. Present it on the opaque projector, and give students three minutes to write a paragraph on what is happening and what mood or idea the picture expresses. Share their responses, and discuss the differences and similarities.

Explore and Develop

1   Focus on the discussion of Russell's   R 5
painting on Student Edition pages 201–202. Call attention to the use of social context knowledge about conflicts between Indians and settlers; and historical context knowledge about the Old West with cowboys, cattle drives, horses, and so forth. Point out that they may use things they know in addition to what they see when interpreting an artwork.

2   Refer to the biography of Grant Wood on Student Edition page 115 for some contextual information.

3   Distribute copies of the Interpretation Guidelines on page T 228. Have students quickly review their descriptions from Chapter 3 and their analyses from Chapter 9 before starting the interpretation.

4   Students may work individually or in   R 5
small groups to develop interpretations? If they work in groups, one person should write the group's ideas down.

5   Metaphors can help with interpretations. Encourage students to try them. Examples are included in the guidelines.

6   Share the interpretations.

Evaluate and Reflect

1 Were students able to complete interpretations that explain the meaning of the artwork?

2 Ask them how they feel about their interpretations? Are they satisfied? Why or why not?

3 How did they use information from their descriptions and analyses in developing the interpretation?

4 Have them describe the use of any historical information or personal experience they were able to use in the interpretation.

Reteach

To help students analyze how compositional organization contributes to the meaning of an artwork, have them look at Russell's *The Toll Collectors* in figure 15–1. Ask students to write how the meaning of the painting would change if:

a. the cowboy and American Indian rode side by side

b. the American Indian was charging with a spear at the cowboy

c. four American Indians were blocking the cowboy's path

Extend the Lesson

Beyond the Basics

EE 4 Students can collect critical analyses from the newspapers and magazines. They may be for the visual arts, theater, or movies.
R 3 Discuss the criticisms. How do they compare to the four-stage analysis they are using?

EE 4 Students can write critical analyses of one
W 4 of their own artworks.

EE 4 Suggest students browse through current issues of art magazines and journals such as *ARTnews* to find criticism written by a
R 5 professional critic. Instruct students to
W 4 describe, analyze, and interpret the work of art before reading any of the comments written by the professional. When finished, read the critique and compare their responses with the professional critic's article. Ask students to discuss points with which they agree and disagree. Did the professional critic bring up things students may have overlooked? Did the student notice something the critic did not address? Try to find another viewpoint of the same work written by a different critic.

Cultural Connections

EE 4 Suggest students describe, analyze, and interpret several sculptures of the human form, including one from prehistory, ancient Greece, and the twentieth century.
R 5 At which stage in the process are the works most different? most alike? Have students write an article summarizing their findings and comparing the results.

Connecting with Other Subjects

Science, Music, Language Arts Suggest students talk with the science teacher to compare steps used in art criticism with the process of scientific inquiry. Assign other students to speak with the music and language arts teachers regarding similar processes.

Language Arts Direct students' attention
R 5 to the example of interpretation on page 201 of the student text. The writer is interpreting *The Toll Collectors* by Charles M. Russell. The writer states "The scene becomes a symbol of a much greater confrontation — a territorial struggle between two cultures with extremely different lifestyles and histories." After students have examined this painting suggest they read the essay, "Remarks Concerning the Savages of North America" in which Benjamin Franklin questions who the savages really were.

Interpretation Guidelines

Interpretation is the third phase of the criticism process. To interpret an artwork is to explain the meaning of it. Interpretation builds on description and analysis. There are two more sources of information you can use for interpretation, your own knowledge and experience, and art history for background about periods and styles of art, and social conventions relevant to the work in question.

1 Look for clues in your description and analysis to help guide your interpretation, such as dominant elements, repetitions, similarities, lines that direct vision, moody colors, subtle or strong contrasts, and so on. The artist had reasons for including these things. What does it all mean?

2 Describe the expressive quality of the work: happy, sad, serious, lighthearted, calm, chaotic, depressing, ominous, sensual, joyful, angry, aggressive, passive, tense, relaxed, restful, threatening, and so on.

3 What is happening? Even if the work is nonrepresentational, try to answer this question. Draw on your own knowledge and experiences related to the subject matter, forms, shapes, and colors in the work. Have you seen, read, or studied about situations or things similar to what you see in the artwork? Are there things in the artwork that remind you of things you have experienced?

Metaphors may help to get at the meaning of the work. Is there something in the work that makes you think of another, different thing? For example, the man has a poker face. Her lips are a sealed envelope. The pitchfork is a three-pronged spear.

4 Form a **hypothesis** about what the work means. A hypothesis is an assumption or guess based on evidence you have collected. It can't be just personal opinion. When you have generated a hypothesis, ask:

   a. Does evidence from the description and analysis support this hypothesis?
   b. Does evidence based on personal knowledge and experiences support the hypothesis?

5 If your evidence does not support the hypothesis, try another one. It is not unusual to generate more than one hypothesis for an artwork.

Examples of Responses for Interpretation of *American Gothic*

1   Hypothesis (an assumption or informed guess about the meaning of the work)
- The painting expresses the belief of Midwestern farmers in the 1930s in early American values such as religion, hard work, frugality, and perseverance.
- The painting is a criticism of the deeply religious (pious) beliefs of people who live in small Midwestern rural areas and towns.
- The painting is about a man's right to own property and protect it from outsiders.
- The painting records the grim realities of an "all work and no time for play" philosophy of people living on small Midwestern farms.

2   Defend your hypothesis with evidence from description and analysis information. **The first hypothesis is used for this example.**

a. Description Information
- The title of the work includes the term *Gothic,* which is a historical term associated with the pointed arches of medieval churches.
- The figures have stern expressions and stiff poses.
- The man's deeply lined face has a toil-worn look.
- The subjects' clothing has an old-fashioned unpretentious look: their high-buttoned collars, his wire-rim glasses, her patterned apron, the style of the house.
- The man's high collar and black jacket are similar to those of a preacher.
- The pitchfork and the man's overalls are symbols for work.

b. Analysis Information
- The pattern of the woman's apron and the curtain are similar.
- The pitchfork shape is repeated in the man's clothing, windows, barn siding.
- There is a great size contrast between the figures and objects in the middle ground.
- The man is the dominant form because of size, position and line of sight.
- The diagonal rooflines and horizontal porch roof direct vision to the figures' heads.
- The strong vertical lines of the figures dominate the work's curves and diagonals.

c. Other Sources (personal knowledge, experiences, and art history)
- The pointed gable and the window in the gable look like church gables and windows.
- The house looks like old houses located in the rural Midwest, and in fact is an example of Carpenter Gothic. Such houses included the pointed arches and gables of Gothic churches built of stone throughout France and Germany in the 13th and 14th centuries. The houses were constructed of wood throughout Iowa in the 1860s.
- Many of the early settlers in rural Iowa communities were deeply religious.
- The painting is dated 1930, which was the time of the Depression in the United States.

Chapter 15
Interpretation: There Is More to It Than Meets the Eye

In Chapter 5, you learned how to describe an artwork. In Chapter 9, you learned how to analyze an artwork. You have been introduced in other chapters to the visual elements, principles of design, and the major two-dimensional and three-dimensional media. At the same time, you discovered a new vocabulary to help you describe and analyze art.

Interpretation and Meaning

Now that you are able to describe and analyze, you are ready to *interpret*. To interpret an artwork is to explain the *meaning* of it. What does it express? What is its content? You have already had some experience in interpretation. For example, you have seen how lines can be nervous or relaxed, how colors can be warm or cool. Shapes can be closed or open. Positive and negative areas of a carved sculpture can flow into one another. Those qualities expressed certain feelings or ideas that you, the viewer, could interpret. The focus of this chapter is on the interpretation and meaning of artworks.

An Example of Interpretation

Imagine being asked to interpret *The Toll Collectors* (fig. 15–1) by Charles M. Russell. First of all, you would describe and analyze it.

As you can see, the subject is a landscape containing people and animals. In the foreground are a cowboy and a Crow Indian. Both are mounted on horses, both are carrying weapons, and both look serious. In the middle ground are cattle, a cowboy on the left, and more Crow Indians on the right. In the distance are more cattle. A large herd seems to be headed this way. In the far distance are the faint outlines of a mountain range. You might have guessed from the title and the gesture of the Crow Indian that a *toll*, or payment, is involved. (Indeed, the Crow Indian warrior is demanding payment before he will allow the cattle and cowboys to cross tribal land. His raised finger indicates a toll of $1.00 per head.) With just the information provided so far, you may be ready to offer an interpretation.

However, your observations would not stop at just the subject matter and the title. You would also note the visual elements, the principles of composition, and the oil medium. You would note that Russell's style is basically realistic. Animals, men, and land are quite natural looking; the sense of open land is especially convincing. The artist skillfully used colors and values to suggest that the time is early morning (or late afternoon) and that the atmosphere is hazy. (Note the effective use of aerial perspective.) Russell used the oil medium much as Renoir did in *Luncheon of the Boating Party* (fig. 3–1). He used short brushstrokes, which you can see clearly in the distant herd. Several lines of continuation unite the scene horizontally. Look at the broad sweep of the hill in the foreground as well as the mountains on the horizon. The cowboy and Crow Indian are painted in warm colors. They overlap the bluish shapes of the mountains and unite foreground and background.

Of course, much more could be said about Russell's painting. For this example, only the main features have been noted. Now you are ready to interpret the work. Like the description and analysis, the interpretation that follows is not intended to be complete.

You might begin by saying that *The Toll Collectors* is about a meeting between a cowboy and a Crow Indian. However, because the Crow Indian is demanding a toll, this meeting could mean a challenge, even

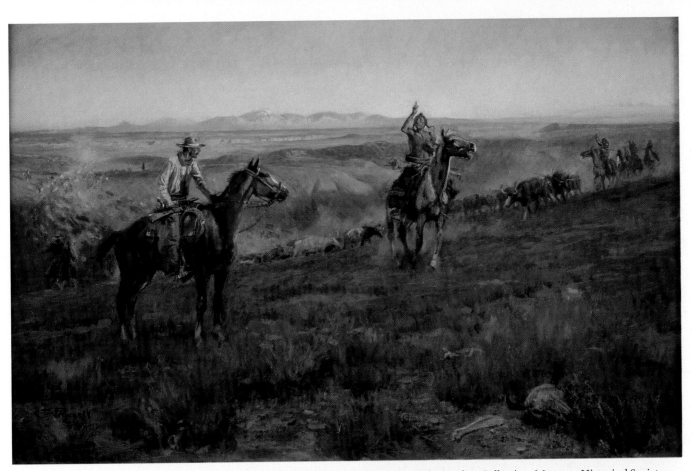

15-1 Charles M. Russell, *The Toll Collectors*, 1913. Oil on canvas, 24″ x 36″ (61 x 91 cm). The Mackay Collection, Montana Historical Society.

danger. Perhaps the meeting should be called a *confrontation*. The confrontation itself, however, is not overly dramatic. The men seem ordinary in appearance. Russell's earthy realism tends to downplay a sense of drama or heroics. Except for the presence of weapons, there is no indication of violence. Except for the cattle in the background pushing ever closer, there is very little movement.

But there is more to consider than the men, their weapons, and the cattle, important as these are. The setting is a vast wilderness—the "Old West." This wilderness stands for more than just the land used for cattle drives. It adds a sense of scale that enlarges its meaning. The scene becomes a symbol of a much greater confrontation. It expresses a territorial struggle between two cultures with extremely different lifestyles and histories.

Sources of Meaning

The meaning we have discussed so far is based on things you see in the picture and information in the title. The tasks of describing, analyzing, and interpreting helped you to bring out the most from these seen things.

But the meaning of Russell's picture is also based on things you do *not* see. For example, you do not actually see a "territorial struggle between two cultures." This part of the interpretation is based on what you *know*. You have learned in school about conflicts between American Indians and the white settlers. Cowboys, cattle drives, sagebrush, and the semi-arid landscape of the western territories are all a part of your knowledge of the Old West, an American legend.

You also probably learned about cowboys, American Indians, and outlaws through movies and TV. Most of those stories were exaggerated and very misleading about the true conditions of the western territories. However, they did make you familiar with the facts and legends of the Old West. Without this knowledge, Russell's painting would have had little meaning. Indeed, you probably would not even have

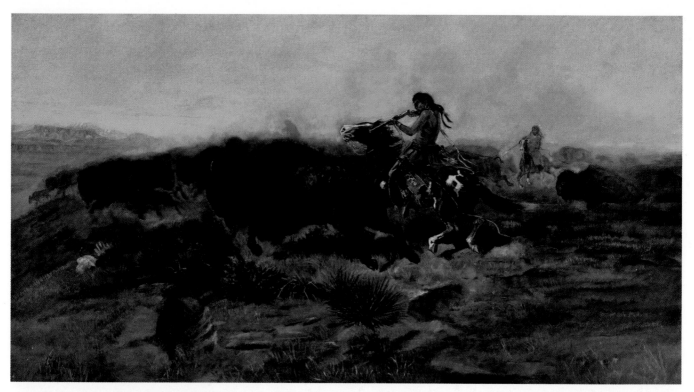

15-2 Charles M. Russell, *Wild Meat for Wild Men*, 1890. Oil, 20 ¼″ x 36 ⅛″ (51 x 92 cm). Amon Carter Museum, Fort Worth, Texas.

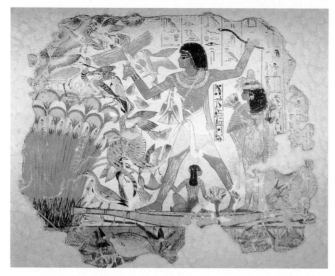

15-3 *Fowling the Marshes*, wall painting, ca. 1400 BC. Reproduced by Courtesy of the Trustees of the British Museum.

recognized the two people as being a cowboy and an American Indian!

Russell based *The Toll Collectors* on memories of his own experiences in the Montana Territory in the 1880s. (This was about the time that Renoir painted *Luncheon of the Boating Party* in France.) Russell spent a winter with the Blackfoot Indian tribe. He developed an admiration for the American Indian that lasted the rest of his life. Russell paid tribute to his "red brothers" by painting their exploits (fig. 15–2). If you knew more about the artist and had seen many of his paintings, you no doubt would have discovered even deeper meanings in this work.

Unfamiliar Art from Unfamiliar Places

Now, imagine being asked to interpret a mural (fig. 15–3) painted on a limestone wall of a 1400 BC Egyptian tomb.

Some things you can identify right away: A man is standing, legs spread, on what appears to be a boat. With one hand he is grabbing two birds by their feet, in the other he holds an odd staff. Also in the boat are two females, both much smaller than he. In front of the man are swarms of birds and a cat gripping one bird in its teeth and clinging to another with its front claws. Directly in front of the boat are what appears to be strange plants. Directly below the boat are some fish.

Sokari Douglas Camp
1958–

Strips of steel are bound together to form the structure of a bed. The metal frame sags with the weight of a body which is not there. Only the spirit of a person remains behind. Surrounding the bed are huddled figures drawn in ribbons of steel. *Church Ede* is a memorial to the father of Sokari Douglas Camp, the artist who created this unusual sculpture. It reconstructs the Nigerian funerary ceremony which honored her father's death. Turn on the electric motor that operates this moving work of art, and the grieving figures begin to move. As they fan the missing body with fly whisks, the bed begins to shake, symbolizing the continuing vitality of the afterlife. The sound of the whirring motors, the shaking fans held by the mourners, the rattling metal strips which form the bed, and the partially complete figures compel your imagination to complete this scene. At once, the viewer captures a glimpse of the Kalabari culture in which this ceremony originated.

Sokari uses the materials and techniques of contemporary Western art to create sculptures that tell of the Kalabari people among whom she was raised. Though Sokari's early life was spent in the Niger Valley of southern Nigeria, she moved to England as a child to live with her sister.

Sokari's experiences in Africa and in the Western world have had unique influences on her

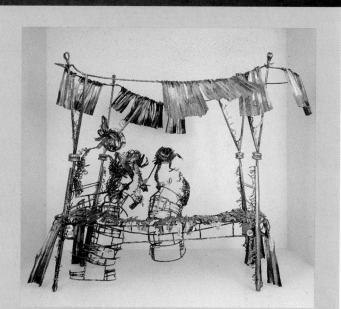

Sokari Douglas Camp, *Church Ede (Decorated Bed for Christian Wake)*, 1984. Steel, cloth, H. 8″. Collection of the artist, courtesy the National Museum of African Art, Smithsonian Institution, Washington, DC. Photograph: Jeffrey Ploskonka, Eliot Eliscfon Archives.

life and art. Her early exposure to the ceremonies and festivals associated with Kalabari culture were significant to Sokari. Her schooling in England and later in the United States influenced the methods and materials she uses to express these early memories of Nigeria. Sokari Douglas Camp combines Western art with the traditional culture of the Kalabari people to express ideas and communicate stories in an art which is uniquely her own.

(We might be able to see more fish if that part of the mural were not damaged.)

The images of the people are flat and relatively stiff. Compared to them, the birds, cat, and fish are very lifelike and active. There is even some overlapping among the birds. You can almost hear them screeching and flapping their wings as they are being atteecked by the man and the cat.

Other than the overlapping, the mural is almost completely lacking in depth. Notice that the boat is *on* the water and not *in* the water.

Beyond these few impressions, there is little else that you can get out of this work, leaving you with little

to say about it by way of interpretation. Indeed, the more you study the mural, the more questions it raises. Among the many questions you may have are: What is the purpose of the mural? Who are the people? Why is the man so much bigger than the women? Why is the picture located in a tomb? Who was the artist? Why are the people so flat, and the whole picture lacking in depth.

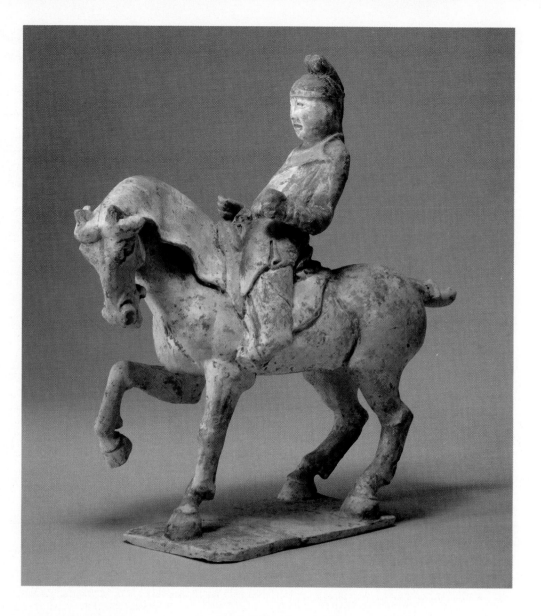

Unlike your interpretation of *The Toll Collectors,* your interpretation of the Egyptian mural depends almost entirely on what you *see.* What you *know* about ancient Egypt and its art, compared to what you know about the Old West and its legends, is obviously limited.

Now, look at the small statue in figure 15–4. You recognize this as a man on a horse. In a captured moment, the rider is restraining the horse with his reins (now missing). The posture of the horse, which seems to have come to a sudden stop, is in rhythm with the posture of the man, who is leaning back sharply. You may have recognized that the sculpture is ceramic. Its rough textures are suited to the forms of the stocky horse and rider.

You can get meaning from this sculpture from the forms. But without additional knowledge, that meaning is rather limited. The sculpture was made in China during the T'ang dynasty (600s AD). This bit of infor-

mation helps you to locate it in time and place. Perhaps it helps you understand the costume of the man. But think how much richer the meaning would be if you knew something of the history and culture of China, especially during the T'ang dynasty.

As stated earlier, meaning is based on things you see, but also on things you do not see, that is, things you know. The images, colors, and shapes in a work are not always enough to help you understand its meaning. If the images do not "connect" with your own experiences, background and education, you may be unable to discover sufficient meaning. This is especially true for a work from an unfamiliar time and place, such as ancient Egypt or T'ang dynasty China. This would even be true for a work like *The Toll Collectors* if a viewer had little knowledge of American history.

Art History

Art history is the study of art within a *social* and *historical context.* That means studying the art of a particular time by also studying the history and social customs of the time. Art history provides information about periods of history, periods of art, and changing styles. Knowing about the period in which an artwork was created can help you understand the work.

Like an archeologist, an art historian sifts through the evidence. He or she looks at other artworks, books, and records of the period. Like a storyteller, he or she attempts to "re-create" an artwork in the context of its original time and place. How did people who were living at that time experience the art? As writer Gerald Brommer explains, "Art history adds personality to works of art."

Knowledge like this can bring an ancient mural and a Chinese sculpture back to life. Of course, you can never experience the mural exactly as the citizens in Thebes, Egypt, did in 1400 BC, or experience the statue the way people in Hsian, China, did in the 600s AD. But by using art history, you can reconstruct some of those experiences, and thus better understand the meaning of these works.

The next four chapters, which discuss non-Western and Western art history, will provide an overview of China and Egypt, among other cultures.

Criticism Experience 15.1

Interpreting *American Gothic*

Interpret *American Gothic* by Grant Wood. Use your earlier description (Criticism Experience 3.1: Describing an Artwork) and your analysis (Criticism Experience 9.1: Analyzing *American Gothic*). In addition, you can rely on what you have already learned in your own experiences. Use the following guidelines (or those provided by your teacher) for interpretation.

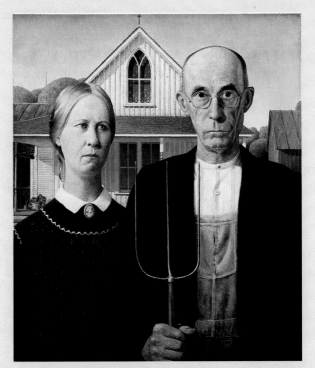

Grant Wood, *American Gothic,* 1930. Oil on beaver board, 30″ x 25″ (76 x 63 cm). Friends of American Art, The Art Institute of Chicago.

1. Organize information from your description and analysis to help you identify what the artwork expresses or means. If you did not do a description or analysis, complete them now. The guidelines for Criticism Experiences 3.1 and 9.1 will be helpful.

2. To identify what the artwork means, add what you already know about the subject matter, the elements such as form, shapes and colors, and the theme of the work.
   a) Does the work remind you of anything?
   b) Have you seen, read, or studied about situations or things like those you see in the artwork?

3. Form a *hypothesis* about what the work means. A hypothesis is an assumption, or an informed guess based on evidence you have collected.
   a) Do your description and analysis support your hypothesis?
   b) Does the information you bring to this work support your hypothesis? Consider knowledge you have picked up from personal experiences, studies, travels, and reading.

4. If your evidence does not support your hypothesis, try another one.

Chapter 16
Non-Western Art I

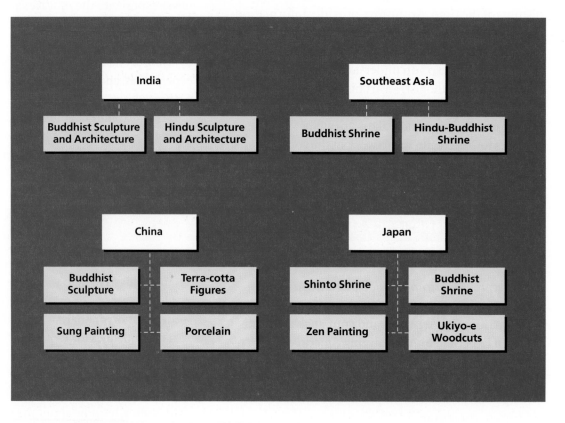

Overview

Chapter Objectives

Students should be able to:

1 understand that there have been cross-cultural influences between the arts of many non-Western and Western cultures   EE 3

2 understand that most non-Western art was created primarily for religious or utilitarian reasons rather than for aesthetic reasons   EE 3

3 understand that non-Western art is most meaningful when studied in the context of its culture   EE 3

4 identify by subject matter or style the art of at least two cultures   EE 3

5 emulate in their own work the style of a non-Western work from one of the cultures in this chapter   EE 3

6 demonstrate an appreciation of the contributions to world culture of the non-Western cultures   EE 3

Rationale

Art history is an important component of art education. The text material and lessons include some references to art history and/or examples of historical art. However, formal coverage of art history can increase students' literacy in the subject. To that end, Chapters 16 through 19 provide an overview of the historical development of art in different parts of the world. Chapters 16 and 17 cover the art of several non-Western cultures; Chapters 18 and 19 review major periods in Western art.

Essential Concepts

• A relationship exists between the forms of art and the important cultural events that occur during a period of time.

• Modern India is one of the oldest continuing civilizations.

• The principal religious architecture of Buddhism is the stupa, a form that evolved out of a burial mound. One of the famous stupas is the Great Stupa at Sanchi.

• Early Buddha images show signs of Greek influence. In later images of Buddha, the Greek influence diminished. Typically, these sculptures consist of a seated figure with a passive face, gentle features, and stylized hand gestures. Their serenity was intended to represent the spirit of Buddha and the state of nirvana.

• Modern China can also claim to be one of the oldest continuing civilizations.

• The earliest art of historic China consists of bronze vessels dating to the Shang dynasty (18th-12th centuries BC). During the Zhou dynasty, the mystical philosophy *Taoism* was founded.

• The Sung dynasty (960-1279 AD) saw the flowering of Chinese landscape painting. Sung artists were inspired by a cult of nature based on a combination of Taoism, Confucianism, and Chan Buddhism. Using ink wash on silk or rice paper, they created airy, panoramic landscapes that express a deep respect for nature.

• Occasionally, both Chinese and Japanese paintings exhibit a type of perspective referred to as "isometric perspective," in which the lines go back in space but do not converge.

• Zen Buddhism in Japan appealed to a warrior class known as samurai. Zen artists made landscape paintings similar to Sung art, but with a special flourish reminiscent of a samurai brandishing a sword.

• Ukiyo-e art consisted of scenes of everyday life produced by color woodcuts.

Vocabulary

non-Western	Hinduism	stupa
Taoism	Shintoism	culture
polytheism	masonry	dynasty
ukiyo-e	civilization	Buddhism
post and lintel	porcelain	

Lesson Plans

16.1 A Watercolor Wash Landscape

> Page **T 232**   Time: 1 period

16.2 Report: Non-Western Art Forms

> Page **T 236**   Time: 1 period

Handouts

Guidelines for a Report on an Art Form

Page **T 238**

Study Questions   Page **T 239**

Test Questions   Page **T 242**

Chapter Closure
Evaluation

1 *Production:* Are students able to emulate the style of Chinese Sung landscape watercolor painting in their own wash experiments?

2 *Art history/Criticism:* Are students able to write an analysis of an art form of one of the cultures in this chapter?   W 2, W 4

3 *Art history:* Can students cite at least one example of cross-cultural influence— either between two of the cultures in this chapter or between one of the cultures and Western culture?   R 5

4 *Art history:* Can students explain the characteristics, religious functions, and histories of the art of two cultures in this chapter?   R 5

5 *Art history:* Are students able to recognize typical examples of art of at least two of the cultures in this chapter?   R 5

A Watercolor Wash Landscape

Time: 1 period

Preparation

Rationale

Students can learn a great deal about how artists control the medium and the elements of art in a style of painting by working with the medium and emulating procedures to produce artworks of a similar nature. This experience requires students to use gradations of value and value contrasts to produce landscape paintings in the style of the Sung dynasty masters. The manner in which Sung artists used voids to hold masses in balance is one of China's great contributions to painting.

Studio Materials

watercolor paints, pointed hair brushes, water containers, paper towels, 9" x 12" white paper appropriate for watercolor, pen and ink, India ink wash (optional)

Enrichment Materials

Slides:
• Tohaku, *Monkey Screen,* 10

Overhead Transparencies:
• Ma Yuan, *Bare Willows,* 20

Large Reproductions:
• Yan, *Brushfire with Animals Fleeing,* 16

Teach the Lesson

Objectives

Students should be able to:

1   use watercolors to emulate the style of Sung dynasty landscape paintings   EE 2, 3

2   explore value gradations and contrasts to produce mystical aerial perspective effects   EE 2

Vocabulary

Sung dynasty refers to a period in China's history extending from approximately 960 to 1279 AD.

Dynasty is the period when a certain family rules.

Warm Up

1   Display *Bare Willows* or other Sung style landscapes. Discuss how value is the dominant art element in the painting. Gradations of value from light to dark make it seem to have depth.

2   Provide students with 3" x 5" pieces of paper. Have them moisten the black pan of watercolor paint and mix three washes — low dark, low medium, and light. Tell students to wet one piece of paper, dampen another piece, and leave one dry. Have them experiment with gradations of wash from black to low dark to medium to light.

3   Have students try another set of three and try to catch some white areas between the value areas. Have them go back to the first set, which should have dried a bit, and use the tip of the brush to paint in some black figures in the foreground.

Explore and Develop

Return to *Bare Willows* shown in figure 7–26. Point out that a typical Sung landscape is asymmetrical and composed on a diagonal. The landscape consists of three distinct parts—foreground, middle ground, and background—which are separated from each other by mist. There is something large in the foreground and there are generally mountains in the background, which are tinted with pale blue to emphasize deep space.

Begin Studio Experience 16.1

You may want to provide photocopies of landscapes with foreground, middle, and background areas for students to refer to. Have students use light pencil line to sketch a landscape with foreground, middle, and background on a piece of 9" x 12" white paper. Suggest they place a large object in the foreground, some trees in the middle, and hills or mountains and sky in the background. Ask them to plan for some misty space between the three areas as in *Bare Willows*.

2 Have them dampen the entire surface and begin the painting with black watercolor washes. Explain that they will develop the composition with value contrasts. You may list the following guidelines:

a. Distant objects vary in size and in distinctness in proportion to their distance.

b. Foreground objects are done in dark values with definite details and strong contrasts.

c. Things in the middle ground are painted in middle values with less detail.

d. Things in the background are painted with light values and no detail so they don't stand out.

e. Gradations of values from dark to light suggest that space goes back into the picture.

f. Emphasis or dominance is achieved with a large form or by including more detail in a portion of the painting than in others.

g. Misty voids between foreground and middle, and between middle and background unite the three areas.

3 Once value gradations are established in the three areas, black line details can be added to the large foreground object and other foreground details. Students may use the tip of the brush or pen and ink.

4 Blue wash may be added to the sky and hill areas. Limited brown wash may be added to some of the foreground. Since these paintings are developed rapidly, students may work back and forth between two paintings during the session.

Evaluate and Reflect

1 Have students analyze their compositions. Is there a gradation or progression of values that implies depth in the painting?

2 Can students emulate the style of Sung dynasty masters?

3 Did students include a dominant object or area? How was it established?

4 Have students discuss where they used strong and subtle contrasts. How were contrasts created?

5 Can students create paintings that suggest a mood?

Reteach

Have students review the section on aerial perspective on Student Edition page 86 and the section on Chinese landscape painting on Student Edition pages 217–218. Have them outline a photocopied landscape and develop it with value contrasts.

Extend the Lesson

Beyond the Basics

EE 2 Watercolors were suggested for this studio experience. Have students use ink washes and add details with brush and pen. Pale tones of color can be added to enhance the near-far aerial perspective appearance.

EE 2 Many of the Chinese landscapes were painted on longs strips of paper mounted to sticks on either end to form scrolls. The scrolls, held by the viewer, were intended to be unrolled slowly and details observed carefully. Suggest interested students make a scroll painting. They will need a strip of paper and two dowel rods slightly longer than the width of the papers. Use paper as large as possible and cut into strips approximately 5" x 30". Suggest attaching a bead to each end of the dowel rods and paint with glossy enamel. When rods and paintings are thoroughly dry attach the paper to the rods with white glue. Roll up the scroll and tie a ribbon around it to hold it closed.

EE 3 Direct students attention to the red stamps and calligraphy found on the Chinese paintings. Suggest students investigate to
R 3, 4 find why these marks are there and what they mean.

Cultural Connections

EE 4 Suggest students use interpretative studies of the local landscape in their Sung style painting. Have students describe, analyze,
W 3 and interpret a Sung painting and their own work. Compare the two.

Connecting with Other Subjects

History In previous chapters students have   EE 3
examined the work of contemporary artists who have used their work as forms of protest. During the Ming Dynasty the artist   R 3, 4
Zhou Chen painted *Beggars and Street Characters*. Some people believed this work was a protest against government indifference to poverty and suffering. Suggest students look for examples of Zhou Chen's artwork. Interested students may want to research this period in Chinese history.

Report: Non-Western Art Forms

Time: 1 period

Preparation

Rationale

Much non-Western art was created primarily for religious, social, or utilitarian purposes rather than for aesthetic reasons. Students should be able to identify some significant forms of art from major historical periods in non-Western cultures. They should also be aware of how significant artworks can reflect societies and cultures, past and present.

Research Materials

Guidelines for a Report on an Art Form (Handout 16.2), library resources

Enrichment Materials

Slides:
- Broken Nose Mask, Onandaga, N. America, 3
- *Venus of Willendorf*, 42
- T'ang Horse, China, 54
- *Shiva Nataraja*, India, 56
- Bronze Vessel, China, 57
- Mosque of Mutawakkil, Kuang, 61
- Machu Picchu, South America, 64
- Double Face Mask, Africa, 66

Overhead Transparencies:
- Oni (King) of Ife, 8
- Raphael, *The School of Athens*, 10
- *Maria Bowl*, 16
- Tamilnada, *Siva, King of the Dancers*, 19
- Ma Yuan, *Bare Willows*, 20

Large Reproductions:
- Statue of Mitry, 6
- *Plate—Hunting Rams*, 7
- Prow ornament, Tlingit war canoe, 17
- *Nubian Wall Painting*, 5

Teach the Lesson

Objectives

Students should be able to:

- write a report on an art form of a non-Western culture that reflects the culture's beliefs and values   **EE 3, W 3**

- identify artworks from non-Western cultures and discuss how they reflect the beliefs and values of the cultures   **EE 3**

Vocabulary

Culture refers to the attitudes, values, beliefs, patterns of behavior, social organization, and concepts of reality of a group of people that persists through time.

Subculture is a group of people who share in part the culture of a larger group to which they belong nationally, socially, or ethnically, but who have identifiable differences as a group.

Warm Up

Ask the students to indicate what they think is one of the most significant forms of visual art produced in our culture today. Ask them to identify the medium and style. Why do they feel the art form is representative of our culture? Can they think of some beliefs and values common to our society that are reflected in this kind of art? Does the art fulfill a social function or need? Can they think of any social, political, or philosophical ideas that contributed to the development of the form and style?

Explore and Develop

1   Show examples of significant artworks from different cultures and time periods. Indicate that these examples are characteristic of other works done in the same medium, style, and time period.

2   Refer to *Bare Willows and Distant Mountains* (figure 16–16). This Chinese landscape painting is similar in medium and style to all ink wash paintings created during the Sung dynasty in the 12th and 13th centuries. The form and style reflected the leading philosophy of Confucianism. The paintings portrayed an intimate relationship between nature and man, which was part of the religious philosophy.

3   You may want to take the class through the study questions prior to assigning the report. Divide the class into groups, and assign a segment of questions to each.

4   Distribute the Guidelines for a Report on an Art Form on page T 238. Make any necessary explanations. You may have students work on the reports individually or in small groups.

5   Share the finished reports. Ask students to bring texts with pictorial examples. Present them on the opaque projector.

Evaluate and Reflect

1   Did students identify any instances of cross-cultural influences in the art form they researched?

2   Can students discuss some of the symbolic and utilitarian purposes of art in non-Western cultures?

3   Are students better informed about how the beliefs and values of non-Western cultures relate to their significant art forms?

4   Have students discuss the need to withhold judgments about another culture's art until they know something about that culture's aesthetic preferences, the meanings they attach to symbols, and the values and purposes they associate with their art forms.

Reteach

Have students work in small groups and go through Chapter 16 to list as many kinds of cross-cultural influences as they can find in twenty minutes (for example, the spread of Hinduism, the effects of Greek sculpture on the style of early sculptures of Buddha).

Extend the Lesson

Beyond the Basics

Suggest students enhance their art history report by using maps and creating a timeline. Suggest using a map with colored pins to indicate where artists lived and worked, where significant events took place, and the places where influences originated. Creating a timeline showing how the art form fits within the flow of history and its relationship to events and lives happening at the same time in the same place and in other places is an important part of understanding the significance of the art form and its impact.

EE 3

R 2

Cultural Connections

Suggest students prepare a display and demonstration of materials, techniques and tools used in a particular art form. Although basic processes may be similar there may be unique variations in the approach taken by different cultures.

EE 2

Connecting with Other Subjects

All Subjects Have students create a diagram illustrating how the art form connects to other subjects and to the timeline. Suggest they place the art form at the center of a hub with spokes branching out in many different directions. Each spoke could represent a different subject such as dance, theater, language arts, mathematics, social studies, etc. Have them fill in the specific connections as they research the art form and how it connects to and impacts other arts, events, people, etc.

Guidelines for a Report on an Art Form

These guidelines can be used to gather information about an art form that is significant to any culture. Artworks are very significant when they reflect the attitudes, values, beliefs, and behaviors of a group of people over an extended period of time.

1 What is the art form? (architecture, painting, metal work, ceramics, print, sculpture, etc.)

2 What culture developed it? What country is the culture a part of?

3 When was the artwork developed? Is there a time period when the work was most significant?

4 What materials were used to produce the artwork?

5 Were there any special or unique procedures? Did the unique procedures influence later artworks?

6 Is the art form associated with a dynasty, kingdom, religion, social function, or need?

7 Does the art form follow a particular style? What are the identifying characteristics of the style?

8 Were there cross-cultural influences on the style of the art form?

9 What social and historical events influenced development of the art form and its style? (for example: war, a period of peace, inventions and technology, religion, philosophy)

Name: _____   Course: _____

Study Questions
Chapter 16–Non-Western Art I

1 What is meant by the term *non-Western culture?*

_____

_____

2 What is the one factor that all non-Western cultures have in common?

_____

3 Attitudes, values, and beliefs are reflected in a culture's _____ and _____.

4 Where and when did the earliest Indian civilization develop? Where were three other civilizations emerging at about the same time?

_____

_____

5 What are the two dominant religions of non-Western cultures?

_____

6 Identify the architectural form that is a symbol of the Buddhist faith.

_____

7 How were third century AD sculptors expected to sculpt the image of Buddha, as is shown in text fig. 16–4? Compare this to the sculpted image of Buddha in the fifth century (fig. 16–5).

_____

_____

_____

8 Describe the architecture of the Hindu temple in Khajuraho, India (text fig. 16–6).

_____

_____

9 Draw an example of post-and-lintel, the principle of construction of most ancient temples. Why is the inside of a masonry post-and-lintel building so small compared to the amount of material used to build it? (Use separate sheet of paper.)

10 What characteristics of the sculpture of Siva (text fig. 16–8) show the power of this Hindu god?

_____

_____

11 What is one way that historians can tell that Buddhism and Hinduism took root in Southeast Asia?

_____

12 How do the architecture and sculpture of the stupa at Borobodur, Java, symbolize Buddhism?

_____

_____

_____

13 What circumstances allowed China to develop and maintain common cultural traditions for such a long time?

_____

14 What is a dynasty?

_____

15 What empire in the West was contemporary with the Han dynasty?

_____

16 How does the Western belief about nature differ from that of the Chinese?

_____

_____

17 Why did the arts flourish during the T'ang dynasty?

_____

_____

18 What three elements of China's spiritual heritage are apparent in Ma Yuan's landscape painting _Bare Willows and Distant Mountains_ (text fig. 16–16)?

_____

_____

19 How did the showing of a Chinese painting differ from that of a Western painting?

_____

_____

20 What kind of clay did the Chinese use that European potters successfully imitated by the seventeenth century?

_____

21 According to the Chinese, which dynasty produced the most "classical" examples of ceramic ware?

_____

22 Which Asian country greatly influenced Japanese art and architecture?

_____

23 What materials were used to build the Ise Shrine (text fig. 16–19)? What ancient building technique was used?

_____

24 Identify two forms of art that flourished under the Fujiwara family.

_____

25 Describe the preferred subject and painting style of Sesshu, the most famous of the Zen painters.

_____

_____

26 For what main purpose was pottery made during the time that Zen Buddhism became an important influence?

_____

27 During the Shogun period of rule, the separation between the social classes was very distinct. What kind of artwork was favored by the aristocracy?

_____

28 What were the favored subjects of the Japanese merchant class? What was this style called?

_____

_____

29 Why was the woodcut a favored medium of the ukiyo-e artists?

_____

_____

Non-Western Art I

Test Questions
Chapter 16–Non-Western Art I

For questions 1 through 5, select from the following countries.

1. China	4. Java
2. Japan	5. Burma
3. India	6. Russia

_____ **1** Developed one of the earliest non-Western civilizations.

_____ **2** Nine-level stupa at Borobodur.

_____ **3** Geographic isolation helped preserve cultural traditions.

_____ **4** Greatly influenced Japanese art and architecture.

_____ **5** Where Hinduism began.

For questions 6 through 9, select from the following religions which influenced the art and architecture.

1. Hinduism	3. Shintoism
2. Buddhism	4. Christianity

_____ **6** The Ise shrine, which used post-and-lintel construction.

_____ **7** The stupa, an architectural form that evolved out of a burial mound.

_____ **8** Sculptures showing the gods Brahma, the creator, and Siva, the destroyer.

_____ **9** To reach nirvana, a state of eternal bliss (two answers).

For questions 10 through 15, select from the following ruling powers and leaders who controlled/influenced art and architecture.

1. Dynasty	4. Confucius
2. Shogunate	5. Lao-Tzu
3. Kamakura	6. Zen

_____ **10** Pottery made during the Ming _____ became popular among Westerners in the sixteenth and seventeenth centuries.

_____ **11** _____ developed Taoism, which advocated obedience to the laws of nature.

_____ **12** Sesshu, the most famous of the _____ painters created his landscape paintings with just a few brushstrokes.

_____ **13** Under the Tokugawa _____, each social class developed its own culture and style of artwork.

_____ **14** _____, whose teachings promoted humility, patience, and respect for nature, recommended an active role in society rather than withdrawing from it.

_____ **15** _____ is a succession of rulers from the same family.

16 The merchant class of seventeenth and eighteenth century Japan preferred the woodcut which was used to produce a popular art called

a. Zen.   c. Horyu-ji.

b. Ukiyo-e.   d. Chen.

17 The cult of Zen encouraged potters to make ceramic vessels

a. for display only.

b. only for the aristocracy.

c. to be used in tea ceremonies.

18 Attitudes, values, and beliefs are reflected in a culture's _____ and _____.

19 Name two ways in which the attitudes of Western peoples differ from those of many non-Western peoples.

_____

_____

While viewing the transparency or text fig. 16–8 of *Siva, King of the Dancers,* answer the following question.

20 Name at least two ways that Hindu sculptors symbolized Siva's power in their works.

_____

_____

While viewing the transparency or text fig. 7–26 of *Bare Willows and Distant Mountains,* answer the following question.

21 The artist Ma Yuan used ink wash on silk, a technique that requires the respect of the artist. How is this like the Eastern philosophy about nature?

_____

_____

_____

_____

Study Answers
Chapter 16
Non-Western Art I

1. Any culture not related to Western Civilization (the people of America and western Europe).

2. All produced art.

3. Symbols and art.

4. Mohenjo-daro on the Indus River around 5,000 years ago (3000 BC); Nile River (Egypt); Yellow River (China); between the Tigris and Euphrates river (Sumeria, [modern Iraq]).

5. Buddhism and Hinduism.

6. The stupa.

7. They were expected to express the qualities of inward peace and release from desire. The Seated Buddha, third century AD, is shown quietly meditating while seated with legs crossed in a yoga position, with signs of super-human perfection, elongated ear lobes, a protrusion from the head and a dot between the eyes. The Seated Buddha, fifth century AD, bears the same features as the earlier Buddha, but his body is more softly curved and is covered with a thinner gown.

8. It has several conical domes and richly carved surfaces. The construction is post-and-lintel, so there are open rooms within.

9. A masonry ceiling is so heavy, the supporting posts have to be large enough to hold the masonry beams.

10. The god's extraordinary grace is signified performing a dance within a flaming arch while balancing on one foot and executing delicate mudras with each of his four hands.

11. By looking at the styles and symbols in Southeast Asian art.

12. The stages of enlightenment progress from the bottom rectangular base covered with relief sculptures that show people caught in the grip of desire and the endless hell of birth, death, and rebirth that Buddha warned about. The next four rectangular levels illustrate a variety of Buddha's teachings. The circular levels have seventy-two miniature bell-shaped stupas, each with a seated Buddha. The top level is a single large stupa symbolizing Buddha.

13. Because it was so isolated—surrounded by mountains, the ocean, and desert.

14. Succession of rulers who are members of the same family.

15. The Roman Empire.

16. Chinese believe in submission to nature; Westerners tend to believe that nature should submit to the will of people.

17. The emperor, Tang Tai Zong, encouraged and supported the arts.

18. A reverence for nature, Confucian philosophy, and the serenity of the Buddha.

19. Chinese paintings were stored in scrolls and viewed in private. Western paintings were hung on the wall.

20. Porcelain.

21. Artists of the Sung dynasty.

22. China.

23. Wooden columns and thatched roofs, post-and-lintel.

24. Lacquered wooden carvings and painted scrolls.

25. Landscape painting done with a minimum of brushstrokes.

26. For use in the tea ceremony.

27. Zen landscapes.

28. Popular entertainment, fiction, and scenes of the everyday world. Ukiyo-e.

29. They could make many inexpensive copies of the same print.

Test Answers
Chapter 16
Non-Western Art I

1 3

2 4

3 1

4 1

5 3

6 3

7 2

8 1

9 2 or 1

10 1

11 5

12 6

13 2

14 4

15 1

16 B

17 C

18 symbols and art

19 Answers may include: Western—individualism; non-Western—whatever is better for all is more important than what is better for the individual. Western—nature should submit to the will of people; non-Western—humankind should submit to nature.

20 Possible answers: Sculptors symbolized Siva's powers by having Siva balance on one foot while doing murdas in each of his four hands and dancing with the flaming arch.

21 As the artist respects the delicate handling of the ink wash on silk, man is to respect the delicate balance of nature.

Chapter 16
Non-Western Art I

Introduction

The great *civilizations* of India, the Orient, Islam, and pre-Columbian America, and the tribal societies of Africa and North America are among the many non-Western cultures. Any culture that is not related to Western civilization (the people of North America and western Europe) is referred to as **non-Western.**

As a collection, non-Western cultures represent an incredible variety of geography, peoples, history, beliefs, and art. Indeed, they have little in common with one another—beyond the fact that they all pro-duce (or did produce) art. But some generalizations about them can be made by contrasting them as a group with Western culture.

Consider the theme of *individualism,* for example. Individualism has been a tradition in Western culture for centuries. This tradition is perhaps emphasized more today than it was in the past. Among other things, individualism is responsible for our concepts of free speech, free thinking, and free enterprise. Individualism has no doubt been a source for the creative energy and inventiveness that have distinguished our culture through time. But individualism has also contributed to people leading lives of egotism and greed, and placing self-interest above the common good.

By contrast, people of non-Western societies, especially Asians, believe the opposite. They believe that it is better to place the common good above one's own interests. Such an attitude obviously affects the ways people relate to their jobs, families, nation, and even to nature. This attitude, along with other values, beliefs and themes, also is reflected in a culture's symbols and art.

Another difference between Western and non-Western cultures involves the concept of art itself. In the twentieth-century West, the purpose of art is primarily for aesthetic enjoyment (Chapter 2). In non-Western societies, art has many purposes, including magic, worship, ritual, sacrifice, propaganda, status, and even politics.

India

India can trace its roots to recently discovered settlements near Mohenjo-Daro on the Indus River in what is now Pakistan (fig. 16–1). Excavations there revealed that these settlements go back in time more than 5,000 years. They consisted of cities with hundreds of houses, shops, streets, wells, and drainage systems. There is even evidence that the people of those ancient cities wrote contracts and signed legal documents.

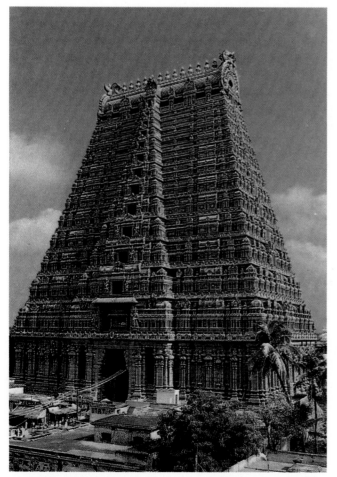

16–0 Ranganathaswanny Temple, Tamilnadi, South India. At 236 feet (78 m) this is the tallest temple tower in Asia. Photograph courtesy James Ellison Thomas.

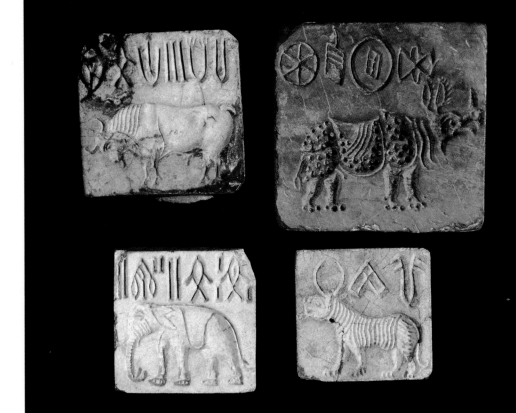

Among the smaller finds were *seals* carved in stone (fig. 16-2). Officials used the seals to stamp (or "sign") documents written on tablets of damp clay.

The Mohenjo-Daro civilization appeared in the fertile valley of the Indus River between 4000 and 3000 BC. Around this same time, other civilizations also emerged in river valleys in different parts of the world. Egypt developed along the Nile River. China developed along the Yellow River. Sumeria, which is now Iraq, developed between the Tigris and Euphrates Rivers.

Modern India has more people than North and South America combined in a space that is not quite half the size of the United States. India can claim to be one of the oldest continuing civilizations. It is a nation of fourteen languages. Although Hinduism is the main religion, there are many others and several ethnic groups. Like its geography of extreme contrasts—from snow-covered mountains to steamy jungles—India has a rich mixture of cultures.

Around 2000 BC a tribal people invaded India from the north. The newcomers not only conquered the native Indians, they introduced their own hymns called the *Vedas.* (These are like the poems of the Jewish Old Testament or the myths of the ancient Greeks.) These hymns marked the beginnings of **Hinduism,** the world's most ancient religion.

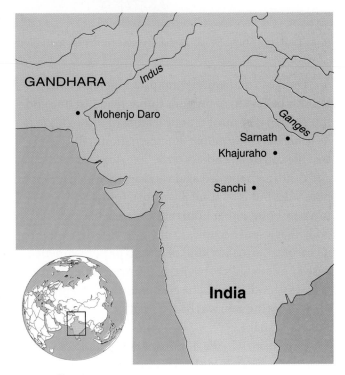

16-1 India.

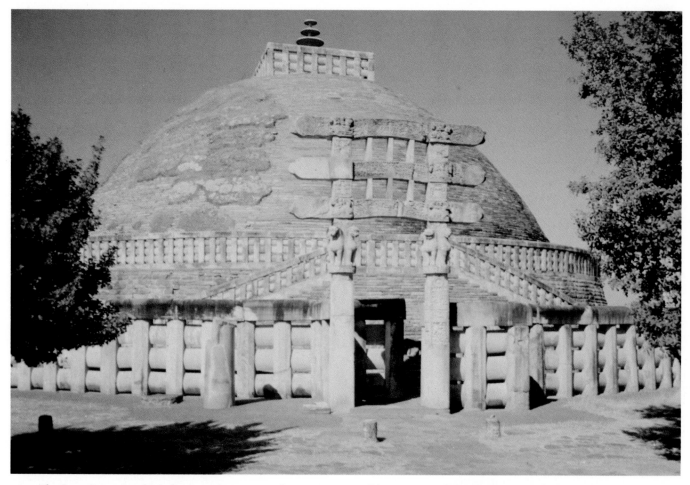

16–3 The Great Stupa, Sanchi, India, second century BC–first century AD. Solid masonry. Scala/Art Resource, NY.

Unlike Christianity, Hinduism is **polytheistic.** Hindus believe in many gods rather than just one god. But perhaps the most unique feature of this religion is its belief in *reincarnation.* Reincarnation is the belief that life can be an endless cycle. The stages of birth, life, and death are repeated again and again. A person's soul never dies but is continually reborn (or reincarnated) in a new body, either human or animal. The type of body that a soul occupies in any given life depends on its *karma.* Karma is a kind of reward or punishment based on the soul's behavior in its previous life. If the soul was good, it might be given the body of a prince or princess. If the soul was bad, it might be given the body of a rat or snake.

Hinduism was the dominant religion for about 1,500 years. Then Buddha was born, about five hundred years before the birth of Christ. During his youth, Buddha (the "enlightened" one) experienced a vision while sitting under a shade tree. He saw the endless succession of birth and death in the stream of life.

From this experience he determined that all evil and suffering were caused by desire, and that human desire started with birth. After seven years of meditation, he proceeded to the city of Sarnath. Here he preached about his insight and founded the new faith of **Buddhism.**

At first, Buddhism was considered just a splinter denomination of Hinduism. However, Buddhism became stronger than Hinduism in India (at least for a while), and then spread to other countries. It became one of the largest religions of the world. The goal of all Buddhists is to achieve *nirvana,* the final state of eternal bliss. To do so, one must conquer not only desire, but the self, and lead a life of perfect justice, patience, and kindness. Only then can the soul break the endless cycle of birth.

A fitting symbol of the Buddhist faith is the **stupa,** a dome-shaped form that evolved out of a burial mound. The best example of this form is the Great Stupa at Sanchi (fig. 16–3). Except for a small burial chamber in the center, the Great Stupa is almost solid

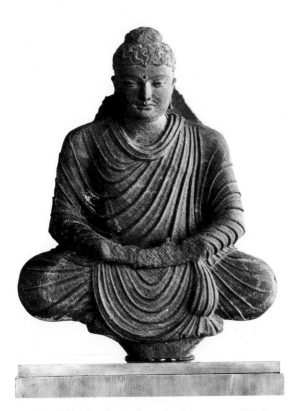

16-4 *Seated Buddha*, Gandhara, first–third century AD. Black schist, 2´ 4¾″ x 22 ½″ (73 x 57 cm). Yale University Art Gallery (Anonymous gift through Alfred R. Bellinger).

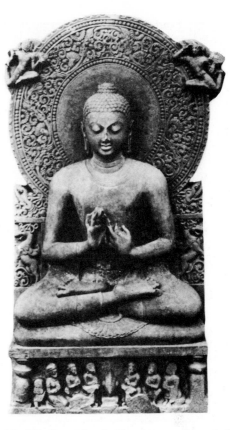

16-5 Seated Buddha Preaching the First Sermon, Sarnath, fifth century AD. Stele, sandstone, 63″ (160 cm) high. Archaeological Museum, Sarnath.

masonry (built of stone, brick or concrete; in this case the material is brick). It was intended to represent the dome of heaven or the world mountain. The little balcony on its top was meant to stand for the home of thirty-three gods. Four ornamental gates were built to face north, south, east, and west. Because the stupa is circular, it is a perfect metaphor for the cycle of life. The simplicity of the dome symbolizes the serenity of nirvana.

There is no image of Buddha himself on the Great Stupa. However, his throne, his shade tree, and even his footprints appear on the gates. Human images of Buddha did not appear until about 100 AD in Gandhara. Gandhara, a northwest region that is now Afghanistan and Pakistan, had once been occupied by the Greeks. Therefore, the style of the early images of Buddha (fig. 16-4) resembled Greek or Roman styles. However, the sculptures express the Buddhist qualities of inward peace and release from desire. Buddha is shown quietly meditating. He is seated with legs crossed in the *yoga* position. The Gandhara sculptors

gave Buddha long ear lobes, a bulge on his head, and a dot between his eyes. These were all meant as signs of Buddha's superhuman perfection.

Later, in areas south of Gandhara, sculptors began to create statues of Buddha in a different style. The new style was more like that of the carvings on the gates of the Great Stupa. The Buddha from Sarnath (fig. 16-5) is wearing a thin gown. The body is curved and feminine. This style became typical of later statues of Buddha. In addition to the signs of perfection found in the Gandhara statue, this one shows Buddha with spoked wheels on the soles of his feet. Buddha is practicing stylized hand gestures called *mudras*.

Buddhism had started out as a reform of Hinduism. As time went on, Buddhism drifted farther away from the humble teachings of Buddha himself. At the same time, Hinduism was experiencing a revival. Buddhism was soon overtaken by its rival religion. Hinduism became stronger in India, although Buddhism was becoming stronger in the rest of Asia.

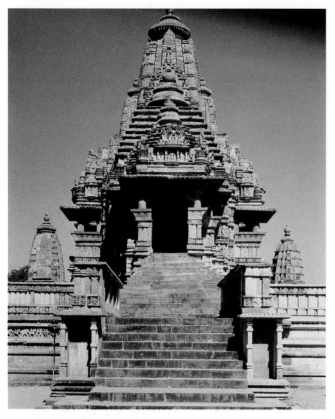

16-6 Temple of Laksmana, frontal view. Khajuraho, India, tenth–eleventh centuries. Scala/Art Resource, NY.

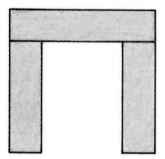

16-7 Post and lintel.

Perhaps as a tribute to Buddhism, Hinduism accepted Buddha as one of its gods. Hinduism's main gods were *Brahma* the creator, *Vishnu* the preserver, and *Siva* the destroyer. To this day, Hindus worship cows as representatives of the divine. They have a strict division of social classes, called a *caste* system. "Brahmans" are at the top and "untouchables" are at the bottom.

Buddhism and Hinduism existed together for many years. Therefore, they often shared the same styles of architecture. In Khajuraho, India, a sacred neighborhood of temples was built around the eleventh century. Some temples are Hindu and some are Buddhist. Yet all are similar. One of the most impressive temples is a Hindu temple dedicated to Siva as Mahadeva, Lord of Lords (fig. 16–6). Because of the cone-shaped domes, the Mahadeva shrine looks like a cluster of beehives. The surfaces are richly carved. Unlike the Great Stupa, this shrine is heavily decorated.

Also unlike the Great Stupa, the Mahadeva shrine is not solid. Inside, there are sanctuaries, aisles, and assembly halls surrounded by porches. But none of these is large. This temple, like most ancient temples, has a post-and-lintel construction. In a **post-and-lintel** building, the walls, posts, or columns support a masonry ceiling (fig. 16–7). Because a masonry ceiling is so heavy, the inside of any post-and-lintel building is very small compared to the mass of material used to build it.

Hindu gods tended to be exotic. Brahma had four faces. Siva had three eyes, and another god had one thousand. Almost all gods had four arms. These extraordinary features were signs of extraordinary knowledge, activity, or power.

The bronze sculpture of Siva (fig. 16–8) shows the god's extraordinary grace. Like Buddha, the god has a feminine body. However, unlike Buddha, the god is not sitting. Within a flaming arch, the god is performing a dance. He is balancing on one foot while performing delicate *mudras* (hand movements) with each of his four hands. This sculpture portrays Siva as Lord of the Dance, one of his many reincarnations. It was made to be placed in a shrine or carried in a procession.

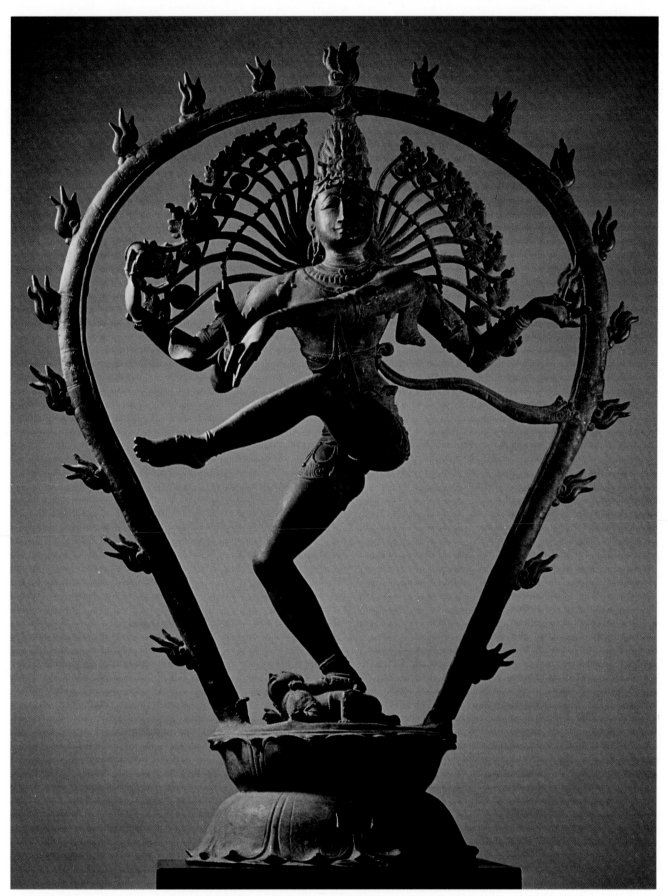

16–8 Tamilnadu, *Siva, King of the Dancers Performing the Nataraja,* Chola dynasty, India, tenth century, bronze, 30″ x 22 ½″ x 7″
(76 x 57 x 18 cm). The Los Angeles County Museum of Art (Anonymous Gift).

Southeast Asia

Indian culture spread to Burma, Thailand, Kampuchea (Cambodia), Sumatra, and Java (fig. 16–9). Buddhism had spread to Tibet, Mongolia, China, and Japan. Buddhism also took root in Southeast Asia. Southeast Asian art has a rich complexity of styles and symbolism. This art reflects the influences of not only Buddhism, but also Hinduism.

Rising on a plain in Java is one of Buddhism's greatest monuments: the stupa at Borobudor (fig. 16–10). The shrine is actually a rounded hill that has been terraced with masonry. Therefore, it effectively embodies the Indian concept of the sky as a bowl covering the world mountain. It consists of ten levels. Of these, the base (which is mostly underground) and first five levels are rectangular. The next three are circular, and the top level consists of a single stupa.

On the base are relief sculptures that show people caught in the grip of desire. They are trapped in the endless hell of birth, death, and rebirth that Buddha warned about. The next five rectangular levels illustrate a variety of Buddha's teachings. The three circular levels contain seventy-two miniature bell-shaped stupas. Each stupa contains a seated Buddha.

Thus, the stages of enlightenment are unfolded as one progresses from the bottom level to the large stupa at the top, the climax of the shrine. The symbolism is Buddhist, but the tropical profusion of architecture and carving is more like Hindu art. Imagine the experience of intrepid pilgrims as they climb the stairs, walk through the corridors, and view this virtual encyclopedia of Buddhist culture.

16–9 Southeast Asia.

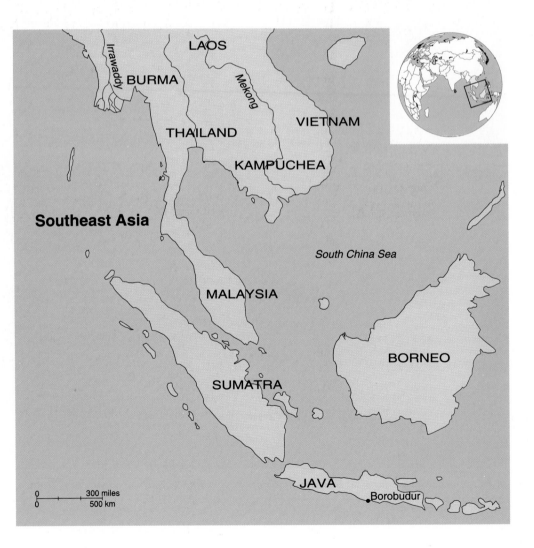

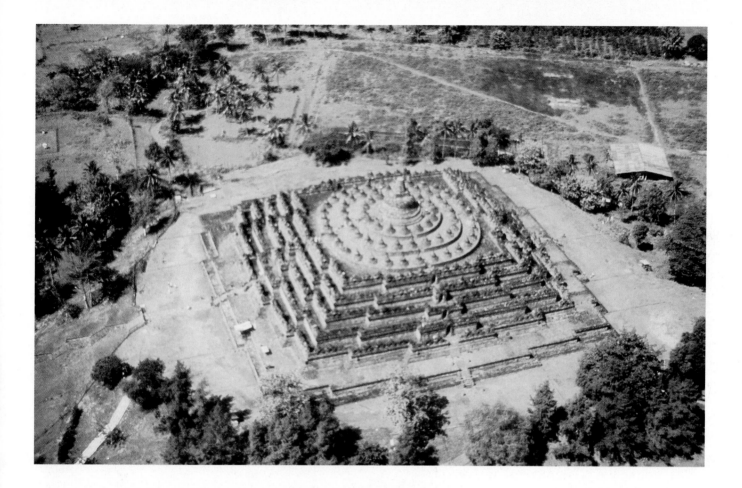

16–10 Stupa, Borobudor, Java, ca.
800 AD. Borromeo/Art Resource, NY.

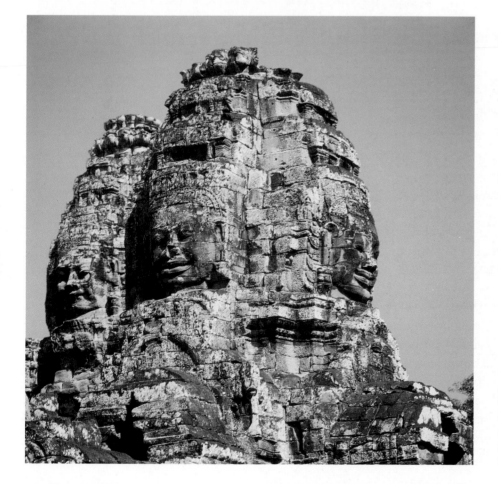

16–10A Rulers in ancient Cambodia were
seen as gods. To make their divinity visible, they constructed huge temples influenced by the Hindu religion. This temple,
Angkor Thom, shows the sculptured
faces of Jayavarmin VII. It was built about
1190 AD. Giraudon/Art Resource, NY.

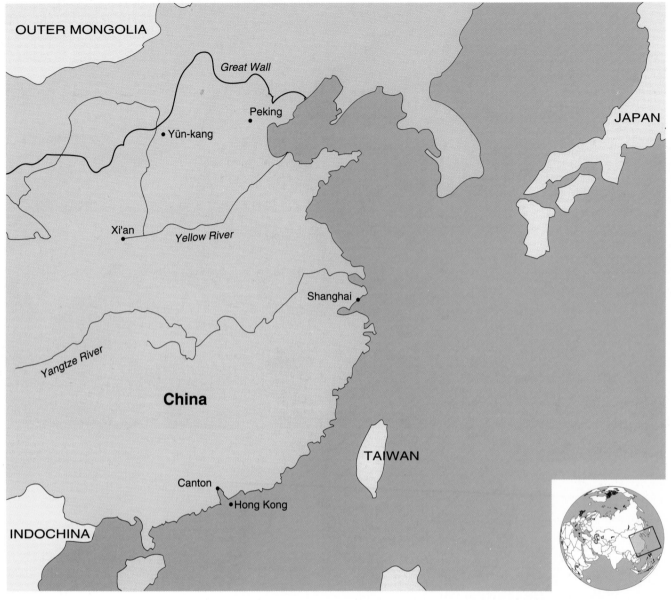

China

Modern China (fig. 16–11) is a country endowed with great rivers, fertile valleys, windswept plains, majestic mountains, and natural harbors. It is remarkably similar to the United States in size and geography, but its population is four times as large. In history, China is twenty times older.

Any country this large is bound to have regional diversity among its people. Nine-tenths of the population is crowded into the eastern sixth of the nation. The spoken language is so varied as to be unrecognizable in different areas. However, the Chinese have a common racial heritage and a culture as old as India's. The written language is understood by everyone. China is hemmed in by the Pacific Ocean on the east,

by high mountains in the south and southwest, and by desert in the west and north. It was splendidly isolated through much of its history. Thus it was able to develop its cultural traditions in relative security.

The earliest art of China that we know about is from the Shang dynasty. **Dynasty** refers to a succession of rulers who are members of the same family. The Shang dynasty thrived from the eighteenth to twelfth centuries BC in the northern part of the country. Remarkable bronze objects were discovered in graves in 1928. The objects were cast by means of piece molds rather than the lost-wax process (Chapter 13). Scholars were so impressed by their craftsmanship that they believed the Shang must have practiced this technique for centuries.

Most of the objects are ritual vessels for holding wine or food used in sacrificial rites (fig. 16–12). Their forms, unlike those of most vessels, tend to be rather angular. The low-relief decorations consist of animal symbols along with spirals, ovals, and zig-zags. These designs are compact and vigorous. In many ways these vessels resemble suits of armor. Perhaps they reflect a militaristic and barbaric society.

The Zhou dynasty saw the flowering of Chinese philosophy and writing. The sixth century BC, the century Buddha was born, was the golden age of Chinese philosophers. (Half a world away in Greece, another age of philosophy was dawning at about the same time.)

Lao-tzu, one of the sages, recommended withdrawal from the hurly-burly of society to become one with nature. A quiet person who distrusted intellectuals, Lao-tzu taught mostly by example. He followed a

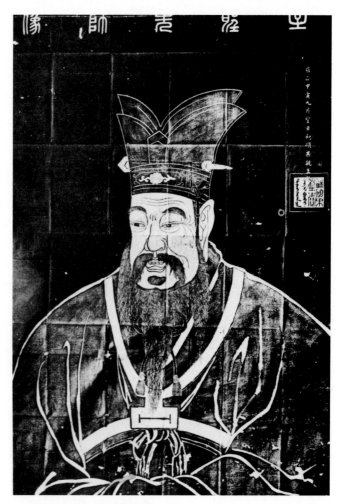

16–13 Portrait of Confucius based on Ancient Traditions. Relief from the Stele in the Pei Lin of Sigan-Fou. The Bettmann Archive, New York.

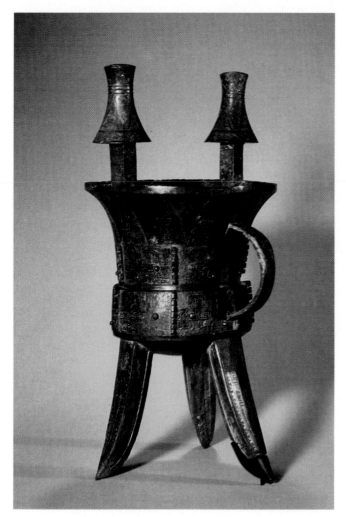

16–12 An example of a vessel used in sacrificial rites. Ceremonial vessel of the type Chia, twelfth century BC, Shang dynasty, China. Bronze, 21″ x 12″ (53 x 30.5 cm). Courtesy of the Freer Gallery of Art, Smithsonian Institution, Washington, DC.

philosophy called **Taoism.** According to Taoism, the secret of wisdom and lasting happiness was to follow a life of simplicity, modesty, patience, and obedience to the laws of nature. To this day, the principle of submitting to nature is deeply ingrained in the minds of the Chinese. By contrast, Westerners tend to believe that nature should submit to the will of people. (This attitude is fostered by the Old Testament teachings of Genesis 1:26 and Psalm 8:6.)

China's greatest thinker was Confucius (fig. 16–13). Like Lao-tzu, Confucius preached humility, patience, and respect for nature. But unlike Lao-tzu, he recommended taking an active role in society rather than withdrawing from it. He came up with the familiar maxim, "Do not do unto others as you would not wish done unto yourself," five hundred years before Christ. Like Christ, he taught by word of mouth rather than by writing. Fortunately his words were recorded by his disciples, and kept alive by scholars down through the

16–14 Bodhisattva from the Yun K'ang temple grotto. Northern Wei Period, late fifth century, Sandstone, 57 ½″ x 29″ (146 x 74 cm). The Metropolitan Museum of Art (Rogers Fund, 1922).

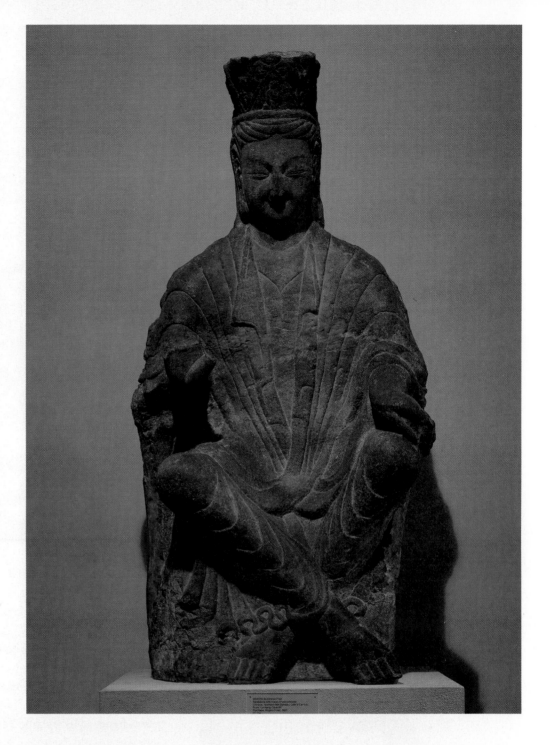

ages. His teachings and sayings, like the Gospels of the New Testament, influenced a whole culture. This culture spread to Korea, Japan, and parts of Southeast Asia.

The Han dynasty took control of China in 206 BC. The Roman Empire in the West existed at the same time. Just as Rome extended its boundaries all over Europe and northern Africa, China, under the Han emperors, extended its boundaries. China included Korea in the north, Vietnam in the south, and Afghanistan in the west. Silk production increased

dramatically, and trade routes penetrated as far as the eastern parts of the Roman Empire. Confucianism was the official policy of the state. Also like Rome, the Han empire experienced chaos and barbaric invasions during its final years. During this time Buddhism was introduced into China. The new religion seemed to answer the needs of the Chinese people during their times of trouble.

The new religion also provided some ready-made subject matter and styles for art. A fifth-century sculpture of a bodhisattva, a type of saint in Buddhism (fig. 16-14), reflects many of the qualities of the Indian statues of Buddha. Its gown is similar to the gown of the Gandhara Buddha (fig. 16-4). Its soft features and gentle mudras are similar to those of the Buddha from Sarnath (fig. 16-5). The bodhisattva's passive face and body capture the spirit of serenity preached by Buddha himself. And yet it was made during the period of unrest after the Han dynasty.

The T'ang dynasty (618–907 AD) ruled during one of China's greatest periods. An enlightened emperor named Tang Tai Zong brought order to the northern borders and led his armies to the ends of the deserts in the west. He reestablished old trade routes. He built libraries and universities, and encouraged the arts and the development of printing. Students from Tibet, central Asia, Korea, and Japan flocked to China's capital.

The non-Buddhist art made at this time, like the ceramic sculpture discussed in Chapter 15 (fig. 16-15), reflected the vigor of the T'ang dynasty. Mounted warriors were important for keeping order and protecting trade routes. The ceramic horse and rider are strong, taut and determined. You can easily imagine the two escorting a caravan of silk merchants across the Gobi desert, a place similar to Russell's desert in the American West (fig. 15-1).

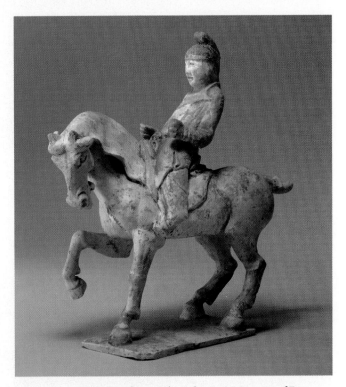

16–15 Terra cotta grave figure, T'ang dynasty. Museum of Far Eastern Antiquities, Stockholm.

The T'ang dynasty, after three centuries of successful rule, ended in a series of civil wars. During this troublesome period, the Chinese turned to a source of hope, just as their ancestors had turned to Buddhism at the end of the Han dynasty. Only this time, the source was nature. The image of this source was a landscape instead of a statue of Buddha or a bodhisattva.

Chinese artists may have painted landscapes even before the T'ang dynasty. However, the finest examples of this art were created during the Sung dynasty (960–1279 AD). Sung artists expressed all three elements of China's spiritual heritage: Taoism, Confucianism and Buddhism. They combined a reverence for nature, Confucian philosophy and the serenity of Buddha. Ma Yuan's *Bare Willows and Distant Mountains* (fig. 16-16) is a good example of this combination. The same work was discussed in Chapter 7 as an example of aerial perspective (fig. 7-26).

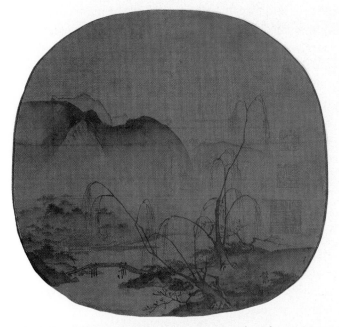

16–16 *Bare Willows and Distant Mountains*, attributed to Ma Yuan, Sung dynasty, twelfth–thirteenth century. Round album leaf, ink and colors on silk, 9″ x 8″ (24 x 21 cm). Chinese and Japanese Special Fund. Courtesy, Museum of Fine Arts, Boston.

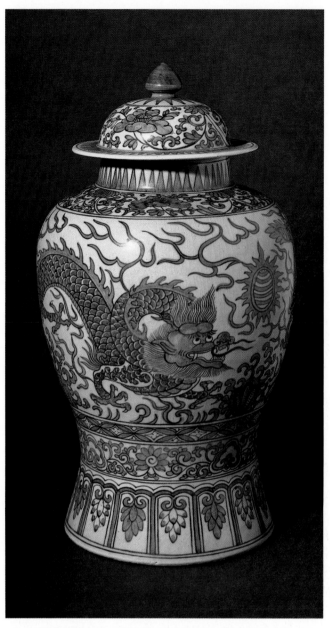

16–17 Underglaze porcelain jar, Chiangning, Kiangsu.

Ma Yuan used the technique of ink wash on silk to create the effects of mist and endless space. This medium requires the respect of the artist, just as nature demands respect. A wash cannot be forced; the artist must literally "go with the flow" as the watery ink glides across the surface and sinks into the fabric. In addition to washes, Ma Yuan used darker lines for detail and to provide focus. A sense of mystical infinity is expressed in the airy landscape.

Western paintings were meant to be hung on walls. Chinese paintings, however, were often stored in scrolls. They were meant to be viewed in private—like reading a book of poems.

Sung landscape paintings expressed the deepest spiritual values of China. They are an excellent example of Chinese civilization. Fine landscapes, and nature studies, like the one shown in figure 4–12, continued to be produced during later dynasties.

But no review of Chinese art would be complete without discussing ceramic art. This art goes back to prehistoric China. Discoveries of excellent pottery at sites in Honan have been dated to 3000 BC or earlier. As we saw in Chapter 13, the Chinese of the Ch'in dynasty (just prior to the Han dynasty) made life-size ceramic sculptures using slab and coil methods (fig. 13–21). Under the T'ang emperors, the Chinese began to produce bowls, plates, jars, vases, bottles, flasks, and pitchers that were both functional and graceful.

Porcelain is a white ceramic that is hard, non-porous and translucent. It may have been invented during the T'ang dynasty. (To a Westerner, the test of porcelain was translucency; to the Chinese, it was the musical note a vessel made when struck.) At any rate, porcelain was produced in quantity by Sung potters. It was not until eight centuries later, in the eighteenth century, that Europeans learned to produce porcelain. Europeans made porcelain in such places as Meissen, Germany and Sèvres, France.

To the Chinese, Sung artisans produced the most "classical" examples of all ceramic wares. But to Westerners, Ming pottery (1358–1644), which tends to be more lavishly decorated, was the most popular. The stately porcelain jar in figure 16–17 is a good example. European potters tried to imitate Ming pottery—mostly without success—in the sixteenth and seventeenth centuries.

A Watercolor Wash Landscape

Create a mystical landscape with a Sung dynasty style. Use gradations of wash to show foreground, middle ground, and background with an aerial perspective effect.

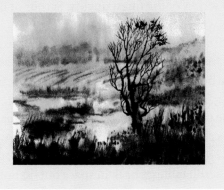

Japan

In many ways, Japanese art was influenced by Chinese art. Buddhism was introduced to Japan in the mid-sixth century; with it came aspects of Chinese culture. But Japan had its own culture even before Buddhism was introduced. Over the centuries, Japan (fig. 16–18) alternated between isolation and interchange with foreign governments. The Japanese had their own independent creativity and imitated the creativity of other cultures. Japan basically has two religions: **Shintoism,** the native religion, and Buddhism.

The facts of early Japanese history are clouded in myth. We do know that Japan was originally settled by a loose collection of tribes and clans. (A clan is a family that claims descent from a common ancestor.) Shintoism, the oldest and still largest religion of Japan, developed out of a form of ancestor worship. Shinto means "the way of the gods." This religion emphasizes reverence for family, race and, above all, the ruling family as a direct descendant of the gods.

Shintoism is also responsible for an early form of Japanese architecture: the Shinto shrine. The main building of the Ise Shrine (fig. 16–19) was originally constructed in the third century. It was, and continues to be, destroyed and rebuilt every twenty years. The structure we see today is a faithful copy of the methods and styles of third-century Japan. The construction is post and lintel. In this case, thick wooden columns (cut from the trunks of cypress trees) support a thatched

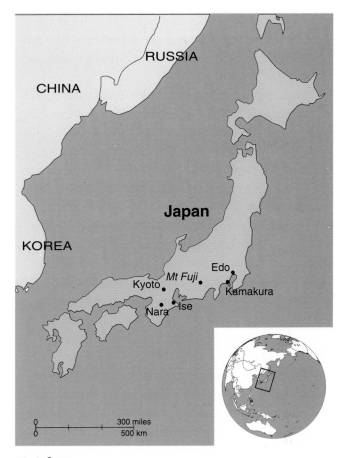

16–18 Japan.

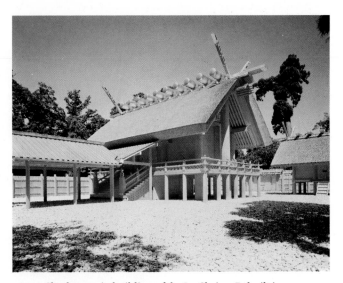

16–19 Shoden, main building of the Ise Shrine. Rebuilt in 1973, reproducing third century type. Art Resource, NY.

roof. Cylindrical weights run the length of the ridge-pole, the horizontal timber at the top of the roof. They provide a distinct rhythmical accent as well as help to stabilize the structure.

Sometime in the 500s, Buddhism was introduced to Japan by a Korean king. After some opposition, the new religion became firmly established. Chinese influence, mostly through Korea, rose dramatically. In 710 the Japanese established a capital at Nara for the imperial family. They began to model their political, economic, and social life on that of T'ang dynasty in China. The extent of this influence can be seen in the Horyu-ji temple complex at Nara. Some of these temples are among the oldest in the world. They follow closely the temples built in China during the T'ang dynasty. Even fourteenth-century buildings, such as the Gold Pavilion in Kyoto (fig. 16–20), provide a glimpse of seventh-century Chinese architecture. Consisting of massive, slightly curved, tiled roofs supported by wooden columns, these structures are basically post and lintel. Yet their openness and complicated system of bracing foreshadow modern frame construction (Chapter 19).

In 784 the capital was moved to Heian (modern Kyoto). Japanese culture entered its golden age. The emperor became the leader in name only. The real power was held by certain clans. The Fujiwara family became the dominant clan. They surrounded themselves and the court with art. Their artists created their own styles of art that were different from the Chinese styles. They produced lacquered wooden carvings and painted scrolls of the finest quality. Scrolls of Buddhist subjects were richly colored and gilded.

Artists also produced inked scrolls that used humor. In one humorous scroll Buddha, in the form of a frog, is being honored by a whimsical collection of monkeys, a cat, a rabbit, and a fox (fig. 16–21). The Japanese used satire, animal caricature, and cartoon styles six centuries before the appearance of American comics. Note that the line of the frog's bench, the altar, and the scroll table go back in space but do not converge. This is sometimes referred to as "isometric perspective."

The leadership of the Fujiwaras was ended by a clique of warriors who created a *shogunate* (military dictatorship). They moved the center of power to the

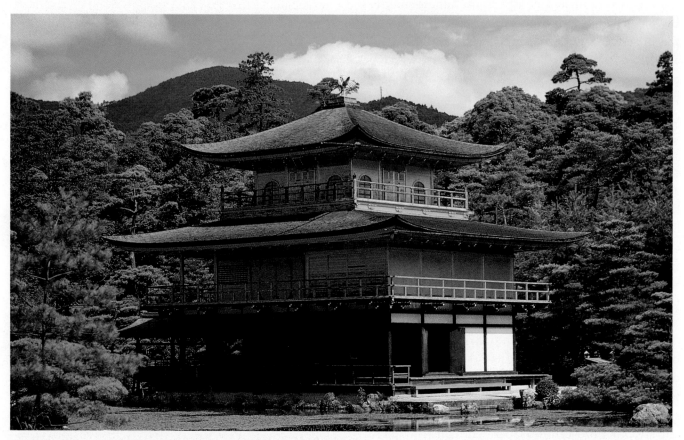

16–20 Japanese Gold Pavilion. Kyoto, Japan. Cooper/Art Resource, NY.

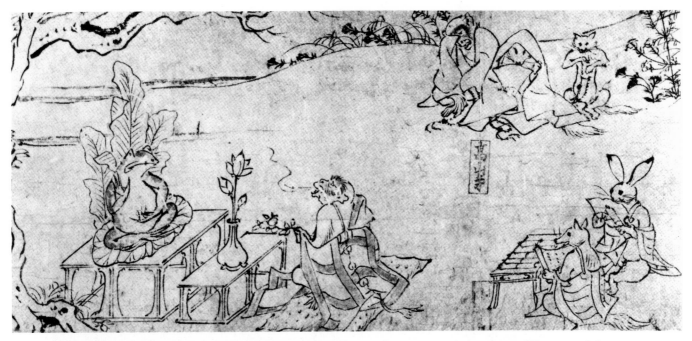

16–21 Animal caricatures, detail of a horizontal scroll attributed to Toba Sojo, later Heian period, ca. late twelfth century. Ink on paper, approx. 12″ (30. 5 cm) high. Kozan-ji.

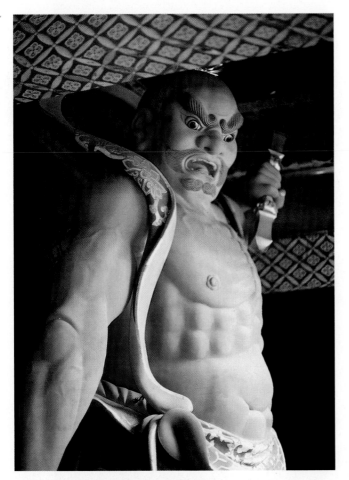

16–22 Temple Guardian, Kamakura period, ca. 1300. Wood, fully painted. Toshogu Shrine, Kyoto.

city of Kamakura. Among other things, the new leaders smashed an invading armada mounted by Kublai Khan in 1274 and 1281.

As a reaction against the refined art of the Kyoto court, Kamakura art was more realistic. Sculpted figures were lifelike and colorful. Sculptors used glass to enliven the eyes. The temple guardian in figure 16–22 was made to ward off demons and evil spirits. With his vivid realism, he could frighten almost anyone—real or imagined.

The Ashikaga shoguns of Kyoto took control in 1392, but were unable to maintain a permanent peace. Therefore, their reign of nearly 200 years is referred to as a "dark age." But the arts thrived during this time. Once again, China was the source. Chan Buddhism, the sect that inspired Sung artists, was known as Zen Buddhism in Japan. Zen Buddhism became an important cultural force. The cult of Zen appealed especially to the aristocracy and a Japanese warrior class called *samurai*. Japanese painters imitated the landscapes of the Sung and Ming masters, but with a personal flourish.

Sesshu was the most celebrated of the Zen painters. He could capture the essence of a landscape (fig. 16–23) with just a few bold strokes. Sesshu applied his brush with the same finesse as a samurai might handle a sword. Do you recall the principle of closure

16–23 Sesshu, *Landscape,*
Ashikaga period, 1495.
Detail of a hanging scroll,
ink on paper. Tokyo
National Museum
(Photograph courtesy of
the International Society
for Educational
Information, Inc.).

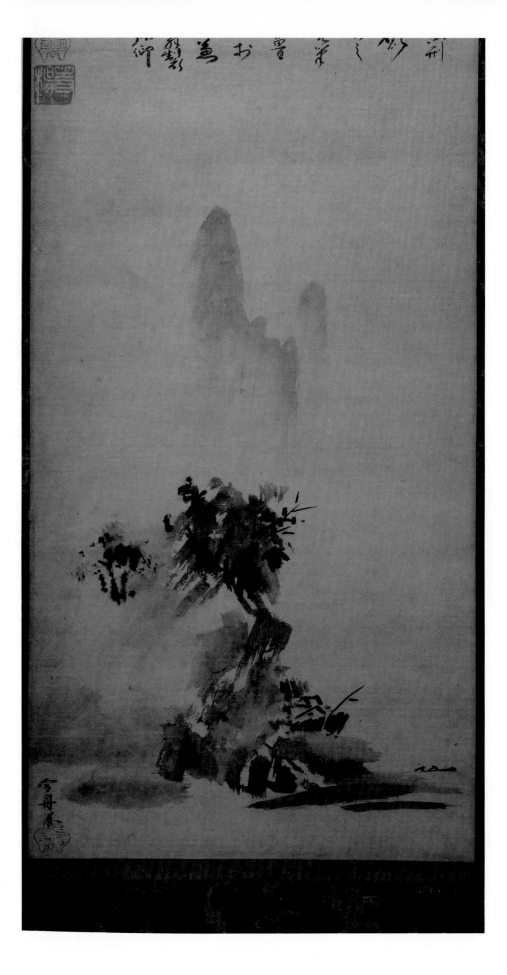

(Chapter 4)? To fully see a Sesshu scene, the viewer must supply the details and contours.

The cult of Zen gave rise to the tea ceremony. The tea ceremony was a major social custom of the aristocracy. It featured many rules and was performed with calculated grace. Supplying tea ceremony needs dominated the art of potters. Their bowls, water jars, and tea-powder jars, like Sesshu's art, attempted to strike a delicate balance between refinement and informality.

Despite its sophisticated art, the Ashikaga shogunate was a political failure. The Tokugawa, an upstart family of shoguns, moved the seat of government to Edo (modern Tokyo) in 1617. To impose order, the new shogunate undertook drastic measures. Christianity, introduced by St. Francis Xavier in 1549, was banned, less for religious reasons than for political reasons. Tokugawa leaders sought to close Japan to all outside influence. Except for a handful of Chinese and Korean traders, no foreigners were allowed on Japanese soil.

The shogunate also tried to freeze Japanese society into separate classes. The samurai were the highest class, followed by farmers, artisans, and merchants. Employees were bound to their employers for life. Because the lines between the social classes could not be broken, each social class developed its own culture.

Zen landscapes, such as the one by Tohaku shown in figure 5–33, continued to be preferred by the aristocracy. But a new kind of picture, known as **ukiyo-e** ("the art of the floating world") became popular with the merchant class. Ukiyo-e art drew its subject matter from popular entertainment, popular fiction, and sight-seeing.

Because of its whimsy, some of ukiyo-e art can be compared to the humorous Heian scrolls (fig. 16–21). The favorite medium was the woodcut. The woodcut was invented by the Chinese during the T'ang dynasty and introduced to Japan during the eighth century. With this method, ukiyo-e artists could make dozens of inexpensive replications.

Scenes such as Hiroshige's *Ohashi, Sudden Shower at Atake* (fig. 16–24) provide vivid glimpses of Japanese life during the Ashikaga period. But they came to be valued in the West during the late 1800s for their aesthetic qualities. European artists of that era, as you will learn in Chapter 19, were influenced by the Japanese aptitude for flat pattern and bold composition.

Art History Experience 16.2

Report on a Non-Western Art Form

Prepare a report on one art form you feel most represents one of the non-Western cultures discussed in Chapter 16. The art form may be architecture, sculpture, metal work, ceramics, painting or printmaking. Ask your teacher for guidelines.

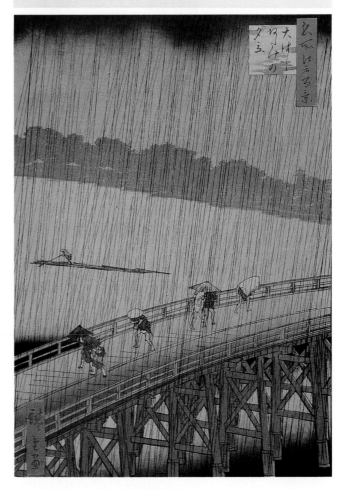

16-24 Ichiryusai Hiroshige, *Ohashi, Sudden Shower at Atake (Storm on the Great Bridge)*. Japanese, Tokugawa period, date of print: 1857. 13″ x 8 11/16″ (33 x 22 cm) The Toledo Museum of Art, Toledo, Ohio (Carrie L. Brown Bequest Fund).

Chapter 17
Non-Western Art II

Student Edition
Pages 224–243

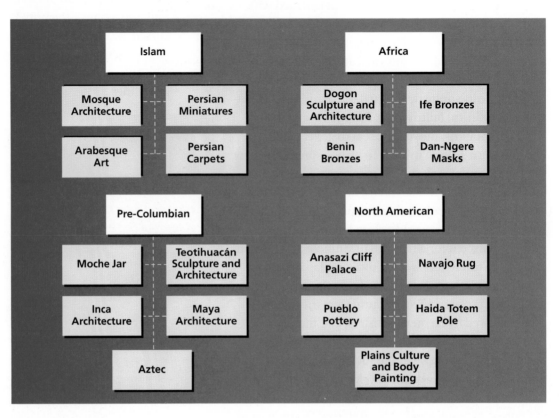

Overview

Chapter Objectives

Students should be able to:

1 appreciate that art can be a primary source of information about past civilizations and non-Western cultures   EE 3

2 discuss a culture's art in terms of its characteristics, religious functions, and history   EE 3

3 write a report on the functions of the art of a culture   EE 3, 4

4 identify by subject matter or style the art of at least two cultures   EE 3, 4

5 produce works of art based on the style of art of two cultures   EE 2, 3

6 demonstrate an appreciation of the contributions of non-Western cultures to world culture   EE 3

Rationale

Chapter 17, a continuation of Chapter 16, resumes the formal coverage of non-Western art history. This chapter reviews the cultures of Islam, Africa, pre-Columbia, and North America.

Essential Concepts

• Islam refers to the Moslem religion and all the nations in which that religion dominates.

• The arch is a masonry construction employing a number of stones in a curve.

• Because Mohammed was opposed to idolatry, the interiors of mosques were not decorated with painted or sculpted imagery of any kind. Instead they were decorated with mosaics and hangings sporting abstract designs.

- Medieval Europeans borrowed many things from the Moslems including the pointed arch, stained glass, arabesque designs, and Arabic numerals.

- Africans do not make sharp distinctions between art and life.

- The Dogon people in Mali are known for their hand-built villages and their sculptures of carved wood.

- The Ife society in Nigeria and the Benin kingdom were famous for their cast bronze.

- The Dan-Ngere people on the Ivory Coast specialized in making masks that were worn as emblems of authority.

- The Moche in South America made refined pottery without using a potter's wheel or glazes.

- The Inca made large masonry structures in which stones, though not cut to uniform shapes and sizes, are closely fitted.

- The Mayas developed writing, a form of arithmetic, a calendar, and the corbeled arch.

- The Pueblo and Navajo cultures are known for their architecture of adobe brick and their crafts of pottery and rugs.

- The Northwest Coast Indians carved wood to create totem poles, canoes, and boxes.

Vocabulary

Islam
monotheism
corbeled arch
pre-Columbian

minaret
arabesque
mosque
totem

Lesson Plans

17.1 Connecting Art and Culture

Page **T 248**   Time: Variable

17.2 A Role Mask

Page **T 250**   Time: 5 periods

17.3 A Personal Totem

Page **T 252**   Time: 3 periods

Handouts

Functions of Art in Culture

Page **T 254**

Study Questions

Page **T 255**

Test Questions

Page **T 258**

Chapter Closure
Evaluation

1 *Production:* Can students make vivid role masks based on their own experiences? Do they voluntarily suggest ideas for skits or tableaus in which to use the masks?

2 *Production:* Do students demonstrate imagination while inventing images and symbols for a totem display?

3 *Art history:* Are students able to explain the characteristics, religious functions, and history of art of at least two cultures?   EE 3   R 3

4 *Art history/Criticism:* Do students willingly seek connections between art and culture? Are they able to apply their knowledge of these connections in a written report?   EE 3   R 3   W 2

5 *Art history/Aesthetic awareness:* Are students able to recognize typical examples of art of at least two cultures?   EE 3   R 2

6 *Art history:* Can students cite at least three examples of cross-cultural influence between the culture of Islam and medieval Europe?   EE 3   R 6

7 *Aesthetic awareness:* Are students showing a greater interest in the art of one or more of the non-Western cultures?

8 *Art history:* Are students demonstrating more appreciation of unfamiliar cultures and their traditions, histories, and art?

Notes

Connecting Art and Culture

Time: Variable

Preparation

Rationale

Art communicates the values, attitudes, and belief systems of people within a society. Among nontechnical cultures, art serves many functions. Art can be an expression of the supernatural or natural world to maintain the sense of reality shared by members of the culture. It can reflect social status of individuals, clans, and regional groups. Art can contribute to political stability through symbolization. Art contributes to entertainment. Students can learn about a culture through its art forms as well as the written word.

Research Materials

Functions of Art in Culture (Handout 17.1), library resources

Enrichment Materials

Slides:
• Chief's Hat, Tlingit, N. America, 1
• Broken Nose Mask, Onandaga, N. America, 3
• Mayan Vase, S. America, 47
• Court of the Lions, Alhambra, 63
• Fang Head, Gabon, Africa, 65
• Feathered Serpent, S. America, 69

Overhead Transparencies:
• Oni of Ife, 8
• *Maria Bowl*, 16

Large Reproductions:
• Stout, *Instructions and Provisions*, 2
• Prow ornament, Tlingit war canoe, 17

Teach the Lesson

Objectives

Students should be able to:

1   prepare a report on the functions of art in a non-Western culture   EE 3, 4

Vocabulary

Culture is a pattern of living among a group of people; the attitudes, values, beliefs, patterns of behavior, social organization, and concepts of reality of a group of people.

Warm Up

Ask students to brainstorm about how art forms are used to influence our concepts of reality. For example, how does art define the "good life"? Discuss the roles of advertisements in magazines, on billboards, and TV commercials in shaping our realities. How does commercial art persuade us that a product is the best of its kind? Make a list on the chalkboard under the heading Art and Concepts of Reality in Our Culture.

Explore and Develop

1   Ask students to list some art forms that help us identify social position and status in our culture (style of dress, jewelry, varsity letters, cars, etc.).

2   Can they think of art forms that help maintain political stability? For example, how do we symbolize authority?

3   What are some art forms associated with entertainment? For examples, costumes are worn for various forms of recreation and games, playing cards, and toys are enhanced with art.

4   Display and discuss the visual examples of art from several non-Western cultures. Where possible, indicate some functions associated with the objects.

W 4   **5**   Pass out copies of the guidelines for the research assignment on page T 254. Explain that in older cultures, and those with less technological development than ours, the functions of art are fairly evident. For example, some African cultures carve ancestor figures that provide a home for the spirit of deceased relatives. Persian paintings such as figure 17–0 recorded historic and romantic stories. The totem poles and boxes made by the Northwest Coast Indians were used as signs of prestige (figure 17–26). The Pueblo Indians produced (and still do) beautiful clay pots for household and ceremonial use (see Student Edition page 240).

Evaluate and Reflect

1   Have students share their findings with the group. What do they feel are some of the most interesting things they learned about the interrelationship between art and culture?

2   Ask them to develop a general definition of art that relates to how it is used in a culture.

Reteach

Organize the class into small groups, and have them complete the study and test questions for Chapter 17.

Extend the Lesson

Beyond the Basics

E 1, 4   Students might apply the guidelines to their own culture to answer questions such as, how does art influence my daily life? How is
R 5   art used as a communication system in our
W 1   society? How does our national culture influence the individual's taste, or aesthetic judgment? How much does mass communication, including TV, influence people's learning about their culture? Suggest students create a diagram showing the answers to these questions for both cultures. Look for similarities and differences.

EE 3   Suggest students reporting on the Islamic culture research to find additional information about current events happening in that
R 3   part of the world at the present time.
W 2   Organize research materials, past and present, using maps and timelines to get a clear picture of what is currently happening and why. Identify current leaders and read about their lives, background, and philosophies. Suggest talking with the social studies teacher to gain additional insight. Have students look at their research of the Islamic culture in light of current events.

Cultural Connections

EE 3   Suggest students research ancient myths and legends from the various cultures. Each culture has stories similar in content. Have
R 3   students look at Michelangelo's *Creation of the Sun and the Moon,* page 273 of the Student Edition. Have students find examples of the same story in non-Western cultures.

Connecting with Other Subjects

R 3, 5   **Language Arts** A thematic approach to
W 2, 3, 4   research and writing the art in culture report can enliven and enrich an activity that students sometimes dread. A culture's beliefs and values can be explored through investigating any significant art form within that culture. Organizing the report thematically helps to maintain focus, direction, and provides insights into the culture that may not be available to researchers who merely string together a list of facts. Suggest students select a theme in light of their interest in a particular subject.

A Role Mask

Time: 5 periods

Preparation

Rationale

Masks are important in many cultures for the part they play in maintaining concepts of what is real, good, or not good. They are also used to project roles and status as in the Dan-Ngere culture. Masks are found in tribal cultures all over the world. Students will experience planning, shaping, and decorating a mask for a specific role.

Studio Materials

plaster gauze or papier mâché, balloons, oak tag, cardboard, shallow pans, paper towels, large cans, scissors, heavy shears, hacksaw blade, plaster bucket, glue, paint and brushes, scrap materials

Enrichment Materials

Slides:
• Broken Nose Mask, Onandaga, N. America, 3
• Mycenaean Funeral Mask, 48
• Fang Head, Gabon, Africa, 65
• Double Face Mask, 66

Large Reproductions:
• Stout, *Instructions and Provisions,* 2
• Prow ornament, Tlingit war canoe, 17
• Swentzell, *The Emergence of the Clowns,* 22

Teach the Lesson

Objectives

Students should be able to:

1   create a full face mask with features in relief by shaping plaster gauze over a balloon   EE 2, 3

2   add descriptive details with found materials and paint to portray a character in a specific role taken from history or from the present, from reality or imagination   EE 2, 3

Vocabulary

Role is a part or character portrayed by an actor.

Warm Up

Ask students what masks are used for. Have them list events and occasions when masks are worn.

Explore and Develop

1   Display examples of masks. Explain that in some cultures masks were or are used to portray roles. The Northwest Coast Indians of North America made spectacular masks with moving parts. A shaman's mask enabled him to impersonate a demon or spirit. Actors in ancient Greece wore masks to establish the character they were playing.

2   Direct attention to the composition of the masks—their symmetry, how unity is achieved, how the shapes of facial features communicate feelings or moods. Note the craftsmanship.

Begin Studio Experience 17.2

1   Direct attention to Student Edition page 233 and the discussion of Dan-Ngere role masks. Have students list roles or characters a mask might portray? Ideas may be taken from history, literature, myths, legends, plays, movies, stories, sports, and politics.

2   Once students have selected a role they wish to play, have them completely cover a balloon inflated to head size with at least two layers of plaster gauze (three if using papier mâché). A gallon plastic jug can be used instead of a balloon. To keep the balloon from rolling about while laying on the strips of plaster cloth, tell students to set it in a large tin can or plastic dish. Students should crisscross the layers of plaster gauze for strength. Work can begin immediately on building and modeling features to portray the chosen role.

3 When the base is dry, students should use heavy shears to cut out the back of the mask so that it can be placed over the head and seal the cut edges with plaster gauze.

4 Have students paint the mask with tempera or acrylic, and glue on objects and materials that contribute to the character of the mask.

Evaluate and Reflect

1 Are students satisfied that their masks portray a role? If not, what could they do differently?

2 Have students discuss the expressive qualities of the masks.

3 Did they model features in relief so that they can be seen from a reasonable distance?

4 How do the students feel about the craftsmanship they exercised in completing the mask?

Reteach

Have students use the guidelines for Functions of Art in Culture in lesson plan 17.1 to outline each of the four cultures covered in this chapter. If several students are involved, assign different cultures to them and have them share information.

Extend the Lesson

Beyond the Basics

W 2 Organize the students in several groups, and have them plan short skits that can be presented to the class while wearing the masks.

R 3, 5 Suggest poetry or short stories as inspiration for the role masks and performing the poem or story while wearing the masks. Students may want to collaborate, each one playing a role in stories with several characters. Suggest students select an ancient myth or legend from one of the cultures studied in this chapter. Create the appropriate masks, select a narrator, and have masked characters act out the story as it is

read. Try acting out the story without the narrator. Use movement and gestures only to tell the story. Some students may be interested in writing an original story to be performed. Suggest writing about an important belief or value in the student's own culture.

Cultural Connections

Masks are a principal art form of African and North American Indian cultures. Have some students obtain information about African masks. Others can gather information about North American Indian masks. Some of these cultures believe in animism —the belief that objects such as masks have a spirit or life force. Have students locate materials that explain these beliefs. Share findings in a discussion on the importance of masks among these cultures. **R 3**

Have students research to find information about the materials and processes used by different cultures in making masks. Have them find examples of traditional masks from each culture studied in chapters 16 and 17. What was the purpose or its intended use? Have students identify the materials used and how the mask was made. **R 3**

Connecting with Other Subjects

Language Arts, Drama Students might seek help from the language arts and drama teachers in planning short presentations with the masks. **R 3**

Drama Interested students might want to consult with district elementary teachers and plan a performance for children. Suggest relating the performances to subjects the children are currently studying. Students may want to act out a story from a reading lesson or an event in history. Another possibility might involve creating a number of masks representing objects, animals, people, or feelings. Show the masks to the children and discuss how each one makes them feel. Have the children write stories or poems and then direct high school students' performances. **EE 2, 3** **R 5** **W 4**

A Personal Totem

Time: 3 periods

Preparation

Rationale

In addition to masks, the Northwest Coast Indians carved poles, chests, and other wooden objects. The poles, carved with the family's totems, were placed in front of the house to identify social status and the family's clan. Creating a small totem pole or box will help students develop more understanding of the Northwest Coast Indians' use of art to communicate beliefs shared by members of that culture.

Studio Materials

clay, tubes about 3" x 8", boxes about 4" x 8", clay boards and tools, rolling pins, table covers, plastic bags, newspaper, engobes, clear glaze

Enrichment Materials

Large Reproductions:
• Prow ornament, Tlingit war canoe, 17
• Lucero, *Zoomorphic Dog Vessel,* 9
• Swentzell, *The Emergence of the Clowns,* 22

Film:
• *The Totem Pole.* University Extension of University of California. 27 min., color. 1964. Rental: University of California.

Teach the Lesson

Objectives

Students should be able to:

1   create a small totem pole or box from clay, using modeled, carved, and incised symbols to represent things of personal meaning to them   EE 2

2   practice analyzing and interpreting the totems   EE 3, 4

Vocabulary

Totem is an animal or natural object considered to be related to a given family or clan, and taken as its symbol.

Warm Up

Display some examples of totem poles, boxes, or carvings by the Northwest Coast Indians. Explain what a totem is. Ask the class to think about how they could use visual symbols to represent ideas that are of personal meaning to them. Have students list things that they value and that are important in their daily lives, such as hobbies, family, pets, school activities, personal achievements, occupations, sports, fashions, and recreational activities.

Explore and Develop

Direct attention to the discussion and pictures of totems on Student Edition pages 241–242. Explain that they will use visual symbols to communicate things of personal interest, concern, and value.

Begin Studio Experience 17.3

1   Have students wrap a tube or small box with newspaper; two layers is enough. The top of the tube should extend beyond the newspaper about ¼" so that it can be pulled with the fingertips. Tell students not to cover the bottom of the tube. They should hold the newspaper with masking tape but should *not* tape the newspaper to the tube or box. The bottom and four sides of boxes must be wrapped. Clay will be formed around the tube or box, which will be pulled out when the clay stiffens up.

2   Have students measure the diameter of the tube, roll out a slab of clay of even thickness, and cut out a piece large enough to wrap around the tube. They should close the seam and smooth it with a paddle. Have them use the slab building method to construct a bottom and four sides for a box.

3   Modeling and adding clay for carving can begin immediately, as the tube or box will support the form. Incising should be delayed until the clay is stiff. Encourage dealing with all sides of the form. If forms are too moist to remove the armatures when the period ends, tell students to wrap the work in plastic. Do not add water or wet towels.

4 During the second period, tell students to pull the tubes and boxes out. Setting the forms in front of a fan will hasten stiffening of the clay, but don't wait too long. Final decoration may be carried out with colored engobes. Students should let the pieces dry.

5 If the clay and clear glaze mature at approximately the same firing temperature, you may have students glaze the dry green ware and conduct only one firing.

Evaluate and Reflect

1 Did students use modeling, carving, and incising procedures to create their symbols?

2 Do students feel they interpreted their ideas satisfactorily with symbols?

3 Ask students to analyze the composition of the form. What makes the totem pole/box visually interesting from all sides? Identify similarities (shapes, colors, lines). Do elements continue around or over the surface? Are there contrasts that add to visual interest? What do you notice first about the artwork? Can students describe the relationship between the subject and the elements of the artwork?

4 Interpret the artwork. How would students describe the expressive quality of the work? Are there things in the work that remind them of personal experiences? Is there an idea or subject that is dominant and supported by all of the parts?

Reteach

Provide teams of two or more students with answers to the study questions for Chapter 17 and have them coach one another in asking and answering questions. The students should change roles every three or four questions.

Extend the Lesson
Beyond the Basics

Organize the class into groups, and have them research information about the different tribes included in the Northwest Coast Indian cultures—Tlingit, Haida, and Kwakiutl. What kinds of art did each tribe create? What are the style characteristics of their artworks? What functions did art fulfill for the members of the tribe? Have the groups compare their findings for similarities and differences.

EE 3

R 3

Some students may be interested in carving a wooden totem. Suggest they find a sturdy walking stick—a fallen tree limb that is fairly straight and has an interesting shape. The stick should be approximately four to six feet long and a comfortable thickness to hold in the hand. Suggest carving the design only on the top portion of the stick above the place where the student finds a comfortable hold. Develop a design and begin carving. Encourage students to try to maintain the natural character of the stick as much as possible.

EE 2

Cultural Connections

Have students investigate the totems made by several different Native American cultures. Did various totems serve different purposes? What symbolic imagery was used? What do the symbols represent? Is the same idea represented by a different image in another culture? What types of wood and tools were used? Share findings with the class.

EE 2

R 3, 4, 5

Connecting with Other Subjects

Language Arts Suggest students read the novel, *The Last of the Mohicans,* and view the film it inspired. Have students research in order to distinguish fact from fiction with regard to the Mohican people. Suggest students compare the culture as presented in the novel and the film with the factual information. Share findings with the class.

R 6

Functions of Art in Culture

Select a culture, and use available resources to identify the functions of art in that culture. Use the following guidelines to structure your report.

1 Name the culture and country.

2 State the time period the report is based on.

3 What kinds of art did the people create?

4 What art forms are used to explain religious beliefs or the supernatural? What art forms are used to interpret the nature of the universe? (for example: masks, sculpture, painted symbols, costumes)
a. What beliefs are associated with the form?
b. How is it used?
c. Who creates the form?

5 How is art used to identify social position or status?
a. What art forms are used (clothes, headdress, weapons, jewelry)?

6 How is art used to maintain political stability? Look for the following purposes:
a. symbolize authority
b. show boundaries of acceptable behavior
c. show consequences of breaking the law
d. induce fear of the supernatural to control behavior

7 How is art used to contribute to or enhance forms of play or entertainment? Look for:
a. costumes for specific activities
b. visual enhancement of game or play equipment
c. cartoons and humorous pictures

8 What do you feel is one of the most representative art forms of this culture?

Study Questions
Chapter 17–Non-Western Art II

1 Who founded the Moslem religion, and where?

_____

2 What is the first year of the Moslem calendar?

_____

3 What does the term *Islam* refer to?

_____

4 How are the writings in the *Koran* similar to the writings of Confucius?

_____

5 What is the design and function of the *minaret*?

_____

6 Why are there no sculptures or pictures of religious images in Islamic buildings?

_____

_____

7 How did Moslem artists decorate the interiors of buildings?

_____

8 Besides the Islamic aversion to idolatry, why did the Arabic people make elaborately decorated carpets and other textiles as well as objects of ceramic, silver, bronze, and glass rather than sculptures and paintings?

_____

9 Name three of the many Arabic/Islamic accomplishments transmitted to the European culture.

_____

_____

10 What is a major difference between the way Africans and Westerners approach art?

_____

11 Name two of the many reasons why Africans create(d) art.

_____

_____

12 Of what material and for what purpose did the Dogon people make their abstracted art objects?

_____

13 How does the structure of the Dogon village reflect its social structure?

_____

_____

14 Name two ways a sculptural portrait from the Ife society differs from a Dogon portrait.

_____

15 State one similarity between the Ife and Benin methods of making sculptural portraits; of the Dogon and Benin methods.

_____

_____

16 What was the major function of the mask in the Dan-Ngere culture of the Ivory Coast?

_____

17 What does the term _pre-Columbian_ refer to?

_____

_____

18 For what three things were the Moche people best known?

_____

_____

19 Describe at least two features of the Incan sun temple at Machu Picchu (text fig. 17–16).

_____

_____

_____

20 Name three Meso-American cultures, and give at least one characteristic of each.

_____

_____

_____

21 Describe and illustrate the corbeled arch. (Use separate sheet of paper.)

22 What is the major source of information about the North American Indians prior to 1500?

_____

23 Why are we able to know so much about the North American Indians since 1500?

_____

24 Even though the North American tribal groups had many different customs, beliefs, languages, and religions, they all practiced some form of _____ _____.

25 Describe the Mesa Verde settlement of the Anasazi culture (text fig. 17–23).

_____

_____

26 For what art form are the Pueblo people known?

_____

27 Describe the ways in which the design of a Navajo rug (text fig. 17–25) is similar to and different from that of a Persian rug (text fig. 17–6).

_____

_____

28 Name at least three items the Northwest Coast Indians made with wood. How were many of the objects decorated?

_____

_____

29 What is a totem? Why were totem poles displayed in front of family homes?

_____

_____

30 What materials did the Plains Indians use for their clothing and art?

_____

31 State three reasons why it is important to study non-Western art.

_____

_____

_____

_____

Test Questions
Chapter 17–Non-Western Art II

For questions 1 through 6, select from the following religious or cultural groups.

1. Islam	5. Pueblo
2. Dogon	6. Mayas
3. Incas	7. Dan-Ngere
4. Northwest Coast Indians	8. Benin

1 _____ African peasant-village people known for their wood sculptures.

2 _____ North American Indians who have preserved some of their pottery-making skills to this day.

3 _____ Faith centered around the *Koran*.

4 _____ Pre-Columbian culture that developed the corbeled arch, invented a calendar, and used hieroglyphic writing.

5 _____ An African people who used masks to express roles in everyday life.

6 _____ South American civilization that built sun temples to worship the sun god.

For questions 7 through 12, select from the following terms.

1. Minaret	5. Tiered pyramids
2. Arabesque	6. Radial symmetry
3. Totems	7. Mosque
4. lost-wax	8. Masonry

7 _____ Bronze-casting process used by Benin and Ife people.

8 _____ Design seen in Navajo and Persian rugs.

9 _____ Displayed on poles in front of homes of Northwest Coast Indians.

10 _____ Faithful were called to prayer from here.

11 _____ Built by Meso-American cultures.

12 _____ Islamic place of worship.

13 The interiors of Islamic buildings were lavishly filled with
    a. abstract designs.
    b. religious statues and pictures.
    c. objects of ceramic, bronze, silver, and glass.
    d. a and b.
    e. a and c.
    f. a, b and c.

14 The architecture of the Dogan village

  a. related to the natural contours of the hillside.
  b. symbolized the human body.
  c. reflected the Dogon social structure.
  d. a and c.
  e. b and c.
  f. a, b and c.

15 The Teotihuacáns, a Meso-American civilization that dominated the region from 300 BC to 800 AD

  a. practiced human sacrifice.
  b. worshiped nature.
  c. built tiered pyramids.
  d. a and b.
  e. a and c.
  f. a, b and c.

16 The Anasazi, a North American culture,

  a. were nomadic.
  b. were potters and weavers.
  c. lived in multileveled and interconnected structures.
  d. a and b.
  e. b and c.
  f. a, b and c.

17 What is the main difference between African art and Western art?

18 Name two of the reasons why Africans create(d) art.

19 Define the term *pre-Columbian*.

20 Name one similarity and two differences among the North American tribal groups.

21 Give two reasons why it is important to study non-Western art.

22 Illustrate:

  post-and-lintel,
  the rounded arch,
  and the corbeled arch.

While viewing the overhead transparency or text fig. 17–11 *Oni (King) of Ife*, answer the following question.

23 This sculpture is an example of an African tribal society's

  a. representation of a power figure.
  b. degree of technology with the lost-wax casting process.
  c. skill in working fine detail.
  d. all of the above.
  e. none of the above.
  f. b and c.

Study Answers
Chapter 17
Non-Western Art II

1 Mohammed, Mecca (on the west coast of Arabia).

2 622 AD, the year of Mohammed's flight from Mecca to Medina.

3 Refers to the Moslem religion and all the nations in which that religion predominates.

4 The *Koran,* like the writings of Confucius, is a collection of one man's teachings recorded by disciples and followers.

5 A slender tower from which a crier calls the faithful to prayer.

6 Mohammed opposed idolatry and forbade the use of all religious images.

7 With lavish abstract designs (later named *arabesque*).

8 Like all nomadic cultures, the Arabs preferred portable art objects.

9 Answers may include Arabic words and numerals, pointed arches, stained glass, arabesque designs, porcelain and silk.

10 Africans did not (and still do not) separate art and life as Westerners do.

11 Answers may include: to appease spirits, to honor ancestors, to ensure fertility, to symbolize authority, to frighten enemies, to celebrate.

12 Wood, for ritual purposes.

13 The interlocking of houses within the village reflects the interlocking of the Dogon social structure, in which families are linked by marriage and collective ownership.

14 Ife: made of cast bronze, naturalistic. Dogon: made of carved wood, abstracted.

15 Ife/Benin: Both used the lost-wax bronze casting process. Dogon/Benin: Both exaggerated the proportions of the body.

16 To express the personality of a particular role, e. g., teacher, doctor, farmer, executioner.

17 To the history of those people who settled in North and South America prior to the time of Columbus.

18 Work with metals, brick pyramids, and hand-built ceramics.

19 Answers may include: Temple was located on top of a high mountain (to be close to the sun god, whom they believed was their ancestor); settlement included over 200 buildings; remarkable masonry (stones are fitted so closely together a knife blade cannot fit between).

20 Answers may include: Olmec—oldest MesoAmerican culture; Teotihuacán—worshiped nature, practiced human sacrifice, built five-tiered pyramids; Toltec—similar to Teotihuacán except for language; Aztec—warlike, empire included all of Mexico, sculptures were monumental; Mayan—developed writing, a form of arithmetic, a calendar, the corbeled arch, astronomy, tiered pyramids, relief carvings.

21 Uses short stones like the round arch, spans an opening by means of succeeding rows of stones projecting inward until they meet at the top.

22 Their graves and burial mounds.

23 Their cultures were not immediately destroyed or absorbed by conquerors.

24 Nature worship.

25 Settlement is multileveled and interconnected; made of stone.

26 Pottery; designs include abstracted figures and repeated patterns.

27 Similarity: radial symmetry. Differences: Persian design—stylized images of leaves, flowers, and geometric shapes; more complicated design of arabesque interlacing of figures, shapes, and lines. Navajo design—starkly abstract, precisely outlined, flat shapes, subtly related colors, careful balance of positive and negative shapes.

28 Houses, sea-going canoes, totem poles, wooden boxes with designs of stylized animals and humans.

29 An animal or object and its representation believed to be related to a family or clan. As signs of prestige and to display the family's hereditary emblems or totems.

30 Buffalo hides, deer hides, feathers, beads, thongs, hair, bones, claws, horns.

31 1) Non-Western cultures have influenced our own art and daily life; 2) Non-Western art can be a source of inspiration; 3) Knowledge of non-Western artworks helps us see our own culture from a different perspective; 4) Understanding the cultural products of other people helps us understand the people themselves.

Test Answers
Chapter 17
Non-Western Art II

1 2.

2 5.

3 1.

4 6.

5 7.

6 3.

7 4.

8 6.

9 3.

10 1.

11 5.

12 7.

13 E.

14 F.

15 F.

16 E.

17 Africans did not (and still do not) separate art and life as Westerners do.

18 Answers may include: to please spirits, to honor ancestors, to ensure fertility, to symbolize authority, to frighten enemies, to celebrate.

19 Refers to those people who settled in North and South America prior to the time of Columbus.

20 All worshiped nature; had different beliefs, customs, languages, religions.

21 Answers may include: has influenced our own art and daily life, can be a source of inspiration, helps us see our own work from a different perspective, and understanding art products of another culture helps us understand the people themselves.

22 Check students' drawings for accuracy.

23 d.

Chapter 17
Non-Western Art II

This second chapter on non-Western art looks at the art of Islam, tribal Africa, pre-Columbian America, and North America.

Islam

Islam is the religion of the Moslems. Islam also refers to the nations that practice the Islamic religion. Islam is one of the five major living religions. (The others are Hinduism, Buddhism, Judaism, and Christianity.) It is also the newest.

The Prophet Mohammed was born in Mecca (on the west coast of Arabia) 570 years after Christ, and over 1,100 years after Buddha. Like Buddha, Moham-

med had a vision. He was told by the angel Gabriel that he was the messenger of Allah (God). The people of Mecca did not believe him, and even threatened his life. In 622 he was forced to flee from Mecca to Medina.

Eight years later Mohammed returned to his hometown of Mecca in triumph, and most of Arabia was converted. Not long after his death, his followers converted the peoples of the Middle East, North Africa, and Spain in a lightning series of conquests (fig. 17–1).

The teachings of Mohammed were collected in the *Koran*, the Moslem's sacred book. The content of the Koran is closely related to the Christian Bible. It teaches **monotheism,** or the belief in one god. Stories about the Jewish prophets of the Old Testament are included in the Koran. Jesus, however, is identified as

17–1 Islam.

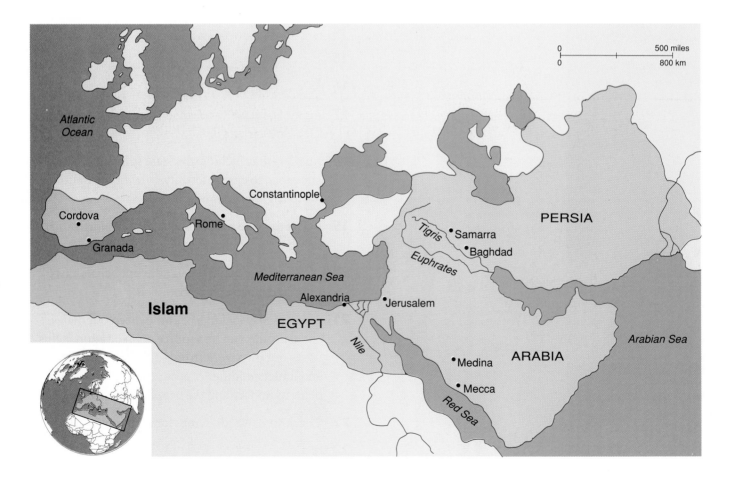

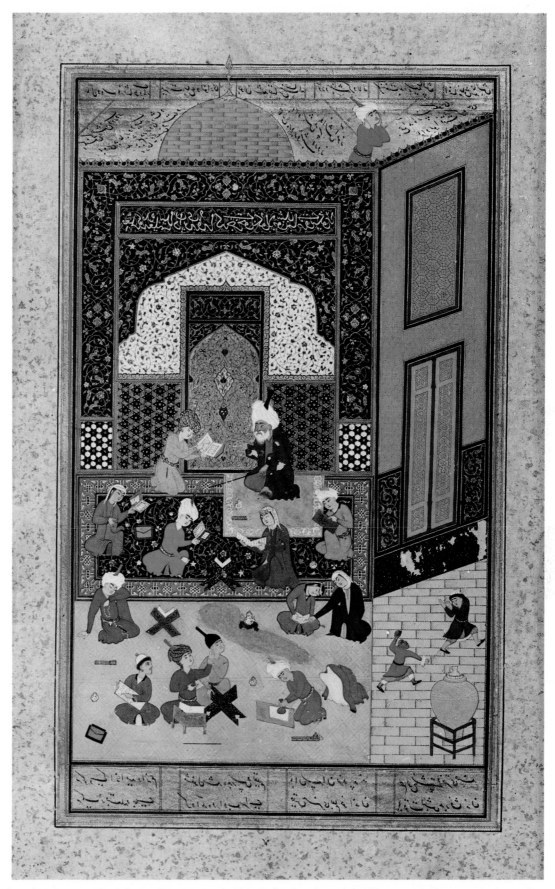

17-0 Artist Unknown, *Layla and Majnun at School*, sixteenth century, Safavid Period. Ink, colors, and gold on paper, 4¾″ x 7½″ (12 x 19 cm). Khamseh (Quintet) of Nizami, style of Shaykh Kadeh. The Metropolitan Museum of Art, Gift of Alexander Smith Cochran, 1913.

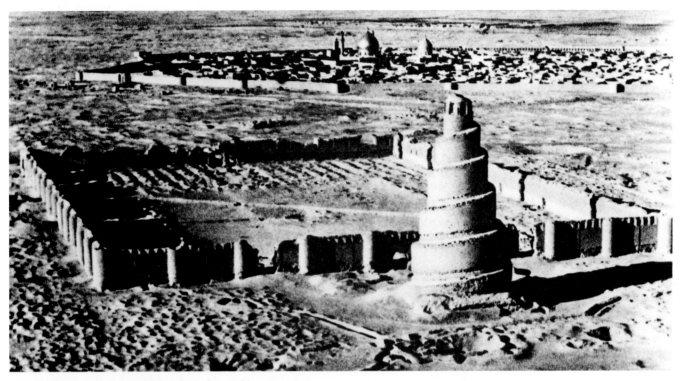

17-2 Mosque of Mutawakkil (view from the north), 848-852 AD, Samarra, Iraq.

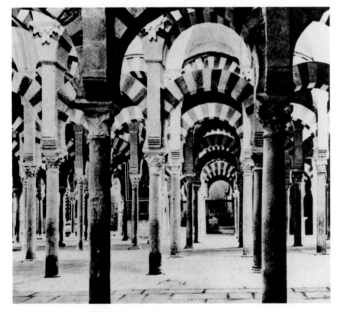

17-3 Interior of the Sanctuary (view from the east), Mosque, Cordova.

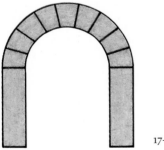

17-4 Arch.

one of the prophets rather than as the Son of God. Moslems believe that Mohammed is the last of the prophets. Moslems must pray in the direction of Mecca five times a day. There are no priests. The only public worship is Friday noon.

The Moslem place of worship is called a **mosque.** Early mosques were very simple. The one at Samarra, Iraq (fig. 17-2), was simply a walled rectangle. It covered ten acres and was large enough to contain all the worshippers of Samarra. It faces south, the direction of Mecca. The *qibla*, or wall on the Mecca side, has a small prayer niche called a *mihrab* in the center. Opposite the qibla is the **minaret,** or prayer tower. A *muezzin* (myoo EZ in), or crier, called the faithful to prayer from the minaret. Later minarets were slender and resembled a medium-range ballistic missile. Today, little is left of the mosque at Samarra. Nothing remains of the roof and the 464 pillars that supported it.

Fortunately, the mosque at Cordova, Spain, is still standing (fig. 17-3). Its interior, with its many arches and pillars, is very dramatic. The pillars are spaced to create multiple aisles. Notice how the pillars and arches draw the eye to the qibla wall.

Arches support the ceiling above the pillars. An arch (fig. 17-4) is a masonry curve made of stones or bricks. The wedge-shaped blocks press against one another instead of falling. The arches in the Cordova mosque are made with stones of contrasting colors.

Arches are placed one on top of the other. These double-tiered arches add complexity and drama.

Like the mosque at Cordova, the Court of Lions of the Alhambra, a palace in Granada, Spain (fig. 17–5), is an outstanding example of Islamic arch construction. An Alhambra arch is richly decorated with stucco and tile reliefs. These reliefs are delicate and create an airy effect. The arches themselves seem almost to hang from, rather than support, the ceiling.

Granada was the last Islamic city on the European continent to fall to the Christians. In 1492 it surrendered to the armies of Spain's Ferdinand and Isabella.

But the splendor of its Islamic heritage, especially its architecture, left a lasting impression on the European imagination.

Mohammed was very opposed to *idolatry,* the worship of idols. He smashed all of Mecca's sculptures of gods and goddesses. Indeed, he did not allow the use of religious images of any kind. To this day, the walls of mosques, unlike those of Buddhist temples or Christian cathedrals, have no statues or pictures of human or animal figures.

17–5 Court of Lions, The Alhambra, 1354–1391, Granada.
© Joe Viesti/Viesti Associates, Inc.

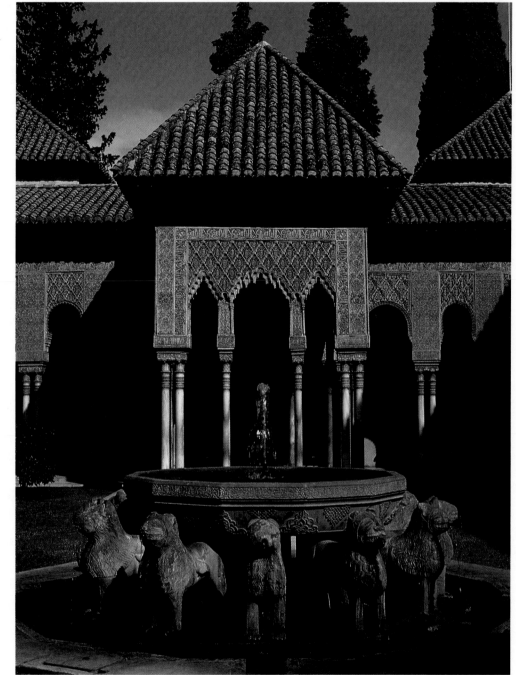

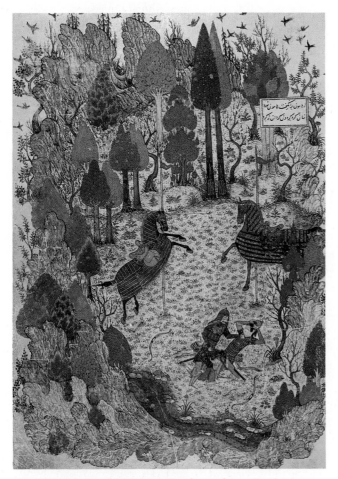

17-7 *Two Warriors Fighting in a Landscape,* from a Persian manuscript, 1396. Reproduced by Courtesy of the Trustees of the British Museum.

intricate design must have been a moving experience.

The absence of human or animal figures in the carpet is due in part to the Islamic aversion to idolatry, mentioned earlier. Another reason is that Arabian culture tended to specialize in craft objects instead of sculptures and painting. Islamic artists did not specialize in pictorial art. Even in Islamic provinces that were not Arab, pictorial skills were never developed.

Book illustration was an exception, however. Islamic artists, especially in Persia, illustrated poems and books with miniature paintings. Persia, which is now Iran, had a highly developed culture. It was also a crossroads for traders and invaders from east and west. In the 1200s Persia was invaded by the Mongols under the notorious Genghis Khan (the grandfather of Kublai Khan). The Persian illustration *Two Warriors Fighting in a Landscape* (fig. 17-7) shows how Persian painting was influenced by the Mongols. Like Sung painters, the artist chose a landscape setting. The rocks and mountains are somewhat Chinese in style. But the delicate details and two-dimensional design are definitely Islamic.

For centuries Islam led Christian Europe in government, philosophy, literature, science, mathematics, and medicine, in addition to architecture and crafts. Many Islamic contributions entered European culture during the Crusades (Chapter 18). The extent of the Islamic legacy is reflected in our language. Many Arabic words have entered our vocabulary: alcohol, bazaar, caravan, check, chemistry, nadir, satin, tariff, and zenith, among others. Arabic numerals (1, 2, 3, 4, etc.), together with the concept of zero and algebra, replaced Roman numerals. (Imagine trying to divide XLV by IX!)

European builders enriched their cathedrals by borrowing the pointed arch, stained glass, and arabesque designs from the Moslems. And European craftspersons learned the secrets of porcelain and silk—which came from China through the Moslems.

However, abstract decorations were allowed. Moslem artists covered the insides of Islamic buildings with inventive designs. The term **arabesque,** meaning "in the Arab style," was coined to describe the complex designs. The designs featured patterns of intertwined lines and shapes.

The kind of lacework arabesques seen in the Alhambra are also found in Islamic crafts. Objects of ceramic, bronze, silver, and glass were all richly covered with arabesque decoration. These objects were used to furnish mosques and palaces.

But the most highly valued Islamic craft was textiles, especially the weaving of carpets. The Ardabil Carpet (fig. 17-6) may have as many as three hundred knots to the square inch. The carpet was probably made by a group of weavers and intended to cover a floor or hang on a wall of a mosque. The medallion design in the center is surrounded by stylized and interlaced leaves and flowers. Even to study such an

Art History Experience 17.1

Connecting Art and Culture

Prepare a report on the meanings, functions, social and religious values of art in one of the non-Western cultures discussed in this chapter.

17–6 Maqsud of Kashan, *The Ardabil Carpet,* 1540, Safavid dynasty, Persia, Tabriz. Silk and wool, 23′ 11″ x 13′ 5″ (729 x 409 cm). The Los Angeles County Museum of Art, Gift of J. Paul Getty.

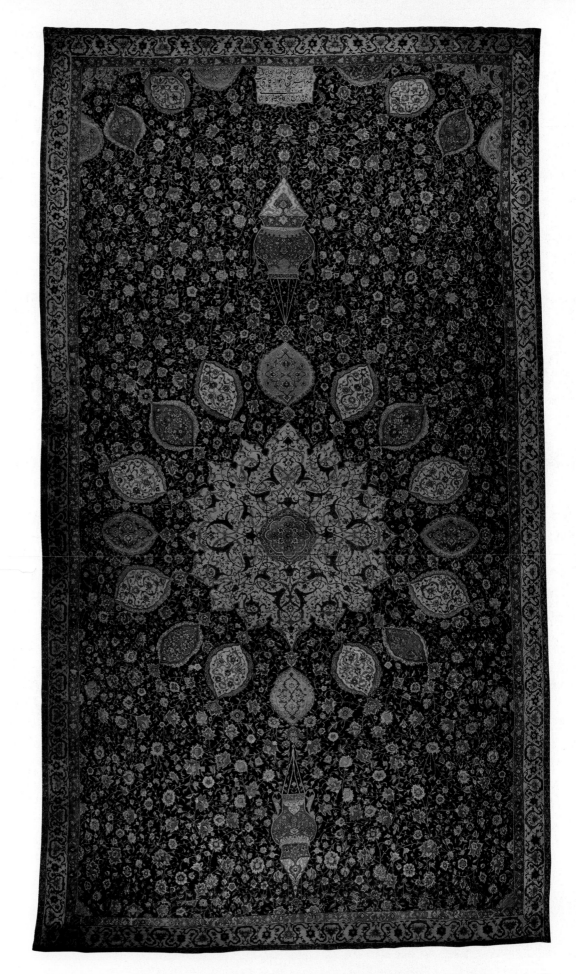

Africa

Africa is a checkerboard of religions and belief systems. The African continent has deserts, highlands, grassy savannas, and river forests. The African population is divided among nomadic tribes, farming villages, and great kingdoms—each with its own language.

There is no such thing as a single style of African art. The style of an object depends on the culture, its purpose, or sometimes the individual artist. African art can be realistic or abstract. It can be highly structured or relatively formless. African art does not always fall into the typical categories of sculpture or craft. For example, a footstool can look like a human figure. A jar handle can be shaped like a crocodile, and a hat can look like a pair of antlers.

Africans did not (and still do not) make sharp distinctions between art and life, as Westerners do. Some of their art, like Western art, was intended to be permanent. But much of it was made to be used for a special occasion and then thrown away. Its functions are as varied as Africa's different beliefs. The art may be intended to appease spirits, to honor ancestors, to ensure fertility, to symbolize authority, to frighten enemies, or simply to celebrate. (Recall the memorial sculpture of Sokari Douglas Camp in Chapter 15.) For these reasons, African art is difficult to analyze. Yet this art, as a class of objects, has captured the imagination of modern artists and collectors. With this in mind, we

will look at a sampling from those regions of Africa (fig. 17–8) that are especially noted for their art.

The Dogon are a peasant-village people in Mali. They are well known for their imaginative wood sculptures. Dogon carvers whittled bowls, jars, stools, masks, granary doors, and figurines in human and animal form. They sometimes even combined both forms.

Although Dogon styles vary, their human figures exhibit a sensitive blend of organic and geometric forms. The ancestral couple in figure 17-9 have long bodies and egg-shaped heads. Their surfaces are engraved with complex geometrical designs. This sculpture expresses a tender, almost wistful, relationship between a man and woman. The abstractness of its style appealed to early twentieth-century artists and collectors. We must remember, however, that Dogon images were made for ritual purposes and not to be admired as art objects.

The Dogon are also known for their architecture. The houses and granaries of the Dogon village in figure 17–10 are organically related to the natural contours of the hillside. They provide an interesting variety of levels and spaces. The buildings themselves, which were built by hand, have the qualities of sculptures.

However, it is the plan of the houses and layout of the village that interests twentieth-century sociologists and city planners. Each house is intended to symbolize a human body. The kitchen area is the head. On a larger scale, the arrangement of houses and granaries in a village is also intended to represent a human body. The symbolic connection between the houses and the village reflects a sense of community that is a part of the Dogon culture. In the Dogon society, families are linked both by marriage and by collective ownership. Each Dogon citizen is connected socially and symbolically to the village.

Unlike the village culture of the Dogon, the Ife society in Nigeria was aristocratic. This society flourished between the 1100s and the 1300s. Its art is lifelike, not abstract, as shown by the bronze head of a king in figure 17–11. The facial features are correct and realistic. The details of his royal headgear are faithfully drawn. Even the tattoos, which follow the contours of his face, seem accurate.

Ife bronzes were made by the lost-wax method of casting (Chapter 13). Some experts have speculated that Ife artists learned this technique from Egyptian

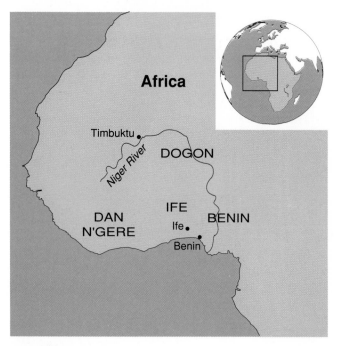

17–8 Africa.

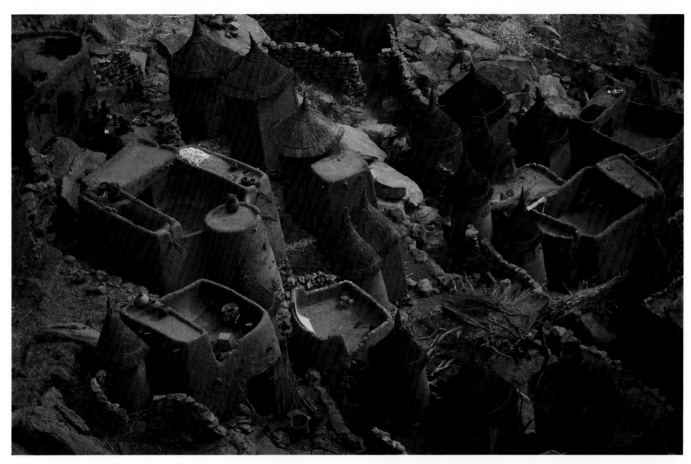

17–10 Dogon village, Mali, West Africa. Courtesy Woodfin Camp & Associates, Inc. New York.

17–9 *Seated Man and Woman,* Dogon origin, Mali. Wood, 30″ (76 cm) high. Photograph ©1989 by The Barnes Foundation.

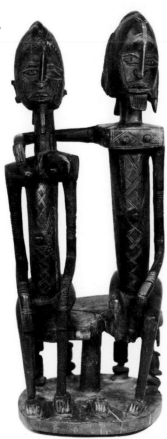

Studio Experience 17.2

A Role Mask

Create a mask with features in relief. Produce relief effects by shaping plaster gauze over a balloon or large plastic jug. The role you create for the mask may come from your own time and experience, or from a play, movie, story or legend.

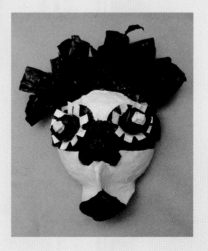

sculptures. Because the bronze portrait of the king has a classical air, others have speculated that the Greeks may have influenced the Ife artists. Today, however, most experts agree that Ife art was not influenced by other cultures. Still, the superb craftsmanship and aesthetic qualities of Ife art call to mind the art of ancient Egypt, classical Greece, and Renaissance Italy (Chapter 18).

A little to the south of Ife was the Benin kingdom, which flourished between the 1400s and 1700s. Possibly, the Ife and Benin kingdoms had historical ties. At any rate, Benin sculptors shared with their Ife neighbors the method of lost-wax. They created bronze castings of a high technical level.

The body of the little flute player in figure 17–12 neatly combines realism with caricature. His propor-

17–11 Oni (King) of Ife, twelfth–fourteenth centuries. Bronze, 14 ½″ (37 cm) high (life-size). Reproduced by Courtesy of the Trustees of the British Museum.

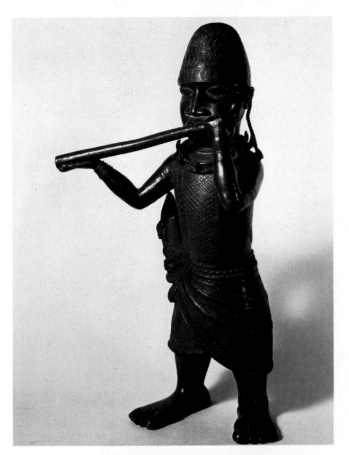

17-12 Flute player, fifteenth–sixteenth centuries. Benin culture, Nigeria. Engraved bronze, 24 ½″ (62 cm) high. Reproduced by Courtesy of the Trustees of the British Museum.

tions (the relationship of a part to a whole) are obviously exaggerated. His overall height is about three times the height of his head. An average man's height is about seven times. The proportions in his face, compared to those in the Ife bronze, are also exaggerated. Nevertheless, there is something very lifelike about him. Look at his large almond-shaped eyes, the folds of his kilt, his stubby legs, and, especially, the way his little arms support the flute. His body and clothes, like the Ife king's, are heavily decorated with engraved designs.

Masks are found in tribal societies all over the world. Perhaps wearing a mask satisfies a universal urge to change identity, be anonymous, or assume the power of another person or animal. This may explain the thrill of wearing masks on Halloween. In tribal societies, masks were usually used in dances and rituals. The purpose of a ritual could vary from a sacrificial offering to entertainment.

Masks were used differently among the Dan-Ngere people of the Ivory Coast. Masks were emblems of authority, much like a police uniform. A person wearing the mask of a judge was not pretending, but being a real judge who could try and convict people. (Imagine, for example, being issued a parking ticket by a person wearing the mask of a meter maid.) Each Dan mask expressed the personality of a particular role. Roles could vary from teachers to executioners. Thus, mask carvers were challenged to come up with a range of forms and styles. Some masks were smooth, highly polished, and with delicate features. Perhaps these were intended to express pleasant roles. Some, like the one in figure 17-13, were coarse with enlarged features. With its large nose, staring eyes, gaping mouth, and fur, the mask is very striking. Was it intended to represent a shaman, a witch doctor, a philosopher, a hermit, a cranky old man, or all of the above?

In Africa, art is not separated from life, as it often is in the West. It is an essential part of the way of life of a tribe. It expresses the social and spiritual values of each culture. Daily living, the natural, and the supernatural are all mingled in African art.

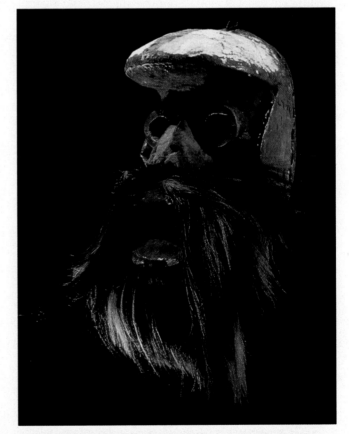

17-13 Mask, Dan-Ngere people, Ivory Coast. Wood, animal hair, copper and pigment, 11″ x 6 ½″ x 8″ (28 x 16.5 x 20 cm). Collection, The University Museum, Illinois State University, Normal, Illinois.

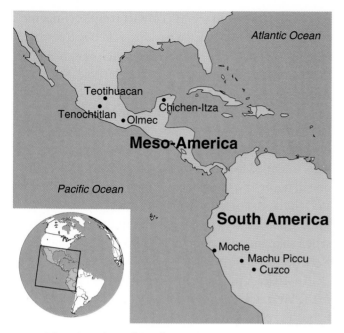

17-14 Meso-America and South America.

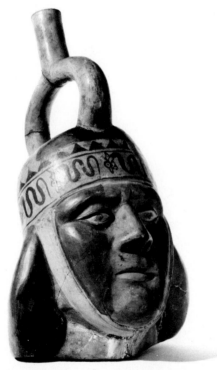

17-15 Portrait jar, Moche, Peru, fifth–sixth centuries. Ceramic, 11 ½″ (29 cm) high. Neg./Trans. No. 121197. Photo by T. L. Bierwerx. Courtesy Department Library Services. American Museum of Natural History.

Pre-Columbian

Around 4000 BC, people of Asian stock began migrating to the New World. They came from Asia to Alaska by crossing the Aleutian Islands. They began to settle in both North and South America. *Pre-Columbian,* as the name implies, refers to the history of those people up to the time of Columbus. However, the term is most often used to mean the Indian civilizations that flourished in Mexico, Central America, and South America (fig. 17–14) before the arrival of the Spanish conquistadors in the 1500s.

South America

The civilizations of South America developed mostly in the central Andes Mountains. The earliest civilization was fully developed by 700 BC (around the time of China's Chou dynasty). This civilization was known for its irrigation canals. The Moche culture arrived on the scene somewhat later. Thriving from AD 1 to 800, the Moche people were known for their metallurgy and sun-dried brick pyramids. They were also known for their remarkable ceramics.

No pre-Columbian culture used a potter's wheel, so all pottery was hand-built or cast from molds (Chapter 13). Glaze also was unknown, so their pots were decorated only with slip (Chapter 13). However, Moche potters were so skilled that their round vessels appear wheel-thrown. The surfaces of their pots resemble those of glazed ware. The portrait jar in figure 17–15 is obviously not wheel-thrown. However, it is an example of their superb craftsmanship. The dual function of portrait and storage vessel is in itself a skillful achievement. As a portrait, it is as solemn and dignified as the Ife bronze. As a vessel, it is both functional and lightweight. Note especially the slenderness of the stirrup spout, one of the unique features of Moche pottery.

Around 800, the Moche kingdom, along with other groups in the highlands and along the coast of modern Peru and Bolivia, came to an end. They may have been conquered by a people known as the Tiahuanacons, but this is not certain. It is certain, however, that around 1400, another ambitious group started from Cuzco (Peru), and rapidly overran all the Peruvian kingdoms. Named for the title of their leader, Inca, these people proceeded to establish an empire that stretched over 2,000 miles from northern Ecuador to Chile.

The main regions of their empire were scattered along the most rugged mountains of the world. To connect Cuzco to these regions, the Incas strung hanging bridges across rivers, and built solid roads. To grow crops, they learned to terrace and irrigate. They also domesticated the llama and the alpaca. To record their business transactions, they used a unique system of knotted cords for numerals. They worshiped gods of thunder, earth, sea, mountains, and rivers. Of these, the most important was the sun god, who they believed was their ancestor. Sun temples were built all over the empire, including one at Machu Picchu (fig. 17–16).

Located on top of a high mountain, Machu Picchu is an extraordinary place to locate a temple, let alone a whole settlement. Its construction must have been a severe challenge to Inca builders. The site has some two hundred buildings. Incan masonry is remarkable. Stones are fitted so closely that a knife blade cannot be run between them. This is even more remarkable because the stones were not cut to uniform sizes.

Today Machu Picchu is sometimes called the City in the Sky or the Lost City. Since it was rediscovered in 1911, it has raised more questions than answers. Was it primarily a religious sanctuary? Was it also a fortress? Why was it built there? And why was it suddenly abandoned? The answers died with the Inca civilization itself when Atahalpa, the last great Inca ruler, was executed by conquistador Pizarro.

Meso-America

Meso-America refers to the area of modern Mexico and the northern countries of Central America. The pre-Columbian civilizations that arose there differed from the Incas and the others of South America. They developed mainly in the central highlands of Mexico, the lowlands along the Gulf of Mexico, and the lowlands of the Yucatán Peninsula.

The oldest civilization was centered at Olmec around 600 BC. The culture of Olmec influenced later civilizations in Meso-America. The Olmecs settled in the swampy lowlands along the coast (in the Mexican states of Tabasco and Vera Cruz).

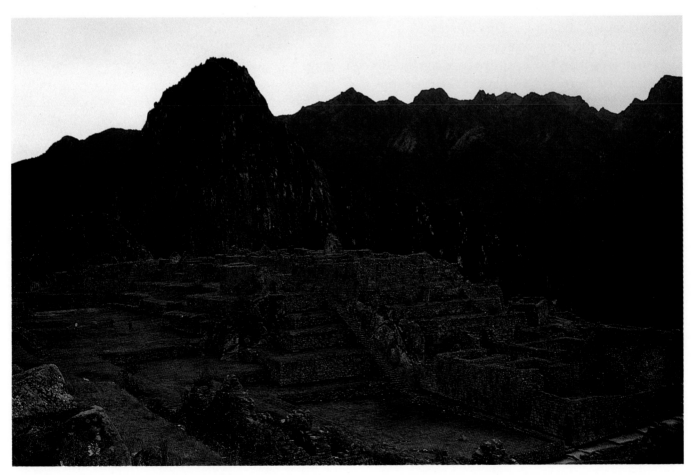

17–16 Machu Picchu, Peru. Art Resource, NY.

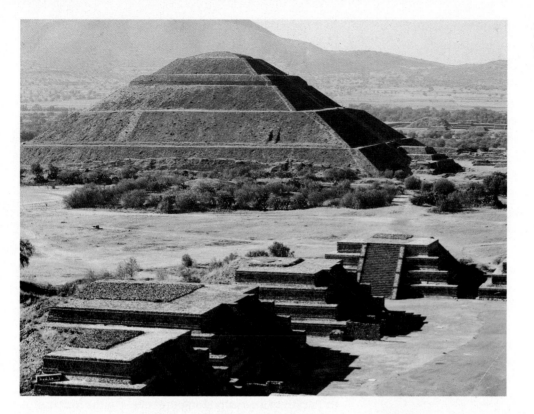

17–17 The Pyramid of the Sun, Teotihuacán, Mexico. Werner Forman/Art Resource, NY.

Another group, called the Teotihuacán, was just beginning to get organized in the central highlands north of modern Mexico City. They dominated the region from 300 BC to 800 AD. (This was roughly the same time as the Han and T'ang dynasties combined.) Like the Incas, they worshiped nature. Their worship centered around *Tlaloc*, god of rain, and *Quetzalcoatl*, a culture hero who was later deified as a feathered serpent. To feed their gods and produce unity between the gods and the people, the Teotihuacán practiced human sacrifice. These rituals occurred frequently at their capital, Teotihuacán, which meant "place of gods." It was perhaps the largest city in pre-Columbian America. Estimates of its peak population range from one hundred thousand to almost one million.

The ritual center of the city had many temples and palaces, and was planned around a broad avenue (fig. 17–17). The largest temple, dedicated to the sun, was a five-tiered pyramid with a broad stairway. A smaller temple was decorated with sculptures of the heads of Quetzalcoatl and Tlaloc. The name Quetzalcoatl comes from the word *quetzal,* meaning "a brilliantly plumed bird" and *coatl,* meaning "snake." Judging by the fierceness of his image (fig. 17–18), Quetzalcoatl clearly commanded respect.

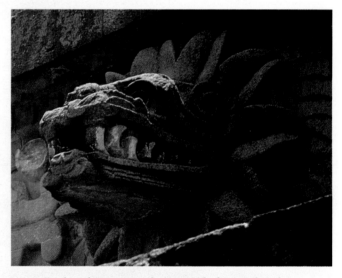

17–18 Feathered Serpent on the Pyramid of Quetzalcoatl, ca. 500 AD. Art Resource, NY.

The downfall of the Teotihuacáns, around 800, coincided with the rise of the Toltecs. The Toltecs took over many aspects of Teotihuacán culture, though their language (Nahuatl) may have been different.

Around 1300, the Aztecs, another Nahuatl-speaking group, came to power. The Aztecs established Tenochtitlán (modern Mexico City) as their capital. A very warlike people, the Aztecs expanded their empire to include all of Mexico. However, despite their skills as warriors and empire builders, they fell to the Spaniards in 1520 when Cortez conquered Tenochtitlán.

While the Teotihuacáns were building their civilization in the highlands, the Mayas were building theirs in the lowlands of Guatemala and Honduras. Of all the pre-Columbian cultures, the Mayan culture was perhaps the finest. Between AD 300 and 900, they developed writing, a form of arithmetic, a calendar, and the corbeled arch. Mayan numerals—a dot (equal to the number 1), a bar (equal to five dots), and a crescent (equal to four bars)—have been compared to Arabic numerals for simplicity and effectiveness.

The Mayan year was divided into eighteen twenty-day months, with five extra days for special religious observations. This resembles a modern calendar in principle. The relief carving in figure 17–19 illustrates not only the Aztec version of the Mayan calendar, but also an example of Aztec carving. To the Mayas, the calendar and the related science of astronomy were so important that many of their priests were astronomers.

The **corbeled arch** allowed Mayan builders to make rooms and hallways within their stone buildings. Like a round arch, a corbeled arch uses short stones. However, the arch is created by projecting succeeding rows of stones inward until they reach the top. This kind of arch cannot span a wide area, and it requires a lot of masonry material for support. Therefore, the rooms in a Mayan temple were narrow (no more than fifteen feet wide) and dark.

Around 900, the Mayas abandoned their sites in Guatamala and Honduras and moved to the Yucatán Peninsula. We still do not know why. Was it due to drought, crop failure, foreign intervention, or perhaps a combination of these? While in Yucatán, the Mayas were invaded by peoples of Toltec affiliation. But this did not prevent them from building some of the finest architecture in pre-Columbian Mexico. Mayan temples were usually built on tiered pyramids, similar to those at Teotihuacán. They were richly decorated with relief carvings and covered with stucco. The major temple at Chichén Itzá (fig. 17–21), rises grandly from the Yucatán plain. It stands not only as an example of handsome Mayan architecture, but also as a reminder of a once-proud culture.

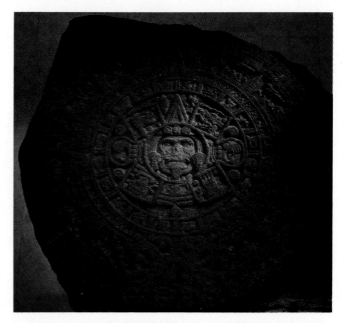

17–19   The Aztec Calendar Stone: Mask of Tonatiuh at Center. National Museum Anthropology. Werner Forman/Art Resource, NY.

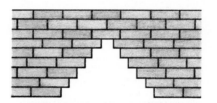

17–20   Corbeled arch.

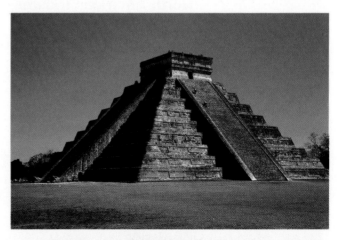

17–21   El Castillo, Mayan pyramid temple of the Toltec period, at Chichén Itzá, Yucatán, dedicated to the Feathered Serpent, patron deity of Chichén Itzá.

North America

The previous review of South American and Meso-American cultures looked at their history before Europeans came. The review of North American Indians in this section looks at their development after Europeans came. Little is known about the histories of North American Indians prior to the 1500s. Unlike the Mayas, they left behind no writing, and few monuments of architecture and sculpture. What we do know of their precontact days comes mostly from graves and burial mounds.

We do know a great deal about their histories since the 1500s, however. Unlike the Incas, Toltecs, Aztecs, and Mayas, their cultures were not immediately destroyed or absorbed by conquerors. Despite displacement and massacres by the white settlers, most of them managed to maintain their cultural identities through the 1800s. (Some held on to their culture through the 1900s.) Since the late 1800s, native North Americans have been the object of intense study by historians and anthropologists.

North American tribal groups (fig. 17–22) had very different customs and beliefs. One expert counted fifty-six different languages. But all groups, except perhaps the Plains Indians, lived near rivers and lakes. They raised corn (maize), beans, and squash. Although they had different religions, all practiced a form of nature worship. They honored such gods as the sun, morning star, south wind, water spirit, and rabbit.

Southwest

One early culture, the Anasazi, did leave a substantial record of their existence. Located in the plateau country of what is now New Mexico, northern Arizona, and southwestern Colorado, the Anasazi made pottery and weavings. They built masonry-walled structures as

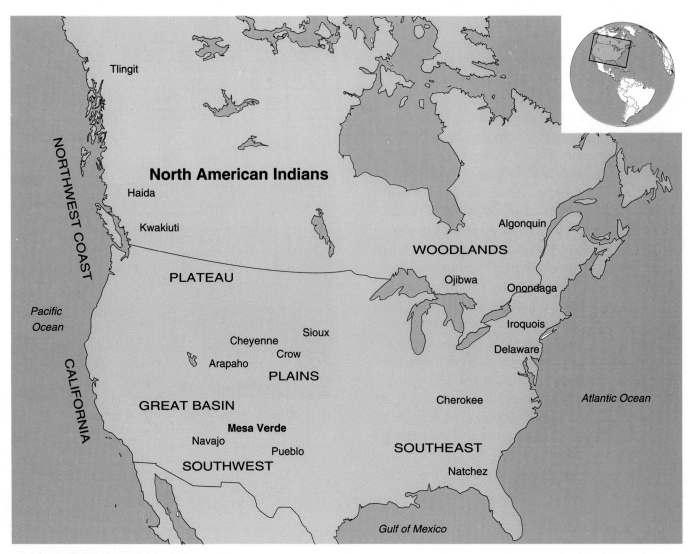

17–22 North America.

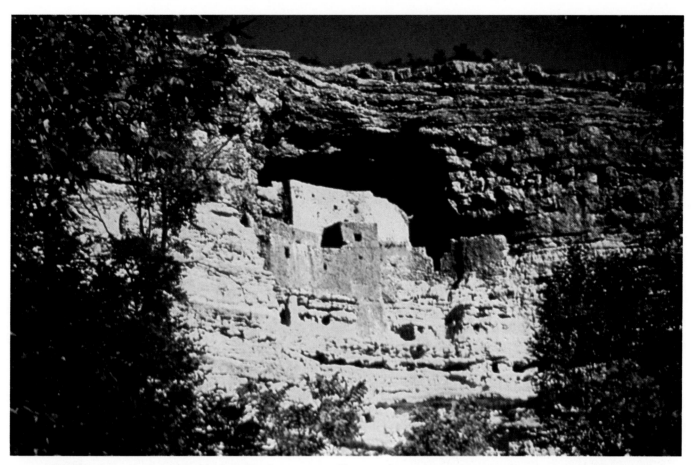

17–23 Cliff Palace, Mesa Verde National Park, Colorado, ca. 1100 AD. Photograph courtesy Department of Interior, Bureau of Reclamation.

early as the first century AD. Chapels, called *kivas*, were built partially underground.

The Anasazi also built cliff dwellings at Mesa Verde (fig. 17–23). The Mesa Verde dwellings are similar to the Dogon village. They are multileveled and interconnected. The cliff dwellings are made of stone, timber, and some *adobe* (sun-dried bricks). The settlement at Mesa Verde has over two hundred rooms and twenty-three sacred kivas. At one time, at least twenty-three clans lived here. The cliff dwelling was like a modern condominium, with an excellent view of Mesa Verde National Park.

The Pueblo Indians were a farming culture made up of the Zuni and Hopi tribes. They came after the Anasazi people. The Pueblo lived in traditional adobe dwellings. Although the Pueblo still live in New Mexico and Arizona, they have lost many of their traditional skills. Some Native American artisans, however, are reviving some of the skills. They are using traditional skills to make pottery like the handmade Acoma vase in figure 17–24. The vase is symmetrical, smooth, and thin-walled. It is ornamented with stylized parrots enclosed by leaves, arches, and geometric

designs. The Pueblo used abstract designs and repetition in their decoration. This preference is typical of nearly all tribal cultures.

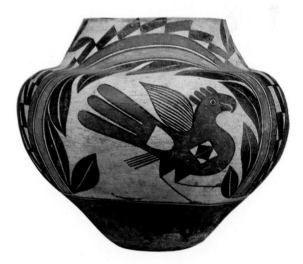

17–24 Acoma Pueblo Water Jar, ca. 1900, 13 ¾″ (35 cm) diameter. Each Pueblo potter develops characteristic shapes and designs. Courtesy of Sotheby's, Inc.

Maria Martinez

ca.1900–1980

Some of the most refined pottery ever produced in the United States has been made without the use of high technology, machinery, or even the potter's wheel. A unique technique for creating "black-on-black" pottery was developed by Maria Montoya Martinez, a Native American artist.

This remarkable pottery is made by hand-pinching thick coils of clay together to create delicate forms. Simple tools made from vegetable gourds are used to smooth and shape the wet clay before the pots are placed in the sun to dry. The dried pots are then covered with a thin layer of liquified clay called "slip." Special river-smoothed stones are used to polish or "burnish" the surface to create a glossy shine. Good polishing stones are highly valued and are often passed on from one generation of potters to another. In the final step, the pots are fired in a fire fueled by wood and manure. To achieve their characteristic rich black coloring, the fire is smothered with manure and covered with wood ashes to prevent air from escaping. The smoke which is produced carbonizes the clay pots, darkening the vessels and leaving a silvery-black sheen.

Maria Martinez was born at San Ildefonso Pueblo in New Mexico. She lived and worked in this small Native American community for over eighty years. There, Maria ritually collected sacred

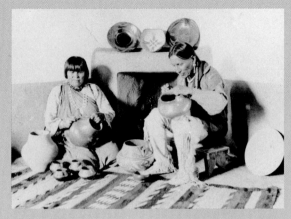

Maria and Julian Martinez, ca. 1920. Photograph: Pedro de Lemos.

clay from special sources in the surrounding mountains. Mixing these clays with proportions of water and volcanic ash, she produced a workable material appropriate for potting.

During her lifetime, Maria worked very closely with her husband, Julian, and her son, Popovi Da, to create these unique vessels. Both were responsible for decorating Maria's pots with carefully painted designs of a matte or dull finish, created before the pot was smoke-fired. Brushes made from pieces of yucca plant are dipped in the slip and used to paint this type of unique pattern on the polished surface of the pot. Once the vessel is heated and the smoke-firing process complete, the polished surface shines, while the painted surface remains matte.

Today, Maria is known worldwide for the highly skilled method of pottery production which established San Ildefonso as a leading pottery producing community. By developing a method for creating black-on-black pots, Maria Martinez was able to revive the art of pottery making in the Pueblo community of the Southwest. Her knowledge and expertise has been passed on to other generations of potters in her community, enlivening the economy and culture of the Pueblo people.

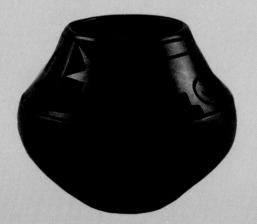

Maria bowl. Collection of Gilbert and Jean Davis.

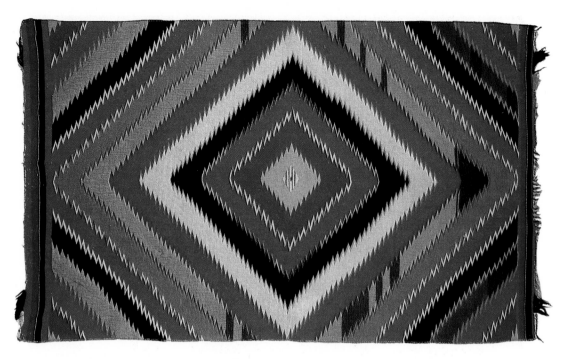

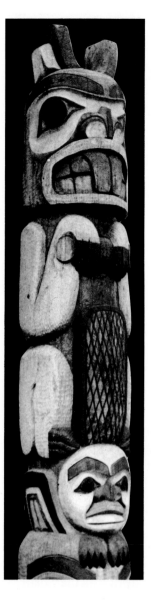

17–25 Navajo rug, 1850–1880. Wool. The Indian Art Center of California, Studio City.

17–26 Haida totem pole. Tlingit Indians of Southeast Alaska.

Although the Navajo were originally a hunting tribe from a different language group, they became associated with the Pueblo in the 1600s. They learned many of their customs from the Pueblo, including the art of weaving. Navajo blankets and rugs are among the finest in the world. Compare the design of the Navajo rug in figure 17–25 with that of the Persian rug (fig. 17–6). The Persian design contains stylized leaves, flowers, and geometric shapes. And, because of its arabesque interlacing of figures, shapes, and lines, it is much more complicated than the Navajo example. On the other hand, the Navajo design is starkly abstract. It contains precisely outlined, flat shapes. The colors of the shapes are subtly related and keenly balanced between positive and negative.

Northwest Coast

The Northwest Coast is made up of the Indian tribes of the Tlingit, Haida, and Kwakiutl. These tribes lived along the Pacific coast from Alaska to California. They depended mainly on food from the ocean, but they also farmed and hunted. Unlike the Pueblo, who built boxy houses of adobe brick, the Northwest Indians built gable-roofed houses of cedar planks. Wood was their most important raw material. In addition to houses, wood was used to make canoes, totem poles, and boxes—all without the help of metal tools.

A *totem* is an animal believed to be related by blood to a family or clan. A totem animal also symbolizes a family or clan. A totem pole (fig. 17–26) is simply a tall post carved with the clan's symbols. Totem poles stood in front of houses as signs of prestige and to showcase the family's totems.

Other objects were often decorated with totems. Haida artists, for example, carved reliefs of clan symbols on the outside of the wooden chest in figure 17–27. There are two central figures, shown facing forward. The largest may be a bear, and the smaller seems to be a human. Beside them are profiles of the heads of other animals—perhaps birds or fish. Although their heads are in profile, their eyes are facing front. The design is perfectly symmetrical. One side is a mirror image of the other.

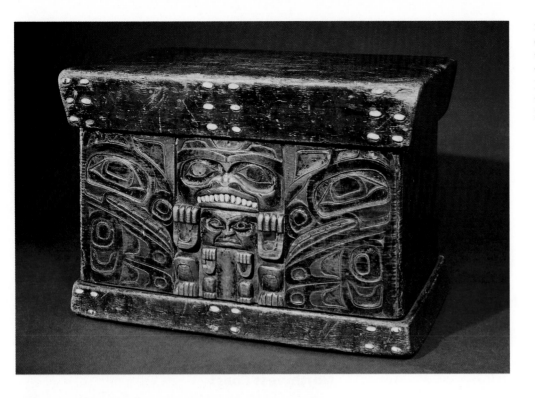

Studio Experience 17.3

A Personal Totem

Invent your own totem. Form clay around a newspaper-wrapped cardboard tube or milk carton. Symbolize your hobbies, interests and achievements, or those of your family.

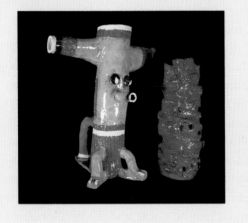

In addition to totem poles and chests, Northwest carvers decorated their canoes and houses, and made masks, rattles, charms, and wooden dishes. Like the chest and the totem pole, all of these have exuberant designs of stylized animals and humans.

Plains

Such tribes as the Crow, Sioux, Comanche, Cheyenne, and Arapahoe roamed the great plains, which stretch from the Mississippi to the Rockies. Of all the North American peoples, the Plains Indians are the most legendary. It was they who hunted buffalo, fought the white man, and defeated General Custer. Paradoxically, there was no Plains culture before the arrival of the Europeans, who brought with them the horse and rifle. Without these, American Indians were unable to hunt buffalo efficiently. Once horses and rifles became available, the buffalo became their source of food, clothing, and shelter. They ate its flesh, and they fashioned shirts, leggings, robes, shields, thongs, and cone-shaped tents called tepees from its hide.

Buffalo hides were even the source of Plains art. Buffalo-skin robes, tepees, and tepee linings were painted with geometric designs. Leather shirts were decorated with feathers, beads, thongs, and hair. The shirt worn by a Plains Indian chief discussed in Chapter 1 (fig. 1–3) is an example. (However, that shirt was made from deer hide rather than buffalo hide.) Plains Indians assembled headgear out of pelts and feathers. They made necklaces out of beads, bones, claws, or horns, and vests out of fur and leather thongs. Add face painting to all of this, and the resulting costume is truly a mixed media work of art. The artist George Catlin visited some forty-eight tribes and persuaded warriors and chiefs to sit for portraits (fig. 17–28). His pictures provide us with a priceless record of this now-extinct Plains art.

Conclusion

As you have seen, non-Western cultures represent an incredible variety of geography, peoples, history, beliefs, and art. Why is it important to study non-Western art?

One reason is that it has influenced our own art and daily life. Chinese porcelain, Japanese woodcuts, Islamic arabesques, and African sculpture have enriched our lives as well as theirs. Non-Western art can continue to be a source of inspiration. Studying the works of others helps us to see our own culture from a different perspective. Finally, and perhaps most importantly, understanding the cultural products of other people helps us to understand the people themselves. By seeing the world through their eyes, we learn to accept other people and other points of view. All of which emphasizes that we belong to one race—the human race—riding through time on a single spaceship called Earth.

17–28 Although George Catlin, who painted this portrait, was not himself a Native American, his painting allows us to see for ourselves the decorated clothing and striking face paint of the Plains Indians. George Catlin, *The White Cloud, Head Chief of the Iowas,* 1844–45. Canvas, 28″ x 22 7/8″ (71 x 58 cm). ©National Gallery of Art, Washington, Paul Mellon Collection.

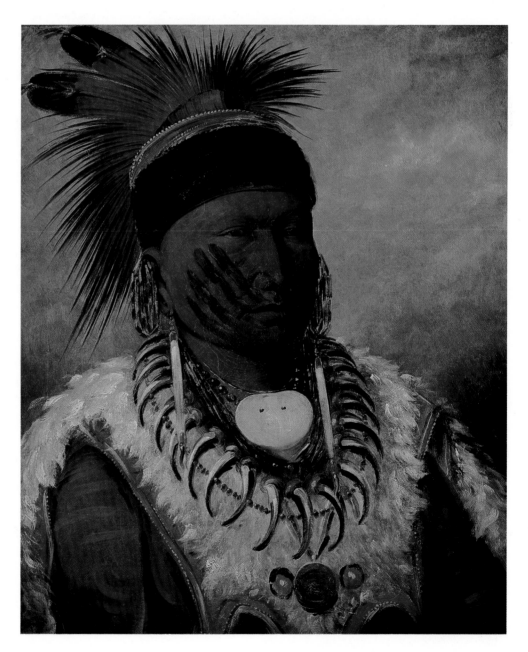

Chapter 18
Islands of Time I

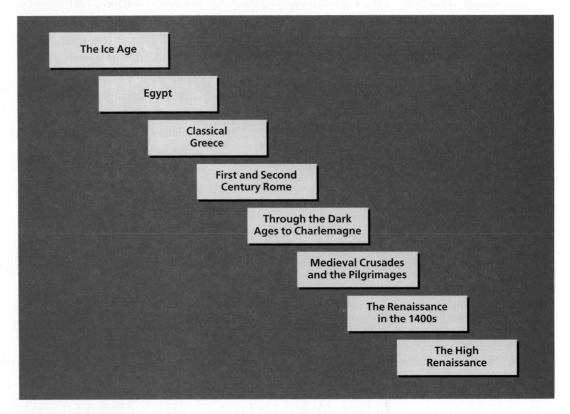

The Ice Age

Egypt

Classical Greece

First and Second Century Rome

Through the Dark Ages to Charlemagne

Medieval Crusades and the Pilgrimages

The Renaissance in the 1400s

The High Renaissance

Overview

Chapter Objectives

Students should be able to:

1 demonstrate knowledge of the art of the eight periods reviewed in this chapter **EE 3**

2 identify by subject matter or style the art of at least three of those periods **EE 3**

3 see connections between the art of the ancient civilizations, particularly that of Greece and Rome, and later developments in Europe **EE 3**

4 prepare a report about the connections between the art of the Renaissance and the changing social and intellectual values of the period **EE 3, W 4**

5 produce a painting using the Renaissance principles of chiaroscuro, linear perspective, and aerial perspective **EE 2, 3**

Rationale

Chapters 16 and 17 covered non-Western cultures to give students a multicultural perspective. In Chapters 18 and 19, students learn more about the Western heritage. The art of today, much as it may seem to be a repudiation of traditional styles, is very much a product of Western art history. Many students from non-Western cultures are learning about Western art (and may know more about the Western heritage than most American students).

Essential Concepts

• Egyptian art and architecture were related to the concept of immortality. This art followed strict rules and changed little over 3,000 years.

• Greek civilization, unlike the Egyptian, evolved and changed its forms.

• The great era of Greek culture, known as the Classical Period, lasted from about 480 BC to 323 BC In addition to the creation of idealized and humanistic figure sculptures, this period saw the rebuilding of the Acropolis and the Parthenon.

• The Romans copied Greek statues and imitated Greek styles in their sculptures and paintings. However, the Romans were very original in their architectural forms and used stone and concrete to construct arches.

• The Gothic style of architecture, which emerged in the late 1100s, employed the pointed arch, ribbed vaulting, and flying buttresses. Producing a great deal of space per pound of material, the Gothic system allowed for large windows, which were filled with stained glass.

• Florentine architects looked to Roman ruins for their models and Florentine sculptors looked to Roman sculpture. Florentine painters were the first to develop a true theory of linear perspective.

• Art flowered during the High Renaissance (c. 1495–1520). Leonardo da Vinci, Michelangelo, and Raphael were the most famous artists of that period.

Vocabulary

classical	aqueduct
Middle Ages	Gothic
humanism	round arch
medieval	Renaissance
idealism	barrel vault
pointed vault	High Renaissance
Doric	cross vault
ribbed vault	forum
arcade	flying buttress

Lesson Plans

18.1 Renaissance Influences

Page **T 264**   Time: Variable

18.2 A Renaissance-Style Landscape

Page **T 266**   Time: 2 periods

Handouts

Notes

Guidelines for a Renaissance Art History Report

Page **T 268**

Study Questions

Page **T 269**

Test Questions

Page **T 272**

Chapter Closure
Evaluation

1 *Production:* Can students successfully synthesize in a painting the illusion of light, space, movement, and depth?

2 *Art history/Criticism:* Are students able to prepare a report on how the works of Renaissance artists reflected the intellectual, cultural, and social developments of their time? R 4 W 2

3 *Art history:* Are students able to demonstrate knowledge of at least four periods reviewed in this chapter?

4 *Art history:* Are students able to characterize some of the changes that took place in European culture during the Renaissance?

5 *Art history:* Can students cite at least two similarities and connections between the art and architecture of the classical civilizations and that of the Renaissance? R 3

6 *Art history:* Are students beginning to appreciate that art can be a major source of information about past cultures and periods of time?

7 *Art history/Aesthetic awareness:* Are students able to recognize typical examples of art of at least three periods reviewed in this chapter?

8 *Aesthetic awareness:* Are students voluntarily seeking to know more about the art of any of the periods of Western history?

Renaissance Influences

Time: Variable

Preparation

Rationale

The Renaissance in Italy was a revival of cultural awareness and learning that emphasized human beings and their environment, science, and philosophy. Renaissance scholars revived interest in ancient Greece and Rome. Renaissance art was an outgrowth of the new humanism that replaced medieval religious authority. Students will develop a better understanding of Renaissance art if they also understand the context in which it developed.

Research Materials

Guidelines for a Renaissance Art History Report (Handout)

Enrichment Materials

Slides:

• Brunelleschi, Dome of Florence Cathedral, 89

• Masaccio, *The Tribute Money,* 90

• Raphael, *The School of Athens,* 91

• da Vinci, *The Last Supper,* 92

• Michelangelo, *Moses, Creation of the Sun and the Moon, Dome of St Peter's,* 93, 95, 96

Teach the Lesson

Objectives

Students should be able to:

1 prepare a report on how the artwork of the Italian Renaissance reflects the religion, science, teachings, philosophy, politics, and discoveries of the period   EE 3

Warm Up

Ask students what they know about the Renaissance. Have they heard of Leonardo da Vinci or Michelangelo? Direct attention to Student Edition pages 266–273, which deal with the Renaissance. Divide the class into three groups. Assign three of the nine study questions (26–34) to each group. Have the groups share their answers with the class.

Explore and Develop

1 Display and discuss examples of Renaissance artwork.

2 Explain the research assignment and   R 3
provide copies of the guidelines. Ask students to find out what important events took place during the period 1400 to 1520 that might have influenced Renaissance artwork. Perhaps the world history or humanities teacher will visit your class or provide information about Renaissance science, exploration, music, and literature. The following are some examples.

• Columbus discovered America.

• Magellan found a passage from the Atlantic to the Pacific (Straits of Magellan).

• Machiavelli wrote a first theory of politics and advocated republican government.

• Erasmus, a Catholic priest and teacher, was one of the greatest humanists.

• Copernicus founded a system on which modern astronomy is based.

3 List the major artists of the period: Brunelleschi, Masaccio, Donatello, Titian, da Vinci, Raphael, Michelangelo, Bramante, Tintoretto, Correggio.

4 In addition to library resources, students may seek help from teachers in other subject areas. Have students share finished reports.

Laser Discs:

daVinci, Ginevra de'Benci, c 1480

Search Frame 168

daVinci, detail

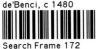

Search Frame 170

daVinci, Reverse of Ginevra de'Benci, c 1480

Search Frame 172

daVinci, segment

Search 7343, Play To 8873

Angelico, The Healing of Saint Cosmas, c 1438-1443

Search Frame 118

Bacchiacca, The Flagellation of Christ, c 1500/1550

Search Frame 244

Evaluate and Reflect

1 Can students relate Renaissance art to the culture and events of the period?

2 Ask students to describe the Italian Renaissance and the concept of "Renaissance Man."

3 What were some developments in painting that affected art long after the Renaissance?

4 Ask students to list what they feel are some of the greatest cultural and artistic accomplishments of the Italian Renaissance.

Reteach

Have students look for structures in the community that reflect the influence of classical Greek and Roman, and Italian architecture. Tell them to pay particular attention to domes, columns and capitals, arches, entry ways, pediments, porches, windows and lintels, entablatures, and roof styles. Have them look for Gothic influences too.

Show the film *The Renaissance.* Encyclopaedia Britannica Films. 26 min., color. Rental: Encyclopaedia Britannica Films.

Extend the Lesson

Beyond the Basics

(See lesson 18–2 which is an extension, as well as a synthesis experience.)

EE 3 During the Renaissance many ideas from the Greek Culture were rediscovered. Renaissance artists were concerned about **R 3** creating realistic images in paintings and sculpture and studied the human form extensively. Proportion and scale were of great importance to Renaissance artists and to the Greeks. Direct students' attention to the Greek architecture shown in this chapter. Designs were created based on mathematical concepts regarding proportion. Have students research the golden mean as expressed philosophically by Aristotle and its mathematical counterpart known as the golden section. What is the formula and how was it used in Greek architecture? Was this concept known to Renaissance artists?

Cultural Connections

Have students identify other parts of **EE 3** Europe that were affected by Renaissance ideas—Flanders, Germany, England, France, Spain. Who were some of the major **R 4** artists during that period of time in those countries? Have students brainstorm different ways that Renaissance ideas may have been spread throughout Europe. Have interested students research to find out.

Direct students' attention to figure 18–14 **EE 1, 3** on page 252. Suggest students interested in sports look for examples of artwork from various cultures showing people as athletes and game players. Greek vase paintings often depict athletic events. Dancing figures can also be found in the art from most cultures and throughout history.

Connecting with Other Subjects

Music Ask the music teacher, or university music department, to provide examples of Italian Renaissance music. Perhaps information about composers can also be provided.

All Subjects Suggest students work to- **EE 3** gether to create a multidisciplinary display about the Renaissance. If possible use a showcase in a main hallway of the school. **R 3** Display examples of Renaissance art, maps, timelines, written information explaining major concepts, magazine photos, Leonardo da Vinci's inventions and writings, illustrations showing how people dressed, architecture, literature, etc. Include a continuous play tape recording of Renaissance music. Use the lowest volume setting so music is heard only when standing close to the showcase. What other items might students include in the display?

A Renaissance-Style Landscape

Islands of Time I

Time: 2 periods

Preparation

Rationale

Renaissance artists made a lasting contribution to all two-dimensional forms of art through their experiments with controlled light and shadow, implied movement, atmospheric effects, and one- and two-point linear perspective. In this lesson, students create the appearance of depth in a painting, using the various techniques of Renaissance artists. Students have explored these techniques in previous studio experiences.

Studio Materials

pencils, 12" x 18" white all-purpose paper, assorted brushes, mixing trays, water containers, paper towels (Other media is optional.)

Enrichment Materials

Slides:
• Masaccio, *The Tribute Money,* 90
• Raphael, *The School of Athens,* 91
• da Vinci, *The Last Supper,* 92

Teach the Lesson

Objectives

Students should be able to:

1 paint an outdoor scene using aerial and linear perspective and creating three-dimensional forms through bold light and shadow due to a controlled light source   **EE 2**

2 describe what they did to suggest depth, analyze the organization of their pictures, and interpret the mood of the paintings   **EE 4**

Vocabulary

Aerial perspective is the diminishing of color intensities to lighter and duller hues to give the illusion of space.

Chiaroscuro is a technique for modeling forms in painting that makes lighted parts seem to advance from darker areas. It is the use of strong light and shadow.

Warm Up

Display paintings by Masaccio, da Vinci, and Raphael. Ask students to identify the strategies used in the paintings to give the illusion of spatial depth. Ask what was done to make the figures appear three-dimensional. Have them identify the direction that light comes from.

Explore and Develop

1 Continue examining the Renaissance paintings. Have students explain how aerial perspective is achieved in a painting. Do they recall how linear perspective works?

2 Have them note how the artists used lighter, duller tones for objects and areas in the background of the paintings. Have them explain how the intensity of a color is reduced; how the value of a color is raised or lowered.

3 Do not overlook other depth devices: overlap, diminishing size, position in space.

Begin Studio Experience 18.2

1 Ask students to lay out a light line sketch of an outdoor scene that includes foreground, middle, and background areas. The picture should include a building in linear perspective; some animate form in the foreground; objects in the middle ground, such as a few trees; and background subject matter, such as hills and sky.

Laser Discs:

Raphael, The Alba Madonna, c 1510

Search Frame 214

Raphael, detail

Search Frame 216

Raphael, segment

Search 9093, Play To 10540

Lotto, A Maiden's Dream, c 1505

Search Frame 321

Lotto, Allegory, 1505

Search Frame 317

Conegliano, Saint Helena, c 1495

Search Frame 313

2 Ask them to concentrate on using all of the strategies they have read about and experimented with to imply spatial depth and three-dimensional forms in their paintings. You may wish to list the devices on the chalkboard: aerial perspective, linear perspective, value contrasts, intensity variations, dark and light modeling of figures, high/low placement, diminishing size, and overlapping.

Evaluate and Reflect

1 Do students feel they were successful in using the Renaissance strategies to suggest space and three-dimensional forms in their paintings?

2 Can students describe the different strategies for implying depth that are evident in the paintings?

3 Analyze the compositions. Do the different strategies suggest depth and three-dimensionality effectively? How do they contribute to the unity of the painting? Is movement implied in the painting because of the perspective devices used? Where is the dominant area in the painting? Why is it dominant? Is direction of light consistent in the painting? Are there strong and subtle contrasts? How are they used? Does the composition seem stable or chaotic? Why?

4 Interpret the mood of the painting. What effects do the color variations have? How can the space be interpreted?

Reteach

Have students locate pictures in which they can identify examples of the strategies used to imply spatial depth and three-dimensional forms.

Ask them to do an outline drawing from one of the pictures. Have them use pencil or pen and ink to deal with everything but aerial perspective, which can be added with watercolor washes.

Extend the Lesson

Beyond the Basics

Have students look for contemporary artworks that include the space and depth devices developed by Renaissance artists, and contemporary works that do not use those devices. Compare and discuss.

EE 2, 3

Suggest students study the paintings of Raphael. His shading techniques create the illusion of volume and deep space. Raphael improved his painting techniques by studying the works of Michelangelo and da Vinci. Examine the works of all three artists and identify elements that are similar. Have students analyze their own painting to determine how it could be improved. Suggest they try using shading techniques they observed in the work of Raphael.

EE 2, 3

Cultural Connections

Michelangelo and Greek architects exhibited a common concern over the effects of optical illusions that occur when a viewer looks at something as monumental in size as the Sistine Chapel ceiling paintings and the Greek architectural forms. Greek architects knew that very long lines would appear to bow and that the tops of very tall columns would appear to diminish in size. The forms they built were slightly distorted to compensate for the effects of optical illusion. Michelangelo made the same kinds of adjustments in his paintings to counteract the effects of viewing the ceiling from the floor below. Suggest students research to find other interesting facts connecting the concerns of Renaissance artists and the Greek culture.

EE 3

R 4

Connecting with Other Subjects

Language Arts The ideas of Charlemagne in the 9th century seem somewhat out of place in time. Ask students why it might be appropriate to call Charlemagne a "renaissance man." Suggest interested students research this period in history and the Empire of Charlemagne.

R 3, 5

Islands of Time I

Guidelines for a Renaissance Art History Report

Use these guidelines to gather information on how the work of major artists reflected or was affected by the social organization of a specific period. Discuss the impact of great scholars, religion, inventions, science, philosophy, exploration and discoveries, politics, and major events on the arts. Use only those items for which you can find information. In addition to library resources, you may wish to consult with teachers of world history, humanities, literature, music, and dramatic arts.

1 State the period of art you are working with.

a. dates of the period
b. country
c. major artists of the period

2 How does the art reflect the religion of the period and the political power structure?

a. Who or what was controlling power vested in?
b. Was there political support, censorship, or neglect of art?

3 Was the primary philosophy of the period supportive of art? Was it reflected in art-works?

4 Who were the primary scholars and writers of the period? Did they affect the art forms of the period?

5 What explorations and discoveries occurred during this period?

6 Were there significant inventions and advancements in scientific research during this period?

7 Include other major events (war, invasion, religious reform).

8 What do you feel was one of the most significant achievements in the visual arts during this period? Did the achievement influence art in following periods? How, and for how long?

Study Questions
Chapter 18–Islands of Time I

1 What media did the Ice Age people probably use to paint animal images on the walls of caves? State at least two of the characteristics of the animal pictures.

_____

_____

2 What do scientists speculate was the purpose of the cave paintings?

_____

3 Why do we know so much about the ancient Egyptians?

_____

_____

4 Why were ancient Egyptians able to develop such a complex society?

_____

_____

5 What are two main features of the Egyptian religion?

_____

6 Name at least four items that an important man might have buried with him in his mastaba.

_____

_____

7 Describe at least two characteristics of Egyptian art.

_____

8 Why didn't the Egyptian art style change for thousands of years?

_____

9 Compare the main difference in style between Egyptian and Classical Greek sculpture.

_____

10 Classical Greek philosophy emphasized *humanism* and *idealism*. Define those two terms.

_____

_____

11 What are two features of Classical Greek sculpture that have affected the art of portraying the human figure since that time?

_____

_____

12 Name three architectural features of the Parthenon (text fig. 18–16).

_____

_____

13 Give three examples of Greek influence on Roman art and architecture.

_____

_____

14 In which of the visual arts were the Romans most original?

_____

15 What two Roman technologies did most buildings employ?

_____

16 Illustrate the post-and-lintel, arch, barrel vault, and cross vault. (Use a separate sheet of paper.)

17 What is the "key" stone?

_____

18 Describe the architecture of the Colosseum (text fig. 18–27) and the Pantheon (fig. 18–28).

_____

_____

19 What was the principal kind of artwork produced for people living during the first 400 years of the medieval era?

_____

20 Who was responsible for bringing artists to his court in an attempt to end the Dark Ages?

_____

21 What was the major difference in point of view between the Greeks and Romans and the medieval Christians? How is this represented in their sculptural forms?

_____

_____

22 What three features did the Gothic style add to architecture?

_____

_____

23 Which was the first major church structure to employ entirely Gothic construction?

_____

24 How were Gothic cathedral interiors enhanced?

_____

25 State two ways in which a Gothic cathedral expresses the "Age of Faith."

_____

26 What does the term Renaissance mean?

_____

_____

27 Give one example of the "rebirth" of classical styles in Renaissance architecture.

_____

28 Name three ways that Donatello's _St. Mark_ resembles Greek sculpture. What is the main difference?

_____

_____

29 Why was Leonardo da Vinci considered a "Renaissance Person"?

_____

30 Identify one reason why da Vinci's painting _The Last Supper_ is considered such a great painting.

_____

31 Explain why Raphael's fresco _School of Athens_ (text fig. 18–47) is considered one of the best examples of Italian High Renaissance painting.

_____

32 In what three artistic areas did Michelangelo excel? Give one example of each.

_____

_____

33 Select one of Michelangelo's artworks, describe it, and explain why it is representative of the High Renaissance. (Use a separate sheet of paper.)

34 Even though the High Renaissance ended in the mid-1500s, how long did its basic ideals dominate Western art?

_____

_____

_____

Name: _____   Course: _____

Test Questions
Chapter 18–Islands of Time I

For questions 1 through 10, which refer to reasons and motivations for creating, select from the following periods of Western art.

1. The Ice Age	5. Medieval
2. Egyptian	6. Gothic
3. Greek	7. Renaissance
4. Roman	

1 _____ Animal paintings possibly created for magical purposes.

2 _____ Referred to as "The Age of Faith" (two answers).

3 _____ Created a set of proportions for the ideal human figure.

4 _____ Painted images and sculptures were made to accompany rulers, priests, noblemen, in their life after death.

5 _____ Focused on humans and the natural world (three answers).

6 _____ Polytheistic religion, belief in immortality, large tomb architecture.

7 _____ Part of this period is referred to as "The Dark Ages."

8 _____ Meaning "rebirth."

9 _____ Focused on God and the divine world (two answers).

10 _____ The beginning of European scientific investigation.

For questions 11 through 21, which refer to significant artworks, terms, styles, and artists, select from the following periods of Western art.

1. The Ice Age	3. Greek
2. Egyptian	4. Roman

11 _____ Parthenon.

12 _____ Caves in Altamira; Spain, and Lascaux, France.

13 _____ Representation of the human form follows a strict formula: head, legs, feet are shown from the side; one eye and shoulders are shown frontally.

14 _____ Colosseum.

15 _____ Pyramids, mastabas.

16 _____ Hieroglyphs.

17 _____ "Weight shift" posture.

18 _____ Aqueducts.

19 _____ Ideal proportions in sculpture and architecture.

20 _____ Solid concrete dome covering the Pantheon.

21 _____ Myron's sculpture of Athena.

For questions 22 through 29, which refer to significant artworks, terms, styles, and artists, select from the following periods of Western art.

     1. Early medieval   3. Renaissance
     2. Gothic   4. High Renaissance

22 _____ Pointed arches, ribbed vaulting, flying buttresses.

23 _____ Michelangelo's Sistine Chapel Ceiling.

24 _____ Cathedrals with intricately designed stained glass windows.

25 _____ The development of linear perspective.

26 _____ Elaborately decorated helmets, sword handles, cape fasteners.

27 _____ A peak development of European art.

28 _____ Very little painting, sculpture, or significant architecture produced.

29 _____ Brunelleschi's dome.

30 Classical Greek sculpture reflected the philosophy of the period, which emphasized

a. humanism and polytheism.
b. humanism and idealism.
c. God and the divine world.
d. idealism and religion.

31 The stone placed at the top of an arch is called the

a. corner stone.
b. top stone.
c. key stone.
d. none of the above.

32 The Egyptian art style didn't change for thousands of years because

a. of the close relationship between art and government.
b. art wasn't important to the Egyptian rulers, so change wasn't necessary.
c. of the Egyptian belief in immortality and in the rule that the human image had to be portrayed in a certain way.
d. a and c.
e. none of the above.

33 One idea that the Romans did *not* borrow from the Greeks was the

a. use of the arch principle to build non-religious structures such as aqueducts and stadiums.
b. method of portrait sculpture.
c. subject matter in their paintings.
d. post-and-lintel construction used in temples.

34 The person credited for attempting to bring cultural rebirth to Europe during the medieval period was

a. Napoleon.
b. Charlemagne.
c. Chartres.
d. St. Sernin.

35 A radial form of the arch is a

a. cross vault.
b. barrel vault.
c. dome.
d. arcade.

36 What was the main difference between Egyptian and Classical Greek sculpture?

37 In what three artistic areas did Michelangelo excel?

38 Why was Leonardo da Vinci considered to be a "Renaissance person"?

39 How long did some of the basic ideals of the sixteenth century High Renaissance dominate Western art?

While viewing the overhead transparency of *The School of Athens*, answer the following question.

40 Raphael used _____ perspective in this picture.

Study Answers
Chapter 18
Islands of Time I

1 Pigments (gypsum and iron oxide) from the ground, charcoal from campsites mixed with animal fat or blood serum. Answers may include: colorations, details, movement and forms of real beasts; chiaroscuro usage found in some cave paintings; only side views of animals shown.

2 Magical—painting an animal meant gaining power over that animal.

3 Many of their monuments still survive, and their written language was decoded in the early 1800s.

4 The fertile Nile River Valley produced a surplus of food so that all the people did not hunt or farm, allowing some to become engineers, teachers, priests, artists, laborers, etc.

5 Polytheism and belief in immortality.

6 His mummified body, earthly belongings, statues, and painted images of himself, of his wife and of his servants.

7 Answers may include: flat images shown only in profile, minimal overlapping, size of people dependent on importance, and little or no depth.

8 Because art played an important role in their belief in immortality, the human image had to be portrayed in a "correct" way.

9 Egyptians—static, Greek—natural actions.

10 Humanism—view of life based on nature, dignity, and interests of people; Idealism—concept of perfection.

11 "Weight shift" (i.e., one hip is higher than the other, upper body is bent so one shoulder is higher than the other) and "ideal proportions."

12 Answers may include: built on human scale, post-and-lintel construction, proportional relationships used throughout, use of Doric columns.

13 Roman sculptures resemble Greek sculptures; Roman paintings were based on Greek scenes; many Roman temples used the post-and-lintel system.

14 Secular (non-religious) architecture, e.g., the forum (commercial district and civic center), water-related structures (harbors, bridges, aqueducts, recreational structures (gymnasiums, public baths, race tracks, stadiums).

15 Arch principle of construction and the use of concrete.

16

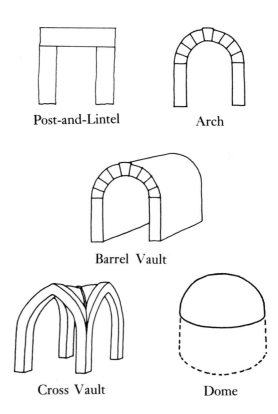

Post-and-Lintel   Arch

Barrel Vault

Cross Vault   Dome

17 The middle stone of an arch.

18 Answers may include: Colosseum—uses every variation of the arch system except the dome; has three levels of arcades, barrel-vaulted ramps, and cross-vaulted corridors; vaults support stadium seats; cells located beneath the arena; 620 feet long, 513 feet wide, 157 feet high. Pantheon—solid concrete dome (largest in world for thirteen centuries), massive Corinthian-columned porch.

19 Craft objects and ornaments for their weapons, their horses and themselves.

20 Charlemagne.

21 Greeks and Romans focused on humans and the natural world: medieval Christians focused on God and the divine world. Greek and Roman sculptures were naturalistic, three-dimensional; medieval sculptures were stylized, floating, lacking in three-dimensional appearance, with folds in clothing appearing decorative rather than natural.

22 The pointed arch, ribbed vaulting, and the flying buttress.

23 Chartres Cathedral.

24 With pointed arches, vaulted ceilings, and elaborate stained glass windows.

25 Answers may include: Architecture symbolizes soaring toward heaven; abstract and symbolic patterns and stylized figures of Christ and the saints represent the spiritual world rather than the earthly world.

26 Rebirth.

27 Answers may include: Brunelleschi's Pazzi Chapel or the dome of the Florence Cathedral.

28 Greek characteristics include: human proportions, weight-shift posture, natural relationship between clothing and body underneath. Greek sculptures have an idealistic calm; St. Mark's face expresses passion and seriousness.

29 He was capable in many fields: painting, architecture, engineering, physics, biology.

30 It is recognized as the first painting to successfully integrate active figures in a realistic spatial world.

31 It incorporates classical Greek elements—Greek philosophers, idealized bodies, and graceful gestures—in a Renaissance setting.

32 Painting: ceiling of the Sistine Chapel. Sculpture: *The Pietà, Moses.* Architecture: the west end of St. Peter's Basilica.

33 Answers will vary.

34 Until the later part of the nineteenth century.

Test Answers
Chapter 18
Islands of Time I

1 1.

2 5, 6.

3 3.

4 2.

5 3, 4, 7.

6 2.

7 5.

8 7.

9 5, 6.

10 7.

11 3.

12 1.

13 2.

14 4.

15 2.

16 2.

17 3.

18 4.

19 3.

20 4.

21 3.

22 2.

23 4.

24 2.

25 3.

26 1.

27 4.

28 1.

29 3.

30 B.

31 C.

32 D.

33 A.

34 B.

35 C.

36 Egyptians—static; Greek—natural actions.

37 Painting, sculpture, and architecture.

38 Excelled in so many things; he was a painter, sculptor, architect, engineer, scientist, inventor.

39 Until the later part of the nineteenth century.

40 One-point.

Chapter 18
Islands of Time I

The history of Western art begins with the earliest of cultures and ends with the present. This is such a big subject that only a few periods, or *islands of time,* will be reviewed. This chapter will review islands of time from the prehistoric era (12,000 BC) to the High Renaissance (1500s AD). Chapter 19 will survey the history of art from the 1600s to the present.

The discovery of the world's oldest painting marks our first island in time. In 1897 in northern Spain, Marcelino de Sautuola, an amateur archeologist, took his five-year-old daughter with him to explore a cave near their home. Because the cave was so full of rubbish accumulated over thousands of years, the ceiling was low, and the father had to stoop. His daughter, who did not have to stoop, was delightfully surprised to see pictures of animals on the ceiling. Sautuola was also surprised, for he believed they were, in fact, a very ancient art. But when he announced this amazing find to scientists, he was met with disbelief.

Later, other cave paintings were discovered in northern Spain and southern France. Some were partially covered by calcium deposits that scientists knew were thousands of years old. Eventually everyone realized that these paintings were the world's oldest known art. They probably had been made by people who lived at the end of the last glacial age.

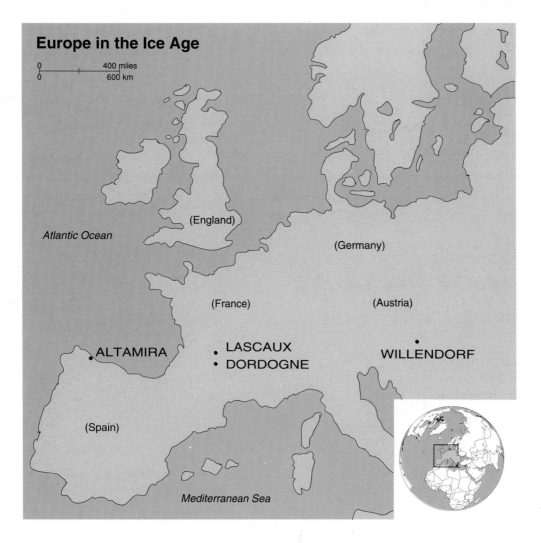

Europe in the Ice Age

0 — 400 miles
0 — 600 km

(England)

Atlantic Ocean

(Germany)

(France)

(Austria)

• ALTAMIRA   • LASCAUX   • WILLENDORF
             • DORDOGNE

(Spain)

Mediterranean Sea

18–2 Europe during the Ice Age.

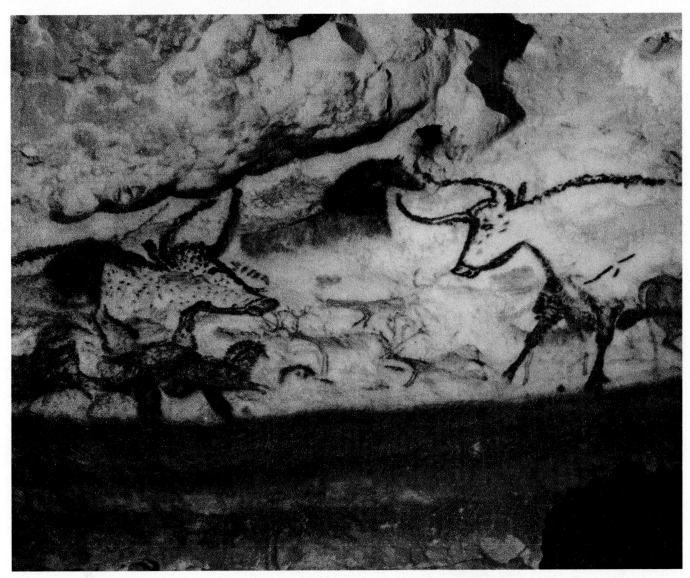

18–1 *Hall of Bulls*, left wall, Lascaux, ca. 15,000–13,000 BC. Dordogne, France. Courtesy of Scala/Art Resource, NY.

The Ice Age

What kind of place was Europe during the Ice Age (fig. 18–2)? England was still covered with ice. The rest of the continent was as cold as Siberia and forest-covered. Bison, wild horses, reindeer, elk, and wild goats, in addition to now-extinct beasts like woolly rhinos and woolly elephants, roamed the land. Europe was also populated with a race of people. These people hunted the animals, using spears made of shafts of wood tipped with animal bone, and knives made of chips of flint. Animals were a source not only of meat, but of hides for clothes and shelter, of bones, horns, and tusks for tools, and perhaps even of tails for paintbrushes.

These Ice Age people sculpted in clay, wood, bone, ivory, and stone. (Recall the little stone Venus of Willendorf, fig. 13–5.) However, they are best known for their animal paintings on the walls of limestone caves (fig. 18–1). They probably obtained pigments, such as gypsum (white) and iron oxide (brownish reds and yellows), from the ground and charcoal (black) from campsites. Then they mixed the pigments with animal fat or blood serum, and applied the mixture to the walls with animal tails or sticks frayed at one end.

Given their crude technology, along with the poor working conditions of a cave, it is a wonder that these hunter-artists were able to produce any art, let alone such vivid images. Ice Age animal pictures capture not only the forms of real beasts, but also their colorations,

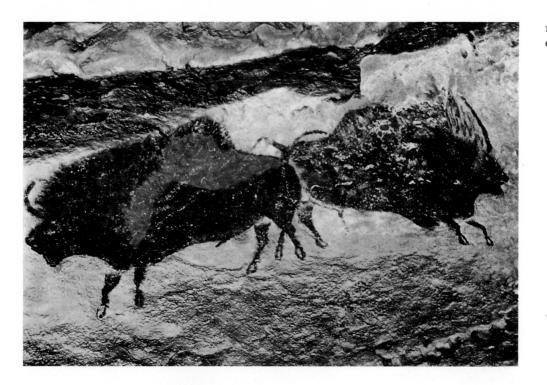

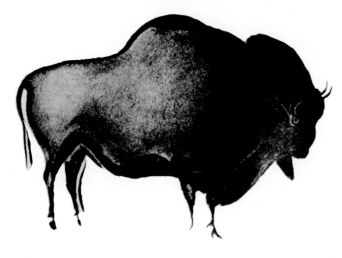

18–4 *Standing Buffalo*, ca. 12,000 BC. Cave painting. Font-du-Gaume, France.

their details, and even their movements (fig. 18–3). In some caves, shading was used to suggest an animal's roundness (fig. 18–4). Thus, Ice Age art reached a level of quality close to that of modern cultures.

However, Ice Age art does have its limitations. Animals are shown in side view only. Little, if any, foreshortening was used to suggest an angle view of an animal. Rarely are two or more animals shown together in any purposeful way. An animal was painted on a wall regardless of the locations of other images on that same wall. Some animals are overlapped without any apparent reason. Apparently hunter-artists were not interested in organizing these images into a unified composition. Furthermore, they did not seem interested in depicting other subjects: trees, plants, ponds, rocks, even people.

What was the purpose of these paintings, many of which are located in cramped, inaccessible places? Scientists speculate that the purpose was magical. Painting an animal was equated with gaining power over that animal. The caves may have been temple-sanctuaries. Hunter-artists gathered there to paint animals and magically ensure their success in the hunt. But no one knows for sure.

Egypt

Much more is known about the art and beliefs of the ancient Egyptians. Many of their monuments are still standing (fig. 18–5). Their written language, a form of picture writing called *hieroglyphic* (fig. 18–6), was decoded by members of Napoleon's army in 1799.

By 2500 BC, Egypt had been a civilization for nearly 1000 years. Just as India's civilization began along the banks of the Indus (Chapter 16), Egypt's developed along the banks of the Nile (fig. 18–7). Nile farms became so successful that Egyptians were able to produce a surplus of food. People were freed to do other things besides farming or hunting. They gathered in large settlements that turned into cities. This development called for new jobs such as mayor, priest, judge, engineer, teacher, laborer, and, of course, artist.

Object Depicted	Egyptian vulture	Flowering reed	Flowering reeds	Forearm	Stool	Quail or chick	Foot	Horned viper	Owl	Water	Mouth	Reed sheltering field
Sign												
Translation	A	I	Y	A	P	W	B	F	M	N	R	H
Sound	A as in FAT	Y	Y as in Hebrew YODH	AH as in FATHER (guttural)	P	W	B	F	M	N	R	H as in ENGLISH

Object Depicted	Wick of twisted flax	Placenta	Animal's belly with teats	Bolt folded cloth	Pool	Hillslope	Basket with handle	Stand for jar	Loaf	Tethering rope	Hand	Snake
Sign												
Translation	H	CH	CH	S	SH	Q	K	G	T	CH	D	J
Sound	Emphatic H	CH as in Scottish LOCH	CH as in German ICH	S	SH	Q as in QUEEN	K	Hard G	T	CH as in CHEST	D	Emphatic S

18–6 Hieroglyphic writing with ink on papyrus, ca. 1025 BC. Courtesy of the Egyptian Tourist Authority.

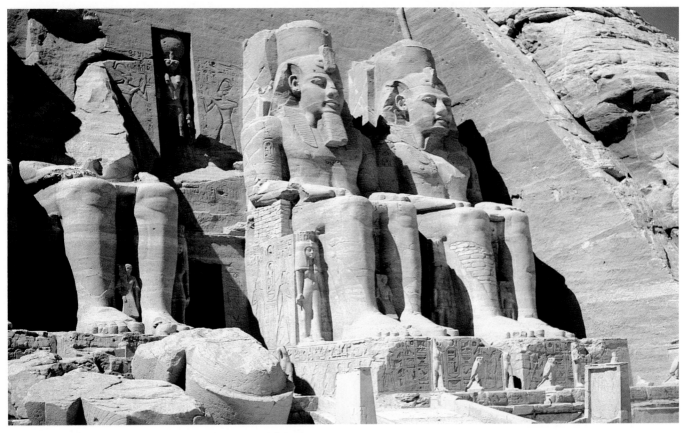

18–5 South Temple, Ramses II. Abu Simbel. Courtesy of Art Resource, NY.

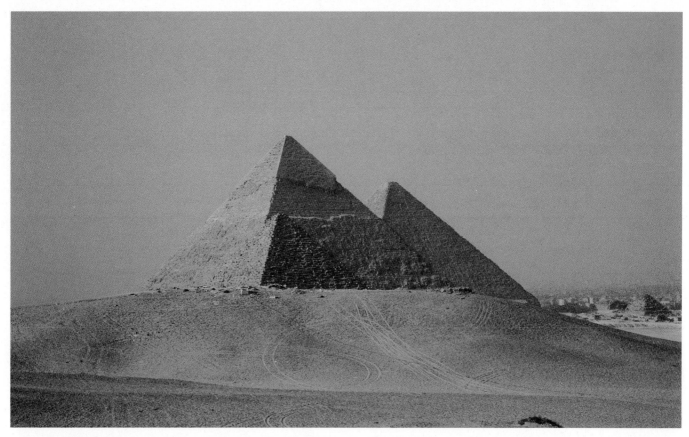

18-8 Pyramids of Gaza, Egypt. Courtesy of Goodfriend/Art Resource, NY.

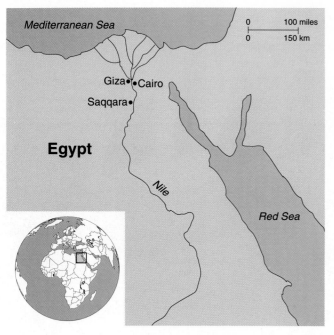

18-7 Ancient Egypt.

Egypt's civilization was very organized with high levels of mathematics, engineering, and construction skills. These skills are evident in the scale of its surviving architecture and sculptures (figures 18–5 and 18–8).

The Egyptian religion was polytheistic. Egyptians also believed in *immortality,* or life after death, especially for such people as the pharaoh (king), priests, and noblemen. Egyptians took great care to make sure that the soul of an important man would live forever. The man's body was embalmed and mummified. He was buried in a solid tomb with all his earthly belongings and statues. (For an example, see the statue of Mycerinus and his queen, fig. 13–6.) Also included were painted images of the deceased, his wife, servants, maids, laborers, and even animals. It was believed that these images participated magically in his eternal happiness. The most impressive tombs are the pyramids for the pharaohs Khufu, Khafre, and Menkaure at Gizeh (fig. 18–8). But most of Egypt's surviving art is found in *mastabas* (fig. 18–9). Mastabas were relatively modest tombs for people below the rank of pharaoh.

In the mastaba of Nebamun (fig. 18–10) is a mural that was discussed briefly in Chapter 15. Nebamun, a nobleman from Thebes, is wearing the hairstyle, necklace, and kilt that signify his rank. He is also shown hunting on the River Nile. Because Egypt was a rich agricultural society, men like Nebamun hunted for pleasure not for survival. During his earthly life, he often went down to the river, at times accompanied by his wife (shown behind him) and his daughter or a maidservant (shown kneeling beneath him).

While Nebamun would catch birds, the women gathered lotuses. Papyrus plants, seen in front of the boat, grew abundantly along the banks of the Nile. These plants may have been harvested by Nebamun's workers and sold on the market to be used for writing material (paper was invented much later by the Chinese: chapter 16). Wildcats may have lurked among the papyrus stalks to challenge Nebamun in the hunt. Or, since Egyptians had domesticated cats, this one may have been trained by Nebamun to help in the hunt.

The Egyptians, as we saw, believed in immortality. They also believed that pictures played a magical role in the afterlife. Whatever was in a picture was believed to exist in the afterlife. Accordingly, this mural guaranteed that Nebamun would enjoy hunting with his family (and his cat) for eternity.

So, why is Egyptian art so flat, especially with regard to depictions of people? One reason had to do with the magical role of art. The figure of the nobleman, for example, follows a strict formula: his head, legs, and feet are shown from the side while one eye and his shoulders are shown frontally. This style was intended to convey the main features of the human body as clearly as possible. Over time, it became the "correct" way to show important people. To depart from this formula would have done magical harm to the soul of the dead man. The figures of the women also reflect this formula, but theirs show more variety. They are also much smaller. Is this because they were such small people in real life? No, it is because they were less important. Also, because they were less important, the artist was allowed some leeway in giving their bodies more variety of pose and movement.

Egyptian society, like Egyptian art, was very conservative. All of its cultural forms changed little over thousands of years. Egyptian art was almost as eternal in fact as it was in intent.

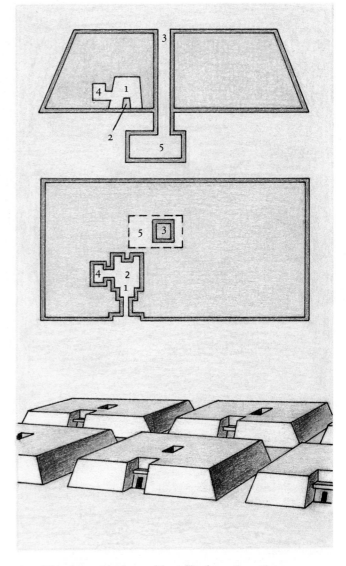

18-9 Mastabas, with plan and (at top) schematic section.

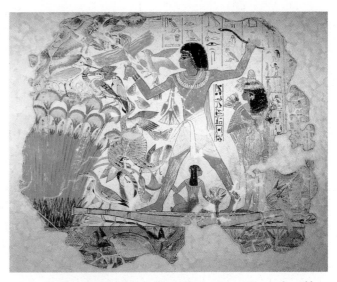

18-10 *Fowling the Marshes*, wall painting, ca. 1400. Reproduced by Courtesy of the Trustees of the British Museum.

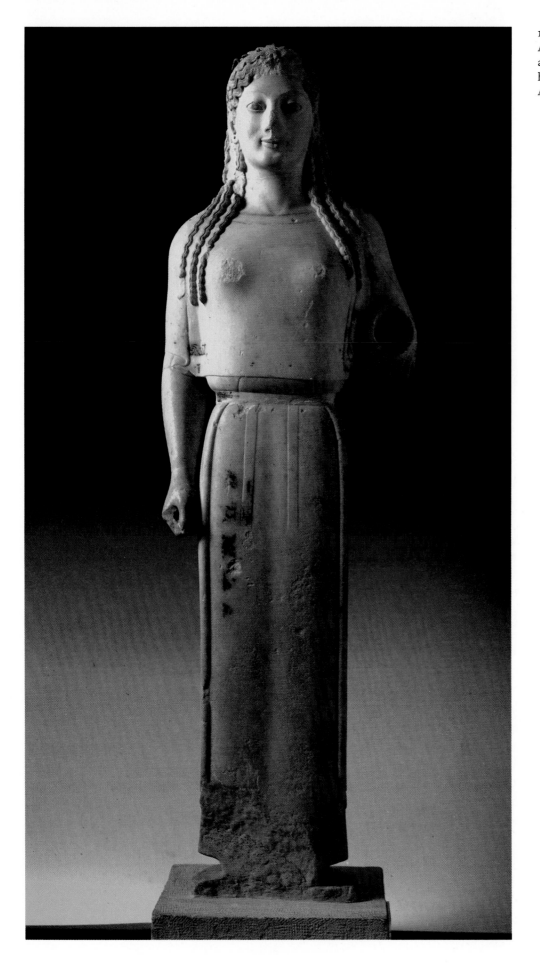

18–11 *Peplos Kore*, Acropolis, Athens, ca. 530 BC. Marble, approximately 48″ (122 cm) high. Acropolis Museum, Athens.

Classical Greece

Unlike Egyptian civilization and art, Greek civilization changed over time. Look at two statues separated by less than one hundred years. The sculpture of the young maiden sculpted in 530 BC (fig. 18–11) is simple and stiff. It contrasts vividly with the naturalness of the goddess Athena, a Roman copy of a statue sculpted by Myron in 450 BC (fig. 18–12).

The great era of Greek culture, known as the Classical Period, lasted from about 480 to 323 BC. Around 450 BC (the year of the *Athena* statue), the citizens of Athens began rebuilding a fortified hill called the *Acropolis* (fig. 18–15) and the temple of Athena called the *Parthenon* (fig. 18–16). Both had been destroyed by the Persians. This was not only the time of Myron, but also of philosophers Protagoras and Socrates; Sophocles and Euripides, the writers of famous Greek tragedies; and Pericles, the leader of Athens. Athens became the center of art and culture in the Greek world.

Myron's statue, like all Greek sculpture of this time, expresses two principles: humanism and idealism. **Humanism** is defined as a view of life based on the nature, dignity, and interests of people. Other societies in the ancient world, like Egypt and pre-Islamic Persia, were dominated by superstition. However, the Greeks were beginning to investigate the workings of the world and to question old ways of thinking. They believed the investigation should begin with humans. As Protagoras stated, "Man is the measure of all things."

The realism of Myron's statue reflects this humanistic tendency. In contrast to the puppetlike maiden of 530 BC, the *Athena* has the form and posture of a real woman. Her gown, which gathers at the waist and hangs in natural-looking folds, suggests the presence of a real body underneath. Her weight is placed more on her right foot than on her left. This causes a subtle movement throughout the body. The right hip is higher than the left. The upper body is bent so that the left shoulder is higher than the right (fig. 18–13). This movement, sometimes called "weight shift," was a real breakthrough in the art of representing the human figure.

The statue by Myron also reflects an idealistic tendency. **Idealism** has to do with a concept of perfection. *Athena* is obviously young, athletic, and beautifully proportioned. Greek philosophers reasoned that there was a perfect form for everything: a perfect woman,

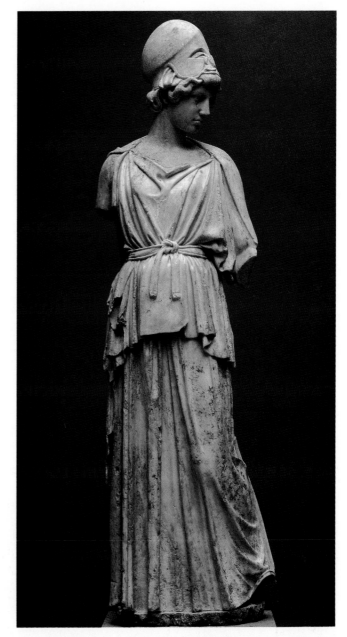

18–12 Myron, *Statue of Athena*. Liebighaus Museum, Frankfurt am Main, Germany. Eric Lessing/Art Resource, NY.

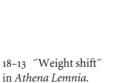

18–13 "Weight shift" in *Athena Lemnia*.

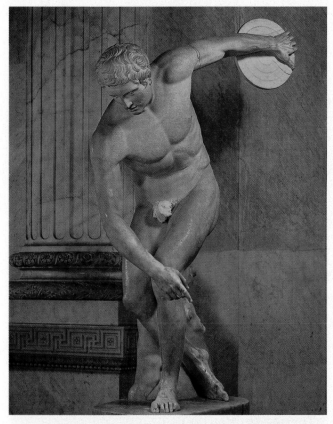

18-14 Myron, *Discobolus,* Imperial Roman. Copy. Marble, 60″ (152 cm) high. Museo Nazionale Romano, Rome. Scala/Art Resource, NY.

perfect man, perfect horse, perfect tree, and so forth. This statue is Myron's attempt to portray ideal womanhood as well as the goddess Athena.

Ideal manhood received equal attention from the Greeks. The *Discobolus* (fig. 18–14) is another copy of a bronze sculpture by Myron. A young athlete is poised to hurl a discus. The suggestion of movement was especially daring for the 400s. The statue must have seemed incredibly lifelike to the Greek public. Still, as with *Athena,* realism is tempered by idealism. Idealism is seen in the *Discobolus*'s proportions, its balanced posture, and its passive face.

Greek architecture of the time also expresses humanism and idealism. The Parthenon (figures 18–15 and 18–16), unlike an Egyptian pyramid or an American skyscraper, is built on a human scale. Although it is grand, it is not overwhelming. The method of its construction, as you can see, is post and lintel. Idealism is reflected in the proportional relationships between the columns and the rest of the temple. Column width and height, column height and the height of the temple, and even column width and the spaces between

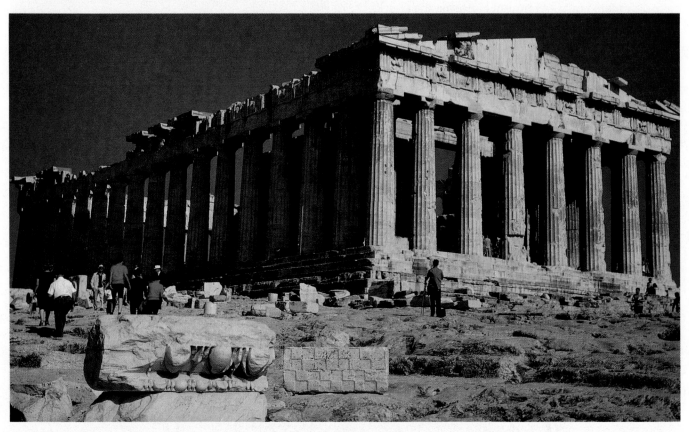

18–16 The Parthenon, Athens, 448–432 BC. Northwest view. Scala/Art Resource, NY.

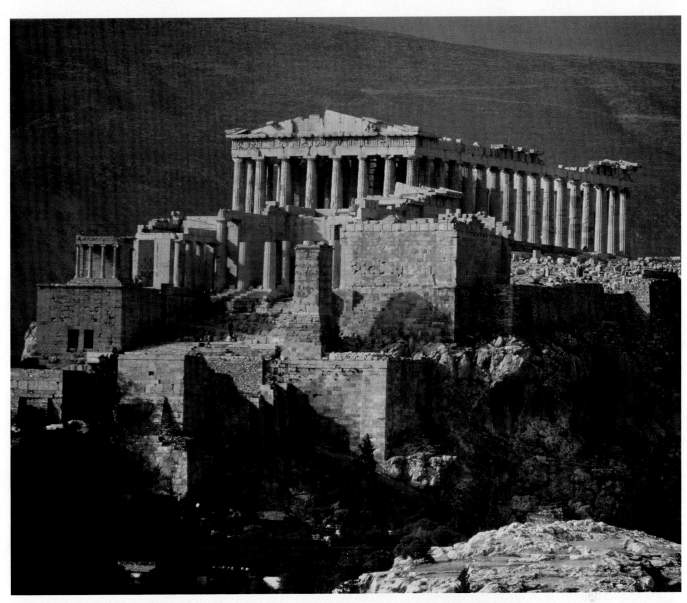

18–15 View of Acropolis, Athens. Scala/Art Resource, NY.

columns are proportional. These proportions represent a refinement of the **Doric** style of temple that took place over hundreds of years. The steps in this process (reading from left to right) are illustrated in figure 18–17.

The entire ancient world was in awe of Greek achievements, not only in sculpture and architecture, but in literature, philosophy, and human rights. Later generations of Europeans shared this awe. As we shall see in this chapter, much of European art bears the influence of Greek artistic styles.

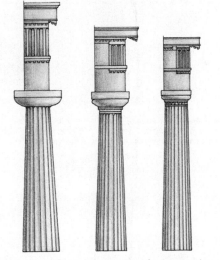

18–17 Changes in Doric order proportions.

First and Second Century Rome

The Romans were the principal heirs of Greek culture. They copied Greek statues by the thousands. (Myron's *Athena* and *Discobolus* are known to us only through Roman copies.) Original Roman sculptures resemble Greek sculptures. Roman paintings were largely based on Greek paintings. As you can see, the pleasant scene in figure 18–18 creates pictorial depth by using several methods. The painting includes foreshortening, shading, placement, variations of scale, and aerial perspective. Notice, however, that the eye levels of the various walls, temples, and monuments are inconsistent. Linear perspective was not applied consistently. Neither the Greeks nor the Romans had developed a system of one- or two-point perspective. Finally, Roman temples, which were also made with post-and-lintel methods, resemble Greek temples (fig. 18–19). Most Roman temples, however, are in the *Corinthian* style rather than the Doric.

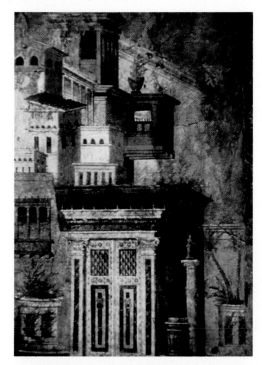

18–18 Wall painting transferred to panel, from a villa near Pompeii, 79 AD.

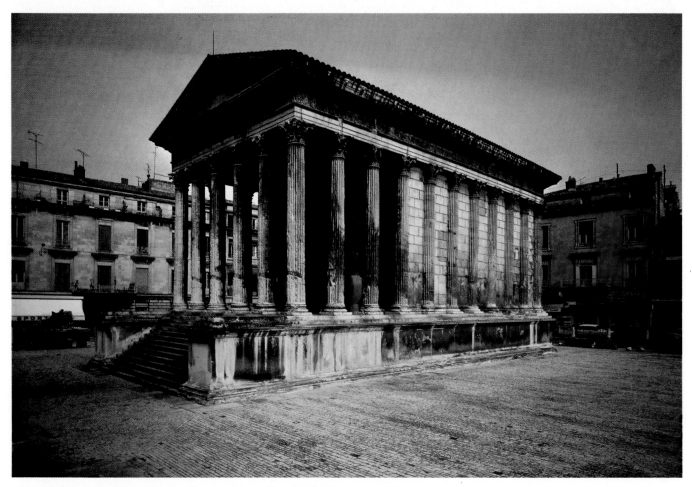

18–19 Maison Caree, Nîmes, France, first century BC. Giraudon/Art Resource, NY.

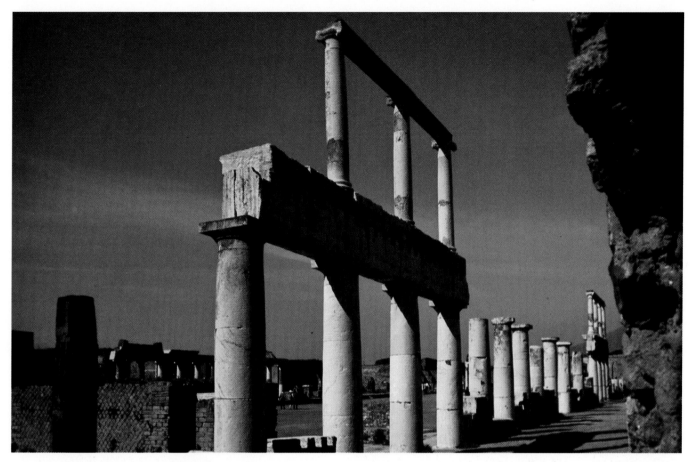

18-20 The Forum of Pompeii. Scala/Art Resource, NY.

In architecture, however, the Romans were original and unsurpassed in the ancient world. In the center of every major city was a **forum,** a combination of commercial district and civic center. A forum contained law courts, money exchanges, record offices, and assemblies. Today these forums are in ruins (fig. 18-20). Romans built harbors, bridges, sewers, and gigantic water conduits called **aqueducts** (fig. 18-21) that still line the landscape of Europe. They also built imposing gymnasiums, public baths, race tracks, and stadiums like the Roman *Colosseum* (fig. 18-27). Most of these structures employ one or both of two Roman technologies: the arch principle of construction, and concrete.

Just about all of the surviving architecture of the Egyptians, Greeks, and Romans were made of masonry materials. A masonry lintel, however, lacks *tensile* strength, the ability to withstand stress (fig. 18-22). A masonry lintel longer than twenty feet is apt to crack of its own weight. A temple with a masonry ceiling has to be supported by a forest of columns. A wooden lintel, which is lightweight and has tensile strength, needs less support. But wood is not a good material for public buildings because it rots or burns.

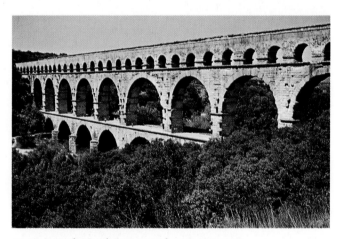

18-21 Pont du Gard. Roman arch, near Nîmes, France, first century BC. Giraudon/Art Resource, NY.

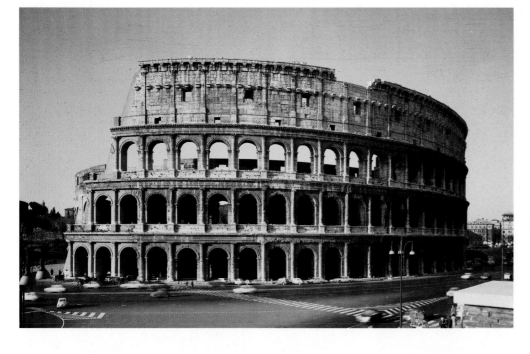

18–27 Colosseum, Rome ca. 70–82 AD. Scala/Art Resource, NY.

Cross section of the Colosseum.

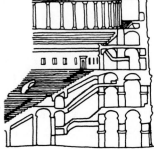

A *round arch* (fig. 18–23), as opposed to either a post and lintel structure or a corbeled arch (see Chapter 17), solves the problem of masonry's tensile weakness. During construction, the stones of an arch are supported by a temporary wooden framework until the last stone (the keystone) is in place. Once it is finished, an arch is extremely strong and can span more than one hundred feet. A *barrel vault* (fig. 18–24) is an arch extended in depth. Like a ceiling, it can be used to cover a rectangular area. A *cross vault* (fig. 18–25), formed by two intersecting barrel vaults, can cover a rectangular area while remaining open on all four sides. A *dome* (fig. 18–26) is simply a radial form of the arch, and can be used to cover a circular area.

The Romans developed concrete as early as the second century BC. They used concrete as well as stones to make barrel vaults, cross vaults, and domes. Concrete resembles a thick sludge before it hardens. It can be poured into forms of almost any shape. Like stone, concrete is much stronger as an arch than as a horizontal lintel.

The legendary Colosseum (fig. 18–27) was begun under the emperor Vespasian and dedicated by his son Titus in 80 AD. It has every kind of arch except the dome. Three levels of repeated arches, called *arcades,* ring the outside. Barrel-vaulted ramps lead to the arena, and cross-vaulted corridors circle the entire stadium on all levels. In addition to covering the ramps and corridors, these vaults supported the stadium seats. The stadium could hold 50,000 spectators. Beneath the arena were cells for wild animals and locker rooms for the gladiators. At the dedication, more than 5,000 animals were killed. At one performance, the arena was flooded to stage a mock naval battle involving thousands of actors. Over 620 feet (189 meters) long, 513 feet (156 meters) wide, and 157 feet (47 meters) high, the Colosseum is ten times the size of the Parthenon.

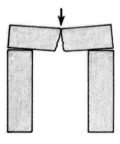

18–22 Post and lintel.

18–23 Arch.

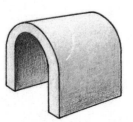

18–24 Barrel vault.

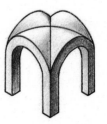

18–25 Cross vault.

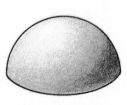

18–26 Dome.

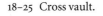

For thirteen centuries the solid concrete dome covering the Pantheon (fig. 18–28) held the record for being the largest in the world. (The view of the dome is obscured by the massive columned porch in the front.) Finished in 125 AD during the reign of Hadrian, the Pantheon was dedicated to the seven planetary gods— a legacy of the Greek religion. In the 600s it was converted to a Christian church. Because of this, the Pantheon was spared the dismantling that marred or ruined almost all other Roman buildings. Today it is a shrine for tourists. On clear days the sun streams through a round hole at the top. A bright disk of sunlight moves across the surface of the floor and walls with the speed of the rotation of the earth (fig. 18–29).

The architecture of Rome was a symbol of the power as well as the splendor of the ancient world until Rome's decline in the 300s and 400s. Christianity replaced the religious system of Greece and Rome. Almost all of the culture of the Roman Empire was rejected as pagan, if not immoral.

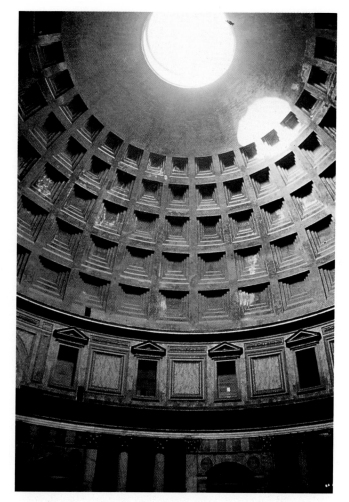

18–29 Pantheon, interior dome. Photograph: Jan Lukas. Scala/Art Resource, NY.

18–28 Pantheon, Rome, ca. 118–128 AD. Photograph: Nimatallah. Scala/Art Resource, NY.

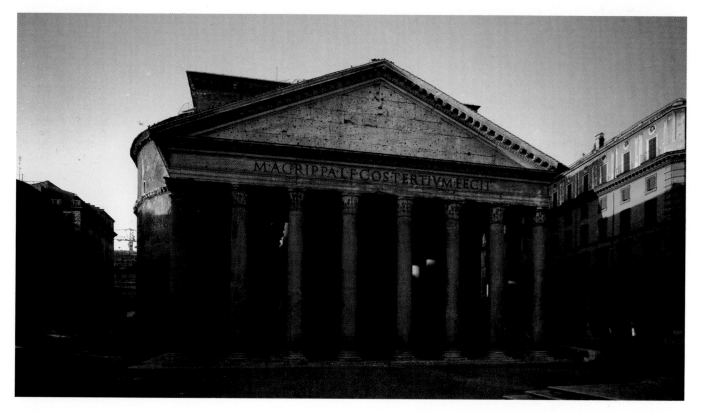

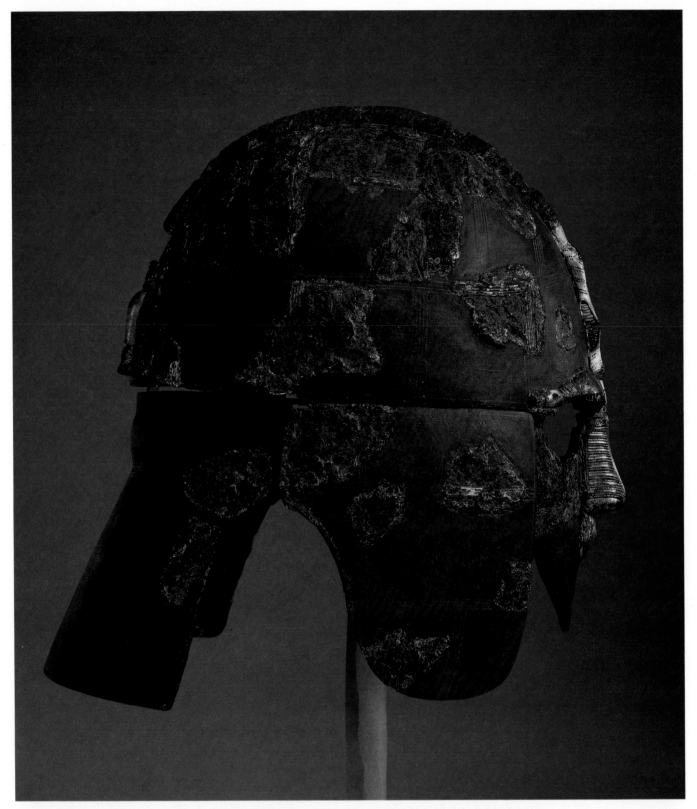

18–30 Sutton–hoo Helmet, seventh century, Saxon. Reproduced by Courtesy of the Trustees of the British Museum.

18–31 Frankish ornaments, (right) sixth century. Silver and paste, 1 1/8″ (10 cm) each. Photograph by Bobby Hansson. (Gift of J. Pierpont Morgan, 1917.) (left) Langobardic ornament, seventh century. Silver-gilt and niello, 6 5/16″ x 3 3/4″ (16 x 10 cm). The Metropolitan Museum of Art, Purchase, 1955, Joseph Pulitzer Bequest.

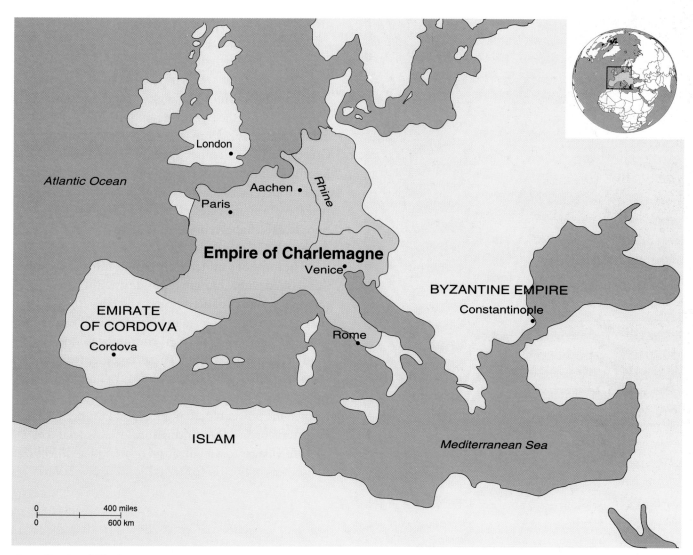

18-32 Empire of Charlemagne.

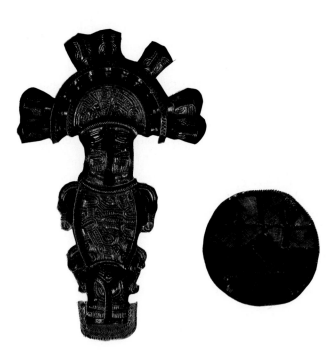

Through the Dark Ages to Charlemagne

During the 400s, western Europe entered the *medieval* era, literally, the *Middle Ages.* This term applies to the long period of time between the Fall of Rome and the Renaissance (to be discussed). During the early part of this period, civilized life had all but disappeared. The people of Europe were illiterate and largely nomadic. They produced little painting, no large buildings, and no in-the-round sculptures. However, they did make such things as military helmets (fig. 18–30) and attractive ornaments for their weapons, their horses, and themselves. You may recognize the technique of cloisonné (Chapter 13) in the fancy pins (fig. 18–31) used to fasten their garments.

In the 800s, a Frankish king named Charlemagne united most of the continent into a Holy Roman Empire (fig. 18–32). Charlemagne was a patron of the

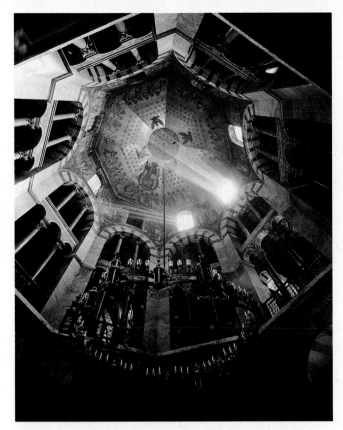

18–33 Aachen Cathedral, view into octagonal dome. Aachen, Germany, Europe. Erich Lessing/Art Resource, NY.

arts as well as a great military leader and statesman. He attempted to bring Europeans out of the Dark Ages by stimulating a rebirth of culture. He imported scholars, architects, and craftspersons from all over, but primarily from Constantinople. Constantinople was the headquarters of the Byzantine Empire. The forerunner of Eastern Christendom (modern Russia, Armenia, Greece, Serbia, and other parts of eastern Europe), the Byzantine Empire was much more civilized than western Europe. Charlemagne's private chapel (fig. 18–33) may have been modeled after a chapel in Constantinople. His chapel represents the beginning of medieval masonry architecture.

The hope of a united Europe and cultural growth was dashed with Charlemagne's death. But two political units grew out of his empire. The Holy Roman Empire, a cluster of German kingdoms in the east, and a French kingdom in the west continued to survive, though somewhat shakily. These, together with the states owned by the Catholic church in Italy and the Anglo-Saxon kingdoms across the English Channel, formed the power blocks of medieval Europe. Together they transformed the continent from a wasteland of peasant villages to a civilization of art and architecture. France was in the forefront of this transformation.

Medieval Crusades and Pilgrimages

By the 1000s and 1100s, large churches with vaulted ceilings were beginning to spring up all over Europe, particularly in France. This was the time of the *Crusades,* when knights and peasants traveled to Palestine to recapture Jerusalem from the Moslem Saracens. In 1189, Richard the Lion-Hearted, king of England, met the king of France in the church at Vézelay to begin the Third Crusade. They probably led their troops through Vézelay's doors under a relief carving of Christ and the apostles (fig. 18–34). Christ, in the center, is giving the apostles their spiritual assignments. The scenes in the eight side compartments show the apostles healing the sick. The scenes on the lintel below show them preaching the gospel to all nations. The knights who passed through the door and glanced up at this relief believed that they, like the apostles, had received a spiritual assignment.

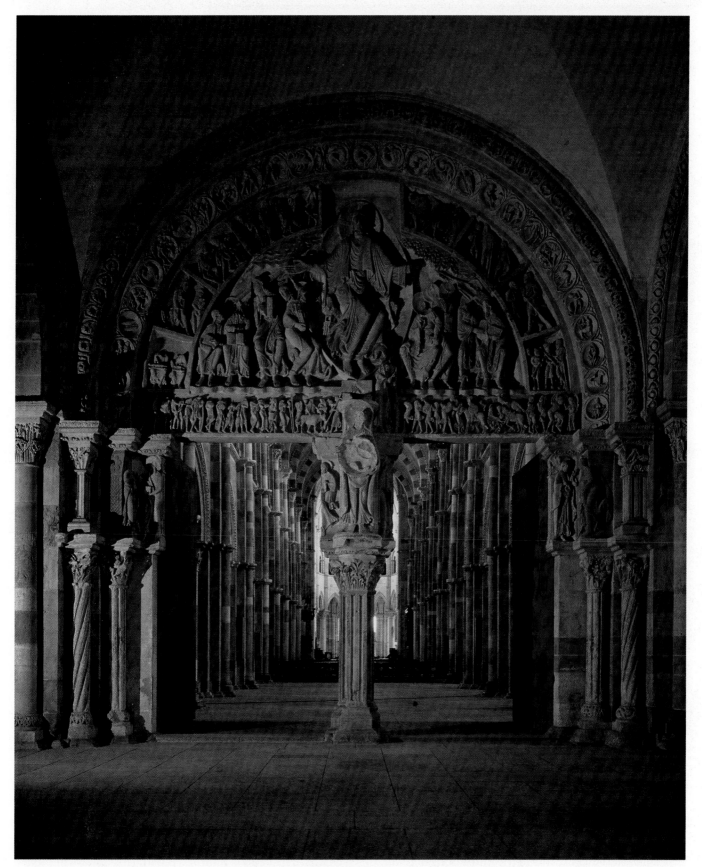

18–34 Central portal of La Madeleine, Vézelay, 1120–1132. Scala/Art Resource, NY.

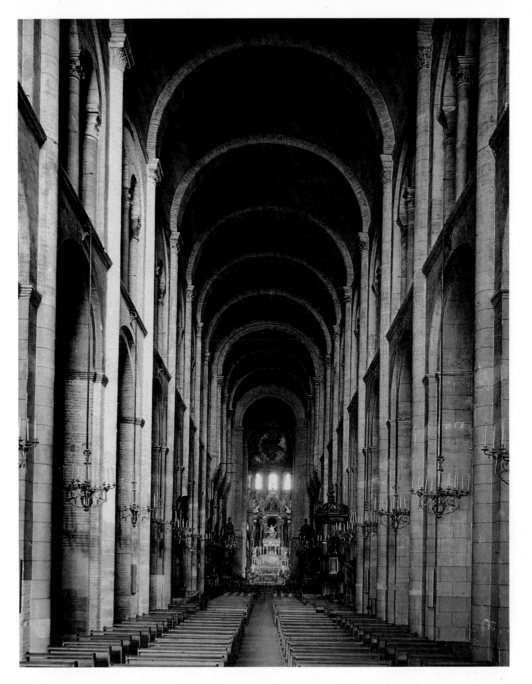

Compare the style of this relief to the classical examples reviewed earlier. Unlike the bodies of the Greek sculptures, these are stylized and unnaturally slender. The figures seem to be floating rather than standing firmly on the ground. The folds of their gowns are more decorative than natural-looking, though they do reveal their bodies to some extent. Unlike Roman murals, the scenes of this relief are completely lacking in three-dimensional space. Some of these characteristics are due to the limitations of relief carving, but most are due to a dramatic difference in point of view. The Greeks and Romans focused on humans and the natural world. The medieval Christians focused on God and the divine world.

The 1100s were also a time when pilgrims traveled to major shrines to see a *relic*. A relic is a remnant of a saint's clothing, hair, or even bones. People believed that a relic had the power to cure disease, forgive sins, and perform miracles. One of the churches on the pilgrimage route was St. Sernin in Toulouse (fig. 18–35). Imagine how pilgrims must have felt as they marched in a procession beneath the barrel vault of St. Sernin's main aisle, while listening to choirs of monks intoning chants. The vault is reinforced with ribs that form their own rhythmic procession as they lead the eye to the rear of the church. Notice also the heaviness of the supports and the relative darkness of the interior.

Gothic France

Although the Crusades were military failures, Europeans gained a great deal from their Moslem adversaries (Chapter 17). Among other things, they learned how to build pointed arches and make stained glass. These important lessons were applied to the *Gothic* style of church architecture. Gothic builders added three important features to Christian architecture: the pointed arch (fig. 18–36), pointed vaulting (fig. 18–37), and the flying buttress (fig. 18–38).

Ceilings based on the ***pointed vault*** are more stable than ceilings based on the round vault. Reinforcing the vaults with ribs makes them even more stable. Because vaulted ceilings are heavy, the walls holding them must be very thick so that they do not bow outward. ***Flying buttresses,*** or stone supports on the outside of the building, add support at those critical points where the ceiling joins the wall. Flying buttresses surround Chartres Cathedral (fig. 18–39), the first major church to use Gothic construction throughout.

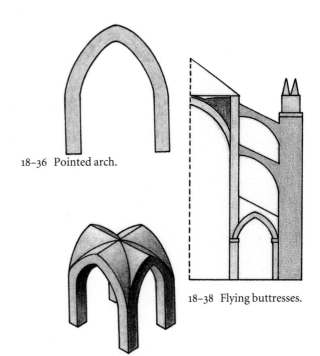

18–36 Pointed arch.

18–38 Flying buttresses.

18–37 Pointed vaulting.

18–39 Chartres Cathedral, France, twelfth–sixteenth centuries. Scala/Art Resource, NY.

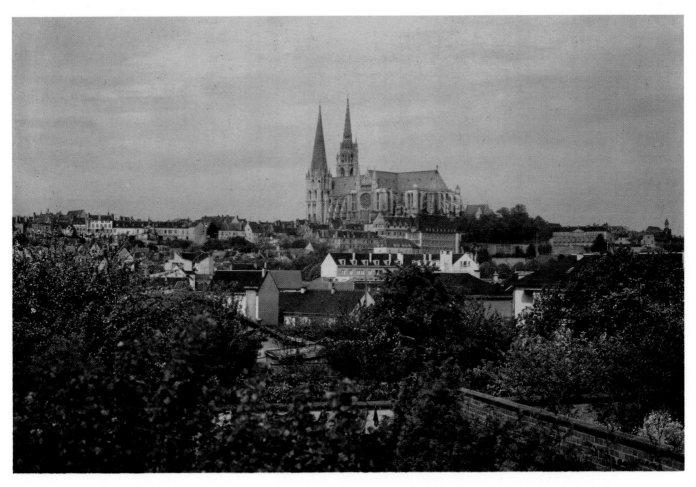

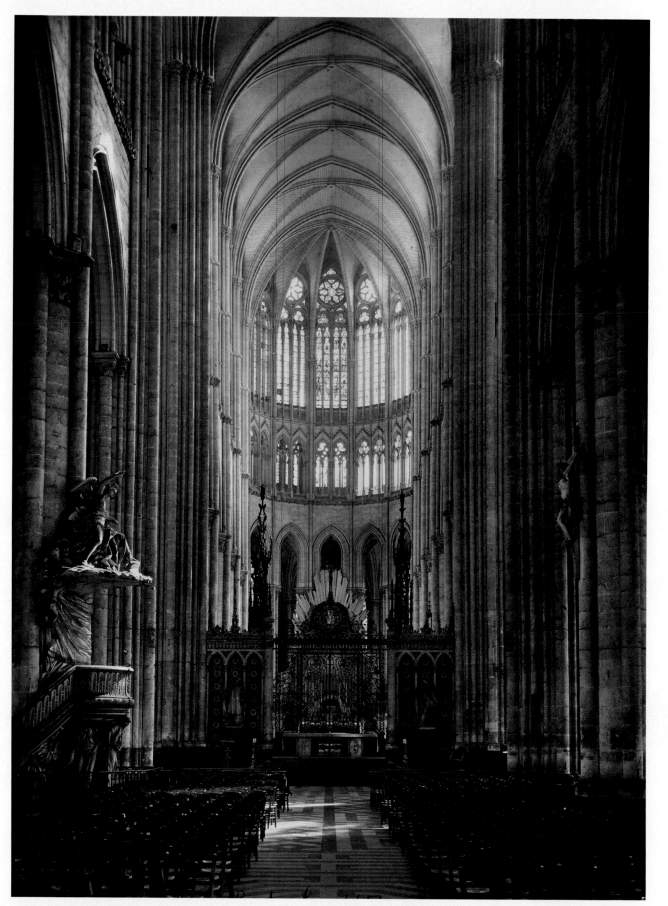

18–40 Nave of Amiens Cathedral. Scala/Art Resource, NY.

With Gothic construction, churches could have very high ceilings. Amiens Cathedral is typical of a church of this type. Notice the pointed arches on the left and in the windows at the rear of the cathedral (fig. 18–40). The soaring vaults in figure 18–41 are based on the pointed arch. Notice in both figures the ribs outlining the contours of the vaults. In what ways do you think a Gothic cathedral expresses the Age of Faith?

Gothic construction produced more space per pound of material than any other kind of masonry construction. It allowed for large windows that could flood the interior with light. However, the brightness of this light was tempered by the used of stained glass. (Recall the methods of making stained glass windows in Chapter 13.) A window from Reims Cathedral (fig. 18–42) illustrates the splendor of this glass. The bodies of Christ and the saints are stylized. The space around them is abstracted into symbols and patterns of color. Some of these characteristics were due to the demands of the stained glass medium. However, this art also reflects the spirituality of medieval life. An abstract and symbolic art is often more appropriate than a realistic art to express the world of faith.

The Gothic style of architecture, which spread to other parts of Europe, flourished in the 1200s and 1300s. After that, it began to be challenged by architects working in Florence, Italy.

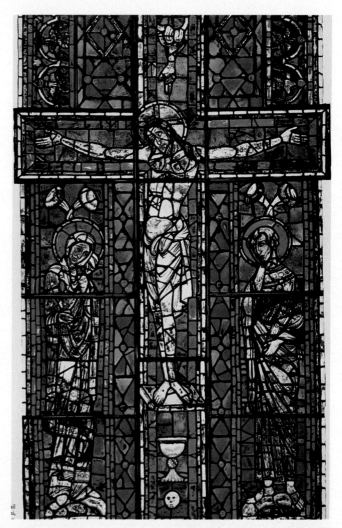

18–42 *Crucifixion*, detail of a window from St. Remi, Reims, ca. 1190. Stained glass, approx. 12´ (366 cm) high. Art Resource, NY.

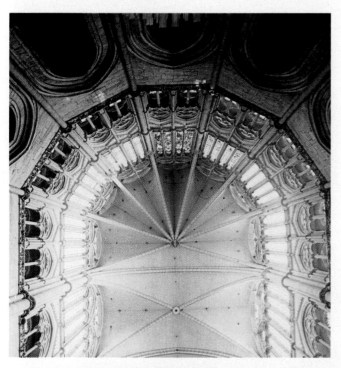

18–41 Choir vault, Amiens Cathedral. Scala/Art Resource, NY.

The Renaissance in the 1400s

Renaissance literally means *rebirth*. It refers to a period of time when attitudes changed dramatically, particularly in Florence, Italy. The spirit of humanism, which had ignited the achievements of the Greeks some 1900 years earlier, was being revived. Like the Greeks, Florentine thinkers focused on people and earthly life. Their questioning lead to major advances in science. At the end of the 1400s, Leonardo da Vinci began exploring the fields of optics, mechanics, and human anatomy, and Christopher Columbus began exploring the world. In the next century, Nicolaus Copernicus, a Polish astronomer, theorized that the earth revolved around the sun. For centuries people had believed that the sun revolved around the earth. These researchers, and others who followed, helped to create the scientific explosion that has affected all of our lives—intellectually, materially, and spiritually.

Renaissance scholars also revived an interest in the classical civilizations. In medieval times, the writings of people like Sophocles, Plato, and Virgil (Roman poet) gathered dust or were interpreted solely in light of Christian doctrine. Now these writings were studied for whatever universal truths they might contain. Earlier, Greek statues, Roman statues, and Roman copies of Greek statues were ignored or destroyed; now they were preserved and admired by artists. Earlier, Roman buildings had been robbed of their stones to construct churches; now they were studied by architects.

Florentine architect Filippo Brunelleschi admired the Pantheon (fig. 18–28), one of the few intact buildings. Brunelleschi's interest in Roman architecture is reflected in the small domed chapel (fig. 18–43) he designed for the wealthy Pazzi family. Notice that its spatial relationships, in contrast to those of a Gothic cathedral, are relatively simple. The use of the round arch, in addition to plain walls, is a change from the Gothic. The color accents were inspired by classical decorations.

18–43 Filippo Brunelleschi, interior of Pazzi Chapel, South Croce. Scala/Art Resource, NY.

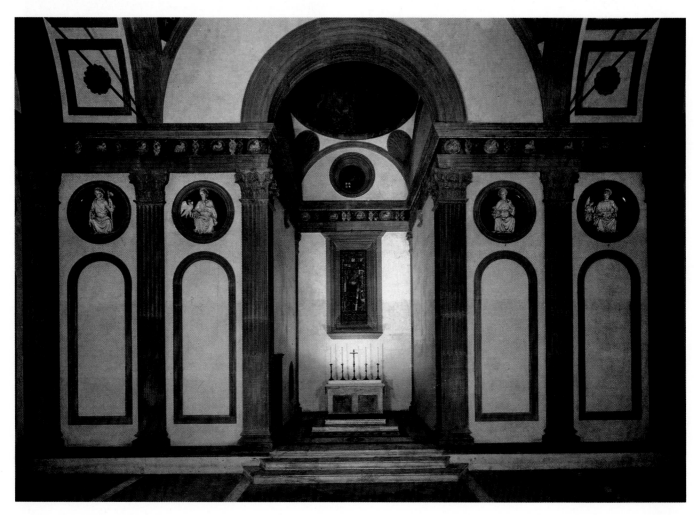

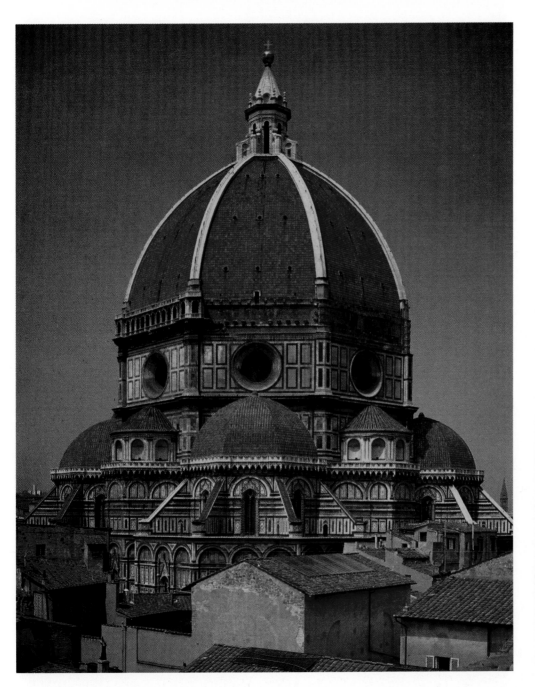

18-44 Filippo Brunelleschi, dome of Florence Cathedral, 1420–1436. Scala/Art Resource, NY.

18-45 Donatello, *St. Mark the Evangelist*. 1411–1413. Marble, approximately 7′ 9″ (236 cm) high. Or San Michele, Florence. Scala/Art Resource, NY.

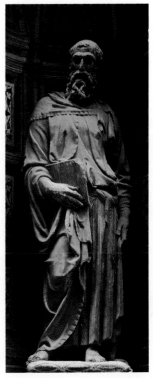

Brunelleschi's most ambitious project was the dome of the Cathedral of Florence (fig. 18-44). The dome is very Renaissance in its boldness. Spanning a diameter of 140 feet (43 meters), it is 300 feet (93 meters) high (351 feet high including the decorative "lantern"). No dome this wide had been built since the Pantheon. No dome this high had even been built in the world. Despite its size and originality, however, this dome is Gothic in its construction. Unlike the dome on the Pantheon, Brunelleschi's is pointed and ribbed.

The change away from medieval styles is clearly reflected in Renaissance sculpture. Donatello shared Brunelleschi's interest in classicism. Donatello's *St.* *Mark* (fig. 18-45) shows many similarities to Greek sculpture. The sculpture has human proportions and weight-shift posture. The clothing is natural-looking. Indeed, St. Mark's gown looks as though the apostle had slept in it. The principal difference between Myron's *Athena* and the *St. Mark*—aside from their gender—is in their faces. Athena's face expresses classical calm. St. Mark's face expresses the passion and seriousness of a Christian evangelist.

The men in *The Tribute Money* (fig. 18–46), a fresco by Masaccio (Tommaso Guidi), also look serious. They are as weighty and solid as sculptures, and they look as intense and serious as St. Mark. Here, Jesus and his disciples confront a tax collector in Capernaum (from St. Matthew 17:24–7). Jesus is in the center telling St. Peter to obtain a coin from the mouth of a fish. Peter is shown in three places. He is standing with the disciples; obtaining the coin on the left; and paying the collector on the right. The men's bodies are shaded on the left with bold strokes of chiaroscuro and illuminated from the right. They appear quite three-dimensional. The space they are in has depth. The building on the right may be the first in art history to have been rendered in one-point perspective. The hills in the background are shrouded in aerial perspective. *The Tribute Money* served as a textbook of pictorial techniques for later Renaissance artists like da Vinci and Michelangelo.

The High Renaissance

At the end of the 1400s, art entered a phase called **High Renaissance,** which lasted about twenty years. This phase brought to perfection the experiments and discoveries of artists like Donatello and Masaccio. A good example of High Renaissance art is Raphael's *School of Athens* (fig. 18–47).

The subject is obviously classical. Famous philosophers from the ancient world, including Socrates, Plato, and Aristotle are assembled. More importantly, the men have idealized bodies and graceful gestures, and a beautiful, spacious environment to move about in.

Raphael's mural, finished in 1511, was not the first successful High Renaissance work. Sixteen years earlier, in 1495, Leonardo da Vinci began *The Last Supper* (fig. 18–48) on the wall of a Milan monastery. Painting was only one of Leonardo's skills. The great artist was also a sculptor, an architect, an engineer, a scientist,

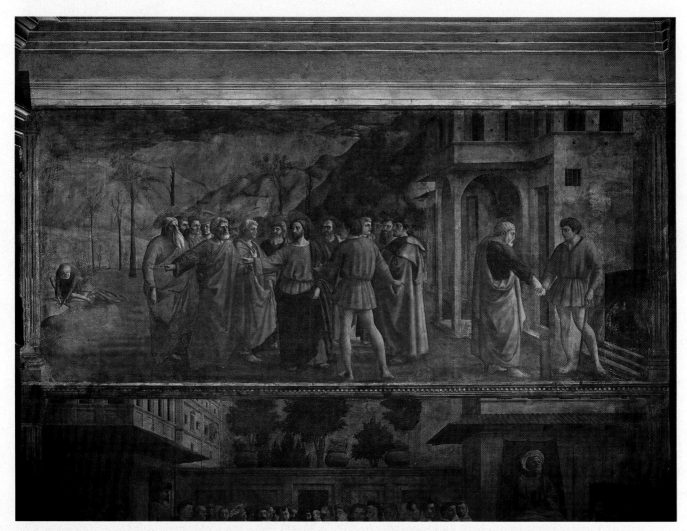

18-46 Masaccio, *The Tribute Money*, fresco, ca. 1427. Branacci Chapel, Santa Maria del Carmine, Florence. Scala/Art Resource, NY.

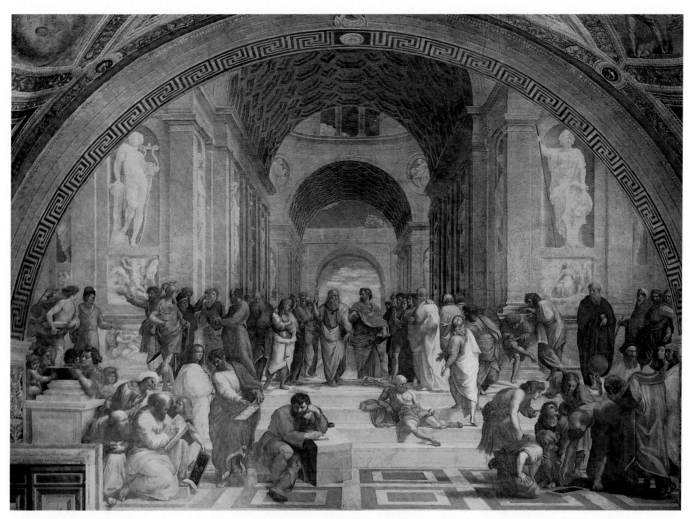

18-47 Raphael, *The School of Athens*, Stanza della Segnatura, The Vatican, Rome. Fresco in lunette: 25´ 3 ¼″ at base. ©1985 Scala/Firenze. Scala/Art Resource, NY.

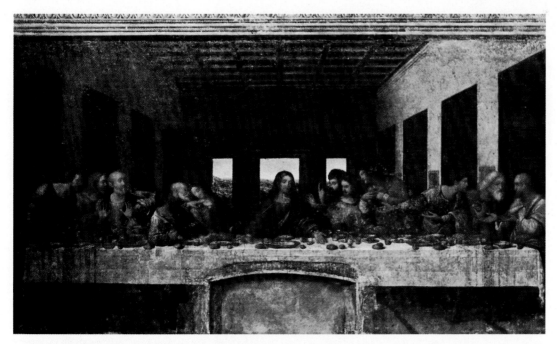

18-48 Leonardo da Vinci, *The Last Supper,* ca. 1494. Oil and tempera on plaster. 14´ 5″ x 28´ ¼″ (4.39 x 8.54 m). Santa Maria delle Grazie, Milan.

and an inventor who filled notebooks with descriptions of everything from armored vehicles to parachutes. He was ahead of his time in the fields of astronomy, hydrology, sound, optics, and especially anatomy (fig. 18–49). He is said to have dissected as many as fifty cadavers in his search for knowledge. More than any man in history, Leonardo was a Renaissance Person—an individual skilled and well versed in many fields.

Before Leonardo started painting, artists were unable to show people moving about in a picture without sacrificing stability. In Masaccio's *The Tribute Money,* for example, the composition is stable, but the men are relatively static. *The Last Supper* is the first major painting to successfully reconcile movement and stability. One reason is that the composition is deceptively simple. The picture is horizontal. The long table is symmetrical and parallel to the picture plane. Jesus is not only located at the middle of the table; his head is at the center of the picture and at the vanishing point. The rectangular space is defined by one-point perspective. These aspects provide stability. Movement is seen in the twelve disciples. They are all reacting to the statement, "One of you will betray me." Despite

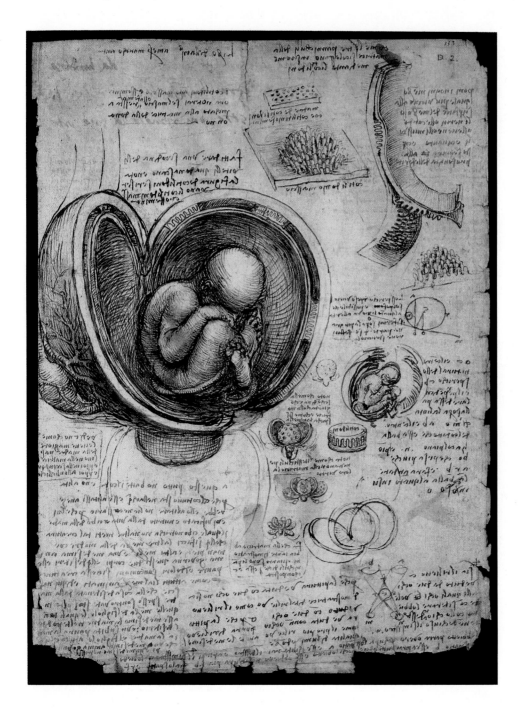

18–49 Leonardo da Vinci, *Embryo in the Womb*, ca. 1510. Pen and ink. Royal Collection Enterprises Limited, Windsor Castle. Copyright reserved. Reproduced by gracious permission of H. M. Queen Elizabeth II.

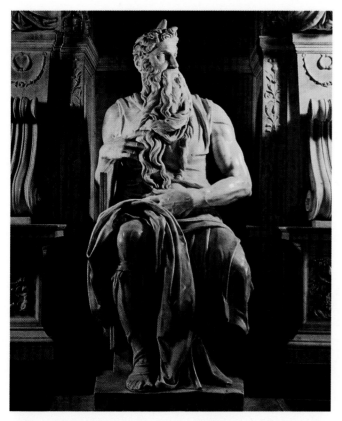

18–50 Michelangelo, *Moses*, 1513–1515. Marble, approximately 8′ 4″ (254 cm) high. San Pietro in Vincoli, Rome.

their agitation, all have idealized bodies and graceful gestures. The one on the left who is leaning back with his face in shadow is Judas. All fit comfortably in the rectangular space. *The Last Supper* was the first painting to successfully integrate active figures in a realistic spatial world. It has been popular from the time it was completed in 1498.

The works of Leonardo's younger contemporary, Michelangelo Buonarroti, have also continued to be popular through time. Like Leonardo, Michelangelo was broadly skilled in the arts: sculpture, painting, architecture, even poetry. However, he was not involved in scientific pursuits. Both artists branched out to other cities: Leonardo to Milan, Michelangelo to Rome.

In the early 1400s, Rome was a collection of old ruins, dirt roads, and cow pastures. When Michelangelo came of age as an artist, Rome was beginning to rival Florence in development and culture. By the time Michelangelo died, Rome had surpassed Florence and went on to become the thriving city and center of culture that it is today.

Michelangelo first began to produce art for the Vatican, a special area in Rome for the headquarters of the Catholic church. The *Pietà* (fig. 8–10), which was

discussed briefly in Chapter 8, was Michelangelo's first work for the Vatican. It is also an excellent example of High Renaissance sculpture. The figures of Jesus and Mary are extremely beautiful and harmoniously related. The *Moses* (fig. 18–50), begun some fifteen years later, falls within the High Renaissance period, and is definitely grand and monumental. But in this case, beauty has given way to righteous anger.

The *Moses* is too awesome to be included in the same category with *School of Athens, The Last Supper,* and the *Pietà.* Michelangelo, a man of strong passions, revered Moses and other heroes of the Old Testament. He aimed to glorify the people of the Bible, often by giving them superhuman proportions. Michelangelo's feelings (which were often disturbed) frequently found their way into his later works. More than anything, it is the psychological power of these works that has fascinated the public for centuries. The *Moses* was originally intended to be part of a grandiose tomb for Pope Julius II. The project was never completed because Julius himself lost interest in it.

One project that Julius did not lose interest in was the ceiling of the Vatican's Sistine Chapel (fig. 18–51).

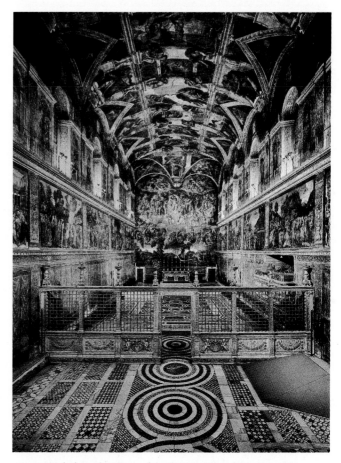

18–51 Michelangelo, View of the Sistine Chapel, Vatican City. Scala/Art Resource, NY.

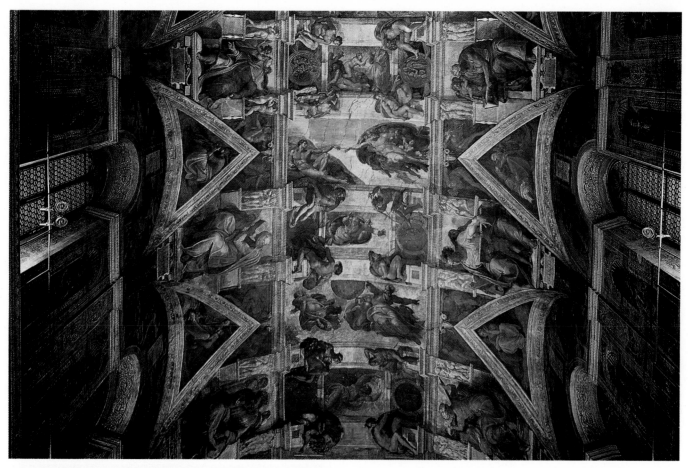

18–52 Michelangelo, ceiling of the Sistine Chapel, 1508–1512. The Vatican, Rome. Only five of the nine panels from Genesis are shown. Scala/Art Resource, NY.

He wanted Michelangelo to cover its vast surface with a mural. In 1508, Michelangelo began the fresco on the subject of God's creation. Covering 5,800 square feet (537 square meters), 70 feet (21 meters) above the floor, Michelangelo's creation itself was almost godlike. It took him four years, but in the end, the weary artist had transformed the surface of a vaulted ceiling into a complex pictorial drama (fig. 18–52).

The triangular spaces (called *lunettes*) around the perimeter of the mural are filled with figures representing the ancestors of Jesus, the Jewish people of the Old Testament. Between the lunettes are niches containing the largest figures, who were supposed to have predicted the birth of Jesus. Old Testament prophets alternate with female oracles (fortune tellers) from Greek myth. The nine panels running the length of the ceiling in the center contain episodes from the Old Testament book of Genesis: the Creation, the Fall, and the Flood. (Recall the scene of God separating light and dark in fig. 6–1.)

God is in each of the Creation episodes. In the *Creation of the Sun and the Moon* (fig. 18–53), God is represented by two figures. Clothed in loose-fitting,

billowing gowns, these figures have massive, muscular bodies like that of Moses. Although they resemble Greek gods, the face of the figure on the right is fierce, like *Jehovah*, God of the Old Testament. Throughout the fresco, Michelangelo borrowed from Greek sources as well as Jewish and Christian sources for his ideas. The use of oracles and heroically proportioned bodies is Greek. The Old Testament themes are Jewish. The predictions of the coming of Jesus, which are symbolized throughout the mural, are Christian.

The imagery and subject matter of the Sistine ceiling successfully bring together ideas from different sources. The composition is also successful in reconciling movement and stability. The mural contains more than 300 energetically moving figures. It could have become a teeming confusion of humanity. Not only that, scenes take place on different planes and in different directions, and are drawn to different scales. Worlds being created, prophecy, sin, worlds being destroyed are all scenes that coexist in the same mural. Michelangelo prevented chaos, however, by dividing each scene into its own rectangular or triangular space. The final effect is both energetic and composed. The

Sistine ceiling is considered by some to be the greatest masterwork of the Western world.

Like his sculpture and painting, Michelangelo's architecture came to represent both the High Renaissance and the Catholic church. The west end of St. Peter's basilica (fig. 18–54), the principal church of the Vatican, was designed by Michelangelo and completed after his death. (Although based on Michelangelo's design, the dome itself was modified by Giacomo della Porta.) The use of a pointed dome surmounted by a lantern recalls Brunelleschi and the Cathedral of Florence. But the sense of mass, and the unity of windows, columns, and ribs is Michelangelo's (and High Renaissance). Like the statue of *Moses*, St. Peter's is truly monumental and a fitting symbol for the headquarters of the Catholic church. It is the ancestor of all of the famous domes in the world, including the Capitol dome in Washington, DC.

The High Renaissance represents a peak development in European art. Although the movement itself ended in the mid-1500s, its basic ideals continued as touchstones of Western art. In the late 1800s, most of these ideals were rejected by the modern movement. But that is a story for Chapter 19.

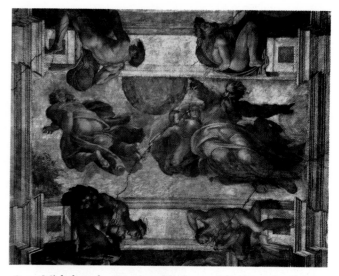

18–53 Michelangelo, *Creation of the Sun and the Moon*, detail from the Sistine Chapel ceiling. 1508–1512. Fresco, approximately 9′ 2″ x 18′ 8″ (3 x 5.5 m). The Vatican, Rome. Scala/Art Resource, NY.

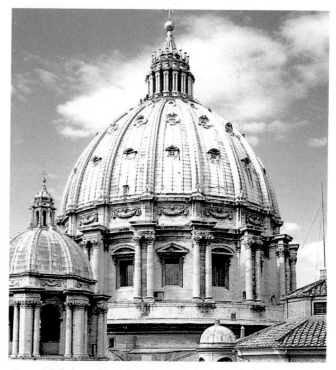

18–54 Michelangelo, *St. Peter's*, 1546–1564 (view from the west). Dome completed by Giacomo della Porta, 1590.

Integration Experience 18.1

Renaissance Influences

Use library resources and contact your history teacher to prepare a report on how the work of Renaissance artists was influenced by the inventions, scientific discoveries, political and religious values of that time period (1400s–1500s).

Studio Experience 18.2

A Renaissance-Style Landscape

Create a landscape painting, using tinting, shading and intensity variations to create the illusion of light, space, movement and depth, that many Renaissance artists tried to perfect in their paintings.

Chapter 19
Islands of Time II

19 Islands of Time II

Student Edition
Pages 274–305

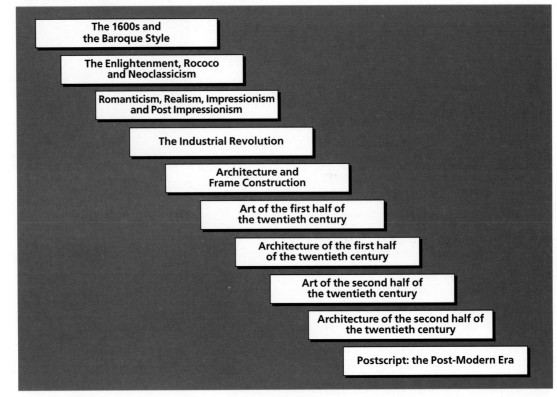

The 1600s and
the Baroque Style

The Enlightenment, Rococo
and Neoclassicism

Romanticism, Realism, Impressionism
and Post Impressionism

The Industrial Revolution

Architecture and
Frame Construction

Art of the first half of
the twentieth century

Architecture of the first half
of the twentieth century

Art of the second half of
the twentieth century

Architecture of the second half of
the twentieth century

Postscript: the Post-Modern Era

Overview

Chapter Objectives

Students should be able to:

1 demonstrate knowledge of the history of art from the Renaissance through the modern age   EE 3

2 understand that Baroque subject matter and styles were affected by the political pressures and differences between Catholic and Protestant patronage   EE 3

3 capture the spirit of the highly ornate Baroque style in creating a Baroque pocket pot   EE 2

4 understand the relationship between changes in society and styles in art   EE 3

5 understand that art styles also develop as reactions to, or extensions of, existing and past styles   EE 3

6 describe changes that led to the outbreak of modernism in the early twentieth century   EE 3

7 explain the relationship between the Industrial Revolution and changes in architecture

8 prepare a report on an art style

9 identify examples of art from at least four periods reviewed in this chapter

Rationale

Chapter 19, which covers developments from the 1600s to the present, completes the overview of Western art history. Baroque, Rococo, Neoclassical, and Realistic styles and developments in architecture (especially frame construction) are briefly summarized. The modern movement is examined, starting with examples of Impressionism and ending with examples of early Abstract Expressionism.

Essential Concepts

• In Catholic Europe the Baroque style, known for complexity, drama, and grandeur, is typified by the paintings of Rubens.

• Because the Dutch Reformed church discouraged the making of religious art, Dutch artists turned to genre subjects.

• Rococo, the major style of the 1700s, represented the views and lifestyles of the aristocracy.

• Neoclassicism, which arrived at the end of the century, is exemplified in painting by David's *Oath of the Horatii* and in architecture by Jefferson's Virginia State Capitol.

• Romanticism, which emphasized emotion and the worship of nature, replaced Neoclassicism.

• Impressionism featured urban scenes painted with bright daubs of paint. The works of the Post Impressionists, which went beyond Impressionism in defying traditional realism, signaled a turning point in art.

• The first half of the twentieth century witnessed the outbreak of many new styles and movements in art.

• Architecture in the first half of the century is represented by the designs of Wright and those of the architects associated with the Bauhaus. Until recently, much post-war architecture reflected the influence of either Mies van der Rohe or Le Corbusier.

• At the end of World War II and the introduction of Abstract Expressionism, leadership in international art began to be shared by American artists.

• Art and architecture are so pluralistic today that it is difficult to identify a leading style or dominant direction.

Vocabulary

Reformation	Enlightenment
ferroconcrete	Counter-Reformation
Industrial Revolution	aristocrats
wood frame	metal frame
Postmodernism	

Lesson Plans

19.1 A Baroque Pocket Pot

Page **T 280** Time: 3 periods

19.2 A Style Report

Page **T 282** Time: Variable

Handouts

Guidelines for a Style Report Page **T 284**

Study Questions Page **T 285**

Test Questions Page **T 290**

Chapter Closure
Evaluation

1 *Production:* Can students simulate the highly ornate decoration of the Baroque style in the surface treatment of a clay pot?

2 *History/Criticism:* Can students prepare a report of an art style that occurred in the 17th to 20th century? **W 2**

3 *History:* Do students demonstrate a basic knowledge of at least five styles or movements reviewed in this chapter? Do they understand similarities and differences among these styles? **R 3**

4 *History:* Can students cite at least two watersheds of change in the art and/or culture of Europe between the Renaissance and the middle of the 1800s, such as the Reformation, the Enlightenment, the French Revolution, Romanticism, Realism? **R 3**

5 *History:* Are students able to describe the changes that led to the outbreak of modernism and some of the major art movements of the 20th century? **R 4**

6 *History:* Can students explain the relationship between the Industrial Revolution and changes in architecture? **R 4**

7 *History/Aesthetic awareness:* Can students recognize typical examples of art of at least five styles reviewed in this chapter?

8 *Aesthetic awareness:* Are students voluntarily seeking to know more about the art of any of the styles reviewed in this chapter?

Notes

Islands of Time II

A Baroque Pocket Pot

Time: 3 periods

Preparation

Rationale

The Baroque style evolved out of the church's demand for artworks that emphasized complexity, drama, and grandeur. As a result, Baroque works became highly ornate, exuberant, and filled with swirling lines. In this lesson, students create a pocket pot for the wall and fill the surface with decorative elements in the spirit of the Baroque style.

Studio Materials

clay, assorted clay tools, clay boards, table covering, water containers, plastic bags, engobes, clear glaze

Enrichment Materials

Examples of Baroque metal work, jewelry and ceiling frescoes.

Teach the Lesson

Objectives

Students should be able to:

1　build a wall pocket pot out of clay slabs and decorate the surface in the highly ornate manner of the Baroque style　EE 2, 3

Vocabulary

Baroque is a 17th century style in which artists used dramatic light, movement, soaring spatial illusions, and ornate detail to encourage emotional involvement.

Warm Up

Show examples of Baroque metalwork, jewelry, reliefs on building facades, cathedral sculpture, and ceilings. Direct attention to the complex, surface-filling designs of the style.

Explore and Develop

1　Explain that a pocket pot is a small container to hang on a wall, made by attaching a pocket to a flat slab of clay. Direct attention to student examples in Studio Experience 19.2.

Begin Studio Experience 19.1

1　Have students roll out slabs of clay and cut out a shape about 7" x 5" for the back of the pot. Then have them roll out a second slab a bit wider and not quite as long to form a pocket with.

2　Tell students to shape a piece of newspaper, place it on the back slab, and drape the pocket slab over it. Have them use slip to knit the edges of the slabs where they join. A coil of clay can be worked into the seam from inside the pot when the paper is pulled out at the leather-hard stage.

3　Encourage students to be imaginative in decorating the pot surface. Some may work with a theme, such as leaves, vines and flowers, or a central figure cut out in relief and added to the pocket.

4　Assorted objects, including pasta shells, may be used to impress motifs into the clay. Line and pattern can be incised. Clay shapes can be pressed on. Encourage students to fill available space with decoration. Remind students to consider similarity and repetition, and perhaps a dominant element for unity.

Laser Discs:

David, Napoleon in His Study, 1812

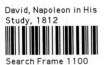

Search Frame 1100

Ingres, Pope Pius VII in the Sistine Chapel, 1810

Search Frame 1116

Turner, Junction of Thame and Medway, c 1805/1808

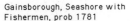

Search Frame 1709

Gainsborough, Seashore with Fishermen, prob 1781

Search Frame 1615

Courbet, Boats on a Beach, Etretat, 1869

Search Frame 1222

Corot, Ville d'Avray, c 1867/1870

Search Frame 1152

5 Tell students to drape the pots with plastic so some air will circulate and stiffen them up overnight. Have them carefully pull out the paper form and work a coil into the seam between the slabs for strength. Students should make a hole in the back piece for hanging. Let them use engobes to decorate with dramatic contrasts of color. Let the pots dry slowly to avoid cracking.

6 After a bisque fire, have students apply liquid glaze and fire to maturity.

Evaluate and Reflect

1 Ask students to describe the Baroque style and the meaning of the term today.

2 Did students decorate their pots in the spirit of the highly ornate Baroque style?

3 Have them explain how they achieved some of the decorative effects.

4 Are they satisfied with their surface treatments? Did they maintain unity?

5 Did their pots and all added parts hold together throughout the drying and firing process?

6 Ask students to find examples of popular or commercial art that could be called Baroque.

Reteach

To help students understand how style affects the meaning and expressive qualities of artworks, refer them to figures 19–2, 19–28, and 19–29, which demonstrate different styles. Discuss how styles of Nolde and Kandinsky differ. Make sure that students understand *style,* the distinguishing characteristics of the artwork, and *characteristics,* those things that are distinctive and usually present in an artist's work.

Extend the Lesson

Beyond the Basics

Students might vary the form of the pocket pot. Try rolling the slab over a textured surface before assembling. Have them explore indenting the pocket form and placing a figure in it. Experiment with things growing out of the pot, and through the pocket slab. **EE 2**

Suggest students who finish early use clay to construct a piece of jewelry in the Baroque style. Suggest designing a pin or a pendant. Point out to students that ceramic jewelry can be heavy. Keep it small and delicate. Suggest they review the characteristics of Baroque art before designing the jewelry. **EE 2**

Cultural Connections

Have students find examples of Thomas Jefferson's architecture. Suggest they research to learn more about Jefferson, the architect and the statesman. Have them examine his work and philosophy that had such an impact on our cultural heritage. Investigate how Neoclassicism and other European architectural styles became popular in America. Jefferson's writings were printed in numerous publications. Several books containing letters written by Jefferson and books written about him are available in most libraries. **R 3, 4**

Connecting with Other Subjects

History Have students browse through history books and talk with teachers to gather information about the industrial revolution and its impact on various cultures. When and where did it occur? What were its causes and effects in a rapidly changing world? How was art affected and what changes may have been brought about by artists? Set up a diagram of events and art connected to this period. Identify dates, places, events and people of importance. Have students organize the information in order to increase understanding of this complex period in world history. **EE 3**

R 3, 4
W 2

Art Style Report

Time: Variable

Preparation

Rationale

Chapter 19 provides an overview of Western art from the 17th to the 20th century, beginning with the Baroque style and ending with directions in the 1980s. Each style has special characteristics, context relationships, and artistic accomplishments. Learning about these styles will increase students' aesthetic awareness and ability to analyze modern artworks. In this lesson, students assemble information about art styles from the 17th to the 20th century into a classroom file.

Research Materials

library resources, Guidelines for a Style Report (Handout), assorted visual aids showing a variety of styles

Enrichment Materials

Slides:

• Rembrandt, *The Mill*, 8
• Cézanne, *Still Life*, 102
• Dali, *The Persistence of Memory*, 112

Teach the Lesson

Objectives

Students should be able to:

1   create a classroom file of art styles from the 17th to the 20th century using library resources and Guidelines for a Style Report   EE 3

Vocabulary

Style refers to the identifying characteristics of the artwork of an individual, a group of artists, a period of time, or an entire society.

Warm Up

Refer to the artworks in figures 19–12, 19–15, and 19–17 to explain and demonstrate styles and their distinguishing characteristics.

Laser Discs:

Rubens, Daniel in the Lion's Den, c 1615

Search Frame 776

Rubens, detail

Search Frame 778

Rembrandt, The Mill, c 1645/1648

Search Frame 856

Rembrandt, detail

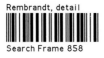
Search Frame 858

David and Neoclassicism: Use of Greek and Roman sculptures as models to depict contemporary events. Stress on balanced composition. Hard edges, subdued colors, flowing contour lines, noble gestures and expressions. Closed space.

Delacroix and Romanticism: Use of rich, dramatic color. Works often charged with movement. Back-to-nature themes. Contour lines not so evident; edges appear softer. Open space with action seeming to extend out of the picture.

Courbet and Realism: Use of contemporary scenery and objects. Images as close to reality as possible without idealizing them. Glorified the working class and its activities. Portrayed life as it is without dramatization.

Explore and Develop

1   Show examples by Caravaggio, Georges de la Tour, and Gentileschi. These works demonstrate the use of dramatic light and pronounced chiaroscuro that is characteristic of Baroque painting.

2   Direct attention to the differences between the Rococo painting by Fragonard (fig. 19–11) and the Neoclassical work by David (fig. 19–12). Explain that Neoclassical art developed during a period of political upheaval in France, which led to the French Revolution and the dictatorship of Napoleon. It was a time for a "no nonsense art."

3   Review the study questions with the group. Most of them are concerned with art styles.

4   Distribute Guidelines for a Style Report on page T 284. Have students choose a style to research.

Evaluate and Reflect

1 Can students identify art styles that developed from the 17th to the 20th century?

2 Can students identify some characteristics associated with these art styles?

3 Can students describe circumstances that contributed to the development of some of the styles?

4 Have students discuss why group styles develop and how individual artists use the styles.

Reteach

Have students work in groups to answer the study questions. You may want to give students the answers. Let students draw a question number and attempt the answer. Group members may prompt. Record a point if correct. Review the answer if wrong.

Extend the Lesson

Beyond the Basics

EE 3

R 3

Direct students attention to *A Mother's Duty* by Pieter de Hooch on page 278. It is a scene of everyday life, an example of genre painting. Remind students of earlier lessons concerning Baroque artists and their dramatic use of light and shadow. Recall how the Baroque painters seemed to capture a moment in time suspended for a second between what had just happened and what was about to happen. The merger of genre painting and the Baroque style was an interesting development. Suggest students research other artists working with similar ideas and subject matter.

Cultural Connections

EE 3, 4

W 1

The introduction of genre painting contributed significantly to our knowledge of life in European countries during this period of history. Through examination of these works we learn about the homes, clothing styles, customs, beliefs and values of the people represented in the paintings. Suggest students critique *A Mother's Duty* on page 278. Find an example of a similar work from a different country. Have students critique the work and compare the two paintings.

Connecting with Other Subjects

Music Ask the music teacher to help select records of Baroque music that represent the period. The music might be played along with a slide presentation of Baroque art. Composers of the period include Bach, Handel, Monteverdi, Scarlatti and Vivaldi.

Music The same might be done with the Romantic period between 1800 and 1850. Composers were Beethoven, Chopin, Mendelssohn, Brahms, and Schubert.

Music Have students analyze several Baroque paintings. Have them listen to the Baroque music and try to match the music to paintings that express similar moods or feelings. Have students collaborate to create a slide show of Baroque art and music. Talk with the music teacher about collaborating on lessons about other periods in history. Suggest having music students perform music from various periods at an upcoming concert and have art students prepare a slide show to accompany each musical selection.

EE 3, 4

Islands of Time II   Criticism Experience 19.1

Guidelines for a Style Report

Use library resources, magazines, and newspapers to gather information about an art style. Use the following questions to write your report. If possible, support your report with pictures and examples.

1 What is the style?

2 What are the dates of the style?

3 Where did the style begin? How widespread was, or is, it?

4 What social or world events occurred during the time of the style? How did they influence the style?

5 What are the main purposes of the style?

6 What are the characteristics of the style?

7 Was the style influenced by preceding styles?

8 Did the style affect a whole culture or just a group of artists?

9 List several artists (architects, painters, sculptors, ceramists, printmakers) and examples of their works in this style.

Name	Medium	Work
_____	_____	_____
_____	_____	_____
_____	_____	_____
_____	_____	_____
_____	_____	_____

Study Questions
Chapter 19–Islands of Time II

1 What did the Baroque style emphasize? Name and describe one example of Baroque art.

_____

_____

2 In sixteenth century Europe, how did the Protestant view of religious art differ from the Catholic view?

_____

_____

3 Who were the main clients of artists in Catholic Europe? In the Dutch Republic?

_____

_____

4 Give one example of an artist and his/her painting using a genre subject.

_____

_____

5 What does the term *The Enlightenment* refer to?

_____

_____

6 What was the major art style of the 1700s? Whose views and lifestyles did the style reflect?

_____

7 Define *Neoclassicism*. What French painter is credited for beginning this style?

_____

_____

_____

8 Who brought Neoclassical architecture to the United States? Name two buildings in the United States built in the Neoclassical style.

_____

_____

_____

9 Give three characteristics of Romanticism.

_____

_____

10 Who was a leader of the Realist movement? How did the Realists portray life?

_____

11 How did the Impressionist painter Claude Monet use the method of _broken color_?

_____

12 How did the Post Impressionist artist Vincent van Gogh use color?

_____

13 By the end of the nineteenth century, what did artists consider to be more important than realism?

_____

_____

14 What art forms were most influenced by the industrial revolution?

_____

15 What was the most significant development in architecture during the nineteenth century?

_____

16 Describe the Crystal Palace.

_____

_____

17 Who was the leader of the _Chicago school_? What did the motto "Form Follows Function" mean?

_____

_____

18 How did the Fauves use color and shape? Give one example.

_____

_____

_____

19 What did the German Expressionists consider to be the most important usage of color and pattern? What are the names of two groups of these artists?

_____

_____

_____

20 Who developed analytical Cubism? Name one similarity of, and two differences between, analytical and synthetic Cubism.

_____

_____

_____

_____

21 Name two artists who were influenced by analytical Cubism.

_____

22 What was the title of the first collage?

_____

23 What were two factors that influenced Surrealism?

_____

24 How was the Dada art movement named?

_____

_____

25 What was the most innovative architecture developed in the early 1900s? Who was the architect?

_____

26 Describe one example of *eclectic* architecture.

_____

_____

_____

27 What was the *Bauhaus*? For what was Walter Gropius known?

_____

_____

_____

28 What event, and when, marked a turning point in twentieth century art history? What was the change in location of artistic leadership at this time?

_____

_____

_____

29 What was the most popular American art style prior to World War II?

_____

30 What American art style was developed by artists including Jackson Pollock and Franz Kline?

_____

31 The variety of experimentation led to pluralism of styles in the contemporary art world. Name three of these styles.

_____

_____

_____

32 What was Mies van der Rohe's motto? In what American city may we find many of his major works?

_____

33 What architect developed the use of ferroconcrete? In what country can his works be seen?

_____

_____

_____

34 Listed below are some of the artists presented in this chapter. Name one of his/her artworks, and state the most appropriate style. (One example is provided.)

Artist	Title of Artwork	Style
Peter Paul Rubens	*Massacre of the Innocents*	Baroque
Rembrandt van Rijn		
Jean-Honoré Fragonard		
Jacques Louis David		
Thomas Jefferson		
Eugene Delacroix		
Gustave Courbet		
Edouard Manet		
Claude Monet		
Mary Cassatt		
Paul Cézanne		
Paul Gauguin		
Henri Matisse		
Emil Nolde		
Paula Modersohn-Becker		
Pablo Picasso		
Georges Braque		
Salvador Dali		
Marcel Duchamp		
John S. Curry		
Jackson Pollock		
Franz Kline		
Louise Nevelson		
Marisol		
Christo		

Test Questions
Chapter 19–Islands of Time II

For questions 1 through 7, select from the following art styles.

1. Baroque	4. Romanticism
2. Rococo	5. Realism
3. Neoclassical	

1 _____ Artists were inspired by the themes and styles of ancient Greece and Rome.

2 _____ *The Swing,* a painting by Jean-Honoré Fragonard, portrays a scene of fun-loving aristocrats in

a makebelieve world.

3 _____ Artists trusted their hearts rather than their heads, painted inspiring scenes of nature.

4 _____ Artists supposedly portrayed life exactly as it was.

5 _____ King Louis XIVs palace in Versailles, France, is an example of this style.

6 _____ Architecture of Washington, DC, is in this style.

7 _____ Elaborate dramatized situations in ornate detail are portrayed on the painted canvas.

For questions 8 through 15, select from the following art styles.

1. Impressionism	4. German Expressionism
2. Post Impressionism	5. Cubism
3. Fauves	

8 _____ *Luncheon of the Boating Party* by Auguste Renoir.

9 _____ Name given to artists of this style by critics who felt they used color in a violent, uncontrolled way.

10 _____ Subject matter is broken up and recombined in an abstract form, emphasizing geometric shapes.

11 _____ Artists concerned with effects of reflected light in nature, attempted to "capture the moment."

12 _____ Artists expressed intensely personal emotions.

13 _____ Artists originally associated with the Impressionists but broke away and went off in their own
individual directions.

14 _____ "The Wild Beasts."

15 _____ Includes analytical and synthetic versions.

For questions 16 through 20, select from the following art styles.

1. Surrealism   4. Abstract Expressionism
2. Dadaism   5. Pop Art
3. Regionalism   6. Op Art

16 _____ Little if any subject matter, emphasis on accident and chance.

17 _____ Most popular American art prior to World War II.

18 _____ "Hobbyhorse."

19 _____ Artists explored the mysterious world of dreams.

20 _____ Artists used familiar symbols, such as grocery store products and comic strips.

21 Since seventeenth century Protestant churches did not commission artists to make murals or sculpture, artists

a. focused on architecture.
b. chose genre subjects.
c. chose elaborate, complex scenes.
d. worked for the aristocracy.

22 The Impressionist painter Claude Monet constructed his entire painting using daubs of paint, a method known as

a. broken color.
b. blending.
c. chiaroscuro.
d. closure.

23 A German design school which influenced modern architecture:

a. Crystal Palace
b. Mondrian
c. Bauhaus
d. Gropius

24 A composition made by gluing varied materials such as paper, cloth, and cardboard onto a flat, firm surface:

a. assemblage
b. fresco
c. collage
d. cloisonné

25 Art forms most influenced by the Industrial Revolution were

a. painting and sculpture.
b. sculpture and architecture.
c. architecture and crafts.
d. crafts and painting.

26 The Chicago fire in 1871 created a need for new commercial buildings. Chicago architects like Louis Sullivan

a. developed skyscrapers.
b. used frame construction.
c. included many towers, arches, and domes.
d. a and b.
e. a and c.
f. none of the above.

27 The architect Frank Lloyd Wright was best known for his

a. commercial buildings.
b. home designs.
c. cathedrals.
d. bridges.

28 What development in the 1500s affected European religion and culture? How is this reflected in the art of the next century?

29 What event marked a turning point in twentieth century art history? What was the change in location of artistic leadership at this time?

30 Many different art styles have developed on the American art scene since 1960. Name two of those styles.

Match the art period or style in the right hand column to the artist in the left hand column.

Artist	**Art style, period or movement**
31 _____ Rembrandt	a. Cubism
32 _____ Eugene Delacroix	b. Dadaism
33 _____ Mary Cassatt	c. Post Impressionism
34 _____ Paul Gauguin	d. Baroque
35 _____ Henri Matisse	e. Fauvism
36 _____ Pablo Picasso	f. Abstract Expressionism
37 _____ Salvador Dali	g. Surrealism
38 _____ Marcel Duchamp	h. Pop Art
39 _____ Jackson Pollock	i. Impressionism
40 _____ Marisol	j. Romanticism

While viewing the indicated overhead transparency for questions 41 through 47, choose the art style that describes it most accurately.

1. Pop Art	3. Folk Art	5. Op Art	7. Cubism
2. Regionalism	4. Fauvism	6. Surrealism	8. Impressionism

Overhead transparency	**Overhead transparency**
41 _____ Picasso, *Still Life with Chair Caning*	**45** _____ Vasarely, *Edetta*
42 _____ Renoir, *Luncheon of the Boating Party*	**46** _____ Oldenburg, *Floor Cake*
43 _____ Dali, *The Persistence of Memory*	**47** _____ Evans, *Design Made at Airlie Garden*
44 _____ Wood, *American Gothic*	

Study Answers
Chapter 19
Islands of Time II

1 Complexity, drama, grandeur. Answers may include: King Louis XIVs palace at Versailles, France; Peter Paul Rubens' *Massacre of the Innocents.*

2 Catholics preferred art with a religious theme; Protestants considered religious art to be idol worship.

3 The Catholic churches and the aristocracy; wealthy middle class (merchants, bankers, lawyers, doctors).

4 Answers may include: Pieter De Hooch's *Mother and Child,* Maria van Oosterwyck's *Vanitas,* Rembrandt's *The Mill.*

5 A philosophy of life that flourished in the 1700s: people placed their faith in reason and science more than in religion.

6 Rococo; pleasure-seeking aristocracy.

7 A late eighteenth century style that found inspiration in the themes and principles of Classical Greek art. Jacques Louis David.

8 Thomas Jefferson; Virginia State Capitol, University of Virginia, architecture of Washington, DC.

9 Answers may include: Major scenes were from nature, full of emotion, dramatic action created from the heart, exotic settings.

10 Gustave Courbet; portrayed life as it really was.

11 Painted entire paintings with daubs of paint.

12 To express emotion.

13 Compositional structure, expressing emotion, color, and pattern.

14 Crafts and architecture.

15 Frame construction.

16 A vast network of wood and iron beams and panes of glass that housed the first world's fair.

17 Louis Sullivan; buildings reflected function and method of construction.

18 In brilliant, daring combinations; shapes were flat, simple. Answers may include Henri Matisse, *The Red Room.*

19 To express personal feelings about life; *Die Brücke* ("The Bridge"), *Der Blaue Reiter* ("The Blue Rider").

20 Pablo Picasso and Georges Braque. Both have sharp angles and interlocking design. Analytical—objects were broken up and recombined in a network of semi-transparent, tilted planes; synthetic—used a variety of colors and textures within shapes.

21 Answers may include: Marc Chagall, Joseph Stella, Piet Mondrian, Umberto Boccioni, David Smith.

22 *Still Life with Chair Caning.*

23 The paintings of Giorgio De Chirico and the writings of Sigmund Freud.

24 Supposedly by placing a knife in a French-German dictionary and selecting the first word that appeared: Dada ("Hobbyhorse" in French).

25 Home architecture; Frank Lloyd Wright.

26 Answers may include the Chicago Tribune Tower (text fig. 19–39); It is a modern skyscraper in Gothic style including even flying buttresses.

27 A German design school; director of Bauhaus, designed world's first multi-storied permanent building with continuous walls of glass.

28 End of the Second World War (1935–1945); passed from Europe to America.

29 Regionalism.

30 Abstract Expressionism.

31 Answers may include: Abstraction, Assemblage, Pop Art, Performance, Environmental, Conceptual, Realism.

32 "Less is more"; Chicago.

33 Le Corbusier, France.

34 Artist

Artist	Title of Artwork	Style
Rembrandt van Rijn;	*Adoration of the Shepherds;*	Baroque
Jean-Honoré Fragonard;	*The Swing;*	Rococo
Jacques Louis David;	*The Oath of the Horatii;*	Neoclassical
Thomas Jefferson;	Virginia State Capitol;	Neoclassical
Eugene Delacroix;	*Arabs Skirmishing in the Mountains;*	Romanticism
Gustave Courbet;	*Burial at Ornans;*	Realism
Edouard Manet;	*Gare Saint-Lazare;*	Realism
Claude Monet;	*La Gerenouillère;*	Impressionism
Mary Cassatt;	*The Bath;*	Impressionism
Paul Cézanne;	*Still Life with Apples and Peaches;*	Post Impressionism
Paul Gauguin;	*The Vision after the Sermon;*	Post Impressionism
Henri Matisse;	*The Red Room;*	Fauves
Emil Nolde;	*Masks;*	German Expressionism
Paula Modersohn-Becker;	*Old Peasant Woman Praying;*	German Expressionism
Pablo Picasso;	*Les Demoiselles d'Avignon;*	Cubism
Georges Braque;	*Violin and Palette;*	Cubism
Salvador Dali;	*The Persistence of Memory;*	Surrealism
Marcel Duchamp;	*Fountain;*	Dada
John S. Curry;	*Baptism in Kansas;*	Regionalism
Jackson Pollock;	*Cathedral;*	Abstract Expressionism
Franz Kline;	*Mahoning;*	Abstract Expressionism
Louise Nevelson;	*Sky Cathedral;*	Assemblage
Marisol;	*Women and Dog;*	Pop Art
Christo;	*Wrapped Coast;*	Environmental

Test Answers
Chapter 19
Islands of Time II

1. 3.
2. 2.
3. 4.
4. 5.
5. 1.
6. 3.
7. 1.
8. 1.
9. 3.
10. 5.
11. 1.
12. 4.
13. 2.
14. 3.
15. 5.
16. 4.
17. 3.
18. 2.
19. 1.
20. 5.
21. B.
22. A.
23. C.
24. C.
25. C.
26. D.

27. B.

28. Reformation. The difference in Catholic and Protestant patronage affected Baroque artists' style and subject matter. Artists in Catholic countries created complex, dramatic works with great detail for rulers, aristocrats, and the church. Their subject matter included portraits of famous people, classical myths, heroic battles, and scenes from the Bible. Protestant churches did not encourage religious art, so artists in the Dutch Republic painted subjects and scenes from everyday life (genre). Clients were professional people from the middle classes.

29. World War II; From Europe to America.

30. Answers may include: Pop Art, Op Art, Environmental, Performance, Conceptual, etc.

31. D.
32. J.
33. I.
34. C.
35. E.
36. A.
37. G.
38. B.
39. F.
40. H.
41. 7.
42. 8.
43. 6.
44. 2.
45. 5.
46. 1.
47. 3.

Chapter 19
Islands of Time II

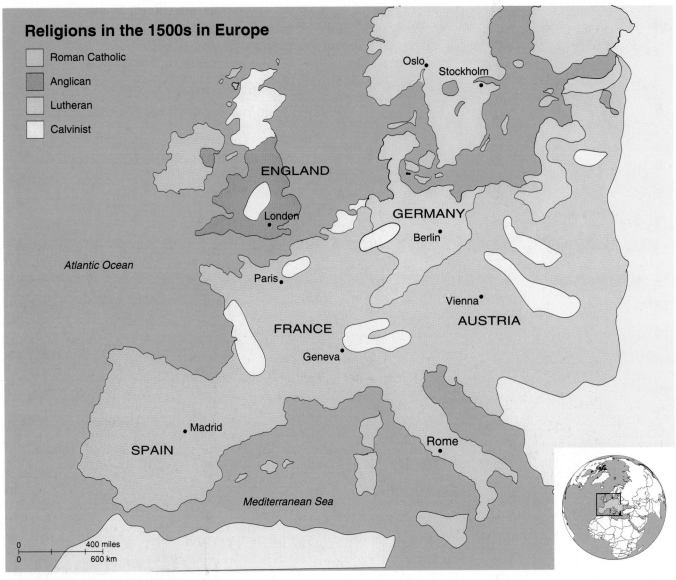

Religions in the 1500s in Europe

- Roman Catholic
- Anglican
- Lutheran
- Calvinist

Oslo
Stockholm
ENGLAND
London
Atlantic Ocean
GERMANY
Berlin
Paris
Vienna
AUSTRIA
FRANCE
Geneva
Madrid
Rome
SPAIN
Mediterranean Sea

0   400 miles
0   600 km

19-1 Religious divisions in sixteenth century Europe.

Chapter 18 ended with a discussion of High Renaissance art in the early 1500s. The 1500s was also the century in which the split in Christianity between Protestant and Catholic began. This development, known as the **Reformation,** affected not only religion but European culture in general. In 1517, just five years after Michelangelo completed the Sistine ceiling,

Martin Luther (fig. 19–2), a German monk, prepared a long list of criticisms of the Catholic church. He nailed the list to the door of a church in Wittenberg. More importantly, the list was printed and circulated throughout Germany. (The printing press had just been developed.) His act eventually led to a revolt against the pope and the Catholic church. New denominations, such as Lutheran, Anabaptist, Mennonite, Calvinist, and Anglican, sprang up in Germany, Scandinavia, Switzerland, the Netherlands, and England.

Meanwhile, Catholics responded with a **Counter-Reformation** led by Ignatius Loyola (fig. 19-3) and his order of monks called the Jesuits. Although Loyola and the Jesuits helped to change many of the practices of the Catholic church, they also helped to harden its doctrines against the Protestants. By the 1600s, the split in Christianity, which had become quite bitter, divided Europe into Catholic and Protestant factions (fig. 19-1). This split is reflected in the art of the 1600s.

The 1600s and the Baroque Style

Italy, as we learned in the previous chapter, was the center of developments in Renaissance art. By 1600 the ideas of this art had spread to other parts of Europe. Gothic styles were abandoned completely. Architects, painters, and sculptors in northern Europe, as well as those in Italy, developed a style called *Baroque*. This new style emphasized complexity, drama, and grandeur. The style was especially popular in Catholic countries. Baroque style was very ornate. To this day, the term baroque is often applied to anything that is excessive or pompous. King Louis XIV's palace at Versailles, France (figures 19-4 and 19-5), is probably the most baroque project ever undertaken. The palace was built by an army of architects, landscape designers, sculptors, stonecutters, and decorators. During the peak of construction, they numbered 36,000 men plus

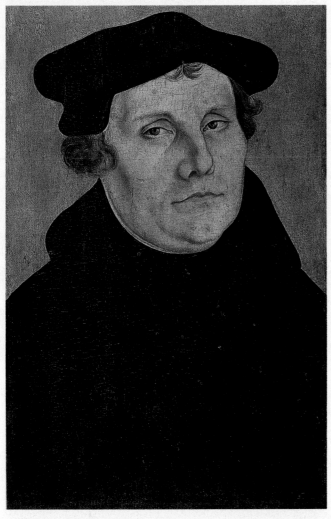

19-2 Lucas Cranach, *Martin Luther.* Galleria degli Uffizi, Firenze.

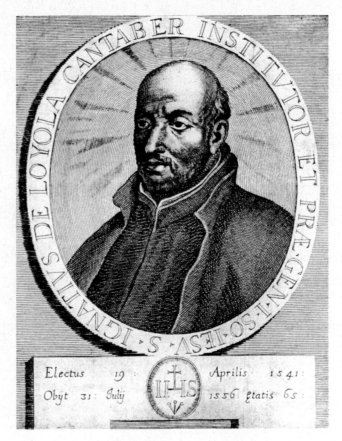

19-3 St. Ignatius Loyola, engraving.

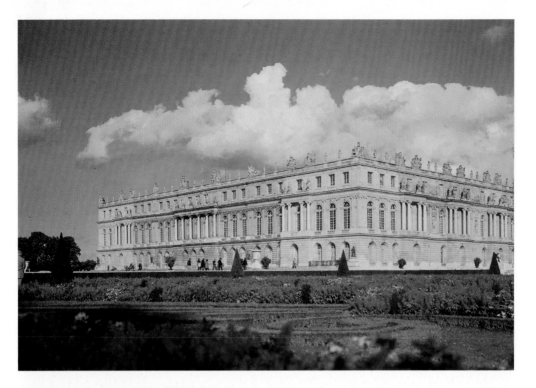

19–5 Louis Le Vau and Jules Hardouin–Mansart, Garden façade, Versailles Palace. 1669–1685. Giraudon/Art Resource, NY.

19–4 Versailles Palace (aerial view), 1661–1688. Palace 1935´ (589 m) wide. Scala/Art Resource, NY.

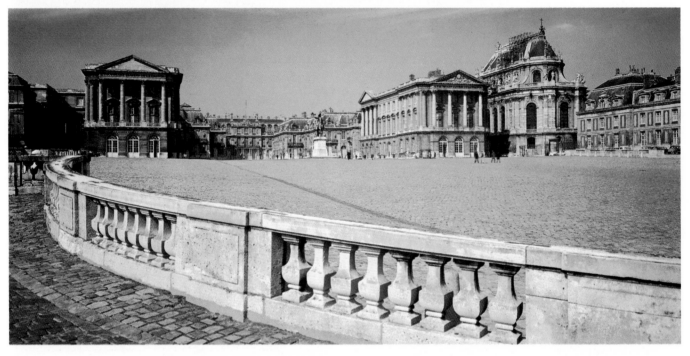

Studio Experience 19.1

A Baroque Pocket Pot

Use clay slabs and various surface decoration techniques to construct a Baroque pocket pot to hang on your wall. Refer to the complex and very ornate style of Baroque metalwork, jewelry, and ceiling frescoes for ideas.

6,000 horses. The palace and its gardens stand as a colossal monument to France's most famous king.

The most popular Catholic painter of the early 1600s was Peter Paul Rubens from Flanders (now Belgium), a small country on the North Sea. Rubens painted for rulers and **aristocrats** (a privileged class with inherited wealth) all over Europe. His subjects included portraits of famous people, classical myths, heroic battles, and scenes from the Bible. His *Massacre*

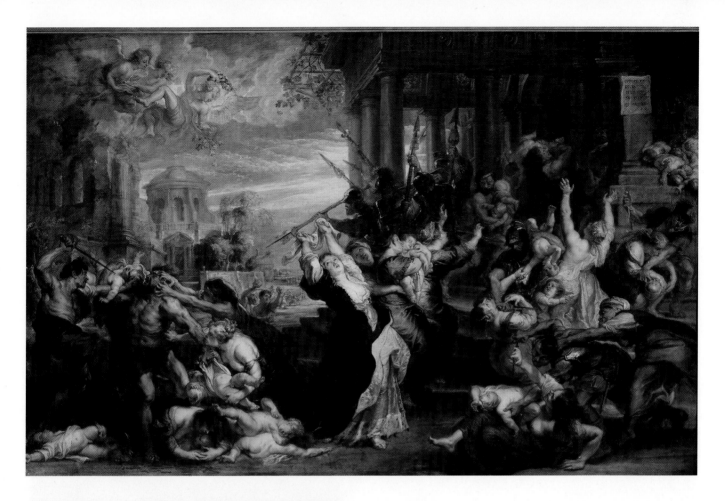

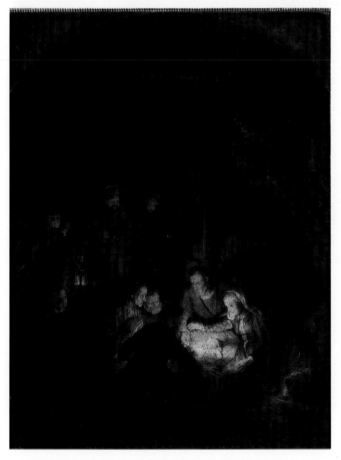

19-6 Peter Paul Rubens, *Massacre of the Innocents*, ca. 1621. Oil on panel, 6´ 6 ¼˝ x 9´ 11˝ (199 x 302 cm). Alte Pinakothek, Munich.

19-7 Rembrandt van Rijn, *Adoration of the Shepherds*, ca. 1646. Oil on canvas rounded at the top, 38 ¼˝ x 24 ¼˝ (97 x 62 cm). Alte Pinakothek, Munich.

of the Innocents (fig. 19–6) is based on the Gospel of Matthew (2:16). It illustrates the killing of all children under the age of two by King Herod's soldiers, after the infant Jesus had been taken to safety in Egypt by Mary and Joseph. It is a vigorously painted commotion of figures charging, fleeing, struggling, and falling. Although true to its subject and full of horror and anguish, *Massacre of the Innocents* is also full of high drama and grandeur. It is set on the steps of a Greek temple, with classical ruins just visible in the distant haze. All of the soldiers, men, women, and children have handsome, robust bodies. Even their costumes, torn or otherwise, are splendid. The painting looks like a scene from an opera. One can imagine hearing a soprano in center stage sing a tragic aria.

Compare Rubens's painting to Rembrandt's *Adoration of the Shepherds* (fig. 19–7), which is based on a different episode of the Christmas story. The Rembrandt is not at all theatrical. Instead of handsome, athletic bodies, all of the people have ordinary bodies. All, including Joseph and Mary, are dressed in peasants' clothes. The setting—as dark, rustic, and dirty as any stable at night—is anything but grand. The newborn child and the intimate group around him are set aglow by the lantern held by Joseph. The faces of the shepherds in the outer circle reflect the radiance of the child. Because *Adoration* is not theatrical, it more successfully captures the mystery of this sacred moment in the Christmas story.

Rembrandt, a Dutchman, made over eight hundred paintings, drawings, and etchings of religious subjects. In this respect, he differed from his fellow Dutch artists. A small country on the North Sea just north of Flanders, the Dutch Republic was predominately Protestant. The Dutch Reformed church, unlike the Catholic church, did not commission artists to make murals or sculptures. Unlike Catholics, Protestants tended to look upon religious art as idol worship, and akin to magic or superstition. Dutch artists turned to other subjects, particularly scenes of everyday life like *Mother and Child* (fig. 19–8) by Pieter de Hooch and still lifes like *Vanitas* (fig. 19–9) by Maria

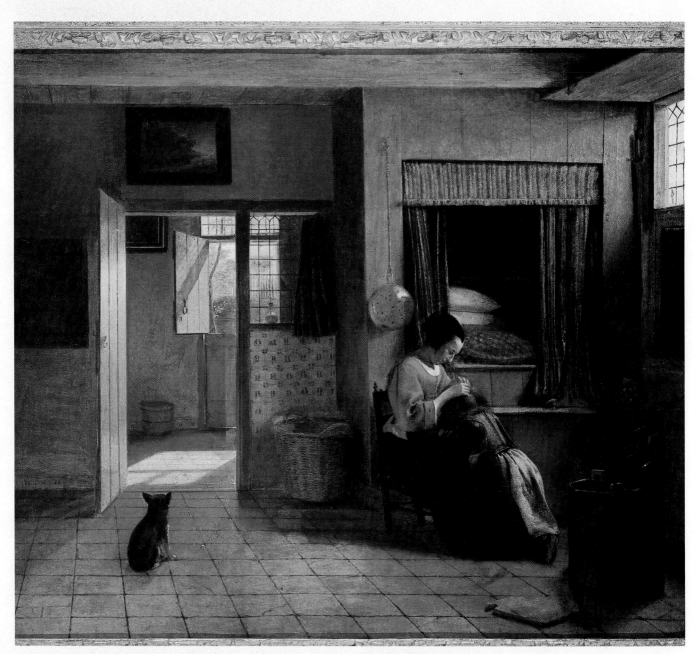

19–8   Pieter de Hooch, *A Mother's Duty*, ca. 1660. Oil on canvas, 4′ 8″ x 6′ 2 ¼″ (142 x 189 cm). Rijksmuseum-Stichting, Amsterdam.

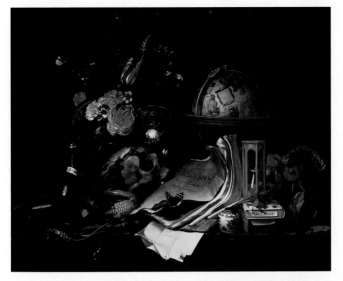

19-9 Maria van Oosterwyck, *Vanitas*, 1668. Oil on canvas, 28 ¾″ x 34 ⅞″ (73 x 89 cm). Kunsthistorisches Museum, Vienna.

van Oosterwyck. The clients of Dutch artists were the wealthy middle classes—merchants, bankers, burgomasters, lawyers, doctors.

Rembrandt painted religious and nonreligious works. (Recall *The Mill,* his somber landscape discussed in Chapter 5, fig. 5–31.) His clients bought both kinds, although his art was not appreciated then as much as it is now. Rembrandt was unique in his time. Unlike most Dutch painters, he continued to make religious art; unlike most Baroque painters in Catholic Europe, he filled his pictures with ordinary people in ordinary settings. In other words, Rembrandt illustrated the stories of the Bible in the context of everyday life. He is perhaps the only artist, certainly the greatest, to express Christian content from a Protestant perspective.

Meanwhile, in the century of Rubens and Rembrandt, the field of science was gaining momentum. Francis Bacon, an English philosopher, outlined a method of science based on observation. Galileo Galilei, a Florentine astronomer, constructed a telescope that was able to verify Copernicus's theory that the earth revolves around the sun (Chapter 18). Johannes Kepler, a German mathematician, improved on Copernicus's idea by determining that the planets traveled in elliptical orbits. Isaac Newton, an English mathematician and inventor of calculus, brought together the research and thinking of the century and devised the law of gravity. This principle explains the movements not only of the planets, but of the whole universe.

The Enlightenment, Rococo, and Neoclassicism

The scientific boom of the 1600s led to the **Enlightenment,** a philosophy of life that flourished in the 1700s. Conservative Catholics and Protestants objected to the new science because they felt it challenged the beliefs and doctrines of the Bible. Enlightenment philosophers, however, believed that science not only revealed the secrets of nature, but improved people's lives. These philosophers (fig. 19-10) placed their faith in reason and science more than in religion. They thought of the universe as an intricate machine, like a huge clock. According to them, God started the clock, but then got out of the way. This concept of the universe was known as *Deism.* This religious view influenced America's founding fathers, including Benjamin Franklin and Thomas Jefferson.

Meanwhile, the major art style of the 1700s seemed to be going in a direction all its own. Called *Rococo,* this style did not reflect the views of Catholics, Protestants, or the Enlightenment. Instead, it reflected the views and lifestyles of the pleasure-seeking aristocracy. *The Swing* by Jean-Honore Fragonard (fig. 19–11) is typical of the style. Here is a scene of aristocrats at play

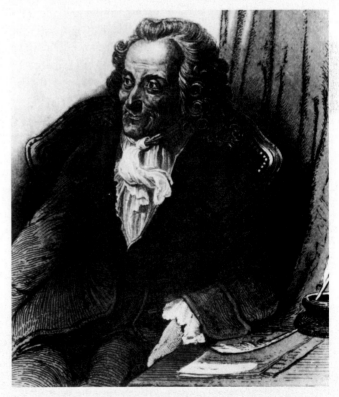

19–10 Voltaire.

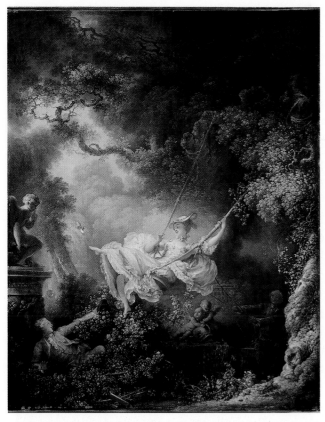

19–11 Jean-Honoré Fragonard, *The Swing*, 1766. Approx. 32″ x 35″ (81 x 89 cm). Reproduced by permission of the Trustees of the Wallace Collection, London.

in a make-believe world. *The Swing* shares with Baroque art fluid brushwork and lively movement. However, its pastel hues, satiny textures, and delicate figures are much lighter in spirit. Its content is also lighter, if not "light-headed."

Later in the century, a reaction set in against Rococo. The **middle classes,** a segment of society that grew dramatically in size and power during the 1700s, felt that Rococo art did not represent their values. Johann Joachim Winckelmann, a German art historian, said that Europe needed an art of "noble simplicity and calm grandeur" to replace Rococo. The hopes of the public and Winckelmann were fulfilled in 1784 when Jacques Louis David unveiled his *The Oath of the Horatii* (fig. 19–12). Painted only eighteen years after *The Swing*, David's picture could not be more different. Rather than fun-loving aristocrats, *The Oath* features Roman warriors swearing an oath to fight a duel to the death. Off to the right their women are slumped in despair. Rather than a beautiful garden, it is set in a severely simple Roman court. It is also very different in style. Its darks and lights are strong. Its colors are

mostly primary. All of its forms, including the people, are starkly defined. They seem to be sculpted in stone.

The Oath of the Horatii was the first painting of a new style. Like Renaissance art (Chapter 18), this style was inspired by the themes and principles of classical art. Indeed, this new art became known as *Neoclassical*. Intellectuals approved of it as a symbol of seriousness and reason. The French middle classes saw it as an allegory of honor and patriotism. It also became a symbol of the French Revolution. David, who was personally active in the French Revolution, eventually became Napoleon's court painter.

Meanwhile, another revolutionary, Thomas Jefferson, was attracted to Neoclassicism when he was ambassador to France (1785–89). Jefferson was an architect as well as a statesman. He admired the Neoclassical buildings that were being erected in Paris (fig. 19–13) as part of Napoleon's grandiose plans to redesign the city. But Jefferson especially admired the Roman temple in Nîmes (fig. 18–19). He used this temple as a model for the Virginia State Capitol (fig. 19–14). Later, he used classical models for the campus of the University of Virginia. Thus Neoclassicism, the art of "noble simplicity and calm grandeur," was brought to America, where it became very popular. Architecturally, Washington, DC is the most Neoclassical city in the world. (Recall the design of the rotunda of the National Gallery, fig. 7–6.)

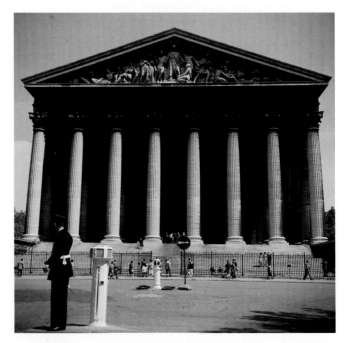

19–13 Pierre–Alexandre Vignon. Façade, La Madeleine, Paris, 1762–1829. 350′ (107 m) long, 47′ (14 m) wide, podium 23′ (7 m) high. Giraudon/Art Resource, NY.

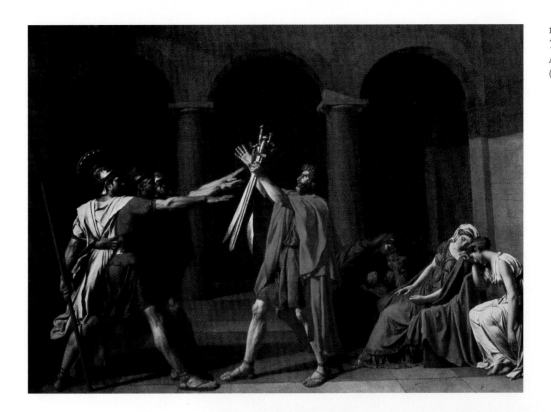

19-12 Jacques Louis David, *The Oath of the Horatii*, 1784. Approximately 14´ x 11´ (4.2 x 3.3 m). Louvre, Paris.

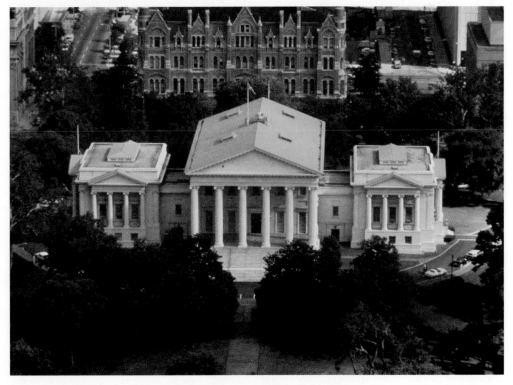

19-14 Thomas Jefferson, State Capitol, Richmond, Virginia, designed 1785–1789. Metropolitan Richmond (VA) Chamber of Commerce.

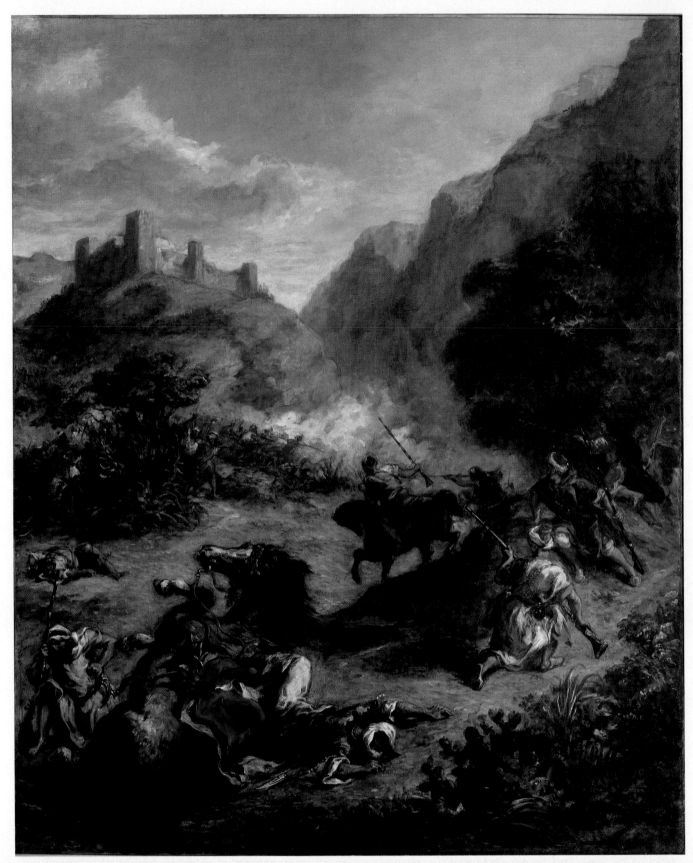

19–15 Eugène Delacroix, *Arabs Skirmishing in the Mountains*, 1863. Canvas, 36 ³⁄₈″ x 29 ³⁄₈″ (92 x 75 cm). The National Gallery of Art, Washington, DC (Chester Dale Fund).

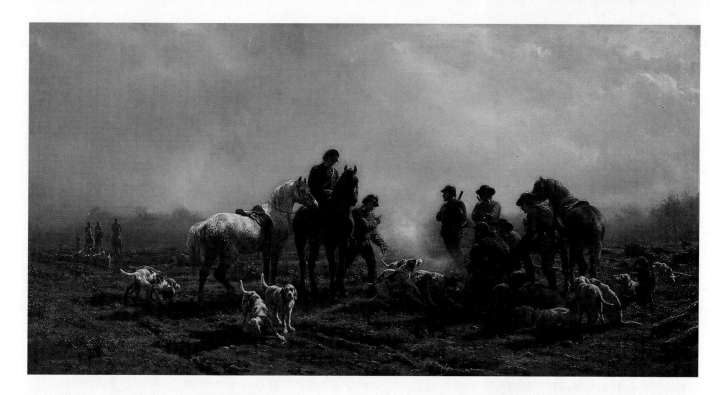

Romanticism, Realism, Impressionism, and Post Impressionism

As we have seen, cultural styles occur in cycles. The closer we get to the present, the shorter the cycles seem to become. The hopes of the Enlightenment and the artistic and philosophical ideals of Neoclassicism were dashed by the atrocities of the French Revolution and the failure of the Napoleonic Wars. Faith in reason was replaced by renewed faith in God, and especially by faith in emotion. This broad cultural movement was called *Romanticism.* Romanticism peaked in the first half of the 1800s. It could be said that Romantic writers and artists trusted their hearts rather than their heads.

Eugène Delacroix, a colorful man with strong emotions, was the idol of Romantic painters and poets. He loved the outdoors and wild animals. He preferred the simple life of rural peasants, especially the Moslem Arabs of North Africa. Ironically, Delacroix himself was considered a "man-about-town" in Paris. Paris, the capital of French culture, was anything but rural. But to Delacroix, Arabs were not only close to nature, but fierce and courageous warriors. Many of his attitudes are expressed in *Arabs Skirmishing in the Mountains* (fig. 19–15). The painting portrays a fierce battle in the wilderness at the foot of a mountain crowned with an ancient fortress. The colors—shades

19–16 Rosa Bonheur, *Gathering for the Hunt,* 1856. Oil on canvas, 30 ½″ x 58 ⅛″ (77 x 148 cm). Haggin Collection, The Haggin Museum, Stockton, California.

of red and orange set against a bright sky—are vivid. Delacroix's brush strokes, unlike David's, are as lively as the battle.

Marie Rosalle (Rosa) Bonheur's *Gathering for the Hunt* (fig. 19–16) expressed Romanticism and the love of the outdoors in more subdued ways. Instead of Arabs, guns, or falling horses, her picture contains a group of French farmers, horses, and dogs on a hazy autumn morning. The brushwork is calm. The colors are balanced between warm and cool. The composition is horizontal, stressing nature's breadth and continuity. Although *Gathering for the Hunt* is much less dramatic than *Arabs Skirmishing in the Mountains,* it is no less a tribute to nature. It also shows tendencies of another movement of the 1800s: *Realism.*

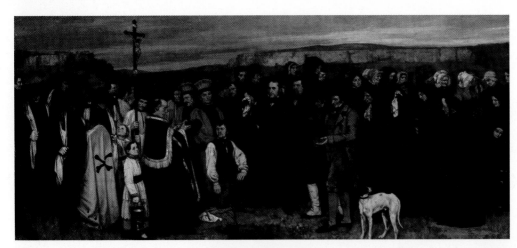

19–17 Gustave Courbet, *Burial at Ornans*, 1849. Approx. 10″ x 22″ (26 x 56 cm). Courtesy The Louvre, Paris and Réunion des Musées Nationaux.

19–18 Edouard Manet, *Gare Saint-Lazare*, 1873. Oil on canvas, 36 ¾″ x 43 ⅞″ (93 x 111 cm). National Gallery of Art, Washington, DC (Gift of Horace Havemeyer in memory of his mother, Louisine W. Havemeyer).

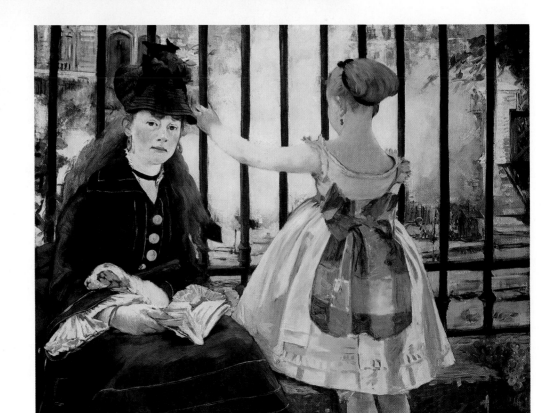

At mid-century, Gustave Courbet became the leader of the Realist movement. This movement, unlike either the Neoclassical or Romantic movement, portrayed life as it is, without nobility, drama, or condescension. His *Burial at Ornans* (fig. 19–17) is typical of Realism. In this homely scene, townspeople are gathered around a grave. There is no trace of beauty or sentiment. The public at the time thought that such a subject and treatment was too commonplace to be considered art.

Edouard Manet, another Realist, focused on the modern city and its people, especially the well-to-do middle class. Like the woman in *Gare* [Railroad Station] *Saint Lazare* (fig. 19–18), Manet's people often have the offhand look of someone caught in a moment of casual activity. The woman will go back to reading her book. The small girl gazing through the iron bars will lose interest as soon as the cloud of steam fades. Manet not only captured the spirit of everyday city life, he pioneered a fresh approach to painting. The figures, unlike those of David, Bonheur, and even Courbet, appear rather flat. As an American critic said, they look as if they had been clipped out of a sheet of tin. Their sense of flatness is partly due to a lack of shading. It is also due to the brightness of the colors and the bold pattern of the bars directly behind the figures.

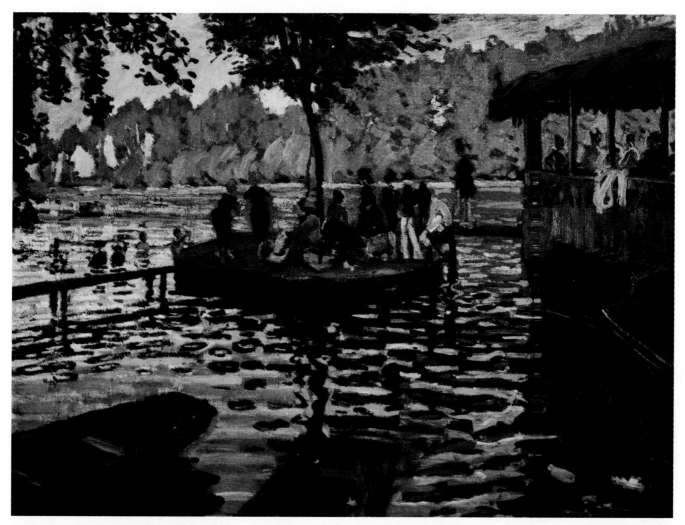

19–19 Claude Monet, *La Grenouillère*, 1869. Oil on canvas, 29 ⅜″ x 39 ¼″ (75 x 100 cm). The Metropolitan Museum of Art, H.O. Havemeyer Collection (Bequest of Mrs. H.O. Havemeyer, 1929).

Manet's subject matter and style influenced still another art movement of the 1800s: *Impressionism.* You have already seen examples of Impressionism in this book: *Luncheon of the Boating Party* by Auguste Renoir (fig. 3–1), *The Bath* by Mary Cassatt (fig. 5–25), and *Waterloo Bridge* by Claude Monet (fig. 10–8). Monet's *La Grenouillère* (fig. 19–19), even more than those, illustrates the characteristics of the style. Like Manet's scene at the railroad station, *La Grenouillère* shows an offhand moment in the lives of some city dwellers, in this case at a river marina. But Monet went beyond Manet in his treatment of the subject. He constructed the entire picture out of nothing more than bright daubs of paint, a method known as *broken color.* When viewed at close range, the daubs tend to be more apparent than the forms. But when viewed at a proper distance, the daubs merge into recognizable trees, people, restaurant, and boats. This kind of painting is often more fresh and vibrant than traditional paint-

ings in which the forms are carefully drawn and the colors are carefully blended. The sensation of rippling water is especially effective.

In many ways Monet's real subject matter was light and color, or as he explained, "to reveal no more of reality than the shifting flux of appearances." Some of Monet's fellow painters broke away to become known as *Post Impressionists.* Although they learned about color from the Impressionists, these artists did not accept the idea that art was a "shifting flux of appearances." Paul Cézanne, in particular, desired a more structured art, "something solid and durable, like the art of the museums." The fruit and objects in his *Still Life with Apples and Peaches* (fig. 19–20) seem indeed to be solid and durable. Furthermore, Cézanne took pains to balance the visual weights and directions so that the composition would be as solid and durable as the fruit.

Georges Seurat, another Post Impressionist, admired the Impressionists' broken color. He tried to use it more systematically while composing his pictures with utmost care. (Recall his *Bathing at Asnières,* fig. 10–1.) Still another Post Impressionist, van Gogh, admired the brightness of Impressionists' colors. Unlike Monet, however, van Gogh used color to express emotions rather than just the changing qualities of reflected light. (Recall his paintings, figures 6–32 and 6–33.) Edvard Munch, like van Gogh, often used acrid color and rhythmical lines to express despair, as in his work *The Scream* (fig. 10–7).

The works of the Post Impressionist Paul Gauguin display the flatness of form found in the works of both Manet and Monet. But in Gauguin's paintings, such as his *The Vision After the Sermon* (fig. 19–21), this flatness is much more decorative. Like Cassatt and van Gogh, Gauguin was influenced by Japanese woodcuts (fig. 19–22). Japanese woodcuts had crisp outlines, flat patterns, and bold designs. (These woodcuts were of the ukiyo-e variety discussed in Chapter 16.) Japanese prints, which had been used by the Japanese to wrap their exports, were avidly collected by both Impressionists and Post Impressionists.

Thus by the end of the 1800s, art had reached a turning point. Specifically, it was turning away from the principles of pictorial realism that had been introduced by Donatello and Masaccio (Chapter 18) and that had dominated European art ever since. Instead of

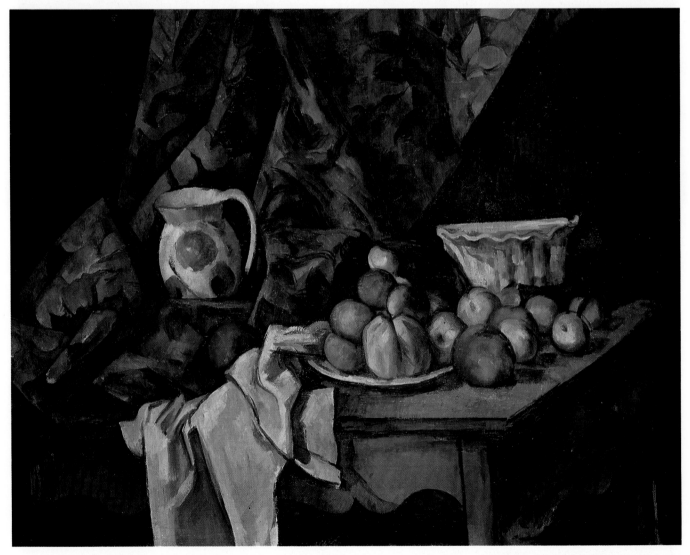

19–20 Paul Cézanne, *Still Life with Apples and Peaches,* ca. 1905. Oil on canvas, 32″ x 39 9/16″ (81 x 101 cm). National Gallery of Art, Washington, DC (Gift of Eugene and Agnes Meyer).

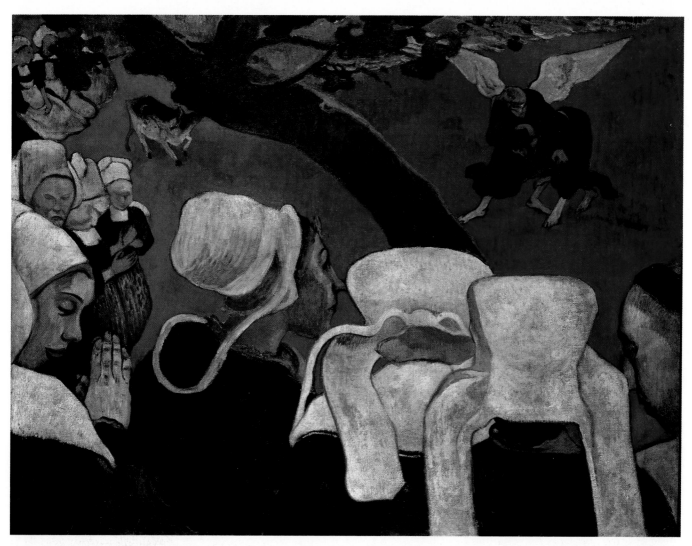

19–21 Paul Gauguin, *The Vision After the Sermon (Jacob Wrestling with the Angel)*, 1888. Oil on canvas, 28 ¾″ x 36 ¼″ (73 x 92 cm). National Gallery of Scotland, Edinburgh.

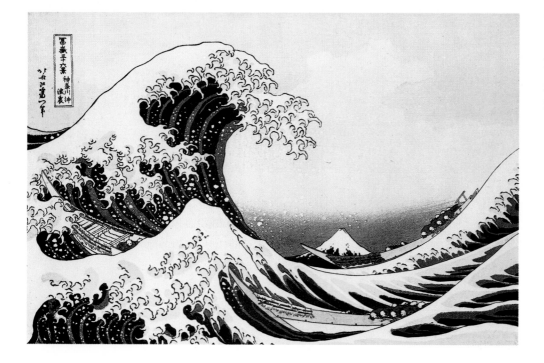

19–22 Katsushika Hokusai, *The Great Wave* from *Thirty-six Views of Mt. Fuji*, Tokugawa period. Woodcut, 10″ x 14 ¾″ (25 x 37 cm). Spaulding Collection, Courtesy, Museum of Fine Arts, Boston.

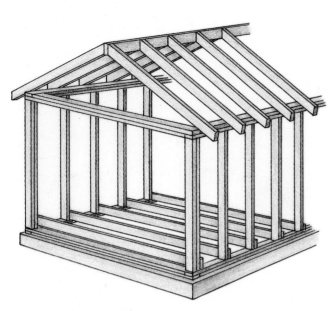

19–23 Frame construction.

realism, the values of compositional structure, of expressing emotion, and of pattern and color were beginning to take priority. These values were to be asserted with even greater force in the twentieth century.

The Industrial Revolution

In addition to art movements, the 1800s also witnessed the *Industrial Revolution.* Large industries replaced small shops, leading to a rapid changeover from hand-made goods to mass production. People had more material things, like clothes, and more leisure time. Post-industrial society also seemed to experience boredom and a sense of rootlessness. All of these side effects of the Industrial Revolution are reflected in Manet's and Monet's people. Note the detached look of the woman at the railroad station and the impersonality of the people at the marina. The impact of the Industrial Revolution, however, was felt more directly in crafts (Chapter 13) and in architecture.

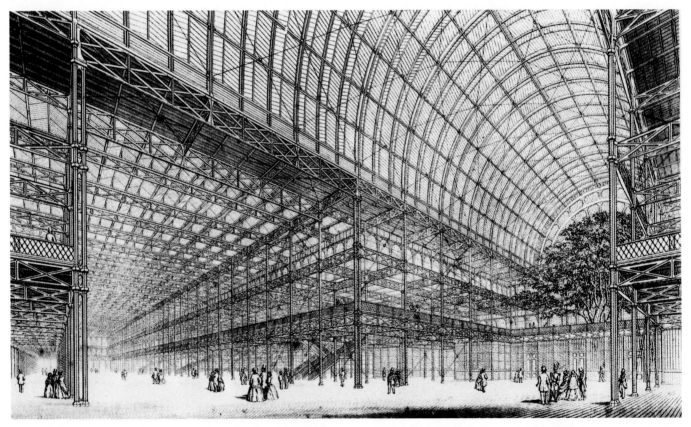

19–24 Joseph Paxton, interior view of the Crystal Palace, Hyde Park, 1851. From a print by R. Cuff after W. G. Brounger.

Architecture: Frame Construction

Up to the 1800s, major public buildings were mainly cathedrals, palaces, theatres, and town halls. All were built according to post-and-lintel and arch methods of construction (Chapter 18). The new industries of the 1800s required new kinds of buildings: factories, massive warehouses, railroad stations, department stores, and office buildings. Masonry architecture was too costly and inefficient for such buildings. Meanwhile, the new industry itself produced such things as standardized nails, rivets, boards, metal beams, and glass panes in huge quantities. This made possible a new method of construction: *wood frame* and *metal frame.*

In masonry methods of construction, walls, columns, buttresses, and so forth are used to support floors and ceilings. By contrast, in frame construction, many thin, relatively lightweight beams are joined to form a rigid framework like a cage. Walls are added to the framework as needed. The walls do not have to support the floors and ceilings. Therefore, these walls may be of any material, even glass. The earliest examples of frame construction were probably wood-frame houses (called "balloon-frame") that sprang up in the boom towns of the American Midwest in the early 1800s (fig. 19–23).

But the most significant early example was the Crystal Palace (fig. 19–24). This vast network of wood and iron beams and panes of glass housed the first World's Fair. Erected in 1851 in less than six months (compared to six decades for some Gothic cathedrals), this enormous glass-enclosed shed covered 800,000 square feet (74,000 square meters). The name Crystal Palace was invented by the fairgoers themselves, who had never seen anything so large or so radiant.

The next stage in the development of frame construction took place not in London or Paris, but in Chicago. During the 1880s, when Post Impressionists were pioneering new styles of painting, Chicago builders were pioneering new kinds of commercial construction. Because of the fire of 1871, new buildings were needed in Chicago's Loop (downtown). However, real estate prices in the Loop were extremely high. So, using the technology of metal-frame construction and the newly invented passenger elevator, Chicago architects developed a new type of building. This new construction took advantage of the inexpensive vertical

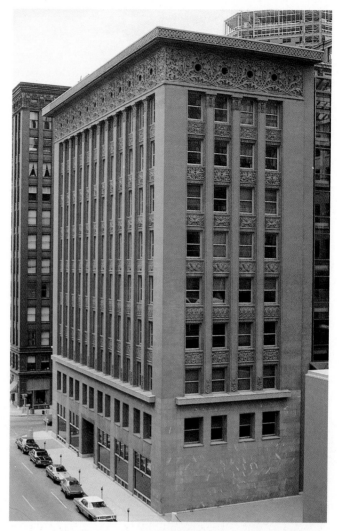

19–25 Louis Sullivan, Wainwright Building, St. Louis, Missouri, 1890–1891. Photograph: George Barford.

space of the sky instead of the costly horizontal space of the ground. It was called the skyscraper.

The style of this architecture was called the *Chicago School.* Significantly, it was relatively lacking in columns, arches, arcades, pediments, towers, and domes that people had grown to expect in public buildings. Louis Sullivan, the leader of the Chicago School, coined the motto "Form Follows Function." The design of a building would reflect its function and method of construction. His design for the Wainwright Building in St. Louis (fig. 19–25) became a classic for downtown office buildings. It is a simple cube with a two-story base, a middle section, and an ornate top. Sullivan never intended his motto to mean the complete elimination of ornament, however. He added his own decorative accents to all of his buildings. In the Wainwright, these are visible not only on the ornate top but also beneath each window and around the main entrance.

Art of the First Half of the Twentieth Century

The twentieth century, the century of two world wars, mass genocide, inflations, depressions, and "future shock," has also been a tumultuous one for art, especially during the years before World War I (1914–18). More changes occurred during that period than had occurred collectively in the previous four hundred years.

In 1905 a show in Paris contained such provocative paintings that a critic referred to them as fauves (French for *wild beasts*). They featured brilliant colors and simple shapes, like those in Henri Matisse's *The Red Room* (fig. 19–26). The paintings in that exhibit were truly "modern." In our day, they would not be out of place at all. But they seemed very wild to the 1905 public. Today, *Fauvism* refers to an important break-through in the modern movement, and bright colors, like those in *The Red Room*, are considered beautiful. Matisse took red, the most stimulating hue of all, and tempered it with the cool colors in the window, the color of the woman's blouse, and the blue of the many decorative lines. He thus brought the powerful forces of brilliant color under control. Matisse was a master at making balanced paintings with daring color combinations.

At about the time the Fauvists were shocking Paris, artists in Germany were beginning to rebel against traditional art and traditional ways of thinking about art. Some even organized into groups. One group in Dresden was called *Die Brucke* (The Bridge). Another in Munich was called *Der Blaue Reiter* (The Blue Rider). These artists and others active in the modern movement prior to the Nazi takeover (1933) were called *German Expressionists*.

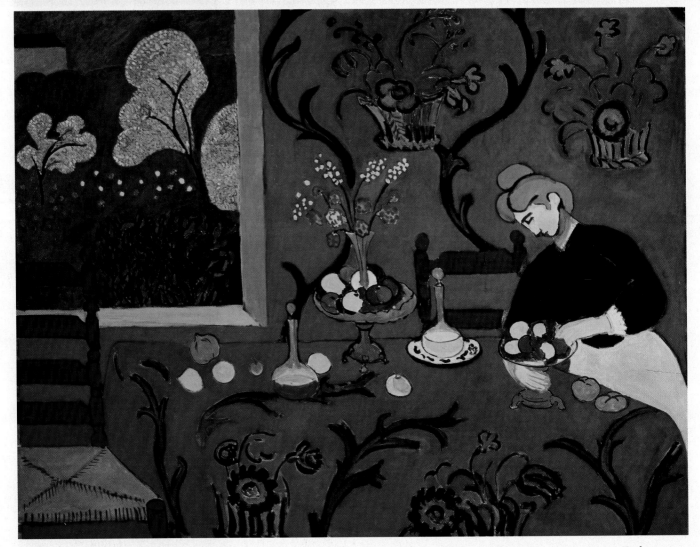

19-26 Henri Matisse, *The Red Room*, 1908–1909. Oil on canvas, 71″ x 97″ (180 x 246 cm). ©1993 Succession H. Matisse/ARS, New York.

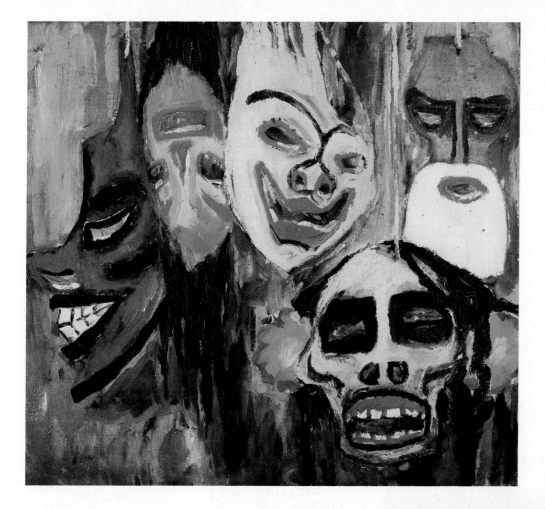

19-28 Emil Nolde, *Masks,* 1911. Oil on canvas, 29″ x 30″ (73 x 77 cm). The Nelson-Atkins Museum of Art, Kansas City, Missouri (Gift of the Friends of Art).

German Expressionists tended to use bright color and flat pattern to express personal feelings about life. Sometimes these feelings were sad or disturbing. As its title suggests, *Old Peasant Woman Praying* (fig. 19-27) by Paula Modersohn-Becker expresses melancholy as well as sympathy for peasant life. Its sincerity of expression is reminiscent of the work of van Gogh, who was one of the German Expressionists' heroes. If she had not died at age 31, Modersohn-Becker would probably have become a dominant figure in the Expressionist movement. *Masks* (fig. 19-28) by Emil Nolde, a member of Die Brucke, represents the German interest in primitive art and the grotesque. Serious themes drawn in harsh styles are typical of twentieth-century German art. For example, see Käthe Kollwitz's *Death Seizing a Woman* (fig. 12-24) and Ernst Barlach's *The Vision* (fig. 13-9).

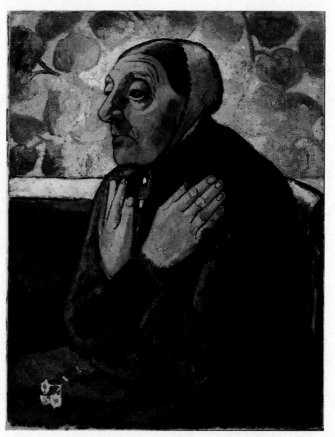

19-27 Paula Modersohn-Becker, *Old Peasant Woman Praying,* ca. 1906. Oil on canvas, 29 ¾″ x 22 ¾″ (76 x 58 cm). The Detroit Institute of Arts (Gift of Robert H. Tannahill).

Although Wassily Kandinsky was Russian-born, he was the leader of Der Blaue Reiter and a highly respected member of the German Expressionist movement. Most significantly, Kandinsky was the first artist to pursue total abstraction. As early as 1910, he made a watercolor that was completely without subject matter and recognizable imagery. His *Sketch I for "Composition VII"* (fig. 19–29) is suggestive of turbulent emotion. The painting is typical of the freeform, coloristic abstractions that Kandinsky had developed out of the tradition of German Expressionism.

In 1905, the year of the Fauvists' show in Paris, Pablo Picasso was a struggling young painter in that city. His *The Old Guitarist* (reviewed in Chapter 6, fig. 6–30) is typical of his early work. Inspired by the success of Fauvism, Picasso embarked on a groundbreaking project of his own in 1906. The result of these efforts, *Les Demoiselles d'Avignon* (fig. 19–30), was

unveiled in 1907. In this painting, the human form is savagely distorted. Imagine how radical this painting must have seemed to the 1907 public. Even Matisse was shocked, calling it a mockery of the modern movement. Today, after nearly a century of modern art, it still looks disturbing. But *Les Demoiselles* is not without purpose. The figures and the background are consistently distorted to create a system of shallow peaks and valleys—as if the whole canvas had been wadded and then spread flat. *Les Demoiselles* became the prototype of a significant early twentieth-century style: Cubism.

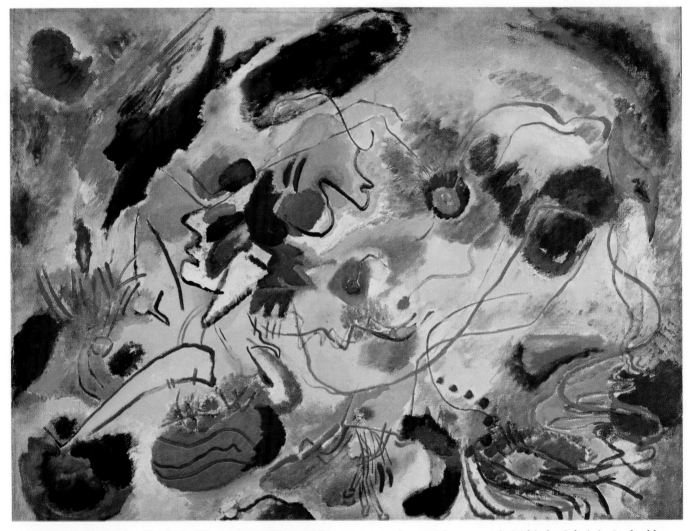

19–29 Wassily Kandinsky, *Sketch I for "Composition VII"*, 1913. Oil on canvas, 30 ¼″ x 39 ⅜″ (77 x 100 cm). Städtische Galerie im Lenbachhaus, Munich.

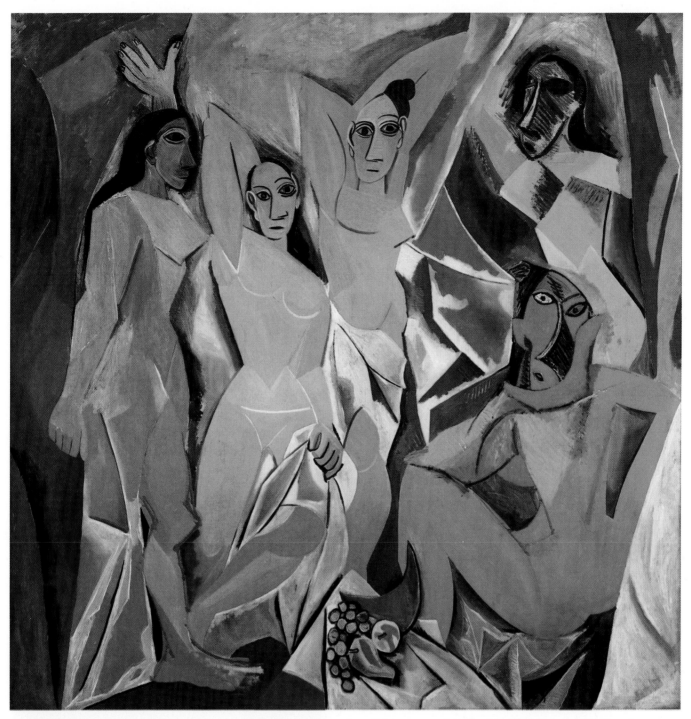

19–30 Pablo Picasso, *Les Demoiselles d'Avignon*, 1907. Oil on canvas, 96″ x 92″ (2.24 x 2.34 m). Collection, The Museum of Modern Art, New York (Acquired through the Lillie P. Bliss Bequest).

Try it Yourself

Can you think of any images on MTV that were inspired by early twentieth century art?

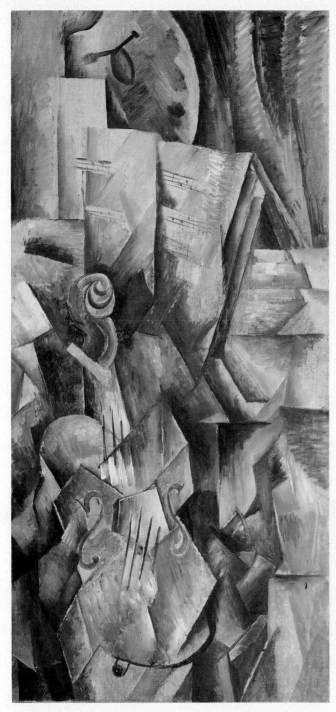

The first variety of Cubism was called *analytical* or *facet* Cubism. Picasso and French artist Georges Braque developed it between 1909 and 1912. A good example is Braque's *Violin and Palette* (fig. 19-31). In this painting, still life objects are broken up and recombined to fashion a network of semitransparent, tilted planes or *facets*—like the surface of a gem. Almost from the time it was introduced, facet Cubism influenced other artists. In *I and the Village* (fig. 19-32), Marc Chagall interspersed images from his memories of rural Russia among the transparent planes of facet Cubism. In *Brooklyn Bridge* (fig. 19-33), Joseph Stella used interlocking facets to express a kaleidoscopic impression of urban America.

In addition to these, we have seen examples in earlier chapters. Piet Mondrian's *Composition in Black, White and Red* (fig. 7-10) is an outgrowth of facet Cubism. Even sculpture was affected by Cubism. Recall Umberto Boccioni's *Unique Forms of Continuity in Space* (fig. 8-15) and David Smith's famous *Cubi* series (fig. 13-32).

Despite their success with facet Cubism, Picasso and Braque continued to experiment. In 1913, the two artists created the first collage (Picasso's *Still Life with Chair Caning*, fig. 12-41). Out of the collage medium, Picasso and Braque developed the second variety of

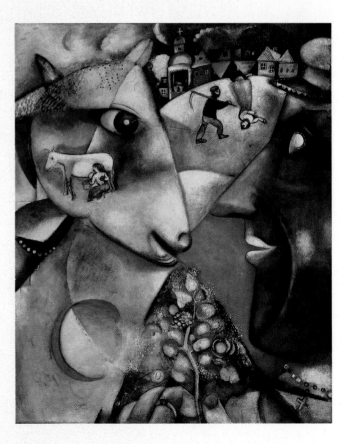

19-31 Georges Braque, *Violin and Palette*, 1909–1910. Oil on canvas, 36 ¼″ x 16 ⅞″ (92 x 43 cm). Guggenheim Museum, New York. Photograph: David Heald.

19-32 Marc Chagall, *I and the Village*, 1911. Oil on canvas, 6′ 3″ x 59″ (192 x 151 cm). Collection, The Museum of Modern Art, New York (Mrs. Simon Guggenheim Fund).

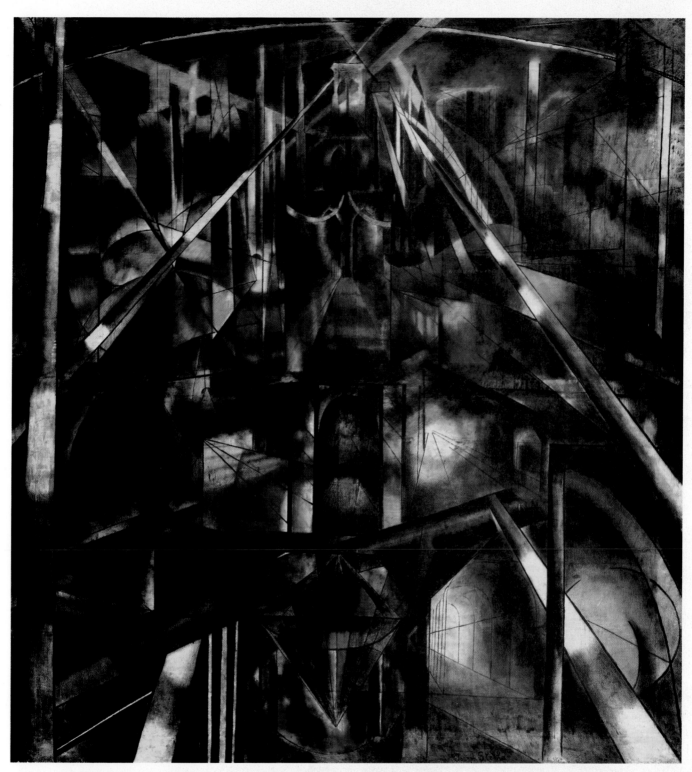

19-33 Joseph Stella, *Brooklyn Bridge,* 1917–1918. Oil on canvas, 84″ x 76″ (213 x 193 cm). Yale University Art Gallery (Gift of Collection Societe Anonyme).

Cubism, called synthetic Cubism. Unlike facet Cubism, *synthetic* Cubism features flat shapes and a variety of colors and textures, as in Braque's *The Table* (fig. 19–34). Picasso's whimsical *Three Musicians* (fig. 5–10) is another good example of the style.

About the only things the two varieties of Cubism share are sharp angles and interlocking design. Picasso often returned to Cubism, using a combination of facet and synthetic methods. He also experimented with a variety of styles, including a kind of realism (*A*

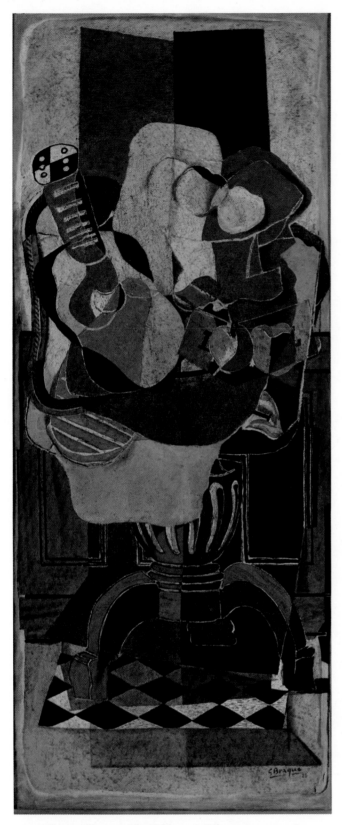

Woman in White, fig. 6–8). Meanwhile, Braque spent the rest of his career making still lifes like *The Table*.

Picasso and Braque had experimented with new approaches to style and media in the second decade of the century. At the same time Giorgio de Chirico experimented with a new approach to subject matter. The style of *The Mystery and Melancholy of a Street* (fig. 19–35) is not particularly new, especially for 1914. But the subject matter is new and unusual. There is a peculiar mix of figures and objects. A deserted square contains a child with a hoop, a gypsy wagon, and a long shadow. It is also strange, like a bad dream. Notice how the exaggerated perspective makes the square appear longer, and, therefore, emptier.

The paintings of de Chirico, along with the writings of Sigmund Freud, the father of modern psychology, influenced *Surrealism*. This art movement specialized in unconscious experiences and dreams. *The Persistence of Memory* (fig. 19–36) is a haunting painting by Salvador Dali. It is a good example of an art that often used extremely realistic methods to portray the mysterious and sometimes foreboding world of dreams. Dali's *Mae West* (fig. 10–12) is mysterious, but not necessarily foreboding.

Dada is the final early twentieth-century movement we will review. Dada was born in 1916, when the

19–34 Georges Braque, *The Table*, 1928. Oil on canvas, 70 ¾″ x 28 ¾″ (180 x 73 cm). Collection, The Museum of Modern Art, New York (Acquired through the Lillie P. Bliss Bequest).

19–35 Giorgio de Chirico, *The Mystery and Melancholy of a Street*, 1914. Oil on canvas, 34 ¼″ x 28 ⅛″ (87 x 71 cm). Private Collection. Photograph courtesy Aquavella Galleries, Inc., New York.

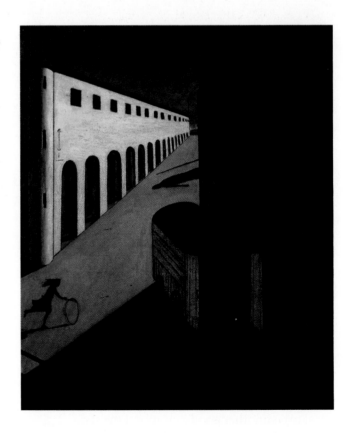

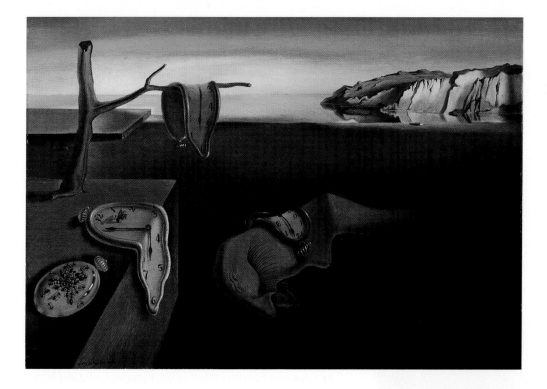

19-36 Salvador Dali, *The Persistence of Memory*, 1931. Oil on canvas, 9 ½″ x 13″ (24 x 33 cm). Collection, The Museum of Modern Art, New York (Given anonymously).

First World War was raging. A small collection of artists, poets, and refugees had gathered in a cafe in neutral Zurich, Switzerland. Relatively sane at first, their activities soon became preposterous. They wrote poetry by cutting words out of seed catalogs, recited two or three poems simultaneously, wore silly costumes, danced to the sounds of a barking dog, and made collages out of random arrangements of garbage. The name Dada (French for *hobbyhorse*) was supposedly discovered by sticking a knife into a French-German dictionary and selecting the first word that appeared. Dadaists tended to thumb their noses at everything.

Dada spread to Paris, Cologne, Barcelona, and New York. The movement died in 1922 and left few lasting works of art. However, it did inject into the art world a taste for the absurd and ironic. (Some would say that Dadaists were simply reflecting the absurdity of modern life, especially the existence of war.) One artwork has become a symbol of the Dada spirit: *Fountain,* a urinal laid on its back and signed "R. Mutt" by Marcel Duchamp (fig. 19-37). Duchamp, a Frenchman who was working in New York at the time, tried to enter *Fountain* in a show, only to have it rejected. Today, however, Duchamp's artwork is part of a distinguished art collection.

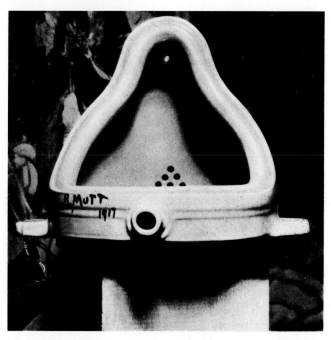

19-37 Marcel Duchamp, *Fountain* (photograph by Alfred Steiglitz, reproduced in *The Blind Man, No. 2,* May 1917). Porcelain, 24 ⅝″ (63 cm) high. The Philadelphia Museum of Art (Louise and Walter Arensberg Collection).

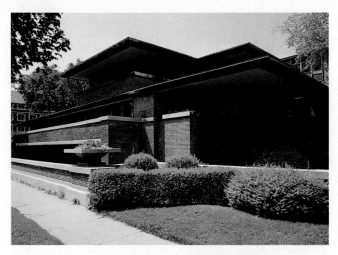

19-38 Frank Lloyd Wright, Robie House, Chicago, 1909. Photograph: Thomas A. Heinz.

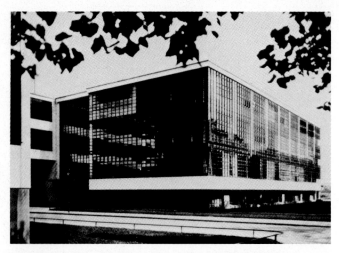

19-40 Walter Gropius, Shop Block, The Bauhaus, Dessau, Germany, 1925–1926. Photograph: George Barford.

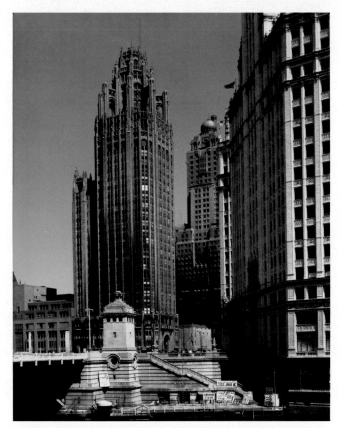

19-39 Tribune Tower, 1925. North Michigan Avenue at the River (north bank). Architects: Hood and Howells. Rosenthal Art Slides, Inc. (Chicago).

Architecture of the First Half of the Twentieth Century

The Chicago School style of commercial building continued into the first decade of the 1900s. However, the most innovative architecture of this period came from a man who specialized in designing homes: Frank Lloyd Wright. His remarkable Robie House (fig. 19–38) has dramatic overhangs and horizontal lines. The house was designed to blend with the prairie landscape of northern Illinois. An apprentice of Louis Sullivan, Wright was the first architect, European or American, to create a distinctive style out of frame construction. The Robie House, like Matisse's *The Red Room* or Kandinsky's *Sketch I for "Composition VII,"* looks modern even today.

By 1910, the Chicago style of architecture was "out of style." The imagination of the American public had been captured by New York architects who were designing skyscrapers in various *eclectic* styles. Eclectic means borrowing from various sources, usually historical. Despite the fact that their buildings were modern metal-frame structures, New York designers decorated them with styles borrowed from Greek, Gothic, or Renaissance sources. The prime example of eclectic architecture is the Chicago Tribune Tower (fig. 19–39), designed by a New York architectural firm. This skyscraper was made to look like a Gothic tower, even including flying buttresses! Ironically, it was completed in 1924, the year of Sullivan's death. That year also marked the end of Sullivan's principle, "Form Follows Function" (at least for the time being).

While architects in America were rejecting Sullivan's principle, those in Europe were discovering

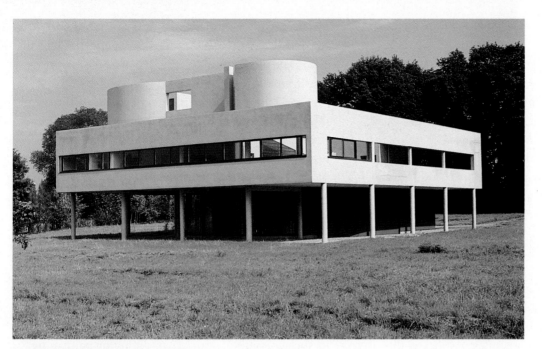

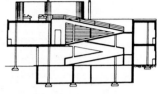

19-42 Le Corbusier Villa Savoye, Poissy–sur–Seine, France, 1929–1930. Photograph: George Barford.

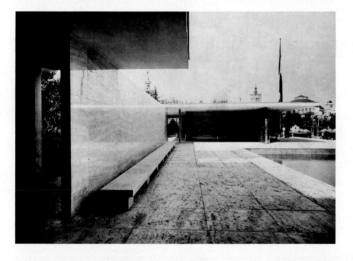

19-41 Ludwig Mies van der Rohe, *German Pavilion at the International Exhibition, Barcelona, Spain*, 1929. Demolished. Photograph courtesy Mies van der Rohe Archive, The Museum of Modern Art, New York.

it. In 1919, a special German design school called the *Bauhaus* (German for house of building) was established. Walter Gropius designed the school's main building, called The Shop Block (fig. 19-40). This building was the world's first multistoried permanent building to be faced with continuous walls of glass. Gropius was also the school's first director. Some of Europe's most famous modern painters, including Kandinsky and Mondrian, lectured there. Mondrian's style (Chapter 7) was especially influential in the design of modern architecture. The simple geometry of his art is reflected in the sleek lines of the German Pavilion (fig. 19-41). For 1929, this was a very modern-looking building. The architect was Ludwig Mies van der Rohe, a friend of Mondrian who became Bauhaus director after Gropius.

Also in 1929, construction began on Villa Savoye (fig. 19-42), designed by Le Corbusier (born Charles Eduoard Jeanneret). This multilevel house consisted of little more than a box on stilts. The forms of both the German Pavilion and Villa Savoye are simple, unadorned, and *modern.* Thus the legacy of modernism and design honesty, originally championed by Sullivan and Wright, had been passed on to European architects.

Art of the Second Half of the Twentieth Century

The end of the Second World War (1939–1945) marked a turning point in twentieth century history. The war ushered in the nuclear age. America and Russia—the so-called superpowers—took over the world stage. Since then many things have happened: the cold war, baby boom, arms race, space race, Korean and Vietnam wars, détente, budget deficit, the breakup of the Soviet Union, and others that we read and hear about daily.

The end of the Second World War also marked a turning point in the modern movement. Artistic leadership passed from Europe to America. Up to this time, American involvement in modern art was weak and tentative. No American had pioneered a new movement, invented a new medium, or even shocked the world with daring color. Only in the field of architec-ture had Americans demonstrated unusual creativity. Even this creativity, as we saw, was replaced by eclecti-cism. The most popular American art before the war was *Regionalism*. Regionalism was a conservative style that specialized in local themes, particularly the simple lifestyles of rural Americans. A good example is John S. Curry's *Baptism in Kansas* (fig. 10–6). Such a style, however, was inappropriate for the 1940s. Americans had been thrust into world leadership. They needed an art that would match this role.

In the mid-1940s, young American artists like Arshile Gorky began experimenting with abstract styles. His *The Liver Is the Cock's Comb* (fig. 19–43) rep-resents the beginnings of a new American abstract art. However, the real breakthrough came in 1947 when Jackson Pollock began his famous "drip" paintings. Pollock would lay a canvas on the floor and walk across its surface spilling, pouring, and flinging paint as he went along (fig. 19–44). The dancing lines and rhythms

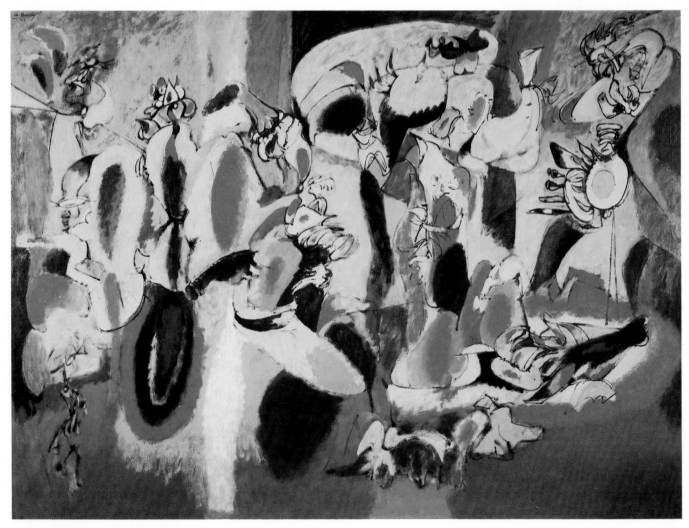

19–43 Arshile Gorky, *The Liver Is the Cock's Comb*, 1944. Oil on canvas, 6′ x 8′ 2″ (1.83 x 2.49 m). Albright-Knox Art Gallery, Buffalo, New York (Gift of Seymour H. Knox, 1956).

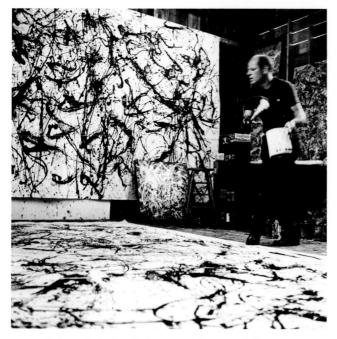

19-44 Jackson Pollock painting, 1950. Photograph ©1990 Hans Namuth.

in *Cathedral* (fig. 19-45) reflect the rhythms of Pollock's bodily movements as he produced the work.

No artist, European or American, had ever made a painting this way on such a scale and with such energy. Other American painters also began making bold abstract canvases. They did not necessarily use Pollock's methods, however. Their style was called *Abstract Expressionism* or *Action Painting*. An example is Hans Hofmann's *Flowering Swamp* (fig. 7-28). Abstract Expressionism was a new style on the world scene. Even European critics were impressed by this American creativity. Since that time American art has continued to rival, if not dominate, European art.

The spirit of American creativity did not end with Abstract Expressionism. Even as that style flourished, artists continued to experiment. They generated a seemingly endless supply of ideas. By the end of the 1960s, many different styles and kinds of art existed. You may recall the discussion of today's artistic variety in Chapters 1 and 2. You have already encountered many examples of postwar art in previous chapters. We will now summarize that art under a few headings and refer back to some of those examples.

Abstraction

Not all postwar abstract painting contains free forms made with bold gestures. In contrast to Abstract Expressionism, much Abstraction is geometric. It reflects an interest in principles of design, color effects,

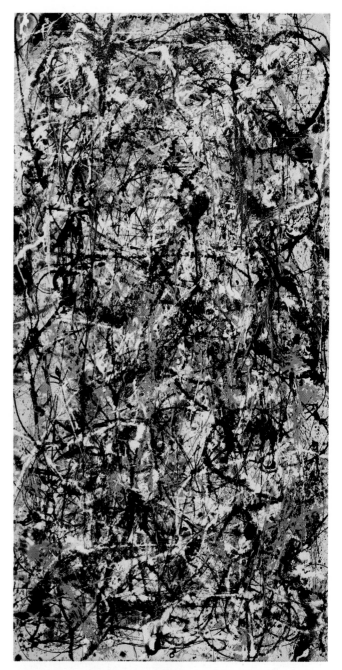

19-45 Jackson Pollock, *Cathedral*, 1947. Oil, 75″ x 35″ (191 x 89 cm). Dallas Museum of Art (Gift of Mr. and Mrs. Bernard J. Reis).

and even optical effects. See, for example, Josef Albers' *Homage to the Square: Glow* (fig. 1-6), Irene Rice Pereira's *Oblique Progression* (fig. 7-29), Bridget Riley's *Current* (fig. 8-17), and Tadasky's *A-101* (fig. 10-14). Abstraction was also expressed in postwar sculptures: Alexander Calder's mobile (fig. 9-1), Donald Judd's *Untitled* (fig. 9-3), Richard Lippold's *Number 7: Full Moon* (fig. 13-27), and Frank Stella's *Katsura* (fig. 13-30).

Assemblage

The art of assemblage, invented by Picasso and Braque around the time of the First World War, experienced a revival after the Second World War. See Robert Rauschenberg's *Monogram* (fig. 1–11), Louise Nevelson's *Sky Cathedral* (fig. 13–28), and Joseph Cornell's *Object (Roses des Vents)* (fig. 10–4).

Pop Art

The *Pop Art* movement emerged in the 1960s. It satirized popular culture by borrowing themes from comics, advertising, and ordinary life. Examples are Roy Lichtenstein's *Whaam!* (fig. 1–7), Andy Warhol's *100 Cans* (fig. 10–3), Claes Oldenburg's *Falling Shoestring Potatoes* (fig. 13–52), and Marisol's *Women and Dog* (fig. 13–29).

Related to Pop Art are environment artworks like Red Grooms's *Ruckus Rodeo* (fig. 13–33) and George Segal's *The Diner* (fig. 13–37). Because of their humor

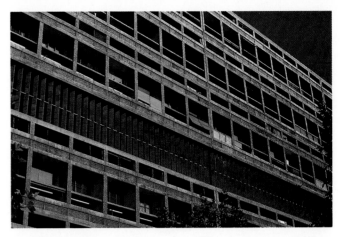

19–47 Le Corbusier, Unité d'Habitation, Marseilles, France, 1952. Art Resource, NY.

and nose-thumbing stance, Pop Art and related styles are sometimes called *neo-Dada* (new-Dada). They recall the spirit of the Dada movement.

Performance, Environment, and Concept

Some untraditional forms of art can also be seen as legacies of Dada: Joseph Beuys's *I Like America and America Likes Me* (Chapter 1), Christo's *Wrapped Coast* (Chapter 1), Mary Miss's *Field Rotation* (Chapter 13), and John Baldessari's *Cremation Piece* (Chapter 12).

Realism

Paradoxically, there has been a significant revival of realistic art (though not the same as the Realistic movement of the 1800s). Examples of this can be seen in Don Nice's *Longhorn Steer, Western Series, American Predella #6* (Chapter 8), Richard Estes's *Nedick's* (Chapter 10), and even in the sculptures of Marilyn Levine (Chapters 1 and 8) and Duane Hansen (Chapter 13).

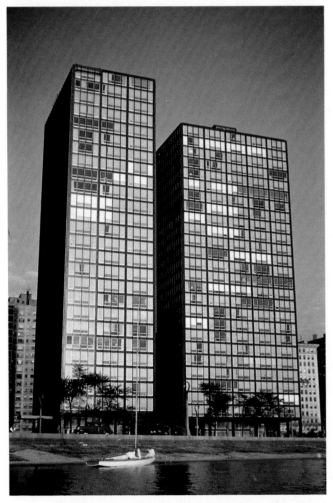

19–46 Ludwig Mies van der Rohe, Lake Shore Drive Apartment Houses, Chicago, 1950–1952. Photograph: George Barford.

History/Aesthetics Experience 19.2

Art Style Report

Select an art style from this chapter. Research the art style and prepare a short style report. Include information such as where and when the style began, its purposes, possible influences, and characteristics, and world events and artists that helped shape it.

Architecture of the Second Half of the Twentieth Century

Major buildings require large investments of time, materials, and capital. Architects are less free to experiment than artists. Until very recently, postwar architecture has been dominated by Mies van der Rohe and Le Corbusier. These are the two European architects who were so inventive in the 1920s (see earlier discussion).

Fleeing the German Nazis, Mies moved to Chicago in the 1930s, where he taught architecture and received commissions for buildings. Living by his own motto, "Less Is More," he designed starkly simple, glass-enclosed towers, like the Lake Shore Drive Apartment Houses (fig. 19-46). Some praised him for returning the principle "Form Follows Function" to the city of its birth. Others criticized him for carrying it to extremes. Today, the Chicago skyline is dominated by buildings designed by either Mies, his students, or his imitators, like the architects of the Sears Tower (fig. 4-17). Indeed, skylines around the world have been affected by Mies's philosophy of less is more. In downtown Chicago that philosophy has been applied with taste and imagination. But in many other cities, it has resulted in glass-coated monotony and architectural boredom.

Contrast Mies's apartment towers with Le Corbusier's Marseille Apartments (fig. 19-47). Instead of narrow steel columns, the Le Corbusier building is supported on massive concrete buttresses. Rather than being on the same plane as the wall, its windows are deeply recessed. Rather than a smooth envelope of metal and glass, the wall itself is unadorned concrete.

Le Corbusier pioneered the use of *ferroconcrete* (concrete reinforced with metal rods). Like metal-frame, ferroconcrete has tensile strength; but like sculpture, it can be cast into a variety of forms. Notre-Dame-du-Haut Chapel (fig. 19-48), one of Le Corbusier's more dramatic projects, demonstrates the sculptural possibilities of ferroconcrete. Le Corbusier's style provided a postwar alternative to Mies's glass box.

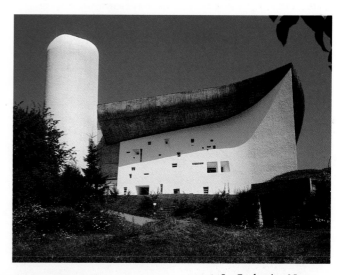

19-48 Le Corbusier, Notre-Dame-du-Haut Chapel, Ronchamp, France, 1955. Photograph: George Barford.

19-49 Alternate view of Notre-Dame-du-Haut Chapel. Photograph: George Barford.

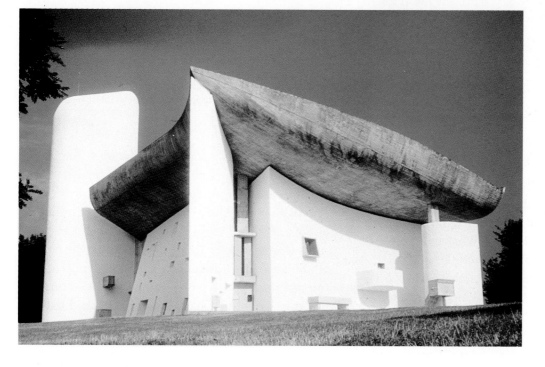

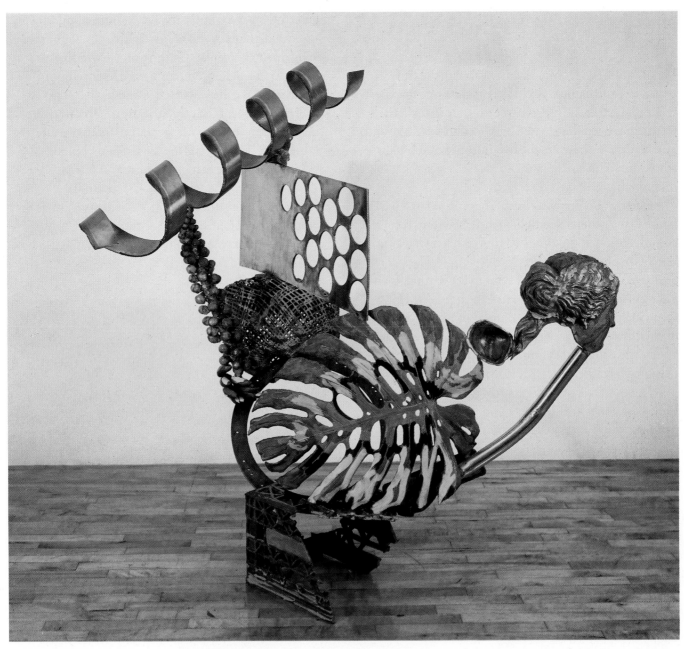

19–50 Eclecticism in art means combining elements of several different styles within one work of art. What is recognizable in this sculpture? How many different kinds of artistic techniques and materials has the artist used? Nancy Graves, *Akroterion*, 1989. Iron, stainless steel, carbon steel, aluminum, bronze, 60 ½″ x 56″ x 47″ (154 x 142 x 119 cm). Courtesy M. Knoedler and Co., New York.

Postscript: The Post-Modern Era

This chapter, starting where Chapter 18 ended, has reviewed the history of art from the 1600s to about 1980. You learned that the period known as Modernism started in the late 1800s. What about the present, though? Many people who study art and culture are saying that Modernism is over, that we live in a *postmodern* period. They believe that modern art, for example, has run out of steam, that it has not produced any significantly new ideas for two decades. The only rules left now are those that Modernism created, and even those are being broken. Look at the satire of Pop Art and other neo-Dada examples, and at the indications of a revival of Realism. In architecture, many young designers are rejecting the modern styles of both Mies van der Rohe and Le Corbusier. Indeed, some architects are even reviving eclecticism—one of Modernism's taboos. Charles Moore's Piazza d'Italia

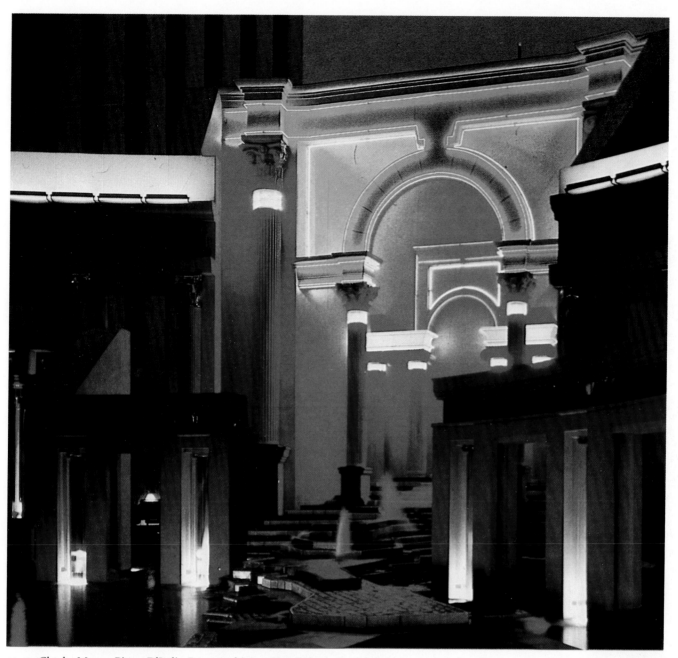

19–51 Charles Moore, Piazza D'Italia. Perez Architects, New Orleans, Louisiana.

(fig. 19–51), a public square in New Orleans, is a fantastic collection of columns and arches reminiscent of Classical, Renaissance, and Neoclassical architecture.

Now, we are at the end of a century. Maybe this is not the time for new ideas; culture is being put on "hold." Unconsciously, perhaps, people are waiting for the beginning of the twenty-first century, when, like the beginning of the twentieth century, the mood will be right for cultural rebirth. Think how exciting it was for people like Henri Matisse, Paula Modersohn-Becker, and Pablo Picasso! Weren't they fortunate to be the right age for the beginning of this century? Have you ever stopped to consider that you are the right age for the beginning of the next century? Some people in your generation will be the famous artists of the 2000s. Maybe one of them will be you.

Part VI
In the Final Analysis

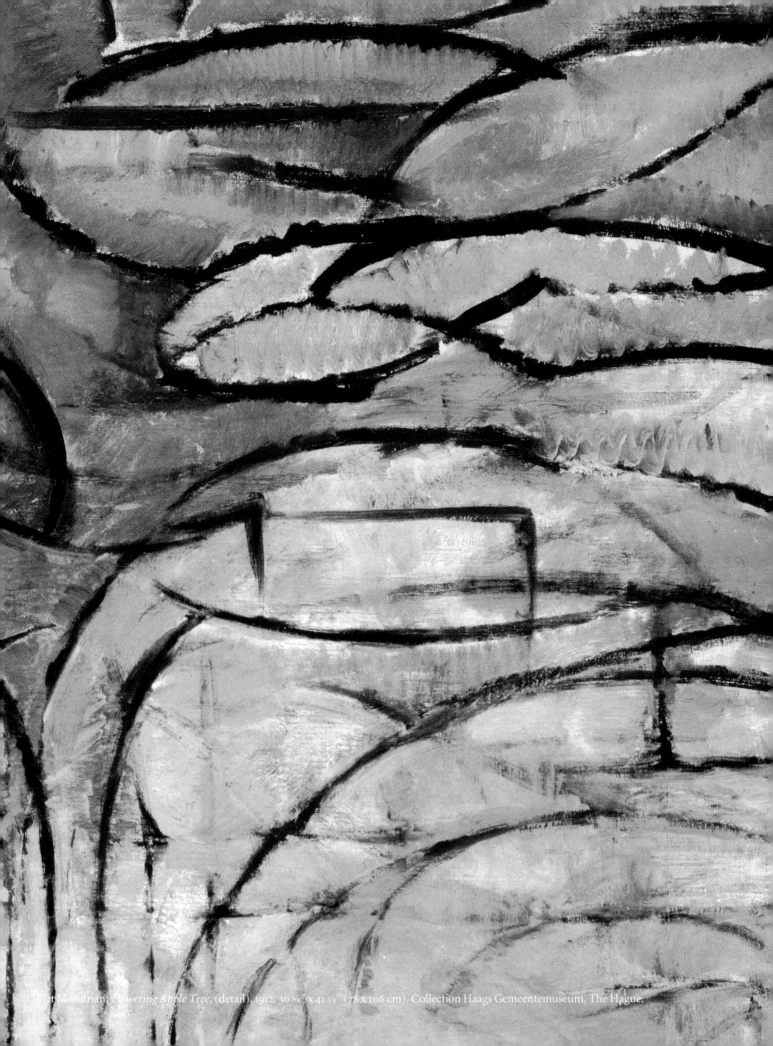

Piet Mondrian, *Flowering Apple Tree*, (detail), 1912, 30 ¾″ x 41 ¾″ (78 x 106 cm). Collection Haags Gemeentemuseum, The Hague.

Chapter 20
Criticism and Critics

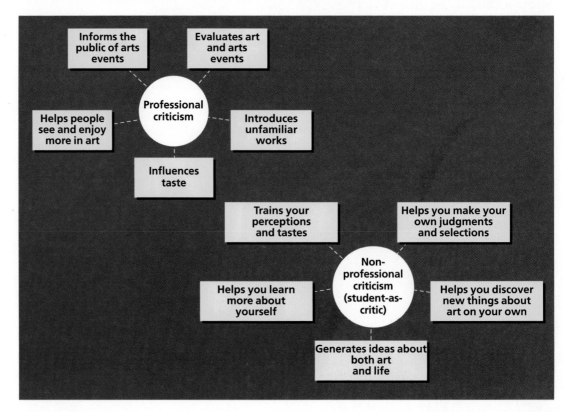

Overview

Chapter Objectives

Students should be able to:

1 define art criticism, identifying four stages of inquiry   EE 3, 4

2 become aware of the different kinds of professional criticism available through magazines, newspapers, radio, and TV   EE 3,4

3 understand that professional critics describe and interpret, and support their interpretations and evaluations with reasons   EE 3, 4

4 appreciate contributions that professional critics make to their awareness and understanding of the visual arts   EE 3, 4

Rationale

This is not the first chapter to deal with the subject of art criticism. Description, the first step of criticism, was introduced in Chapter 3, analysis in Chapter 9, and interpretation in Chapter 15. Most of the lessons so far have included some exercises in criticism. At this point, near the end of the book, students are ready to engage fully in the act of criticism. This is because they have been exposed to the necessary art concepts and vocabulary for such a task. Art criticism, then, becomes the culminating learning experience of this book.

Chapter 20 is designed to "whet the appetite" of the students by explaining the purposes of criticism, presenting examples of art criticism at the professional level, and demonstrating that criticism can play a significant role in students' personal lives. Chapter 21, the last chapter in the book, details all the stages of art criticism.

Essential Chapter Concepts

• Art criticism is a systematic discussion of an artwork, usually involving four stages: description, analysis, interpretation, and evaluation.

• Criticism is not a negative act but rather a process for learning what something is about, what it means, and how significant it is.

• Professional art criticism serves many functions: informing the public about art events, providing evaluations of events, introducing unfamiliar works, and influencing taste.

• The personal benefits of learning to criticize art include learning more about art, developing taste, sharing experiences with others, and making objective judgments about art.

Vocabulary

criticism

Lesson Plans

20.1 Critique a Critic

Page **T 298**   Time: 1 period

Handouts

Study Questions

Page **T 300**

Chapter Closure

Evaluation

1   *Criticism:* Do students demonstrate an awareness of the availability of professional criticism in local media and specialty magazines?

2   *Criticism/Aesthetic awareness:* Do students show an interest in following and considering reviews?

3   *Criticism:* Are students developing an appreciation for the contributions of critics in their daily lives? Can they identify ways in which professional criticism is useful to them?   R 6

Notes

Critique a Critic

Time: 1 period

Preparation

Rationale

Criticisms of art, music, theater, books, and plays appear frequently in magazines and newspapers, and may be heard on radio and TV. Students can learn about the process of criticism by studying the work of professionals. They may also begin to differentiate between objective and subjective criticism.

Discussion Materials

clippings of reviews or criticisms from local newspapers and magazines, videotapes of critics (optional)

Teach the Lesson

Objectives

Students should be able to:

1 select a criticism of art, music, a film, or a play and look for description, interpretation and evaluation; reasons that support the judgment; and objectivity and subjectivity in the statements   EE 3, 4

2 share their findings with classmates

Vocabulary

Criticism involves the analysis and evaluation of artworks, books, film, plays, and entertainment.

Warm Up

Have students bring a criticism to the class.   R 6
Ask if any of the students were familiar with the work before they read a criticism of it. If so, do they agree or disagree with the criticism? Why? Who read a criticism that convinced them they should see or buy the work?

Explore and Develop

1 List the different kinds of criticism students found. What were their sources?

2 List the different kinds of things the critics discussed in the examples.

3 Ask who thinks they have the most   R 6
objective criticism; the most subjective; the most convincing; the least convincing. Make comparisons.

4 Have students point out description,   R 5
analysis, and interpretation in the professional examples.

Evaluate and Reflect

1   Have students discuss ways in which criticisms published in the media can be helpful.

2   Ask them to discuss things for which the reader of criticisms should be alert.

3   Are students learning that good criticism requires sound analysis rather than heated argument and subjective opinion?

4   Which of the criticism did they most prefer?

Reteach

Review the five study questions for the chapter. Have students list characteristics of artworks that can be discussed in criticism, such as art elements, design principles, media, style, historical associations, and context.

Name: _____   Course: _____

Study Questions
Chapter 20–Criticism and Critics

1 What is the general definition of criticism given in chapter 20?

_____

_____

_____

2 Define art criticism.

_____

_____

_____

3 List the areas of professional criticism described in chapter 20.

_____

_____

_____

4 If you know of another kind of professional criticism that is not mentioned in the text, describe it and if possible bring an example to class.

_____

_____

_____

5 How can developing skills in art criticism be of benefit to people who are not professional critics?

_____

_____

_____

_____

Study Answers
Chapter 20
Criticism and Critics

1 Criticism is a discussion of the characteristics of something.

2 Art criticism is a systematic discussion of an artwork, usually involving four stages: description, analysis, interpretation, and evaluation.

3 Film, music, television, books or literature, theater or plays, art shows, architecture.

4 Answers will vary.

5 Answers may vary. Possible answers include: learning about art and art criticism, organizing knowledge about art and sharing it with others, and developing taste, discovering new things about art, exploring unfamiliar works of art, evaluating the writing of critics, learning about one's self, ideas and feelings.

Chapter 20
Criticism and Critics

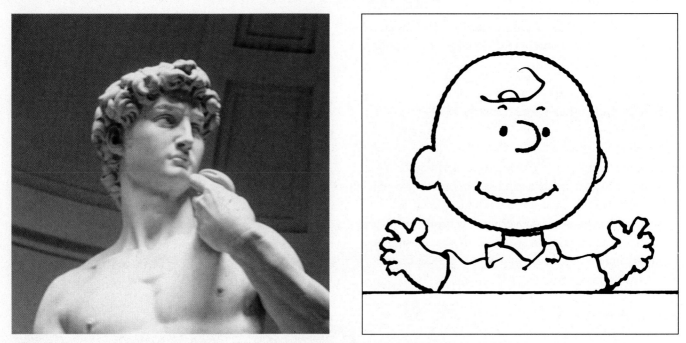

20–1 One is a famous sculpture of a biblical hero by Michelangelo; the other is a popular comic by Charles Schulz. Although vastly different in form and content, both have a lot to offer if we take time to examine them critically. (left) Detail of Michelangelo's *The David*, 1501–1504. Marble. Gallery of the Academy, Florence. (right) Charles M. Schultz, *Charlie Brown*, 1973. *Peanuts* reprinted by permission of UFS, Inc.

We tend to think that **criticism** means disapproval. For example, if we don't like something, we "criticize" it. This use of the term is very limited, however. Have you ever thought that criticizing something can involve saying positive things about it? For example, when criticizing one of your drawings, your teacher may point out just its good qualities. In one sense, criticism is simply a discussion of the characteristics of something—particularly if that something is a work of art.

For our purposes, we will say that **art criticism** *is a systematic discussion of an artwork, usually involving four stages: (1) description, (2) analysis, (3) interpretation, and (4) evaluation.* Sometimes a criticism involves only the first three stages. Recall that in Chapter 3, you described Renoir's *Luncheon of the Boating Party*. In Chapter 10, you analyzed Seurat's *Bathing at Asnières*. In Chapter 15, you interpreted Russell's *The Toll Collectors*.

The next chapter will review evaluation, the fourth stage. Evaluation is something like judgment. Chapter 21 will also explain how to put the stages together to do a criticism.

In this chapter, we will examine several kinds of *professional* criticism, as well as the *critics* who write it. We will also discuss the reasons why we, who are not professional critics, should get involved in criticism.

Professional Criticism

Most of the movies you see were recommended to you by something or somebody. For example, an advertisement may have made a film sound exciting. You may have heard your friends say good things about the film. Usually, when you see the film, you are satisfied, but sometimes you are not. You soon learn that advertisements can be misleading. You also learn that just because other people like a film does not mean that you will.

Yet, to avoid wasting your time and money on every film that comes to town, you need to have some kind of information. One source of information is film criticism. Unlike an advertisement, film criticism does not always try to make you think a movie is exciting. Film critics are not obligated to sell movies, and they say negative things about them as well as positive things. Unlike the opinions of your friends, which are often very limited, professional criticism usually explains a great deal about a particular film. A criticism (sometimes called a *review*) will give you a better basis on which to make up your mind.

Most newspapers have film critics on their staffs who criticize the films playing in the local theatres. Each of the major networks has a film critic who reviews films, usually on the morning show. Even the cable networks and the public networks have such critics. These critics not only discuss the current films, but also show "clips" of those films. No doubt you have seen some of these critics. The interesting thing about all of them is that they often disagree.

Disagreement is especially apparent with two critics—Gene Siskel and Roger Ebert—who appear on camera together (fig. 20–2). Perhaps the most famous of all the national critics, Siskel and Ebert have their own half-hour show in which they criticize (or review) about five or six films. In addition, they write film criticism for two different newspapers. Siskel's column is in the *Chicago Tribune* and Ebert's is in the *Chicago Sun-Times*.

Newspapers like the *Tribune* and *Sun-Times* also contain reviews of art shows, books, musical programs, plays, and even architecture. In fact, every major city newspaper, and many smaller newspapers, review these kinds of things fairly regularly. If your hometown newspaper does not carry such reviews, you can find them in weekly newsmagazines like *Time* and *Newsweek*.

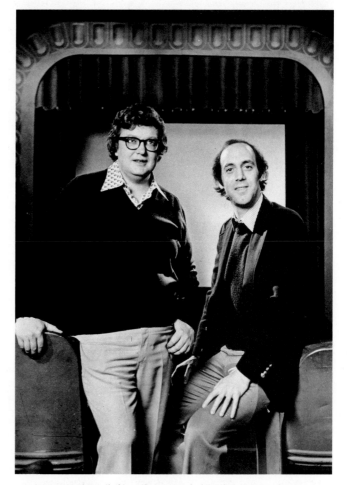

20–2 Roger Ebert (left) and Gene Siskel (right). Scenic design: Michael Loewenstein. Courtesy Public Broadcasting System.

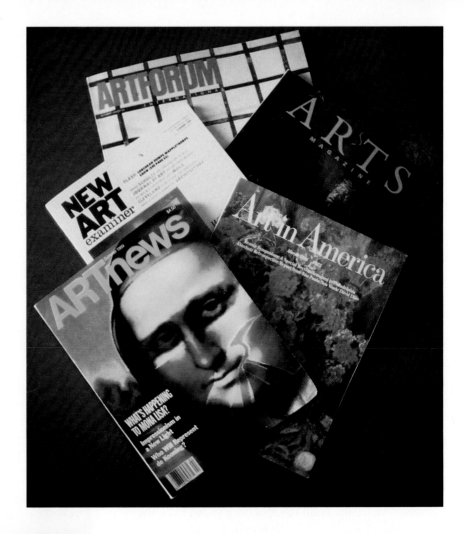

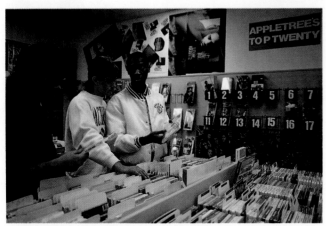

20-4 When you talk about your favorite rock bands, do you ever think that you might be engaged in a form of criticism?

Many publications specialize in just one of the arts. For those interested in the visual arts (painting, sculpture, photography, etc.), there are many magazines to choose from: *Arts, Artforum, Art in America, Art News,* and others (fig. 20-3). Those who want advice about recent books can read the *Saturday Review of Literature* and the *New York Review of Books. Downbeat* and *Rolling Stone* inform readers about the latest in jazz and rock music. *TV Guide* provides information and critical reviews about television programs. There are even publications for criticizing things that are not considered the arts. *Motor Trend* magazine, for example, offers critical reviews of the latest cars.

What is the purpose of all this criticism? We have already suggested a reason for reading film criticism. By providing information and an evaluation, a film criticism helps us decide whether or not we want to spend our own time and money on a film. If we read one of Mr. Ebert's criticisms, we benefit from the time he has taken to see and criticize a particular film. In a sense, a criticism is a *preview* that helps us make a more intelligent decision.

But there are other reasons for criticism besides saving us time and money. Good criticism also educates. It can point out things that we might overlook. It can encourage us to see artworks that are unusual or unfamiliar. In the long run, it can influence our taste. If the influence is good, we may grow to like more difficult things and to dislike childish things.

Professional criticism:

1. informs the public of ongoing artistic events—movies, art shows, musical programs, plays, books, and so forth;

2. provides information and evaluations of particular events so that people have a basis for making selections;

3. points out things in an artwork that might be ignored, thereby helping people to see more and enjoy more about a work;

4. introduces unfamiliar artworks, thereby encouraging people to see and enjoy things that they would ordinarily miss;

5. influences taste so that people may grow in their likes and dislikes.

Criticism Experience 20.1

Critique a Critic

Find a critical review of art, film, music or drama in a local or national publication. Critique the review, and write down what you think about it. Were the reviewer's arguments sound? Discuss your impressions in class.

Nonprofessional Criticism

As long as there are people who are paid to criticize artworks, why should other people—such as you and I—do it also? The rest of this chapter will be devoted to answering that question.

First, criticizing art is good training. Have you ever heard the saying: To learn physics, be a physicist? In this case, it would be: To learn about criticism, *be a critic,* or to learn about the field of art, *be an art critic.*

Second, the reasons for professional criticism that were mentioned earlier also apply to doing your own criticism. In this case, however, you would be making selections, discovering new things in familiar works of art, exploring unfamiliar works of art, and developing your taste without the help of professionals.

Third, criticism enables you not only to discover new things about artworks. It also helps you to organize this knowledge so that you can share it with others. Have you ever written about a popular song or talked about it with a friend? Did writing or talking about it increase your understanding of it?

Fourth, artworks, like good films, often deal with attitudes or ideas about life. Have you and your friends ever analyzed a good film? If so, you probably came up with a lot of interesting things to discuss. Analyzing an artwork can also generate ideas for sharing and discussion.

Finally, the more you learn about art and the ideas it expresses, the more you learn about yourself and your own ideas and feelings.

Summary

Art criticism, as defined here, is a systematic description, analysis, interpretation, and evaluation of an artwork. Sometimes criticism includes just the first three stages. A specific method of criticism will be explained in the next chapter.

Professional criticism of the arts can be found in newspapers, magazines, radio, and television. Basically, professional critics inform and educate the public through studying and writing about works of art.

People who are not professional critics can benefit from criticizing art in many ways: learning more about art and criticism, developing their own taste, and sharing experiences with others.

Chapter 21
A Critical Method

Student Edition
Pages 312–323

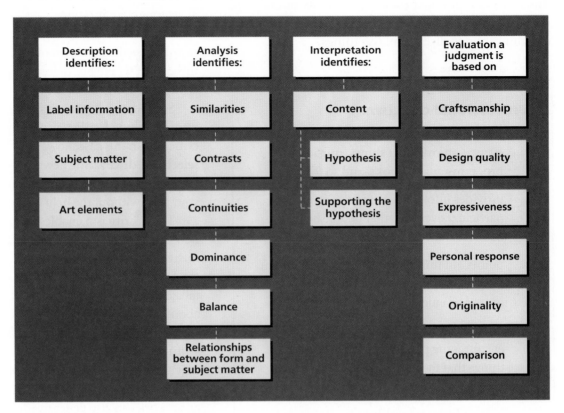

Description identifies:	Analysis identifies:	Interpretation identifies:	Evaluation a judgment is based on
Label information	Similarities	Content	Craftsmanship
Subject matter	Contrasts	Hypothesis	Design quality
Art elements	Continuities	Supporting the hypothesis	Expressiveness
	Dominance		Personal response
	Balance		Originality
	Relationships between form and subject matter		Comparison

Overview

Chapter Objectives

Students should be able to:

1 use the four-stage criticism model to make independent, objective judgments about artworks and products of commercial or industrial design   EE 3, 4

2 use appropriate vocabulary to describe the composition of artworks   EE 3, 4

3 analyze how the art elements interact in artworks using the principles of design as guidelines   EE 3, 4

4 explain the value of art criticism in organizing thoughts and making objective judgments about artworks   EE 3, 4

5 discuss how sensory, formal and technical qualities of an artwork interact to express ideas.   EE 3, 4

Rationale

A goal of long standing in most art programs is to have the students appreciate the important human activities of making and responding to art. The criticism process involves questioning what artworks mean, how they are made, how they are composed, and how significant they are. Once students have acquired the skills for criticizing artworks, they will find those skills useful throughout their lives in learning about and enjoying art, and making judgments about various images and forms that affect daily living.

Essential Chapter Concepts

• Art criticism is a systematic discussion of the characteristics of an artwork, usually involving four stages: description, analysis, interpretation, and evaluation.

• There are distinct differences between description, analysis, interpretation, and evaluation.

• Evaluation is the most difficult and complex of all stages of criticism. It is based on factors such as craftsmanship, design, quality, expressiveness, personal response, originality, and comparison.

• Criticism must be objective; judgments of artworks should be based on rational reasons.

• The meaning of artworks is accessible through the criticism process.

• The knowledge and skills for art criticism are useful in all areas of the art program.

• Art criticism is done in a positive manner, avoiding negative derogatory remarks.

Vocabulary

art criticism	analysis
evaluation	hypothesis
description	interpretation
content	

Lesson Plans

21.1 Analyzing an Artwork

Page **T 304** Time: 1 period

Handouts

Study Questions

Page **T 306**

Test Questions

Page **T 308**

Chapter Closure

Notes

Evaluation

1 *Criticism:* Can students complete an objective criticism of an artwork using the four-stage model?   R 5 W 2

2 *Criticism:* Do students differentiate between objective and subjective statements, and use them at appropriate places in the criticism process?   R 1

3 *Criticism:* Do students use the criticism method to make independent evaluations of popular arts, entertainment, advertising, and commercial products?   R 6

4 *Criticism:* Can students discuss how the concepts and skills necessary for art criticism help them in the areas of art production, art history, and aesthetic awareness?   R 5

5 *Criticism/Aesthetic Awareness:* Do students use appropriate vocabulary to describe the organization of sensory elements in artworks?   R 1 W 2

6 *Criticism/Aesthetic Awareness:* Do students use appropriate vocabulary to describe the organization of sensory elements in artwork?   R 1 W 2

A Critical Method

Analyzing an Artwork

Time: 1 period

Preparation

Rationale

The concepts and skills necessary for art criticism apply to all areas of the art program, including production, history, and aesthetic awareness. In addition, students will find these concepts and skills useful throughout their lives in learning about and enjoying art.

Criticism Materials

Outline provided in Chapter 21, Student Edition pages 312–315

Teach the Lesson

Objectives

Students should be able to:

1 write a critical analysis of an artwork using the four-stage model   EE 3, 4

2 learn the necessary concepts and skills for objective art criticism   EE 3, 4

Vocabulary

Art criticism is a systematic discussion of the characteristics of an artwork, involving four stages: description, analysis, interpretation, and evaluation.

Content in criticism refers to the meaning of the artwork. Content is distinct from *subject matter,* which is what the artist uses as a source of stimulation or what the artwork includes.

Warm Up

Place the waste can on a pedestal and announce that it has been donated to the nearest art museum by a local artist who says it is an artwork. The students are local art critics who must decide if the object is a significant art form and should be purchased by the museum. Divide them into small groups. Assign each group a belief about art:

a. Art is anything that is made of traditional materials and that has interesting lines, shapes, colors, textures, and patterns.

b. Art is anything that gives pleasure and communicates some kind of message.

c. Great art does something useful. It is functional. It functions to show us a better world, to help promote a great idea.

d. Significant artworks are realistic. They show us the world the way we know it.

e. Great works of art demonstrate good formal organization of the art elements. They don't have to deliver a message if they are well composed.

Give each group a few minutes to organize an argument, then have them present their arguments. Let the class decide which argument was most convincing. Have them discuss the objectivity of their arguments. Lead them into the use of the formal analysis process.

Explore and Develop

1 If students have done the criticism exercises throughout the text, this is a synthesis activity. You may want to have students complete a written analysis of an artwork individually or in small groups.

2 You may want to introduce the process by leading students through the four stages and demonstrating proper questions for each phase. Make sure that students read through the examples in Chapter 21 before trying the entire criticism model.

3 Although subjectivity enters into stage three, students should base their judgments on what they know from description and analysis, relevant personal knowledge, and art history.

Laser Discs:

Mondrian, Lozenge in Red, Yellow, and Blue, c 1925

Search Frame 2255

Kline, C & O, 1958

Search Frame 2321

Cassatt, Little Girl in a Blue Armchair, 1878

Search Frame 2000

Rousseau, Tropical Forest with Monkeys, 1910

Search Frame 1588

Gaughin, Fatata te Miti (By the Sea), 1892
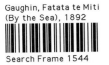
Search Frame 1544

Toulouse-Lautrec, Quadrille at Moulin Rouge, 1892

Search Frame 1560

Describing the mood of an artwork and using metaphors can be helpful in getting at meaning.

4 Students should know that there are often several meanings for an artwork. They are not held accountable for finding the one best meaning.

Evaluate and Reflect

1 Do students feel they were successful in completing a criticism of an artwork?

2 What did they learn about the work that they did not know before the critical analysis?

R 1 **3** Can students differentiate between subject matter and content of an artwork?

4 Do students support their interpretations and judgments with evidence and reasons?

5 Ask students to state the major question to be answered for each of the four stages of critical analysis.

6 Display an artwork and ask the group to explain how the sensory elements contribute to both unity and variety.

Reteach

Review the study and test questions with students.

Extend the Lesson

Beyond the Basics

EE 4 Students will become comfortable with the criticism process only if they practice it. Have them periodically analyze their own artwork. Ask students to apply the procedure to utilitarian objects—products of industrial design. Have them select an advertisement from a magazine, poster, or product package for analysis.

R 5 Ask students to look for criticisms in newspapers, and magazines of movies, plays, sports, art, music. Analyze the criticisms for reasons and evidence to support judgments.

Direct students' attention to Robert Stefl's R 5
Illinois Landscape #14 on page 318 and the W 1
sample criticism written about the work. Involvement with a work of art through art criticism offers students the opportunity to make many meaningful connections for further study and integration of the curriculum. For example, the hypothesis that the work "…expresses the wonder of the trees' survival under very threatening conditions" leads to any number of connections with environmental issues and possible connections to nearly every subject in the school. Suggest students read the sample criticisms in this chapter and write down any possible connections that come to mind.

Cultural Connections

A thematic approach to learning about dif- EE 3, 4
ferent cultures may be helpful. Have students look again at figures 21–2, 21–3, 21–4 and 21–5. The selection of these four works W 1
of trees could be the starting point for many different connections. Consider finding a tree painting from each culture, critique each one, compare the findings and follow the lead.

Connecting with Other Subjects

History/Humanities The world history R 5
teacher may help explain how different cultures use monumental sculpture, reliefs, public buildings and war memorials to communicate beliefs and values to others. For example, the Bayeux Tapestry represents a human need to record accomplishments in war and conquest. How or why do these artworks evoke emotional responses? Introduce mythology, folklore and fairy tales that exemplify human needs and values. How have archaeologists and historians used myths and legends to learn about the past?

Study Questions
Chapter 21–A Critical Method

1 What are the four stages of the art criticism method presented in the text?

_____

_____

2 What are the four aspects of an artwork that can be examined through art criticism?

_____

_____

3 Explain the difference between *subject matter* and *content* in an artwork.

_____

_____

4 What is the major question answered in the first stage of art criticism?

_____

_____

5 What is the major question answered in the second stage of art criticism?

_____

_____

6 What is the major question answered in the third stage of art criticism?

_____

7 What is the major question answered in the fourth stage of art criticism?

_____

_____

8 Which is the most subjective stage of art criticism?

_____

_____

9 What are some criteria your evaluation in stage four can be based on?

_____

_____

10 Sometimes metaphors help with interpretation of the meaning in an artwork. Look up the definition of *metaphor*. Find an example of a metaphor in one of the interpretations in chapter 21. Try writing one of your own.

_____

_____

_____

11 What is a hypothesis in art criticism?

_____

_____

12 What effect may the personal experiences of people in a group have on their interpretation of the same painting?

_____

_____

13 During which stage of criticism would you consider similarities and contrasts of elements in an artwork?

_____

_____

_____

14 What are some factors not seen in artworks that affect the judgment of professionals when purchasing artworks?

_____

_____

_____

Test Questions
Chapters 20 and 21–Criticism and Critics, A Critical Method

A Critical Method

1 List the four stages of art criticism presented in Chapters 20 and 21.

_____

_____

_____

_____

2 List four areas of professional criticism available to thc public that were described in Chapter 20.

_____

_____

_____

_____

3 Which of the following is cited as a general purpose of criticism in Chapter 20.

a. To express dislikes about something.
b. To discuss the characteristics of something.
c. To discuss good and bad qualities of something.

4 Which of the following was NOT listed in Chapter 20 as a reason for criticism.

a. To learn about art.
b. To discover new things in artworks.
c. To determine what kinds of art to reject.
d. To organize and communicate knowledge about art.

5 What the artwork expresses about human experience is referred to as

a. subject matter.
b. content.
c. an hypothesis.
d. speculation.

For questions 6 through 11, select from the following stages of criticism.

1. Description   3. Interpretation
2. Analysis   4. Evaluation

6 _____ The most subjective stage of art criticism.

7 _____ The stage in which you identify the meaning of the artwork.

8 _____ The stage in which a statement about movement resulting from the placement of elements should occur.

9 _____ In which stage would you place statements like "a figure straight as a flagpole," "the ghost-like shapes of the trees," and "the lifting sweep of the hills"?

10 _____ The stage in which you list the objects and elements included in an artwork.

11 _____ The stage in which you determine the quality or success of an artwork.

12 List four things, other than the work of art, that were discussed in Chapter 21 that might affect a museum director's decision about purchasing a work of art.

_____

_____

_____

_____

Study Answers

Chapter 21

A Critical Method

1 Description, Analysis, Interpretation, Evaluation.

2 Describable elements, organization, expressive content, and quality.

3 *Subject matter* refers to those things represented in an artwork: figures, objects and other representational things, or the art elements in completely abstract works. *Content* refers to what the artwork expresses about human experience—the meaning or message communicated by a work of art.

4 What can you see and describe in the artwork?

5 How are things organized and interrelated in the artwork?

6 What does the artwork express about human experience? Or, what is the meaning of the work?

7 How successful do you think the work is?

8 The interpretation stage.

9 Craftsmanship, design quality, expressiveness, personal response, and originality. (Comparison may be included.)

10 *Metaphor* is an implied comparison: one thing is likened to a different thing by being described as if it *were* that other thing; a word or phrase ordinarily used for one thing is applied to another. Example: "…the green of the hemlock is a promise of continuing life." Students may also write their own metaphors.

11 An assumption or informed guess about the meaning of an artwork.

12 The personal experience of different people may result in different interpretations of the same artwork.

13 Analysis, or stage two.

14 The artist's reputation and achievements, importance of the work in art history, recognizability of the artist's style, demand for the artist's work, lasting value of the work, opinions of experts, freshness of treatment.

Test Answers

Chapters 20 and 21

Criticism and Critics,

A Critical Method

1 Description, Analysis, Interpretation, Evaluation.

2 Answers may include: art, film, theater, music, television, literature, architecture, cars.

3 B.

4 C.

5 B.

6 3.

7 3.

8 2.

9 3.

10 1.

11 4.

12 Answers may include: how well known the artist is (reputation), importance of artist's achievements, importance of artwork in art history, recognizability of artist's style, demand for artist's work, opinions of experts, freshness of treatment.

Teacher Lesson Notes

Chapter 21
A Critical Method

Chapter 20 explained the purposes of art criticism. Developing your own critical skills will contribute to your enjoyment and understanding of art.

In earlier chapters, you learned about the three stages in the critical analysis of artworks: *description* (Chapter 3), *analysis* (Chapters 9 and 10), and *interpretation* (Chapter 15). Criticism may include a fourth stage, *evaluation*. This process is explained at the end of this chapter.

The four stages of criticism are outlined here. The outline can help you understand and talk about art.

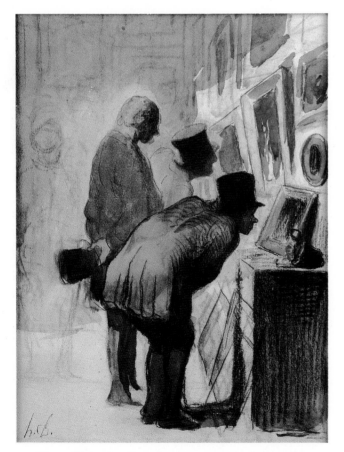

21-1 Honoré Daumier, *Connoisseurs,* ca. 1862–64. Crayon, charcoal, wash and watercolor. © The Cleveland Museum of Art, Dudley P. Allen Fund.

Description

Identify things about the work that you can see, name, and describe with certainty. Be sure your statements do not include opinions, evaluations or interpretations. Just record what is there.

Label Information

1. Title of work and artist's name.

2. When and where the work was created.

3. The medium (or media) used.

Subject Matter

1. Recognizable images such as people, buildings, trees, and other things.

   a) Describe what living forms are doing

   b) What is large/small, near/far, in front/behind

2. If the work consists of geometric shapes or free forms, indicate that and then go on to Art Elements.

Art Elements (Chapters 4–8)

1. **Line**

   Straight, curved, dotted, broken, wavy, swirling, jagged, textured, horizontal, vertical, diagonal, continuous, heavy, thin, etc. Are there lines that direct your attention from place to place?

   Contour lines or outlines.

   Implied by abrupt color, value, or texture changes.

2. **Color** and **Value**

   Are colors warm, cold, bright, dull, dark, light, opaque, transparent? Are they like or unlike real world colors? Is there a dominant color?

   Do values result from combinations of black and white, or shades and tints of color? Are value contrasts strong, soft, or both?

3. **Shapes** (two-dimensional) and **Forms** (three-dimensional)

   Are shapes representational, abstract, non-objective, organic, geometrical, open, closed.

4. **Textures**

   Are they visible in the work? Where? Are they rough, smooth, coarse, soft, bumpy, hairy, sandy?

   Are they *simulated* (you can see, but not feel it) or *real* (an actual part of the work you can feel)?

   Don't confuse texture with *pattern,* which is the repetition of some design in a recognizable order, such as polka dots or a checkerboard. Identify patterns.

5. **Space**

   Two-dimensional art (implied depth): Does space appear shallow or deep? Due to shading, colors that seem to advance/recede, foreshortening, linear perspective, aerial perspective, overlap, high-low placement?

   Three-dimensional art (real depth): Due to voids, concaves, convexes, volumes?

Analysis

How have the things listed under Subject Matter and Art Elements been organized or inter-related? How do they work together?

Similarities

1. Are some things similar in shape, color, texture, form, or size?

2. Are some lines similar in direction or kind?

Contrasts

1. Are there contrasts in color such as dull/bright, cool/warm, dark/light?

2. Are there contrasts of shape, form, texture, movement, size, complexity, simplicity?

Movement and Continuation

1. If movement is suggested in the work, which of the following devices is it due to: Repetition of something, alternating elements, progression from large to small, dark to light, etc., living forms doing something?

2. Are there elements that lead your eye through the composition—edges, rows of things, continuous lines, directional shapes, figures painting, or eyes looking in a particular direction?

Dominance

1. Is there some area, element, or arrangement that seems most important?

Balance

1. What contributes to balance in the composition?

2. Is balance symmetrical, asymmetrical, or radial?

Relationships

1. What are the relationships between the subject of the artwork and the art elements?

2. What are the relationships between the subject of the artwork and the medium or procedure used to produce it?

Interpretation

Use the information from your description and analysis to help you identify the *meaning* of the work (what it expresses about human experience).

Describe the expressive mood of the work: sad, happy, serious, lighthearted, calm, chaotic, depressing, ominous, sensual, somber, joyful, angry, aggressive, passive, tense, relaxed, etc.

Metaphor may help to get at meaning: In a metaphor, one thing is spoken of as if it is another, different thing, e.g., "He is a bull in a china shop." "Her voice is music." "Colors roll across the canvas in thunderous waves." "The red shape is a loose cannon among misty greens."

Hypothesis (an assumption or informed guess, about the meaning of the work)

Defense

1. Defend your hypothesis with evidence from your description and analysis.

2. Defend your hypothesis with evidence from other sources such as art history, past experiences the work reminds you of, or presumed purposes: to praise, criticize, predict, record an event, make a political or social statement, ridicule, and so on.

Evaluation

Based on your analysis in the first three stages, how would you judge the quality or success of the work? Judgment may be affected by the following criteria.

Craftsmanship—the degree of skill in use of media and procedures, and how well the medium relates to the subject matter and purpose of the artwork.

Design Quality—the degree of visual organization of the materials and elements that make up the work. Consider unity, variety, proximity, balance, dominance, and rhythm.

Expressiveness—how well the work expresses its subject, idea, or theme.

Personal Response—the extent to which the artwork provokes a personal response, one that could be shared with others.

Originality—the degree of uniqueness, imagination, and freshness in the artwork.

Comparison—how the work compares with other artworks of similar kind.

Using the First Three Stages of the Critical Analysis Model

The following examples will provide you with some guided practice in art criticism. This guided practice will help you learn how to gather facts about a work of art before you draw conclusions. Once you have learned the process, you will feel more confident in your ability to discuss and enjoy artworks.

An adequate analysis can be based on completion of the first three stages of the model. Because the last stage, evaluation, is difficult even for art professionals, it will be discussed separately.

Hemlock in November

Description. You will find it easy to describe this work by Charles Burchfield, a well-known Regionalist painter. It is a watercolor of a wooded grove. It includes an evergreen tree identified as a hemlock in the title (fig. 21–2). The hemlock is surrounded by trees that are losing their leaves. The forms of the tree and stump in the foreground appear three-dimensional. These forms are emphasized by warm, dark colors and strong textures. The clearing in the background contains some different varieties of evergreens. It is flooded with white light that filters down through the trees. The painting includes a mixture of warm and cold, transparent and opaque colors. Colors have been tinted and shaded. The space in this painting appears deep because of overlapping, the diminishing sizes of the trees, and aerial perspective.

Analysis. The first thing you see in this painting is the hemlock. The hemlock contrasts with the surrounding trees because of its size, textures, green needles, and dark colors. The entire tree is silhouetted against a cool, silvery light. The rhythm of the branches and needles causes a lively upward movement. Due to these factors and its slightly off-center placement, the hemlock is the dominant form in the composition.

Light is everywhere, filtering down through the branches and giving the tree trunks a silvery glow. Clusters of the evergreen's needles reflect the light. The light becomes a background haze into which distant trees disappear. The brown, gold, yellow, and white foreground colors are repeated in the fallen leaves, the leaves on the trees at each side of the picture, and in the top branches of the hemlock. These colors produce a framing effect around the painting.

The bases of the trees on each side of the hemlock are progressively higher on the picture plane as they go back in the distance. This progression causes a directional flow from the foreground to the background. The triangular shape of the leaf-covered foreground reinforces this flow and leads to a small evergreen shimmering with light.

Relationships between subject and elements can be seen in the artist's use of predominantly cool colors and the transparent gray washes to suggest a cold fall day. Relationships between subject and procedure are seen in the heavy lines, warm colors, and rhythmical brushstrokes applied to the hemlock.

Interpretation. Our description and analysis suggest several meanings for *Hemlock in November*.

1. It is about the effects of seasonal change upon the natural environment.

2. It is about the mood of a cold fall day in a wooded grove.

3. It is about the hemlock's defiance of approaching winter.

We will defend the first hypothesis for our example of interpretation. The picture is filled with a cool, hazy kind of light that we associate with cold fall days and the feeling that winter is in the air. The trees have lost or are losing their leaves, which have been transformed from green to the colors of fall. Even the trunks of the bare trees and some of the hemlock's needles have been transformed to a silver-white color by the light. However, the green of the hemlock and the lively upward movement of its branches are a promise of continuing life. These are all effects that we associate with seasonal change.

What description and analysis information would you use to support either of the other hypotheses?

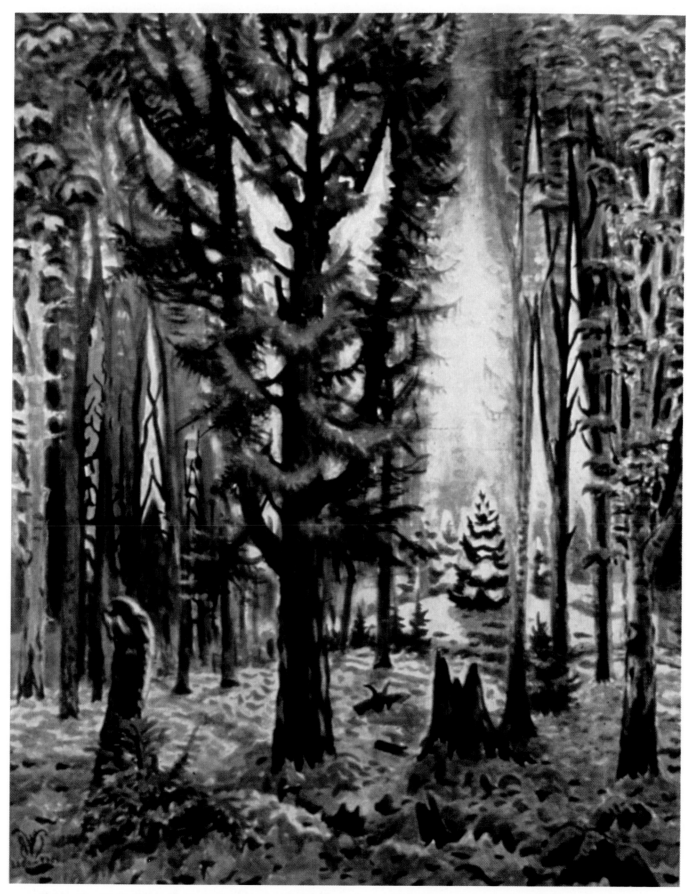

21–2 Charles Burchfield, *Hemlock in November*, 1947–66. Watercolor, 42″ x 32 ½″ (107 x 83 cm). Private Collection. Kennedy Galleries.

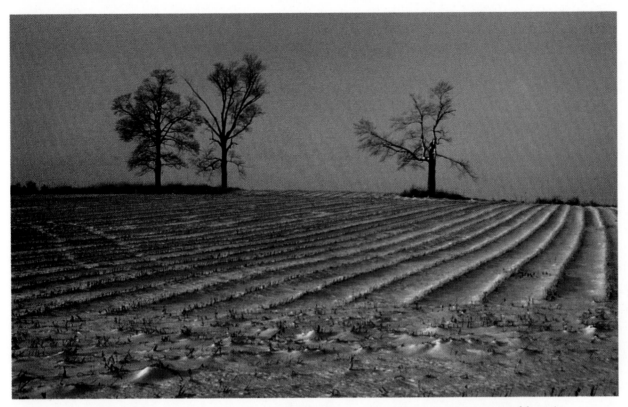

21–3 Robert Stefl, *Illinois Landscape,* 1988. Color photograph cibachrome, 11″ x 14″ (28 x 36 cm). Courtesy of the artist.

Burchfield's painting expresses the effects of fall and a seasonal change upon the environment. *Illinois Landscape #14* (fig. 21–3) by Robert Stefl, a contemporary photographer, refers to the effects of winter on the land. Like a painting, a photograph can express ideas and feelings that may be teased out in the process of critical analysis.

Illinois Landscape #14

Description. This photograph by Robert Stefl depicts a gently rolling field lined with rows of corn stubble that pokes through and casts shadows on wind-packed snow. On the horizon are three leafless black trees and several clumps of grass. Warm browns appear in the rows of stubble that extend in rough lines across the field, and in the clumps of grass on the horizon. The distant trees support angular branches that end in a maze of feathery lines. The sky and the snow-covered field are filled with light values of gray-blue and white. There is an illusion of deep space.

Analysis. When you first look at *Illinois Landscape #14,* your eyes follow the converging lines of corn stubble. These lines direct your attention to the tree on the right. The branches of the lone tree seem to point toward the two trees on the left. The spaces between the rows of stubble become progressively wider from the left to right. They cause a wave-like flow across the foreground to the widest rows on the right. These rows then direct your eyes back to the lone tree.

The warm browns of the corn stubble and grass contrast with the cold colors in the field and sky. However, the cold colors dominate the warm colors. The linear movement of the rows and one-point perspective direct our attention to the trees and the empty space between them. The silhouetted trunks of the trees and the fragile lines of their branches contrast with the cold gray-blue of the sky. The texture of the snow looks crisp and crunchy to the step.

Interpretation. We will hypothesize that *Illinois Landscape #14* expresses the wonder of the trees' survival under very threatening conditions.

The composition of this photograph directs our attention to the trees. The most obvious hardship they must endure is the cold grip of winter, which is evident in the bleakness of the land and the isolation of the trees. A second threat comes from man, who continually clears the land for farming. The rows and furrows extend up to and beyond the trees. The trees are the last sentinels of a grove that existed before the field was cleared. They too may feel the axe.

Before you read the title of figure 21–4, can you guess what the subject matter is? Abstract works of art may change the form of the object to emphasize qualities that you normally might not see. Even though a work is not representational, you can respond to its visual forms. The critical analysis process can help you explain the organization of abstract works and propose meanings for them.

Flowering Apple Tree

Description. This oil painting by Mondrian, a major figure in the Modern movement, consists of lines and primarily geometric shapes, rather than recognizable objects. The lines vary in thickness and intensity. They are mostly curved or arched. Some are horizontal and

vertical. The colors are dull grays, blue-greens, and brownish hues with black line. The outlined shapes are flat, and some are leaflike. There is a minimal sense of spatial depth and no perspective depth, which you can see in *Hemlock* and in *Illinois Landscape #14.*

Analysis. You can identify similarities and contrasts in this work. The orderly, repeated lines create rhythmical movements up, down, left, and right on the surface of the painting. The vertical lines in the lower central area direct your attention to the enclosed leaflike shapes. An area in the center, with lines radiating from it, tends to be a focal point, creating a feeling of formal balance. The two-dimensional shapes and the colors are all at about the same value level, making the composition appear relatively flat. One-half of the painting is approximately the same as the other, so the work is basically symmetrical.

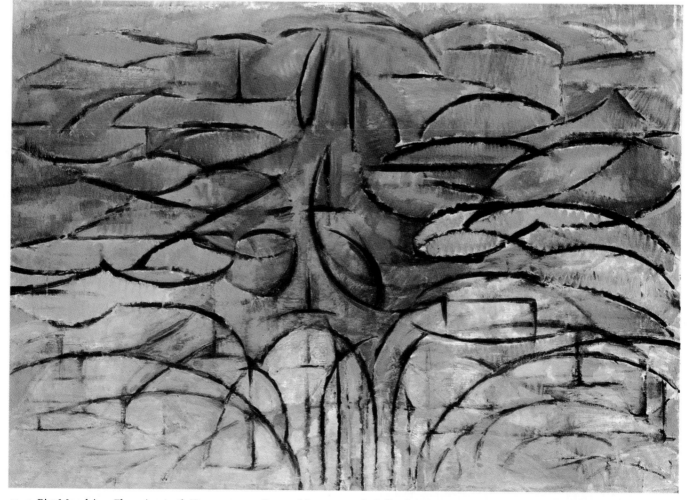

21–4 Piet Mondrian, *Flowering Apple Tree*, 1912. 30 ¾ ″ x 41 ¾ ″ (78 x 106 cm). Collection Haags Gemeentemuseum, The Hague.

Interpretation. *Flowering Apple Tree* is about the rhythm, movement, and balance that can be found in the structure of a tree. The title indicates that the painting is based on a tree. Knowing that, we can relate the central vertical and upward curving lines to a tree trunk and branches, and the outlined shapes to leaves. Since there is no definite tree form in the work, we can concentrate on the rhythmical movements caused by the lines and shapes.

Evaluation

So far, our examples of critical analysis have covered the first three stages of the critical analysis outline. Often, these stages are enough to allow you to explain and understand a work of art. However, evaluation (refer to part IV of the outline) is a step that can let you estimate the quality or lasting importance of an artwork. We will use *Hemlock in November* to illustrate the process of evaluation.

Craftsmanship. Craftsmanship is demonstrated by the artist's skillful control of washes. The washes effectively suggest the changing light in a heavy growth of trees. To suggest deep space, Burchfield used contrasts of opaque and transparent colors and aerial perspective. The forms are crisp and the colors are fresh—a favorable characteristic of watercolor.

Design quality. Our analysis of *Hemlock* indicated that all of the parts are effectively organized around the dominant evergreen tree. The stronger the design of an artwork is, the less aware we are of individual parts, and the more we can focus on the meaning of the work.

Expressiveness. This area of evaluation involves a judgment about the strength of human feelings aroused by the work of art. Sometimes our reactions to an artwork are based on what it reminds us of. Our feelings are related more to that experience or event than to the art form. A successful work should arouse feelings that come from the work itself. The artist organizes symbols and forms to express human feelings that are connected to some experience. For example, assume that *Hemlock in November* is about the effects of seasonal change upon the natural environment. How successful do you feel the painting is not only in arousing your feelings about seasonal change, but in providing you with fresh insights about this theme?

Originality. Originality is closely associated with expressiveness, and involves a judgment about the uniqueness or freshness of an artwork. Is the hemlock tree in Burchfield's painting an unusual interpretation? Or is it what you would expect to see in a calendar or greeting card picture of the same subject? Have you seen similar approaches to lighting, color, and form in other pictures representing late fall? Are there unique qualities here?

Comparison. Comparing an artwork with historical examples is more a task for art professionals such as museum directors and art critics than it is for nonprofessionals. Well-known works that have stood the test of time provide touchstones for judging the quality of other works with similar subjects in similar styles.

Pine Trees with Setting Sun (fig. 21–5) by Vincent van Gogh is a work that has many similarities to *Hemlock in November*. Although the paintings were done with different media (the van Gogh is oil, the Burchfield is watercolor), they are similar in subject and style. Both are landscapes with trees as a principal subject. Both emphasize the vertical. Both emphasize the effects of light, and both employ lively brushwork and exaggeration— seen particularly in the trees—to make the picture vivid.

Art professionals would probably prefer the van Gogh for a number of reasons. The brushwork is more animated. It seems to come from within the forms and to enliven the whole picture. The painting also contains more variety. Notice the asymmetrical composition and the different directions of the branches. Note especially the way in which the diagonal and horizontal branches of the near tree provide a counterpoint to the vertical emphasis. Despite its variety, the van Gogh is at least as well organized as the Burchfield.

Still, on the grounds of craftsmanship, design quality, and expressiveness, you might prefer the Burchfield. This is your right. However, imagine you are a museum director with a large budget to spend on art, and can afford the best. You no doubt would select the van Gogh over the Burchfield for a number of reasons not seen in the works themselves. Some things that professionals consider before purchasing an artwork are:

1. how well-known the artist is;

2. the importance of the artist's achievements;

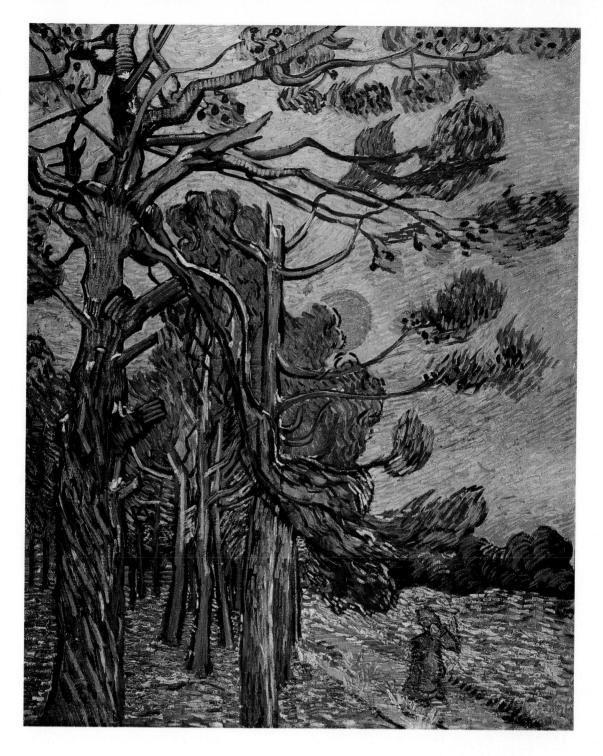

3. the importance of the artwork in the history of art;

4. the recognizability of the artist's style;

5. the demand for the artist's work;

6. the probable lasting value of the work;

7. the opinions of other curators, art dealers, collectors, and investors; and

8. the freshness of treatment of an idea, a medium, a style, or a technique.

Given these reasons, the van Gogh wins easily. Consider reason 8, for example. Van Gogh pioneered an expressionistic style in the late 1880s when such a style was not popular. For all of his efforts, he received almost no recognition during his lifetime. His style was too fresh for the times. But in the early part of this century, his work became celebrated. Van Gogh influenced and paved the way for artists like Burchfield in this century. Reasons 1, 2, and 3 also weigh heavily in the choice of the van Gogh over the Burchfield.

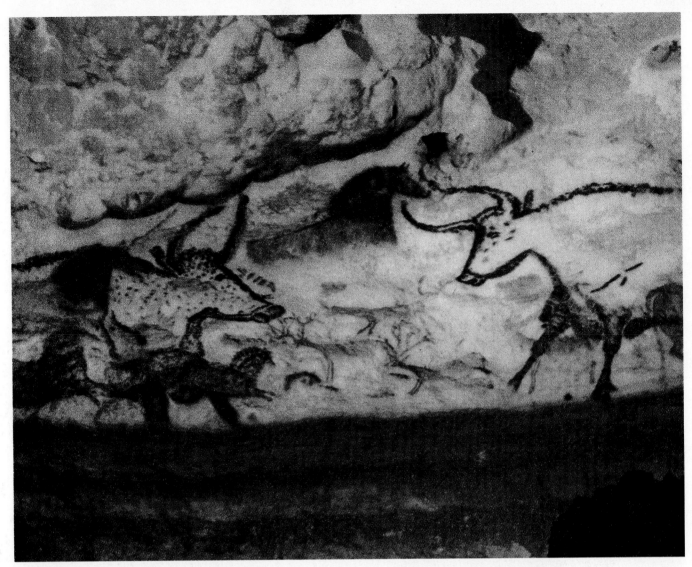

21-6 *Hall of Bulls,* left wall, Lascaux, ca. 15,000–13,000 BC. Dordogne, France. Courtesy of Scala/Art Resource, NY.

Conclusion

We have reached the end of our text, but we have not concluded the story of art. That story begins with the images made on cave walls by prehistoric people, and continues through the cultures of the world, past, present and future. We began with questions about what art is, how and why it is created. In the process of answering these questions, you learned about the elements and principles of design and how the artist uses these elements to create art. You have learned about the wide variety of art forms and art media, and seen how artists use them in their work.

As an art student, you have learned how to use the elements and principles and some art media in your own artwork. You have been introduced to the art history of both Western and non-Western cultures to help you learn about works of art: where, when and why they were created, the style of art, and cultural influences upon artists. Throughout the text, you have used information obtained from all of these experiences to practice art criticism. As you have learned, art criticism is concerned with questions such as: What should I look for in the work? How is it organized? What does it mean? How successful is the work? Most importantly, you have discovered how to learn from the nonverbal language of art. Art provides all civilizations of the world with a means of communication.

Now that you have completed the book, we are certain that you not only know more about art, but also are better prepared to continue learning from it. No one can predict just what forms art will take in the future, or what social functions it will serve. However, art has been important in human affairs over the past 3,000 years. The diversity of forms it has taken suggest that the art of your future will be both exciting and important. We hope that you'll continue to look for ways art can help you learn about and enjoy the world around you.

Criticism Experience 21.1

Analyzing an Artwork

Write a critical analysis of an artwork that has not been discussed in class. Use the four-stage model provided in your text.

Try it Yourself

Continue your role as a museum director. How would you choose between the Burchfield and the Stefl? Between the Burchfield and the Mondrian? You may have to do a little research.

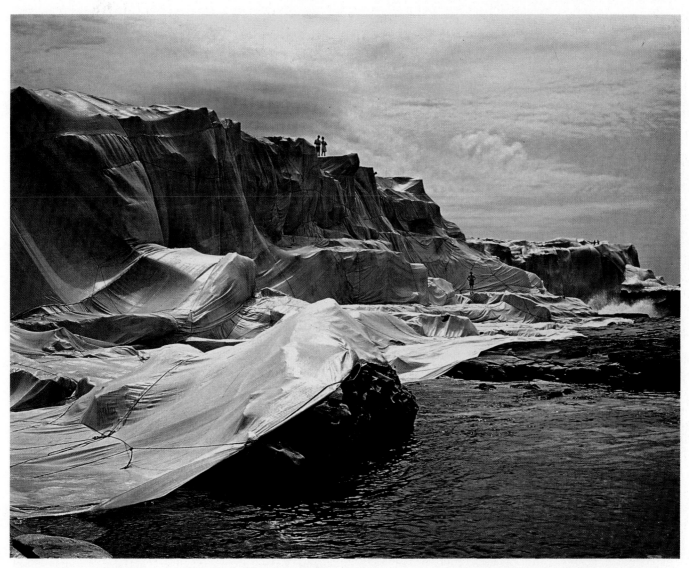

21–7 Christo, *Wrapped Coast, One Million Square Feet, Little Bay, Australia,* 1969. Erosion control fabric and 35 miles of rope. Photograph: Harry Shunk. ©Christo 1969.

Glossary with Pronunciation Guide

abstract art Art stressing the form of its subject rather than its actual appearance. The subject is broken down into elements: line, shape, etc., not necessarily resembling the subject itself.

Abstract Expressionism A twentieth century style in which feelings and emotions are emphasized. Accident and chance are stressed rather than accurate representation of subject matter.

abstract line Lines found in very abstract and nonobjective artworks which do not describe anything. They are meant to be seen only as line.

acrylic paint A synthetic painting medium in which pigments are mixed with acrylic, a plastic emulsion that acts as a vehicle and a binder.

aerial perspective The diminishing of color intensity to lighter and duller hues to give the illusion of distance.

aesthetic (es-*thet*-ik) The theory of perceiving and enjoying something for its beauty and pleasurable qualities. This theory tries to explain and categorize our responses to art forms.

aesthetic response A response that occurs when something is seen and enjoyed for its own sake, or for its beauty and pleasurable qualities.

analogous colors Colors that are next to each other on the color wheel and are closely related, such as yellow, yellow-orange, yellow-green and green.

approximate symmetry The use of forms which are simillar yet different, on either side of a vertical axis.

aquatint A form of intaglio printmaking in which resin is melted on the metal plate to resist the biting action of acid so that tonal areas can be produced when the plate is printed. May be combined with engraving and etching on the same plate.

arabesque (*air*-uh-besk) A flowing, intricate pattern of stylized organic motifs arranged in symmetrical designs.

arcade A series of repeated arches, in some cases supported by columns.

arch A masonry construction in which a number of wedge-shaped stones, held in place by pressing against one another, form a semicircular curve.

architect A person who designs and directs construction of buildings and environmental areas.

architecture The art and science of designing and constructing buildings.

aristocracy A privileged class whose wealth and priveleges are inherited from previous generations.

armature A framework used to support material being modeled in sculpture.

art criticism A systematic discussion of the characteristics of an artwork, usually involving four stages: description, analysis, interpretation and judgment.

art education An area of education which provides programs in art production, art history, aesthetics and art criticism for students in the public schools.

art elements The sensory elements including line, shape, form, color, value, texture and space that are used to create artworks.

artist A person who makes artworks and is skilled in composing subject matter and the art elements with a variety of art materials and procedures.

artwork An object or performance that satisfies conditions or requirements recognized by the art world as necessary for an artwork.

assemblage An artwork composed of objects, parts of objects or materials originally intended for purposes other than art.

asymmetrical balance A feeling of balance attained when the visual units on either side of a vertical axis are actually different but are placed in the composition to create a "felt" balance of the total artwork.

aqueduct A Roman masonry structure supporting a trough for carrying water.

balance A principle of design referring to the arrangement of visual elements to create stability in an artwork. There are three kinds of balance: symmetrical, asymmetrical and radial.

Baroque (bar-*oak*) A period and style in seventeenth century European art in which painters, sculptors and architects used dramatic movement, light, soaring spatial illusions and ornate detail to encourage emotional involvement.

barrel vault A semicircular masonry ceiling.

bas relief (*bah* ree-*leef*) See *low relief*.

batik (ba-*teek*) A method of dyeing cloth using removable wax to repel the dye on parts of the design where dye is not wanted.

Blaue Reiter, Der (*blah*-way *right*-er, dehr) (The Blue Rider) A group of Munich artists including Käthe Kollwitz, Oskar Kokoschka and expatriates such as the Russian Wassily Kandinsky, and the Swiss born Paul Klee. Concems were with presentation of subjective feelings toward reality, and imagination. This group greatly influenced the development of Modern art.

Brücke, Die (*broock*-eh, dee) (The Bridge) A small group of German artists led by Ernst L. Kirchner who emphasized violent color and distortion of features in their paintings and woodcuts in protest of the economic and social conditions in Germany prior to World War I. Other members included Emil Nolde and Wassily Kandinsky.

Buddha (*boo*-dah) Any Buddha sage who has achieved enlightenment in accordance with the teachings of Gautama Siddhartha, founder of Buddhism.

Buddhism (*boo*-dizm) A religious belief based on the teachings of Gautama Siddhartha, who held that suffering is a part of life but that mental and moral self-purification can bring about a state of illumination carrying the believer beyond suffering and material existence.

calligraphy Handwriting or letters formed by hand. Elegant penmanship usually featuring a flowery, precise line.

came Channeled lead strips, either H or U shaped, used in stained glass windows to join the pieces of glass together. The U shape is used on outer edges of the design and the H for all other purposes.

caricature A likeness of a person, distorted by exaggerated features or mannerisms.

cartoon A comic strip or caricature showing some action, situation or person. May be single or multiple frame. In painting, a full-size preliminary drawing from which a painting is made.

carving The process of producing a sculpture by cutting, chipping or hewing wood or stone.

casein (*kay*-seen) A type of paint made from milk or cheese protein used to achieve a transparent or opaque effect.

casting The process of making forms by pouring a fluid substance such as molten metal, liquid plaster or plastic into a mold.

ceramics Objects made of clay and fired in a kiln to a permanent form. Ceramics are often decorated with glazes and fired again to fuse the glazes to the clay body.

chalk A stick of color including a binder, preservative, chalk and pigment, mixed with water, formed into sticks and dried.

chiaroscuro (key-ah-ross-*kyoo*-roh) From the Italian meaning "light-dark." The use of value contrasts to represent the effects of light and shadow.

cire perdue (sear per-*dew*) See *lost-wax process.*

Classical The art of ancient Greece produced in the 400s and 300s BC. Any art form influenced by ancient Greek or Roman examples.

cloisonné (kloy-soh-*nay*) A decorative enameling technique in which thin metal strips are attached to a metal base to outline design areas, or cloisons, which are then filled with enamels and fired.

close-up In the graphic arts (including comic strips) figures and objects are made large to appear close to the viewer. Also a film shot.

closed form Forms in painting and sculpture that have few or no openings, or negative shapes.

closure The tendency to complete partial forms or shapes by seeing lines that do not exist.

collage A two-dimensional composition made by gluing various materials such as paper, fabric, etc., on a flat, firm surface. Introduced by the Cubist artists Picasso and Braque.

color An element of design with three properties, hue, value and intensity. Also the character of surfaces created by the response of vision to wavelengths of reflected light.

commemorative art Art that is produced in remembrance of something or someone.

complementary colors Two colors which are directly opposite each other on the color wheel, meaning they are in extreme contrast with each other.

composition The act of organizing the elements of an artwork into a harmoniously unified whole.

concave Surfaces that are hollow or curved inward.

concept art A style of the 1970s emphasizing the idea behind the work of art rather than the work itself. Artists tried to deemphasize the artwork in favor of the concept to demonstrate that the conception of the work is more imponant than the product.

conditions Requirements that philosophers and critics of art generally agree something must fulfill to be an artwork.

construction A sculpture built by connecting several or many parts to one another. The parts may be made of a single material or of a variety of materials. *Number 7: Full Moon* by Richard Lippold (p. 168) is an example.

contemporary art Artworks created in our own time.

content The essential meaning of an artwork interpreted by an individual or critic.

continuation An element or series of elements that passes through a composition that may direct the viewer's attention, and contribute to unity.

contour line Lines that define the outer edges of forms and surfaces within a form such as shapes or wrinkles and folds. Used in contour drawings to suggest depth in addition to height and width.

contrast A principle of design that refers to differences between elements such as color, texture, value and shape. A painting might have bright colors contrasted with dull or angular shapes contrasted with round ones.

converging lines In perspective, lines that represent the parallel edges of an object are drawn to converge to a vanishing point.

convex Surfaces that curve outward.

cool colors Those colors in which blue is dominant found on the right side of the color wheel.

corbeled arch An arch constructed from an overlapping arrangement of stones, each layer projecting a bit beyond the row beneath it, and held in place by the pressure of the stones against one another.

Corinthian One of the classical styles of ancient Greek architecture featuring tall, slender columns topped with ornate capitals.

Counter-Reformation The reform movement in the Catholic Church following the Reformation.

crafts Works of art that may be expressive, but generally have utilitarian purposes. This includes fiber arts, ceramics, metalsmithing, fabrics, fumiture, basketry, etc.

crosshatching Shading created by crossed parallel lines.

cross vault A masonry ceiling consisting of two barrel vaults intersecting at right angles.

crusade A military expedition of Christian knights against the Moslems in Palestine and/or other parts of the Near East from the eleventh through the thirteenth century.

Cubism A twentieth century art movement developed mainly by Picasso and Braque in which the subject matter is broken up, analyzed and reassembled in an abstract form, emphasizing geometric shapes.

culture The attitudes, values, beliefs, patterns of behavior, social organization and concepts of reality of a given people which persists through time.

descriptive lines Lines created with a variety of tools; can be outlines, contour lines, single lines or hatching.

design The plan the artist uses to organize the art elements (line, shape, form, space, etc.) in a work of art to achieve a unified composition.

dome A hemispherical vault or ceiling over a circular opening.

dominance A concept of design which suggests that one element, or a combination of elements, attracts more attention than anything else in a composition. The dominant element(s) is usually a focal point in a composition and contributes to unity by suggesting that other elements are subordinate to it.

Doric The earliest of the classical styles of ancient Greek architecture.

dynasty The period of time when a certain family ruled.

earthenware Ceramic ware that is made from natural clay. It is soft, porous and fired at low temperatures.

eclectic Borrowing from many sources, particularly of architecture, which imitates styles of the past.

edge Where one shape ends and another begins, resulting in implied line.

elements of design Space, line, shape, form, color, value and texture. The tools the artist works with to create an artwork according to the principles of design.

ellipse An oval shape produced by drawing an elongated circle so that it appears to be viewed from an angle. A foreshortened circle that is longer in one dimension than it is in the other.

emulsion A liquid in which droplets of a second liquid are suspended until painted on a surface where they dry and bond together.

engraving A technique in which a design is incised in a plate of metal, wood or plastic. A print is then made from the plate.

Enlightenment A philisophical movement of the eighteenth century marked by faith in science and reason.

environmental art An artwork which is part of the environment surrounding it, or which provides an enclosed environment that viewers can enter; or an arrangement which the viewer can walk around or through.

etching A technique in which a metal plate covered with an acid-resistant coating is incised by needle scratches. The plate is then immersed in acid and a print is made from the plate.

Expressionism An art movement developed at the end of the nineteenth and the beginning of the twentieth century in Germany. This style emphasized the expression of the artist's emotions through the use of strong color, exploitation of media and the use of suggestive and symbolic imagery.

expressive lines Lines that are produced to express an idea, mood or quality (e.g., graceful, nervous, delicate, aggressive, etc.).

eye level A horizontally drawn line that is even with the viewer's eye. In landscape scenes it can be the actual horizon line, but can also be drawn in still life.

façade (fah-*sahd*) The front of a building. The façade accents the entrance and usually prepares the viewer for the architectural style inside.

fashion design Creating and producing apparel for every occasion.

Fauvism (*foe*-vizm) An early twentieth century style of painting developed in France. The artists, led by Matisse, used brilliant and explosive color to express the inner quality of their subjects rather than how they appeared in nature. They were called Fauves, or "Wild Beasts" because critics thought they used colors in a violent uncontrolled way.

ferroconcrete A principle of construction employing concrete reinforced with steel rods.

figure-ground The perceptual tendency to divide visual patterns into two kinds of shapes with the figure(s) appearing to be on top of, and surrounded by, the ground. In the pictorial arts, the relationship between images and the background. Figure and ground are often referred to as positive shape and negative shape.

film and television graphics The design and production of films and tapes.

fine artist Person skilled in the making of symbols, the use of media and techniques, and one who creates compositional arrangements that demonstrate uniqueness of interpretation and individuality of technique.

flat wash An area of thin paint that is uniform throughout.

flying buttress An external support for the wall of a Gothic cathedral consisting of a half arch connected to a narrow masonry pier outside the building.

foreground The area of a picture that appears to be closest to the viewer.

foreshortening A method of applying perspective to an object or figure so that it seems to recede in space by shortening the depth dimension, making the form appear three-dimensional.

form An element of design that appears three-dimensional and encloses volume such as a cube, sphere, pyramid or cylinder. The term may also refer to the characteristics of an artwork's visual elements (lines, color, textures, etc.) as distinguished from its subject matter.

forum In a Roman city, a center of civic, legal and commercial activity.

frame Each individual drawing in a sequence such as a comic strip or a story board.

frame construction A method of construction in which a skeleton of studs and joists is erected as in a new house. An exterior of wood, brick, metal or plaster is added.

framing Once the artist decides on the horizontal and vertical borders of a picture, framing determines the space and point of view for a picture.

fresco A method of mural painting in which pigments are applied to a thin layer of wet plaster so that they will be absorbed.

Futurism A style of art originating in Italy during the early twentieth century that emphasized representation of a dynamic, machine-powered world.

genre (*jsahn*-ra) A type of localized art that depicts realistic scenes or events from everyday life.

genre subjects Subject matter of ordinary people in ordinary settings.

geometric shapes (rectillinear) Mechanical, humanmade shapes such as squares, triangles, circles, etc. Geometric shapes have regular edges as opposed to the irregular edges of organic shapes.

glaze A thin coating of minerals which gives the surface a glass-like quality. Used in painting and ceramics.

good design A condition that is fulfilled when a logical and harmonious relationship exists among all the parts of an object.

Gothic A style in European art and architecture that prevailed from the twelfth through the fifteenth century. Gothic architecture, specifically in cathedrals, was characterized by pointed arches, ribbed vaults, flying buttresses.

gouache (gwash) A form of water-soluble paint used to create opacity.

graded wash An area of thin or transparent paint that increases or decreases in intensity from dark to light, light to dark, or both.

graphic art The art of printmaking in any form. In commercial art, advertising, book and magazine illustration, cartoons and signs, etc., for commercial purposes.

graphic design Creating visual communications with two-dimensional media and images.

ground The treated surface on which a painting or drawing is made. A coating such as priming or sizing is used to prepare a support (e.g., bare canvas or wood) for a painting.

harmony A condition in which the elements of an artwork appear to fit well together.

hatching Shading using closely spaced, parallel lines used to suggest light and shadow.

hieroglyph (high-row-*gliff*) A form of ancient writing in which pictures or symbols are used to represent sounds, words or ideas.

High Renaissance In art and architecture, the flowering of the Renaissance (c. 1495–1525).

Hinduism (*hin*-doo-izm) The world's most ancient religion. It is polytheistic (worshipers believe in many gods). Hindus believe in reincarnation, that life is an endless cycle of birth and death.

historical context The historical circumstances of an artwork, periods of history and style prevalent when the work was created.

hue The property of color that distinguishes one gradation from another and gives it its name.

humanism Devotion to human concerns; the study of humanity.

hypothesis An informed assumption proposed for the purpose of argument.

idealism A concept of perfection, particularly in the treatment of the human figure.

idolatry The worship of an image.

illustration A drawing with any medium used to clarify ideas.

implied line Lines that are indicated indirectly in artworks at edges where two shapes meet, where a form ends and the space around it begins, or by positioning several objects or figures in a row.

implied movement The appearance of movement in a static artwork resulting from an artist's use of elements such as: subject matter, line, shape, progression, repetition and alternation, running or pointing figures, etc.

impressing Figures and shapes made by stamping or pushing patterns and symbols into soft surfaces such as clay, leather or copper foil.

impressionism The first of the Modern art movements developed in France during the second half of the nineteenth century which emphasized the momentary effects of light on color in nature.

incising Making lines and figures by cutting into a surface with a sharp tool.

industrial design Conceiving of, and designing objects which meet the needs of people.

Industrial Revolution A significant change in the economies of Western Europe and the United States during the ninteenth century marked by the introduction of power-driven machinery and mass production.

intaglio (in-*tahl*-ee-oh) A technique of printmaking where lines and areas are etched, engraved or scratched beneath the surface of a metal or plastic plate. Ink is then transferred from the plate onto paper.

intensity The degree or purity, saturation or strength of a color. High intensity colors are bight; low intensity colors are dull.

interior design Planning space inside a house or building, including furnishings.

intermediate colors Colors produced by mixing a primary color and the adjacent secondary color on the color wheel. (For example, yellow and green for yellow-green.) They are also made by mixing unequal amounts of two primaries. (For example, adding more yellow to a combination of yellow and blue produces yellow-green.)

Ionic (eye-*ahn*-ik) Classical Greek architecture characterized by slender, elegant columns with spiral device capitals and fluted shafts.

Islam (is-*lahm*) The Moslem religion and all the nations in which that religion dominates.

isometric perspective A method of applying perspective by drawing the height, width and depth of an object or figure on the same scale at equal angles of 120° with one another. Planes recede on the diagonal, but the parallel lines along edges remain parallel rather than converging as in linear perspective.

kiln (kill) A furnace capable of controlled high temperatures used to fire ceramic ware and sculpture.

kinetic art Any art construction that contains moving elements which can be set in motion by the action of gravity, air currents, motors, springs or magnets.

line An element of art which is used to define space, contours and outlines, or suggest mass and volume. It may be a continuous mark made on a surface with a pointed tool or implied by the edges of shapes and forms.

line of sight Implied lines suggested by the direction in which figures in a picture are looking, or from the observer's eye to the object being looked at.

linear perspective A technique of creating the illusion of depth on a flat surface. All parallel lines receding into the distance are drawn to converge at one or more vanishing points on the horizon line. In one point linear perspective receding lines converge to one vanishing point. In two point perspective receding lines converge to two vanishing points.

lithography A method of printing from a flat stone or metal plate. A drawing is made on the stone or plate with a greasy crayon and chemically treated so that only the greasy drawing will hold ink while the remaining surface resists it. A print is then made from the plate.

load carrying Pertaining to a wall or post that supports a ceiling, as distinguished from a nonload-carrying wall or post.

lost-wax process (cire purdue) A method of casting metal in which a mold is lined with wax, filled with a solid core of heat resistant materials (vestment) and heated to melt the wax leaving a thin cavity between mold and core into which metal is poured.

low relief (bas relief) Sculpture that projects slightly from the surface.

Mannerism A sixteenth century European art style that rejected the calm balance of High Renaissance art in favor of emotion, distortion of the figure, exaggerated perspective views and crisp treatment of light and shadow.

masonry A medium of architecture consisting of stone or brick.

mastaba (mah-*stah*-bah) A low, rectangular Egyptian tomb made of mud brick with sloping sides and a flat top.

medieval (mee-*dee*-vuhl) Pertaining to the Middle Ages.

medium (pl. media) The materials used to create an artwork such as oil, watercolor, etc., or a category of art such as drawing, painting or sculpture.

metal frame A principle of construction in which narrow light-weight members of iron or steel are joined to form a framework to which walls and ceiling can be attached.

Middle Ages The period of Western European history from the decline of the Roman Empire to the beginning of the Renaissance (476 AD to 1400 AD).

middle classes The class of society between the upper class and the lower class. In pre-industrial Europe, the class of merchants, traders and professionals that were beneath the aristocracy and above the peasant class.

minaret (min-ar-*et*) A high, slender tower attached to or near a mosque with balconies from which a crier calls the people to prayer.

minimal art A twentieth century style that stressed reducing an artwork to minimal colors, simple geometric forms, lines and textures.

mixed wash Transparent colors are placed on a damp paper and allowed to flow together, resulting in mixed colors.

mobile A kinetic sculpture, invented by Alexander Calder in 1932, constructed of shapes that are balanced and arranged on wire arms and suspended from above so as to move freely in air currents.

mold A hollow container that produces a cast by giving its form to a substance (molten metal, plastic or plaster) placed within it and allowed to harden.

monochromatic One color which is modified by changing the values and saturation of the hue by additions of black or white.

monotheism Belief in one God.

mosaic A mural technique formed by placing colored pieces of marble or glass (tesserae), small stones or ceramic tiles in a layer of adhesive material.

mosque (mahsk) A Moslem house of worship.

movement A principle of design associated with rhythm, referring to the arrangement of parts in an artwork to create a sense of motion to the viewer's eye through the work. (See *implied movement, optical movement.*)

mural A large design or picture created directly on the wall or ceiling.

negative space The space not occupied by an object or figure but circulating in and around it, contributing to the total effect of the composition.

Neoclassicism ("New Classicism") A style of art in the nineteenth century in which artists and critics sought inspiration from the classical art of ancient Greece and Rome and imitated its themes, simplicity, order and balance.

neutral colors Colors not associated with any hue such as black, white and gray and are neither warm nor cool. Also colors which have been "grayed" or reduced in saturation by mixing them with a neutral or complementary color.

nonload carrying Pertaining to a wall attached to a frame structure. A wall that does not support a roof.

nonobjective art Artworks that have no recognizable subject matter such as figures, flowers, buildings, etc.

Nonwestern Civilization Any culture that is not related to Western Civilization (the people of North America and Western Europe).

one-point perspective A way to show three-dimensional objects on a two-dimensional surface, using one vanishing point. One object faces the viewer; the lines defining other objects in the artwork recede at an angle to a single vanishing point on the horizon line. (See *perspective.*)

Op art A twentieth century style in which artists sought to create an impression of movement by means of optical illusion.

opaque (oh-*payk*) In the two-dimensional arts, an area that light does not pass through. The opposite of transparent.

open form Forms in paintings and sculpture which emphasize openings.

opinion Personal belief or impression which may be true for the individual but not for other people.

optical mixing Colors or black and white laid side by side seem to blend together; mixing takes place in the eye.

optical movement An illusion of movement, or implied movement caused by the response of the eye to lines, shapes and colors arranged in artworks. (See *Op art.*)

organic shapes (bimorphic) Free forms, or shapes and forms that represent living things having irregular edges, as distinguished from the regular edges of geometric shapes.

outline Lines with little variation that describe the outer edges of shapes which appear flat.

pan Moving a camera from side to side in a stationary position.

papier-mâché (*pay*-per ma-*shay*) A technique of creating three-dimensional or relief sculpture by molding strips of paper soaked in glue or paste.

pastel A chalky, colored crayon consisting of pigment and adhesive gum. Also paintings done with such crayons.

patina (pah-*tee*-nah) The surface coloration on metal caused by natural oxidation. This effect can also be produced by the application of heat, chemicals and polishing agents.

pattern The repetition of elements or combinations of elements in a recognizable organization.

performance art Works of a theatrical nature performed by the artist before an audience. A performance may involve props, lights, sound, dialogue, etc.

perspective The representation of three-dimensional objects on a flat surface to produce the same impression of distance and relative size as that received by the human eye.

photography The art of making photographs for fine art or commercial purposes.

picture plane The flat surface or plane that the artist organizes the picture in.

piece mold A mold with sections completely free of undercuts. It may consist of two or more pieces and is generally made from plaster.

pigment A powdered coloring material for paint, crayons, chalks and ink.

pilgrimage The journey of a pilgrim to a shrine; in the Middle Ages, the journey to a cathedral to see and be in the presence of a relic.

plane A flat, two-dimensional surface.

planographic print Prints made from a flat surface area on which ink is placed. The lithograph is planographic as are monoprints made from ink spread on a flat, nonporous surface.

pluralism A condition of art or culture in which many styles and doctrines of taste coexist.

pointed arch A masonry construction in which a number of wedge-shaped stones form curves that come to a point.

polytheism The belief in many gods.

Pop art An art style, also known as neo-Dada, developed in the 1950s. Pop artists depicted and satirized popular culture such as mass media symbols, comic strips, fast foods, billboards and brand name products.

porcelain Ceramic ware made from a specially prepared, fine white clay that fires at the highest temperatures. Porcelain is hard, translucent, thin walled and rings when struck.

positive and negative shapes In pictures, positive shapes are the figures and negative shapes make up the ground.

positive space The enclosed areas or objects in an artwork. They may suggest recognizable objects or nonrepresentational shapes.

post and lintel A method of construction in which two vertical members (posts) support a horizontal member (lintel) to create a covered space.

Post Impressionism A style developed in the 1880s in France in reaction to Impressionism. It included artists such as Cezanne, Seurat, Gauguin and van Gogh. The first two artists explored the formal structure of art while the other two championed the expression of personal feelings.

Post Modernism A loosely defined term referring to a new cycle in art history and culture in general.

pottery Ceramic ware made of clay and hardened by firing at low temperatures.

Pre-Columbian The history of the peoples living in Central and South America before the time of Columbus.

primary colors The three basic colors, red, yellow and blue, from which it is possible to mix all other colors. The primaries cannot be produced by mixing pigments.

principles of design Balance, emphasis, rhythm, movement, repetition, contrast and unity. The methods or techniques that artists use to organize or design artworks by controlling and ordering the elements of design.

proximity The placement of objects very near to each other to make them look related.

radial balance A composition based on a circle with the design radiating from a central point.

Realism A mid-nineteenth century style in which artists turned to painting familiar scenes and events as they actually appeared in nature in the belief that subject matter should be shown true to life, without stylization or idealization as in Neoclassicism and Romanticism.

Reformation A sixteenth century religious movement marked by the establishment of the Prostestant Church.

relic An object that is worshiped because it is believed to be associated with, or part of the remains of, a Christian saint or martyr.

relief A type of sculpture in which forms project from a background. It is classified according to the degree in which it is raised from the surface: high relief, low relief, etc.

relief print A print produced when raised surfaces are inked and applied to paper or other materials. Woodcuts, linocuts and collographs are examples of relief prints.

Renaissance (ren-eh-*sahnss*) A period in Western history (ca. 1400–1600) marking a "rebirth" of cultural awareness and learning, founded largely on a revival of Classical art and writing.

repoussé (ree-*pooh*-say) A metalworking process of hammering or pressing sheet metal into relief on one side to create shapes or patterns on the other side.

rhythm A principle of design that refers to ways of combining elements to produce the appearance of movement in an artwork. It may be achieved through repetition, alternation or progression of an element.

ribbed vault A cross vault reinforced at the intersections with ribs.

Rococo (roh-*koh*-koh) An eighteenth century style of art and interior decoration which emphasized portraying the carefree life of the aristocracy. Love and romance were portrayed rather than historical or religious subjects.

Romanticism A style of art that flourished from the middle of the eighteenth century and continued well into the nineteenth century. Romanticism emphasized personal emotions, dramatic action and exotic settings using literary and historical subject matter.

saturation The purity, vividness or intensity of a color.

screen print Stencils are attached to porous fabrics such as nylon and polyester. Ink is squeezed through openings in the stencil to produce a print. Originally called silkscreen because that was the fabric first used for the process.

sculpture Three-dimensional forms (sculpture in the round) or forms in relief created by carving, assembly or modeling.

secco (*se*-koe) A mural technique created by painting on a dried lime-plaster wall with pigment ground in casein.

secondary colors Colors that result from a mixture of two primary colors. On the twelve-color wheel, orange, green and violet.

sequence In the popular arts of comics and movies, the following of one event or image after another in logical ordering.

serigraph (sehr-*ig*-raff) A term originated to refer to the screen process when done by an artist rather than commercially. It means "drawing on silk."

sgraffito (skrah-*fee*-toe) Decorating a surface such as clay, plaster or glass, by scratching through a surface layer to expose a different color underneath.

shade Variations in the dark and light of color made by adding black to the color.

shape An element of art. An enclosed space defined by other art elements such as line, color and texture.

shape constancy The tendency to see the shape of a three-dimensional object as unchanging regardless of any change in position or angle from which it is viewed.

Shintoism (*shin*-toe-izm) A Japanese religion which emphasizes reverence for family, race and above all, the ruling family as direct decendents of the gods.

shot and sequence An unbroken segment of a scene or action in a film or videotape; a series of shots.

similarity Making components of an artwork alike in one or more ways such as color, shape, texture, size or form.

simulated texture An artist may use color and value contrast to give a painting or drawing the appearance of texture as distinguished from the texture of the artwork itself.

size constancy The tendency to see the size of an object as unchanging regardless of the distance between the viewer and the object.

social context The environment in which the artwork was created, and how it was experienced by people of that time and place; their aesthetic preferences.

space An element of art that indicates areas between, around, above, below or within something.

split complementary On the color wheel, a hue which is combined with hues on either side of its complement.

stabile A term adopted by Alexander Calder to identify standing constructions that emphasize space, similar to the mobile, but do not have moving parts.

stoneware Ceramic ware made from clay that is fired at a relatively high temperature (2200°F). It is hard and nonporous.

storyboard In filmmaking, a series of pictures that resemble comic strips, corresponding to a sequence. Each illustration represents a shot.

stupa (*stew*-pah) A large, mound-shaped Buddhist shrine.

style The identifying characteristics of the artwork of an individual, a group of artists, a period of time or an entire society.

subculture A group of people who share in part the culture of a larger group to which they belong nationally or ethnically, but who have identifiable differences as a group.

subject matter Things that are represented in an artwork such as people, buildings, trees, etc.

symmetrical balance The organization of the parts of a composition so that one side duplicates or mirrors the other.

tactile The sensation of touch. Some surfaces may be perceived through touch.

Taoism (*dow*-izm) A philosophy based on the belief that to achieve lasting happiness one must follow a life of simplicity, modesty, patience and obedience to the laws of nature.

tempera A technique of painting in which the waterbase paint is mixed or tempered with egg yolk.

tesserae (*tess*-ah-ree) The small cubes, usually pieces of glass or clay, used in making mosaics.

texture The surface quality of an artwork usually perceived through the sense of touch. However, texture can also be implied; perceived visually though not felt through touch. (See *simulated texture*.)

three-dimensional Having height, width and depth.

tilt A movie camera can tilt, or move up and down in a stationary position.

tint A lighter value of a hue made by adding a small amount of another color to it.

totem (*toe*-tem) An object, such as an animal or a plant, that serves as an emblem of a family or clan.

track In filmmaking, to move or follow an action.

traditional art Works that have form, style and subject matter that are familiar to the public as art.

trapezoid A shape with four angles and four sides only two of which are parallel.

triadic color scheme Any three colors equidistant on the color wheel.

two-dimensional Having height and width.

two-point perspective A way to show three-dimensional objects on a two-dimensional surface, using two vanishing points and two sets of converging lines to represent forms. These forms are seen from an angle and have two receding sides. Two dimensions appear to recede: width and depth. (See *perspective*.)

ukiyo-e (oo-key-oh-eh) ("the art of the floating world") Japanese art that centered around the district of Edo and popular culture. Commonly produced in woodcuts.

unity A principle of design related to the sense of wholeness which results from the successful combination of the component elements of an artwork.

value An element of design concerned with the degree of lightness of colors. Darker colors are lower in value.

vanishing point A point on the eye-level line, toward which parallel lines are made to recede and meet in perspective drawing.

variety A principle of design concerned with the inclusion of differences in the elements of a composition to offset unity and make the work more interesting.

vault An arched roof or covering made of brick, stone or concrete. (See *barrel vault* and *cross vault*.)

vehicle A liquid binding agent in paint such as water, oil, or egg yolk that allows the paint to adhere to the painting surface.

viewers For purposes of this program, people who look at and analyze artworks.

warm colors Those hues in which yellow and red are dominant and are located on the left side of the color wheel.

wash A transparent layer of color applied to a surface allowing underlying lines, shapes and colors to show through. Watercolor or ink that is diluted with water to make it lighter in value and more transparent.

waste mold A plaster mold from which one cast is taken. The mold is formed around a clay model in two or three removable parts which are reassembled and filled with liquid plaster that is allowed to harden. The mold is broken away (wasted) to reveal the cast.

wood engraving A technique of relief printmaking in which a design is cut into the end grain of a wooden block with gravers like those used for metal plates. Wood engravings contain more detail than woodcuts.

wood frame A principle of construction in which narrow lightweight members of wood are joined to form a framework to which walls and ceiling can be attached.

woodcut A technique of relief printmaking in which a design is cut into a block of plank wood with knives and gouges leaving raised shapes to receive ink. A print is then made from the block.

zoom In filmmaking, to make an image appear nearer or farther by means of a zoom lens.

Index with Pronunciation Guide

Bibliography

Part I Introduction

Books

Beardsley, Monroe C. *Aesthetics: Problems in the Philosophy of Criticism.* 2nd ed. Indianapolis: Hackett Publishing Co., 1981.

Blocker, H. G. *Philosophy of Art.* New York: Charles Scribner's Sons, 1979.

Congdon, Kristin G., and Doug Bland. *Pluralistic Approaches to Art Criticism.* KY: The Bowling Green State University Popular Press, 1991.

Dickie, George. *Aesthetics: An Introduction.* Indianapolis: Pegasus, 1971.

———. *Art Aesthetics: An Introduction.* Indianapolis: Pegasus, 1981.

Dissanayake, Ellen. *Homo Aestheticus: Where Art Comes From and Why.* New York: The Free Press, 1992.

Hobbs, Jack A. *Art in Context.* 4th ed. San Diego: Harcourt Brace Jovanovich, 1990.

Kaelin, Eugene F. *An Aesthetics for Art Education.* New York: Teachers College Press, 1989.

Wollheim, Richard. *Art and Its Objectives.* 2nd ed. New York: Cambridge University Press, 1980.

Videodiscs

The National Gallery Videodisc and Companion Software for the Macintosh. New York: Videodisc Publishing, Inc., 1983. Manufactured by Pioneer Video, Inc. Distributed in the U.S.A. and Canada by The Voyager Company.

Part II What To Look For

Books

Albers, J. *Interaction of Color.* Rev. ed. New Haven: Yale University Press, 1975.

Arnheim, R. *Visual Thinking.* Berkeley and Los Angeles: University of California Press, 1960.

Auvil, Kenneth. *Perspective Drawing.* Mayfield Publishing Co., 1990.

Birren, F. *Principles of Color.* Rev. ed. West Chester, PA: Schiffer Publishing Ltd., 1987.

Bobker, Lee R. *Elements of Film.* 3rd ed. New York: Harcourt, Brace, and World, 1979.

Brommer, Gerald F. *Movement and Rhythm.* Book 4 of *Principles of Design.* Worcester, MA: Davis Publications, Inc., 1975.

Cheatham, F., and J. Cheatham. *Design Concepts and Applications.* 2nd ed. Englewood Cliffs, NJ: 1983.

D'Amelio, J. *Perspective Drawing Handbook.* New York: Van Nostrand Reinhold, 1984.

De Saino, Michael. *The Principles and Elements of Art & Design.* New York: Trillium Press, 1991.

Doblin, J. *Perspective: A New System for Designers.* 11th ed. New York: Whitney Library of Design, 1976.

Ellinger, R. G. *Color, Structure and Design.* New York: Van Nostrand Reinhold Co., 1980.

Enstice, Wayne, and Melody Peters. *Drawing: Space, Form & Expression.* Englewood Cliffs, NJ: Prentice-Hall, 1990.

Feldman, Edmund B. *Varieties of Visual Experience.* 3rd ed. Englewood Cliffs, NJ: Prentice-Hall, Inc., 1987.

Gatto, Joseph A., Albert W. Porter and Jack Selleck. *Exploring Visual Design.* 2nd ed. Worcester, MA: Davis Publications, Inc., 1987.

Gibson, James J. *The Ecological Approach to Visual Perception.* Hillsdale, NJ: Lawrence Erlbaum Assoc., 1986.

Gill, Robert W. *Basic Rendering.* New York: Thames & Hudson, 1991.

Gleason, Roger. *Seeing for Yourself — Techniques & Projects for Beginning Photographers.* IL: Chicago Review Press, 1993.

Goldstein, Ernest, Theodore Katz, Jo Kowalchuk and Robert Saunders. *Understanding and Creating Art.* Dallas: Garrard Publishing, 1986.

Gombrich, E. *Art and Illusion: A Study in the Psychology of Pictorial Presentation.* 2nd ed. Princeton: Princeton University Press, 1961.

Gordon, Louise. *The Figure in Action.* London: Batsford Ltd., 1989. Distributed by Trafalgar Square.

Horn, George F. *Texture: A Design Element.* Book 5 of *Elements of Design.* Worcester, MA: Davis Publications, Inc., 1974.

Lauer, David A. *Design Basics.* 2nd ed. NY: Holt, Rinehart and Winston, 1985.

Larsen, Karl V. *See & Draw.* Worcester, MA: Davis Publications, Inc., 1993.

Leland, Nita, *Exploring Color.* OH: Northlight Books, 1991.

Nigrosh, Leon. *Claywork: Form and Idea in Ceramic Design.* 3rd ed. Worcester, MA: Davis Publications, Inc., 1994.

Richardson, John A., Floyd W. Coleman and Michael J. Smith. *Basic Design: Systems, Elements, Applications.* Englewood Cliffs, NJ: Prentice-Hall, Inc., 1987.

Richmond, Wendy. *Book Design & Technology — Erasing the Boundaries.* New York: Van Nostrand Reinhold, 1990.

Panofsky, Erwin, and Christopher S. Wood, trans. *Perspective as Symbolic Form.* Cambridge: MIT Press, 1991.

Stoops, Jack, and Jerry Samuelson. *Design Dialogue.* 2nd ed. Worcester, MA: Davis Publications, Inc., 1990.

Zelanski, Paul, and Mary Fisher. *The Art of Seeing.* Englewood Cliffs, NJ: Prentice-Hall, Inc., 1988.

Videos

If You Paint, You See More. Agency for Instructional Technology. Teacher's guide included.

Masters of Illusion. Home Vision. 30 minutes. Color.

Painting with Light. Media for the Arts. 70 minutes. Color.

Price, Gail. *Pencil Drawing.* Crystal Productions. 20 minutes. Color.

Quiller, Stephen. *Composition.* Crystal Productions. 16 minutes. Color.

Watercolor Workshop — Simplified Technique for the Classroom. Alarion Press. 120 minutes. Color.

What's in a Painting? Teacher's guide included. J. Weston Walch. 60 minutes. Color.

Software

Color Ware. The Detroit Institute of the Arts. Designed for 128K Apple II with color monitor.

MacDraw, Macintosh.

Part III How Is It Organized?

Books

Appleton, Jay. *The Symbolism of Habitat — An Interpretation of Landscape in the Arts.* WA: University of Washington Press, 1991.

Glassner, Andrew S. *3-D Computer Graphics: A User's Guide for Artists & Designers.* 2nd ed. New York: Design Press, 1991.

Itten, J. *Design and Form: The Basic Course at the Bauhaus.* New York: Van Nostrand Reinhold, 1975.

Mason, Kathy. *Going beyond Words: The Art & Practice of Visual Thinking.* AZ: Zephyr Press.

Roukes, Nicholas. *Design Synectics: Stimulating Creativity in Design.* Worcester, MA: Davis Publications, Inc., 1988.

Zelanski, Paul, and Mary Fisher. *Design Principles and Problems.* New York: Holt, Rinehart and Winston, 1984.

Software

Fontographer. Altsys Corp. Plano, TX.

Adobe Illustrator. Adobe Systems. Mountain View, CA.

QuarkXPress. Quark, Inc. Denver, CO.

Aldus PageMaker. Aldus Corp. Seattle, WA.

Aldus FreeHand. Aldus Corp. Seattle, WA.

Part IV What Is It Made Of?

Books

Anderson, K., ed. *Education and the Art Teaching Profession.* Reston, VA: NAEA, 1980.

Bontemps, Arna Alexander, ed. *Forever Free: Art by African American Women 1862-1980.* Alexandria, VA: Stephenson, Inc., 1981.

Brommer, Gerald F. *The Art of Collage.* Worcester, MA: Davis Publications, Inc., 1978.

Brommer, Gerald F., and Joseph A. Gatto. *Careers in Art: An Illustrated Guide.* Worcester, MA: Davis Publications, Inc. 1984.

Brommer, Gerald F. *Discovering Art History.* 2nd ed. Worcester, MA: Davis Publications, Inc., 1988.

———. *Exploring Drawing.* Worcester, MA: Davis Publications, Inc., 1988.

Brommer, Gerald F., and Nancy Kinne. *Exploring Painting.* Rev. ed. Worcester, MA: Davis Publications, Inc., 1994.

Brown, Erica. *Interior Views, Design at Its Best.* New York: Viking Press, 1980.

Casewit, Curtis. *Making a Living in the Fine Arts: Advice from the Pros.* New York: Macmillan, 1981.

Chaet, B. *The Art of Drawing.* 3rd ed. Fort Worth: Holt, Rinehart and Winston, 1993.

Constantine, M., and J. Larsen. *The Art Fabric: Mainstream.* New York: Kodansha, 1986.

Davis, Virginia. *Crafts: A Basic Survey.* Dubuque: Wm. C. Brown, 1988.

Evans, Chuck. *Jewelry: Contemporary Design and Technique.* Worcester, MA: Davis Publications, Inc., 1983.

Fixman, Adeline. *Aim for a Job in Cartooning.* New York: Richards Rosen Press, 1976.

Fonvielle-Bontemps, Jacqueline. *Choosing: An Exhibit of Changing Perspectives in Modern Art and Art Criticism by Black Americans, 1925-1985.* Washington, DC: Museum Press, 1985.

Gatto, Joseph A. *Drawing Media & Techniques.* Worcester, MA: Davis Publications, Inc., 1987.

Geahigan, G., ed. *Career Education in the Visual Arts: Representative Programs and Practices.* Reston, VA: NAEA, 1980.

Goldstein, N. *Painting: Visual and Technical Fundamentals.* Englewood Cliffs, NJ: Prentice-Hall, Inc., 1979.

Greh, Deborah. *Computers in the Artroom: A Handbook for Teachers.* Worcester, MA: Davis Publications, Inc., 1990.

Hall, Carolyn Vosburg. *Soft Sculpture.* Worcester, MA: Davis Publications, Inc., 1981.

Holden, D. *Art Career Guide: A Guidance Handbook for Art Students, Teachers, Vocational Counselors and Job Hunters.* 4th ed. New York: Watson Guptill, 1983.

Ito, Dee. *The School of Visual Arts Guide to Careers.* New York: McGraw-Hill, Visual Arts Press, 1987.

James, J. *Perspective Drawing: A Point of View.* 2nd ed. Englewood Cliffs,NJ: Prentice-Hall, Inc., 1988.

Joel, Seth. *Photographic Still Life.* New York: Watson-Guptill Publications, 1990.

Kingman, Dong, and H. K. Kingman. *Dong Kingman Watercolors.* New York: Watson Guptil, 1980.

Krauss, R. *Passages in Modern Sculpture.* Cambridge: MIT Press, 1981.

Laybourne, K. *The Animation Book: A Complete Guide to Animated Film Making.* New York: Crown Publications, 1988.

Mayer, Barbara. *Contemporary American Craft Art: A Collector's Guide.* Layton, UT: Gibbs Smith Publishers, 1987.

Mendelowitz, Daniel M. *Drawing.* Stanford: Stanford University Press, 1980.

Nelson, G. *Ceramics: A Potter's Handbook.* 5th ed. New York: Holt, Rinehart and Winston, 1984.

O'Brien, Michael F., and Norman Sibley. *The Photographic Eye.* Rev. ed. Worcester, MA: Davis Publications, Inc., 1994.

Porter, Albert W. *Expressive Watercolor Techniques.* Worcester, MA: Davis Publications, Inc., 1982.

Rosenthal, H. *Job Descriptions in the Business World of Art and Design.* Reston, VA: NAEA, 1978.

Silverman, R., ed. *Art Education and the World of Work: A Handbook for Career Education in Art.* Reston, VA: NAEA, 1980.

Smith, E. *Sculpture Since 1945.* New York: Universe Books, Inc., 1987.

Smith, Paul J. and Edward Lucie-Smith. *Craft Today: Poetry of the Physical.* New York: American Craft Museum, 1988.

Sprintzen, Alice. *Crafts: Contemporary Design and Technique.* Worcester, MA: Davis Publications, Inc., 1987.

Toale, Bernard. *Basic Printmaking Techniques.* Worcester, MA: Davis Publications, Inc., 1992.

Williams, Arthur. *Sculpture: Technique, Form, and Content.* Rev. ed. Worcester, MA: Davis Publications, Inc., 1994.

Videodiscs

Exploring Photography: The History of Photography. Teacher's guide included. McIntyre Visual Publications, Inc. 43 minutes.

The Louvre: Painting & Drawing. Vol. 1. Produced by ODA, 1989. Distributed in the U.S.A. and Canada by The Voyager Company.

The Louvre: Sculptures & Objects. Vol. 2. Produced by ODA, 1989. Distributed in the U.S.A. and Canada by The Voyager Company.

Videos

The Art of Creating Monotypes. HR Productions. 120 minutes. Color.

The Classroom Collection. Brooks Institute of Photography. Six-tape set. Color.

Computer Magic: The World of Computer Imagery. Cinemagic Productions. 58 minutes. Color.

Drawing Landscapes with Pencil & Ink. Crystal Productions. 45 minutes. Color.

Drawing: Learning Professional Techniques. Crystal Productions. 45 minutes. Color.

The Expanding Universe of Sculpture. Jacoby/Storm. 12 minutes. Color.

The Mind's Eye. Abstract computer art. Mirimar. 40 minutes. Color.

Siegel, Arlene. *Sculpture in the Classroom.* Videocine Services, Inc. 53 minutes. Color.

Software

MacPaint. Claris Corp. Mountain View, CA.

Videoworks. Animation software. Chicago, IL.

Part V What Is It Saying?

Books

Aldrich, J., ed. *The Western Art of Charles M. Russel.* New York: Ballantine, 1988.

Anfam, David. *Abstract Expressionism.* New York: Thames & Hudson, 1990.

Arnason, H. *History of Modern Art: Painting, Sculpture, Architecture, Photography.* New York: Harry N. Abrams, 1986.

Ashton, R., and J. Stuart. *American Indian Art.* Cambridge: Peabody, Harvard, 1973.

Atkins, R. *Artspeak: A Guide to Contemporary Ideas, Movements, and Buzzwords.* New York: Abbeville Press, 1990.

Bazin, G. *Baroque and Rococo.* New York: Thames & Hudson, 1985.

Brommer, Gerald F. *Discovering Art History.* 2nd ed. Worcester, MA: Davis Publications, Inc., 1988.

Burn, Lucilla. *The British Museum Book of Greek & Roman Art.* New York: Thames & Hudson, 1992.

Bussabarger, R., and B. Robins. *The Everyday Art of India.* New York: Dover Publications, Inc., 1977.

Chanda, Jacqueline. *African Arts & Cultures.* Worcester, MA: Davis Publications, Inc., 1994.

D'Alleva, Anne. *Native American Arts & Cultures.* Worcester, MA: Davis Publications, Inc., 1993.

De la Croix, Horst, and Richard Tansey. *Gardner's Art through the Ages*. 8th ed. New York: Harcourt Brace Jovanovich, 1986.

Emmerich, Andre. *Art before Columbus*. New York: Simon and Schuster, 1983.

Encyclopedia of World Art. Vols. 1–15. Palatine, IL: Publishers Guild, 1959–68.

Feest, Christian F. *Native Arts of North America*. New York: Thames & Hudson, 1992.

Fletcher, B. *A History of Architecture*. 18th ed. New York: Charles Scribner's Sons, 1975.

Fitzpatrick, Virginia. *Art History: A Contextual Inquiry Course*. Reston, VA: NAEA, 1992.

Furst, J., and P. Furst. *North American Indian Art*. New York: Rizzoli International, 1984.

Harris, Ann S. *Women Artists: 1550-1950*. New York: Alfred A. Knopf, Inc., 1977.

Hobbs, Jack A., and Robert L. Duncan. *Arts, Ideas and Civilization*. Englewood Cliffs, NJ: Prentice-Hall, Inc., 1989.

Hughes, J. *Imperial Rome*. Rev. ed. New York: Franklin Watts, Inc., 1985.

Hunter, S., and J. Jacobus. *American Art of the Twentieth Century*. Englewood Cliffs, NJ: Prentice-Hall, Inc., 1974.

Huntington, Susan L., and John C. Huntington. *The Art of Ancient India: Buddhist, Hindu, Jain*. New York: Weatherhill, 1985.

Janson, H. *History of Art*. 3rd ed. New York: Harry N. Abrams, 1986.

Jensen, Vickie. *Where the People Gather — Carving a Totem Pole*. WA: University of Washington Press, 1992.

Ketchum, R., ed. *The Horizon Book of the Renaissance*. New York: American Heritage Publishing, 1961.

Nuttgens, Patrick. *The Story of Architecture*. Englewood Cliffs, NJ: Prentice-Hall, Inc., 1984.

Panofsky, E. *Meaning in the Visual Arts*. Chicago: University of Chicago Press, 1983.

Paz, O., et al. *Mexico: Splendors of Thirty Centuries*. Boston: Bulfinch Press, 1990.

Peterson, Susan. *Lucy M. Lewis: American Indian Potter*. New York: Kodansha International, 1992.

Rice, David T. *Islamic Painting*. New York: Columbia University Press, 1972.

Sear, Frank. *Roman Architecture*. Ithaca: Cornell University Press, 1983.

Smith, B. *Japan: A History in Art*. Garden City, NJ: Doubleday and Co., 1971.

Willett, Frank. *African Art*. London: Thames & Hudson, 1985.

Wilson, Christopher. *The Gothic Cathedral*. New York: Thames & Hudson, 1991.

CD-I

Philips/Treasures of the Smithsonian, Renaissance Gallery, French Impressionists, World of Impression, Art of the Czars

Films

African American Art: Past & Present. Reading & O'Reilly. Three 30-minute videos and guide.

African Art and Sculpture. Philadelphia: WCAU-TV, 1971. Rental: Carousel Films and Association Films. 21 minutes. Color.

The Age of Rococo: From Divine Right to Equality. Aleman Films, 1961. Canadian rental: International Tele-Film Enterprises. 17 minutes. Color.

American Realists (Part I: 18th–19th Centuries). AZ: University of Arizona Radio-TV Bureau, 1965. Rental: McGraw-Hill Films. 23 minutes. Color.

The Ancient Chinese. International Film Foundation, 1974. 24 minutes. Color.

The Ancient Peruvian. International Film Foundation., 1968. 27 minutes. Color.

The Architecture of Frank Lloyd Wright. NVC. 75 minutes. Color.

Arts of Village India. British Film Institute, 1970. Rental: Films Incorporated. 26 minutes. Color.

Charles Burchfield: Fifty Years of His Art. AZ: University of Arizona Radio-TV Bureau, 1966. Rental: International Film Bureau. 14 minutes. Color.

The Eye of Thomas Jefferson. Washington, DC: National Gallery of Art. 27 minutes. Color.

Expressionism. International Film Bureau, 1971. 26 minutes. Color.

Fauvism. International Film Bureau, 1971. 17 minutes. Color.

A Floating World of Japanese Painting. American Educational Films. 20 minutes. Color.

From Foric to Gothic (Architecture). Paris: Atlantic Films, 1954. Canadian loan: Canadian Film Institute. 20 minutes. Black and white.

Gardonyi, Frank, and Clifford Janoff. *African Craftsmen: The Ashanti*. 1970. Rental: BFA. 11 minutes. Color.

Goya. National Gallery of Art, Washington, DC.

Greek Sculpture. London: Marsden Film Productions, 1959. Rental: New York University Film Library. 25 minutes. Color.

Herzog, Milan. *In Search of Rembrandt*. 1972. Rental: Films Incorporated. 28 minutes. Color.

The Impressionists. Flag Films, 1966. Rental: FACSEA or Macmillan. 26 minutes. Color.

Le Corbusier. Museum without Walls. 26 minutes. Color.

Leonardo: To Know How to See. Washington, DC: National Gallery of Art, 1969. Rental: Time-Life. 55 minutes. Color.

Michelangelo: The Last Giant. NBC News, 1967. Rental: McGraw-Hill Films. 67 minutes. Color.

Mona Lisa Descending a Staircase. Pyramid Film & Video. 9 minutes. Color.

Monet: Legacy of Light. Boston: WGBH, Malone Gill Productions, Museum of Fine Arts. 27 minutes. Color.

Claude Monet — The Man Who Gave Birth to the Impressionist School. Independent Television Corp., 1972. Loan: National Gallery of Art, Washington, DC. 40 minutes. Color.

Robert Motherwell: Storming the Citadel. RM Arts. 56 minutes. Color.

New Ways of Seeing Picasso, Braque, and the Cubist Revolution. Phillip Morris Companies, Inc. 66 minutes. Color.

Notre Dame de Paris. Paris: Pathe Cinema, 1961. Rental: FACSEA. 20 minutes. Color.

Painting in America: Copley to Audubon. Detroit Institute of Arts, 1957. Rental: Film Images. 21 minutes. Color.

Picasso: From 1900 through Cubism. Filmsonor Marceau, 1973. Rental: Macmillan. 12 minutes. Color.

Picasso: The Volcanic Thirties. Filmsonor Marceau, 1973. Rental: Macmillan. 17 minutes. Color.

The Precursors: Cezanne, Gaugin, van Gogh. International Film Bureau, 1970. 26 minutes. Color.

Prehistoric Images: The First Art of Man. Les Films de Saturne and Renaissance des Film, 1954. Rental: Macmillan. 17 minutes. Color.

The Renaissance. Encyclopedia Britannica Films. 26 minutes. Color.

Rubens. Resobel, Brussels: 1973. Rental: International Film Bureau. 26 minutes. Color.

Sentinels of Silence (Ruins of Ancient Mexico). Produciones Concord, 1971. Rental: Encyclopedia Britannica Educational Corporation. 19 minutes. Color.

Surrealism (and Dada). Texture Films., 1970. 18 minutes. Color.

The Totem Pole. CA: University Extension of University of California, 1964. 27 minutes. Color.

Ukiyo-e: The Fabulous World of Japanese Prints. NHK (Japanese Broadcasting System), 1972. Rental: Films Incorporated. 30 minutes. Color.

The Worship of Nature (Civilization series). BBC-TV, 1969. Rental: Time-Life. 50 minutes. Color.

Vincent: A Dutchman. Premiere Programming, Inc. 26 minutes. Color.

Videodiscs

The Mystery of Picasso, Image Entertainment.

Voyager/van Gogh Revisited, Michelangelo, The Orsay Museum, Exotic Japan (CD-ROM)

Andrew Wyeth: The Helga Pictures. Videodisc Publishing.

Videos

Art & Architecture of Japan. Alarion Press, Inc.

Art History: A Survey of the Western World. Agency for Instructional Technology. Twelve 15-minute programs and teacher's guide.

The Art of Africa. Teacher's guide included. J. Weston Walch. 35 minutes. Color.

The Art of Mexico, Central America, and South America. Teacher's guide included. J. Weston Walch. 77 minutes. Color.

The Caves of Altamira. Films of the Humanities & Sciences. 26 minutes. Color.

Crete and Mycenae. Museum without Walls. 54 minutes. Color.

The Greek Temple. Museum without Walls. 54 minutes. Color.

Legacy of the Mamluks. Savin, ArtsAmerica. 29 minutes. Color.

Light of the Gods. National Gallery of Art. 28 minutes. Color.

Maria! Indian Pottery of San Ildefonso. Holiday. 27 minutes. Color.

The Origins of Art in France. ORTF–The Roland Collection. 38 minutes. Black and white.

Picuris Indians. Heese/Waldrum. 60 minutes. Color.

Pre-Columbian Art & Architecture. Alarion Press, Inc.

Reid, Bill. *The Spirit of Haida Gwaii.* Deluxe Productions, Vancouver, BC. 45 minutes. Color.

Stairways to the Mayan Gods. The Hartley Film Foundation. 28 minutes. Color.

A Thousand and One Years Ago: Inca Art of Peru. Deutsche Condor Films. 13 minutes. Color.

Part VI In the Final Analysis

Books

Cincinnati Art Museum. *Improving Visual Arts Education.* Art Specialists Seminar Level 1. A project of the Getty Center for Education in the Arts. Cincinnati: Cincinnati Art Museum, 1992.

Ebert, Roger. *Roger Ebert's Movie Home Companion.* Kansas City: Andrews and McMeel, 1989.

Feldman, Edmund B. *Varieties of Visual Experience.* Englewood Cliffs, NJ: Prentice-Hall, Inc., 1987.

Feldman, E. *Thinking About Art.* Englewood Cliffs, NJ: Prentice-Hall, Inc., 1985.

Timeline of Artworks
in *The Visual Experience*

Pg.	Title, Artist	Culture, Style, Date
213	Angkor Thom	Southeast Asia, 1190
263	Chartres Cathedral	Medieval, France, 1194
232	Oni (King) of Ife	Africa, Ife, 1200
217	*Bare Willows*	China, Sung, 1200
265	Choir vault of Amiens	Medieval, France, 1220
264	Nave of Amiens Cathedral	Medieval, France, 1220
221	Temple Guardian	Japan, Kamakura, 1300
227	Court of the Lions	Islam, Spain, 1354
228	Two Warriors	Islam, Persia, 1396
218	porcelian jar	China, Ming, 1400
267	*St. Mark,* Donatello	Renaissance, Italy, 1411
268	*The Tribute Money,* Masaccio	Renaissance, Italy, 1420
266	Pazzi Chapel, Brunelleschi	Renaissance, Italy, 1420
233	Flute player	Africa, Benin, 1450
222	*Landscape,* Sesshu	Japan, Ashikaga, 1495
269	*The Last Supper,* da Vinci	High Renaissance, 1498
235	Machu Picchu	South America, Inca, 1500
269	*The School of Athens,* Raphael	High Renaissance, 1508
273	*Creation,* Michelangelo	High Renaissance, 1508
272	Sistine ceiling, Michelangelo	High Renaissance, 1508
270	*Embryo in the Womb,* da Vinci	High Renaissance, 1510
271	*Moses,* Michelangelo	High Renaissance, 1513
52	*Pine Trees,* Tohaku	Japan, Momoyama, 1539
229	*The Ardabil Carpet*	Islam, Persia, 1540
273	*St. Peter's,* Michelangelo	High Renaissance, 1546
225	*Layla and Majnun,* Unknown	Islam, Persia, 1550
277	*Massacre,* Rubens	Baroque, Flanders, 1621
277	*Adoration,* Rembrandt	Baroque, Dutch, 1646
278	*A Mother's Duty,* de Hooch	Baroque, Dutch, 1660
276	Versailles Palace	Baroque, France, 1661
276	Versailles Palace	Baroque, France, 1661
279	*Vanitas,* van Oosterwyck	Baroque, France, 1668
280	La Madeleine, Vignon	Neoclassical, France, 1762
280	*The Swing,* Fragonard	Rococo, France, 1766
281	*Oath of the Horatii,* David	Neoclassical, France, 1784
281	State Capitol, Richmond, Jefferson	Neoclassical, America, 1785
287	*The Great Wave,* Hokusai	Japan, Tokusawa, 1823
243	*The White Cloud,* Catlin	American, 1845
317	*Hemlock in November,* Burchfield	American, Regionalism, 1846
284	*Burial at Ornans,* Courbet	Nineteenth century, 1849
125	Pomo storage basket	American Indian, 1850
241	Rug	North America, Navajo, 1850
241	Totem pole	North America, Haida, 1850
242	Inlaid chest	North American, Haida, 1850
288	The Crystal Palace, Paxton	Nineteenth century, 1851
16	*Blue Hole, Flood,* Duncanson	African American, 1851
283	*Gathering for the Hunt,* Bonheur	Nineteenth century, 1856
223	*Sudden Shower,* Hiroshige	Japan, Tokusawa, 1857
282	*Arabs Skirmishing,* Delacroix	Nineteenth century, 1863
285	*La Grenouillére,* Monet	Nineteenth century, 1869
90	*The Country School,* Homer	American, 1871
284	*Gare Saint-Lazare,* Manet	Nineteenth century, 1873
287	*The Vision after,* Gauguin	Nineteenth century, 1888
289	Wainwright Building, Sullivan	Nineteenth century, 1890

Artwork by Subject

Two-Dimensional

People	Landscape	Still Life	Abstract
Duncanson, 16	Duncanson, 16		Albers, 17
Renoir, 21	Renoir, 21		
Comic, 23			
Renoir, 23			
Wood, 25			
Schulz, 28			
Persian, 29			
Wyeth, 30	Wu Chen, 30		
Ingres, 31			
Levine, 31			
Mokuan, 34			
			Aguilar, 36
			Espada, 37
			Tanahashi, 36
			Feltner, 37
	da Vinci, 39		
	van Gogh, 39		
Escher, 41			Picasso, 43
Picasso, 43			
Bouts, 45			
White, 46			
Cassatt, 47			
	Rembrandt, 51		
	Hopper, 51		
	Tohaku, 52–3		
Michelangelo, 56	Stanton, 57		
Tanner, 59			
Picasso, 61			
Unknown, 61			
Picasso, 69			Frankenthaler, 67
		van Gogh, 70	
		van Gogh, 71	
	Monet, 74		Mondrian, 80
Oloyede, 80			
Hogarth, 85	Hogarth, 85		
Bingham, 86	Bingham, 86		
	Ma Yuan, 87		
Tsinahjinnie, 88	Tsinahjinnie, 88		Hofmann, 89
			Pereira, 88
Homer, 90			
Lange, 93			

Artwork by Subject

Three-Dimensional

Artwork by Medium

Two-Dimensional

Artwork by Medium

Three-Dimensional